SPORTING ARMS OF THE WORLD

An Outdoor Life Book

SPORTING ARMS
OF THE WORLD

RAY BEARSE

OUTDOOR LIFE / HARPER & ROW
New York, Evanston, San Francisco, London

This Book Is For

LILLIAN

With Love

CONTENTS

APPENDIX

INDEX

INTRODUCTION

Almost any tool for shooting at game or targets can be classified as a "sporting arm." Archers certainly classify the bow as a sporting arm, and possibly a slingshot or fishing rod might be so classified by some people. It's safe to assume, though, that anyone who buys this book is interested in shooting and has in mind a comprehensive book on firearms designed for game or targets. *Sporting Arms of the World* is indeed comprehensive—the most comprehensive book of its kind.

It lists and describes all of the currently manufactured production-line sporting firearms made in the United States. It also lists and describes those made abroad and sold in the United States, whether they are designed here and produced specifically for the American import market, or designed in the country of manufacture for sale here and perhaps elsewhere. Specifications are provided; background data and comment are provided; clear photographs of most of the guns are provided; and there are even exploded views and cutaway or other technical illustrations of some of them.

This is not to say that it includes every sporting firearm in the world. No book will ever succeed in doing that, and in any case it would be pointless in a work of this kind to include arms that are rarely if ever available or are available only overseas. Neither does it include custom-made arms which are produced only on special order; after all, no one has ever compiled a complete list of gunsmiths who offer such arms, much less a list of all the kinds of guns they offer. Moreover, there would be no reliable way to describe the specifications, which generally change for every customer. What I *have* included is a collection of all the normally and currently available guns (including a few that are in the process of being phased out of production but can still be bought)—all of the many guns a shooter might want to know about.

My definition of sporting arms includes those rifles, shotguns, and handguns designed for hunting small and big game, for shooting upland game birds and wildfowl, and for match rifle and pistol shooting and skeet and trap matches.

I have omitted semiautomatic versions of full-automatic military arms and all semiautomatic military arms save the M1 Carbine, Caliber .30, and pistols such as the .45 Colt Automatic.

With minor exceptions, only those handguns with sporting-length barrels and sporting sights are included. The handguns without micrometer sights can be fitted with them.

The book is divided into arms types. A major exception is the bolt-action centerfire rifle, which is divided into categories like (a) basic rifle; (b) varmint rifle; (c) big-bore rifle for dangerous African and Asiatic game; (d) single-shot match rifle.

Since this book deals with arms employing modern firing systems, muzzleloading replicas—flintlocks and caplocks—are not included. In addition to arms of modern design, however, there will be listings and descriptions of currently available replicas of a number of famous old breechloading firearms employing self-contained ammunition.

There was a time when a shooter could take for granted that a gun stamped with the name Winchester or Savage or Ithaca—to name but a typical few—was made in America. (A major exception was Browning, of course.) This is no longer true. Many American arms companies make some of their products in this country and have some of them made abroad. Those produced in the United States are simply listed in the specification tables by brand and model name. For those made abroad, I have included the name of the manufacturer and the country of origin as well as the name of the American importer/distributor. This is a kind of information that most shooters would like to have, and it is not always readily available—especially for those guns stamped with an American brand name but nonetheless manufactured abroad. Names and addresses of manufacturers and importers are listed in the Appendix. With a few exceptions (such as the British manufacturers of double rifles) the address of the sole or primary American importer is given, rather than that of a foreign manufacturer from whom it would be difficult if not impossible to order the gun.

Many foreign manufacturers owe their existence large to the United States market. Some would go out of business if they could not sell in the U.S.

Major arms exporters to the United States include Belgium, England, Italy, Japan, Spain, Sweden, and West Germany. Austria, France, and the USSR export limited types and quantities to the United States. The Mauser Mark X action, imported largely through Interarms, is manufactured by the Yugoslavian State Arsenal. Few Musgrave rifles are imported from the Union of South Africa, which only recently entered the arms business.

This book employs the decimal rather than fractional system—4.25 inches, for example, rather than 4¼ inches. The decimal system is more precise and is often used in firearms literature. With regard to certain specifications, however, it may be misleading to those not accustomed to it. For example, the weight of any firearm is apt to vary by several ounces from factory specifications. This is primarily because wood density varies, and another factor is introduced if there are options such as a cheekpiece. In addition to variations in the stock, there may be a choice of sights—open, receiver, scope blocks, etc.—each of which has a different weight. As a rule, the weight comes within about 4 oz. of the factory specification. On a shotgun, a ventilated rib generally adds about that amount —4 oz.

Some manufacturers refuse to specify trigger pull. This is not because a particular arm may have a poor or heavy trigger pull but because many purchasers fail to understand that the pull of a given model is likely to vary from arm to arm. The pull is adjustable on many of the finer bolt-action centerfire rifles and rimfire match rifles. Most bolt-action centerfire sporters have an average pull of 4.5 lbs. The single-action pull of a double-action revolver is usually much, much lighter than the double-action pull; where possible, both are listed.

Some trap shooters put great emphasis on trigger pull but, generally speaking, it is not as important with shotguns as with rifled arms, and it is not included in the book's smoothbore specifications. It is quite rare, incidentally, for a side-by-side or over/under to have an identical trigger pull for each barrel, even if the gun has a single selective trigger.

The trigger-pull weights given in this book are mostly nominal. In some cases they have been specified by the manufacturer. In others, they were not specified but were calculated by using a trigger gauge on several sample guns of the same model and taking the average. For those guns that could not be tested and for which the maker specified no pull weight, the trigger pull is simply listed as "not specified." Where it is specified, it is not intended to be interpreted as precise, particularly for the many arms with adjustable pulls.

Overall lengths are given for rifled arms and for magazine shotguns but not for side-by-side or over/under shotguns. In the latter two instances the maximum takedown length is the same as the barrel length. It is important to know the takedown length or, for a gun that cannot be taken down, the overall length. The need becomes obvious when ordering a gun case for travel, shipment, or simply carrying. (Unfortunately, some of the cheaper gun cabinets are made more skimpily than they should be, so it can also be important to know the length of your longest gun when judging the suitability of such a cabinet.)

I intended to maintain consistency throughout the technical data section of each type of firearm. However, when there was an opportunity to provide additional information I opted to sacrifice consistency for the sake of the additional data.

The section titled "Data" was designed to provide additional facts. The section titled "Comment" was designed to provide personal observations on a particular firearm. It sometimes proved impossible to maintain a distinct line between the sections.

After nearly fifty years' involvement with firearms and firearms research, I have some strong opinions. Because I like or dislike a particular firearm does not mean that my preference is to be interpreted as Gospel.

Some of my opinions are obvious. I like traditional contours, oil-finish stocks, hand checkering and finely finished arms. Such features don't mean that a particular firearm is going to function better, last longer or shoot straighter. These matters are purely esthetic and personal.

Within two weeks before the manuscript went to the printers, I contacted by mail or phone every manufacturer and importer/distributor to ensure that the book would be up to date. The current state of imported firearms is very fluid. Many first-rate foreign arms are being discontinued because of the rapid and steep increase in prices. This is partly due to increasing cost of foreign labor and materials, and the decrease of the dollar's value on the international currency market. Many foreign bolt-action rifles are no longer imported because of the improved quality of American commercial arms. Today, unless one wants a specific caliber like the .416 Rigby, virtually no imported rifle offers anything that is not provided by an American commercial bolt-action sporting rifle. There are rifles for those who like the distinctive Weatherby stock and for those who prefer the classic English sporter type stock with a dull oil finish.

As for shotguns, there are plenty of magazine guns—that is, repeaters—in both the American-made and imported categories. But the doubles are another matter. It is possible to buy an inexpensive but sturdy American-made side-by-side or over/under, but most such guns, whether cheap or expensive and whether or not they are stamped with an American brand name, are made in other countries.

Sporting handguns, like magazine shotguns, come in a wide enough array of types, both domestic and foreign. (An exception is the free pistol, used for highly specialized match shooting; no free pistols are now made by American manufacturers, and not many are made in other countries.)

A final note: Manufacturers frequently make minor changes in stock design and sighting equipment. The specifications presented here are the latest available, but some of them will change from time to time. When buying a gun, check on the specifications with the dealer so you'll know precisely what you're getting.

Good shooting.

Ray Bearse
Bristol, Vt.

ACKNOWLEDGMENTS

The writing and publication of *Sporting Arms of the World* would not have been possible without the assistance of the following friends:

Howard Walzer, Beretta Arms and Sloans Sporting Goods, Inc.; Val Browning, Bruce Browning, and Harmon Williams of Browning Arms Co.; Robert Greene of Charter Arms Co., Inc.; Thomas Turner and Thomas Thornber of Colt Industries, Firearms Division; Richard Wulff of Garcia Corporation; Jack Sharry of Harrington & Richardson; Gil Hebard of Gil Hebard Guns; Eric Brooker and James Reardon of High Standard Sporting Arms; Carl Ring of Interarms; Kristin Driscoll Colongeli of Ithaca Gun Co.; Wayne L. Johnson of Jana International Co.; Viktor Brandl of Krieghoff Gun Co.; William Lawrence III of George Lawrence Co.; Robert Behn of Marlin Arms Co.; Carl H. Benson and Carl Liedke of Mossberg Co.; Val Forgett of Navy Arms Co.; Myron Charness of Nikon (Ehrenreich Photo-Optical Company); Ted MacCauley and Richard Dietz of Remington Arms Company, Inc.; Earle Harrington of Savage Arms Division, Emhart Corporation; James McClellan of Smith & Wesson; Jon Sundra of Stoeger Industries; Edward Nolan and Stephen Vogel of Sturm, Ruger Company, Inc.; Warren Center of Thompson/Center Arms Company, Inc.; the late Carl Walther of Carl Walther Waffenfabrik; Roy Weatherby of Weatherby's Inc.; Dan Wesson of Dan Wesson Arms Company; John Faulk of Winchester-Western Division, Olin Industries.

Also, I wish to thank Angus Cameron, Wilton, Conn., a master voyageur and hunter/rifleman, and one of my best friends for more than thirty years. Wynn Underwood, Middlebury, Vt., friend and hunting *campañero* since 1936. William Dickinson, Street, Md., formerly with Aberdeen Proving Grounds and former director, H. P. White Laboratory, Bel Aire, Md., a good friend who supplied much technical data, fine wine and stimulating conversation. J. Trevor Underwood, Middlebury, Vt., a fine hunting friend who shoots and hunts in the grand old British tradition. Ernest Taylor, longtime Vermont neighbor, a fine shot and very knowledgeable woodsman. Donald Davis, Brandon, Vt., my first hunting and fishing *campañero*. That was in the early 1930s. The greatest debt is to my friend Lili Capra Woodard who supplies companionship, good conversation, gourmet meals and encouragement.

Ray Bearse

SPORTING ARMS OF THE WORLD

PART I

CENTERFIRE RIFLES

CHAPTER / 1

SINGLE-SHOT CENTERFIRE RIFLES

The single-shot metallic centerfire cartridge rifle—the legend, Hollywood, television, and Winchester advertising notwithstanding—was the basic arm that "won the West."

The Winchester and its parent, the Henry rifle, played a considerable role, but its users were largely ranchers, rustlers, civilian army scouts, and peace officers.

The U.S. Army—save for limited use of experimentals—fought the Indian Wars (1866–90) with single-shot trapdoor Springfields, first in caliber .50 Government (.50–70 rifle/carbine) and later with the .45 Government (.45–70 rifle/carbine).

The bison (buffalo is a misnomer) were nearly wiped out with big-bore single-shot rifles like the .45–120–550 Sharps and the shorter-ranged Big Fifty Sharps.

The most popular single-shot action among non-bison-hunting civilians was probably the Remington rolling block. This was Lieutenant Colonel George Armstrong Custer's favorite hunting-rifle action. Unlike most officers, he carried a rifle in addition to his sixguns.

Meanwhile the British Indian Army controlled a continent with the single-shot .577 Snider and the later .577/450 Martini-Henry rifle (the .577/.450 is a .45 caliber bullet in a necked-down .577 case).

British sportsmen after big game—big game to the British means dangerous game, like elephant, rhino, Cape buffalo, lion, and leopard—used the magnificent single-shot falling-block Farquharson rifle. This rifle was less expensive than a double rifle and was available in a wide range of calibers. Big-bore Farquharsons were also used in India.

William B. Ruger's Number One and Number Three single-shot rifles use a vastly improved Farquharson action.

The author's late friend John "Pondoro" Taylor, one of Africa's most experienced dangerous-game hunters for more than forty years, used a .577/.450 Martini-Henry single-shot for several years. He took more than 100 elephants with this rifle.

The Sharps rifle, made in places like Windsor, Vt. and Hartford and Bridgeport, Conn., was the nemesis of the bison. The Sharps was a favorite of meat and hide hunters. Some had 34-inch barrels. Its accuracy has been well proved, but never better than by the 1100-yard shot made by buffalo hunter Billy Dixon at the Battle of Adobe Walls. He dropped a Comanche at that measured distance. Most Adobe Walls riflemen, including future New York City newsman William Barclay "Bat" Masterson, were skilled buffalo hunters. This was the Sharps' finest hour.

1

Meanwhile, back in the East, Sharps-armed shooters successfully engaged in prosaic marksmanship on paper targets.

Though the single-shot .45–70 was used by state militia in the Spanish-American War and the Philippine Insurrection, and by home guards during World War I, its last major use against the Indian came at the Battle of Wounded Knee (1890), where the pungent bark of the Springfield was heard against the stutter of the rapid-firing Hotchkiss, which had been invented in France by an American, Benjamin Hotchkiss.

The .45–70 Springfield, both carbine and rifle, was officially replaced by the U.S. Magazine Rifle 1892, better known as the .30–40 Krag. But as noted above, the .45 Springfield lingered in the service for nearly thirty years.

The Remington rolling block was used by several countries, including Denmark, Egypt, and Spain, as their standard military rifle.

In 1866, Nelson Story, a native of Ohio, made the first trail drive from Texas to the meat-hungry miners of Montana's gold fields. Story armed each of his thirty-two Texas cowhands with several Remingtons. There was plenty of ammunition. Arriving in Wyoming, Story and his outfit, including 3000 longhorns, headed up "Bloody" Bozeman Trail to Montana. Colonel Henry Carrington, commanding officer, Fort Phil Kearny, denied him passage on the grounds that there were too many Indians for Story to make safe transit and that he could not spare escort troopers. The fort and environs were under daily harassment by the Indians.

"To hell with you," Story said. "I'm going anyway." Carrington, who admired the brash promoter, wished him well.

Carrington's men were armed with single-shot muzzleloaders. He had asked for single-shot breechloaders but had not received them.

Story and his hands were attacked repeatedly, but fast accurate fire from breechloading Remingtons proved sufficient deterrent.

Some years before the Indian Wars ended, the Winchester M85 single-shot rifle, designed by John Moses Browning, appeared. This was available with six types of barrels and three sizes of frame. The rifle was available in every caliber, about fifty, for which Winchester chambered its other rifles. Those ranged from .22 Short to .50–110 Win. It was also made in 20-bore shotgun. A full-stocked version in caliber .22 Short—the Winder Musket—was used by the thousands of trainees during World War I.

Chief of Ordnance General Edward Ripley consistently opposed the adoption of a magazine rifle. He preferred the single-shot muzzleloader. His influence lingered for nearly a quarter-cen-

tury after Appomattox. Because of the direct intervention of Abraham Lincoln, reportedly an able rifleman, there were a few magazine rifles, mostly Spencer carbines, used by Union troops.

Despite the superior firepower of the lever-action magazine rifles, there were times when the single-shot breechloader was a heaven-sent weapon compared to clumsy muzzleloaders.

In June 1867 a thirty-two-man woodcutting detachment from Fort Phil Kearny, in the Dakota Territory (now Montana), was attacked by more than 1000 Sioux and Cheyenne. Forming an oval with wagons, the party, using breech-loading single-shot .50–70 carbines and rifles, successfully stood off the attackers.

The Indians, who expected their enemies to be armed with muzzleloaders, were appalled at the rapidity of fire. The better shots among the whites were armed with several rifles. These were kept loaded by the poorest shots. One man, an old frontiersman, estimated he kept eight rifles "pretty well het up" for six hours.

In the early 1900s, target riflemen racked up impressive scores with Stevens-made Walnut Hill single-shot rifles. Today's riflemen who consider the .32–40 and .38–55 to be short-range obsolete cartridges would be surprised by 200-yard targets with all holes of a 10-shot group cutting each other. The Walnut Hill model was named after a famed Boston suburban range.

During the 1920s and early 1930s the single-shot fell into disrepute because hunters wanted the magazine capacity of a lever- or bolt-action.

The 1930s saw the advent of medium- and long-range varmint cartridges: .22 Hornet, .257 Roberts, .220 Swift, .218 Bee, and .219 Zipper. Many varmint shooters, especially wildcatters, had heavy-barreled rifles made up on reliable Sharps, Winchester M85, or other single-shot actions.

In the 1950s, Vermont gunsmith Wilbur Hauck manufactured a few single-shot rifles using an action of his own design but it was not until 1967, when Bill Ruger began manufacturing the Number One, which he designed himself, that the real revival set in.

Today there are the modern single-shots like the Ruger and the Browning—a modified version of John Moses Browning's M85 Winchester—and single-shot replicas like H&R Springfields.

In the late 1960s, Arthur Swenson of Salt Lake City, Utah, redesigned the famed Sharps-Borchardt and then organized the Sharps Arms Company to manufacture this well-designed rifle. Colt Industries acquired the firm's assets in 1970 but as yet has not gone into production. The future of the new Sharps is uncertain.

BROWNING M78 SINGLE-SHOT

Manufacturer: Miroku, Japan

Importer/distributor: Browning Arms

Action type: falling block; exposed hammer; S-type lever

Safety: half-cock hammer

Barrel length: 26 inches; round or semi-octagon

Stock: 2-piece fancy walnut; well-executed (20 lines to the inch) hand checkering on full pistol grip and fore-end

Buttplate: shotgun type with solid recoil pad

Overall length: 42.0 inches

Length of pull: 13.5 inches

Drop at comb: 1.5 inches

Drop at heel: 2.5 inches

Weight: semi-octagon, 7.625 lbs.; round, 7.925 lbs.

Trigger pull: 3.0–4.5 lbs. (adjustable)

Sight, rear: none

Sight, front: none

Scope adaptability: receiver drilled and tapped for scope bases; Browning scope bases and 1.0-inch-diameter scope rings furnished with each rifle

Caliber: .22–250, .25–06, .30–06, 6mm Rem.

Data: This well-designed and finely made rifle is a direct descendant of the Winchester M85 single-shot designed by John Moses Browning. Though the M85 (1885–1920) did not appear until near the end of the single-shot's heyday, about 140,000 were sold.

GARCIA-STAR ROLLING BLOCK CARBINE

Manufacturer: Star B Echeverria, Spain

Importer/distributor: Garcia Corp./Firearms International

Action type: rolling block (reproduction of Remington rolling block)

Safety: half-cock

Barrel length: 20.0 inches

Stock: 2-piece walnut; uncheckered; barrel band on fore-end

Buttplate: crescent (rifle) type; serrated steel

Overall length: 35.0 inches

Length of pull: 13.75 inches

Drop at comb: 2.5 inches

Drop at heel: 3.0 inches

Weight: 6.0 lbs.

Trigger pull: 4.50 lbs.

Sight, rear: folding leaf

Sight, front: blade on ramp

Scope adaptability: no provision

Caliber: .30–30 Win., .357 Magnum, .44 Magnum

Comment: This is a well-made replica of the Remington rolling-block. Forged steel receiver. Although the stock has excessive drop, recoil with these mild cartridges is not excessive.

The .30–30 and .44 Magnum chamberings are adequate for short-range deer hunting. The .357 Magnum is an inadequate deer cartridge. Receiver bridge and barrel should be tapped and drilled for scope mount. A 2.5× scope with a wide field of view would be ideal for this carbine.

HARRINGTON & RICHARDSON LITTLE BIG HORN COMMEMORATIVE CARBINE

Action type: Springfield trapdoor; top loading and ejection; outside hammer

Safety: half-cock hammer

Barrel length: 22.0 inches

Stock: 1-piece plain American walnut with removable metal pistol-grip adaptor

Buttplate: rifle type; metal

Overall length: 41.0 inches

Length of pull: 13.25 inches

Drop at comb: 2.0 inches

Drop at heel: 3.0 inches

Weight: 7.25 lbs.

Trigger pull: 6.0 lbs.

Sight, rear: folding tang, adjustable for windage and elevation

Sight, front: blade

Scope adaptability: no practical adaptation

Caliber: .45–70 Gov't.

Data: This is a reproduction of the standard M1873 U.S. Springfield cavalry carbine (1873–90). The Little Big Horn Commemorative has three features not on the original of 1873: folding tang sight, removable metal pistol grip, and case-hardened receiver. The first two items appeared on the officer's rifle.

This H&R carbine — 5000 were made — was introduced at the centennial of the carbine, not the centennial of Custer's demise at the Little Big Horn in 1876. Purchasers receive a 128-page book describing Custer's blunder and the gallant death of his men at the Little Big Horn.

Comment: Though made from much better steel than the original, this carbine should *not* be used with maximum smokeless-powder loads. The trapdoor-type action is not safe for these loads. It is entirely safe with currently manufactured (Remington/Winchester-Western) smokeless loads and full (70-grain) black-powder loads.

HARRINGTON & RICHARDSON 1873 COMMEMORATIVE RIFLE (M1873 U.S. SPRINGFIELD REPLICA)

Action type: Springfield trapdoor type; top loading and ejection; outside hammer

Safety: half-cock hammer

Barrel length: 32.0 inches

Stock: 1-piece plain American walnut; straight grip; ramrod carried beneath barrel in stock

Buttplate: rifle type; metal

Overall length: 52.0 inches

Length of pull: 13.25 inches

Drop at comb: 2.0 inches

Drop at heel: 3.0 inches

Weight: 8.625 lbs.

Trigger pull: 6 lbs.

Sight, rear: leaf, adjustable for elevation

Sight, front: blade

Scope adaptability: no practical adaptation

Caliber: .45–70 Gov't.

Data: Classic Springfield trapdoor action. Similar to M1873 carbine except for barrel length, full-length stock, and sight. The metal finish is blue-black with a case-hardened breechblock and buttplate. This is a limited-production rifle, with serial numbers running from SPR1 to SPR1000.

Comment: Same as for carbine M1873. Odd as it may seem today, there was a time when these rifles, using the full .45–70–500 loading, were used on 1000-yard targets.

HARRINGTON & RICHARDSON CAVALRY MODEL (M1873 U.S. SPRINGFIELD REPLICA)

Action type: Springfield trapdoor; top loading and ejection; outside hammer.

Safety: half-cock hammer

Barrel length: 22.0 inches

Stock: 1-piece plain American walnut with saddle ring; straight grip

Buttplate: rifle type; metal

Overall length: 41.0 inches

Length of pull: 13.25 inches

Drop at comb: 2.0 inches

Drop at heel: 3.0 inches

Weight: 7.0 lbs.

Trigger pull: 6 lbs.

Sight, rear: standard battle sight, adjustable for elevation only (deluxe version has sight adjustable for windage and elevation)

Sight, front: blade

Scope adaptability: no practical adaptation

Caliber: .45–70 Gov't.

Data: Many owners of M1873 carbines are somewhat reluctant to fire their original. This replica gives them a functional carbine.

Comment: Should *not* be used with maximum smokeless-powder loads.

HARRINGTON & RICHARDSON SHIKARI RIFLE/CARBINE

Action type: top-break (shotgun type)

Safety: half-cock hammer

Barrel length: rifle (.45–70 Gov't. only), 28.0 inches; carbine, 24.0 inches

Stock: 2-piece plain hardwood with walnut finish

Buttplate: shotgun type; plastic

Overall length: 28-inch barrel, 43.0 inches; 24-inch barrel, 39.0 inches

Length of pull: 13.5 inches

Drop at comb: 1.5 inches

Drop at heel: 2.5 inches

Weight: 28.0-inch barrel, 7.5 lbs.; 24.0-inch barrel, 7.0 lbs.

Trigger pull: not specified

Sight, rear: folding leaf, crudely adjustable

Sight, front: blade

H.&R. SHIKARI RIFLE (continued)

Scope adaptability: not readily adaptable

Caliber: .44 Magnum, .45–70 Gov't.

Data: H&R for many years has made sturdy utilitarian single-shot break-open shotguns, and in more recent years has offered interchangeable rifle-shotgun barrels for at least one break-open.

Comment: This is a good economical buy for single-shot buffs who cannot afford a more expensive single-shot like the Ruger Number One or Three, or for .45–70 or .44 Magnum buffs who likewise cannot afford more expensive rifles. The author would rather face a giant Alaskan brown bear with a single-shot .45–70 Shikari rifle (holding a spare cartridge between the fingers of the right hand—an old African hunter's trick) than with a full 5-shot magazine of .30–06s in a semi-automatic rifle.

RUGER NUMBER ONE SINGLE-SHOT RIFLE

Action type: general characteristics of the fine British Farquharson rifle but thoroughly modernized, improved, and strengthened

Safety: top tang; slide safety functions only when arm is cocked; arm may be opened or closed with safety either on or off

Barrel length: 22.0 inches, 24.0 inches, or 26.0 inches

Stock: American walnut; hand-checkered full pistol grip and fore-end; fore-end either slim British Alexander Henry type or semi-beavertail type

Buttplate: shotgun type; solid recoil pad

Length of pull: 13.5 inches

Drop at comb: 1.75 inches

Drop at heel: 2.75 inches

Overall length: 26-inch barrel, 42.5 inches; 24-inch barrel, 40.5 inches; 22-inch barrel, 38.5 inches

Weight: see model variations below

Trigger pull: 4.0 lbs.

Sight, rear: folding leaf, adjustable for windage and elevation; can be ordered without sights; varmint model fitted with scope bases

Sight, front: flat-faced gold bead on ramp with removable sight protector

Scope adaptability: all rifles except varmint version fitted with quarter rib which provides base for tip-off scopes; varmint rifle fitted with scope blocks

Caliber: .222 Remington (discontinued), .243 Win., .22–250, .25–06, .270 Win., .30–06, .300 Win. Magnum, .375 H&H Magnum, .458 Win. Magnum, .45–70 Gov't., 6mm Rem., 7mm Rem. Magnum

Model Variations

Number One Light Sporter. Barrel: 22 inches. Calibers: .243 Win., .270 Win., 30–06. Sights: open and quarter-rib. Alexander Henry fore-end is standard. Front sling swivel mounted on barrel band forward of fore-end tip. Weight: 7.25 lbs.

Number One Medium Sporter. Barrel: 26 inches. Calibers: .300 Win. Magnum, 7mm Rem. Magnum. Sights: open with quarter-rib. Alexander Henry fore-end is standard. Front sling swivel mounted on barrel band forward of fore-end tip. Weight: 8.0 lbs.

Number One .45–70 Gov't. version. Not illustrated. Barrel: 22 inches. Caliber: .45–70 Gov't. Alexander Henry fore-end is standard. Front sling swivel mounted on barrel band forward of fore-end tip. Weight: 7.25 lbs.

Number One Standard Rifle. Barrel: 26 inches. Calibers: .22–250, .243 Win., .25–06, .270 Win., 30–06, .300 Win. Magnum, 6mm Rem., 7mm Rem. Magnum. Sights: quarter-rib with 1.0-inch tip-off rings. Semi-beavertail fore-end. Weight: 8.0 lbs.

Number One Special Varminter. Barrel: 24.0 inches. Calibers: .22–250, .25–06, .300 Win. Magnum, 7mm Rem. Magnum. Semi-beavertail fore-end. Sight: scope blocks (designed for target or varmint scopes with internal adjustments). Weight: 9.0 lbs.

Number One Tropical Rifle. Barrel: 24 inches. Calibers: .375 H&R Magnum, .458 Win. Magnum. Alexander Henry fore-end. Swivel attached to barrel band forward of fore-end tip. Sights: open and quarter-rib. Weight: .375 H&R, 8.25 lbs.; .458 Win. Magnum, 9.0 lbs.

Data: The finely made British Farquharson rifle —calibers ranging from varmint to elephant stoppers—was until its discontinuance the standard by which all other single-shot actions were judged. Arms designer Bill Ruger took the original Farquharson, left the outside lines largely intact, and completely redesigned and rebuilt the inner mechanism.

A major improvement over the original Farquharson is the increased strength of the action walls. The large dangerous-game calibers so beloved by British African and Indian hunters actually had much lower breech pressures. Though the .458 Win. Magnum case is much smaller than the dangerous-game British cases it has a much higher breech pressure, as do several other of the cartridges for which the Number One is chambered.

Ruger increased the thickness of the exterior walls to 0.218 inch. Directly behind the breech-block, the side walls are joined by a massive piece of steel. The original Farquharsons, designed in the black-powder era and for low-pressure smokeless cartridges, had but a thin steel web protecting the shooter. The stock is securely attached to the receiver itself.

The ejector is fully automatic, but for those who do not need this automatic feature, the ejector spring may readily be removed. Some professional African hunters do not want their exact shooting site revealed to dangerous beasts, and so remove the automatic ejector. (An ejected case might strike a rock, thus sounding an alarm.) The removable ejector is also of interest to hand-loaders who don't want to lose their fired cases.

Barreled actions are available.

Comment: This is the finest single-shot rifle it has ever been the author's privilege to own and shoot. It is also the quickest-handling and best-looking rifle he has ever owned. The original Farquharson was a beautiful and utilitarian rifle, and this is an improvement with its rugged, well-designed mechanism.

The .458 Tropical Rifle should weigh at least 11.0 lbs. Inasmuch as at least eight out of ten varmint-rifle owners use scopes with internal rather than external adjustments, the Special Varminter version should be fitted with a quarter-rib. Scope bases (blocks) should be optional.

Shooters who can afford the luxury of engraving and gold inlay will find that the receiver walls provide adequate space for an artist's creativity.

RUGER NUMBER THREE SINGLE-SHOT CARBINE

Action type: same as Ruger Number One

Safety: top tang (sliding)

Barrel length: 22.0 inches

Stock: 2-piece plain well-finished American walnut

Buttplate: semi-rifle type, metal

RUGER NUMBER THREE CARBINE (continued)

Overall length: 38.5 inches

Length of pull: 13.5 inches

Drop at comb: 1.75 inches

Drop at heel: 2.75 inches

Weight: 6.0 lbs.

Trigger pull: 4.0 lbs.

Sight, rear: folding leaf, adjustable for windage and elevation

Sight, front: flat-face gold bead on barrel band

Scope adaptability: .22 Hornet fitted with scope blocks; others require fitting

Caliber: .22 Hornet, .30–40 U.S. Army (.30–40 Krag)

Data: The Number Three Carbine uses the same action as the Number One, but costs about $100 less. Most of the savings are effected in the stock. The Number Three also uses the traditional American-style lever rather than the more expensive Farquharson lever of the Number One.

Comment: It's good to see the old reliable .30–40 Krag—one of our best deer and black-bear cartridges—return to life. No rifle has been chambered for the .30–40 Krag since the M95 Winchester was discontinued in 1931. The Hornet has not been available since the late 1950s.

We cannot have everything, and so it is a pleasure to welcome old friends like the .30–40 Krag and .22 Hornet back to the land of the living. Who knows? Someday Bill Ruger may even chamber his Number One Rifle for these excellent cartridges.

CHAPTER 2

LEVER-ACTION CENTERFIRE RIFLES

The lever-action magazine rifle (and carbine) has been the most celebrated American repeater for more than a century. Though outsold in recent years by the bolt-action magazine rifle, the lever-action, thanks to motion pictures and television, remains *the* American rifle to most Americans, including nonshooters.

The best-selling centerfire lever-action of a century ago was the lever-action M73 Winchester. Today, the best-selling rifle, regardless of type, is the lever-action M94 Winchester, introduced more than 80 years ago. Both models have tubular magazines, top ejection, and exposed hammers.

Lever-action rifles can be classified in several ways: by type of magazine, by type of ejection (top or side), by type of hammer (exposed or concealed), and type of stock. These variations will be discussed below.

Magazine type

1. *Tubular magazine beneath barrel.* The oldest (Volcanic, 1849) and the most popular type even today. All great Winchester lever-actions, except the nondetachable-box-magazine M95 and the recently discontinued detachable-box-magazine M88, have had tubular magazines.

The classic tubular magazine, either rifle or carbine, is the full-length magazine – that is, it is about the same length as the barrel. Magazines one-third, one-half, and two-thirds barrel length have never been as popular. This preference, obviously, is based on a desire for the greatest possible magazine capacity.

Carbine magazines for cartridges like the .38–40 Win. and the .44–40 Win. hold 13 cartridges, and rifle magazines (26-inch barrel) hold 16.

2. *Nondetachable box magazine.* The M95 Winchester is the only lever-action rifle with a nondetachable straight-line box magazine. Care has to be exercised in loading rimmed cartridges, or jams result. This was the first lever-action magazine to handle spitzer bullets. The .30–06 Springfield cartridge is usually considered a bolt-action or semiautomatic load, but the M95 was the first sporting rifle chambered for this round.

Both rimmed and rimless cartridges have to be singly loaded. There was one exception: the M95 chambered for the 7.62mm Russian cartridge had a charger clip slot like that of M1903 Springfield.

3. *Detachable box magazine.* The M88 Winchester (1955–74) was probably the first lever-action rifle to use this type of magazine. The rarely seen Sako Finnwulf uses it, and some current-production M99 Savage lever-actions are available with box-type magazines.

This is the quickest reloading method, and in states where only unloaded rifles may be carried in a car, speed in loading and unloading can be important. It has disadvantages, though: an overly hasty hunter may attempt to insert the magazine wrong end to, or the magazine may be improperly secured (catch not completely locked) and the magazine will fall out.

4. *Rotary magazine.* This type, to the author's knowledge, has been used only in the M99 Savage and its predecessor, the M96. It is easy to load, though not as fast as the detachable box magazine. It is practically jamproof.

5. *Tubular magazine in buttstock.* This type, used in the short-lived Spencer-action rifle and carbine, has not been made in many years.

Ejection type

1. *Top ejection.* This system has been used on all Winchester lever-actions save the short-lived M88. Not until the advent of the telescopic sight did top ejection become a disadvantage: scopes must be offset or set forward of the receiver. Nevertheless, the top-ejection lever-action M94 Winchester continues to sell better than all other action types.

2. *Side ejection.* Current-production Marlins, the M99 Savage, the M88 Winchester, and the Sako Finnwulf use side ejection, which creates no scope-mounting problems.

Hammer types

1. *Exposed hammer.* All Winchester lever-action centerfire rifles except the M88 have exposed hammers. This is by far the most popular type. An exposed hammer can slip and fall forward while the shooter is trying to thumb the hammer back into full-cock position, and it can also be accidentally cocked if caught on a branch or other object, but these mishaps rarely occur. Most lever-action users apparently feel safer because they can tell at a glance if the action is cocked or in the safety position (half-cock).

2. *Hammerless.* The Savage M96 and M99 were the first successful hammerless lever-action rifles. The Sako Finnwulf and Winchester M88 have concealed hammers. Some M99 Savages have a cocking indicator.

Stocks

1. *One-piece stock.* The one-piece stock provides greater rigidity, and thus, in theory, superior accuracy, but has been used only on the M88 Winchester and Sako Finnwulf lever-actions. Most lever riflemen do not need minute-of-angle accuracy for their relatively short-range shots.

2. *Two-piece stock.* Nearly all lever-action rifles have two-piece stocks. These are adequate for most tasks demanded of the lever action.

Other lever-action characteristics

Most lever-action users are once-a-year deer hunters. They want a very inexpensive rifle — that's one reason so many buy M94 carbines — and this means no frills like pistol grip and checkering. No lever-action, regardless of type or make, fitted with a pistol grip and with checkering has ever outsold a plain rifle or carbine. Winchester at one time offered such lever-action frills as fancy walnut, hand checkering, and set triggers. None of these features was popular for very long. Pistol grips on rifles or carbines chambered for big-bore cartridges — .40 caliber and up — do provide somewhat better control.

Most carbines — like the M94 — have 20-inch barrels. The traditional 26-inch rifle barrel ceased to be popular about the turn of the century. The 24-inch barrel also falls way below the 20-inch barrel in popularity, and even the 22-inch barrel is less popular. The lever-action today is mostly a brush-country firearm. During the heyday of the cowboy and Indian the rifle was popular because of its greater magazine capacity, and also because it had somewhat more velocity and thus a slightly flatter trajectory over the long ranges in open country.

EARLY HISTORY OF THE LEVER-ACTION

The great-granddaddy of the M73 Winchester (1873) was the tubular-magazine Volitional Repeater of 1849, which was soon renamed the Volcanic. The granddaddy was the Henry rifle (1860), designed by Vermont-trained designer and machinist Benjamin Tyler Henry. Confederates called the Henry "that damned Yankee rifle you load on Sunday and shoot all week." The immediate ancestor of the M73 was the improved Henry known as the M66 Winchester (1866). This was the first rifle to bear the Winchester name. It was named after financial backer Oliver P. Winchester, who switched from shirts to shooting irons.

Manufacture of the M66 Winchester was discontinued in 1898 after 170,101 had been made. It was chambered only for the .44 (Henry) Flat Rim Fire and the .44 (Henry) Pointed Rim Fire. These were interchangeable. The rifle and musket versions held 16 cartridges, the carbine 14. The Henry was not adopted by the U.S. Army during the Civil War, but several states purchased Henry rifles for their militia, and the Federal Government bought a small number which saw action in the Petersburg Campaign of 1864.

The M73 rifle and carbine were discontinued in 1919 after more than 720,000 had been manufactured. Rifles and carbines made up from parts on hand were sold until the final cleanup in 1924–25. The M73 was chambered for .32–20 Win. (1882), .38–40 Win. (1880), and .44–40 Win. (1873). A special version of the M73 was chambered for the .22 Short and later the .22 Long and .22 Long Rifle. Barrel lengths ranged from a 32-inch musket to a 14-inch carbine. Standard barrel length was 22 inches for the carbine and 26 inches for the rifle.

The popularity of the M73 created an immediate demand for a lever-action arm chambered for more powerful cartridges. Winchester responded with the M76 rifle and carbine. Chamberings included .45–75 Win. (1876), .50–95 Win. Express (1879), .45–60 Win. (1879) and .40–60 Win. (1884). The M76 carbine in .45–75 Win. was the official arm of the North West Mounted Police for many years. The M76 was discontinued in 1897 after 63,871 had been manufactured. The M76 was the last Winchester centerfire lever-action tubular-magazine rifle that was not designed by John Moses Browning.

The M76 did not meet the demand of riflemen who wanted a lever-action that would handle even more powerful cartridges. The .45 Government cartridges (.45–70–500 and .45–55–405) were widely distributed along the frontier and used in both infantry rifles and cavalry carbines.

Winchester purchased rights to John Moses Browning's and Matthew Browning's U.S. Patent 306,577 for a long-receiver lever-action. Winchester shop superintendent William S. Mason improved the original Browning feed mechanism (U.S. Patent 311,079). The M86 Winchester (1886) and its improved version the M71 (1937) were the strongest and smoothest-operating tubular-magazine lever-actions ever made.

The M86 was chambered for the .45–70 Gov't. (1886–1919, 1928–31), .45–90 Win. (1886–1919), .40–82 Win. (1894–1911), .40–65 Win. (1887–1911), .38–56 Win. (1887–1911), .50–110 Win. (1887–1911), .40–70 Win. (1894–1911), .50–100–450 Win. (1895–1911), and .33 Win. (1903–35).

This was a very popular rifle—popular not among deer hunters, but among riflemen like Theodore Roosevelt, who went up against big game that could strike back. The M86 remained in production until 1935, when it was about to be replaced by an "improved" version, the M71 (1936–57). This was chambered for .348 Win. only. More than 47,000 M71s and about 160,000 M86s were manufactured.

The M86 was the first lever-action to employ the Browning-designed vertical sliding locks. This feature made it possible for the action to handle long, powerful cartridges.

The next Winchester lever-action rifle—the second Winchester whose sales would exceed a million—was the M92 (1892). This action, a modified and scaled-down M86, was designed to replace the M73. It was chambered in 1892 for the .32–20 Win., .38–40 Win., and .44–40 Win. The .25–20 Win. cartridge, designed especially for the M92, was introduced in 1895. A very few M92 carbines were chambered for the .218 Win. Bee (1936–38).

The M92 rifle was discontinued in 1932 and the carbine in 1941. About 1,004,000 M92s were manufactured. This production figure includes about 25,000 M53s (1924–32) and about 5,700 M65s; both used the M92 action.

The M53 had a 6-shot magazine and 22-inch barrel and was chambered for .25–20 Win., .32–20 Win., and .44–40 Win. The M65, which succeeded the M53, had a 7-shot magazine and 22-inch barrel and was chambered for .25–20 Win. (1935), .32–20 Win. (1933), and .218 Bee (1939–47). Most M65s were made for the .218 Bee.

The M94 was followed in 1895 by Browning's M95 rifle with nondetachable box magazine. At the time of its initial release it was chambered only for roundnose or flatnose bullets—the spitzer (pointed) type was a decade away—but it was the first lever-action to handle spitzer bullets. In a tubular magazine, a pointed bullet theoretically could detonate the primer of the cartridge in front of it when jarred by recoil. The M95's box magazine avoided this problem.

M95 calibers included two black-powder cartridges, the .38–72 Win. and .40–72 Win. The most popular civilian caliber was the .30 U.S. Army (.30–40 Krag). Lever-action-oriented cowboys in Teddy Roosevelt's First Volunteer Cavalry (the Rough Riders) armed themselves with M95s in this caliber.

In 1915–16 Czar Nicholas' army purchased 293,816 M95s in caliber 7.62mm Russian (see Chapter 12). The U.S. Army purchased a few M95s (.30–40 Krag) for use in the Philippine Insurrection, but it is not known if these carbines reached the islands before the fight ended. noncompetitive with Winchester. But the Win-

The most famous M95 was the .405 Win. carried by T.R. on his African safari. This was his favorite "big bad medicine gun" for lion. The Roosevelt safari also carried a M86 Winchester (.45–70) and a M94 Winchester (.30–30 Win.). In addition, the battery included a Holland & Holland double rifle for use on elephant, Cape buffalo, and rhino and the first semi-sporterized M1903 Springfield.

Until the advent of the Charles Newton bolt-action .30–06 Springfield, just before World War I, the only regular sporting rifle available to the general public in caliber .30–06 was the M95. Stewart Edward White used a M95 on his African safari. He was also one of the first to have a custom-sporterized M1903 Springfield.

In the World War I era, an early *Outdoor Life* editor carried two M95s chambered for the .30–03 and .30–06 Springfield on a long and successful Yukon hunt.

The M95 was also chambered for the .303 British and .35 Win. The .30–03 cartridge was discontinued shortly after the appearance of its .30–06 successor. The M95 was the only lever-action rifle with a receiver long enough for the .30–06 and capable of handling that cartridge's 50,000 p.s.i. pressures. The M95 chambered for the .30–06 Springfield was discontinued early in the 1920s, because many shooters tried to load it with the 7.92mm German service cartridges, which were available through surplus outlets and also had been brought home by returning dough-

The Winchester 1873 Action

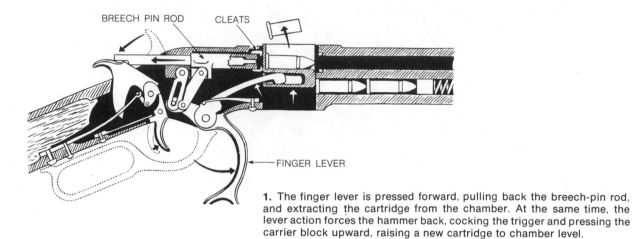

1. The finger lever is pressed forward, pulling back the breech-pin rod, and extracting the cartridge from the chamber. At the same time, the lever action forces the hammer back, cocking the trigger and pressing the carrier block upward, raising a new cartridge to chamber level.

2. Returning the lever to its original position sends the breech-pin rod forward, pushing the cartridge into the chamber and lowering the carrier block to receive a new cartridge.

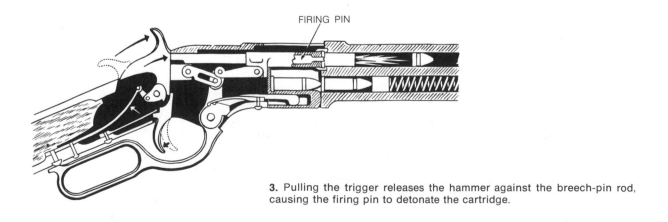

3. Pulling the trigger releases the hammer against the breech-pin rod, causing the firing pin to detonate the cartridge.

How A Modern Lever-Action Rifle Works *(Marlin Model 336)*

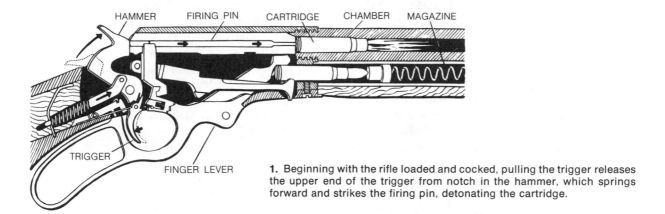

1. Beginning with the rifle loaded and cocked, pulling the trigger releases the upper end of the trigger from notch in the hammer, which springs forward and strikes the firing pin, detonating the cartridge.

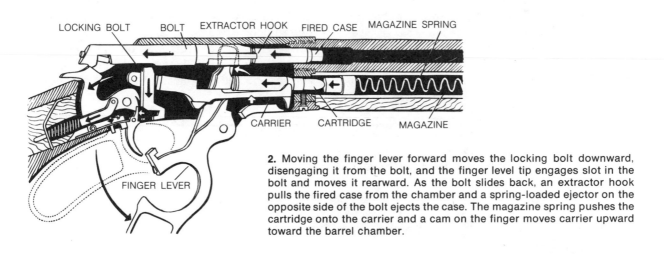

2. Moving the finger lever forward moves the locking bolt downward, disengaging it from the bolt, and the finger level tip engages slot in the bolt and moves it rearward. As the bolt slides back, an extractor hook pulls the fired case from the chamber and a spring-loaded ejector on the opposite side of the bolt ejects the case. The magazine spring pushes the cartridge onto the carrier and a cam on the finger moves carrier upward toward the barrel chamber.

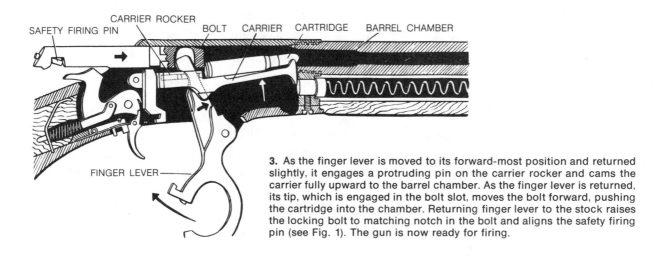

3. As the finger lever is moved to its forward-most position and returned slightly, it engages a protruding pin on the carrier rocker and cams the carrier fully upward to the barrel chamber. As the finger lever is returned, its tip, which is engaged in the bolt slot, moves the bolt forward, pushing the cartridge into the chamber. Returning finger lever to the stock raises the locking bolt to matching notch in the bolt and aligns the safety firing pin (see Fig. 1). The gun is now ready for firing.

boys. When the German cartridge was fired in the M95, or even in the 1903 Springfield, the action was nearly wrecked. Sixty years would pass between the appearance of the M95 and the next Winchester lever-action type, the M88 (1955).

There have been, of course, lever-action rifles other than Winchesters, but their total production, Spencer, Marlin, Stevens, Savage, and even Colt, has not exceeded the production of one Winchester—the M94.

The lever-action Spencer, with its tubular magazine in the buttstock, saw service during the Civil War. It, too, was sometimes praised as the gun that could be "loaded on Sunday and shot all week"—but in reality that would have meant shooting it only once a day as it held only 7 rounds. There was an understandable preference for the 16-shot Henry. Spencer sales declined swiftly after the war, and in 1869 the manufacturer went out of business.

During the Indian Wars, Colt marketed a lever-action rifle. Immediately after its public appearance Winchester announced that it was going into revolver production, and exhibited prototypes. Colt's Hartford boys got the message. They dropped the lever-action and substituted a slide-action—one of our first—which was noncompetitive with Winchester. But the Winchester lever-action was too firmly imbedded in the American tradition to be seriously threatened by a new and untried type of magazine rifle, and Colt soon withdrew the centerfire slide-action from production.

Marlin entered the lever-action field with a few top-ejection models, but these failed to achieve popularity. Marlin later developed a solid-top side-ejection model. Variations of the original model are still available. Despite the superiority of the side-ejection Marlin over the top-ejection Winchester for scope mounting, the M94 Winchester still remains almost supreme in terms of sales after more than 80 years of production.

Stevens and Bullard lever-actions never seriously challenged Marlin's sales.

The M99 Savage rotary-magazine (1899; more recently the M99 is available with detachable box magazine), is the only lever-action to challenge the sales of the M94 Winchester, and even the Savage is outsold by the M94 by more than two to one.

In 1976, Navy Arms was offering reproductions of the M66 Winchester lever-action rifle and carbine and a replica of the M73 Winchester rifle and carbine.

BROWNING LEVER RIFLE (BLR)

Manufacturer: Fabrique Nationale, Belgium

Importer/distributor: Browning Arms

Action type: lever; exposed hammer

Magazine type: detachable box

Magazine capacity: 4-shot

Safety: half-cock hammer (inertia firing pin)

Barrel length: 20.0 inches

Stock: 2-piece checkered walnut with oil finish; straight grip; forward barrel band

Buttplate: recoil pad

Overall length: 39.75 inches

Length of pull: 13.75 inches

Drop at comb: 1.75 inches

Drop at heel: 2.375 inches

Weight: 6.925 lbs.

Trigger pull: 4.0 lbs.

Sight, rear: modified Rocky Mountain (buckhorn), crudely adjustable for elevation

Sight, front: bead on ramp with removable sight protector

Scope adaptability: receiver drilled and tapped for standard scope bases

Caliber: .243 Win., .308 Win. (7.62mm NATO)

Data: This modern-design—despite exposed hammer—lever-action rifle might technically be considered a bolt-action, since it has a rotary bolt with multiple locking lugs. The designer was Val Browning. In addition to the half-cock hammer safety—typical of exposed-hammer arms—the BLR has an inertia firing pin. The pin doesn't rest on the cartridge primer when the firing pin is in the forward position. The pin in this position is retracted by a spring. It is perfectly safe for a hunter to carry this rifle with the firing pin in the forward position, rather than with the hammer at half-cock. Should the hunter accidentally strike the hammer a sharp blow, as by dropping the rifle on a rock, the firing pin will not move forward with force sufficient to ignite the primer. The trigger, housed in the lever, disconnects when the lever is operated.

Comment: This rifle should be chambered for a wider range of cartridges.

GARCIA-ROSSI LEVER-ACTION RIFLE

Manufacturer: Rossi Arms, Brazil

Importer/distributor: Garcia Corp.

Action type: lever; exposed hammer; top ejection

Magazine type: tubular; beneath barrel

Magazine capacity: 10-shot

Safety: half-cock hammer

Barrel length: 20.0 inches

Stock: 2-piece straight grip, uncheckered walnut; forward barrel band

Buttplate: rifle type

Overall length: 39.0 inches

Length of pull: 13.50 inches

Drop at comb: 2.0 inches

Drop at heel: 4.0 inches

Weight: 5.75 lbs.

Trigger pull: 5.0 lbs.

Sight, rear: Rocky Mountain (buckhorn), crudely adjustable for elevation

Sight, front: blade

Scope adaptability: not readily adaptable to scope

Caliber: .357 Magnum, .44 Magnum

Data: This carbine has a strong resemblance to the Winchester M92.

Comment: The author cannot see why anyone would select the .357 Magnum over the .44 Magnum for a carbine cartridge. The Marlin M94, in the same price range, is a better buy.

GARCIA-SAKO M73 FINNWULF LEVER-ACTION RIFLE

Manufacturer: Sako, Finland

Importer/distributor: Garcia Corp.

Action type: lever-actuated cams; side ejection; concealed hammer

Magazine type: detachable box

Magazine capacity: 4-shot

Safety: crossbolt in trigger guard

Barrel length: 23.0 inches

Stock: 1-piece walnut; hand-checkered; sling swivels; Monte Carlo comb; pistol grip

GARCIA-SAKO M73 FINNWULF RIFLE (continued)

Buttplate: rifle type; plastic

Overall length: 42.5 inches

Length of pull: 13.625 inches

Drop at comb: 1.5 inches

Drop at Monte Carlo: 1.5 inches

Drop at heel: 2.625 inches

Weight: 6.75 lbs.

Trigger pull: 4.5 lbs.

Sight, rear: none

Sight, front: bead on forged ramp with removable sight cover

Scope adaptability: dovetail blocks for tip-off mount

Caliber: .243 Win., .308 Win. (7.62mm NATO)

Data: This short-stroke lever-action rifle has an unusual action operated by gears. It is the only current lever-action with hand checkering.

Comment: This fine rifle is not popular on the American market. It costs more than twice as much as a Winchester M94. Most lever-action owners are economy-minded and prefer the less-expensive Winchester, Marlin or Savage lever-actions.

MARLIN M444 (1895) SPORTER REPEATING RIFLE

Action type: lever; exposed hammer; side ejection

Magazine type: tubular; beneath barrel

Magazine capacity: 4-shot

Safety: half-cock hammer

Barrel length: 22.0 inches

Stock: plain uncheckered American walnut; semi-pistol grip (composition cap with white spacer); fluted comb; fore-end with barrel band

Buttplate: shotgun type; ventilated recoil pad with white spacer

Sling: 1.5-inch leather carrying sling; forward sling swivel attached to barrel band

Overall length: 40.5 inches

Length of pull: 13.25 inches

Drop at comb: 1.75 inches

Drop at heel: 2.5 inches

Weight: 7.5 lbs.

Trigger pull: 5.0 lbs.

Sight, rear: Rocky Mountain (buckhorn) modified to fold down, crudely adjustable for elevation

Sight, front: bead

Scope adaptability: receiver top drilled and tapped for scope sight, and sandblasted to reduce sun glare when using open or receiver sight

Caliber: .444 Marlin in this updated version of M95, but straight-gripped M95 is chambered for .45–70 (.45 Gov't.)

Comment: This semi-pistol-grip version of the revived Marlin M95, a solid-frame lever-action originally designed by John Marlin, is adapted to the .444 Marlin cartridge, which is adequate for all but the heaviest North American game such as the polar bear and Alaskan brown bear.

MARLIN M336 (1893) SERIES—REPEATING RIFLES AND CARBINE

Action type: lever; exposed hammer; side ejection

Magazine type: tubular; beneath barrel

Magazine capacity: M336C-M336T, 6-shot (full); M336A, 5-shot

Safety: half-cock hammer

Barrel length: M336C and M336T Carbines, 20.0 inches, round; M336 Octagon, 22.0 inches, octagonal; M336A Rifle, 24.0 inches, round

Stock: M336C and M336A have semi-pistol grip with cap and plain uncheckered American walnut stock; M336C and M336T have blued steel forward barrel bands; M336A and M336 Octagon have blued steel fore-end tips; M336T and M336 Octagon have straight plain stocks and plain fore-ends of uncheckered American walnut

Buttplate: M336A, M336C, and M336T, modified rifle-shotgun type; M336 Octagon, hard rubber; other current M336s, composition with white spacers

Overall length: M336C and M336T, 38.50 inches; M336 Octagon, 40.50 inches; M336A, 42.50 inches

Length of pull: 13.25 inches

Drop at comb: 1.75 inches

Drop at heel: 2.5 inches

Weight: about 7.0 lbs. for all M336 variations

Trigger pull: 4.5 lbs.

Sight, rear: Rocky Mountain (buckhorn) modified to fold down, crudely adjustable for elevation

Sight, front: bead (not on ramp)

Scope adaptability: receiver top drilled and tapped for scope sight, and sandblasted to reduce sun glare when using open or receiver sight

Caliber: M336A and M336C; .30–30 Win., .35 Rem.; M336 Octagon and M336T; .30–30 Win.; discontinued calibers include .38–55 and .25–36 Marlin

Data: This is the oldest centerfire lever-action still in production. It was designed by John Marlin and introduced in 1893—the year before Winchester's famed M94. More than 2,000,000 have been manufactured. This Marlin is competitively priced with the M94, probably because of its high production rate.

Comment: Lever fanciers who want to use a .30–30 Win. cartridge in a tubular-magazine carbine would do well to select this side-ejecting model over the M94 if a scope is to be used.

MARLIN 1894 REPEATING RIFLE

Action type: lever; exposed hammer; side ejection

Magazine type: tubular; beneath barrel

Magazine capacity: octagon barrel, 10-shot; sporter barrel, 6-shot

Safety: half-cock hammer

MARLIN 1894 REPEATING RIFLE (continued)

Barrel length: octagon, 20.0 inches; sporter, 22.0 inches

Stock: plain uncheckered American walnut; straight grip

Buttplate: modified rifle-shotgun type; hard rubber with Marlin monogram

Overall length: octagon barrel, 37.5 inches; sporter barrel, 39.5 inches

Length of pull: 13.25 inches

Drop at comb: 1.625 inches

Drop at heel: 2.5 inches

Weight: octagon barrel, about 6.0 lbs.; sporter barrel, about 6.0 lbs.

Trigger pull: 4.5 lbs.

Sight, rear: Rocky Mountain (buckhorn) modified to fold down, crudely adjustable for elevation

Sight, front: bead (not on ramp)

Scope adaptability: receiver drilled and tapped for scope sight, and sandblasted to prevent or reduce glare when using open or receiver sight

Caliber: .44 Magnum (.44–40 Win. and .38–40 Win. discontinued)

Data: The M1894 short-action Marlin was John Marlin's answer to John Moses Browning's M92 Winchester. This is an excellent, well-designed rifle. Once discontinued, it was revived to handle the popular .44 Magnum handgun-rifle cartridge.

Comment: The large-caliber .44 Magnum cartridge is a much better deer killer than the .30–30 Win. at ranges not exceeding 75–100 yards.

MARLIN M94 REPEATING RIFLE

Action type: lever; exposed hammer; side ejection

Magazine type: tubular; beneath barrel

Magazine capacity: 4-shot

Safety: half-cock hammer

Barrel length: 22.0 inches; round

Stock: plain uncheckered American walnut; straight grip; blued steel fore-end tip

Buttplate: modified rifle-shotgun type with hard rubber plate bearing Marlin monogram

Overall length: 40.5 inches

Length of pull: 13.25 inches

Drop at comb: 1.625 inches

Drop at heel: 2.5 inches

Weight: 7.0 lbs.

Trigger pull: 5.0 lbs.

Sight, rear: folding Rocky Mountain (buckhorn), crudely adjustable for elevation

Sight, front: bead (not on ramp)

Scope adaptability: receiver top drilled and tapped for scope sight, and sandblasted to eliminate or reduce glare when using open or receiver sights

Caliber: .45–70 Gov't.

Data: One year before the .45–70 (.45 Gov't.) cartridge celebrated its 100th birthday, Marlin reintroduced its M95 for hunters who want a big-bore cartridge suitable for the largest North American timber-country game. (For .45–70 data see Chapter 11.)

Comment: Since rifles are no longer made for the .348 Win. or .358, the .45–70 — in selected handloads — is our most powerful short-range timber cartridge. This rifle and caliber make a first-rate hunting outfit for deer, black bear, and larger game such as elk. The 1895 Marlin with handloaded .45–70 cartridges using a 405-grain bullet is an excellent combination for very big North American game — up to and including the big Alaskan brown bears. Scope power should not exceed 2.5×.

MOSSBERG 472 SERIES LEVER-ACTION

Action type: lever; exposed hammer; side ejection

Magazine type: tubular; beneath barrel

Magazine capacity: carbine, 6-shot; rifle and brush gun, 5-shot

Safety: pistol-grip models have hammer block safety which prevents accidental discharge when hammer is cocked; straight-grip models have traditional half-cock hammer safety

Barrel length: carbine, 20.0 inches; rifle, 24.0 inches; brush gun, 18.0 inches

Stock: 2-piece American walnut; straight-grip and pistol-grip models available

Buttplate: straight-grip versions have rifle type; pistol-grip versions have shotgun type with recoil pad

Overall length: carbine, 38.5 inches; rifle, 42.5 inches; brush gun, 36.5 inches

Length of pull: 13.25 inches

Drop at comb: 1.75 inches

Drop at heel: 2.5 inches

Weight: 6.5–7.0 lbs.

Trigger pull: 4.5 lbs.

Saddle ring: standard feature on straight-grip versions

Sight, rear: Rocky Mountain (buckhorn), crudely adjustable for windage, elevation

Sight, front: gold bead on ramp; rifle has sight protector

Scope adaptability: receiver drilled and tapped for scope sight

Caliber: .30–30 Win., .35 Rem.

Data: This recent addition to the Mossberg line is a solid-frame lever-action that bears a strong resemblance to the side-ejection Marlins.

Comment: Like other side-ejection lever-actions, the Mossberg 472 series are well adapted for scope sights.

SAVAGE M99 HAMMERLESS LEVER-ACTION

Action type: lever; hammerless

Magazine type: rotary or detachable box (recently introduced)

Magazine capacity: rotary, 5-shot; detachable box, 4-shot

Safety: top tang (sliding); original type (discontinued) was right-side lever

Cutaway Views of Savage 99 Lever Action

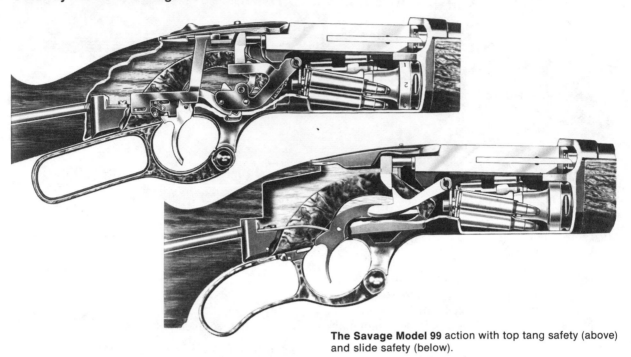

The Savage Model 99 action with top tang safety (above) and slide safety (below).

Safety features: all of today's M99s except 99C box-magazine and 99E rotary-magazine have a visible counter window showing the number of cartridges remaining; all models have a cocking indicator

Barrel length: current M99DL, M99C, M99F, 22.0 inches; current M99A, M99E, 20.0 inches; longer barrels (24.0 inches, 26.0 inches, 28.0-inch Military) have all been discontinued

Stock: 2-piece American walnut (except 99E, which has hardwood stained with walnut finish). All current models have pistol grip. Plastic grip caps on all models except 99E. Earliest M99s had no checkering, but Grade A hand checkering cost $5 and Grade B hand checkering cost $8. In later years, machine checkering was substituted. Today's checkering is the "impressed" or "reverse" type, which provides no grip in humid or rainy weather, and lacks the handsome appearance of hand checkering. Most American manufacturers (Ruger is an exception) have been forced by rising costs to use impressed checkering.

Buttplate: shotgun type; plastic. (Original buttplates were rifle type of uncorrugated steel; only the 22-inch round-barrel rifle was regularly fitted with a steel shotgun-type buttplate. The author remembers seeing M99 buttplates of the shotgun type in the 1930s. Factory records do not indicate when the shotgun type became standard.)

Overall length: 22.0-inch-barrel models (99DL, 99C, 99F), 41.75 inches; 20.0-inch-barrel models (99A, 99E), 39.75 inches

Stock dimensions (except 99DL)

Length of pull: 13.5 inches

Drop at comb: 1.5 inches

Drop at heel: 2.5 inches

Stock dimensions (99DL)

Length of pull: 13.5 inches

Drop at Monte Carlo: 1.5 inches

Drop at comb: 1.5 inches

Drop at heel: 2.5 inches

Weight: 22.0-inch barrel, 7.25 lbs.; 20.0-inch barrel, 7.0 lbs.; discontinued longer-barreled models, up to 8.75 lbs.

Trigger pull: 5.0 lbs.

Sight, rear: folding leaf on all current versions except 99E, which uses a modified Rocky Mountain (buckhorn)

Sight, front: bead on ramp with removable sight cover on current versions

Scope adaptability: all current production M99s drilled and tapped for standard scope sights

Caliber: .243 Win., .250–3000 (.250 Savage), .300 Savage, .308 Win. (7.62mm NATO); discontinued chamberings include .22 Hi-Power (IMP), .284 Win., .30–30 Win., .303 Savage, .32–40, .358 Win.

Data: More than 1,000,000 have been made; this was the first successful hammerless lever-action. It was designed by Arthur Savage, originally for rimmed cartridges like the .303 Savage and the look-alike-shoot-alike .30–30 Win.; a successful transition was made to rimless rounds like the .250–3000 Savage and the .243 Win.

The first M99 the author ever saw was a .300 Savage in the takedown version, which has long been discontinued. A .410 (2.5-inch case) barrel could be fitted into the frame when the .300 barrel was removed. The .410 was single-shot only.

The M99 ushered three notable cartridges onto the American hunting scene: the .22 Savage Hi-Power, which was the first high-velocity .22 centerfire; the .250–3000 Savage, our first high-velocity .25; and the .300 Savage, the first high-velocity short-case .30. The first two cartridges were designed by high-velocity pioneer Charles Newton. Both the .250 and the .300 have been with us for more than half a century.

M99 shooters are protected by a thick piece of steel that lies between them and the cartridge head.

There have been numerous variations of butt-stocks and fore-ends in the past 75 years.

Comment: This is one of the finest lever-actions extant. It was the first, and for more than 50 years the only, lever-action capable of handling cartridges with breech pressures approaching 50,000 p.s.i. The .250–3000 and the .300 Savage calibers have long been popular with Western riflemen for their saddle guns. With the advent of the .243 Winchester, Savage dropped (in about 1960) the .250–3000 Savage from the M99 line. The caliber was restored in 1970, and continues to be in demand.

WINCHESTER M94 REPEATING CARBINE

Action type: lever; exposed hammer; top ejection

Magazine capacity: all calibers except discontinued .44 Magnum (which held 10 shots): full, 6-shot; one-half, 3-shot; two-thirds, 4-shot

Safety: half-cock hammer

Barrel length: 20.0 inches; round only. Sole known exception was octagonal barrel of Winchester '66 Centennial Carbine (1966 only). Barrel lengths shorter than 20 inches were available on special order until about 1924.

Trigger pull: 5.0 lbs.

Saddle ring: 1895–1925; revived and brass-plated in 1966 for '66 Centennial Carbine and Antique Model M94; saddle ring has since been used on other M94 commemorative editions

Stock: 2-piece (buttstock and fore-end); plain uncheckered American walnut; straight grip. Some M94 stocks were reportedly made in the mid-1960s of a light-colored hardwood other than walnut, an economy move later discontinued.

Buttplate: 1937 to date, shotgun-type; hard rubber or plastic. Rifle type (1894–1937) was metal at first, later changed to hard rubber. Shortly after the M94's introduction

WINCHESTER M94 REPEATING CARBINE (continued)

shotgun-type buttplates were available on special order.

Overall length: 37.75 inches (M94 carbines with rifle-type buttplate average 38.5 inches)

Length of pull: 13.0 inches

Drop at comb: 1.75 inches

Drop at heel: 2.5 inches

Following dimensions for pre-1937 and Winchester '66 Centennial carbines with rifle-type buttplate

Length of pull: 13.125 inches

Drop at comb: 2.0 inches

Drop at heel: 2.75 inches

Weight: 5.75–6.5 lbs. ('66 Centennial Carbine with full octagon barrel weighs about 7.0 lbs.)

Trigger pull: 5.0 lbs.

Sight, rear: Rocky Mountain (buckhorn), crudely adjustable for elevation

Sight, front: Bead on ramp; sight (cover) removable protector added 1931

Scope adaptability: top ejection precludes normal scope mounting, and M94's greatest popularity is for deer hunting in brush and timber where shots are usually over short ranges; however, long-eye-relief scopes are available for special mounting forward of ejection port

Caliber: .30 Win. (.30–30, 1895 to date), .25–35 Win. (1895–1936, 1940–50), .32 Win. Special (1902–73), .32–40 (1894–1924), .38–55 (1894–1924), .44 Magnum (1970–71); manufacture of .32–40 and .38–55 barrels was reportedly discontinued in 1924 but carbines in these calibers were sold until about 1936, when the barrel supply was exhausted

Data: Winchester Repeating Arms Company had by 1893 two excellent lever-action carbine/rifles. These were the long-action M86 for powerful cartridges like the .45 Gov't. (.45–70) and the short-action M92 for the .44–40 Win. and .38–40 Win. John Moses Browning designed both actions.

In 1893 Browning offered Winchester what he called the M93 medium-length action for cartridges like the popular black-powder .38–55. Sometime in the next few months Winchester decided to develop two cartridges specifically designed for smokeless powder: .25–35 Win. and .30 Win. (.30–30). Both new cartridges were necked-down .38–55 cases. Meanwhile, Browning's new action became the M94. On August 21, 1894, it was assigned Patent No. 542,702.

The M94 (carbine and rifle) was the first American sporting magazine rifle chambered for smokeless cartridges. (The Winchester M85, also designed by John Moses Browning, was chambered for the smokeless .30–40 Krag, but it was a single-shot rifle.)

Production and/or design difficulties delayed M94 manufacture for the two smokeless cartridges until August, 1895. The first M94s, chambered for the .32–40 and .38–55, appeared on the market in late 1894.

The .32 Winchester Special M94—first marketed in 1902—originally had a special front sight. The rifle was designed to be first fired with Winchester factory ammunition and then with black-powder reloads. At a later date, unknown, a standard front sight was fitted.

The serial numbers on the M94 and its close relatives are located on the underside of the receiver. The numbers reportedly began with 1. Their range includes M94 carbines and rifles (except the specially numbered commemoratives) plus 20,580 M55s (except the first 2,870) and all M64s and M64As.

Comment: The M94 Carbine is the most popular sporting arm ever manufactured. This includes rifles, carbines, handguns, and shotguns. At least 3,000,000—probably more—of the 3,500,000 M94s made were carbines. At this writing (1975) nearly 4,000,000 have been manufactured, and unless Americans are deprived of their Constitutional and traditional right to own firearms, we may well see the M94's centennial with possible production approaching 6,000,000. Production and sales are increasing. It took 33 years to sell the first million but only 10 years to sell the last million.

The 1,000,000th M94 was presented to President Calvin Coolidge in 1927. Carbine number 1,500,000 was presented to President Harry S. Truman in 1948. Five years later, President Dwight David Eisenhower was presented with the 2,000,000th M94. The Carbine number 2,500,000 was produced in 1961, and number 3,500,000 in the mid-1970s.

CHAPTER 3

SLIDE-ACTION CENTERFIRE RIFLES

The slide action (also called "pump" or "trombone") is the fastest of the three manually operated types of magazine-rifle actions. It is about as fast as the semiautomatic action; in the fraction of a second it takes for the semiautomatic's barrel to return from its recoil position, the slide action can be operated. Yet the slide action is the least popular rifle action (though it is the most popular shotgun action).

Caliber .22 rimfire slide-action rifles were common for 70-odd years. Except for a few experimentals—a Colt of a century ago and a current Savage .30–30—the one name in slide-action centerfire rifles has always been Remington.

Danish-born John Douglas Pedersen, a long-time Wyoming resident, was the genius responsible for Remington rimfire and centerfire slide-action rifles as well as for the Remington M51 semiautomatic pistol (1918–34) and the "Pedersen device" of World War I fame. He also designed several semiautomatic rifles during the 1920s which, despite excellent possibilities, were edged out by the M1 Garand. It was cheaper, thought some authorities, to adopt the design of a Springfield Armory salaried employee (he got $3,500 annually) than to pay royalties to an outside designer, and a foreigner at that.

The Remington M14 was manufactured (1912–35) in .25 Rem., .30 Rem., .32 Rem. and .35 Rem. The barrel was 22.0 inches long, and the stock was available with or without a pistol grip. The M14R (1912–34) had an 18.50-inch barrel and a straight-grip stock.

The Remington M14½ (1912–25) had a 22.0-inch barrel and was chambered for the .38–40 Win. and the .44–40 Win. The M14½R (1912–25) was a carbine version of the M14½.

The .25 Rem. was a rimless .25–35 Win. The .30 Rem. is a rimless .30–30 Win. The .32 Rem. is a rimless .32 Win. Special. These cartridges and the original .35 Rem. were designed for the semiautomatic Remington M8 (Woodsmaster).

Remington officially discontinued the M14 and M14½ on December 31, 1935. On the following day the company announced the "improved" M141 and M141½. These were available in .30 Rem., .32 Rem., and .35 Rem., had a barrel length of 24.0 inches, and had a pistol grip. They were discontinued in 1950.

Two years later, Remington brought out the M760, the first slide-action designed for .30–06-length cartridges and capable of handling pressures in the 50,000 p.s.i. class.

REMINGTON M760 GAMEMASTER

Action type: slide; concealed hammer

Magazine type: detachable box

Magazine capacity: 4-shot

Safety: crossbolt on right (or left in lefthand versions, available in .270 Win., .30–06 Springfield, and .308 Win.)

EXPLODED VIEW OF SAVAGE M170 AND SPRINGFIELD M174 SLIDE-ACTION RIFLES

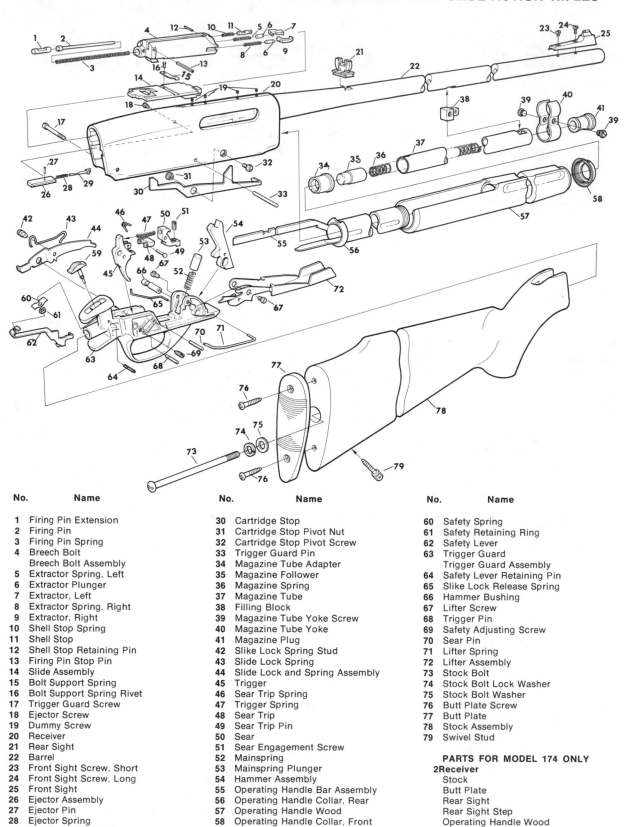

No.	Name	No.	Name	No.	Name
1	Firing Pin Extension	30	Cartridge Stop	60	Safety Spring
2	Firing Pin	31	Cartridge Stop Pivot Nut	61	Safety Retaining Ring
3	Firing Pin Spring	32	Cartridge Stop Pivot Screw	62	Safety Lever
4	Breech Bolt	33	Trigger Guard Pin	63	Trigger Guard
	Breech Bolt Assembly	34	Magazine Tube Adapter		Trigger Guard Assembly
5	Extractor Spring, Left	35	Magazine Follower	64	Safety Lever Retaining Pin
6	Extractor Plunger	36	Magazine Spring	65	Slike Lock Release Spring
7	Extractor, Left	37	Magazine Tube	66	Hammer Bushing
8	Extractor Spring, Right	38	Filling Block	67	Lifter Screw
9	Extractor, Right	39	Magazine Tube Yoke Screw	68	Trigger Pin
10	Shell Stop Spring	40	Magazine Tube Yoke	69	Safety Adjusting Screw
11	Shell Stop	41	Magazine Plug	70	Sear Pin
12	Shell Stop Retaining Pin	42	Slike Lock Spring Stud	71	Lifter Spring
13	Firing Pin Stop Pin	43	Slide Lock Spring	72	Lifter Assembly
14	Slide Assembly	44	Slide Lock and Spring Assembly	73	Stock Bolt
15	Bolt Support Spring	45	Trigger	74	Stock Bolt Lock Washer
16	Bolt Support Spring Rivet	46	Sear Trip Spring	75	Stock Bolt Washer
17	Trigger Guard Screw	47	Trigger Spring	76	Butt Plate Screw
18	Ejector Screw	48	Sear Trip	77	Butt Plate
19	Dummy Screw	49	Sear Trip Pin	78	Stock Assembly
20	Receiver	50	Sear	79	Swivel Stud
21	Rear Sight	51	Sear Engagement Screw		
22	Barrel	52	Mainspring		**PARTS FOR MODEL 174 ONLY**
23	Front Sight Screw, Short	53	Mainspring Plunger	**2**	**Receiver**
24	Front Sight Screw, Long	54	Hammer Assembly		Stock
25	Front Sight	55	Operating Handle Bar Assembly		Butt Plate
26	Ejector Assembly	56	Operating Handle Collar, Rear		Rear Sight
27	Ejector Pin	57	Operating Handle Wood		Rear Sight Step
28	Ejector Spring	58	Operating Handle Collar, Front		Operating Handle Wood
29	Ejector Plunger	59	Safety		

REMINGTON M760 GAMEMASTER (continued)

Barrel length: Carbine, 18.5 inches (chambered for .30–06 Springfield and .308 Win. only); rifle, 22.0 inches

Stock: 2-piece impressed checkered American walnut; pistol grip with white line spacer and plastic cap

Buttplate: rifle type; plastic with white spacer

Overall length: 18.5-inch barrel, 38.5 inches; 22.0-inch barrel, 42.0 inches

Length of pull: 13.25 inches

Drop at comb: 1.625 inches

Drop at heel: 2.125 inches

Weight: rifle, 7.5 lbs.; carbine, 6.75 lbs.

Sight, rear: modified Rocky Mountain (buckhorn), crudely adjustable for windage and elevation

Sight, front: flat-faced gold bead on ramp

Scope adaptability: receiver tapped and drilled for standard scope bases

Caliber: .222 Rem., .243 Win., .270 Win., .30–06 Springfield, .308 Win. (7.62mm NATO), 6mm Rem.; discontinued chamberings include .244 Rem., .257 Roberts, .280 Rem., .300 Savage; .35 Rem.

Data: This model replaced the tubular-magazine M141 and M141½.

Comment: The M760, as of 1975, was the first and only slide-action rifle chambered for cartridges in the .30–06 Springfield class. It is a very well-made rifle. It is the only box-magazine slide-action centerfire rifle.

The designation "Gamemaster" was also used for the M141 and M141½.

SAVAGE M170 PUMP-ACTION

Action type: slide; concealed hammer

Magazine type: tubular

Magazine capacity: 3-shot

Safety: top tang; slide

Barrel length: 22.0 inches

Stock: 2-piece impressed checkered American walnut; pistol grip with no cap; fluted foreend

Buttplate: shotgun type; plastic

Overall length: 41.5 inches

Length of pull: 13.5 inches

Drop at comb: 1.5 inches

Drop at Monte Carlo: 1.5 inches

Drop at heel: 2.5 inches

Weight: 6.75 lbs.

Sight, rear: folding leaf

Sight, front: gold bead on removable ramp

Scope adaptability: receiver drilled and tapped for standard scope bases

Caliber: .30–30 Win.

Data: This is the only currently available slide-action centerfire rifle with a tubular magazine, and the only slide-action rifle chambered for the .30–30 Win.

CHAPTER 4

SEMIAUTOMATIC CENTERFIRE RIFLES

The most recently introduced sporting-rifle action type has passed its 75-year mark. This is the semiautomatic. John Moses Browning patented his recoil-operated sporting-rifle action in 1900. It was the same basic action used in his popular autoloading shotgun. The gas-operated semiautomatic action, currently the standard type for semiautomatic sporting and military rifles, had been adapted to machine guns some years earlier.

For sporting rifles the semiautomatic action ranks third in popularity behind the lever action and bolt action. The lever action predominated from its Civil War inception through World War II. Since then the bolt action has been in the ascendancy.

Between 1905 and 1950 there were only two American-made semiautomatic rifles, a Remington and a Winchester. First came the Browning designed Remington M08 (1906–36) and its successor the M81 Woodsmaster (1936–50). The M81 was identical to the M8 except for an improved stock. This was a recoil-operated rifle. The Winchester M05 series was the second.

Though Browning patented his long-recoil action in 1900, the rifle was not manufactured until 1906. Winchester designer Thomas Crossley Johnson, who had a hard act to follow when Browning severed his Winchester connection, designed the Winchester M05 Self-Loading Rifle. Two other versions, the M07 and M10, followed. They were virtually identical to the M05 except in caliber; all three were blowback-operated.

Before delving further into the development of semiautomatic sporting rifles, let's define the crucial terms "semiautomatic," "automatic," and "selective-fire."

1. *Semiautomatic*. This designates a rifle, pistol, or shotgun which fires one shot when the trigger is depressed; the trigger must be released and then depressed again to fire another shot.

Manufacturers and frequently users often miscall the semiautomatic action "automatic," or "auto" for short. There is a difference between "semiautomatic" and "automatic."

2. *Automatic*. This designates a rifle, pistol, shotgun, machine gun, submachine gun, or light machine rifle which continues to fire as long as the trigger is depressed. Firing stops when the trigger is released. Except with heavy and light machine guns, firing is usually done in "bursts" of 3-5 shots. Sustained firing of a fully automatic weapon that is not mounted on a tripod, bipod, or monopod causes the barrel to rise, thus causing misses on the target.

3. *Selective-fire*. Some weapons, classified as "capable of full automatic fire," have selector switches so the firer can select semi- or full automatic fire. Most shoulder arms — including submachine guns, which are often fired from the hip — are more effective when fired "semiauto" or in short bursts.

Laws regarding automatic and semiautomatic weapons

Discussion of full automatic weapons is largely academic, because U.S. residents, except for military and police on duty, are effectively prohibited from owning or using full automatic weapons.

It is possible for a U.S. resident — under federal law — to possess and use full automatic weapons provided he pays the Bureau of Alcohol, Tobacco and Firearms (an IRS unit) a $200 transfer fee. The fee is paid by the purchaser (in addition to purchase price). The purchaser must be fingerprinted. His character is checked by FBI and BATF agents. Some states outlaw automatic weapons. A potential purchaser may comply with BATF regulations — i.e. pay transfer tax — and have an "acceptable character," but ownership could still be outlawed by state statute. Jail plus a multi-thousand-dollar fine are potential penalties that can be invoked against violation of the "full automatic weapons" law.

Selective-fire weapons are subject to the same restrictions as full automatic arms. Furthermore, any arm designed as a semiautomatic weapon is illegal if it can be readily converted to full automatic fire.

Obviously, the truly automatic weapons are designed for military and police use. Anyone interested in guns and their mechanisms can get a lot of pleasure out of informal target shooting with the full automatics, but they are not sporting arms in the normal sense, and certainly they have no place in hunting. Since this book is devoted to sporting arms, data will be listed for semiautomatics but not for full automatics.

Commercially available semiautomatic military rifles include the Colt AR-15 (semiautomatic version of the full-automatic M16) and the semiautomatic versions of the German-made Heckler & Koch and Swiss-made SIG. These are legal because they have been modified so that they cannot be readily converted to full automatic fire.

Most semi- or full-automatic military rifles have at least a 20-shot detachable magazine (the M16 has a 30-shot magazine), but state laws often limit semiautomatic magazine capacity to 5 shots. Manufacturers usually meet this challenge in two ways: a special 5-shot magazine, or a magazine filler block that reduces capacity to 5 shots.

Though state laws usually limit semiautomatic magazines for hunting, there is rarely a restriction on target shooting or plinking. If manufacturers sell only 5-shot magazines for military-design semiautomatics, those who wish a greater capacity can purchase surplus military magazines.

Canadians can own and shoot full automatic weapons. Canadian owners of full automatic weapons just register them at their local police station. A Canadian friend of the author owns Thompson submachine guns, a BAR, a Lewis light machine gun, and several other light and heavy machine guns. The author occasionally visits his friend for a real *schutzenfest*.

Early problems of the semiauto

Semiautomatic Remingtons and Winchesters did not become popular for several reasons. For one thing, most hunters until after World War II (with some exceptions in the plains states) were firmly wedded to the lever action. And with one brief unsuccessful exception, the .300 Savage, cartridges chambered in these semiautomatic rifles were strictly short-range. The .32 Win. S.L.R., .35 Win. S.L.R., and .351 Win. S.L.R. were barely adequate for deer at ranges exceeding 75 yards. The .401 Win. S.L.R. cartridge was a good whitetail and black-bear killer at 100–125 yards.

Remington M8 and M81 cartridges—.25 Rem. (rimless .25–35 Win.), .30 Rem. (rimless .30–30 Win.), .32 Rem. (rimless .32 Win. Special) and the .35 Rem.—were also brush cartridges for deer and bear. The M81 was briefly chambered for the .300 Savage. The cartridge generated a high breech pressure and malfunctions occurred, so this fine cartridge was dropped from the M81 list.

Winchester's blowback action had severe limitations. The weight of the breechbolt has direct relationship to the pressure generated by the cartridge. To chamber a .30–06 in a blowback action would require a breechbolt weighing 27 lbs. The double-barrel 4-bore elephant rifles of black-powder days were caliber 1.052, used 14 drams of propellant behind a 1882-grain projectile and generated 158.4 lbs. of recoil—and weighed only 24 lbs. That included lock, stock, and barrel!

While the long-recoil action of the Remington M8 and M81 series could use somewhat more effective cartridges than Winchester's blowback, there were disadvantages. The barrel recoiling inside an outer sleeve (some folks thought the M8 and M81 could be used as a shotgun by removing the rifle barrel) made minute-of-angle accuracy impossible. The Remington was cumbersome and heavy. Time lapse between shots was a fraction of a second less with the semiauto than with the lever action, but the time required to pull the barrel down from recoil made the time difference between *aimed* shots with a semiautomatic and with a lever-action virtually nonexistent.

Weight was another factor. The light, handy, 20-inch-barrel Winchester M94 carbine weighs about 6.5 lbs. The M8 and M81 weighed 8.0 lbs. Why use a heavier, bulkier, longer-barreled rifle for a rimless .30–30 Win. when the handier, reliable M94 was available in .30–30 Win., and at considerably less cost?

In the late 1930s the Remington M81 in standard (cheapest) grade was $69.95. The Winchester M94 sold for $30 or less. The author remembers several mid-Depression sales of new M94s for $19.95. Dealers could slash M94 prices because of sales volume. The M81 price was rarely slashed, but even on these occasions it still cost more than twice as much as the M94.

Western and Canadian hunters pursuing elk, grizzly, or moose could find no reliable killer cartridge among the semiautomatics.

Lever-action buffs had suitable calibers ranging from .33 Win. to "Big Fifty" Winchesters (these calibers were discontinued in the M86 Winchester but secondhand rifles were available and Winchester made ammunition up to World War II).

Lever-action devotees stalking antelope, caribou, and sheep had the .30–06 in the M95 Winchester, the .250–3000 and .300 in the M99 Savage.

The lever-action was (as it still is) primarily the rifle of the man who hunted in his own bailiwick. The few hunters — mostly well-to-do Easterners — who traveled a fair piece to hunt sheep, elk, grizzly, caribou, and moose toted bolt-action rifles. It was not until after World War II that the average American could afford such hunts.

Thus semiautomatic sales were restricted by cartridge limitations, weight, accuracy, price, and sometimes handiness.

Winchester M05, M07, and M10 series

These rifles weighed 7.5–7.75 lbs. Barrel length was 22.0 inches except in the .351 W. S. L. R. (20.0 inches). A 5-shot detachable box magazine was standard. In October 1911, detachable 10-shot box magazines became optional as an extra-cost item. It has been reported that some manufacturer, not Winchester, made 20-shot .351 W.S.L.R. magazines available (supposedly for use with the 1907 Police Model); the author has never seen one.

Though the M10 in .401 W.S.L.R. caliber only was the most effective combination, the M07 in caliber .351 W.S.L.R. was the most popular. Several thousand M07s were purchased by the French Air Force during World War I. These rifles were used by pilots and observers, in the days before aerial machine guns, to potshot enemy pilots and observers. The .351 was popular with police, if only because it was a short, handy semiautomatic with extra-capacity magazine.

The M05 was discontinued in 1920 after about 29,000 had been made. The M07 was discontinued in 1936. About 20,775 were sold. The M10 was discontinued in 1957. About 58,000 were made. The M07 was replaced (1960) by the Winchester gas-operated M100.

Remington M8 and M81 series

The M8 was available with straight stock or pistol grip. The nondetachable box magazine had a 5-shot capacity. The barrel length was 23.0 inches.

The M8 was replaced by the M81 Woodmaster. The walnut stock has a pistol grip, and the M8's splinter fore-end was replaced with a semi-beavertail type. In addition to the M8 and M81 rifles made in America by Remington, the M8 was also manufactured in Belgium (1910–1931) by Fabrique Nationale under the name "Browning Hi-Power Rifle." It was made in metric-designated calibers comparable in power to their American counterparts. Remington agreed not to sell the M8 in Europe, and FN agreed not to sell its version in America.

Total production figures for either model are not available, but the Remington/Browning was far more popular than the Winchesters.

The M8 was the first semi-automatic sporter with a locked breech. This feature allowed the action to be chambered for more powerful cartridges than the straight (unlocked-breech) blowback Winchesters.

Remington M740 series

Five years after Remington discontinued the M81 (1950), it introduced the Model 740 Woodsmaster gas-operated semiauto sporting rifle. This was the first semiautomatic sporting rifle to handle cartridges of .30–06 length and pressure. It was later replaced by the improved Model 742, which handles cartridge lengths from .223 Rem. through .30–06.

OTHER SEMIAUTO DESIGNS

Between the advent of the long-recoil-operated Remington/Browning and its contemporary Winchesters and today's gas-operated semiautomatic sporting rifles were a series of semiautomatic designs. Some were — and are — civilian semiautomatic versions of military rifles. Some were experimentals.

Johnson semiauto rifles

In 1936 a Boston attorney, Capt. Melvin Johnson, U.S.M.C. (Res.), designed a caliber .30–06 short-recoil semiautomatic rifle with a 10-shot rotary magazine. It featured a quick (30-second) barrel change. Barrels of different calibers — provided they had .30–06 Springfield head size — could be interchanged. The rifle was reliable, accurate, and easier and cheaper to make than the M1 (Garand), which was the gas-operated semiautomatic rifle adopted in 1936 by the U.S. Army.

Johnson designed his rifle so that many of its parts could be manufactured by machine shops on standard lathes and presses. The rotary magazine was stamped metal. Conventional military men, including Ordnance folk, disliked stamped and punch-press components. Germany was rearming its troops, and many successful *Abwher* weapons like its machine guns and Schmeisser machine pistol were made by methods similar to Johnson's. He was way ahead of the U.S. military mind. But the services had already adopted the M1, and the Johnson was rejected.

The Marine Corps, however, purchased thousands of Johnson rifles and Johnson M1941 light machine guns. Johnsons were used by Army Ranger units. The Dutch adopted the Johnson rifle and the light machine gun.

It was easy for Johnson to make Dutch rifles. Rifle components were identical to the .30–06 version. Only the 7×57mm barrels were different; these were made for Johnson on contract.

The Dutch were good volume customers, but in 1940 the Nazis overran the Netherlands, and in 1942 the Holland Pacific Island Empire was overrun by the Japanese.

After the war, thousands of Johnson/Dutch rifles were returned to the United States and sold as surplus. Some Johnsons were sold with 7mm barrels and stocks. Others fitted with .30–06 or .270 Win. barrels of commercial manufacture. Some rifles had "sporterized" stocks.

A major advantage of the Johnson over the M1 was in the magazine system. The M1 uses an *en bloc* magazine. It holds seven cartridges. When the last shot is fired the magazine is ejected from the rifle. Many times loose ammunition—usually in boxes for the M1917 Browning heavy machine gun or the M1919 Browning light machine gun—was available. Unless empty M1 clips were available the rifle had to be single-loaded; thus the firing rate was no greater than Custer's troopers could achieve at the Little Big Horn in 1876. Ejected M1 clips cannot always be salvaged. Frequently they are dented or battered beyond use after striking a rock or other object. It is almost impossible to locate them at night.

The Johnson rifle can be loaded with 10 single cartridges or by using two 5-shot Springfield stripper clips or with 5 single rounds and one stripper clip.

In 1945–47 the author was informally associated with Johnson through a mutual friend, the late Charles T. Haven, military arms authority. He fired more than a quarter-million cartridges through Johnson semiautomatic rifles and M1941 and M1944 Johnson light machine guns. Few problems were encountered. Among rifles suitable for civilian use, the Johnson is the only one known to the author using the short-recoil system.

Johnson's competitors' assertion that the short-recoiling barrel would not function with its bayonet in position was not true. The Johnson functioned equally well with service ammunition—M1(172 grains), M2(152 grains), and armor-piercing, incendiary, and grenade-launching cartridges—and with sporting cartridges.

Developments in military arms

During the 1920s, Canadian John Garand, a hired hand at Springfield Armory, designed an experimental rifle. The cartridge primer moved rearward out of the case to actuate the semiautomatic action. The project was dropped as unfeasible.

In 1915, Comdr. Blish, U.S.N. (Ret.), received U.S. Patent 1,131,319 for a "delayed blowback" action. Thompson submachine guns M1921, M1928 and M1928A1 used a brass H-block, sometimes called a Blish adhesion block. It was discovered that the arm functioned as effectively without the block as with it. The Thompson without the block was easier, cheaper, and quicker to manufacture. World War II Thompsons without Blish's block were the M1 and M1A1 Thompsons.

During the 1920s a Thompson Autorifle (*sic*) using the Blish principle was tested at Springfield Armory. The Garand semiautomatic rifle was selected over all comers, including the John D. Federsen retarded-blowback rifle.

In 1941 the U.S. Army adopted the Winchester carbine, later known as "U.S. Carbine, Caliber .30M1." Several million were made. This carbine utilized the short-stroke piston as designed by ex-convict David "Carbine" Williams, one of this nation's great arms designers. This method eliminated the necessity for a long operating rod like that of the Garand. The first major U.S. use of gas-operated (long-stroke) action was the M1917 Browning Automatic Rifle (BAR), the basic automatic Squad weapon in two world wars and Korea.

M1 Garand. The U.S. Army, after more than a dozen years of experimentation, adopted John Garand's M1 rifle in 1936. Garand designed not only the M1 but also jigs and dies necessary to

How A Modern Pump-Action Rifle Works *(Remington Model 760)*

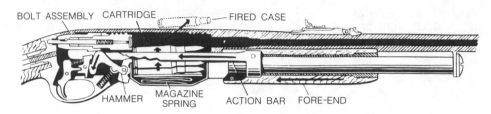

BOLT ASSEMBLY CARTRIDGE   FIRED CASE

HAMMER MAGAZINE ACTION BAR FORE-END
        SPRING

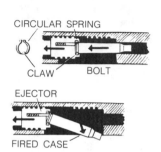

CIRCULAR SPRING

CLAW   BOLT

EJECTOR

FIRED CASE

1. Moving the fore-end rearward pushes back the action bar and the bolt assembly, which in turn moves the hammer downward and ejects the empty case. Ejection is accomplished by a circular spring in the end of the bolt (see detail, showing top view) with a claw which hooks under rim of the cartridge and pulls it out of the chamber. When the case clears the chamber, the ejector spring in the bolt flips the case out. Then the magazine spring moves a new cartridge upward.

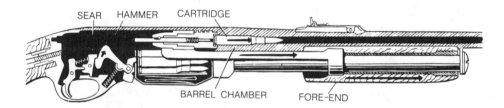

SEAR   HAMMER   CARTRIDGE

BARREL CHAMBER   FORE-END

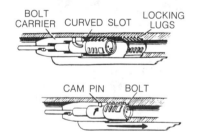

BOLT   LOCKING
CARRIER CURVED SLOT LUGS

CAM PIN   BOLT

2. Moving the fore-end forward locks the cartridge in the barrel chamber. The notch in the sear holds the hammer so that the rifle is cocked. As the bolt carrier is moved forward, the threads on the bolt contact the locking lugs (see detail). Continued movement of the bolt carrier causes the cam pin on the carrier to engage a curved slot in the bolt, turning the bolt and threading it into locking lugs.

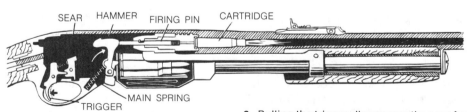

SEAR HAMMER FIRING PIN CARTRIDGE

MAIN SPRING
TRIGGER

3. Pulling the trigger disengages the sear from notch on the hammer. The main spring forces the hammer against the firing pin, detonating the cartridge. The safety lock and a disconnecting device, which prevents the rifle from going off until the action is closed, is not shown to allow maximum clarity.

How An Autoloading Rifle Works *(Remington Model 742)*

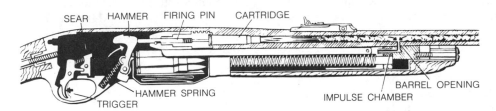

SEAR HAMMER FIRING PIN CARTRIDGE
BARREL OPENING
IMPULSE CHAMBER
HAMMER SPRING
TRIGGER

1. Beginning with rifle loaded and cocked, pulling the trigger disengages the sear from notch on the hammer. The hammer spring forces the hammer against the firing pin, exploding the cartridge. After the bullet passes the port, residual gases are metered downward through the barrel opening into the impulse chamber in the fore-end.

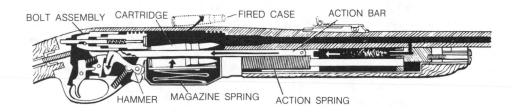

BOLT ASSEMBLY CARTRIDGE FIRED CASE ACTION BAR
HAMMER MAGAZINE SPRING ACTION SPRING

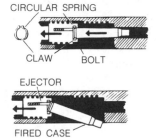

CIRCULAR SPRING
CLAW BOLT

EJECTOR
FIRED CASE

2. Gases force the action bar and bolt-assembly rearward, compressing the action spring, pushing down the hammer and ejecting the empty case. Further rearward travel of the bolt permits the next cartridge to raise into the path of the returning bolt. The ejection mechanism (see detail, showing top view) is the same as in the pump action.

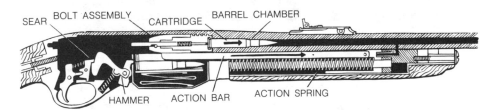

SEAR BOLT ASSEMBLY CARTRIDGE BARREL CHAMBER
HAMMER ACTION BAR ACTION SPRING

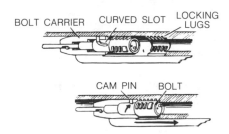

BOLT CARRIER CURVED SLOT LOCKING LUGS

CAM PIN BOLT

3. Compressed action spring moves the action bar and bolt-assembly forward, causing multiple lugs to lock the bolt into place (see detail also), sealing the cartridge tightly in the barrel chamber. The notch in the sear holds the hammer in cocked position. Pulling the trigger sets the weapon in motion as in the first diagram. The safety lock and a disconnecting device, which prevents the rifle from going off until the action is closed, is not shown to allow maximum clarity.

put the rifle into production. At the time he completed his successful design his annual government salary was $3,500. Despite his major contributions to America's victory in the war, some of the Army Ordnance hierarchy in Washington wanted him fired on the basis that he had "already served his usefulness." Major General Julian Hatcher, one of the nation's leading riflemen and handgunners and an expert on semiautomatic and automatic weapons and firearms identification, threatened to raise hell if Garand's services were terminated. They were not.

In its initial stages the M1 had to overcome prejudice from Army men and Marines reared on the familiar M1903 Springfield. Ultimately the M1 on target range, on training field, and in combat proved itself superior to the M1903.

Tens of thousands of M1s were sold through the Director of Civilian Marksmanship to National Rifle Association members. Included were carefully tuned National Match M1s, which proved themselves superior in accuracy to National Match M1903 Springfields.

The M1, however, has not been popular in the hunting field. Most big-game hunters are bolt-action advocates, and probably will be for a long time to come. New cartridges—many with more punch and longer range than the .30–06—appeared after World War II and Korea, and many could not be chambered in the M1. It is much more expensive to rebarrel an M1 with its gas system than to rebarrel or rechamber a bolt-action rifle. Only a few M1's have been sporterized.

M14. In 1957 the United States began a gradual replacement of the M1 with the M14. The M14 is capable of full or semiautomatic fire. None can be sold to civilians. The rifle was not an unqualified success, and while still used in Europe it was replaced by the M16 in Vietnam.

Meanwhile the M14 is being phased out. A Texas firm purchased remaining M14 components, except what the military kept for current service maintenance and repair, and created a semiautomatic rifle called the M14A1. When used as a semiautomatic the M14 is a remarkably accurate rifle. It is this version that will be used in military matches requiring this type of rifle and ammunition.

Gas-operated sporting rifles of recent years

The first gas-operated semiautomatic sporting rifle to appear on the American market was the German Krieghoff. It resembled the Browning semiautomatic, with a big square-shouldered receiver. What appeared to be a full-length tubular magazine beneath the barrel contained the operating rod. The magazine resembled the Krag series. Cartridges were inserted one by one through a left-side loading port. There was, however, no external box like the Krag's. The rifle weighs about 7.0 lbs. The Krieghoff was the first sporting gas-operated semiautomatic available for the "caliber .30–06 U.S. or any other rimless cartridge." Not many of these rifles sold here. They were first advertised in Stoeger's 1939 catalog, which appeared a few months before the Nazis invaded Poland. Even had war not come it is doubtful that many would have sold, at $500 each.

Winchester discontinued the M07 in 1958 and brought out the gas-operated M100 in 1960. This fast-handling, accurate rifle was chambered in .243 Win., .284 Win., and .308 Win. It was discontinued in 1974.

Browning brought out the first—and to date only—gas-operated rifle for short magnum cartridges like the 7mm Rem. Magnum, .300 Win. Magnum, and .338 Win. Magnum.

BROWNING HIGH-POWER AND MAGNUM AUTO RIFLE

Manufacturer: Fabrique Nationale, Belgium

Importer/distributor: Browning Arms

Action type: semiauto; gas-operated

Magazine type: detachable box

Magazine capacity: standard calibers, 4-shot; magnum calibers, 3-shot

Safety: crossbolt

Barrel length: standard calibers, 22.0 inches; magnum calibers, 24.0 inches

Stock: five grades of stock and engraving available, French walnut; Grades I and II, machine-checkered; Grades III through V, finely hand-checkered

Buttplate: shotgun type; plastic; recoil pad with white line spacer on magnum calibers

Overall length: standard calibers, 43.25 inches; magnum calibers, 45.25 inches

Length of pull: 13.625 inches

Drop at comb: 1.625 inches

Drop at heel: 2.0 inches

Weight: Magnum calibers, 8.4 lbs.; standard calibers, 7.4 lbs.

Trigger pull: 5 lbs.

Sight, rear: Rocky Mountain (buckhorn), crudely adjustable for elevation (no open sights on Grades III through V).

Sight, front: Bead on ramp (none on Grades III through V).

Scope adaptability: receiver drilled and tapped for standard scope bases

Caliber: .243 Win., .270 Win., .30–06, .308 Win. (7.62mm NATO), 7mm Rem. Magnum, .300 Win. Magnum, .338 Win. Magnum

Data: The full name of this model is the Browning High-Power Auto Rifle or Browning Magnum Auto Rifle, depending on the chambering, but it's often called the Browning Automatic Rifle, or BAR. It's strictly a sporter and not to be confused with the BAR light machine rifle which won a well-deserved reputation in two world wars and Korea. This is the only semi-automatic rifle chambered for belted magnum cartridges. It was designed by Val Browning and associates.

Comment: This rifle, from the standpoint of quality, is *the* current production semiautomatic sporter.

HARRINGTON & RICHARDSON M360/361

Action type: semiauto; gas-operated; side ejection

Magazine type: detachable box

Magazine capacity: 3-shot

Safety: slide on trigger guard

Barrel length: 22 inches; tapered

Stock: 1-piece hand-checkered American walnut; pistol grip with rosewood cap; rollover cheekpiece; sling swivels

Buttplate: shotgun type; solid recoil pad with white line spacer

Overall length: 43.5 inches

Length of pull: 13.5 inches

Drop at Monte Carlo: 1.75 inches

Drop at comb: 1.5 inches

Drop at heel: 2.625 inches

Weight: 7.5 lbs.

Trigger pull: not specified

Sight, rear: improved Rocky Mountain (buckhorn), adjustable for windage and elevation

Sight, front: gold bead on ramp

Scope adaptability: receiver drilled and tapped for standard scope bases

Caliber: .243 Win., .308 Win. (7.62mm NATO)

Data: M361 is identical to M360 except that it has a full rollover cheekpiece for left- or right-handed shooters. Gas piston and cylinder are machined from stainless steel.

Comment: This is a high-quality semiautomatic. It is notable for its hand checkering and the precision machinework.

PLAINFIELD U.S. CARBINE, CALIBER .30 M1

Action type: semiauto; gas operated

Magazine type: detachable box

Magazine capacity: 5-shot (to comply with magazine capacity laws for semiautomatic shoulder arms in many states); 15-shot and 30-shot also available

Safety: crossbolt

Barrel length: 18.0 inches

Stock: 1-piece uncheckered walnut-stained hardwood; fitted with sling

Buttplate: black plastic

Overall length: 35.5 inches

Length of pull: 13.6 inches

Drop at comb: 1.5 inches

Drop at heel: 2.75 inches

Weight: 5.5 lbs.

Trigger pull: 5.0 lbs. minimum; 7.0 lbs. maximum

Caliber: .30 M1 Carbine

Data: This carbine, originally designed by Winchester in 1941, was intended to replace the service pistol and submachine gun. It didn't. The M1 carbine is not to be confused with the M1 Rifle, Caliber .30 (Garand Rifle) or the M14.

It is also not to be confused with the M2 Carbine, which is a full automatic shoulder arm.

Comment: This arm was rarely popular with front-line troops. It was a favorite of many rear-echeloners.

It is light and handy but its cartridge is ineffective against medium game (deer class). Most Marines in Korea abandoned their M1s and M2s in favor of almost any other service arm, including the Colt .45 Automatic pistol.

Some states have outlawed the use of the .30 carbine cartridge for use on deer-class game.

REMINGTON M742 (WOODMASTER) AUTOMATIC RIFLE

Action type: semiauto; gas operated; side ejection

Magazine type: detachable box

Magazine capacity: 4-shot

Safety: crossbolt in rear portion of trigger guard.

Barrel length: 22.0 inches on all versions except 18.5 inches on carbine

Stock: 2-piece walnut; impressed checkering; pistol grip with cap; BDL custom Deluxe has Monte Carol with cheekpiece; left-hand BDL has right-side cheekpiece

Buttplate: shotgun type; plastic with white spacer

Overall length: 42.0 inches on all versions except 38.5 inches on carbine

Stock Dimensions (except BDL)

Length of pull: 13.24 inches

Drop at comb: 1.625 inches

Drop at heel: 2.5 inches

Stock dimensions (BDL)

Drop at Monte Carlo: 1.625 inches

Drop at comb: 1.625 inches

Drop at heel: 2.5 inches

Weight: 7.0 lbs. all versions except carbine, 6.75 lbs.

Trigger pull: 4.0 lbs.

Sight, rear: Rocky Mountain (buckhorn), crudely adjustable for elevation

Sight, front: bead on ramp

Scope adaptability: receiver drilled and tapped for standard scope bases

Caliber: .243 Win., .244 Rem. (discontinued), .280 Rem., .30–06 Springfield, .308 Win. (7.62mm NATO), 6mm Remington; carbine available in .308 and .30–06 only

Data: This model replaced the recoil-operated Remington M08 and M81 designed by John Moses Browning. This is the first American semiautomatic rifle chambered for standard-length cartridges like the .30–06. The name "Woodsmaster" is a carryover from the M81.

Comment: Those who like semiautomatic hunting rifles will find this a fast-handling, reliable rifle.

RUGER M44 AUTOLOADING CARBINE

Action type: semiauto; short-stroke piston; side ejection

Magazine type: tubular (inside fore-end)

Magazine capacity: 4-shot

Safety: crossbolt in forward portion of trigger guard

Barrel length: 18.5 inches

Stock: 1-piece uncheckered American walnut; semi-pistol grip; forward barrel band

Buttplate: semi-rifle type; steel

Overall length: 36.75 inches

Length of pull: 13.5 inches

Drop at comb: 1.5 inches

Drop at heel: 2.625 inches

Weight: 5.75 lbs.

Trigger pull: 4.5 lbs.

Sight, rear: folding leaf, crudely adjustable for windage and elevation

Sight, front: flat gold bead on forged ramp

Scope adaptability: receiver drilled and tapped for standard scope bases

Caliber: .44 Magnum

Data: This is the lightest, shortest, and least expensive of all current sporting (as opposed to semimilitary) semiautomatic rifles. Recoil for the revolver cartridge is slight. Breech remains open after the last shot is fired. Two-stage unserrated trigger is 0.635 inch wide. A button readily releases loaded cartridges from the magazine.

Comment: This uniquely designed semiautomatic by Bill Ruger is, despite its low cost, as sturdy as any other sporting semiauto on the market. A highly specialized arm, it is designed for deer and black-bear hunting at ranges not exceeding 75–100 yards. Most whitetail deer are taken within this range.

We would like to see a fuller and capped pistol grip with the same quality checkering as on the bolt-action M77 Ruger. The flat-face Redfield Sourdough front sight on early production models was a much better sight than the present one. This is Redfield's fault, not Ruger's, inasmuch as Redfield ceased making what was the best front sight ever produced for sporting rifles.

UNIVERSAL U.S. M1 CARBINE, CALIBER .30 M1

Action type: semiautomatic; gas operated

Magazine type: detachable box

Magazine capacity: 5-shot (to comply with magazine capacity laws for semiautomatic shoulder arms in some states); 15-shot and 30-shot also available

Safety: crossbolt

Barrel length: 18.0 inches

Stock: 1-piece uncheckered American walnut

Buttplate: black plastic

Overall length: 35.5 inches

Length of pull: 13.6 inches

Drop at comb: 1.5 inches

Drop at heel: 2.75 inches

Weight: 5.5 lbs.

Trigger pull: 5.0 lbs. minimum; 7.0 lbs. maximum

Caliber: .30 M1 Carbine

Data: See Plainfield M1 Carbine

Comment: Except for optional decorative features, this is almost identical to Plainfield M1 Carbine.

CHAPTER 5

DOUBLE-BARREL RIFLES

The big-bore double-barrel rifle is the weapon of romance and adventure for those yearning to hunt dangerous African game. For more than a century this rifle—first in muzzleloading and then in metallic-cartridge versions—has been the rifle of the professional hunter, elephant poacher, white hunter, tropical planter; and British civil servants; military men on leave, wealthy American sportsmen, and maharajahs have traditionally favored it.

Usually considered an African rifle, the double has also seen service against the tiger and buffalo of India and Southeast Asia. It is used by tea and rubber planters on islands like Ceylon.

The best-quality double rifle is strictly a British arm. Colt once made a few double-barrel hammer rifles in .45–70, and before World War II Winchester chambered one M21 shotgun for the .405 Winchester.

Until the late 1950s nearly every American on safari purchased a double rifle or rented one. But the wonderful, trusty double rifle is passing from the scene in dangerous-game country.

Once the sun never set on the British Empire. Now there is no longer a British Empire for it to shine on, and the British sportsmen and colonials who were major purchasers of double rifles have departed. This exodus from Empire lands has placed double rifles on the secondhand market. There remain only a few *pukka* sahibs affluent enough to keep their doubles—in racks bracketed with 100-pound elephant tusks—to gaze at or occasionally to fondle with affection.

Fifteen years ago the author purchased a Westley Richards double rifle, .458 Win. Magnum caliber, for $750 (new price with import duty was $1000). Today a similar rifle costs about $4000. Some best-quality doubles cost about $5000.

DOUBLE-RIFLE DESIGN AND FEATURES

Double-rifle safeties, triggers, locks, and bolting systems are identical to those of the side-by-side double-barrel shotgun. Over-and-under rifles have the characteristics of over-and-under shotguns. There are three basic double-barrel action types:

1. *Anson & Deeley box locks.* This is found on 95 percent of side-by-side double-barrel rifles and shotguns. It is a very sturdy action. The buttstock must be dismounted before examining the action. The stock "small" is sturdier than that of the sidelock action.

2. *Side lock.* This is the easiest to inspect, clean, and repair. It is not as sturdy as the Anson & Deeley box lock. A side plate, usually with Holland & Holland side levers, is easily removed. Side plates offer an additional area for engraving.

3. *Hand-detachable box lock.* Inaugurated by Westley Richards, this action combines the advantages of the Anson & Deeley box lock and the side lock. The trigger system is removed from the bottom of the action. Inspection, cleaning, and repair is quite easy, and the mechanism doesn't have the weakness inherent in the sidelock system.

Safety

Double-barrel rifle safeties, like double-barrel side-by-side or O/U shotgun safeties, are of the sliding type, located on the tang. All tang safeties should be nonautomatic. When barrels are closed, thus cocking the hammers, the safety should not automatically go on. It should require a manual effort to put the safety on. A double-rifle user with an automatic safety may easily forget to push the slide forward to the firing position. In the time it takes to realize the gun has not gone off and to push the automatic safety to firing position, a charging elephant, buffalo, or rhino can trample a man to death—and frequently this has happened.

Double rifles with factory-installed automatic safeties can readily be converted to nonautomatic. Your gunmaker should do this without charge.

Many experienced old hunters—and they got to be old because they used their heads—were contemptuous of safeties. They believed a man should be able to handle his gun properly without benefit of mechanical devices.

The fictional Henry McKenzie, millionaire—through his own efforts—and onetime ivory poacher in the late Robert Ruark's *Something of Value* (Doubleday & Co., New York, 1955), was based on a real character. Ruark, a hunter of dangerous big game, noted:

> None of his double rifles had a safety or an automatic ejector. Henry McKenzie did not believe in over-complication of weapons, nor did he believe that any man fit to carry arms was milksop enough to need protection against himself. The purpose of a gun, Henry McKenzie thought, was to shoot as fast and accurately as possible, with a minority of potential mechanical breakdowns.

Trigger systems

The double-barrel rifle, like the side-by-side or over-and-under scattergun, has two basic trigger systems.

Twin triggers. These are still standard on most double rifles and some shotguns. Many double-rifle and shotgun shooters consider twin triggers the most reliable trigger system. Ninety-nine percent of the time if one trigger fails—which is rare—the other trigger remains operational. Some smokeless-powder double rifles are more than 70 years old. Metal fatigue may cause one trigger to fail. Firing-pin crystallization is one of the more common failings.

Single trigger. Westley Richards introduced the single trigger for double rifles. WR also introduced the detachable-trigger system for boxlock doubles. (Another WR innovation—and it was a radical—was chambering double rifles for rimless cartridges. Westley Richards was the first to chamber the .458 Win. Magnum in double rifles.)

The author has a wide acquaintance and an even wider correspondence with double-rifle users. He has not found one case of single-trigger failure on WR rifles. This doesn't mean that there have been no WR failures, but they must be rare. The Westley Richards reputation for reliability is so great that the author doubts he would ever purchase a single-trigger double made by anyone other than Richards. He certainly would not purchase a non-British-made double with a single trigger, at least not for use on dangerous game.

Recoil Pads

These are live rubber on best-quality British doubles (and on other British doubles, too). The price difference between a best-quality double and the least expensive one by the same gunmaker is largely in engraving, etc., and not in mechanism. (The Westley Richards White Hunter—the economy rifle of the WR line—has double triggers rather than the WR single trigger.)

Pads are always solid. Ventilated pads are for shotguns, even though some American gunmakers, like Winchester, fit their .458 Win. Magnums with them. The 158-lb. recoil of the 4-bore is a thing of the past, but the .470 #2 Nitro Express produces about 70 ft.-lbs. Tropical shooters have little clothing to provide additional padding against recoil.

Sights

A non-British rifle buyer who is pursuing British arms literature will encounter some words or phrases which seem a bit odd. As British automobile lingo differs from American, so does British gun talk. The American "rear" sight is the British "back" sight; the American "front" sight is the British "fore" sight. Sights, recoil pads, and trigger systems are "furniture."

Back sight Usually this is a quarter-rib mounting three sight series. Standard leafs are frequently marked from 100 to 300 yards in 100-yard increments. Some knowledgeable shooters prefer leafs ranging from 50 to 150 yards marked in 50-yard increments. The latter figures are probably more realistic for the short ranges at which dangerous game is generally bagged. Considerable firing is required to properly adjust each leaf. Shots are fired for each range. The sight is then filed. Firing and filing continues until the proper adjustment is established.

Typical sights have wide, shallow V-notches. Aiming is aided by a vertical line from sight base to the V-notch base. This line is etched or filed and then filled with white platinum.

Fore sight. Fore sight beads are gold, silver, or ivory. The author likes the Redfield Sourdough tipped with copper and the sight blade at a 45° angle. This sight is no longer made. Scope-minded Americans neglect to learn front and rear sight design and use. Williams makes a similar sight, though the author believes it is not as well designed or as effective.

The standard double-rifle fore sight for many years was a reversible—or tip-up—sight. A shooter could select an ivory or gold bead by flipping it into position. Silver and ivory show up badly against a light background. Copper is the best compromise.

Ejectors

Most double rifles have automatic ejectors which throw empties clear of the rifle. When a rifle chambers one fired cartridge case and one loaded cartridge, the empty is ejected and the live round remains in the chamber. This seems like a great advance over the nonejector, where empty cases are but slightly elevated to be plucked out with fingers. But Ruark's Henry McKenzie, as many other experienced dangerous-game hunters, had his own method:

> Holding two extra heavy express cartridges in his left hand, he was able to fork them into a double rifle, after shaking out the expended cases, so swiftly he could fire four shots out of his doubles more rapidly than most men could shoot a half a magazine from a rifle with a bolt action.

John "Pondoro" Taylor usually removed the automatic ejectors from rifles so fitted. He did not want an empty case clanging off a nearby rock. The sound might alert his quarry. This could be fatal, or at least diminish his ivory haul.

Carrying straps

British double-rifle users rarely use carrying straps on double rifles. Most strap-equipped rifles seen in British Africa were originally brought by German planters, who were used to the Continental custom fitting their double-barrel shotguns or drillings with carrying straps. The British did not need slings, as their heavy rifles were carried by gunbearers until the actual moment of closing on their quarry. Carrying straps should be fitted with quick-detachable swivels. A strap should be removed before advancing into the brush where it might catch at a crucial moment on brush or creepers.

Double-rifle cartridges

The double-barrel rifle is usually considered by non-Britishers as strictly a big-bore rifle for dangerous game. However, doubles have regularly been made in calibers as small as .256, and possibly smaller on special order. The .375 H&H Flanged (rimmed) Magnum was a popular double cartridge for many years. Ammunition is no longer made. Once rimless and belted cartridges were chambered in double rifles the demand for the .375 H&H fell off.

Where two cartridge types are available—rimmed for double rifles and rimless for magazine rifles—the double-rifle load has somewhat less authority. Tropical temperatures sometimes exceed 115 degrees. The British worry about high temperatures raising chamber pressures (which they quote in long tons rather than foot-pounds). Increased pressures could create excessive obturation, causing cases to stick in the chamber. The powerful camming action of turn-bolt rifles is rarely affected to the extent that extraction problems occur.

Over-and-under rifles

The conservative British maintain that the O/U is slower to reload than the traditional side-by-side double because the lower chamber has to be elevated. The author has little knowledge of O/U rifles, but he has used O/U shotguns for 40 years and does not believe the slightly greater elevation creates any real time lag.

An O/U rifle advantage is the single sighting plane. Recoil seems less, as it does in an over-and-under shotgun. The recoil comes straight back on the shoulder.

THE DOUBLE'S PRESENT AND FUTURE

The future of double-rifle manufacture is uncertain. It is reliably reported that the great British gunmakers such as Holland & Holland, John Rigby, and Westley Richards are making, between them, less than 25 new doubles a year. Most, if not all, are made to order.

A few doubles are made in Austria, Spain, and possibly elsewhere—the picture is constantly shifting—that sell for as little as $2000 new. Most double-rifle purchasers, however, prefer a secondhand British double by a reputable gunmaker.

Secondhand rifles will be with us for many years. Check with the gunmaker—give him the serial number and he can tell when the rifle was made. With older rifles it is a good idea to replace firing pins and main and ejector springs. Replacement is cheap insurance. Double-rifle stocks have a tendency to work loose; they're subjected to repeated clouts from heavy recoil.

Ammunition is a problem. Kynoch, the sole manufacturer of double-rifle ammunition, has discontinued some older and less popular cartridges. Make sure an adequate supply is available. It could be worthwhile to secure extra bullets and primers. American custom bullet makers can supply steel-jacketed bullets.

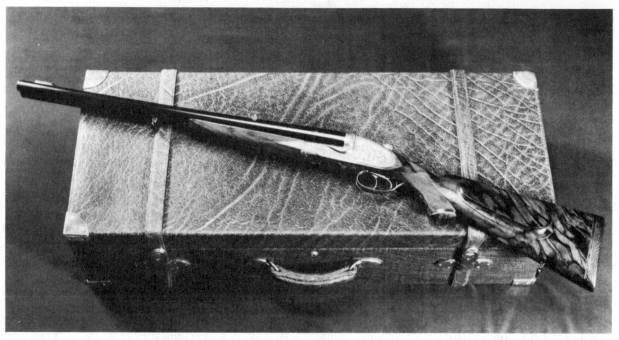

Ferlach double rifle in .300 caliber with H&H style action. Automatic ejectors, 24″ barrels, and Circasian walnut stock with horn fittings, scroll and hand engraving.

The last .600 Bore Holland & Holland Double Rifle. This fine custom-made gun is the last of a series of only six made by the company. It features 24″ barrels with a platinum-tipped foresight bead with fold-over "night" sight inset with a diamond. Exquisite engraving decorates the action, barrels, trigger guard and pistol grip cap. This gun is the epitome of fine custom firearms, which are not covered in this book, but can be ordered through custom gun makers.

The medium-bore double rifle may become a thing of the past sooner than the big-bore rifle. A few who can afford it will pay up to $5000 for a double rifle that is life insurance in the face of dangerous game. Not many will pay almost as much for a .375 H&H Magnum when they can buy the same caliber in a Winchester M70 for $350.

Popular big-bores today for collectors and shooters alike are the big-bore black-powder hammer express rifles. Calibers include the .577/.450, .500 Black Powder Express, and the .577 Black Powder Express.

There are hammer doubles for smokeless-powder loads. Some are still used in Africa and Asia along with big-bore single-shot rifles.

If you want a double-barrel big-bore rifle, whether to hunt with in Africa, admire in your gunroom, or shoot on the nearby rifle range, then go ahead even if you have to save up for the purchase. Abercrombie & Fitch and their affili-

ate Griffin & Howe are good starting places for anyone seeking secondhand double rifles of assorted vintages. Except for a very few new double rifles in some gunshops, all double rifles are made to order.

Shooters who are interested in ordering a double rifle may want to contact one of the following makers:

Holland & Holland
13 Bruton St.
London W 1, England

John Rigby & Co., Ltd.
13 Pall Mall
London SW 1, England

Westley Richards & Co., Ltd.
Grange Road, Bournebrook
Birmingham 29, England

PART II

BOLT-ACTION CENTERFIRE RIFLES

CHAPTER / 6

BOLT-ACTION MAGAZINE RIFLES

The turnbolt-action centerfire magazine rifle is the world's most versatile sporting rifle. Calibers range from the tiny .17 Rem. with its 25-grain varmint bullets to the mighty .458 Win. and .460 Weatherby Magnums with their 500-grain bullets for stopping Cape buffalo, rhino, and elephant in their tracks.

There are cartridges which will harvest woodchucks at 400 yards, and others like the 7mm Rem. Magnum that take light game like pronghorn antelope, mountain goat, sheep, and caribou to ranges like 400 yards. The .375 H&H Magnum, .338 Win., Magnum, and .340 Weatherby Magnum are long-range cartridges for the biggest North American and much African game. The reliable .30–06 Springfield—it's been around for nearly 75 years—will take more than 90 percent of the world's medium and big game at ranges out to 300 yards.

The bolt action—turnbolt version—has since the end of World War II become the pre-eminent rifle action of the American hunter/rifleman. It has displaced the lever action, which reigned supreme for more than three-quarters of a century.

Hundreds of thousands of surplus military turnbolt-action rifles were imported and sold for a few dollars on the American market. Rifles based on the M98 Mauser action could be made into fine sporting rifles. Other rifles were mere junk because of their condition or poor design or workmanship. Many purchasers of these rifles ultimately purchased American or imported turnbolt-action sporters.

Today, fine bolt-action sporting rifles are marketed by a number of American arms companies including Colt, Harrington & Richardson, Ithaca, Mossberg, Remington, Ruger, Savage, Weatherby, and Winchester, among others. Some of these rifles are made domestically, others by foreign suppliers. In addition, various distributors import bolt-action rifles from Austria, Belgium, Denmark, England, Finland, Japan, South Africa, Sweden, West Germany, Yugoslavia, and other countries. Hence the bolt action's popularity—it is versatile and it is available. In addition, it is inherently the most accurate action, and since it is capable of withstanding greater pressures than any other type of rifle action it can handle maximum handloads.

The prime disadvantage of the bolt action is its relative slowness when compared to the lever, slide, and semiautomatic actions. Also, fine bolt-action rifles cost more than any other type except double rifles.

BOLT-ACTION SYSTEMS

There are two types of bolt action, the turnbolt and the straight-pull bolt. We will discuss these in detail, then go on to discuss magazine types.

Turnbolt. This system is nearly universal for today's bolt-action rifles.

1. When the bolt handle turns upward it causes the bolt's locking lugs to turn about 90°, thus unlocking the lugs on the inside of the receiver. Once unlocked, the bolt may be pulled directly to its rearward position. On most current Mauser-derived actions, opening the bolt and pulling it to the rear position cocks the action. The most notable action to cock on the closing stroke of the bolt was the M1914/17 Enfield. Americans are accustomed to the cock-on-opening design, and many purchasers of the Enfield alter the bolt to cock-on-opening. The slight resistance encountered while thrusting the bolt home on the cock-on-closing actions seems to bother riflemen trained on the cock-on-opening system. There is no real difference in the efficiency of the two systems.

2. With the bolt in its most-rearward position, the magazine well and the magazine follower (the platform for cartridges) are open. As each cartridge is inserted, the magazine follower and magazine spring are further depressed. When the magazine is fully loaded the spring follower can no longer be depressed.

It is possible to load a cartridge into the chamber after the magazine is loaded. To do this the thumb holds down the top cartridge in the magazine while the extra round is inserted in the chamber.

Some military rifles, including the M1903 Springfield, the M1917 Enfield, and some M70 Winchesters, chambered for the .30–06, have a clip slot at the inside after end of the receiver. A stripper clip holds five cartridges and is inserted into the magazine. The clip guide cannot be used on a scope-equipped rifle.

3. To load cartridges from the magazine into the empty chamber, the bolt is moved forward. While moving forward, the bottom front face of the bolt catches the upper rear of the top cartridge in the magazine. The cartridge now slides forward into the chamber.

4. Once the cartridge is fully chambered, the bolt handle is turned down. This movement catches the firing-pin extension on the sear, and the pin is thus held in its rearmost position.

5. The thrusting forward of the bolt and the turning down of the bolt handle interlocks the bolt lugs with those on the inside wall of the receiver. The firing pin is now in firing position.

(The safety may deactivate the firing pin.) As the bolt moves into its maximum forward position, the extractor in the bolt face hooks over the cartridge (or into the extractor groove on rimless or belted cartridges).

6. The safety is released (if it was actuated). The trigger is depressed. This removes the sear from engagement with the firing-pin extension. The firing pin is driven forward by the tension of the firing-pin spring. When the firing pin hits the primer the cartridge is fired.

7. The bolt is again drawn to its most-rearward position. The extractor withdraws the fired cartridge case from the chamber. During this process the rear of the fired case contacts the ejector, which ejects the case from the rifle. (Some target shooters or varmint hunters who wish to reload the fired cases either remove or otherwise negate the ejector and pull out the empty cases by hand.) A recent modification of the Mauser ejector system replaces the outside (of the bolt proper) ejector with a plunger. This simplifies production but is not necessarily an improvement.

Straight-pull bolt. This system is usually found on military or sporterized military rifles. It is rarely used on commercial sporting rifles. Exceptions include the Ross Sporting rifle, Remington Keen, and Winchester Lee (all discontinued long ago).

Here's a typical straight-pull operation: The bolt is pulled straight to its rearmost position. As the bolt moves directly rearward, bolt-head locking lugs are disengaged from receiver-wall lugs by a moving cam on the bolt. A reverse action occurs when the bolt is moved to its forward position. Loading, extraction, and ejection are accomplished as in the turnbolt rifle.

A straight-pull rifle can be fired slightly faster than a turnbolt. The turnbolt, however, can be built to withstand higher pressures and thus more powerful cartridges than the straight-pull. The camming action of the turnbolt provides a greater extraction capability.

The straight-pull action should not be confused with the straight (or T-bolt) bolt handle. Many early M98 Mausers had the bolt handle at right angles to the action. The bolt handle stuck straight out. The M83 Winchester Hotchkiss rifle had a similar bolt. Most straight-pull actions had turned-down bolt handles. The straight bolt handle was apparently designed with the idea that it would slightly reduce the time required to manipulate the bolt. The inconvenience created by the protruding handle more than offset any saved time. German Army M98 cavalry carbines had the bolt handle turned down in the conventional manner so the arm would fit scabbards. Most civilian owners of straight-bolt military rifles have the handle bent down by heating. Some gunsmiths cut the handle off and weld it back in a turned-down position.

Magazine types

1. *Nondetachable staggered box magazine.* The Spanish (that is, made for the Spanish army, but not made in Spain) M93 Mauser is the first rifle known to the author to be fitted with this type of magazine. The usual capacity for standard (nonbelted) cartridges is 5-shot. Capacity for belted magnum cartridges is usually 3-shot (this doesn't count a round in the chamber). The staggered box magazine, unlike the straight-line magazine used in Belgian and Argentine Mausers, does not protrude below the stock bottom. The magazine is thus protected from damage.

The nondetachable box magazine is standard on most first-line sporting bolt-action rifles like the Winchester M70, Ruger M77, Remington M700, and Weatherby models.

2. *Blind magazine.* Remington with its M700 ADL was one of the first American manufacturers to offer a rifle with no floorplate. Object: slightly lower cost. Disadvantage: cartridges must be worked through the action for emptying purposes. Loading time is the same as for rifles with nondetachable box magazines.

3. *Mannlicher spool (rotary) magazine.* The Mannlicher-Schoenaur uses a rotary magazine similar to the magazine used in the original M99 Savage rifle. Loading time is about the same as for a nondetachable box magazine. The rotary is probably the most jam-free magazine type.

4. *Straight line en bloc clips.* These are not found in current bolt-action sporters. They are found on surplus military rifles, such as the old Mannlicher-Steyrs once used by Austria, Bulgaria, Hungary, and Rumania. The expendable clip fits into a magazine well. When the final round is fired, the clip drops out of the magazine well. Disadvantage: loose or individual cartridges may be available, but unloaded clips may not be available. Retrieved clips are not always in usable condition. This expendable clip is also a disadvantage of the Garand. If usable clips are not available then the arm must be operated as a single-shot.

5. *Tubular magazine.* This system has rarely been used on centerfire bolt-action rifles. The M83 Winchester, designed by Benjamin B. Hotchkiss, used a seven-shot tubular magazine.

6. *Straight-line magazine.* Some are detachable, some nondetachable. They are basically like the nondetachable staggered box magazine.

THE DEVELOPMENT OF THE BOLT-ACTION RIFLE

Mauser. Peter Paul (1838–1913) and Wilhelm (1834–82) Mauser designed the basic turnbolt action from which nearly every contemporary turnbolt rifle action is derived. Mauser rifle authority Ludwig Olsen estimates that more than 100,000,000 military Mausers have been manufactured.

The first Mauser centerfire-cartridge turnbolt rifle was the single-shot M71. In 1884 the German Army adopted Mauser's tubular-magazine M84. Both rifles were chambered for the rimmed 11mm (.43 caliber) Mauser cartridge.

In 1884, two years after Parisian chemist Paul Vielle invented smokeless gunpowder, the French army adopted the bolt-action magazine Lebel Rifle in caliber 8mm Lebel. The 8mm Lebel was the world's first smokeless-propellant military cartridge and the first cartridge to use a metal-jacketed bullet.

The German army then adopted the M88 Commission rifle. They used the basic Mauser action—without consulting Peter Mauser—but with an expendable Mannlicher *en bloc* clip magazine. The most important feature of the short-lived M88 rifle was its cartridge, 7.92mm (8 × 57) Mauser. This was the granddaddy of the 7mm Mauser, the .30–06 Springfield, and many others.

The M89 Belgian Mauser introduced the rimless 7.65mm Belgian Mauser cartridge and the straight-line box magazine. The M89 was manufactured by Fabrique Nationale, the Belgian National Armory, by Hopkins & Allen, Norwich, Conn., and during World War I by Belgian refugees in England.

The M91 7.65mm Turkish Mauser (same cartridge as Belgian Mauser) was similar to the M89 except that the metal handguard was replaced by a wood handguard.

The M93 Spanish Mauser (made in Germany) introduced the nondetachable staggered box magazine. This magazine, flush with the bottom of the stock, did not project like the straight-line M89 and M90 magazine.

The M93 Mauser (a few M92s had been made for the Spanish navy) introduced the 7mm (7 × 57) Mauser cartridge. The M95 was the first short-action small-ring Mauser (smaller-diameter receiver ring than earlier Mausers). The Mauser plant in Czechoslovakia once made a superb small-ring Mauser action.

How the Mauser Action Works

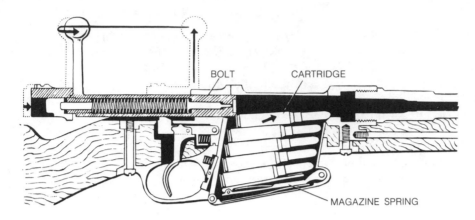

1. The bolt handle is raised and pulled backward, relaxing pressure on the magazine spring which then pushes a cartridge upward into position for loading.

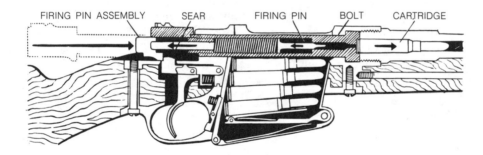

2. As the bolt is moved forward, the end of the firing-pin assembly is engaged by the sear. Moving the bolt fully forward cocks the firing pin and locks the new cartridge in the chamber.

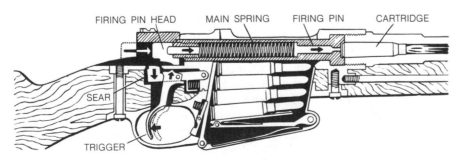

3. Pulling the trigger releases the sear from the notch on the firing-pin head and the main spring drives the firing pin forward, detonating the cartridge primer.

How A Modern Bolt-Action Rifle Works

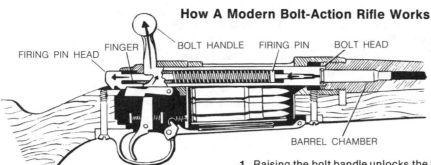

FIRING PIN HEAD FINGER BOLT HANDLE FIRING PIN BOLT HEAD

BARREL CHAMBER

1. Raising the bolt handle unlocks the bolt head from the barrel chamber. At the same time, notch at bottom of the bolt handle catches and pushes up protruding finger of the firing pin head, pushing firing pin to rear.

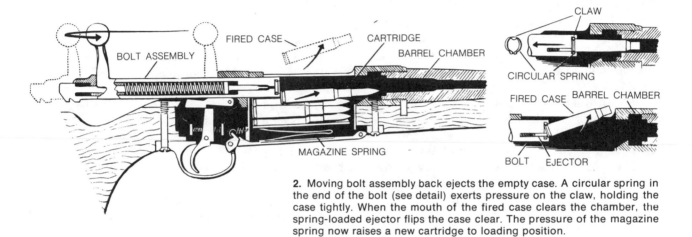

BOLT ASSEMBLY FIRED CASE CARTRIDGE BARREL CHAMBER

MAGAZINE SPRING

CLAW CIRCULAR SPRING

FIRED CASE BARREL CHAMBER BOLT EJECTOR

2. Moving bolt assembly back ejects the empty case. A circular spring in the end of the bolt (see detail) exerts pressure on the claw, holding the case tightly. When the mouth of the fired case clears the chamber, the spring-loaded ejector flips the case clear. The pressure of the magazine spring now raises a new cartridge to loading position.

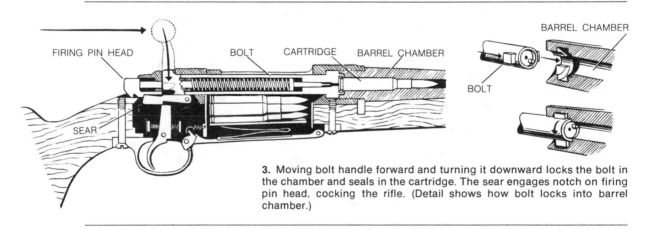

FIRING PIN HEAD BOLT CARTRIDGE BARREL CHAMBER

SEAR

BARREL CHAMBER BOLT

3. Moving bolt handle forward and turning it downward locks the bolt in the chamber and seals in the cartridge. The sear engages notch on firing pin head, cocking the rifle. (Detail shows how bolt locks into barrel chamber.)

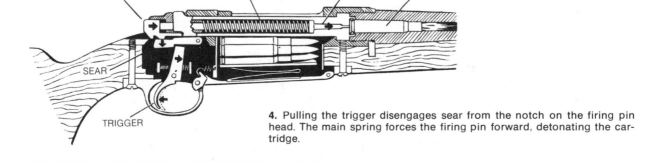

FIRING PIN HEAD MAIN SPRING FIRING PIN CARTRIDGE

SEAR

TRIGGER

4. Pulling the trigger disengages sear from the notch on the firing pin head. The main spring forces the firing pin forward, detonating the cartridge.

The M98 Mauser, as adopted by the German army in 7.92mm, introduced dual locking lugs and cocking on the opening stroke of the bolt. This action is the basis for most of the world's military and commercial sporting turnbolt rifles.

After World War I, when Germany was allowed to produce sporting rifles, the great Mauser Werke at Oberndorf produced sporting versions of the M98 action. Hinged floorplates and trigger-guard floorplate releases were among the refinements.

M1903 Springfield. The first major offspring of the M98 Mauser was the United States Magazine Rifle, Caliber .30, Model of 1903. This was the U.S. Standard rifle in World War I and Limited Standard in World War II.

The United States had fought the Spanish-American War (1898), Philippine Insurrection (1898–1902), and Boxer Rebellion (1899–1901) with the United States Magazine Rifle, Caliber .30, Model of 1892 (and successors), and the single-shot trapdoor U.S. Rifle, Model of 1873 (and successors), caliber .45 (.45–70). U.S. Regulars were armed with the side-loading .30–34 Krag, while Volunteers—except Theodore Roosevelt's First Volunteer U.S. Cavalry—were armed with the trapdoor Springfields. The dense smoke from black-powder .45–70 Springfields revealed the rifleman's position. The smokeless-propellant Krag cartridge did not reveal the rifleman's position, but the Krag had to be loaded one cartridge at a time. American soldiers noted the fast-loading charger (stripper clip) used in the Spanish Mausers.

The U.S. Army, after a series of experiments, adopted the M1903 Springfield. Even today there are those who consider the M1903 Springfield superior to the "German" Mauser. Actually, the M1903 Springfield was a Mauser M98. The U.S. made what they considered to be improvements over the original Mauser: they added a cocking piece, turned the original one-piece firing pin into an inferior two-piece pin, and added a magazine cutoff device. The U.S. Army used magazine rifles as single-loaders, saving the magazine contents for making or repulsing a charge.

The U.S. government acknowledged its design debt to Mauser by paying the Mauser Works 75 cents per rifle until a total of $200,000 had been paid. This included a royalty of 50 cents per 1000 stripper clips. Final royalty payment was made in July, 1909.

The original M1903 Springfield bullet, like that of the .30–40 Krag, was a metal-jacketed 220-grain roundnose bullet. In 1905 the German army adopted a metal-jacketed spitzer pointed bullet. The United States then adopted a 150-grain metal-jacketed spitzer. The new bullet required a shorter-necked case. Existing rifles were rechambered.

Deutsche Waffen und Munitionsfabriken (DWM) sued the United States government, claiming the new service bullet (M1906) violated a U.S. Patent issued to one Henrich Gleinich. The case dragged on. During World War I the U.S. Custodian of Enemy Alien Property took over the patent rights. After the war the International Court at The Hague awarded Gleinich $300,000 for his design plus $112,520.55 interest. Thus, in effect, we paid a German designer for every .30 rifle and machine gun bullet U.S. forces fired at Germans during the war.

A few Springfields found their way into the hands of civilian riflemen/hunters before World War I. Charles Newton, the father of high-velocity cartridges, imported a few rifles, but the war ended his imports. He then designed and made his own rifles in limited numbers.

It was not until after the war (during which several million Americans first encountered the turnbolt rifle) that civilians began purchasing bolt-action rifles in appreciable quantities. National Rifle Association members, through the War Department's Director of Civilian Marksmanship, could purchase M1903 Springfields for about $35. Surplus Krags cost as little as $1.50. M1917 Enfields, superior to the more popular M1903 Springfield, cost $7.50.

M1917 Enfield. The M1917 Enfield was the .30–06 Springfield version of the British P-14 (P for pattern) Enfield. These were made under commercial contract in the United States by Winchester, Remington, and the Remington-operated Eddystone, Pa., plant. When the U.S. entered the war, the combined facilities of Springfield and Rock Island armories were producing only 1400 rifles daily. This production, together with 600,000 M1903s on hand, was far below the requirements of the American Expeditionary Force.

It was discovered that by chambering the .303 P-14 Enfields for the .30–06 cartridge and by changing bore and groove dimensions to our specifications, the rifle could be used by our forces. The P-14 became the M1917. Three M1917 plants produced 11,000 rifles daily. Total World War I M1917 rifle production between August 1, 1917, and November 9, 1918, was 2,193,429. Total M1903 Springfield production for the same period was 296,212 rifles.

Early manufacturers of American bolt-action

sporting rifles found sales slow. No wonder, considering the competition from less expensive — if not so refined — military rifles.

Remington offered a modified civilian M1917 Enfield. Introduced as the M30 (1921–40), it was chambered for cartridges like the .25 Rem., .257 Roberts, .30–06 Springfield, .35 Rem., and 7mm Mauser. Its popularity was retarded by the availability of military arms, commercial Mausers, and the Winchester M54.

M54 Winchester. The M54 Winchester, the first successful American bolt-action sporting rifle, was an improved M98/1903 but without the latter's disadvantages. The M54 (1925–36) introduced three famed Winchester cartridges: .270 Win. (1925), .22 Hornet (1931), and .220 Swift (1935). Other calibers were 7mm Mauser, 7.65mm Mauser, 9mm Mauser (9×57), .30–06 Springfield, .257 Roberts, and even the .30–30 Win. The M54 sold at the rate of 5,000 annually.

Custom bolt-actions. Wealthy or devoted gun buffs who wanted something better than a military rifle or a standard factory rifle ordered custom Mausers or used the M1903 action as the basis for fine custom sporters. Makers like Griffin & Howe, Hoffman, and Neidner and stockers like Bob Owens, Thomas Shellhammer, and Alvin Linden became well known.

M70 Winchester

Winchester improved the M54. The new rifle, the M70, was introduced January 1, 1937. Changes included an improved speedlock (faster ignition time), a bolt stop independent of sear and trigger, a fuller fore-end and better checkering, and a hinged floorplate.

The original M70 (1937–63) was made in 20 calibers. Cartridges for which the pre-64 M70 was chambered throughout its lifetime included .220 Swift, .270 Win., .30–06 Springfield, .300 H&H Magnum, and .375 H&H Magnum. Cartridges which were added to the M70's list and which were still extant in 1963 included .243 Win. (1955), .308 Win. (1952), .458 Win. Magnum (1956), .338 Win. Magnum (1959), .264 Win. Magnum (1960), and .300 Win. Magnum (1963). Cartridges discontinued before 1964 included .22 Hornet, .250–3000 Savage, .257 Roberts, .300 Savage, .35 Rem., .358 Win., 7mm Mauser, 7.65mm Mauser, and 9mm Mauser.

The smooth-working, well-stocked, and well-checkered M70 with a machined receiver and all-steel parts became the standard by which all other turnbolt sporting rifles were judged. Nearly 30 years passed before the M70's pre-eminence

was challenged. No rifle today, except the post–1964 M70, would be offered in such a variety of rifle types: (1) sporting rifle with regular stock, (2) sporting rifle with Monte Carlo stock, (3) carbine with standard stock, (4) standard rifle with Monte Carlo stock, (5) target rifle, (6) Bull Gun, (7) varmint rifle, (8) Featherweight with regular stock, (9) Featherweight with Monte Carlo, (10) .264 Win. Magnum Featherweight.

The M70 introduced several Winchester-originated cartridges. The short-magnum series include .458 Win. Magnum, .338 Win. Magnum, .264 Win. Magnum, and .300 Win. Magnum. Also the .308 Win., and the .243 Win. The .243 is the most popular sporting centerfire cartridge of nonmilitary origin.

Before the introduction of the M70, big-game riflemen desiring a rifle for the .300 H&H Magnum or .375 H&H Magnum had to purchase an expensive custom rifle, or import a European rifle or Mauser magnum action. The M70 action — there was but one length — was designed to handle the long (3.60 inches) .300 H&H and .375 H&H Magnums. During its early years a .375 H&H Magnum M70 cost just the same as one chambered for the .22 Hornet — $61.95.

The .375 H&H gamble paid off. The .375 H&H M70 gained almost immediate favor among African professionals, among safari clients, and oddly enough among many Americans who never expected to hunt in Africa. The .375 H&H also gained popularity among Alaskan guides, who used it as a backup rifle while guiding clients to brown bear.

The M70 Bull Gun and Target Model in caliber .300 H&H Magnum took top honors in the 1000-yard match at Camp Perry for more than a quarter-century.

The date 1964 inevitably comes up in any discussion of the M70. Production costs had risen steadily, and that year Winchester instituted a number of changes in order to economize. The styling of the stock was altered (and its quality lowered) and the machine-cut checkering was soon replaced by impressed checkering. The receiver and bolt design was modified to eliminate as much machining and hand work as possible. The new bolt, with a recessed head, was actually stronger than the old one, though it wasn't quite as smooth-working until an anti-bind device was added in 1968. In '64 the ejector became a spring-loaded plunger in the bolt head, and the old Mauser-type nonrotating extractor was replaced by a rotating one riding in a transverse T-slot in the bolt head.

The new version functioned reliably but it was

no longer the "classic 70" and it was severely criticized. The stock aroused the greatest objections, and Winchester soon revived the old contours. Since '64, machine checkering has been restored and there have been refinements (like that anti-bind device) in the action. Other details are given in the data and comment under the specifications for the M70. Today's M70 is a fine rifle, even though pre-1964 devotees will pay more for an old one in top condition than for a new one.

M70 sporter stocks were not originally designed for use with scope sights. All pre-1964 M70s were drilled and tapped for the fine Lyman 48 micrometer receiver sight. Monte Carlo stocks were soon offered those who wished to use telescope sights.

The pre-1964 M70 was and is one of the strongest rifle actions ever made. Its safety margins can be even further strengthened by drilling a vent hole in the left receiver wall opposite the vent hole in the bolt body. A simple gas shield can be easily installed (*American Rifleman*, p. 73, April 1964).

The M70's single-stage, easy-to-adjust trigger is one of the finest available. It is still used on post-1964 M70s. Riflemen who feel they can improve—this is difficult to do—on the M70 trigger can install the M70 Canjar trigger. The author once installed a Mauser M98 double set trigger on his pre-'64 M70 .243 varmint rifle. It worked very well.

The M70 Featherweight (1952) was the first M70 in which alloy parts were substituted for steel. A slight weight saving was effected by substituting an alloy floorplate and trigger guard and aluminum buttplate for the all-steel versions in other M70s.

Winchester developed an elephant cartridge, the .458 Win. Magnum, and a special M70 to handle it. The M70 African and the magnificent 500-grain full-metal-cased bullet—there's a 510-grain softpoint for big thin-skinned game like tiger, lion, and brown bear—are rapidly replacing the double rifle in the battery of professional African hunters.

About 500,000 pre-1964 M70 Winchesters were made. Post-1964 Winchester serial numbers started at 700,000. On pre-1964 M70s, caliber and the last two digits of the year of manufacture are stamped on the bottom of the barrel.

Remington 700 series

In 1948, Remington introduced the M721/M722 action. The M721 "long" action was chambered for "full" or "Magnum-length" car-tridges like the .270 Win., .30–06 Springfield, and .300 H&H Magnum. The M722 "short" action chambered the .257 Roberts, .300 Savage, .222 Rem., .222 Rem. Magnum, .244 Rem., and .243 Win. In 1962, with minor modifications, the M721/M722 actions were redesignated the M700. Details of the M721/M722 action will be found in this chapter in the section on the Remington M700.

In the March, 1948, issue of *American Rifleman,* the late Major General Julian Hatcher—an authority not given to superlatives—stated that the M721 action was the strongest action then extant. By "the strongest action" he meant that it was capable of withstanding more pounds per square inch breech pressure than any existing action. This did not mean that actions like the Winchester M70 were not safe but that the M721 had a higher safety margin than any other existing action. Any modern rifle is capable of withstanding pressures created by cartridges whose loads are within factory norms.

The Remington M721 had the cartridge head completely surrounded and supported by metal. In typical M98 Mauser actions, notably the M1903 Springfield, part of the cartridge head is unsupported. The M721 with its completely enclosed case head offered a greater margin of safety in event of cartridge case-head failure.

MODERN TRENDS IN DESIGN AND CONSTRUCTION

For many years, actions—including receiver, bolt, magazine, trigger guard, and floorplate—were precision-machined from high-quality steel. The past decade has seen the advent of "investment casting." Some shooters associate "casting" with the cheap cast iron of yore. Actually our finest factory rifles, including the Ruger M77, which some consider our finest domestic rifle, use investment castings. Ruger organized his own investment casting company. Pine Tree Castings, Newport, N.H., supplies Ruger. Investment casting allows precision casting of a rifle's major steel components. So closely to final specifications can an investment casting be made that only minimal machining is required.

The current trend in bolt-action rifles is to reduce costs. Competition is keen and inflation is a major cost factor. Eliminating the Mauser claw extractor and substituting a spring-loaded plunger extractor for the classic Mauser type extractor and ejector are cost-cutting methods. Trigger bows and floorplates, formerly machined steel and blued, are now alloy and are anodized rather than blued. Alloy trigger bows and floorplates are slightly lighter, but are not as rugged as steel.

Action length. The standard-length American action was one which would accommodate a cartridge not exceeding the overall length of the .30–06 Springfield. Shorter cartridges like the .257 Roberts were adapted to the .30–06-length action by using a shorter bolt stop and a magazine spacer. The M70 Winchester was the first American commercial action—barring custom jobs—designed to accommodate cartridges ranging from the .375 and .300 H&H Magnums down to the .22 Hornet. Shorter cartridges were accommodated by varying-length bolt stops and magazine fillers. The .22 Hornet M70 used a magazine system based on the M1922 Springfield. A detachable magazine was inserted through a slot in the magazine floorplate.

Today, action length designation is confusing. Every manufacturer has his own designation. Some makers who do not chamber rifles for the .375 H&H Magnum cartridge call their action for .30–06 Springfield cartridges "Magnums." "Short" magnums like the .458 Win. Magnum, .338 Win. Magnum, .300 Win. Magnum, .264 Win. Magnum, and 7mm Rem. Magnum will function through a .30–06-length action. The M77 Ruger's "magnum"-length action will handle the "short" magnums but not cartridges based on the full-length .375 H&H case. Ruger's short action, designated the "Short Stroke" action, handles cartridges like the .243 Win. and .250–3000 Savage.

"Short" cartridges like the .222 Rem. occasionally jam when used in a long action. This malfunction may be avoided by using a single-shot bolt action like the Savage M12V, or using a true "short" action like the Sako L-461.

Barrels

Winchester used nickel-steel barrels for many years. Some manufacturers use so-called "ordnance" steel. With the advent of high-velocity cartridges like the .220 Swift it became imperative to use harder steel. The author wore out three M70 Winchester .220 Swift barrels in 500 rounds each. The rifle was no longer capable of producing 1-inch 5-shot groups at 100 yards.

After World War II when Winchester introduced its superbly accurate 26.0-inch-barrel M70 varmint rifle, the barrels were stainless steel. .220 Swift barrel life was tripled. Stainless steel is difficult to blue, so Winchester iron-plated stainless steel and then applied a bluing solution. Remington, for a time, used stainless-steel barrels in 7mm Rem. Magnum. Today,

Remington uses unplated stainless-steel barrels for its benchrest rifle, the 40-X BR.

Barrels for Weatherby's magnum cartridges are relatively short-lived. However, the average big-game hunter shoots only a few rounds annually, and replacement barrels, even for Weatherbys, are not too expensive.

Barrel weights. Assuming stock and action weights to be relatively stable, the ultimate weight of a rifle is determined by the barrel weight. Light sporter barrels 22.0 inches long may have a smaller barrel diameter than a 24.0-inch sporter barrel. Barrels for most current varmint rifles are medium heavy (total rifle weight: 9-10 lbs.); total weight of a match rifle is 11.0-12.0 lbs. The bull barrels of yesteryear (12.0–13.0 lbs. plus) are custom-order-only rifles today. There are exceptions to these weight classifications.

Barrel length. The standard sporter barrel of 24.0 inches was derived from the M1903 Springfield. The M1903 was the first military rifle to use a 24.0-inch barrel. This length was a compromise between the 30.0-inch Krag infantry barrel and the 22.0-inch cavalry carbine.

Winchester with its first commercially successful American bolt-action sporting rifle, the M54 introduced in 1925, followed the lead of Springfield and adopted the 24.0-inch barrel as standard. Exceptions to the pre-1964 M70 standard sporter barrel were the .220 Swift and .300 H&H Magnum, with 26.0-inch barrels. The .375 H&H Magnum has a 25.0-inch barrel.

Winchester introduced the first 26.0-inch-barrel medium-weight varmint rifle in calibers .220 Swift and .243 Win. in the late 1950s. This length was dropped for the 24.0-inch barrel in 1964. Except for the Ruger M77 in caliber .220 Swift and the new Savage single-shot varmint rifle (M112V) in calibers .243 Win., .22–250 Rem., and .220 Swift, all other varmint rifles like the M700 Remington have 24.0-inch barrels.

Barrel length affects velocity. The 80-grain .243 Win. has a specified muzzle velocity of 3500 f.p.s. but this velocity is obtained with a 26.0-inch test barrel. For 11 years after Winchester discontinued its 26.0-inch varmint barrel no American bolt-action rifle in .243 Win. had a 26.0-inch barrel. Muzzle velocity in a 24.0-inch barrel, according to factory standards, would be 3350-3400 f.p.s. Velocity in a 22.0-inch barrel sporter would be about 3250 f.p.s. Actual velocity is less in all barrel lengths because factory velocity tests are made in special barrels.

Short barrel lengths—18.0–20.0 inches—have never been popular with bolt-action riflemen. The M70 was available with a 20.0-inch barrel before World War II. Remington's 20.0-inch-barrel models were short-lived.

Several factors depend on barrel length: handiness or convenience, weight, and muzzle blast. Judging the relative importance of these factors is up to the individual buyer. For nearly 25 years the author's long-range rifle was a 26.0-inch-barrel .300 H&H Magnum M70 Winchester. A 22.0-inch barrel would have reduced the muzzle and residual velocities to that of the .30–06 Springfield. Muzzle blast would have been greater than with the .30–06, and ammunition more expensive. But the advent of the .300 Weatherby, .308 Norma, and .300 Winchester Magnums has resulted in velocities in 24.0-inch barrels that are greater than the .300 H&H Magnum with a 26.0-inch barrel.

In calibers .30–06 Springfield and .270 Winchester, the author prefers his pre-1964 M70 to the Ruger M77 simply because the M77 is not available with 24.0-inch barrels in those calibers. This is a matter of personal choice; certainly 22.0-inch-barrel .270 Winchesters are capable of excellent work, as proved by Jack O'Connor's successes on game ranging from antelope through grizzly bears to big African plains game.

The 24.0-inch barrel was standard for cartridges ranging from the .22 Hornet through the .30–06 Springfield until 1951. Winchester introduced its M70 Featherweight in calibers like .243 Win. and .308 Win. Barrel length was 22.0 inches. This M70 version introduced the alloy floorplate and trigger guard. Traditionalists could still purchase standard M70 sporters with the 24.0-inch barrel.

The Featherweight M70 was popular in .308 Win. (7.62mm NATO). This was the first commercial rifle chambered for this cartridge, which replaced the nearly half-century-old .30–06 Springfield as the standard U.S. service cartridge.

When Winchester introduced the post-1964 M70, the barrel length for cartridges like the .243 Win., .270 Win., .30–06, and .308 Win. was standardized at 22.0 inches.

The standard M70 length—which other American manufacturers generally followed—for all magnum calibers except the .458 Win. Magnum (original length 25.0 inches) is 24.0 inches. This includes the .264 Win. Magnum, .300 Win. Magnum, .338 Win. Magnum, .375 H&H Magnum, and 7mm Rem. The current M70 .458 Win. Magnum has a 22.0-inch barrel. This is a proper length for a shorter-range cartridge and for faster handling in the brush.

Weatherby offers options: 24.0-inch or 26.0-inch barrel. At Weatherby prices—about twice what standard Winchester M70, Ruger M77, and Remington M700 rifles cost—there should be options. Not that Weatherby rifles are overpriced; stockwork, action, finish, and bluing are of higher quality than on most standard factory rifles (we except M77 stockwork). You pay for what you get.

Stocks

American black walnut is used for most American rifle and shotgun stocks. Some less expensive rifles use a walnut-stained hardwood. There are many special stock woods; most are available only as custom rifles.

Stock designs. The classic stock is best exemplified by the Ruger M77. This type was developed during the 1920s by stockers like Alvin Linden, Bob Owens, and Griffin & Howe. The M77 has no checkpiece or Monte Carlo comb. The M77 stock is similar to the original standard Winchester stock except that it has a full pistol grip with cap. Riflemen with an eye for the beautiful and graceful prefer the classic design.

The Weatherby stock is distinguished by a flat-bottom slab-sided fore-end fitted with a 45°-angled rosewood tip. Checkering is basketweave. The high comb slants down and forward. The slightly flared pistol grip has a rosewood cap and white line spacer. The stock has a high-gloss finish.

In the past ten years this stock has become the most widely copied design. Even Winchester copied Weatherby. Some manufacturers use tips of material other than rosewood. The author, a longtime admirer of the classic stock, was late to appreciate the advantages of the Weatherby-design comb and pistol grip. No Weatherby copy seems as well done as the original. Price is a factor. Many foreign imports adopted the Weatherby design.

Stock types. The most widely used method of securing stock and barrel is with a screw in the fore-end. Wood is—or should be—closely fitted to the metal except with free-floating barrels. Unless the stock is thoroughly seasoned and properly finished, climatic changes or exposure to moisture may warp the wood and affect the accuracy of the rifle by putting uneven pressure on the barrel.

Free-floating barrels are just that. The barrel projects from the receiver into a barrel channel. The barrel is not attached to the stock; wood doesn't contact the barrel. This method was originally used on varmint and target rifles where extreme accuracy is required.

When Winchester released its post-1964 M70,

devotees of the rifle were appalled at the excessively wide gap between barrel and stock. This was a lamentable, though understandable, attempt to save money by reducing machine and hand labor required to fit barrel and stock. This free- or floating-barrel technique allows manufacturers to use barrels of different diameters with little barrel channeling. Winchester realized its error and offered M70s with better-fitting floating barrels. The original channel was so wide that leaves, pine needles, and other debris collected in the channel.

Comb. There are two basic types: classic and Monte Carlo. The amount of drop between comb and heel has slowly been decreasing during the past 30-odd years. The almost universal use of telescopic sights on bolt-action rifles has been responsible for the decrease. Very few riflemen use both micrometer receiver sights, like the famed Lyman #48 or Williams Foolproof, *and* scopes. In theory, rifles so fitted should have compromise measurements. There would be a very slight neck craning to use the scope, and a slight downward pressure of the cheek to use the receiver sight. A few target rifles are designed for the same position when using either receiver or scope sights.

The classic comb is represented by the standard-stock pre-'64 Winchester M70 and the current Ruger M77. Neither has a cheekpiece. The classic comb with cheekpiece is represented by the pre-'64 M70 Super Grade and some current imports.

Monte Carlo stocks were first used on trap shotguns designed for the famed live-pigeon shoots at Monte Carlo. The Monte Carlo was adopted for rifles to provide a high sight line—for scopes—without increasing buttplate area.

In the late 1930s the Winchester M70 became the first factory rifle to offer purchasers a choice of a standard or a Monte Carlo stock and cheekpiece. Early M70 sporter stocks were designed for a receiver sight only.

The Monte Carlo stocks with cheekpiece includes such widely varying designs as the forward-sloping Monte Carlo of the Weatherby and the near-classic (slight Monte Carlo) of the excellent post-1964 Winchester M70 (Super Grade only) .458 Win. Magnum.

Weatherby stocks with the pronounced Monte Carlo have a forward and downward slope. The forward point of the comb is lower than the after end of the Monte Carlo. Since Weatherby rifles are quite light for the amount of recoil, this forward-sloping Monte Carlo—together with the semi-flared pistol grip—reduces the felt (but not actual) recoil.

Some Monte Carlo stocks have a rollover comb. This is an unneeded comb, but attractive to many shooters. Harrington & Richardson's bolt-action series using the Sako action are examples. This type of cheekpiece comb was useful in the single-shot *schützen* rifle era but not today.

Someone once remarked that *Homo sapiens* is an adaptable cuss. This is borne out by rifle stock variations. The author has used about all variations, from stocks with classic combs to radical Monte Carlos. He seems to use all with equal effectiveness and ease.

The cheekpiece is a European innovation, several centuries old. The late Colonel W. Townsend Whelen devised the first practical cheekpiece for modern American bolt-action rifles, and the style is now classic. The best examples are on the current M700 Remingtons. Many shooters, however, including the author, seem to shoot rifles without cheekpieces like the Ruger M77 as well as those with cheekpieces.

Fore-end

Fore-ends on the original bolt-action rifles were the typical full-length—up to the muzzle. A wooden—or sometimes metal—handguard covered the barrel top. Full-length fore-end and top guard were designed to keep the left hand from being blistered during rapid fire. As the bolt-action evolved into a sporting rifle the top guard was eliminated and except in Mannlicher type the full-length fore-end was shortened. This reduced weight and improved the rifle's locks (though many shooters consider the full-length Mannlicher style most handsome).

1. *Classic fore-end.* Examples include pre-1964 M70 Winchester and current Ruger M77. The round, plain fore-end—no flats and no fore-end tip insert—was standard until the advent of the Weatherby and its imitators. The rounded fore-end is justly popular because it fits the hand.

2. *Classic fore-end with tip inserts.* During the 1920s, Griffin & Howe offered clients a black fore-end tip made of buffalo horn. Inserts were fitted at a 90° angle. These tips were usually fitted on rifles designed for use against dangerous game and chambered for .375 H&H Magnum, .416 Rigby, .425 Westley Richards, .505 Gibbs, and similar cartridges.

The first assembly-line rifle known to the author that was fitted with a fore-end insert was the Winchester Super Grade M70. The insert was molded plastic. The only current Super Grade M70, the .458 Magnum, has an ebony tip.

Other manufacturers use, or have used, plastics like tenite. At least one manufacturer painted a black fore-end tip on .22 rimfire rifles. Fore-end tip inserts have no practical use. They are strictly decorative.

Remington's M700 is the only current production American bolt-action to offer a black fore-end tip fitted at the traditional 90° angle. Most inserts are fitted at a rakish 45° angle.

3. *Weatherby-type fore-end tip.* Roy Weatherby's stockers were apparently the first to introduce the fore-end insert angled at 45°. Weatherby uses rosewood for fore-end tips and pistol-grip caps. Winchester, except on the M70 Super Grade .458 Win. Magnum, copied Weatherby's angled tip and like Weatherby uses white line spacers between tip and main stock, pistol-grip cap and pistol grip, and recoil pad or buttplate and stock. Fanciers of the classic stock feel that angled inserts would not be as ugly if white line spacers were deleted.

By 1970 many American rifles and numerous European sporters had adopted angled fore-end tips and white line spacers. By 1975 the trend may be beginning to change. Savage has returned to the traditional fore-end. The demand for the Ruger M77 is so great that the Newport, N. H., plant is running several months behind on orders —and Ruger never offered any type of fore-end tip, Monte Carlo comb, or cheekpiece. The increasing popularity of the M77 may be forecasting a return to classic stocks. One thing is almost certain. Roy Weatherby won't go classic. He'll find enough customers for his unique rifle stock, which in its own way has become a classic.

Traditionalists prefer the rounded fore-end. The Weatherby slab-sided flat-bottomed fore-end, they say, is not as comfortable to hold, nor, they maintain, can it be held as securely. This may be true, but Weatherby users don't seem to mind and they certainly account for their share of the world's big and dangerous game.

4. *Mannlicher fore-end.* This full-length stock, originally used on sporting rifles based on Ferdinand von Mannlicher's patents, has been used occasionally on American rifles. It's heavier, and being longer is more subject to warpage.

5. *Schnabel fore-end.* This form, of European origin, is rarely seen now. It terminates in a finial lump—a *Schnabel.* In theory the small lump at the fore-end tip aids in steadying the rifle. The theory is not borne out in practice.

6. *Beavertail or semi-beavertail fore-ends.* These, without checkering, are usually found on top-grade match rifles.

Pistol grip

A pistol grip has one primary function: it enables a rifleman to hold his piece steadier. This is very important for long-range shooting. On big-bore rifles designed for use against dangerous game, the pistol grip also snugs the rifle tightly to the shoulder to aid rifle control and reduce felt recoil.

1. *Semi-pistol grip.* The classic example is the pre-1964 Winchester M70. The semi-pistol grip is distinguished from the full pistol grip by the angle of the lower front part of the stock. There is no clear demarcation between this section and the bottom rear of the pistol grip.

2. *Pistol grip (full).* Found on the post-1964 Winchester M70, Remington M700, Ruger M77, and Mauser X. The author considers the pistol grip on the Winchester M70 Super Grade .458 Win. Magnum ideal—at least for his ham-size hands.

3. *Semi-flared pistol grip.* The Weatherby Mark V and Varmintmaster are the classics. This pistol grip, together with the forward-and-down-pitching Monte Carlo comb, is probably necessary to control Weatherby magnum-caliber rifles, which are light for their caliber and generate considerable recoil. Some Weatherby-stock imitators use the down-pitching comb but not the semi-flared pistol grip. They would be well advised to do so.

4. *Flared pistol grip.* This weird design offers no advantages over the standard full pistol grip or semi-flared Weatherby type. Flared grips are often seen in combination with a zebra-type stock (laminated wood with alternating light and dark layers). The result in the author's opinion, is an LSD nightmare.

Pistol-grip cap

Most semi-pistol grips are not capped. Caps, regardless of material, are decoration, but many riflemen, including the author, feel that a cap—preferably blue steel—provides a nice finishing touch to a fine rifle.

Off-the-shelf factory caps may be hard rubber, plastic, rosewood, or steel. Some have white line spacers between the pistol grip and the cap. Spacers seem appropriate on Weatherbys, but admirers of the classic rifle do not like them.

The author replaces non-steel caps with blued steel.

Manufacturers often place their monograms on pistol-grip caps. Some, like the one on the Super Grade Winchester M70 .458 Win. Magnum rifle and the Ruger M77, are relatively subdued. Probably the most garish of all was the big red "W" on early post-1964 Winchester M70s. Monograms are strictly advertising. Why pay money for a rifle and then get stuck with advertising it?

Buttplate

Bolt-action buttplates are the flat (shotgun) type. The deeply curved buttplate of the early lever-action—a heritage from old Pennsylvania flintlocks—was painful when fired with heavy loads and uncomfortable at anytime.

Military buttplates like those of the M98 Mauser and M1903 Springfield were plain steel. They had a trapdoor so an oiler and cleaning thong could be toted within the buttstock. This is not a bad idea. Similar buttplates of checkered steel can be obtained from custom gunsmiths or gunsmith-supply houses.

The checkered steel buttplate of the pre-1964 M70 Winchester type has largely been replaced by high-impact plastic. Surely a man who purchases a rifle costing $250 and up is entitled to a checkered steel buttplate.

Early rifle buttplates were brass, iron, and then plain steel. Winchester used aluminum to reduce weight on its Featherweight M70. An exception was the ventilated recoil pad of the short-lived (too much recoil and muzzle blast) Featherweight M70 in .264 Win. Magnum.

Recoil Pads

There are two types of recoil pad: ventilated for shotguns, and solid rubber for rifles. Unfortunately, most manufacturers use ventilated (shotgun-type) recoil pads even on rifles of moderate (.375 H&H Magnum) to heavy recoil like the .458 Win. Magnum. The difference in cost between ventilated recoil pads and solid recoil pads is infinitesimal. If Bill Ruger can fit solid recoil pads on rifles costing $200, then Winchester and others should be able to fit solid pads to rifles costing $400 plus.

There is a difference between rifle and shotgun recoil. Solid recoil pads seem to absorb big-bore-rifle recoil far better than the ventilated shotgun type. All magnum-caliber rifles should be fitted with solid recoil pads.

Bill Ruger has gone to the other extreme. He fits all M77s with solid pads. There is no need—in terms of recoil—to fit a recoil pad on a .243 or .22–250 or even .30–06 rifle. The advertising gimmick is that a rifle when stood up against a wall, a car, or a tree will not be as likely to slip and fall down when fitted with a recoil pad. Any man who stands a rifle up anytime, anyplace, except in an upright gun cabinet is a fool. The real reason for fitting the same pad type to all rifles is purely economic. Rifle stock blanks are cut to overall length by machines. It is less expensive to set all machines to one length than to set some machines for cutting to steel or plastic buttplate length and other machines for cutting to recoil-pad length. The overall stock length for a rifle with a recoil pad is less (before attaching the pad) than for a rifle with the thinner metal or plastic buttplate.

Recoil pads were formerly made of rubber. Today, many are made of synthetics. Rubber recoil pads ultimately have to be replaced. Synthetic ones may last longer, but the author doubts if they absorb recoil as well. They do not seem to but this may be his imagination.

Swivels and slings

All bolt-action sporting rifles—save the least expensive—are fitted with sling swivels. Detachable swivels are the best type. Permanently attached swivels such as were furnished on most pre-1960 rifles require the complete removal of the sling itself. Quick-detachable (QD) swivels are simple. It takes 15 seconds to remove the swivels and sling. Only an inconspicuous swivel stud remains. Rifles stowed in upright rifle racks look sloppy with slings left on. There are times when slings are a confounded nuisance, as in thick brush. Slings are best removed when firing from a bench (when a rest is used).

On the basis of use, there are two types:

1. *Carrying sling.* This is sometimes called a carrying strap and is what the name implies. Big-bore rifles like the M70 African and Mark V .460 Weatherby Magnum are designed for use at short range against dangerous game. One doesn't get into the prone position and carefully adjust the sling when confronted by a charging Cape buffalo or elephant at 20 feet.

In Alaska, brown-bear hunters tote their own rifles. This is where a carrying sling is useful. In Africa your gun bearer precedes you. Your heavy rifle is carried over his shoulder, stock to the rear, where you can readily grasp it. Slings should be detached in heavy cover.

2. *Standard sling.* For many years the sling used by sportsmen was the surplus or "liberated" M1907 sling as designed for the M1903 Springfield. This was the sling issued during two world wars. Simpler web slings for the M1923 and M1 were also used.

The M1903 sling was useful but cumbersome, slow and heavy. The author's first experiences with the M1907 sling came when undergoing infantry officers' training, and later as a horse cavalry cadet. The sling substantially improved one's chances for a hit at ranges out to 1000 yards, but it is too slow for use while hunting sheep, antelope, caribou. Here the "hasty sling" position should be used. This position is easy to get into though not as effective as the standard position. The time saved may make the difference between bagging and missing your trophy.

The late Colonel Townsend Whelen, a military rifleman and a big-game hunter, devised the lighter, easier-to-use Whelen sling. It costs only a few dollars. Buy one and forget the heavy 1.5-inch-wide military sling.

The author uses a Whelen 0.875-inch sling on rifles (with scope) weighing less than 9.0 lbs. and a 1.0-inch sling for rifles over that weight.

3. *Big-bore rifle slings.* Forward sling swivels for use on rifles of .40 caliber or over (including the .378 Weatherby Magnum) can severely injure or temporarily cripple the left hand if placed in the conventional fore-end position. Such heavy-recoil rifles should have the forward swivel positioned on the barrel ahead of the fore-end with a barrel band or barrel stud fitted with quick-detachable sling swivels. The Winchester M70 African is one of the few .458 Win. Magnum rifles so fitted. It has the forward swivel fitted to a barrel stud. Ruger's superb M77 .458 has a barrel band, as does the Ruger Number One Tropical single-shot rifle in both .375 M&M and .458 Win. Magnums. Some of Weatherby's lightweight smallbore rifles like the .300 and mediumbore .338 Weatherby Magnums could do with a barrel-band or barrel-stud forward swivel mount.

Checkering

Checkering has two functions: to assist in holding the rifle steady (particularly important when hands are sweaty) and to improve appearance. There are three basic checkering types:

1. *Machine checkering.* Until the mid-1960s most off-the-shelf factory rifles were machine-checkered.

2. *Impressed checkering.* Remington in its fight to minimize rising production costs, introduced "reverse" or "impressed" checkering. This "checkering" type is worthless for gripping purposes, and most shooters agree that it looks like hell. Nevertheless, other companies, were also caught in the campaign to increase sales while keeping production costs down. The post-1964 Winchester had reverse checkering for a while. M70 admirers protested. Many turned to Bill Ruger's M77, which not only sells for less money but offers modest hand checkering. By 1975 Remington and Winchester returned to machine checkering on the M700 and M70.

3. *Hand checkering.* This is used by only one of the Big Three. It is the Ruger noted above. Hand checkering, until Bill Ruger trained Newport, N.H., girls to hand-checker stocks (under supervision of top custom stocker Leonard Brownell), was the province of a relatively few craftsmen.

Hand checkering found on factory-stocked rifles cannot, of course, compare with fine custom-stocked rifles, where the cost of checkering may exceed the cost of an entire new M70, M77, or M700 rifle. Roy Weatherby's Mark V rifles—costing nearly twice as much as the Big Three—has hand checkering of the basketweave type.

BSA CF2 HUNTING RIFLE

Manufacturer: Birmingham Small Arms, England

Importer/distributor: Ithacagun

Action type: bolt; modified Mauser

Magazine type: nondetachable staggered box; hinged floorplate

Magazine capacity: 5-shot, except 4-shot capacity in .300 Win. Magnum and 7mm Rem. Magnum

Safety: pivoting side lever

Barrel length: 23.5 inches

Stock: 1-piece walnut; skip-line hand checkering; roll-over Monte Carlo comb; Weatherby-style slab fore-end; flared pistol grip with rosewood cap and white line spacer; rosewood fore-end tip with white line spacer; high-gloss finish; quick-detachable sling swivels

Buttplate: solid rubber recoil pad.

Length of pull: 13.75 inches

Drop at comb: 1.5 inches

Drop at Monte Carlo: 1.5 inches

Drop at heel: 2.25 inches

Weight: 7.75–8.25 lbs., depending on caliber

Trigger pull: 4.5 lbs.

Sight, rear: Williams Guide, fully adjustable

Sight, front: bead

Scope adaptability: receiver drilled and tapped for standard mount

Caliber: .222 Rem., .22–250 Rem., .243 Win., .270 Win., .30–06 Springfield, .308 Win. (7.62mm NATO), .300 Win. Magnum, 7x57 Mauser, 7mm Rem. Magnum

Data: Set trigger available at extra cost.

Comment: A well designed and crafted rifle.

BSA MONARCH DELUXE RIFLE

Manufacturer: Birmingham Small Arms, England

Importer/distributor: J. Galef & Sons

Action type: bolt; modified Mauser

Magazine type: nondetachable staggered box; hinged floorplate

Magazine capacity: 5-shot, except 4-shot capacity in 7mm Rem. Magnum

Safety: pivoting side lever

Barrel length: 22.0 inches, except 24.0 inches in 7mm Rem. Magnum

Stock: 1-piece walnut; machine checkering; Weatherby-style slab fore-end with rosewood tip and white line spacer; flared pistol grip with rosewood cap and white line spacer; Monte Carlo comb; high-gloss finish; quick-detachable sling swivels

Buttplate: solid rubber recoil pad

Overall length: 22.0-inch barrel, 42.0 inches; 24.0-inch barrel, 44.0 inches

Length of pull: 13.75 inches

Drop at comb: 1.5 inches

Drop at Monte Carlo: 1.5 inches

Drop at heel: 2.25 inches

Weight: 7.5 lbs.

Trigger pull: 4.5 lbs.

Sight, rear: folding leaf, crudely adjustable for windage and elevation

Sight, front: bead on ramp with detachable hood.

Scope adaptability: receiver drilled and tapped for standard mount

Caliber: .270 Win., .30–06 Springfield, .308 Win. (7.62mm NATO), 7mm Rem. Magnum

Comment: This is one of the lower-priced bolt-action imports. It offers no unique features, but is well designed and crafted.

BSA MONARCH HEAVY BARREL RIFLE

Manufacturer: Birmingham Small Arms, England

Importer/distributor: J. Galef & Sons

Action type: bolt; modified Mauser

Magazine type: non-detachable staggered box; hinged floorplate

Magazine capacity: 5-shot

Safety: pivoting side lever

Barrel length: 22.0 inches

Stock: 1-piece walnut; machine checkering; Weatherby-style slab fore-end with rosewood tip; flared pistol grip with rosewood cap and white line spacer; high-gloss finish; quick-detachable sling swivels

Buttplate: solid rubber recoil pad

Length of pull: 13.75 inches

Drop at comb: 1.5 inches

BSA MONARCH HEAVY BARREL RIFLE (continued)

Drop at Monte Carlo: 1.5 inches

Drop at heel: 2.25 inches

Weight: 8.25 lbs.

Trigger pull: 4.5 lbs.

Sight, rear: folding leaf, crudely adjustable for windage and elevation

Sight, front: bead on ramp with detachable hood

Scope adaptability: receiver drilled and tapped for standard mount

Caliber: .222 Rem., .243 Win.

Data: same as for standard BSA Monarch except for slightly heavier barrel.

Comment: This would be a better varmint rifle if it had a 24.0-inch barrel and weighed at least 8.5 lbs.

CARL GUSTAV SWEDE RIFLE

Manufacturer: Carl Gustav Stads Gevarskfaktori, Sweden

Importer/distributor: FFV Sports, Inc.

Action type: bolt; modified Mauser; recessed bolt face

Magazine type: nondetachable staggered box with hinged floorplate; inside trigger bow release; interchangeable with detachable box magazine

Magazine capacity: 5-shot

Safety: slide on right side of receiver

Barrel length: 23.5 inches

Stock: Standard Grade: 1-piece European walnut in either classic or Monte Carlo version; hand-checkered pistol grip and fore-end; Schnabel tip, thin white line spacer between pistol-grip cap and pistol grip; oil-rubbed finish. Swede Standard: French walnut stock; hand-checkered pistol grip and fore-end; Schnabel tip

Buttplate: shotgun type; plastic

Overall length: 44.0 inches

Length of pull: 13.5 inches

Drop at comb: 0.625 inches

Drop at Monte Carlo: 0.25 inch

Drop at heel: 1.5 inches

Weight: 7.25 lbs.

Trigger pull: externally adjustable to 3.3-lb. minimum

Sight, rear: standard, open; Deluxe, none

Sight, front: standard, gold bead with removable sight protector; Deluxe, none

Scope adaptability: drilled and tapped for adjustment scope mounts

Caliber: .22–250 Rem., .243 Win., .25–06 Rem., .270 Win., .30–06 Springfield, .308 Win. (7.62mm NATO)

Data: Basic action data is the same as for Carl Gustav Grades II/III. Swede Deluxe has jeweled bolt, engraved bolt plate.

Comment: This is an extraordinarily fine rifle. Superb craftsmanship and design. The Schnabel tip may not appeal to all stateside riflemen.

CARL GUSTAV (FFV-FRANCHI) RIFLE

Manufacturer: Carl Gustav Stads Gevarskfaktori, Sweden

Importer/distributor: Stoeger Arms Corp./FFV Sports, Inc.

Action type: bolt; modified Mauser; recessed bolt face

Magazine type: nondetachable staggered box with hinged floorplate; interchangeable with detachable box magazine

Magazine capacity: standard calibers, 5-shot; Magnums, 3-shot

Safety: 3-position slide on right side of receiver

Barrel length: 23.5 inches

Stock: Grade II (no Grade I): 1-piece European walnut; rosewood tip insert; oil finish; hand-checkered pistol grip and fore-end; Monte Carlo comb and cheekpiece; rosewood pistol-grip cap with white line spacer; sling swivels. Grade III: 1-piece French walnut; hand-checkered pistol grip and fore-end; 5 coats of polyurethane, glossy finish; rosewood tip and pistol-grip cap; white line spacer between pistol-grip cap and grip and between fore-end and fore-tip; cheekpiece and Monte Carlo comb; quick-detachable sling swivels.

Buttplate: shotgun type; ventilated recoil pad on magnum calibers; plastic buttplate with white line spacer

Overall length: 44.0 inches

Length of pull: 13.5 inches

Drop at comb: 0.625 inch

Drop at Monte Carlo: 0.25 inch

Drop at heel: 1.5 inches

Weight: 7.2–7.5 lbs.

Trigger pull: adjustable to 3.3 lbs. minimum

Sight, rear: Grade II, open; Grade III, none

Sight, front: Grade II, gold bead with removable sight protector; Grade III, none

Scope adaptability: both grades drilled and tapped for standard scope mounts

Caliber: .22–250 Rem., .243 Win., .270 Win., .30–06 Springfield. .300 Win. Magnum, .308 Win. (7.62mm NATO), 7mm Rem. Magnum, 6.5×55 Mauser

Data: Action features anti-bind device (bolt guide) and externally adjustable trigger. Bolt handle has short (80°) lift. Chrome bolt handle. Grade III has jeweled bolt body, hand-engraved floorplate.

Grade III in calibers 6.5×55 Mauser, .25–06 Rem., .270 Win., and .30–06 Springfield is available in a left-hand action.

Comment: This is a very fine rifle. Wood and metal unions are perfectly executed. Actions and barreled actions are available.

COLT SAUER SPORTING RIFLE

Manufacturer: J.P.Sauer & Sohns, West Germany

Importer/distributor: Colt

Action type: bolt; shrouded head

Magazine type: detachable box

Magazine capacity: 4-shot, except 3-shot capacity in 7mm Rem. Magnum and .300 Win. Magnum

Safety: slide

Barrel length: 24.0 inches

Stock: 1-piece European walnut; hand checkering; full pistol grip with rosewood cap and white line spacer; rosewood fore-end cap with white line spacer; Monte Carlo comb; high-gloss finish; quick-detachable sling swivels

Buttplate: ventilated rubber recoil pad with white line spacer

Length of pull: 13.75 inches

Drop at comb: 1.5 inches

Drop at Monte Carlo: 1.3 inches

Drop at heel: 2.25 inches

Weight: 7.5 lbs.

Trigger pull: 4.5 lbs.

Open sights: none

Scope adaptability: receiver drilled and tapped for standard mount

Caliber: .25–06 Rem., .270 Win., .30–06 Springfield, .300 Win. Magnum, 7mm Rem. Magnum

Data: The shrouded bolt and locking lugs bear a superficial resemblance to the Weatherby Mark V action, which was formerly manufactured by Sauer.

Comment: This is an excellent action, and the stock work is superior to the average bolt-action rifle.

COLT SAUER SHORT ACTION RIFLE

Manufacturer: J.P. Sauer & Sohns, West Germany

Importer/distributor: Colt

Action type: bolt; shrouded head

Magazine type: detachable box

Magazine capacity: 3-shot

Safety: slide

Barrel length: 24.0 inches

Stock: 1-piece European walnut; hand checkering; full pistol grip with rosewood cap and white line spacer; rosewood fore-end cap with white line spacer; Monte Carlo comb; high gloss finish; quick-detachable sling swivels

Buttplate: ventilated rubber recoil pad with white line spacer

Length of pull: 13.75 inches

Drop at comb: 1.5 inches

Drop at Monte Carlo: 1.3 inches

Drop at heel: 2.25 inches

Weight: 7.25 lbs.

Trigger pull: 4.5 lbs.

Open sights: none

Scope adaptability: receiver drilled and tapped for standard mount

Caliber: .22–250 Rem., .243 Win., .308 Win. (7.62mm NATO)

Comment: Short-action version of Colt Sauer Sporting Rifle.

GARCIA SAKO M74 SPORTER

Manufacturer: Sako, Finland

Importer/distributor: Garcia Corp./Firearms International

Action type: bolt; modified Mauser; recessed bolt face

Magazine type: nondetachable staggered box; hinged floorplate

Magazine capacity: standard calibers, 5-shot; magnum calibers, 4-shot

Safety: slide

Barrel length: 23.5 inches in .222 Rem., .223 Rem. (5.56mm); 23.0 inches in .22–250 Rem., .243 Win., .308 Win. (7.62mm NATO); 24.0 inches in all other calibers

Stock: 1-piece European walnut; hand-checkered fore-end and pistol grip; un-capped full pistol grip; slab-sided, flat-bottom fore-end; crossbolt through stock on magnum calibers; quick-detachable sling swivel studs

Buttplate: shotgun type; plastic with white line spacer on standard calibers; ventilated recoil pad on magnum calibers

Overall length: 43.0–44.0 inches

Length of pull: 13.5 inches

Drop at comb: 1.0 inch

Drop at Monte Carlo: 0.875 inch

Drop at heel: 0.65 inch

Weight: 6.5 lbs. in .222 Rem., .223 Rem. (5.56mm); 6.75 lbs. in .22–250 Rem., .243 Win., .308 Win. (7.62mm NATO); 8.0 lbs. in other calibers.

Action lengths: short in .222 Rem., .223 Rem. (5.56mm); medium in .22–250 Rem., .243 Win., .308 Win. (7.62mm NATO); long in all other calibers

Trigger pull: 3.5 lbs.

Sight, rear: none

Sight, front: none

Scope adaptability: drilled and tapped for standard scope bases

Caliber: .222 Rem., .223 Rem. (5.56mm), .22–250 Rem., .243 Win., .25–06 Rem., .270 Win., .30–06 Springfield, .300 Win. Magnum, .308 Win. (7.62mm NATO), .338 Win. Magnum, .375 H&H Magnum, 7mm Rem. Magnum

Data: The M74 designation covers three action lengths, each of which has had at least one previous designation and which also had names like Vixen, Forrester, and Finnbear. The oldest action dates back to 1949.

The M74 is one of the few rifles that have three different-length actions instead of using one length magazine with magazine fillers for varied cartridge lengths.

GARCIA SAKO M74 SPORTER (continued)

L-46/L-461 (Vixen) action. This action, originally designed for the rimmed .22 Hornet and .218 Bee, was later chambered for the .222 Rem. It was fitted with an almost exact duplicate of the famed Winchester M70 trigger and had a detachable box magazine. When the L-46 was chambered for the .222 Rem. the magazine was lengthened and bolt face altered to handle a rimless cartridge. The .222 Rem. Magnum chambering was not a success. The case was too long to feed and eject properly. The L-46 safety for some reason was located on the left—a damnably inconvenient site. It was later moved to the right side.

In 1964 Sako replaced the L-46 with the L-461. This modification has a nondetachable staggered box magazine with a hinged floorplate. The M70-type trigger was replaced by a Sako trigger. A bolt sleeve uniform in design with that on the Sako L-579 and L-61 was adopted.

Most rifle makers don't make a short action for short cartridges. The M70 Winchester uses the same length action for its .375 H&H Magnum as it does for the .222 Rem. Magazine fillers and bolt stops of varying lengths are used to accommodate different-length cartridges.

If Sako were to chamber its "long" action for short cartridges like the .222 Rem., bolt travel would be increased from 2.925 inches to 4.4635 inches. Action weight would be increased from 33.0 oz. to 44.0 oz.

The use by Winchester of one action length or the use of two lengths by Remington and Ruger doesn't imply that these actions are inferior to the Sako but that for short cartridges the true short action like the L-46 and L-461 is more efficient.

L-57/L-579 (Forrester) action. The increasing popularity of the .243 Win. and .308 Win. cartridges led Sako to introduce the medium-length L-57 (Forrester) action in 1958. The action was fitted with a nondetachable staggered box magazine. Essentially the L-57 was an elongated L-46 action, though the trigger system was different.

In 1960 Sako issued the L-579. This improved version's major change was the altering of the mechanism to accept the Sako Number 4 trigger system or the same as that of the L-461. Action weight is 40 oz.

L-61 (Finnbear) action. This is designed to handle "long" cartridges like the .30-06 Springfield and short magnums like the 7mm Rem. Magnum. It has the Sako Number 4 trigger system. Action weight is 44.0 oz.

Over the years Sako standardized the component design of its three actions. Today, the M74 designation covers three separate length actions, uniform in design. Actions can be purchased separately: L-461, L-579, and L-61.

Several American rifles have used—some still do use—Sako actions. The author recently purchased a Marlin 322 (1954-57). The Micro-Groove Barrel was shot out, but he bought it for its L-46 action. Marlin discontinued the 322 not because of action problems but because the barrel rarely retained minute-of-angle accuracy beyond 500 rounds.

Harrington & Richardson currently uses Sako actions for the 300 series rifles. Coltsman rifles (1957-61 *ca.*) used the L-57 action. Better-grade Browning Hi-Power rifles, (discontinued 1974) used the L-461 action for .222 Rem. chamberings and the L-579 for .22-250 Rem. J. C. Higgins' M52 rifle in .222 Rem., made by Marlin for Sears Roebuck, used the L-46 action.

Comment: The Sako is one of the world's great actions. It ranks with the pre-1964 M70 Winchester—for short cartridges it is better—and with the finest of the Oberndorf Mauser sporters. Some potential purchasers would prefer a classic stock. True, they could have a custom stock, but such stocks are expensive.

For most calibers like the .243 Win., .30-06 Springfield, or 7mm Rem. Magnum, the author can get along with his pre-1964 M70s and Rugers, but for short cartridges he prefers the short Sako action over all others. So do many others, including action expert Frank de Maas, who has evaluated all existing bolt actions.

Actions and barreled actions are available.

HARRINGTON & RICHARDSON M300

Manufacturer: Sako, Finland

Importer/distributor: Harrington & Richardson

Action type: bolt; modified Mauser; enclosed bolt head

Magazine type: nondetachable staggered box; hinged floorplate

Magazine capacity: standard calibers, 5-shot; magnum calibers, 3-shot

Safety: 3-position; sliding

Barrel length: 22.0 inches

Stock: 1-piece American walnut; Monte Carlo comb; rollover cheekpiece; pistol grip with rosewood cap and contrasting wood fore-end insert at 45° angle

Buttplate: shotgun type with solid recoil pad; black and white line spacers

Overall length: 42.5 inches

Length of pull: 13.625 inches

Drop at comb: 1.5 inches

Drop at Monte Carlo: 1.5 inches

Drop at heel: 2.125 inches

Weight: 7.75 lbs.

Trigger pull: 4.5 lbs.

Sight, rear: folding leaf, crudely adjustable for windage

Sight, front: flat gold bead on ramp grooved for sight protector (not furnished)

Scope adaptability: receiver drilled and tapped for standard scope bases

Caliber: .22–250 Rem., .243 Win., .270 Win., .30–06 Springfield, .300 Win. Magnum, .308 Win. (7.62mm NATO), 7mm Rem. Magnum

Data: Fitted with studs for quick-detachable sling swivels. All barrels and actions in the H&R 300 series are made by Sako/Finland.

Comment: Sako actions and barrels are as good as can be found. The 22.0-inch barrels are too short for magnum cartridges. There is velocity loss and excessive muzzle blast. This is one of the few models with a 22.0-inch barrel for magnum cartridges.

HARRINGTON & RICHARDSON M301 (MANNLICHER STOCK)

Manufacturer: Sako, Finland

Importer/distributor: Harrington & Richardson

Action type: bolt; modified Mauser; recessed bolt face

H.&R. M301 (continued)

Magazine type: nondetachable staggered box; hinged floorplate

Magazine capacity: standard calibers, 5-shot; magnum calibers, 3-shot

Safety: slide (just aft bolt handle), 3-position

Barrel length: 19.0 inches

Stock: 1-piece American walnut, Mannlicher-style with flared pistol grip capped by rosewood; Monte Carlo comb; hand checkering

Buttplate: shotgun type with white and black line spacers; thin solid recoil pad (red)

Overall length: 39.0 inches

Length of pull: 13.625 inches

Drop at comb: 1.75 inches

Drop at Monte Carlo: 1.5 inches

Drop at heel: 2.125 inches

Weight: 7.25 lbs.

Trigger pull: 4.5 lbs.

Sight, rear: folding leaf, crudely adjustable for windage and elevation

Sight, front: gold bead on ramp with groove for sight protector (not furnished)

Scope adaptability: receiver drilled and taped for standard scope bases

Caliber: .243 Win., .270 Win., .30–06 Springfield, .300 Win. Magnum, .308 Win. (7.62mm NATO), 7mm Rem. Magnum

Data: No provisions for sling swivels. Medium-length Sako action.

Comment: Except for men who carry a rifle lashed to a packboard or packframe, the 19-inch barrel is too short. There is excessive muzzle blast. Several American manufacturers and importers have offered similar barrel lengths but discontinued them within a year or two.

INTERARMS MAUSER MARK X RIFLE

Manufacturer: Zavodi Crvena Zastava Arsenal, Yugoslavia

Importer/distributor: Interarms

Action type: bolt; modified Mauser

Magazine type: nondetachable staggered box; hinged floorplate

Magazine capacity: 5-shot, except 3-shot capacity in .300 Win. Magnum and 7mm Rem. Magnum

Safety: slide

Barrel length: 24.0 inches

Stock: 1-piece European walnut; hand checkering; Monte Carlo comb; full pistol grip with black plastic cap and white line spacer; black tenite fore-end cap with white line spacer; cheekpiece; quick-detachable sling swivels; high-gloss finish

Buttplate: black plastic with white line spacer

Overall length: 44.0 inches

Length of pull: 13.75 inches

Drop at comb: 1.75 inches

Drop at Monte Carlo: 1.5 inches

Drop at heel: 2.125 inches

Weight: 7.5 lbs.

Trigger pull: not specified

Sight, rear: Williams Guide, fully adjustable

Sight, front: gold bead on ramp with detachable hood

Scope adaptability: receiver drilled and tapped for standard mount

Caliber: .22–250 Rem., .243 Win., .25–06 Rem., .270 Win., .308 Win. (7.62mm NATO), .30–06 Springfield, .300 Win. Magnum, 7× 57 Mauser, 7mm Rem. Magnum

Data: This rifle uses the Yugoslavian-made Mauser Mark X action, which is almost like its illustrious ancestor the M98 Mauser. Single-stage sporting trigger replaces the double-pull military trigger. The triggerbow and magazine floorplate are milled steel rather than the inferior alloys. The action closely resembles the M24 Yugoslav Mauser.

The bolt stop more closely resembles that on the recently deceased FN Browning Hi-Power rifle. It has an almost flush combination stop and ejectors. The ejector and extractor are of the highly desirable classic Mauser design.

Comment: This is an excellent action for those who prefer the classic Mauser rather than the current types which use plunger ejectors and other money-saving devices.

INTERARMS MAUSER MARK X CAVALIER RIFLE

Manufacturer: Zavodi Crvena Zastava Arsenal, Yugoslavia

Importer/distributor: Interarms

Action type: bolt; modified Mauser

Magazine type: nondetachable staggered box; hinged floorplate

Magazine capacity: 5-shot, except 3-shot capacity in 7mm Rem. Magnum and .300 Win. Magnum

Safety: slide

Barrel length: 24.0 inches

Stock: 1-piece walnut with modified Weatherby styling; machine checkering; full pistol grip with rosewood cap; rosewood fore-end tip; high-gloss finish

Buttplate: ventilated black rubber recoil pad

Overall length: 44.0 inches

Length of pull: 13.75 inches

Drop at comb: 1.75 inches

Drop at Monte Carlo: 1.5 inches

Drop at heel: 2.5 inches

Weight: 7.5 lbs.

Trigger pull: not specified

Sight, rear: Williams Guide, fully adjustable

Sight, front: gold bead on ramp with detachable hood

Scope adaptability: receiver drilled and tapped for standard mount

Caliber: .22–250 Rem., .243 Win., .25–06 Rem., .270 Win., .308 Win. (7.62mm NATO), .30–06 Springfield, .300 Win. Magnum, 7×57 Mauser, 7mm Rem. Magnum

Data: For general action data see Interarms Mauser Mark X Rifle.

Comment: A well-designed rifle with classic Mauser 98 action features. Save for stock design, this is same as other Interarms Mark X rifles.

ITHACA-LSA M55 STANDARD RIFLE

Manufacturer: Tikka, Finland

Importer/distributor: Ithacagun

Action type: bolt; modified Mauser

Magazine type: detachable box

Magazine capacity: 3-shot

Safety: thumb slide

Barrel length: 22.0 inches

Stock: 1-piece European walnut; machine checkering; Weatherby-style slab fore-end with rosewood tip and white line spacer; flared pistol grip with rosewood cap and white line spacer; Monte Carlo comb; high-gloss finish; quick-detachable sling swivels

Buttplate: shotgun type; black plastic

Overall length: 42.0 inches

Length of pull: 13.625 inches

Drop at comb: 1.5 inches

Drop at Monte Carlo: 1.375 inches

Drop at heel: 2.0 inches

Weight: 6.5 lbs.

Trigger pull: 4.5 lbs.

Sight, rear: Williams Guide, fully adjustable

Sight, front: bead on ramp with detachable hood

Scope adaptability: receiver drilled and tapped for standard mount

Caliber: .222 Rem., .22–250 Rem., .243 Win., .308 Win. (7.62mm NATO), 6mm Rem.

Data: An improved Mauser action with bolt face completely covering the cartridge head.

Comment: Well-designed and crafted bolt-action.

ITHACA-LSA M55 DELUXE RIFLE

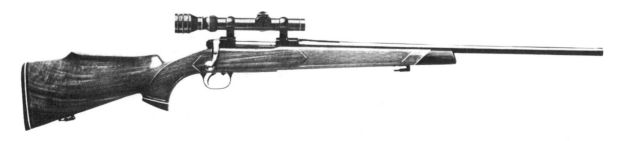

Manufacturer: Tikka, Finland

Importer/distributor: Ithacagun

Action type: bolt; modified Mauser

Magazine type: detachable box

Magazine capacity: 3-shot

Safety: thumb slide

Barrel length: 22.0 inches

Stock: 1-piece walnut; skip-line hand checkering; Weatherby-style slab fore-end with rosewood tip with white line spacer; flared pistol grip with rosewood cap and white line spacer; roll-over Monte Carlo comb; high-gloss finish; quick-detachable sling swivels

Buttplate: solid rubber recoil pad with white line spacer

Overall length: 42.0 inches

Length of pull: 13.625 inches

Drop at comb: 1.875 inches

Drop at Monte Carlo: 1.75 inches

Drop at heel: 2.125 inches

Weight: 6.5 lbs.

Trigger pull: 4.5 lbs.

Open sights: none

Scope adaptability: receiver drilled and tapped for standard mount

Caliber: .222 Rem., .22–250 Rem., .243 Win., .308 Win. (7.62mm NATO), 6mm Rem.

Comment: As the name implies, this is a deluxe version of the M55 Standard.

ITHACA-LSA M55 HEAVY BARREL RIFLE

Manufacturer: Tikka, Finland

Importer/distributor: Ithacagun

Action type: bolt; modified Mauser

Magazine type: detachable box

Magazine capacity: 3-shot

Safety: thumb slide

Barrel length: 23.0 inches

Stock: 1-piece walnut; machine checkering; flared pistol grip with rosewood cap and white line spacer; beavertail fore-end; roll-over cheekpiece; Monte Carlo comb; oil-type finish; quick-detachable sling swivels

Buttplate: solid rubber recoil pad

Overall length: 43.0 inches

Length of pull: 13.625 inches

Drop at comb: 1.875 inches

Drop at Monte Carlo: 1.75 inches

Drop at heel: 2.125 inches

Weight: 8.25 lbs.

Trigger pull: 4.5 lbs.

Open sights: none

Scope adaptability: receiver drilled and tapped for standard mount

Caliber: .222 Rem., .22–250 Rem.

Data: Save for barrel and beavertail fore-end, similar to M55 Standard.

Comment: For varminting, the author would prefer a 24.0-inch barrel and a bit more weight.

ITHACA-LSA M65 STANDARD

Manufacturer: Tikka, Finland

Importer/distributor: Ithacagun

Action type: bolt; modified Mauser

Magazine type: detachable box

Magazine capacity: 4-shot

Safety: thumb slide

Barrel length: 22.0 inches

Stock: 1-piece walnut; machine checkering; flared pistol grip with rosewood cap and white line spacer; Monte Carlo comb; high-gloss finish; quick-detachable sling swivels

Buttplate: shotgun type; black plastic

Overall length: 43.0 inches

Length of pull: 13.625 inches

Drop at comb: 1.5 inches

ITHACA-LSA M65 STANDARD (continued)

Drop at Monte Carlo: 1.375 inches

Drop at heel: 2.0 inches

Weight: 7.0 lbs.

Trigger pull: 4.5 lbs.

Sight, rear: Williams Guide, adjustable for windage and elevation

Sight, front: bead on ramp with detachable hood

Scope adaptability: receiver drilled and tapped for standard mount

Caliber: .25–06 Rem., .270 Win., .30–06 Springfield

Data: Same as for Ithaca-LSA M55 save for chamberings.

Comment: See Ithaca-LSA M55 Standard.

ITHACA-LSA MODEL 65 DELUXE RIFLE

Manufacturer: Tikka, Finland

Importer/distributor: Ithacagun

Action type: bolt; modified Mauser

Magazine type: detachable box

Magazine capacity: 4-shot

Safety: thumb slide

Barrel length: 23.0 inches

Stock: 1-piece walnut; skip-line hand checkering; roll-over cheekpiece; Monte Carlo comb; Weatherby-style slab fore-end with rosewood tip and white line spacer; flared pistol grip with rosewood cap and white line spacer; high-gloss finish; quick-detachable sling swivels

Buttplate: solid rubber recoil pad with white line spacer

Overall length: 43.0 inches

Length of pull: 13.625 inches

Drop at comb: 1.875 inches

Drop at Monte Carlo: 1.75 inches

Drop at heel: 2.125 inches

Weight: 7.0 lbs.

Trigger pull: 4.5 lbs.

Open sights: none

Scope adaptability: receiver drilled and tapped for standard mount

Caliber: .25–06 Rem., .270 Win., .30–06 Springfield

Data: Same as for M55 Deluxe except for chamberings.

Comment: See M55 Deluxe.

MOSSBERG 800 SERIES

Action type: bolt; modified Mauser; six locking lugs

Magazine type: nondetachable staggered box; hinged floorplate; short action

Magazine capacity: 4-shot (except .222 Rem., 3-shot)

Safety: thumb; 3-position; at rear end of bolt

Barrel length: 22.0 inches; 24.0-inch heavy varmint barrel on M800VT (calibers: .22–250 Rem., .222 Rem., .243 Win.)

Stock: 1-piece American walnut with reverse checkering; Monte Carlo comb; cheekpiece; plastic pistol-grip cap with white spacer

Buttplate: shotgun type; plastic with white line spacer

Overall length: 22.0-inch barrel, 42.0 inches; 24.0-inch barrel, 44.0 inches

Length of pull: 14.0 inches

Drop at comb: 1.875 inches

Drop at Monte Carlo: 1.625 inches

Drop at heel: 2.125 inches

Weight: 6.5 lbs.; M800VT (varmint version), 9.5 lbs.

Trigger pull: not specified

Sight, rear: folding leaf, crudely adjustable for windage and elevation; none on M800VT

Sight, front: gold bead on ramp; none on M800VT

Scope adaptability: receiver drilled and tapped for standard scope bases; M800VT has dovetail base for target (external adjustment) scope.

Caliber: .222 Rem. (M800 VT only), .22–250 Rem., .243 Win., .308 Win. (7.62mm NATO); not in varmint version.

Data: Mossberg uses a letter suffix for each variation and caliber in the M800 series — i.e., a .308 Win. M800 is M800A, a .308 Win. with a Mossberg 4× scope is M800ASM, and so on

Comment: One of the most moderately priced rifles on the market. The varmint version is capable of 1-inch 5-shot groups at 100 yards. This is not quite as good as some of the more expensive rifles like the Ruger M77, but considering the price difference, this rifle will supply the accuracy requirements of all but the most exacting shooters.

MOSSBERG 810 SERIES

Action type: bolt; modified Mauser; enclosed bolt head

Frame: solid

Magazine type: nondetachable staggered box with hinged floorplate; or detachable box

Magazine capacity: standard calibers, 4-shot; magnum calibers, 3-shot

Safety: thumb slide at end of bolt

Barrel length: standard calibers, 22.0 inches; magnum calibers, 24.0 inches

Stock: 1-piece American walnut with reverse checkering; Monte Carlo comb; cheekpiece; plastic pistol-grip cap with white line spacer; classic fore-end

Buttplate: shotgun type with white line spacer and rubber recoil pad

Overall length: 22.0-inch barrel, 42.0 inches; 24.0-inch barrel, 44.0 inches

Length of pull: 14.0 inches

Drop at comb: 1.875 inches

Drop at Monte Carlo: 1.625 inches

Drop at heel: 2.125 inches

Weight: 22.0-inch barrel, 7.5 lbs.; 24.0-inch barrel, 8.0 lbs.

Trigger pull: not specified

Sight, rear: folding leaf, crudely adjustable for windage and elevation

Sight, front: gold bead on ramp; no sight protector

Scope adaptability: receiver drilled and tapped for standard scope bases; no open sights provided if rifle is ordered with 4× Mossberg scope

Caliber: .270 Win., .30–06 Springfield, .338 Win. Magnum, 7mm Rem. Magnum

Data: Engine-turned bolt. Standard sling swivels. Adjustable trigger. Mossberg, as with the 800 series, uses letter suffixes for each M810 variation. Thus 810A is .30–06 Springfield with detachable box magazine. M180AH is .30–06 with hinged floorplate. M810ASM is .30–06

MOSSBERG 810 SERIES (continued)

Springfield with detachable box magazine and 4× Mossberg scope.

Comment: This excellent rifle is one of the best buys on the market. It should be made available in a wider range of calibers. It is basically the "standard" or "short-magnum"-length version of the M800 series.

EXPLODED VIEW OF THE MOSSBERG 810 BOLT-ACTION RIFLE

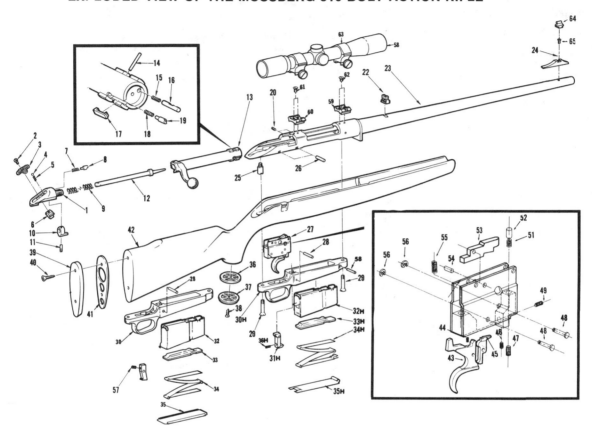

No.	Name	No.	Name	No.	Name
1	Bolt Cap	28	Magazine Latch Retaining Pin	42	Stock Complete
2	Safety Button Screw	29	Take Down Screw	43	Trigger
3	Safety Button			44	Sear & Trigger Spring
4	Click Ball		The Following Parts for Models with Box Magazine	45	Trigger Sear
5	Click Spring	30	Trigger Guard	46	Trigger Sear Adjusting Screw
6	Safety Lock	31	Magazine Latch	47	Trigger Sear Spring Screw
7	Bolt Cap Spring	32	Magazine Assembly	48	Trigger Pin
8	Bolt Cap Lock Plunger		Magazine Shell	49	Trigger Sear Adjusting Screw
9	Mainspring	33	Magazine Follower	50	Trigger Housing Assembly
10	Striker	34	Magazine Spring	51	Trigger Sear Spring
11	Firing Pin & Striker Screw	35	Magazine Bottom Plate	52	Trigger Sear Plunger
12	Firing Pin			53	Sear
13	Bolt and Lever Assembly		The Following Parts for Hinged Floorplate Models	54	Sear
14	Ejector Retaining Pin	30H	Trigger Guard	55	Trigger Spring
15	Ejector Spring	31H	Floor Plate Latch	56	Retaining Ring
16	Ejector	32H	Magazine Assembly	57	Magazine Latch Spring
17	Extractor	33H	Magazine Follower	58	Scope
18	Extractor Spring	34H	Magazine Spring	59	Front Scope Mount Base
19	Extractor Plunger	35H	Floor Plate	60	Rear Scope Mount Base
20	Dummy Screw	36	Stock Grip Spacer	61	Rear Scope Mount Base Screw (2)
22	Barrel Sight Assembly	37	Stock Grip Cap	62	Front Scope Mount Base Screw (2)
23	Barrel and Receiver Assembly	38	Stock Grip Screw	63	Scope Ring (2)
24	Front Sight Ramp	39	Recoil Pad	64	Front Sight Bead
25	Take Down Stud	40	Recoil Pad Screw	65	Front Sight Screw
26	Trigger Housing Retaining Pin	41	Recoil Pad Spacer		
27	Trigger Housing Assembly				

MUSGRAVE PREMIER RIFLE

Manufacturer: Musgrave & Sons, South Africa

Importer/distributor: J. Sherban & Co.

Action type: bolt; Mauser-derived

Magazine type: nondetachable staggered box/ hinged floorplate

Magazine capacity: standard calibers, 5-shot; magnum calibers, 3-shot

Safety: side slide

Barrel length: 25.75 inches

Stock: 1-piece dark walnut with epoxy finish; well-executed borderless hand checkering (22 lines per inch) on fore-end and pistol grip; Monte Carlo comb; cheekpiece; white spacer between butt and recoil pad; rearward-slanting 45° fore-end tip of wild olive wood; wild olive pistol-grip cap; quick-detachable sling swivel studs

Buttplate: ventilated red rubber recoil pad

Overall length: 46.75 inches

Length of pull: 14.875 inches

Drop at comb: 1.625 inches

Drop at Monte Carlo: 1.565 inches

Drop at heel: 2.25 inches

Weight: standard calibers, 7.75 lbs.; 7mm Rem. Magnum, 8.0 lbs.

Trigger pull: 3.5–5.5 lbs.

Sight, rear: none

Sight, front: none

Scope adaptability: drilled and tapped for standard scope mounts

Caliber: .243 Win., .270 Win., .30–06 Springfield, .308 Win., 7mm Rem. Magnum, .458 Win. Magnum (special model)

Data: This rifle incorporates desirable Mauser features like claw extractor and dual opposed front locking lugs. The swept-back bolt handle serves as an extra lug by fitting into a receiver notch.

The long Mauser-type extractor prevents cartridges from being double-loaded, a feature not found on the otherwise excellent Ruger M77.

The Premier has one action length for all cartridges. The .243 Win., tested by the author, as with the .308 Win. has a sheet-metal spacer block to provide proper cartridge functioning.

The barrel fore-tip—just aft of tip insert—rests on two fiber pads. The remainder of the barrel is free-floating, though the space between barrel and stock is slight.

Comment: This is a very well-designed rifle. Workmanship is excellent. One might believe this rifle—it's in the M70/M700/M77 price range—would cost considerably more. The checkering is of much better quality than on most American factory rifles in this price range. Only a few foreign rifles can be purchased for so little, and not all of those are as good as the Premier.

One feature which may not appeal to riflemen accustomed to actions that cock on the opening stroke of the bolt is the resistance felt as the bolt is slammed home on this cock-on-closing action.

PARKER-HALE SUPER RIFLE

Manufacturer: Parker-Hale, England

Importer/distributor: Jana International

Action type: bolt; modified Mauser

Magazine type: nondetachable staggered box; hinged floorplate

Magazine capacity: 4-shot, except 3-shot capacity in .300 Win. Magnum and 7mm Rem. Magnum

Safety: sliding thumb

Barrel length: 24.0 inches

Stock: 1-piece European walnut; skip-line hand checkering; Weatherby-style flat fore-end with rosewood tip; flared pistol grip with rosewood cap; high-gloss finish; quick-detachable sling swivels

Buttplate: ventilated rubber recoil pad with white line spacer

Overall length: 45.0 inches

Length of pull: 13.5 inches

Drop at comb: 1.8 inches

Drop at Monte Carlo: 1.5 inches

Drop at heel: 2.3 inches

Weight: 7.25 lbs.

Trigger pull: not specified

Sight, rear: leaf, crudely adjustable for windage and elevation

Sight, front: gold bead on ramp with detachable hood

Scope adaptability: receiver drilled and tapped for standard mount

Caliber: .22–250 Rem., .243 Win., .25–06 Rem., .270 Win., .30–06 Springfield, .300 Win. Magnum, .308 Win. (7.62mm NATO), 6mm Rem., 7mm Rem. Magnum

Data: Well-finished action. High-luster blue finish. Gold-colored single-stage trigger.

Comment: A rifle that resembles a Weatherby Vanguard in looks and is available in a number of comparable calibers.

REMINGTON M40-XC NATIONAL MATCH COURSE RIFLE

Action type: bolt; modified Mauser; short throw

Magazine type: nondetachable staggered box; stripper clip slot for rapid loading

Magazine capacity: 5-shot

Safety: 3-position thumb slide

Barrel length: 23.25 inches (stainless steel)

Stock: 1-piece uncheckered American walnut; wide, deep fore-end; full pistol adjustable hand stop and grip

Buttplate: 2-position adjustable type, thumb groove

Overall length: 42.5 inches

Length of pull: 13.5 inches

Drop at comb: 0.0 inch

Drop at heel: adjustable

Weight: 10.0 lbs. without metallic sights or scope

Trigger pull: 2.0–4.0 lbs. (adjustable)

Sights: none furnished; receiver and barrel drilled for metallic (peep and target fronts at option of shooter); scope (external-adjustment) blocks furnished

Caliber: 7.62mm NATO (.308 Win.)

Data: Special order requiring 18 weeks, minimum, for delivery. Time period subject to change.

Comment: Obviously, this rifle is designed for competitive target shooters. It's a fine National Match Course rifle. Hand-bedded stock.

REMINGTON M700 ADL/BDL/BDL VARMINT/C

Action type: bolt; enclosed cartridge head

Magazine type: nondetachable staggered box

Magazine capacity: 6-shot in .222 Rem., .222 Rem. Mag., .223 (5.56mm); 5-shot in all other standard calibers; 4-shot in magnum calibers

Safety: modified Mauser thumb type

Barrel length: 20.0, 22.0, or 24.0 inches in standard calibers; 24.0 inches in magnum calibers; 24.0-inch heavy barrel in BDL Varmint Model; 26.0-inch magnum barrel discontinued

Stock: 1-piece checkered American walnut; pistol grip with plastic cap; quick-detachable sling swivels and leather carrying strap except on ADL version. Original finish was replaced with glossy Dupont RK-W (bowling-alley type) in 1965. Original machine checkering with fleur-de-lis patterns was replaced in 1969 with impressed checkering in a stylized "S" design. In 1974 the M700 BDL returned to its original—and much better—machine checkering in a traditional pattern. Monte Carlo stock has a black wood fore-end tip.

Buttplate: shotgun type; plastic with white line spacer except magnum calibers which have solid rubber recoil pad

Overall length: 20.0-inch barrel, 39.5 inches; 22.0-inch barrel, 41.5 inches; 24.0-inch barrel, 43.5 inches; 24.0-inch barrel in magnum calibers (with recoil pad), 44.5 inches; 26.0-inch Magnum barrel (discontinued), 46.5 inches

Length of pull: 13.375 inches

Drop at comb: 1.625 inches (from open sight line) except Varmint Special, 0.5 inches (from center of bore)

Drop at heel: 2.375 inches except Varmint Special, 1.375 inches

Weight: 20.0-inch barrel, 6.75 lbs.; 22.0-inch barrel, 7.0 lbs.; 24.0-inch barrel, 7.5 lbs; M700 BDL Varmint weighs 9.0 lbs.; discontinued versions range from 6.5 to 9.0 lbs.

Trigger pull: 3.5 lbs.

Sight, rear: adjustable for elevation

Sight, front: flat-faced gold bead on ramp with removable sight protector

Scope adaptability: receiver drilled and tapped for standard scope bases; Varmint Special has no sights

Calibers: .222 Rem., .222 Rem. Magnum, .22–250, .223 (BDL Varmint rifle only), .243 Win., 6mm Rem., .25–06, .264 Win. Magnum, .270 Win., .280 (discontinued), 7mm

EXPLODED VIEW OF REMINGTON MODEL 700 BOLT-ACTION RIFLE

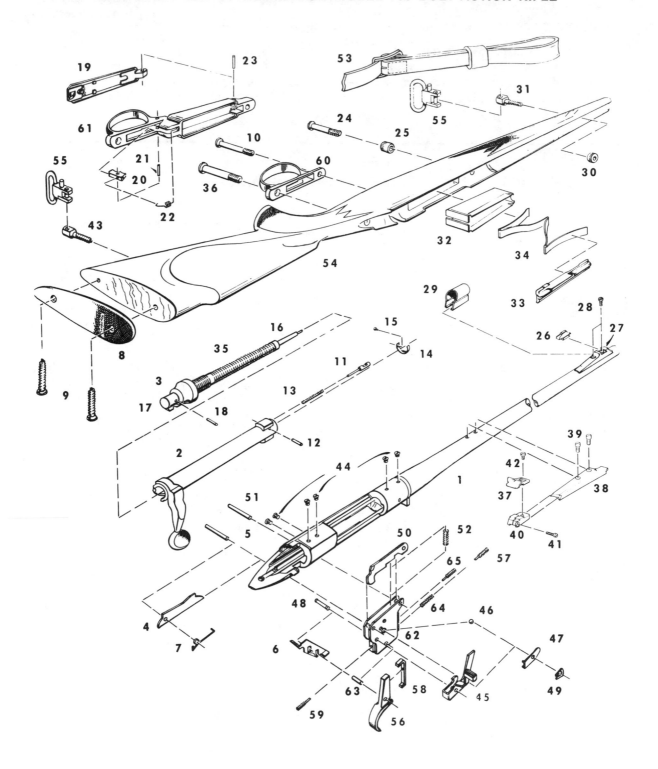

REMINGTON M700 ADL/BDL/BDL
VARMINT/C (continued)

Rem. Magnum, .300 Win. Magnum, .30–06 Springfield, .308 Win. (7.62mm NATO), .350 Rem. Magnum, .375 H&H Magnum, .458 Win. Magnum, .25–06 (1970), .300 Win. Magnum (1964), .350 Rem. Magnum (1969), 6.5mm Rem. Magnum (1969) .17 Rem. (1971)

Data: The cartridge case head is completely enclosed by the shroud of the recessed bolt face. The M700 ADL, the less expensive version, has impressed checkering and no floor plate or sling swivels. The BDL is available with a left-hand action and left-hand cheekpiece in .270, .30–06, and 7mm Rem. Magnum. The M700 Safari is the BDL in .375 H&H Magnum or .458 Win. Magnum, but unlike the smaller bore BDL rifles it has an oil-finished stock and hand checkering. It's more expensive, of course, as is the M700C, or Custom version—the only one presently offered with a 20-inch barrel as well as the 22- or 24-inch options. The C has a hand-lapped barrel, jeweled bolt, select and hand-checkered American walnut stock, and rosewood fore-end tip and grip cap. It can be ordered with or without a hinged floorplate.

Comment: Remington took 25 years to produce a bolt-action rifle that could compete in sales and quality and in a broad range of calibers with Winchester's famed M70. In recent years M700 sales have reportedly been higher than those of the M70. The M70 that the M700 has been competing against since 1964 is not the grand old M70 of the 1937–63 era but the "new" M70.

The M700 (notice resemblance of name to M70), aside from being a well-designed and well-constructed rifle, has certainly gained sales by introducing several original calibers, like the 7mm Rem. Magnum, and a cartridge that had been a popular wildcat, the .25–06. This is partly due to the genius of Remington designer Mike Walker. Aside from the .30–06, which is of military origin, the 7mm Rem. now made by most bolt-action rifle manufacturers is probably the most popular bolt-action caliber for medium to large North American game ever introduced.

Many M700 admirers will applaud the discarding of the impressed checkering on the BDL and the return to machine checkering, which took place in 1973–74. In that period an "antibind" device, or bolt guide, was added to the action.

Parts List For Remington Model 700 Bolt-Action Rifle

No.	Part Name	No.	Part Name	No.	Part Name
1	Barrel Assembly	24	Front Guard Screw	44	Receiver Plug Screw
2	Bolt Assembly	25	Front Guard Screw Bushing, ADL Grade	45	Safety Assembly
3	Bolt Plug	26	Front Sight	46	Safety Detent Ball
4	Bolt Stop	27	Front Sight Ramp	47	Safety Detent Spring
5	Bolt Stop Pin	28	Front Sight Ramp Screw	48	Safety Pivot Pin
6	Bolt Stop Release	29	Front Sight Hood, BDL Grade	49	Safety Snap Washer
7	Bolt Stop Spring	30	Front Swivel Nut, BDL Grade	50	Sear Safety Cam
8	Butt Plate	31	Front Swivel Screw, BDL Grade	51	Sear Pin
8a	Butt Plate Spacer BDL Grade	32	Magazine, ADL Grade	52	Sear Spring
9	Butt Plate Screw		Magazine, BDL Grade (not shown)	53	Sling Strap Assembly, BDL Grade
10	Center Guard Screw, ADL Grade	33	Magazine Follower	54	Stock Assembly, ADL Grade
11	Ejector		Magazine Tab Screw (ADL Grade)	55	Swivel Assembly, BDL Grade (Q.D.)
12	Ejector Pin	34	Magazine Spring	56	Trigger
13	Ejector Spring		Magazine Spring, BDL Grade	57	Trigger Adjusting Screw
14	Extractor	35	Main Spring	58	Trigger Connector
15	Extractor Rivet	36	Rear Guard Screw	59	Trigger Engagement Screw
16	Firing Pin	37	Rear Sight Aperture	60	Trigger Guard
17	Firing Pin Assembly	38	Rear Sight Base	61	Trigger Guard Assembly, BDL Grade
18	Firing Pin Cross Pin	39	Rear Sight Base Screw (2)	62	Trigger Housing Assembly
20	Floor Plate Latch, BDL Grade	40	Rear Sight Slide	63	Trigger Pin
21	Floor Plate Latch Pin, BDL Grade	41	Elevation Screw	64	Trigger Spring
22	Floor Plate Latch Spring, BDL Grade	42	Windage Screw	65	Trigger Stop Screw
23	Floor Plate Pivot Pin, BDL Grade	43	Rear Swivel Screw, BDL Grade		

REMINGTON M788

Action type: bolt

Magazine type: detachable box

Magazine capacity: .222 Rem., 4-shot; all others, 3-shot

Safety: thumb type

Barrel length: 24.0 inches in .222 Rem., .22–250; 22.0 inches in all other calibers

Stock: 1-piece hardwood with walnut stain; no checkering; Monte Carlo comb; uncapped pistol grip

Buttplate: shotgun type; plastic

Overall length: 22.0-inch barrel, 42.0 inches; 24.0-inch barrel, 43.625 inches

Length of pull: 13.625 inches

Drop at comb: 1.875 inches (from line of open sight)

Drop at heel: 2.625 inches

Weight: 22.0-inch barrel, 7.25 lbs.; 24.0-inch barrel, 7.5 lbs.

Trigger pull: 3.5 lbs.

Sight, rear: U-notch, crudely adjustable for windage and elevation

Sight, front: detachable blade on ramp

Scope adaptability: receiver drilled and tapped for standard scope bases

Caliber: .222 Rem., .243 Win., .308 Win., .6mm Rem.; .30–30 Win. and .44 Magnum discontinued

Data: This rifle has been available in left-hand variations in calibers .308 Win. (7.62mm Nato) and 6mm Rem. since 1968. No cost increase over standard M788. Several extra-cost options are available: a Universal 4× scope complete with rings and bases; an extra clip; and a carrying strap, with quick-detachable swivels installed.

Comment: This is a sturdy, reliable rifle for the man who cannot afford a fine rifle like the Remington M700 or Ruger M77. The author suggests the purchase of the sling (it's handy when climbing or toting out deer) and an extra magazine (so-called clip). The 4× Universal scope is not suggested. A scope at this price is not going to last many deer seasons; its waterproofing is not apt to last long. Scope power for short-range deer and bear shooting should be no greater than 2.5×. This gives a wider field of view for running game than the 4×.

RUGER M77

Action type: bolt; modified Mauser

Magazine type: nondetachable staggered box; hinged floorplate operated by release button inside trigger guard

Magazine capacity: standard calibers, 5-shot; magnum calibers, 3-shot

Safety: sliding (top tang)

Barrel length: .220 Swift varmint version, 26.0 inches; magnum calibers and .25–06 Rem., 24.0 inches; other calibers, 22.0 inches

Stock: 1-piece hand-checkered American walnut; capped pistol grip; fitted with eyes for quick-detachable swivels

Buttplate: shotgun type with solid rubber recoil pad

Overall length: 22.0-inch barrel, 42.0 inches; 24.0-inch barrel, 44.0 inches; 26.0-inch barrel, 46.0 inches

Length of pull: 13.5 inches

Drop at comb: 1.5 inches

Drop at heel: 2.5 inches

Weight: 22.0-inch barrel, 7.0 lbs.; 24.0-inch barrel (except .458 Win. and varmint version), 7.5 lbs.; .458 Win., 8.75-lbs.; 24.0-inch barrel varminter versions (.22/.250 Rem., .220 Swift, .243 Win., 25–06 Rem., 6mm Rem.), 9.0 lbs.

Trigger pull: 3.5 lbs.

Sight, rear: Williams folding leaf, adjustable for windage and elevation

Sight, front: flat-faced gold bead on ramp fitted to barrel with band

Scope adaptability: The M77 (except varmint version) is available with or without open sights. Flat Top receiver version is fitted with integral scope bases for 1.0-inch Ruger split scope rings. Open sights optional at extra cost. Round Top receiver is drilled and tapped for standard scope bases. Open sights optional at extra cost. Round Top receiver is available in limited number of calibers. Varmint version is drilled and tapped for scope blocks

Caliber: .22–250 Rem., .220 Swift, .243 Win., .250–3000 Savage, .257 Roberts, .270 Win., .284 Win., .30–06 Springfield, .300 Win. Magnum, .308 Win. (7.62mm NATO), .338 Win. Magnum, .458 Win. Magnum, 6mm Rem., 7×57 (7mm Mauser), 7mm Rem. Magnum; discontinued calibers include .222 Rem., 6.5mm Rem. Magnum, .350 Rem. Magnum

Data: The M77 is available in two action lengths: short-stroke and Magnum.

Short-stroke handles nonmagnum cartridges shorter than the .270 Win./.30–06 Springfield class. These range from the .22–250 Rem. through the .243 Win. and 7×57 Mauser. Magazine box length (interior): 2.920 inches. This is about one-half inch shorter than the so-called magnum length.

Magnum action designation is misleading. This action handles all M77 magnum cartridges, but these are short magnums, which are no longer than the .30–06 case. For many years there have been three basic action lengths: short-action, as described above; standard length, meaning .30–06 length; and magnum, to handle full-length magnums like the .300 H&H Magnum, .375 H&H Magnum, and full length Weatherby Magnums based on the .300 H&H Magnum or .375 H&H Magnum cases. Beginning with the .458 Win. Magnum and short Weatherby Magnums, there has developed a tendency to call the standard-length action a magnum action. To avoid confusion we should term the M77 standard action a short-magnum action and leave the term magnum action in its original meaning. The M77 "Magnum" magazine-box length (interior) is 3.340 inches. The .300 and .375 H&H Magnum case length is 3.60 inches.

The M77 Ruger provides safety in the event of cartridge-head failure (or pierced primer) in several ways. Gas moving rearward along the locking lug channel is largely diverted by the bolt stop. Gas is then vented through a Ruger-designed gas escape port. The usual gas escape port is located on the receiver's right side. The bolt sleeve further diverts gas from the shooter.

Non-M77 barrels may be free-floating (stock not attached to barrel) or may be attached to the stock with a fore-end screw that enters the barrel at right angles. Both methods have advantages and disadvantages. Ruger designed and patented a diagonal-front-mounting-screw system with the advantages of both systems but without their disadvantages. A heavy diagonal mounting screw passes through the stock into the receiver recoil lug at a 45° angle. The mounting screw thus firmly draws the barrel-receiver unit downward to the rear. This seats the barrel solidly in

Ruger Model 77 round-top receiver is tapped to take standard scope mount bases.

its channel. The receiver is now positively positioned against the stock's recoil shoulder.

Ruger bucked the trend of nearly all riflemakers, both American and foreign, toward the Weatherby-type stock. He reverted to the simple classic lines of the stock made famous by noted old-time stockers like Louis Wundhammer, Bob Owens, Thomas Shelhammer, Griffin & Howe, and Nate Bishop. This stock has no cheekpiece, no Monte Carlo comb, no flared pistol grip. There are no white line spacers or fore-end tip inserts.

In a day when most major riflemakers are using "reverse" checkering or machine checkering, Ruger offers 20-line-to-the-inch hand checkering. Heretofore, hand checkering was considered the domain of skilled stockers. Ruger hired leading stockmaker Leonard Brownell to teach a bevy of girls the mysteries of hand checkering. The experiment has proved successful.

Comment: The M77 with its classic stock and features usually found on custom rifles, like the triggerbow floorplate button release and tang safety, offers American riflemen almost a single choice against the overwhelming number of Weatherby copies.

Weatherby's stock style is perfectly functional, but not all riflemen like it. With the advent of the M77 they have two distinct choices.

No manufacturer makes a sufficiently heavy .458 Winchester Magnum. The M77 weighs 8.75 lbs. (the Ruger Number One single-shot .458 weighs 9.0 lbs.), but this is far too light. The .458 Win. Magnum has about twice the recoil of the .375 H&H Magnum, yet most gunmakers offer the .375 H&H Magnum and the .458 Win. Magnum at identical or similar weights.

In most respects the author considers the M77 the equal of the pre-1964 M70 Winchester. Exceptions:

1. The M77 has a plunger ejector rather than the pre-1964 M70's Mauser ejector. Varmint shooters can easily modify their M70 ejector so it does not eject or lightly ejects. This is desirable for handloaders. Violently ejected cases may get lost or battered beyond reuse. This minor point, however, only concerns a few shooters.

2. All calibers should be available in round-top and flat-top with integral mount. A minority of hunters, notably those who trek the outback, want a micrometer receiver sight to back up their scope. The best mount for this purpose is Griffin & Howe's quick-detachable side mount. This mount, as is obvious from its name, doesn't require the integral base. A micrometer receiver sight like the famed and reliable Lyman 48 cannot be mounted on the integral-base M77.

3. The trigger was originally advertised as serrated (grooved), but never has been made that way. The trigger should be serrated and wider to provide a firmer grip.

4. There is no need for a recoil pad on standard calibers. A rifle of this classic design and superb quality should be fitted with a Neidner (checkered steel) buttplate on standard calibers. The theory is put forth that a rubber recoil pad prevents the rifle from slipping when it is stood in a corner or against a tree or car. But no rifleman with any affection for his rifle or shotgun ever stands it up except in an upright gun cabinet. The arm is laid over a chair or across a Stetson or jacket. It is never stood up.

5. The present barrel band securing the fore sight to the barrel should be abandoned. Twice the author has seen Vermont deer hunters turn back M77s which they had just purchased. The gun shop proprietor—a competent gunsmith—fitted scopes to the M77s, and the fore sights showed in the scopes. It was virtually impossible to remove the barrel band. It can be sweated off, but then the barrel has to be reblued.

6. Alloy triggerbow, floorplate, and floorplate hinge frame should be replaced by steel. Alloy doesn't hold its finish. It's poor material for engraving.

7. The bolt must be firmly closed whenever it is turned down; otherwise double feeding can occur. The author greatly admires the M77 in .458 Win. Magnum caliber. It is the handsomest .458 he knows—the M70 is second—but because of the potential double-feeding hazard he'll stay with his M70 African.

8. The so-called bolt guide should be redesigned so that it really functions as an anti-bind device or bolt guide.

SAVAGE M110 SERIES

Action type: bolt; modified Mauser

Magazine type: M110D/M110DL, nondetachable staggered box, hinged floorplate; M110C/M110CL, detachable box; M110E/M110EL, nondetachable staggered box, no floorplate

Magazine capacity: standard calibers, 4-shot; magnum calibers, 3-shot

Safety: sliding (top tang)

Barrel length: standard calibers, 22.0 inches; magnum calibers, 24.0 inches (stainless steel); M110E/M110EL have satin finish; all others blued

Stock: 1-piece American walnut; capped pistol grip; Monte Carlo comb; cheekpiece; reverse checkering; classic fore-end. M110E/M110EL has walnut-stained hardwood and no pistol-grip cap. Many stock variations since the M110 was introduced. At one time a premier grade had a roll-over cheekpiece. Weatherby slab-side fore-ends have also been offered.

Buttplate: shotgun type; plastic

Overall length: 22.0-inch barrel, 43.0 inches; 24.0-inch barrel, 45.0 inches

Length of pull: 13.0 inches

Drop at comb: 1.625 inches

Drop at Monte Carlo: 2.25 inches

Drop at heel: 2.5 inches

Weight: 22.0-inch barrel, 7.0 lbs.; 24.0 inch-barrel, 7.75 lbs.; 24.0-inch barrel (M110E/M110EL), 7.5 lbs.

Trigger pull: 4.5 lbs.; adjustable to 3.0 lbs.

Sight, rear: folding leaf, crudely adjustable for windage and elevation

Sight, front: bead on ramp

Scope adaptability: receiver drilled and tapped for standard scope bases

Caliber: .243 Win., .270 Win., .30–06 Springfield, .300 Win. Magnum, 7mm Rem. Magnum; discontinued calibers include .264 Win. Magnum, .284 Win., .308 Win. (7.62mm NATO), .338 Win. Magnum

Data: Models 110CL/110 DL/110EL have left-hand actions. No M110 is fitted with sling swivels. The M110E formerly had a 24.0-inch barrel and a floorplate. This version of the M110E had no checkering. Rear sights were formerly Rocky Mountain (buckhorn).

Comment: This rifle, while not in the same category as the Ruger M77, Winchester M70, Remington M700, Browning Hi-Power, or the Weatherby Vanguard, is an excellent buy for those who wish to spend less and still have an accurate, reliable rifle.

EXPLODED VIEW OF SAVAGE MODELS 110 C, D AND E, AND SERIES K BOLT ACTION RIFLES.

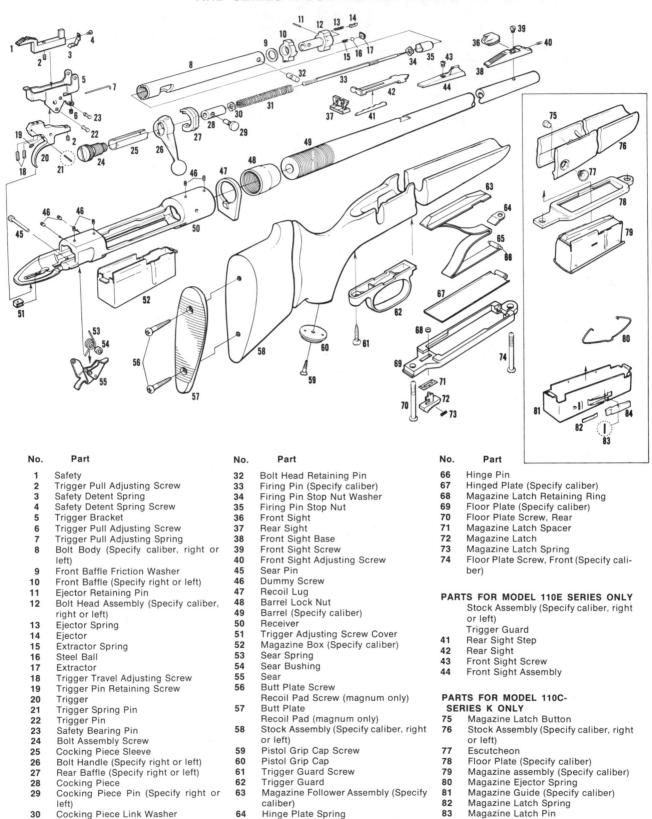

No.	Part
1	Safety
2	Trigger Pull Adjusting Screw
3	Safety Detent Spring
4	Safety Detent Spring Screw
5	Trigger Bracket
6	Trigger Pull Adjusting Screw
7	Trigger Pull Adjusting Spring
8	Bolt Body (Specify caliber, right or left)
9	Front Baffle Friction Washer
10	Front Baffle (Specify right or left)
11	Ejector Retaining Pin
12	Bolt Head Assembly (Specify caliber, right or left)
13	Ejector Spring
14	Ejector
15	Extractor Spring
16	Steel Ball
17	Extractor
18	Trigger Travel Adjusting Screw
19	Trigger Pin Retaining Screw
20	Trigger
21	Trigger Spring Pin
22	Trigger Pin
23	Safety Bearing Pin
24	Bolt Assembly Screw
25	Cocking Piece Sleeve
26	Bolt Handle (Specify right or left)
27	Rear Baffle (Specify right or left)
28	Cocking Piece
29	Cocking Piece Pin (Specify right or left)
30	Cocking Piece Link Washer
31	Mainspring (Specify caliber)

No.	Part
32	Bolt Head Retaining Pin
33	Firing Pin (Specify caliber)
34	Firing Pin Stop Nut Washer
35	Firing Pin Stop Nut
36	Front Sight
37	Rear Sight
38	Front Sight Base
39	Front Sight Screw
40	Front Sight Adjusting Screw
45	Sear Pin
46	Dummy Screw
47	Recoil Lug
48	Barrel Lock Nut
49	Barrel (Specify caliber)
50	Receiver
51	Trigger Adjusting Screw Cover
52	Magazine Box (Specify caliber)
53	Sear Spring
54	Sear Bushing
55	Sear
56	Butt Plate Screw
	Recoil Pad Screw (magnum only)
57	Butt Plate
	Recoil Pad (magnum only)
58	Stock Assembly (Specify caliber, right or left)
59	Pistol Grip Cap Screw
60	Pistol Grip Cap
61	Trigger Guard Screw
62	Trigger Guard
63	Magazine Follower Assembly (Specify caliber)
64	Hinge Plate Spring
65	Magazine Spring (Specify caliber)

No.	Part
66	Hinge Pin
67	Hinged Plate (Specify caliber)
68	Magazine Latch Retaining Ring
69	Floor Plate (Specify caliber)
70	Floor Plate Screw, Rear
71	Magazine Latch Spacer
72	Magazine Latch
73	Magazine Latch Spring
74	Floor Plate Screw, Front (Specify caliber)

PARTS FOR MODEL 110E SERIES ONLY

	Stock Assembly (Specify caliber, right or left)
	Trigger Guard
41	Rear Sight Step
42	Rear Sight
43	Front Sight Screw
44	Front Sight Assembly

PARTS FOR MODEL 110C- SERIES K ONLY

75	Magazine Latch Button
76	Stock Assembly (Specify caliber, right or left)
77	Escutcheon
78	Floor Plate (Specify caliber)
79	Magazine assembly (Specify caliber)
80	Magazine Ejector Spring
81	Magazine Guide (Specify caliber)
82	Magazine Latch Spring
83	Magazine Latch Pin
84	Magazine Latch

SAVAGE M111 CHIEFTAIN

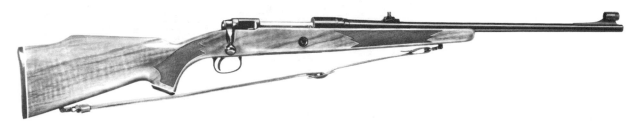

Action type: bolt; modified Mauser; recessed bolt face

Magazine type: detachable staggered box

Magazine capacity: 4-shot in .270 Win., .30–06 Springfield; 3-shot in 7mm Rem. Magnum

Safety: sliding (top tang)

Barrel length: 22.0 inches in .270 Win., .30–06 Springfield; 24.0 inches in 7mm Rem. Magnum

Stock: 1-piece American walnut; hand-checkered pistol grip and fore-end (20 lines to the inch); full pistol grip with plastic cap and white spacer; quick-detachable sling swivels with carrying strap; Monte Carlo fluted comb; crossbolt on 7mm Rem. Magnum

Buttplate: hard rubber with white spacer

Overall length: 22.0-inch barrel, 43.0 inches; 24.0-inch barrel, 45.0 inches

Length of pull: 13.5 inches

Drop at comb: 1.625 inches

Drop at Monte Carlo: 1.5 inches

Drop at heel: 2.25 inches

Weight: standard calibers, 7.5 lbs.; 7mm Rem. Magnum, 8.25 lbs.

Trigger pull: 3.5 lbs.

Sight, rear: Williams Open Guide Sight

Sight, front: bead on ramp with removable sight protector

Scope adaptability: receiver drilled and tapped for standard scope bases

Caliber: .270 Win., .30–06 Springfield, 7mm Rem. Magnum

Data: A relatively deluxe rifle based on the Savage M110.

Comment: This is the finest Savage the author has seen. There are no unsightly gaps between stock and barrel as sometimes occurs—it did with the early post-1964 M70 Winchesters—with free-floating barrels. Adequate safety margins are provided by two gas ports and three safety gas baffles.

This rifle would be almost as good—for the classic-minded—as the Ruger M77 if the white line spacers were eliminated. The author would prefer a nondetachable magazine. The trigger system could be refined.

SAVAGE M340

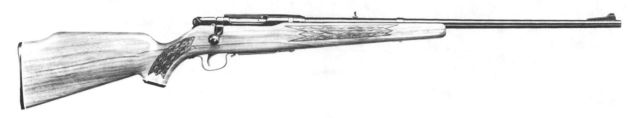

Action type: bolt; modified Mauser

Magazine type: detachable staggered box

Magazine capacity: 4-shot in .222 Rem.; 3-shot in .225 Win. (discontinued), .30–30 Win.

Safety: thumb type; locks bolt and trigger

Barrel length: .30–30 Win., 22.0 inches; .222 Rem. (and discontinued .225 Win.), 24.0 inches; 20.0-inch, .30–30 Win. discontinued

Stock: 1-piece American walnut; plastic pistol-grip cap; Monte Carlo comb; reverse checkering; classic fore-end; earlier stocks had no Monte Carlo comb and no checkering

Buttplate: shotgun type; plastic with white line spacer

Overall length: 22.0-inch barrel, 40.0 inches; 24.0-inch barrel, 42.0 inches

Length of pull: 13.5 inches

Drop at comb: 1.75 inches

Drop at Monte Carlo: 1.75 inches

Drop at heel: 2.5 inches

Weight: .222 Rem., 7.5 lbs.; .30–30 Win., 7.25 lbs.

Trigger pull: 4.5 lbs.

Sight, rear: folding leaf, crudely adjustable for windage and elevation; replaces earlier Rocky Mountain (buckhorn)

Sight, front: bead on removable ramp

Scope adaptability: receiver drilled and tapped for standard scope mount

Caliber: .222 Rem., .30–30 Win.; .225 Win. discontinued

Data: This is the post-World War II version of the old Savage M23 (.22 Hornet, .25–20, .32–20).

Comment: This is an inexpensive rifle designed for casual varmint shooting (.222 Rem.) or for the occasional .30–30 Win. shooter who wants this caliber in a bolt action.

WALTHER KKJ SPORTSMAN CENTERFIRE RIFLE

Manufacturer: Carl Walther Waffenfabriken, West Germany

Importer/distributor: Firearms International

Action type: bolt

Magazine type: detachable box

Magazine capacity: 5-shot

Safety: thumb slide

Barrel length: 22.5 inches

Stock: European walnut; hand checkering on pistol grip and fore-end; cheekpiece; plastic-capped pistol grip; sling swivels; left-hand stock available at extra cost on special order

Buttplate: Shotgun type; hard rubber

Overall length: 41.5 inches

Length of pull: 13.75 inches

Drop at comb: 2.0 inches

Drop at heel: 2.9 inches

Weight: 5.5 lbs.

Trigger pull: not specified; standard or double set trigger available

Sight, rear: military-type leaf, adjustable for windage and elevation

Sight, front: bead on ramp with removable hood

Scope adaptability: receiver dovetailed for scope mounts

Caliber: .22 Hornet

Data: Same basic rifle (except, of course, for the action) is offered in a rimfire version, and is described in the chapter on bolt-action rimfire rifles. Both the centerfire and rimfire are handsomely finished as well as finely crafted for precision shooting, although the cheekpiece is

too small. These Walthers are intended for serious shooters; both are priced at well over $300 with a standard trigger, and about $20 extra with a double set trigger.

Comment: It has become hard to find a rifle chambered, as this one is, for the famous old .22 Hornet. At appropriate ranges, the Hornet is a fine cartridge for woodchucks, prairie dogs, jack rabbits, and other varmint species or fairly small game—even including foxes. However, this Walther KKJ is not a varmint rifle in the traditional sense. A varmint rifle needs plenty of weight for long, deliberate shots. At 5.5 lbs., the Walther is a sporter rather than a true varminter despite its caliber.

WEATHERBY MARK V RIFLE

Manufacturer: Howa Machinery Co., Japan

Importer/distributor: Weatherby, Inc.

Action type: bolt; nine locking lugs

Magazine type: nondetachable box; hinged floorplate

Magazine capacity: 5-shot in .240 Weatherby Magnum; 4-shot in .30–06 Springfield; 3-shot in all other calibers

Safety: horizontal thumb type

Barrel length: 24.0 inches in .240, .257, .270, .300, 7mm Weatherby Magnums; 26.0 inches in .340 Weatherby Magnum (available for same caliber with 24.0-inch barrel at extra cost); 26.0 inches, heavier barrel, in .378 Weatherby Magnum; for .460 Weatherby Magnum, see Chapter 8

Stock: distinctive Weatherby styling; American walnut; flared pistol grip capped by rosewood insert; Monte Carlo comb and cheekpiece; solid rubber recoil pad; rosewood fore-end tip insert at 45° angle; flat sides and

bottom on fore-end; basketweave checkering; high-gloss waterproof and scratch-resistant finish; all stocks individually hand-bedded; cheekpiece slants up to rear; Oregon myrtle stock was formerly offered but has been discontinued.

Buttplate: shotgun type; ventilated rubber recoil pad

Overall length: 24.0-inch barrel, 44.5 inches; 26.0-inch barrel, 46.5 inches

Length of pull: 13.5 inches (except .460 WM); 13.875 inches (.460 WM)

Drop at Monte Carlo: 0.875 inch (front); 0.5 inch (rear)

Drop at heel: 1.5 inches

Weight: 24.0-inch barrel with contour one, 7.25 lbs; 26.0-inch barrel with contour two or three, 8.5 lbs.

Trigger pull: 3.5 lbs. (adjustable)

Sight, rear: none except on special order

Separate view of the Weatherby Mark V action with the one-piece bolt in place. The bolt is machined from chrome moly steel.

WEATHERBY MARK V RIFLE (continued)

Sight, front: none except on special order

Scope adaptability: receiver drilled and tapped for standard scope bases; Weatherby scopes furnished on special order

Caliber: .240 WM, .257 WM, .270 WM, .30–06 Springfield, .300 WM, .340 WM, .378 WM, 7mm WM

Data: This action, designed by Roy Weatherby, was originally made for him by J. P. Sauer & Sohn, Suhl, Germany. It is now produced in Japan.

A major feature of this strong action is not merely that the bolt face is recessed—many other bolt actions have this feature—but that the barrel face is also counter-bored. Thus the bolt head fits into the barrel.

The Mark V action has a combination of features of various actions. The one-piece bolt is machined from chrome moly steel. The receiver is made from a one-piece chrome moly forging.

There are nine locking lugs in contrast to the two of the typical Mauser action. The actual bearing area of the nine lugs is not appreciably greater than the total area of two standard lugs.

The bolt sleeve is entirely enclosed from the rear. The Weatherby was one of the first American sporting rifles to have this feature.

The Mark V action and other parts of the rifle are entirely made of steel. There are no alloy parts.

Comment: This is one of the strongest and most handsome actions made. The barrel and the entire action—save the receiver-ring top and bright bolt—are finished with very high-quality bluing. The streamlined action, despite its massive appearance, weighs only 36 oz.—4.0 oz. less than the short-stroke Ruger action and 6.0 oz. less than the magnum Ruger action.

The well-designed trigger is adjustable.

The author's major criticism concerns the small size of the safety slide. It should be considerably larger even at the expense of breaking up the action's sleek lines.

It is unfortunate that separate Mark V actions are not available. There are many riflemen who have no desire for Roy's fancy stocks but would like to build a rifle around the Mark V action. You have to purchase a barreled action.

WEATHERBY VANGUARD

Manufacturer: Howa Machinery Co., Japan

Importer/distributor: Weatherby, Inc.

Action type: bolt; modified Mauser

Magazine type: nondetachable box

Magazine capacity: 5-shot except .300 Win. Magnum, 3-shot

Safety: thumb type; horizontal

Barrel length: 24.0 inches

Stock: 1-piece American walnut with Weatherby styling; flared pistol grip with rosewood cap; rear of Monte Carlo comb elevated above forward portion; rosewood fore-end tip inletted at 45° angle; cheekpiece; glossy waterproof and scratch-resistant finish; sharp machine checkering

Buttplate: shotgun type; ventilated rubber recoil pad

Overall length: 44.5 inches

Length of pull: 13.5 inches

Drop at Monte Carlo: 0.875 inch (front); 0.5 inch (rear)

Drop at heel: 1.5 inches

Weight: 7.925 lbs.

Trigger pull: 3.25 lbs.

Sight, rear: none; available on special order

Sight, front: none; available on special order

Scope adaptability: receiver drilled and tapped for standard scope bases; Weatherby scopes furnished on order

Caliber: .243 Win., .25–06 Win., .270 Win., .30–06 Springfield, .300 Win. Magnum

Comment: This improved Mauser action offers the economy-minded a genuine Weatherby-type stock in several standard calibers. It is one of the few rifles on the market which offers a 24.0-inch barrel in standard calibers like .270 Win. and .30–06 Springfield. A very well-made rifle.

WHITWORTH EXPRESS RIFLE, AFRICAN SERIES

Manufacturer: Whitworth Rifle Co., England

Importer/distributor: Interarms

Action type: bolt; modified Mauser

Magazine type: nondetachable staggered box; hinged floorplate

Magazine capacity: 3-shot

Safety: slide located behind bolt

Barrel length: 24.0 inches

Stock: 1-piece finely figured European walnut; classic English styling; hand-cut checkering; full pistol grip with plastic cap; black tenite fore-end cap; oil-type finish; quick-detachable sling swivels

Buttplate: solid red rubber recoil pad with black line spacer

Overall length: 44.0 inches

Length of pull: 14.0 inches

Drop at comb: 1.5 inches

Drop at heel: 2.5 inches

Weight: .375 H&H Magnum, 8.25 lbs.; .300 Win. Magnum, 7.5 lbs.; 7mm Rem. Magnum, 7.5 lbs.

Trigger pull: not specified

Sight, rear: three folding leafs, mounted on quarter rib and marked 100 yards, 200 yards, 300 yards

Sight, front: flat gold bead on ramp with detachable hood

Scope adaptability: receiver drilled and tapped for standard mount

WHITWORTH EXPRESS RIFLE, AFRICAN SERIES (continued)

Caliber: .375 H&H Magnum, .300 Win. Magnum, 7mm Rem. Magnum

Data: Action is same type of modified Mauser used in Interarms Mauser Mark X rifle, described earlier in this chapter.

Comment: For hunters who prefer the classic English rifle styling and furniture like leaf sights on a quarter rib, this is an excellent rifle.

The author would like to see this rifle available in such noted big-game calibers as 7×57 Mauser, .270 Win., and .30–06. The fore-end cap should be made of the traditional ebony or Cape buffalo horn rather than tenite. The pistol-grip cap should be steel.

WINCHESTER M70

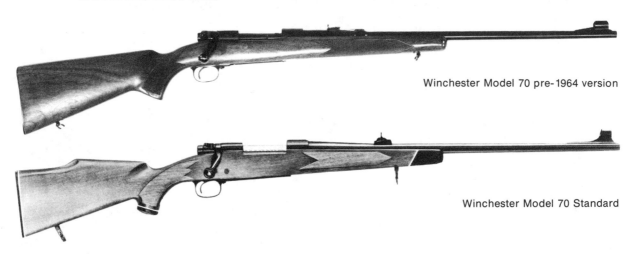

Winchester Model 70 pre-1964 version

Winchester Model 70 Standard

Action type: bolt; cartridge head enclosed

Magazine type: nondetachable staggered box; hinged floorplate

Magazine capacity: standard, varmint, and target, 5-shot; Magnum and African, 3-shot

Safety: 3-position, horizontal; red dot shows when arm is cocked

Barrel length: 22.0 inches for all standard calibers except .25–06 (24.0 inches); 24.0 inches for all magnums except .458 African (22.0 inches); 26.0 inches for M70 target in .30–06 Springfield and .308 Win. (7.62 NATO); 24.0 inches in .308 Army International Match rifle; 24.0 inches for all varmint calibers; 19.0 inches for all calibers with Mannlicher-type stock (discontinued)

Stock: new M70 stock (1964) was a radical departure from its predecessor (1937–63). Machine-cut checkering was replaced by impressed checkering. Secured barrels were replaced by floating (unsecured to stock by screw) barrels. Gap between barrel and stock was considered too large by many leading firearms writers. In 1972 Winchester returned to machine checkering. For several years after its introduction the new M70's Monte Carlo slanted down from the rear. The forward slant has been substantially modified. In 1972 the M70 was given an entirely new stock. It now has a Weatherby-style slab-sided fore-end with a wood insert, slanted at 45°, with a white line spacer. The grip was reshaped with some Weatherby-type flare.

Buttplate: shotgun type; plastic on standard and varmint models; black rubber recoil pad on magnums

Overall length: 19.0-inch barrel, 35.5 inches; 22.0-inch barrel, 42.5 inches; 24.0-inch barrel, 44.5 inches; 26.0-inch barrel, 46.5 inches; 24.0 inch barrel Army International Match in .308 Win. (7.62 NATO), 43.25 inches

Length of pull: 13.5 inches except .308 Win. (7.62 NATO) Army International Match, 12.0 inches

Drop at comb: 1.75 inches except .308 Win. (7.62 NATO), 1.25 inches

Drop at Monte Carlo: 1.5 inches except .458 African, 1.75 inches; none on Army International Match rifle

Drop at heel: 2.125 inches except Army International Match, 1.25 inches, and .458 African, 2.375 inches

Weight: standard, 22.0-inch barrel, 7.5 lbs.; standard, 24.0-inch barrel, 7.75 lbs.; magnums (except .375 H&H), 24.0-inch barrel, 7.75 lbs.; .375 H&H Magnum, 8.5 lbs.; .458 African, 8.5 lbs.; Varminter calibers, 9.75 lbs.; 308 Win. (7.62mm NATO) Army International Match rifle, 11.0 lbs.; target rifle, 26.0-inch barrel, 10.5 lbs.; Mannlicher, 19.0-inch barrel, 7.5 lbs. (discontinued)

Trigger pull: not specified

Sight, rear: target, varmint, and Mannlicher, none; folding leaf all others

Sight, front: target, varmint, and Mannlicher (discontinued), none; others have gold bead on ramp with removable sight protector

Scope adaptability: varmint and target versions have scope blocks; other versions have receiver drilled and tapped for standard scope bases

Caliber: .222 Rem., .22–250, .243 Win., .25–06, .264 Win. Magnum, .270 Win., .30–06 Springfield, .300 Win. Magnum, .308 Win. (7.62 NATO), 7mm Rem. Magnum, .338 Win. Magnum, .375 H&H Magnum, .458 Win. Magnum; .225 Win. discontinued

Basic model variation data

1. *Standard M70.* Calibers: .22–250 Rem., .222 Rem., .225 Win. (1965–72), .243 Win., .270 Win., .30–06, .308 Win. (7.62mm NATO). These calibers have 22.0-inch barrels. Caliber .25–06 (introduced 1972) has a 24.0-inch barrel. Standard M70s now have quick-detachable sling swivels (1972) and a plastic buttplate with white line spacer.

When the new M70 appeared, the Featherweight version with the 22.0-inch barrel (pre-'64) was dropped from the line. Standard calibers like the .243 Win., .270 Win., and .30–06 Springfield that had heretofore been available with 22.0-inch barrel in the Featherweight or 24.0-inch (pre-'64 Standard) are available with 22.0-inch barrels.

2. *Magnum M70.* Calibers: .264 Win. Magnum, .300 Win. Magnum, .338 Win. Magnum, .375 H&H Magnum, 7mm Rem. Magnum. All barrels are 24.0 inches. Butts are fitted with ventilated recoil pads. Quick-detachable sling swivels.

All calibers except the .375 H&H Magnum

Winchester Model 70 Magnum

Winchester Model 70 target rifle

WINCHESTER M70 (continued)

are "short" magnums in that they are .300 H&H or .375 H&H cases shortened and necked up or down. These cases function through a standard (.30–06 length) action. The .375 H&H Magnum is the only M70 cartridge requiring a full-length or true magnum action. The magazine capacity of the .375 H&H post-1964 M70 Magnum is 3-shot; pre-1964 was 4-shot. All Winchester M70 Magnums in current production have 3-shot magazines.

The .300 H&H Magnum cartridge was the only magnum cartridge available in the pre-1964 M70 that was not carried over into the present M70. All new M70 Magnum stocks are reinforced with a steel crossbolt; the .458 African has two.

3. *Mannlicher-stocked M70.* In 1969 Winchester introduced a 19.0-inch barrel M70 with the full-length Mannlicher-type stock. Calibers: .243 Win., .270 Win., .30–06 Springfield, .308 Win. (7.62mm NATO). Steel fore-end cap. Checkering was reverse type (1969–71). Quick-detachable sling swivels. Discontinued 1972.

This variation was probably discontinued because: it cost about $75 more than the Standard M70, and medium- to high-velocity cartridges created about 250 f.p.s. loss of muzzle velocity from the 24.0-inch barrel. The handiness of the short barrel was insufficient compensation.

4. *M70 African.* Discussed in Chapter 8.

5. *M70 Target rifle.* Like the M70 African, the new M70 Target is little changed in stock dimensions from the old M70. (There is, of course, the improved action with recessed bolt head.) Calibers: .308 Win. (7.62mm NATO), .30–06 Springfield. Clip slot in receiver bridge for use with 5-shot Springfield stripper clips. Contoured aluminum hand stop.

We would like to see a return of the Old M70 Bull Gun in either .300 H&H Magnum or .30–06 Springfield or both. This M70 had a 28.0-inch barrel and weighed 13.0 lbs.

6. *M70 Varmint Rifle.* Discussed in Chapter 9. The author would like the 26.0-inch barrel fitted to this rifle. He prefers this rifle weight over any other commercially available rifle in these calibers. Now that Ruger has revived the .220 Swift in his M77, perhaps Winchester will also revive this fine cartridge, which it originated in 1935.

7. *M70 Custom (Super Grade) Rifle.* Introduced in 1964, discontinued in 1973. Its name was changed to Super Grade (after old M70) in 1972. Calibers: .243 Win., .270 Win., .30–06 Springfield, .300 Win. Magnum (with ventilated recoil pad). Receiver bridge matted to prevent glare. Knurled bolt handle. Prior to 1972 the Super Grade had a stock similar to (but better wood) than other M70s.

Data (general): Many modifications were made on the post-1963 M70 during its first 11 years. Many changes involved stock design, and some of these changes were sufficiently unfortunate so that they were later refined or abandoned: reverse checkering, a loss of classic contours, a free-floating barrel which theoretically should have improved accuracy (by eliminating the variable pressure of wood against metal) but — until the design was refined — was floated in too wide a channel. It should be stressed that most of the criticisms no longer apply, although the M70 has not returned to traditional contours but has, instead, incorporated a subtle touch of Weatherby styling.

A major difference between the old and current M70 is the recessed bolt head, which offers additional protection in the event of cartridge-head failure.

Other improvements over the old M70: jeweled bolt, quick-detachable sling swivels, and knurled bolt handle.

Pre 1964 M70s — except Featherweight — had machined-steel trigger guards. M70s now have the old Featherweight aluminum alloy trigger-bow. Early pre-1964 M70s, save those with recoil pads, were fitted with a checkered steel buttplate. The current M70 has a plastic buttplate in standard calibers. The new M70 retained the old M70's hinged floorplate. Trigger pull is adjustable.

In 1968 Winchester added an anti-bind device, or bolt guide. This makes the bolt noticeably easier to operate. This feature was installed on all M70s at serial number 866,000. Purchasers of secondhand post-1964 M70s should endeavor to get one with the serial above 866,000. *Bolts above 866,000 will not fit receivers below that number.*

The alloy floorplate was replaced with one of black chrome steel. Triggerbow and floorplate frame are still alloy. Pre-1964 M70 triggerbows and floorplate frame — both of machined steel — are still available.

Comment: The author, along with many another admirer of the lovable pre-1964 M70, intensely disliked the replacement M70 for a long time after its appearance. This dislike was partly esthetic, partly emotional, and partly technical. Some of the features were mechanically improved, but there were also changes for the sake of economy — cheaper methods of manufacturing the receiver and action by eliminating some machining and meticulous handcrafting. (For further details and comment, see the introductory text at the beginning of this chapter.) While these economy measures did not significantly impair functioning, they were mere changes rather than progress and, as with the stock, later refinements were made.

The recessed bolt head of the new M70 is safer than that of the old M70, but no one who used factory ammunition or sensible reloads could have asked for greater safety with the pre-1964 M70. It was partly Remington's advertising its M700's bolthead safety feature that impelled Winchester to adopt the enclosed bolthead.

Gradually, and especially in the last three or four years, the new M70 has returned to the good graces of some old M70 buffs. Others have been permanently weaned away by the Ruger M77, which bears a strong resemblance to the classic lines and features of the pre-1964 M70.

The new M70 is an even safer rifle than the old M70, but the old M70 was extremely safe. It was primarily the looks, including the useless reverse checkering, that caused old M70 lovers to bewail its fate. Machine-cut checkering has returned.

Many recent M70 changes may well have been effected because the Remington M700 was surpassing the M70 in sales — and because of the appeal of the Ruger M77 to pre-1964 M70 admirers.

WINCHESTER M70A

Winchester Model 70A Sporter

Action type: bolt; modified Mauser; cartridge case head enclosed

Magazine type: nondetachable box; no floorplate

Magazine capacity: standard calibers, 4-shot; magnum calibers, 3-shot

Safety: 3-position

Barrel length: magnum calibers, 24.0 inches; standard calibers, 22.0 inches

Stock: 1-piece Weatherby-style American walnut; plastic pistol-grip cap; machine-cut checkering; Monte Carlo comb; cheekpiece; fluted comb

Buttplate: shotgun type; plastic

Overall length: 22.0-inch barrel, 42.5 inches; 24.0-inch barrel, 44.5 inches

Length of pull: 13.5 inches

Drop at comb: 1.75 inches

Drop at Monte Carlo: 1.5 inches

Drop at heel: 2.125 inches

Weight: 22.0-inch barrel, 7.5 lbs.; 24.0-inch barrel, 7.75 lbs.

Trigger pull: not specified

Sight, rear: folding leaf

Sight, front: gold bead on ramp with removable sight protector

Scope adaptability: receiver drilled and tapped for standard scope bases

Caliber: 1974 .222 Rem., .22–250 Rem., .243 Win., .25–06 Rem., .270 Win., .30–06 Springfield, .300 Win. Magnum, .308 Win. (7.62mm NATO), 7mm Rem. Magnum

Data: This economy version of the M70 is available in all M70 calibers except the .338, .375 H&H, and .458 Winchester magnums. A major economy was achieved by eliminating the hinged floorplate. This reduces the magazine capacity by one round. The M70A has an engine-turned bolt, three-position safety, and wide serrated trigger. No fore-end-tip wood insert, and the rounded, classically plain fore-end may appeal to many old M70 lovers.

Comment: This is Winchester's third economy version of the post-1964 M70. The other attempts, both discontinued, were the M670 and M770.

CHAPTER 7

SINGLE-SHOT BOLT-ACTION CENTERFIRE RIFLES

The single-shot bolt action is the most restrictive of all centerfire rifle categories. There are three basic uses for such an action: match rifles for use in a limited number of matches, varmint shooting, and benchrest shooting. At the present time, one American production-line rifle is manufactured for each of these purposes. (There are, of course, plenty of custom-built single-shot bolt-action centerfires, made by gunsmiths to fill individual orders.)

Despite the limited uses, there is sufficient demand to keep these rifles in production. Before 1975 only two rifles, both using the same basic Remington 40XB action, were available. In 1975 Savage introduced its M112V single-shot varmint rifle.

If Savage and Remington had to design and manufacture actions solely for single-shot use there would be no single-shot bolt rifles. However, the two Remington single-shot rifles are actually one-shot versions of a magazine rifle. The magazine rifle becomes a single-shot by the simple expedient of not cutting a magazine well in the stock. A bolt-action single-shot costs slightly less to produce because the stock-cutting process is simplified and there is no magazine or magazine floorplate. However, a rifle for benchrest shooting, other kinds of target matches, or varminting does have special features and it must be exceptionally accurate. It requires very painstaking manufacture—which means that a single-shot costs the buyer as much or more than its magazine counterpart.

Why a single-shot rifle?

The stiffer a stock is, or the less spring it has, the more accurate the rifle should be, all other factors being equal. The simplest way to stiffen a stock is to delete the magazine well.

The only benchrest rifle from a major manufacturer is the Remington 40XB-BR. This model represents a very small portion of the rifles used by the thousands of benchrest shooters. From personal observation the author estimates that at least 95 percent of benchrest rifles are custom-made. Many of these rifles use modified Remington actions.

One of the most popular actions is the Shilen. This handcrafted action is designed for benchrest shooting. Many benchrest rifles based on a Remington or Shilen action are made up by the shooters themselves.

The benchrest shooter has one ultimate goal. He—or she—wants to put three bullets into one hole, the size of one bullet. Twenty years ago this seemed impossible, though even then pioneer benchresters were hoping to achieve it. The day is approaching when it will happen. After that, what? The clan will probably seek to achieve the same effect at twice the distance.

The original benchrest shooters met informally back in the early 1950s in Johnstown, N.Y. The author's friend, the late Harvey Donaldson, wildcatter and designer of the famed .219 Donaldson Wasp, was largely responsible for the meet. Most of the group were dedicated varmint shooters and wildcat cartridge experimenters.

Today, there are two benchrest shooter organizations. National matches are attended by shooters from all over the United States and Canada. The organizations are International Benchrest Shooters (publication: *Precision Shooting*), 8 Cline St., Dolgeville, N.Y. 13329; and National Bench Rest Shooters Association (publication: *The Rifle Magazine*), Box 3030, Prescott, Ariz. 86301.

There are three basic rifle categories in benchrest matches: (1) Sporting rifle class, not to exceed 8.5 lbs. including scope; (2) Varmint rifle class, not to exceed 11.5 lbs. including scope; and (3) any-weight class. The author once fired a class-three rifle which used a healthy portion of a railroad tie for a stock and weighed 47.0 lbs.

Benchrest bullets are extraordinarily precise affairs. Many benchresters manufacture their own bullets. Others buy them from small-quantity, high-quality craftsmen. Many benchresters load their cartridges at the shooting site. Stationwagon tailgates and the trunk deck become loading benches.

There may be a benchrest group in your area. Even if you're not interested in this type of shooting, you won't regret a few hours' watching

and listening and talking to benchrest shooters—and you might get the bug.

The one single-shot varmint rifle is the Savage M112V, and the position target rifle is the Remington 40XB Rangemaster. Both are described in this chapter.

REMINGTON MODEL 40XB SINGLE-SHOT

Action type: bolt; modified Mauser; recessed bolt head

Safety: 3-position thumb-operated slide

Barrel length: 27.75 inches (round)

Stock: 1-piece American walnut, uncheckered, with full pistol grip; straight comb; hand-bedded free-floating barrel; adjustable front swivel and hand guide

Buttplate: shotgun type; plastic with white line spacer

Overall length: 47.75 inches

Length of pull: 13.5 inches

Drop at comb: 1.25 inches

Drop at heel: 1.25 inches

Weight: standard-weight stainless-steel barrel, 9.75 lbs.; heavy-weight stainless-steel barrel, 11.25 lbs.

Trigger pull: 2–4.0 lbs. (adjustable); 2.0-oz. special trigger available at extra cost

Sights, open: none furnished; receiver drilled and tapped for receiver peep/target sight

Scope adaptability: target scope block installed

Calibers, standard: .222 Rem., .222 Rem. Magnum, .223 Rem. (5.56mm), .22–250 Rem., .243 Win., .25–06 Rem., .30–06 Springfield, .300 Win. Magnum, 7.62mm NATO (.308 Win.), 6mm Rem., 7mm Rem. Magnum

Calibers, wildcat: 6×47mm (6mm Rem. case necked to .222 Rem.), 6mm International, .30–.338 (.338 Win. case necked to .30)

Data: 18 or more weeks for delivery after order date.

Comment: This rifle—one of our best target types—is available in many more calibers than its competitor, the 5-shot M70 target model.

REMINGTON MODEL 40XB-BR BENCHREST RIFLE

Action type: bolt; modified Mauser (short-throw)

Safety: thumb slide

Barrel length: light-varmint class, stainless-

steel, 20.0 inches; heavy-varmint class, stainless-steel, 26.0 inches

Stock: similar to Model 40-XB

Buttplate: special target-type "non-slip"

**EXPLODED VIEW OF
REMINGTON MODEL 40-XE CENTERFIRE RIFLE**

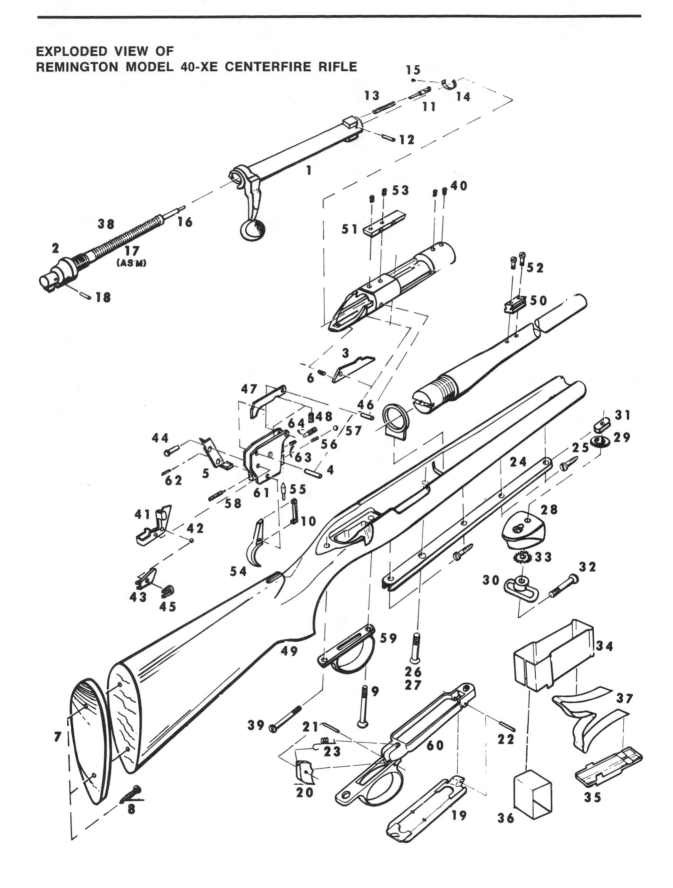

Parts list for Remington Model 40-XE Centerfire Rifle

No.	Part Name	No.	Part Name	No.	Part Name
1	Bolt Assembly	22	Floor Plate Pivot Pin (Repeating)	44	Safety Pivot Pin
2	Bolt Plug	23	Floor Plate Latch Spring (Repeating)	45	Safety Snap Washer
3	Bolt Stop	24	Fore-end Rail	46	Sear Pin
4	Bolt Stop Pin	25	Fore-end Rail Screw (3)	47	Sear Safety Cam
5	Bolt Stop Release	26	Front Guard Screw	48	Sear Spring
6	Bolt Stop Spring	27	Front Guard Screw (Repeating)	49	Stock (H2) (Repeating)
7	Butt Pad	28	Front Swivel Block	50	Telescope Base, Front
8	Butt Pad Screw	29	Front Swivel Block Washer	51	Telescope Base, Rear
9	Center Guard Screw (Single Shot Only)	30	Front Swivel with Bushing	52	Telescope Base Screw, Front
		31	Front Swivel Nut	53	Telescope Base Screw, Rear
10	Connector	32	Front Swivel Screw	54	Trigger
11	Ejector	33	Front Swivel Washer	55	Trigger Adjusting Screw
12	Ejector Pin	34	Magazine (Repeating)	56	Trigger Adjusting Spring
13	Ejector Spring	35	Magazine Follower (Repeating)	57	Trigger Adjusting Ball
14	Extractor	36	Magazine Spacer (Repeating)	58	Trigger Engagement Screw
15	Extractor Rivet	37	Magazine Spring (Repeating)	59	Trigger Guard
16	Firing Pin	38	Main Spring	60	Trigger Guard (Repeating)
17	Firing Pin Assembly	39	Rear Guard Screw	61	Trigger Housing Assembly
18	Firing Pin Cross Pin	40	Receiver Plug Screw	63	Trigger Spring
19	Floor Plate (Repeating)	41	Safety Assembly	64	Trigger Stop Screw
20	Floor Plate Latch (Repeating)	42	Safety Detent Ball		
21	Floor Plate Latch Pin (Repeating)	43	Safety Detent Spring		

REMINGTON MODEL 40XB-BR BENCHREST RIFLE (continued)

Overall length: 20.0-inch barrel, 39.25 inches; 26.0-inch barrel, 45.25 inches

Length of pull: 13.5 inches

Drop at comb: 0.5 inch

Drop at heel: 0.35 inch

Weight: 20.0-inch barrel, 9.24 lbs.; 26.0-inch barrel, 12.5 lbs.

Trigger pull: 2.0–4.0 lbs. (adjustable)

Sights, open: none

Scope adaptability: target scope blocks installed

Caliber, standard: .222 Rem., .222 Rem. Magnum, .223 Rem. (5.56mm), 7.62mm NATO (.308 Win.)

Caliber, wildcat: 6×47mm

Data: Specifications meet the requirements of National Bench Rest Shooters Association (NBRSA). Special order item. Allow 18 weeks minimum for delivery.

Comment: This is the only benchrest rifle regularly available through a manufacturer. Most benchrest rifles are made by custom makers (including action makers like Shilen). This is a superb varmint rifle. The author would like it available in calibers .243 Win. and/or 6mm Rem.

SAVAGE M112V SINGLE-SHOT VARMINT RIFLE

Action type: bolt; Savage M110 action (modified Mauser); enclosed cartridge head

Safety: sliding (top tang)

Barrel length: 26.0 inches

Stock: black walnut; hand-checkered (20 lines per inch); uncapped pistol grip; plain uncheckered fore-end; quick-detachable sling swivels

Buttplate: shotgun type; recoil pad with white line

Overall length: 47.0 inches

Length of pull: 13.5 inches

Drop at comb: 0.625 inch

Drop at heel: 0.625 inch

Weight: 9.25 lbs.

Trigger pull: 4.0 lbs. (adjustable)

Sight, rear: none

Sight, front: none

SAVAGE M112V SINGLE-SHOT VARMINT RIFLE
(continued)

Scope adaptability: receiver drilled and tapped for standard scope blocks

Caliber: .22–250 Rem., .220 Swift, .22–250 Rem., .243 Win., .25–06 Rem.

Data: For basic action data see Chapter 6.

Comment: This is the first American-made bolt-action single-shot varmint rifle. It is the only current-production varmint rifle which offers a 26.0-inch barrel in all calibers including the .220 Swift. It is one of two current production rifles — the other is the Ruger M77 — chambered for the .220 Swift.

The Wundhammer swell of the pistol grip is readily adaptable for either the right or left hand. The M112V is available in right- and left-hand actions.

Many dedicated varmint shooters prefer a single-shot bolt-action rifle because of the increased stock stiffness gained by lack of magazine well. Most custom varmint rifles are single-shots.

The non-Monte Carlo stock and plain fore-end appeal to lovers of the classic stock. One discordant note is the white line in the recoil pad. If Savage wanted to produce a pure classic rifle, a steel buttplate should have been used. Or, if a recoil pad must be used, at least the white line should have been left out. It is, however, no great chore to replace the recoil pad.

This is the only current-production centerfire rifle known to the author which has a checkered pistol grip and a plain — uncheckered — fore-end. This was an economy measure. Most custom varmint rifles have neither the pistol grip nor the fore-end checkered. Because the varmint rifle is usually fired in conjunction with some sort of improvised rest, the grip usually provided by checkering is not so vital.

The trigger pull of the author's two M112V rifles, a .220 Swift and a .243 Win., was a bit heavy upon arrival from the factory. This was readily rectified.

CHAPTER / 8

BIG-BORE BOLT-ACTION RIFLES

The big-bore magazine rifle—caliber .450 and up—did not become a major player on the African scene until the Winchester M70 African and its companion cartridge, the .458 Win. Magnum, appeared in 1956.

There were no magazine rifles in caliber .450. The .500 Mauser (Jeffrey) and .505 Gibbs are ultra-big-bores. The .500 Mauser, never popular because of feeding problems with the rebated case head, is dead. Only the .505 Gibbs is in the general range of the ultra-big-bores like the .500, .577, and .600 Nitro Expresses.

The large-medium-bore class includes .404 Westley Richards, .416 Rigby, and .425 Westley Richards. The .416 Rigby, capable of dropping elephant under all conditions except a charge, was most popular. Its popularity lay in the stoutly constructed steel-jacket solid. Many professional hunters like Harry Selby used the .416 as their personal rifle. The .425 WR acquired a reputation for unreliability for the same reason the .500 Mauser did—rebated-case feed problems.

These two ultra-big-bore and three large-medium-bore rifles, assembled in England, used Mauser actions.

The most popular medium-bore bolt-action cartridge, the .375 H&H Magnum, is more popular than any other bolt-action cartridge, including ultra-large and large-medium bores. The .375 H&H is capable of dropping but not stopping an elephant. It is also an excellent long-range caliber for African plains game. Many British East African and Rhodesian professionals tote a two-gun battery—.375 H&H and large-bore double or magazine rifle.

In the late 1930s when ultra-big-bore and large-medium-bore rifles cost $350 to $500, the .375 H&H Winchester M70 cost $61.96, and it rapidly became popular on the African scene. The M70 acquired a reputation for accuracy and reliability.

Jacques Lott, an experienced dangerous-game hunter, writing in *The American Rifleman*

("Why Big Bore Rifles Are Best," Jan./Feb. 1972), noted that professional white hunters Harry Manners and Wally Johnson "killed between them thousands of elephant and buffalo plus countless antelope and many lions between 1937 and 1960. They used pre-war Model 70 .375s and wore out several stocks apiece."

Trouble came, as it must, to all men who hunt dangerous game long enough with a marginal caliber. Lott noted:

Wally changed his old Model 70 for a .458 after a nasty duel with a snared buffalo which charged his clients. . . .

The buffalo, pain-maddened because his neck had been cruelly cut by a poacher's snare, charged before Wally could get in his third shot. The buff crashed into the muzzle, knocking the rifle from Wally's hand . . . Down went Wally, with the buffalo working on him . . . Wally got a horn through his thigh.

Jerry Knight, manager of Kerr's Sport Shop (Hollywood, California), ran up and pumped a couple of .458 solids, one of which severed the buffalo's spine just forward of the shoulders.

As Roy Weatherby topped the .338 Win. Magnum with his .340 Weatherby Magnum, so he topped the .458 with his .460 Weatherby Magnum. Advertised as the "World's most powerful cartridge"—the custom .475 A&M has more energy, 10,000 ft.-lbs.—the .460 uses the same weight and diameter bullet as the .458 Win. but at a higher velocity.

Some professional hunters believe the .460 Weatherby Magnum is a case of "overkill" while others prefer the .458 Win. Magnum on the grounds that it has better penetration. Some hunters, preferring more bullet weight to high velocity, use a 600-grain bullet.

Experienced elephant hunters like barrelmaker John Buhmuller—he may have killed more elephants than any contemporary American—used a .460 WM with a 600-grain bullet reversed in the case. Buhmuller shot elephants on control—for the government—at his

93

own expense. He was not allowed to keep the ivory.

Two other Weatherby loads are .375 Weatherby Magnum and .378 Weatherby Magnum. The .375 Weatherby Magnum was a .375 H&H case with a Weatherby shoulder. Increased propellant capacity gave the .375 bullets about 200 f.p.s. higher velocity than the .375 H&H. It was a deadly caliber. Unfortunately it was discontinued when Roy brought out his .378 Weatherby Magnum. He added a belt to the .416 Rigby case and necked it down to .375 H&H diameter. In some African countries neither of these cartridges can be used for elephant. Local laws require a .400 caliber minimum for the big stuff.

Most professionals now use the .458 Win. Magnum cartridge, and most are Winchester M70 Africans.

Big-bore design and features

Barrel length. The .458 Win. Magnum M70 originally had a 25.0-inch barrel. Post-1964 M70s have a 22.0-inch barrel. This is ideal. It is handy in bush or jungle. The .458 is a short-range cartridge, so the slight velocity loss is not critical.

Two other pre-1964 M70s had 25.0-inch barrels, the .375 H&H Magnum and .338 Win. Magnum (both are 24.0 inches in post-1964s).

The original Remington M700 in .458 Win. Magnum had a ridiculous—and, in bush or jungle, dangerous—26.0-inch barrel. It is now 24.0 inches; 22.0 inches would be even better. The current M70 is the only .458 with a 22.0-inch barrel.

Stocks. .458s usually have black or European walnut stocks. The .458 Colt Sauer Grand African has a stock of African bubinga wood. Any wood should be close-grained; big-bore rifle stocks take a tremendous pounding, so there can be no coarse-grained or flawed wood. The M70, Remington M700, and Ruger M77 use close-grained wood.

Weatherby's Mark V .460 Weatherby Magnum uses California mesquite. This must be good; Weatherby continues to use it and the author has heard no complaints.

Recoil lugs. First-production .458s had one recoil lug. Splintered stocks were common. A second recoil lug was added. Large recoil lugs are essential on stocks subject to heavy recoil.

Crossbolts. Winchester uses two crossbolts on the current .458 M70. These are essential to avoid stock breakage.

Overall weight. There is only one .458 Win. Magnum rifle which approaches a practical weight for a rifle with nearly 70 lbs. free recoil. This is the 10.5-lb. Colt Sauer. This is about the standard weight for a British magazine rifle with a cartridge with the .458's recoil.

No American riflemaker has a sense of proportion between recoil and rifle weight. Most gunmakers who produce both .375 H&H Magnums and .458 Magnums make them in about the same weight range. The .375 H&H Magnum has about one-half the recoil of a .458 Win. Magnum. The author, who has fired several thousand .375 H&H Magnum cartridges, agrees that the 8.5 lbs. of the .375 H&H is about right, if only because most .375s weigh about 9.5 lbs. with a scope. Most .458 Win. Magnums are not fitted with scopes.

Big-bore rifles are usually toted by a gun-bearer. Such rifles are carried to the hunting area in Land Rovers or jeeps. The .458 could conveniently weigh 10.5 lbs.

The author's present M70 (1974 production) .458 Win. Magnum is catalog-listed at 8.5 lbs. The actual weight, empty without carrying strap or scope, is 8.75 lbs. Because of wood density variation, it could just as readily weigh 8.25 lbs. That's just too light.

There is this point, however. Recoil is usually forgotten when firing at onrushing dangerous game. The author fires his .458 without excessive discomfort, but he has fired big-bore rifles for many years and enjoys it, and he is an unusually large man. Many potential purchasers are scared of .458 recoil. Don't be. A box of 20 solids will last through your sighting-in session and probably through the average elephant-rhino-buffalo safari. You'll only use your 510-grain softpoints on lion, so half a box may do. It is better to have a few left over. You may need to resight your rifle, so take an extra box.

Front sight. The .458 Winchester and most other front-sight-equipped rifles have a damnable microscopic bead. This should be replaced by the superb Redfield Sourdough front (if you can locate one).

Rear sight, open. The author's M70 African is fitted with the best American-made back sight he has ever used: a Williams Open Guide Sight adjustable for elevation and windage.

Rear sight, receiver. Some prefer a micrometer receiver sight. The classic micrometer is Lyman's 48. Inasmuch as long-range shooting is not practiced with the .458 Win. Magnum or .460 Weatherby Magnum, such an advanced sight is not essential. The Lyman #58 is adequate, or even better is Williams' Foolproof receiver sight.

When your receiver sight arrives, unscrew the

disc aperture and pitch it into the junk box.

Scope sight. The man who uses a scope sight on a short-range big-bore rifle against dangerous game is a damn fool. At short range in a scope it's just too hard to tell what you're seeing and get off a fast, accurate shot. The only possible exception is the rare man with one rifle who uses his .458 against nondangerous game. Few men, however, venture into the African bush without gunbearer and trackers. They can tote a second rifle like a .375 H&H or .30–06.

Sanity aside, it is very difficult to find a scope mount that can withstand repeated batterings of a big-bore's recoil. The only one known to the author is the Griffin & Howe quick-detachable mount. If a scope is going to be used on a big-bore then it should be a side mount. Before moving into the brush you quickly detach the scope and slip your micrometer slide into position or look through your Williams Open Guide Sight.

Top mounts such as Roy Weatherby supplies with his fine .460 Weatherby Magnum are to be abhorred. Roy likes to sell one of his superbly made scopes with a rifle. This is all right except in the case of the .460. On request Roy can probably supply a G&H side mount already installed if you insist on a scope.

Only a few scopes can withstand heavy recoil. You never know. A scope that has remained intact after 25 shots may crystalize on the 26th shot. Four inches should be minimum eye relief. Five inches is better.

Floorplate releases. Must be absolutely secure against premature opening. It is not uncommon for a magazine floorplate to open from the recoil of a big-bore. It is rather inconvenient when facing a charging elephant to find your magazine is empty. Loaded cartridges on the ground won't stop a charge.

During the 1930s the author saw a Griffin & Howe Springfield sporter that had its magazine floorplate-release catch inside the lower forward section of the triggerbow. Thirty-five years later he bought a Ruger M77 .30–06 Springfield. It was wonderful after all those years to have a classic-stocked rifle complete with tang safety and triggerbow magazine release. Then came the day while deer hunting the Green Mountains. A gloved finger accidentally moved the catch. The floorplate opened. There was no second shot at the vanishing whitetail.

The Winchester/Weatherby magazine floorplate release located outside and forward of the upper portion of the triggerbow is probably the safest release. It is even safer to pin the catch release permanently shut. The detachable-magazine Colt Sauer can be taped closed.

The big-bore bolt-action has only one barrel, but the action is so well designed and constructed that malfunctions are very rare. You can buy a new .458 Winchester Magnum—or even a .460 Weatherby Magnum—and take a three-week safari or longer for the price of a new best-quality British double.

Thoroughly familiarize yourself with the rifle. Practice loading. Try to create jams. Treat it well and it will not let you down in what matadors and Hemingway term "the moment of truth."

COLT SAUER GRAND AFRICAN

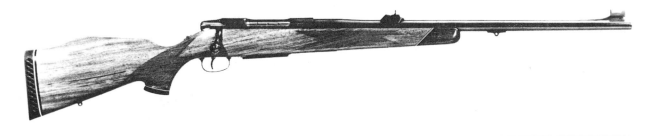

Manufacturer: J. P. Sauer & Sohns,

Importer/distributor: Colt's, Hartford, Conn.

Action type: nonrotating bolt

Magazine type: detachable box

Magazine capacity: 3-shot

Safety: sliding (top tang)

Barrel length: 24.0 inches

Stock: 1-piece African bubinga wood, rosewood fore-end tip at 45° angle with white line spacer; rosewood pistol-grip cap with white line spacer; 18-line-per-inch hand checker-

COLT SAUER GRAND AFRICAN (continued)

ing; rear detachable sling swivel; forward swivel mounted on barrel band

Buttplate: ventilated recoil pad

Overall length: 43.5 inches

Length of pull: 13.5 inches

Drop at comb: 1.75 inches

Drop at Monte Carlo: 1.5 inches

Drop at heel: 2.5 inches

Weight: 10.0–10.5 lbs.

Trigger pull: 4.5 lbs.

Sight, rear: sliding leaf; adjustable for windage and elevation

Sight, front: ivory bead on ramp with removable sight protector

Scope adaptability: receiver drilled and tapped for standard scope bases

Caliber: .458 Win. Magnum

Data: For general data, see Chapter 6.

Comment: This is the most comfortable-shooting rifle in caliber .458 Win. Magnum that the author has fired. About as heavy as the Weatherby .460 Magnum, it weighs more than any other current .458 Win. Magnum rifle, and the forward-slanting Monte Carlo comb helps handle severe recoil. The author does not trust the security of any detachable box magazine rifle, particularly in such a heavy caliber designed for use against dangerous game. He recommends taping or pinning the magazine in place. Like all rifles used against dangerous game, it should be fitted with a magazine follower stop so that the bolt remains open after the last round is fired.

This is an excellent rifle, but except for the heavier barrel and the other factors mentioned above, the author cannot see its advantage over the same caliber in the M70 Winchester.

INTERARMS MARK X ALASKAN RIFLE

Manufacturer: Zavodi Crvena Zastava Arsenal, Yugoslavia

Importer/distributor: Interarms

Action type: bolt; modified Mauser

Magazine type: nondetachable staggered box; hinged floorplate

Magazine capacity: 3-shot

Safety: slide located behind bolt handle

Barrel length: 24.0 inches

Stock: 1-piece walnut; machine-checkered; full pistol grip with black plastic cap; tenite fore-end cap with white line spacer; Monte Carlo comb; high-gloss finish; quick-detachable sling swivels

Buttplate: black rubber recoil pad with white line spacer

Overall length: 44.0 inches

Length of pull: 13.75 inches

Drop at comb: 1.5 inches

Drop at Monte Carlo: 1.25 inches

Drop at heel: 2.35 inches

Weight: 8.25 lbs.

Trigger pull: not specified

Sight, rear: Williams Guide, fully adjustable

Sight, front: flat gold bead on ramp with detachable hood

Scope adaptability: receiver drilled and tapped for standard scope mount

Caliber: .458 Win. Magnum, .375 H&H Magnum

Data: For basic action data see Interarms Mauser Mark X Rifle (Chapter 6).

Comment: This rifle uses the same action as the Whitworth Express Rifle, but costs less and has a stock designed for those who prefer semi-Weatherby styling.

REMINGTON M700 SAFARI GRADE

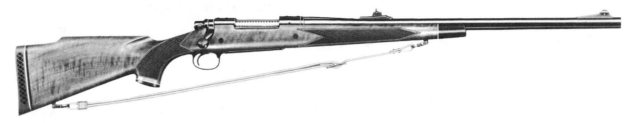

Action type: bolt; cartridge case head enclosed

Magazine type: nondetachable staggered box; hinged floorplate

Magazine capacity: 3-shot

Safety: 3-position vertical

Barrel length: 24.0 inches

Stock: 1-piece American walnut; hand-checkered fore-end and pistol grip; pistol-grip cap with white line spacer; black plastic fore-end tip with white line spacer; Monte Carlo comb; cheekpiece; twin steel reinforcing crossbolts

Buttplate: solid rubber recoil pad with white line spacer (photograph shows ventilated pad used previously)

Overall length: 44.5 inches

Length of pull: 13.375 inches

Drop at comb: 1.75 inches

Drop at Monte Carlo: 1.625 inches

Drop at heel: 2.125 inches

Weight: 9.0 lbs.

Trigger pull: 4.0 lbs., adjustable

Sight, rear: Williams Open Guide Sight, adjustable for windage and elevation

Sight, front: gold bead on ramp with removable sight protector

Scope adaptability: receiver drilled and tapped for standard scope bases

Caliber: .458 Win. Magnum, .375 H&H Magnum

Data: Same as for basic M700 action (Chapter 6).

Comment: This is a well-designed and well-constructed rifle. It has the reliable M700 Remington action. Anyone who owns the earlier version with a 26.0-inch barrel should cut it to 22.0 inches. The present 24.0-inch barrel could be cut to 22.0 inches without adversely affecting velocity/energy.

Remington should have mounted the front quick-detachable sling swivel on either a barrel band or barrel stud (like the Winchester M70 African). This is the standard method of mounting big-bore rifle front swivels.

With the forward swivel in its present position the left hand gets severely bruised from heavy recoil. The author fired more than 100 rounds through this rifle in .458 caliber and knows from experience. Remington probably didn't use the forward stud or barrel band in order to prevent any accusations of imitating the Winchester M70 African too closely, but Winchester just adopted a long-standard practice.

Purchasers of secondhand M700s—in any caliber—should get one that incorporates the bolt guide (anti-bind device) introduced in 1974. For other changes in that year see Chapter 6.

RUGER M77 ELEPHANT RIFLE

Action type: bolt; modified Mauser; recessed bolt face

Magazine type: nondetachable staggered box; hinged floorplate operated by release button inside triggerbow

Magazine capacity: 3-shot

RUGER M77 ELEPHANT RIFLE (continued)

Safety: sliding (top tang)

Barrel length: 24.0 inches

Stock: 1-piece selected dense-grade American walnut; hand-checkered pistol grip and fore-end; capped pistol grip; quick-detachable sling swivel studs

Buttplate: shotgun type; solid red rubber recoil pad

Overall length: 44.0 inches

Length of pull: 14.0 inches

Drop at comb: 1.5 inches

Drop at heel: 2.5 inches

Weight: 8.75 lbs.

Trigger pull: externally adjustable to 3.5-lb. minimum

Sight, rear: Williams Open Guide Sight, adjustable for windage and elevation

Sight, front: bead on ramp with removable sight protector

Scope adaptability: receiver drilled and tapped for standard scope mounts

Caliber: .458 Win. Magnum

Data: For basic action data see Chapter 6.

Comment: For basic action comment see Chapter 6. This rifle, though it costs less than any other .458 Win. Magnum rifle on the market, is as well made as any, and better than some. Actions and barreled actions are available.

WEATHERBY MARK V .460 MAGNUM

Manufacturer: Howa Machinery Co., Japan

Action type: bolt; modified Mauser; recessed bolt face

Magazine type: nondetachable staggered box; hinged floorplate

Magazine capacity: 2-shot

Safety: slide, right side of receiver

Barrel length: 26.0 inches

Stock: 1-piece California mesquite; basket-weave-checkered pistol grip and fore-end; flat-bottom fore-end with slab sides; rosewood fore-end tip insert at 45° angle; rosewood pistol-grip cap with white plastic diamond insert; forward-sloping Monte Carlo comb; cheekpiece; quick-detachable sling swivel studs

Buttplate: shotgun type; ventilated recoil pad with white plastic spacer

Overall length: 46.5 inches

Length of pull: 13.5 inches

Drop at comb: 0.75 inch

Drop at Monte Carlo: 0.5 inch

Drop at heel: 1.5 inches

Weight: 10.5 lbs.

Trigger pull: 3.5 lbs.; adjustable

Sight, rear: none except on special order

Sight, front: none except on special order

Scope adaptability: receiver drilled and tapped for standard scope mounts

Caliber: .460 Weatherby Magnum

Data: For basic action data see Chapter 6.

Comment: This rifle is chambered for the "world's most powerful cartridge." Actually the .475 A&M wildcat has more energy, some

10,000 ft.-lbs. Some experienced dangerous-game hunters prefer the .458 Win. Magnum, which they believe has better penetration. Others prefer the 750-grain bullets of the .577 double rifles to the 500-grain Weatherby Magnum. Some .460 Weatherby Magnum users prefer 600-grain bullets. Weight, they argue, is preferable to velocity.

The 26.0-inch barrel is unhandy in the brush. However, it takes a long barrel to approach advertised velocities. In the author's opinion the maximum barrel length for jungle and bush is 22.0 inches. That extra 4 inches could cost a hunter his life if the gun became entangled on a vine or brush during a critical situation.

The rifle doesn't come fitted with iron sights. This is a mistake. This rifle should not be used on dangerous game with a scope sight.

The .460 Weatherby Magnum produces nearly 100 lbs. of free recoil; the rifle should weigh at least 2 lbs. more than it does.

Barreled actions are available.

WHITWORTH .458 EXPRESS RIFLE, AFRICAN SERIES

Manufacturer: Whitworth Rifle Co., England

Importer/distributor: Interarms

Action type: bolt; modified Mauser

Magazine type: nondetachable staggered box; hinged floorplate

Magazine capacity: 3-shot

Safety: slide located behind bolt

Barrel length: 24.0 inches

Stock: 1-piece finely figured European walnut with classic English styling; hand-cut checkering; full pistol grip with plastic cap; black tenite fore-end cap; oil-type finish; quick-detachable sling swivels

Buttplate: solid red rubber recoil pad with black line spacer

Overall length: 44.0 inches

Length of pull: 14.0 inches

Drop at comb: 1.5 inches

Drop at heel: 2.5 inches

Weight: 8.0 lbs.

Trigger pull: not specified

Sight, rear: three folding leafs, mounted on quarter rib and marked 100 yds., 200 yds., 300 yds. Flat gold bead on ramp with detachable hood

Scope adaptability: receiver drilled and tapped for standard mount

Caliber: .458 Win. Magnum

Data: For general action data see Interarms Mauser Mark X Rifle (Chapter 6).

Comment: This is an excellent rifle for use on dangerous big game. For those who prefer the Mauser sporter action with the classic extractor and ejector this is about ideal. The author's only criticisms are minor. A rifle in this price range should be fitted with an ebony or Cape buffalo horn fore-end tip. Such tips are standard decoration on classic English big-game rifles. The pistol-grip cap should be blued steel. The rifle should weigh at least 3 pounds more to substantially reduce recoil. Still, this is one of the best big-bore bolt-action rifles available.

WINCHESTER M70 AFRICAN

Action type: bolt; cartridge case head enclosed.

Magazine type: nondetachable staggered box; hinged floorplate

Magazine capacity: 3-shot

Safety: 3-position vertical; red dot exposed when arm is cocked

Barrel length: 22.0 inches (25.0 inches on pre-1964 type)

Stock: 1-piece selected black walnut; twin steel reinforcing crossbolts; sharply defined hand-checkered fore-end and pistol grip; ebony fore-tip; slight Monte Carlo stock; well-defined cheekpiece

WINCHESTER M70 AFRICAN

Buttplate: shotgun type; black ventilated rubber recoil pad

Overall length: 42.5 inches

Length of pull: 13.5 inches

Drop at comb: 1.75 inches

Drop at Monte Carlo: 2.0 inches

Drop at heel: 2.6 inches

Weight: 8.5 lbs.

Trigger pull: not specified

Sight, rear: Williams Open Guide Sight, adjustable for windage and elevation; wide shallow V-notch; receiver drilled and tapped for standard receiver sight

Sight, front: silver bead on ramp with removable sight protector

Scope adaptability: receiver drilled and tapped for standard scope bases

Caliber: .458 Win. Magnum

Data: For basic action data see Chapter 6.

Comment: This rifle was the first arm chambered for the .458 Win. Magnum cartridge, and it established standards for future competitors. The author believes that despite higher prices the .458 M70 exceeded those standards. The higher cost of foreign competitors is due to inflation here and abroad, devaluation of the American dollar, and import duties.

The post-1964 Winchester M70 African has not been as subject to the severe criticism that other post-1964 M70s received.

The M70 African in both the old and current versions has been made in Super Grade only. During the lifetime of the pre-1964 M70 all calibers were available in Standard or Super Grade. The present M70 African is the only Super Grade survivor.

Quality of wood, fitting of wood to metal, and excellent hand checkering is as good as or better than found on any American factory rifle today. It is better than most foreign imports. Admirers of fine line (24 to 26 lines per inch) might prefer finer checkering, but in rifles largely designed for use in hot deserts and the humidity of tropical rain forests, excessively fine checkering can be a disadvantage. Hands wet with perspiration or rain can slip more easily on finely checkered stocks.

The M70 African is so well designed and its lines so graceful that there is little need for customization. Even those affluent individuals who can afford the $1000-plus price tag that first-class stocking and metalwork costs today rarely have any gunsmithing done on their M70 Africans.

The M70—like beautiful women—has one flaw, but it is a flaw we can live with. For more comfortable firing, the rifle should be 2 to 2½ pounds heavier.

Achieving this weight increase would mean a new barrel and a new stock. A custom barrel and first-class stock in a fine wood would cost at least $750.

The author would prefer a solid rubber recoil pad to the ventilated one. It's only a matter of a few dollars. He has owned two Africans over the last 20 years and has survived with the factory-installed pad. However, on a relatively expensive production-line rifle it seems that Winchester could install a solid rubber pad.

The M70 African is the only current-production M70 fitted with a steel magazine floorplate and triggerbow. The former is beautifully blued. The words "SUPER GRADE" appear on the barrel. Its appearance on the plate makes engraving nigh impossible. Even if one doesn't intend to engrave the floorplate, the gold-filled letters are gaudy. Only one .458 Win. Magnum rifle—the Ruger M77—currently sells for less than the M70 African.

CHAPTER 9

BOLT-ACTION VARMINT RIFLES

A varmint rifle is any rifle with a cartridge capable of taking varmints. There is, however, a special rifle and cartridge class designed for varmint shooting. A "varmint" — derived from "vermin" — to the Easterner is a woodchuck and to the Westerner is a rock chuck or prairie dog. Coyotes, foxes, crows, and even mountain lions are varmints to some shooters. Many states have no season or limits on certain varmints, but in recent years some of these species have been elevated to the legal status of game animals, with the harvest controlled by season and limit regulations. This trend is apt to continue. It is welcomed by sportsmen who are concerned about the future of wildlife as habitat continues to be depleted by urbanization.

Dedicated varmint shooters are usually chuck shooters. Experienced chuck shooters are deadly long-range riflemen. Rocky Mountain guides and outfitters agree that chuck shooters usually get their sheep or other long-range game like caribou or goat.

The author has fired all varmint rifles on the current market in at least one caliber. He has had the most experience with the pre-1964 Winchester M70. For 27 years the M70 had no production-line competitor, and the post-1964 M70 was on the market for four years before Remington introduced its M700 Varmint Special. This was followed by the excellent Ruger M77 varmint version.

Accuracy of varminters

It is virtually impossible to say one rifle model is more accurate than another. No matter how extensive one man's experience is, it would take the firing of hundreds of rifles over a long period to determine the most accurate.

Any properly scoped rifle with a varmint-weight barrel should make 1.0-inch 5-shot groups at 100 yards. In theory this means a 2.0-inch group at 200 yards, 4.0-inch at 400 yards, etc. It doesn't usually work that way. Beyond 200 yards there is a tendency for groups to open up a bit.

Some rifles are capable of 0.75-inch groups with factory ammunition. The author owns four such rifles: a pre-1964 M70 in .243 Win., two Ruger M77s in .243 Win. and .220 Swift, and a Carl Gustav in .22–250 Rem. Handloads bring groups down to nearly 0.50 inch.

Such accuracy is not good enough for benchrest shooting but is more than adequate for varmints because under field conditions a rifleman cannot utilize all of his rifle's accuracy potential. Benchrest shooters fire at known ranges from sandbagged rests. A paper target won't move, so the benchrest shooter can wait for the wind to die down — except under certain conditions. The chuck shooter has no sandbag. He must use his sling, a bipod or monopod rest, or a binocular case, felt hat, or rolled jacket. Stone walls, as they are called in New England (stone fences elsewhere), provide a good rest but should be covered with a shirt or jacket to protect the rifle's finish.

Varmint cartridges

Varmint hunters are careful handloaders. They experiment to find the best cartridge case and bullet and reject those exceeding allowable tolerances.

Two basic cartridge/caliber types are used by dedicated varmint shooters: .22 centerfire, and 6mm.

.22 centerfire. These include 200-yard cartridges like the .222 Rem. and .223 Rem. (5.56mm). The .222 Rem. Magnum is fading from the scene, not because it is not a good cartridge but because it is identical in performance with the .223 Rem. The latter is now a U.S. service cartridge in the M16 automatic rifle. Surplus cartridges and/or brass will soon become available.

The .22 Hornet, for which American rifles were not made for nearly 20 years, is experiencing a revival. Several bolt-actions are now made for the Hornet. Bill Ruger's Number Three Single-Shot is chambered for the Hornet. The Hornet's maximum range is about 150 yards. It is your best bet for shooting where a low decibel level is appropriate.

.22 centerfire long-range cartridges include the .22–250 Rem. and .224 Weatherby. These cartridges and the dying .225 Win. have almost identical ballistics. The .22–250 is now available in just about all bolt-action centerfire rifles.

The .220 Swift, long-range king of .22 centerfire cartridges, is staging a comeback. It was not available from 1964, when Winchester dropped it from the M70, until 1973, when Ruger revived it. Savage now chambers the M112V single-shot bolt-action rifle for it.

Long-range .22 centerfire rifles are capable of taking chucks out to 400 yards.

6mm cartridges. A disadvantage of the .22s is that they are ultrasensitive to even slight breezes. This is where 6mm class cartridges are useful. They also retain their residual velocities over longer ranges.

6mm-class cartridges include .240 Weatherby Magnum, .243 Win., 6mm Rem., and the dying .244 Rem. (see Chapter 11). These cartridges can be used with 75–80-grain bullets for varmints and with 100-grain heavier-jacketed bullets for deer, antelope, etc. Most hunters who are interested in both use standard-weight sporters rather than the heavier varmint rifle. The author considers his various .243s as strictly for varmints and prefers something heavier for deer and antelope.

The .243 Win. and 6mm (.244 Rem. case) calibers are available in several classic varmint rifles. Many more rifles, sporting and varmint, are chambered for the .243 Win. than for the 6mm Rem. (see Chapter 11). The Weatherby Magnum is available only in sporter weight.

Any 6mm is capable of taking chucks at 400-plus yards. They have better windbucking propensities.

During the years 1935–55 the .257 Roberts—there were no 6mm cartridges in those days—was the most popular dual-purpose varmint/deer cartridge. The advent of the .243 Win. killed off the excellent Roberts. Today's .25–06 Rem. is perfectly capable of harvesting both chucks and deer, but many chuck shooters—the author included—think the .25–06 has disadvantages for regular chuck shooting: it has a high noise level, ammunition is more expensive (the day of cheap surplus .30–06 brass is past), and ideally a true varmint caliber has minimal recoil. Commercial .25–06s have recoil pads and 24.0-inch barrels to reduce muzzle blast. This is indicative of their disadvantages as varmint rifles.

The .264 Win. Magnum and .257 Weatherby Magnum have trajectories flat enough for varmint shooting, but they have a very high noise level and considerable recoil, and magnum cases are far more expensive than .243 cases. Neither cartridge is available in a varmint-type rifle.

In using dual-purpose rifles, always select the proper bullet for the chore at hand. The 80-grain 6mm bullet is designed strictly for varmints and disintegrates on impact with rocks, etc. This reduces ricochet danger. The 100-grain bullet has a heavier jacket for thin-skinned medium-size game like deer. Varmint shooters who prefer the 100-grain weight can purchase custom bullets with light varmint jackets for handloading.

The .30-caliber 110-grain bullets have varmint jackets. The initial 3500 f.p.s. velocity is shed very rapidly. They have poor sectional density, *i.e.,* ratio of width to length.

Barrels

The .220 Swift, ever since its initial appearance in 1936, has always had 26.0-inch barrels. This length has been necessary to develop the advertised 4100 f.p.s. velocity and to reduce muzzle blast. Winchester's pre-1964 M70 varmint and target model in caliber .243 Win. always had a 26.0-inch barrel. The .257 Roberts and the .22 Hornet, in both standard and varmint target barrels, were a standard 24.0 inches.

The post-1964 M70 Winchester—at that time it was the only varmint-type rifle—was fitted with a 24.0-inch barrel in all calibers. The Remington M700, Ruger M77 (except .220 Swift), and Mossberg M800V all have 24.0-inch barrels.

The 1975 introduction of the Savage M112V with a 26.0-inch barrel for all five calibers now gives the varmint shooter something he has not had in a long time: a bolt-action rifle in .243 Win. with a 26.0-inch barrel. Calibers .22–250 Rem. and .25–06 have never been available in a 26.0-inch-barrel varmint rifle.

Make your choice: a 26.0-inch barrel with slightly superior ballistics or the shorter and somewhat handier 24.0-inch barrel. There is no option with .220 Swift. You wouldn't want one.

The medium-heavy-barrel rifles do not necessarily shoot more accurately but they do hold steadier under field conditions.

Scopes

The usual varmint scope of 10–12× requires the steadiest possible hold; wobble is to be kept at a minimum.

From the early 1930s, when modern varminting was born with the .22 Hornet, until the late 1950s varmint shooters used target scopes with micrometer mounts (external adjustments). The situation changed when Lyman brought out its 10× All-American scope with internal adjustments.

The target scope with external adjustments provided finer adjustments but was easier to damage than the lower-mounted internal-adjustment scope. Target scopes are considerably more expensive.

Since about 1960 the internal-adjustment scope has become almost universal for varminters.

The classic varmint rifle has a 26.0- or 24.0-inch barrel and weighs 8.75 to 9.75 lbs. There are, however, included in this chapter several rifles which do not meet the classic standards. Some are called varmint rifles because they are chambered for varmint calibers. In some instances, like the .224 Weatherby Magnum, the particular rifle described is the only one chambered for the cartridge.

The Savage M112V, though essentially a varmint rifle, is covered in Chapter 7 with the other single-shot bolt-action centerfires. The Ruger Number One and Number Three single-shot rifles are covered in Chapter 1.

CARL GUSTAV V/T RIFLE

Manufacturer: Carl Gustav Stads Gevarskfaktori, Sweden

Importer/distributor: F.F.V. Sports

Action type: bolt; modified Mauser; recessed bolt head

Magazine type: detachable staggered box (interchangeable with detachable box)

Magazine capacity: 5-shot

Safety: slide on right side of receiver

Barrel length: 27.0 inches

Stock: European walnut; target type; no checkering; flat-bottom, slab-sided fore-end; fluted comb; Wundhammer-swell pistol grip

Buttplate: shotgun type; checkered steel

Overall length: 47.5 inches

Length of pull: 14.25 inches

Drop at comb: 0.4375 inch

Drop at Monte Carlo: 0.3125 inch

Drop at heel: 1.625 inches

Weight: 9.25 lbs.

Trigger pull: externally adjustable to 18.0 oz. minimum

Sight, rear: none

Sight, front: none

Scope adaptability: receiver drilled and tapped for standard scope bases

Caliber: .22–250 Rem., .222 Rem., .243 Win., 6×55 (Swedish) Mauser

Data: For basic action data see Chapter 6.

Comment: One of the world's most accurate target rifles, the V/T (Varmint/Target) has been introduced to the American shooting public in hopes that it will attract both varmint and match shooters. European shooters—usually Swedes—have won many international and national matches with this rifle. The Swedish Shooting Team established two new world records at the World Shooting Championships in 1970 at Tucson, Arizona. Such matches are usually shot with a very accurate Swedish service cartridge, the 6×55 (Swedish) Mauser.

The wide, flat-bottom, slab-sided fore-end is very popular these days. Actually the classic rounded fore-end is better for sporting rifles. The stock on this rifle is just what is needed for shooting over sandbag rests or for field rests in varmint shooting.

HARRINGTON & RICHARDSON M317/317P ULTRA WILDCAT

Manufacturer: Sako, Finland

Importer/distributor: Harrington & Richardson

Action type: bolt; modified Mauser; enclosed bolt head

Magazine type: nondetachable staggered box; hinged floorplate

Magazine capacity: 6-shot

Safety: sliding (just aft of bolt handle); 3-position

Barrel length: 20.0 inches

Stock: 1-piece American walnut; machine-checkered on M317, hand-checkered on M317P; Weatherby-style slab fore-end with wood insert at 45° angle; flared pistol grip with rosewood cap; selected figured walnut and basketweave hand checkering on M317P; Monte Carlo comb; cheekpiece

Buttplate: shotgun type; solid rubber recoil pad with white and black line spacers

Overall length: 38.5 inches

Length of pull: 13.625 inches

Drop at comb: 1.25 inches

Drop at Monte Carlo: 1.6 inches

Drop at heel: 2.6 inches

Weight: 5.25 lbs.

Trigger pull: 4.5 lbs.

Open sights: none

Scope adaptability: receiver drilled and tapped for standard scope bases

Caliber: .17 Rem., .222 Rem., .223 Rem.; .17/.223 Rem. wildcat discontinued

Data: M317 is standard or Ultra Grade. M317P is Presentation Grade.

Comment: For the varmint shooter who has everything or the tyro varminter who doesn't know any better. A standard-weight varmint field rifle weighs 6.5–7.25 lbs. A standard heavy-barrel rifle weighs 9.0–9.75 lbs. The M317's short barrel reduces the 4000 f.p.s. to less than 3750 f.p.s. or about the same as a .22–250 Rem., .224 Weatherby Magnum, or .225 Win. It is a shame to waste such a fine action and excellent stocking on a too-light rifle.

MOSSBERG M800 VARMINT RIFLE

Action type: bolt; modified Mauser; recessed bolt head

Magazine type: nondetachable staggered box; hinged floorplate

Magazine capacity: 4-shot except .222 Rem., 3-shot

Safety: tang slide

Barrel length: 24.0 inches (straight taper)

Stock: 1-piece American walnut; Monte Carlo comb; cheekpiece; reverse checkering; plastic pistol-grip cap with white line spacer; quick-detachable sling swivels

Buttplate: shotgun type; red rubber recoil pad with white line spacer

Mossberg M800 Varmint Rifle

Overall length: 44.0 inches

Length of pull: 14.0 inches

Drop at comb: 1.875 inches

Drop at Monte Carlo: 1.625 inches

Drop at heel: 2.125 inches

Weight: 9.0 lbs.

Trigger pull: 3.5 lbs.

Sight, rear: none

Sight, front: none

Scope adaptability: scope blocks; receiver drilled and tapped for standard scope bases

Caliber: .222 Rem., .22–250 Rem., .243 Win.

Data: This is a short-action version of the Mossberg 810 series. The bolt has a recessed head. Locking is accomplished by six lugs.

Comment: This rifle, which sells for considerably less than other American-made varmint rifles, is surprisingly reliable and accurate. The M800 is capable of 1.0-inch groups. The trigger may require some easing up. This is an excellent rifle for the economy-minded shooter.

PARKER-HALE M1200V VARMINT RIFLE

Manufacturer: Parker-Hale, England

Importer/distributor: Jana International

Action type: bolt; modified Mauser

Magazine type: nondetachable staggered box; hinged floorplate

Magazine capacity: 4-shot

Safety: sliding thumb

Barrel length: 24.0 inches

Stock: 1-piece European walnut; skip-line hand checkering; flat Weatherby-style fore-end with rosewood tip; flared pistol grip with rosewood cap and white line spacer; Monte Carlo comb with roll-over cheekpiece; high gloss finish; quick-detachable sling swivels

Buttplate: solid rubber recoil pad with white line spacer

Overall length: 45.0 inches

Length of pull: 13.5 inches

Drop at comb: 1.8 inches

Drop at Monte Carlo: 1.5 inches

Drop at heel: 2.3 inches

Weight: 9.5 lbs.

Trigger pull: not specified

Open sights: none

Scope adaptability: receiver drilled and tapped for standard mount; target-scope bases supplied

Caliber: .22–250 Rem., .243 Win., .25–06 Rem., 6mm Rem.

Data: This is a good-quality rifle with a 4.0-lb. target-type barrel. High-luster blue finish. Glass-bedded action.

Comment: An excellent varmint rifle. Inasmuch as many varmint shooters prefer the more classic type of stock, some of us would prefer a comb without the roll-over cheekpiece, but this is of relatively small importance.

REMINGTON M700 BDL VARMINT SPECIAL

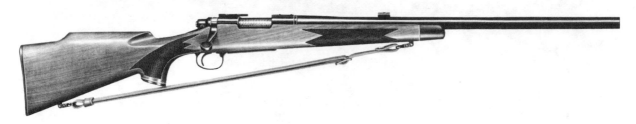

Action type: bolt; modified Mauser; encased cartridge head

Magazine type: nondetachable staggered box; hinged floorplate

Magazine capacity: 5-shot except .17 Rem., 6-shot

Safety: 3-position thumb type

Barrel length: 24.0 inches

Stock: 1-piece American walnut; machine-checkered (formerly reverse-checkered) pistol grip and fore-end; black fore-end tip with white spacer; plastic pistol-grip cap with white spacer; Monte Carlo comb; cheekpiece; quick-detachable sling swivels and sling

Buttplate: black plastic with white plastic spacer

Overall length: 43.5 inches except .25–06 Rem., 44.5 inches

Length of pull: 13.375 inches

Drop at comb: 0.5 inch (from center of bore)

Drop at heel: 1.375 inches

Weight: 9.0 lbs.

Trigger pull: 3.5 lbs.

Sight, rear: none

Sight, front: none

Scope adaptability: scope blocks; receiver drilled and tapped for standard scope mounts

Caliber: .22–250 Rem., .222 Rem., .223 Rem. (5.56mm), .243 Win., .25–06 Rem., 6mm Rem.; .222 Rem. Magnum discontinued

Data: For basic action data see Chapter 6.

Comment: This was the second U.S.-made classic varmint-type rifle to appear on the American scene. It is probably the best-selling varmint rifle today. This is due partly to the wide range of calibers available and partly to its deserved reputation as a very accurate rifle.

RUGER M77 VARMINT RIFLE

Action type: bolt; modified Mauser

Magazine type: nondetachable staggered box; hinged alloy floorplate; release located inside triggerbow

Magazine capacity: 5-shot

Safety: sliding (top tang)

Barrel length: 24.0 inches except .220 Swift, 26.0 inches

Stock: 1-piece American walnut; hand-checkered; plastic pistol-grip cap; quick-detachable swivel studs; classic stock type

Buttplate: shotgun type; solid red rubber recoil pad

Overall length: 24.0-inch barrel, 44.0 inches; 26.0-inch barrel, 46.0 inches

Length of pull: 13.5 inches

Drop at comb: 1.5 inches

Drop at heel: 2.5 inches

Weight: 8.5–8.75 lbs.

Trigger pull: externally adjustable to 3.5-lb. minimum

Sight, rear: none

Sight, front: none

Scope adaptability: scope blocks; fitted with Ruger integral scope base and 1.0-inch Ruger scope rings

Caliber: .22–250 Rem., .220 Swift, .243 Win., .25–06 Rem., 6mm Rem.

Data: For basic action data see Chapter 6.

Comment: The author owns three of these rifles: .22–250 Rem., .220 Swift, and .243 Win. They are among the most accurate varmint rifles he has used.

Several varmint rifles weigh up to a pound more than the Ruger but the Ruger is fully as accurate. It would be interesting to see the results if another pound were added.

SAKO HEAVY BARREL VARMINT RIFLE

Manufacturer: Sako, Finland

Importer/distributor: Garcia Corp./Firearms International

Action type: bolt; modified Mauser

Magazine type: nondetachable staggered box; hinged floorplate

Magazine capacity: 5-shot

Safety: sliding

Barrel length: 23.5 inches in .222 Rem., .223 (5.56mm) Rem.; 24.0 inches in .22–250 Rem., .243 Win., .308 Win. (7.62mm NATO), .25–06 Rem.

Stock: 1-piece European walnut; hand-checkered pistol grip and fore-end; uncapped pistol grip; semi-beavertail fore-end; Monte Carlo comb; quick-detachable sling swivel studs

Buttplate: shotgun type; plastic with white line spacer

Overall length: 23.0-inch barrel, 43.0 inches; 23.5-inch barrel, 43.5 inches; 24.0-inch barrel, 44.0 inches

Length of pull: 14.0 inches

Drop at comb: 1.5 inches

Drop at Monte Carlo: 1.25 inches

Drop at heel: 2.5 inches

Weight: .25–06 Rem., 9.0 lbs.; all other calibers, 8.5 lbs.

Trigger pull: 3.5 lbs.

Sight, rear: none

Sight, front: none

Scope adaptability: receiver drilled and tapped for standard scope bases

Caliber: .222 Rem., .223 Rem. (5.56mm), .22–250 Rem., .243 Win., .25–06 Rem., .308 Win. (7.62mm NATO)

Data: For basic action data see Chapter 6. Cali-

SAKO HEAVY BARREL VARMINT RIFLE (continued)

bers .222 and .223 (5.56mm) use the L-461 short action. Calibers .22–250 Rem., .243 Win., and .308 Win. (7.62mm NATO) use the L-579 me-

dium action. The .25–06 Rem. uses the L-61 long action.

Comment: These are beautifully made varmint rifles. The .308 Win., though not a varmint caliber, is in this instance a lightweight target rifle.

SAVAGE/ANSCHUTZ M1432 HORNET

Manufacturer: Anschutz, West Germany

Importer/distributor: Savage

Action type: bolt; modified Mauser

Magazine type: detachable box

Magazine capacity: 5-shot

Safety: 3-position wing

Barrel length: 24.0 inches

Stock: 1-piece French walnut; hand-checkered pistol grip and fore-end; Schnabel fore-tip; pistol-grip cap with white line spacer; roll-over cheekpiece; Monte Carlo comb; quick-detachable swivel studs

Buttplate: shotgun type; plastic with white line spacer

Overall length: 43.0 inches

Length of pull: 14.0 inches

Drop at comb: 1.25 inches

Drop at Monte Carlo: 1.25 inches

Drop at heel: 1.75 inches

Weight: 6.57 lbs.

Trigger pull: adjustable; minimum, 3.0 lbs.

Sight, rear: folding leaf

Sight, front: bead on ramp with removable sight protector

Scope adaptability: receiver grooved for mount and drilled and tapped for standard scope bases

Caliber: .22 Hornet

Data: This is a well-made rifle for the .22 Hornet which seems to be staging a comeback. Stock features skip-checkering.

Comment: The rifle would have greater appeal if the roll-over comb were eliminated. This type of comb was designed for the old *Schutzen* rifles — and this isn't a *Schutzen* rifle.

WEATHERBY VARMINTMASTER RIFLE

Manufacturer: Howa Machinery, Japan

Importer/distributor: Weatherby, Inc.

Action type: bolt; modified Mauser

Magazine type: nondetachable staggered box

Magazine capacity: .224 Weatherby Magnum, 4-shot; .22–250, 3-shot

Safety: thumb-operated horizontal type

Barrel length: standard, 24.0 inches; semi-target, 26.0 inches

Weatherby Varmintmaster Rifle

Stock: 1-piece American walnut with Weatherby styling; flared pistol grip with rosewood cap; flat-bottom fore-end; rosewood fore-end tip inserted at 45° angle; forward-sloping Monte Carlo comb; cheekpiece; sharpcut basketweave hand checkering; actions individually handfitted to stock; high-gloss finish

Buttplate: rifle type; solid rubber recoil pad

Length of pull: 13.5 inches

Drop at Monte Carlo (front): 0.56 inch

Drop at Monte Carlo (rear): 0.25 inch

Drop at heel: 1.265 inches

Weight: 6.5 lbs. (either barrel)

Trigger pull: 3.5 lbs.

Sight, rear: none

Sight, front: none

Scope adaptability: receiver drilled and tapped for standard scope bases; Weatherby scope available on order

Caliber: .22–250 Rem., .224 Weatherby Magnum

Data: This is a scaled-down version of Weatherby's Mark V action. The stock is classic Weatherby with flaring pistol grip, rosewood cap, rosewood fore-end tip inserted at 45° angle, and white line spacers. Typical Weatherby cheekpiece and Monte Carlo comb.

Comment: This rifle was originally chambered for the .224 Weatherby Magnum (almost identical with the .22–250 Rem.). The .22–250 Rem., at the time the .224 was introduced, was still a wildcat cartridge. In 1966, when .22–250 rifles and cartridges had become available through commercial channels, Weatherby chambered the Varmintmaster for the .22–250 Rem.

WINCHESTER M70 VARMINT RIFLE

Introduced: 1964 (current version)

Action type: bolt; modified Mauser

Magazine type: nondetachable staggered box; hinged floorplate

Magazine capacity: 5-shot

Safety: 3-position thumb

Barrel length: 24.0 inches (pre-1964, 26.0 inches)

Stock: 1-piece American walnut; plastic pistol-grip cap with white line spacer; Monte Carlo comb; fore-tip insert with white line spacer;

WINCHESTER M70
VARMINT RIFLE (continued)

machine-checkered pistol grip and fore-end since 1974, reverse checkering 1964–73; quick-detachable sling swivels

Buttplate: shotgun type; plastic with white plastic spacer

Overall length: 44.5 inches

Length of pull: 13.5 inches

Drop at comb: 0.625 inch (from line of sight)

Drop at Monte Carlo: 0.375 inch (from line of sight)

Drop at heel: 0.0875 inch (from line of sight)

Weight: 9.75 lbs.

Trigger pull: adjustable to minimum of 3.0 lbs.

Sight, rear: none

Sight, front: none

Scope adaptability: scope blocks; receiver drilled and tapped for standard scope mounts

Caliber: .22–250 Rem., .222 Rem., .243 Win.; .225 Win. discontinued

Data: For basic action data see Chapter 6.

Comment: A lineal descendant of the pre-1964 M70 Varmint, this is the oldest—and heaviest—varmint rifle available. Despite criticisms—some unjust—this M70 is as accurate as its predecessor. Most admirers of the pre-1964 M70 Varmint rifle could live with this one if the stock more closely resembled the old one.

The M70 Varmint rifle is available in three calibers, compared to the seven calibers of the Remington M700 and the five calibers of the Ruger M77 and Savage M112V. Those three calibers, however, cover all basic needs of varminters.

It will be interesting to see if Winchester, which originated the .220 Swift—about 95 percent of all .220 Swifts were M70s—will revive the cartridge now that two competitors are chambering rifles for it. At this writing (1976) Winchester doesn't even make .220 Swift ammunition.

PART III

CENTERFIRE RIFLE CARTRIDGES

CHAPTER / 10

DESIGN OF THE CENTERFIRE CARTRIDGE

The centerfire—formerly "centralfire"—cartridge has been with us for slightly more than a century. The .44–40 Winchester (1873) was our first successful centerfire cartridge.

A cartridge consists of case, primer, propellant, and bullet. This chapter will explain the design and function of each component.

CASE TYPES

1. *Bottle (shoulder) case.* This is the most common type for rifles. Most contemporary cartridges are rimless. Any rimless cartridge must have a shoulder to control headspace. Bottleneck cartridges can readily be necked down (closed to a smaller diameter) or opened up (enlarged to a greater neck diameter) to create a cartridge of smaller or larger caliber.

2. *Straight case.* Most cases have a slight taper, but for practical purposes they are considered straight. Straight cases of recent years include the belted .458 Win. Magnum and rimmed .444 Marlin. The .458 Win. Magnum is a straight case because it is the shortened .375 Magnum case opened up to accept .458 caliber bullets.

3. *Straight taper case.* Straight taper cases are

from the black-powder days. They are, of necessity, rimmed.

Case material

Centerfire cartridges have been brass for nearly a century. Cartridge brass is 70 percent copper and 30 percent zinc. No substitute has been found which has the advantages of brass. It can easily be made into cases in large quantities. Brass possesses *obturation*, a quality not found in other usable case material. Cases must be smaller than the chamber into which they are fitted. When fired the case material must expand—obturate—to fill the chamber.

Early centerfire cases and predecessor rimfire cases were copper. The .45–70 and .45 Colt cases used by Custer's troops at the Little Big Horn, June 16, 1876, were copper, not brass. When a trooper fired his single-shot M1873 Springfield carbine the thin copper case too readily transmitted the heat to the chamber walls. At about every fifth shot the heat caused a fired case to expand excessively and stick in the chamber. The extractor usually tore off the case head. Troopers tried to remove ruptured cases with the broken shell extractor. Little Big Horn troopers were dead before they could remove the headless case.

Ordnance knew about the fifth-round problem, but with the slowness as typical of Washington bureaucracy then as now, nothing had been done. The "fatal fifth" sealed the fate of one glory-hunting general, his officers, and more than 200 troopers.

The government nevertheless continued using copper cases until the cartridge was replaced by the .30–40 Krag.

Steel. In wartime, brass is in short supply. Germany experimented with steel cases during World War I. The most successful steel cases — and they were not authorized for use in Thompson or M3 submachine guns — were developed in World War II. Chrysler Corporation's .45 ACP plant in Evansville, Ind., developed a coating which prevented steel cases from rusting, but the inferior obturation of steel was never solved. Chrysler's Kronak process was used on caliber .30 rifle and M1 carbine ammunition.

World War II steel cases in calibers .30 M1 carbine, .30–06, and .45 ACP, readily identified by gray case color, are not suitable for reloading.

Aluminum. Reich Marshal Hermann Goering, in an effort to increase the ammunition load carried by his Luftwaffe fighter pilots, had aluminum cases made. Only a limited quantity were made before the war ended.

The current status of caliber 7.62mm NATO (.308 Win.) aluminum cases, recently made on contract for the U.S. government, is not known.

Plastic. The author knows of no successful cases made from plastic for use in rifled arms, though plastic has become the primary material for shotshell cases.

Caseless. Germany was the first country to experiment with caseless cartridges. There have been several forms. The author is familiar with one that had the propellant pressure-formed into proper case size. The only metal in the complete cartridge — excluding the bullet jacket — was the primer. Experiments have been made with disintegrating primers. About 10 years ago the Daisy Air Rifle Company purchased rights to a caseless cartridge (it was not for air rifles). Little has been heard since then.

Cartridge brass will probably continue as the standard sporting cartridge case material for many years.

Case head types

Rimmed. The first centerfire rifle cartridges were designed for use in lever-action, single-shot, and double rifles. The rim was inherited from the rimfire case. The rim serves two purposes: it headspaces the cartridge — that is, holds it in proper relationship to chamber and bolt face — and it provides a surface for the extractor to grip. A few slide-action rifles like the old Colt and Remington were once chambered for rimfire cartridges like the .38–40 Win. and .44–40 Win.

Very few rimmed cartridges have been introduced in the past 50 years. Except for the .22 Hornet (1930), other rimmed cartridges have been designed for lever-action rifles. These include .218 Bee, .219 Zipper, .348 Win., and .444 Marlin.

The bolt-action, semiautomatic, and full automatic arms have pushed the rimmed cartridge into the background. Existing lever-action cartridges like the 80-odd-year-old .30–30 Win. will be around for a long time.

Three rimmed cartridges are undergoing a revival: .22 Hornet, .30–40 Krag, and .45–70.

Rimmed cases will function in bolt-action rifles, but rimless cases are easier to make and function better through semi- and full automatic arms. A rimmed cartridge requires a bigger bolt face and hence a heavier and bulkier action than a rimless case using an identical-caliber bullet. A .30–30 Win. rimmed cartridge would have required a bigger action for the M81 Remington semiautomatic or the slide-action Remington than the rimless .30–30 Rem.

The M1917 action is bigger than the M1903 Springfield/Enfield action because the M1917 was adapted from the P-14 Enfield originally made for the rimmed .303 British cartridge. In this case there was an advantage — not to M1917 Enfield .30–06 users but to those who built rifles chambered for long cartridges like the .375 H&H Magnum and .416 Rigby. The P-14/M1917 Enfield is an exception.

Rimless. The first successful rimless cartridge was the 8mm Mauser (8×57) developed for the German M1888 Commission rifle. Dozens of cartridges using the same head size are based on this former German army cartridge. Some 8mm-head-based cartridges: 7×57 Mauser, 8×56 Mannlicher, .30–06 Springfield, .308 Win. (7.62mm NATO), .243 Win., .244 Rem., 6mm Rem., .257 Roberts, .300 Savage, .250–3000 Savage, .270 Win., and scores of wildcats.

The first U.S.-designed rimless cartridge was probably the .236 Lee Navy (6mm Lee Navy) in 1895. The M1903 Springfield was the first U.S. service rifle with a rimless cartridge, caliber .30 M1906 (.30–06).

Proper headspace was no problem with the rimmed cartridge. It can be a problem with rimless cartridges. The rimless case is properly positioned in the chamber by its shoulder. Some rimless cases with very little shoulder have caused headspace problems. The excellent .358 Win., a necked-up .308 Win. case, has a very slight shoulder. Other rimless cases have encountered similar problems. The wildcat .400 Whelen, a necked-up .30–06 case, was almost shoulderless.

Modern sporting rifles and cartridges provide virtually no headspace problems. A great deal was heard about headspace in the 1930s and after World War II when many military rifles were converted to sporting cartridges.

Semirimmed. This compromise type, supposed to combine the advantages of the rimmed and rimless types, is nearly obsolete. No rifles have been made for the .351 W.S.L.R. and .303 Savage cartridges for many years.

Belted. This is a rimless case with a belt behind the head that controls headspace. The first commercially successful belted case was probably the .275 H&H Magnum (about 1910).

Belted rifle cases are "magnums." The .275, .375, and .300 H&H were pioneer magnums. Three cartridges today are based on the full-length .375 H&H case: the .375 H&H Magnum and .340 and .300 Weatherby Magnums. Weatherby started the "short magnum" trend with his .257 and .270 Magnum. Winchester then introduced its short-magnum series in 1956 with the .458 Win. Magnum, .338 Win. Magnum (1959), .264 Win. Magnum (1960), and .300 Win. Magnum (1963).

The belted magnum case is very strong. Most magnum cartridges approach the workable safe limit of about 55,000 p.s.i.

Rebated. The only current rebated American case is the .284 Win. (1963). No rifles are now made for the cartridge. Rebated cases were long used in Europe. The .500 Mauser (Jeffrey) was such a case. The .500 Mauser case used a rebated head, so existing Mauser bolts could handle the heavy propellant charges required for a .500 cartridge.

The rebated case body diameter is larger than head diameter. Rebated cases headspace on the shoulder. The extractor on rimless and rebated cases grips an extractor groove located between the head and case body.

The .284 Win. was designed to give .270 Win. ballistics in a cartridge short enough to work through the short lever action. The case had to be larger than the head so that an adequate powder charge could be used.

PRIMERS

For nearly a century American centerfire rifle and handgun cartridges have used the British-designed Boxer primer. For about the same time most English and Continental cartridges have used an American-designed Berdan primer. Boxer was a British Army colonel. General Hiram Berdan was known for his Union Army sharpshooters.

Cartridges using the Boxer primer are easy for handloaders to reprime. Berdan cases can be reprimed but require special repriming tools. (Berdan primer users could say Boxer primers require special tools.) Repriming Berdan cases takes a little more time.

Since World War II some European ammunition manufacturers have produced Boxer-primed cases and loaded cartridges for American shooters. Norma of Sweden, which made American cartridges for the Europeans with Berdan primers, for some time marked cases exported to the United States with the code RE on the headstamp (this practice has apparently been discontinued). This indicated to knowledgeable American shooters that the case could be reprimed with a Boxer primer.

German manufacturers like DWM also load cases with Boxer primers. It is reported that even Britain's conservative Kynoch now loads many cases with Boxer primers.

Primer sizes. Basic primer sizes have a designation of small and large rifle, small and large pistol. For many years handloaders used Remington primers in Remington cases and Winchester primers in Winchester cases, etc. Today, some companies manufacture primers but do not make cartridge cases.

Primer composition. During the black-powder era and for more than 40 years into the smokeless-propellant era all primers—there were German exceptions—were mercuric and corrosive.

In the days when an inexact mixture rather than the later exact composition was the rule, it was believed that mercury was essential to primer performance. The mercury residue in fired cases meant that they had to be cleaned in water almost immediately after use. Buffalo hunters reloaded their Sharps cartridge cases. They carried water containers. Water stopped mercury's immediate reaction upon copper or brass. Later cases were scrubbed with a brush.

Chemical developments eliminated mercury. Until recently the Western Cartridge Company, however, loaded its very accurate .300 H&H Magnum 180-grain boattail load with mercuric priming. This was done because the best accuracy was produced by a particular priming compound.

Mercury was eliminated, but there remained the barrel-corrosion problem because nonmercuric primers still contained a salt (potassium chloride).

Chemist James Burns became a Remington chemist after he developed the first American noncorrosive priming compound with the copyrighted trade name of Kleanbore. This was in the 1920s. Burns based his experiments on work done by the Germans. Lead styphenate replaced potassium chloride.

The U.S. Army—with one exception—used corrosive primers until the early 1950s. This was not a quirk of the conservative military mentality. Military ammunition is subjected to far greater stresses than sporting ammunition. The deer hunter who buys a box of .30–30s doesn't worry about long years of storage or transport under wide climatic changes. Military ammunition must be capable of being stored for at least 20 years without deterioration. Caliber .30 ammunition made in 1918 was used for training purposes in the 1930s.

There was one major exception to the use of corrosive primers in American small-arms service ammunition in World War II. When the Winchester M1 Carbine was developed, Colonel Edward H. Harrison of the Ordnance Department believed the extremely small gas port would readily be fouled by corrosive primer residue. He wrote into the cartridge specifications the requirements for a noncorrosive primer.

Millions of World War II caliber .30 and .45 ACP cartridges are on the market. This is corrosive ammunition. After firing, one either resorts to the traditional method the author used in the infantry and cavalry before World War II or uses the GI Bore Cleaner developed during World War II for the purpose of removing the corrosive residue. Prior to the bore cleaner, rifles, pistols, BARs, machine guns, and submachine guns had to be washed and scrubbed with hot water.

Current American, Swedish, and German ammunition and that of most other countries has nonmercuric, noncorrosive primers. Much of the Kynoch ammunition does, however, have corrosive primers. When in doubt, wash and scrub or use GI Bore Cleaner.

BULLET DESIGN

Lead was the basic bullet material from the day of the first firearm until the twentieth century. Lead, no matter how hard, will fuse at the base if propelled by smokeless propellants at velocities much over 1000 f.p.s. A gas check—metal cap on bullet base—will allow up to about 1500 f.p.s. Above 1500 f.p.s. bullets need semijackets, which puts them into the softpoint category.

Lead bullets, either straight lead or used as the core of solid (full metal-jacketed) bullets or softpoint bullets, are hardened by the addition of tin and/or antimony.

Sixgun—not semiautomatic pistol—bullets are either lead or lead with a semijacket (softpoint). Many sixgun bullets originated in the black-powder days.

Solid. This term when applied to a rifle bullet means a "solid" jacket. "Solids" are used by dangerous-game hunters. Bullets like the 500-grain .458 Win. Magnum bullet are designed for maximum penetration on thick-hided game like elephant, rhino, and Cape buffalo.

Full metal-jacketed military bullets. Colonel Lebel, designer of the French Army Lebel rifle, designed the first metal-jacketed bullet for the first smokeless-propellant military cartridge, the 8mm Lebel. The adoption by major powers of smokeless propellants also led to universal adoption of metal-jacketed bullets. The U.S. adopted its first metal-jacketed bullet, the 220-grain .30–40 Krag bullet, in 1892. The Spanish American War, however, was largely fought with volunteers using lead-bullet .45–55 405-grain (cavalry) and .45–70 500-grain loads with black powder. There were not enough Krags to supply the rapidly expanding army.

In the early 1900s the Geneva Convention outlawed "dumdum" bullets. Full metal-jacketed bullets may make less devastating wounds. The Dumdum Arsenal in British India had made bullets with knife-nicked tips during the Chitral Campaign.

The United States, though not a Geneva signatory, agreed to abide by convention rules. Most powers, by the time of the convention, had already adopted metal-jacketed bullets, not for humanitarian reasons but because smokeless propellants required them. However, effective barrel life is far shorter with metal-jacketed bullets than with lead.

During the Depression years when money was scarce, World War I surplus military .30–06 cartridges sold for two cents apiece. It was a common practice for deer hunters to drill a small hole, a "hollowpoint," in the M1906 bullets. This was a dangerous practice, because no full metal-jacketed bullet is actually fully jacketed. The base is open. When the tip is opened, the jacket

—or envelope, as the British say—becomes a mere tube. Doctored bullets may strip their jackets during barrel passage. The resulting obstruction makes things interesting when the succeeding shot is fired.

Dumdumming has been—and probably still is—practiced by some troops of every nation. But dumdums violate the Geneva Convention. For civilian purposes, dumdums are useless. If one of them causes a barrel obstruction, the firearm will be ruined even if the shooter isn't maimed or killed. And commercial hollowpoints are not only safe to shoot but far more accurate and far more effective on game.

Full metal-jacketed match bullets. Originally these were metal-jacketed military bullets. For many years they were made available without charge to National Rifle Association members through the Director of Civilian Marksmanship.

Before World War I, National Match ammunition was taken from the best of several tested lots. After the war, match ammunition was developed by the Frankford Arsenal. Some years later, lots were again purchased from commercial manufacturers. From 1931 until World War II, National Match ammunition was taken from selected lots of standard service issue. Before 1919 the 150-grain caliber .30 M1906 cupronickel-jacket bullet was used. Beginning in 1920, a 170-grain cupronickel and then gilding-metal bullet was used in match—or selected service—ammunition. A 172-grain and later a 173-grain M1 gilding-metal bullet succeeded the M1906 bullet.

Those and succeeding bullets became the basis for some of the most accurate commercial and military match ammunition ever made. The M1 bullet had a boattail—sometimes called tapered heel—and was extremely accurate at rifle ranges up to 1000 yards. Western Cartridge Company developed the very accurate 180-grain boattail caliber .30 bullet. This was widely used by civilian riflemen in both .300 H&H Magnum and .30–06 matches.

Custom bullet makers developed accurate bullets like the 160-grain and 200-grain Sierra Match Kings. A match bullet will be developed for the 5.56mm (.223 Rem.). The 55-grain full metal-jacketed service bullet has developed surprising accuracy in heavy-barrel AR-15 semiautomatic (civilian) and M16 full automatic (military) rifles.

The most accurate bullets—many are made by shooters themselves—are the .22 caliber (.222 Rem. is popular) bullets for super-accurate benchrest shooting. These are usually 50 or 55 grains.

Hollowpoint bullets. Once known as mushroom bullets, this type lost some of its former appeal after the development of controlled-expansion softpoint bullets. The best hollowpoint bullet known to the author was the Western Open Point Expanding. He used this bullet extensively for many years in the 139-grain 7mm and the 180-grain caliber .30 in both .30–06 Springfield and .300 H&H Magnum. Recently he was fortunate enough to salvage some 139-grain 7mm bullets from old cartridges with cracked necks. The 130-grain .270 Win. Open Point Expanding was a longtime favorite of Jack O'Connor. He also liked the 180-grain Open Point Expanding .30–06 bullet.

Today, the hollowpoint bullet has its widest use among varmint shooters, mostly in .22 caliber. The author uses hollowpoints in his .22 Hornet, .22–250 Rem., and .220 Swift but prefers the 80-grain Winchester-Western Pointed Soft Point in his much-used .243 Win. rifles.

The Remington Bronze Point is a hollowpoint with a spitzer-shaped tip plug which protects the hollowpoint and improves ballistics efficiency. It is made in two calibers and three weights: 130-grain .270 Win., 150-grain and 180-grain .30–06 Springfield. The author found the Bronze Point adequate on open-country game like deer and antelope, but now uses Nosler partition bullets for much of his shooting.

Softpoint bullets

In this broad category calibers range from the .17 Rem. to the .600 Nitro Express. Quarry ranges from woodchucks to elephants. Probably 95 percent of today's game bullets fall in this category.

Original softpoint. Once common to many calibers and originally loaded with black powder, few made the transition to the smokeless era. Early smokeless-propellant cartridges like the .30–30 Win. and .25–35 Win. used this type of bullet for many years.

The factory-loaded 405-grain .45–70 is typical of the few bullets of this type made today. The .38–40 Win. and .44–40 Win. are also typical.

The softpoint lead bullet has a metal base and half jacket. The base is supposed to remain intact while the lead expands.

Dangerous-game softpoints. These bullets are designed for heavy-boned, thin-skinned dangerous game like lion, leopard, and Alaskan bears. An ideal example is the Winchester-Western 510-grain .458 Win. Magnum Soft Point. This bullet has a very heavy base designed to hold together under adverse conditions. The exposed portion is designed to expand slowly while driving through the animal's vitals.

Experienced hunters do not agree on penetration. Some say the bullet should penetrate almost through the animal, ideally stopping at or near the hide on the far side. This means all the bullet's energy is expended within the animal. Other hunters, notably skilled trackers or those who have a skilled tracker (as one does on safari/shikar), like the bullet to exit. If the bullet exits there should be a blood trail.

Nondangerous big-game expanding bullets. This category ranges from deer (not truly big game) through elk, caribou, and grizzly bear and some African plains game like eland.

These bullets, like the dangerous-game softpoint, should have a base that holds together while the exposed lead portion—sometimes covered with a protective tip—expands. Bullets like the 300-grain Silvertip will expand at a slower rate than the 130-grain .270 Win. Silvertip. The same holds true for comparable bullets in Remington's excellent Core-Lokt series.

When a bullet designed for use on big game is used on lighter game like deer, there may be little nor no expansion. Two years ago when the author was experimentally inclined he poured a .510-grain .458 Win. Magnum Soft Point completely through a deer at 35 yards. The great bullet went through the animal and buried itself in a sandbank. The recovered bullet showed little trace of expansion. So great was the force of the bullet—about 5000 ft.-lbs.—at that range, that the deer was slammed off its feet.

During his high school days in the 1930s, the author hunted deer with a .30–40 Winchester M95 carbine. Wanting the heaviest bullet he could get, he purchased a box of 220-grain Winchester Soft Points—this was the pre-Silvertip era—which had only a tiny point of exposed lead. There was virtually no expansion. He went back to 180-grain Western Open Point Expanding bullets.

Deer hunters would be better off with other bullets, but the trade names Silvertip and Core-Lokt are so well known that it became almost imperative for Winchester-Western and Remington to add the Silvertip and Core-Lokt design to deer cartridges like the .30–30 Win. However, as noted above, the .30–30 Win. jackets are much lighter than those for bigger calibers.

A caliber .30 bullet designed for use in a .30–30 Win. has a lighter construction than a caliber .30 bullet for the .30–06 or one of the Big Thirty magnums. The .30–30 Win. 180-grain bullet pro-

pelled at moderate velocities needs a light jacket. The .30–06 and .300 magnum 180-grain bullets need a heavier jacket that will hold together under their much higher velocities.

Nosler partition bullets. During the late 1920s or early 1930s the German small-arms-ammunition firm of RWS—the world's largest sporting ammunition manufacturer at one time—designed its famed Mantle bullet. A cross-section of the bullet looked like the letter H. The portion of the bullet above the crossbar was relatively thin metal. The base below the crossbar was thicker. When such a bullet entered an animal—light or thin-skinned—it expanded back to the metal crossbar. The base remained intact.

This bullet was the basis for the famed American Nosler Partition bullet. This is probably the best-controlled expanding bullet available to North American hunters. Roy Weatherby is the only ammunition manufacturer who uses Nosler Partition bullets for factory-loaded cartridges.

Nosler bullets cost about twice as much as commercial or custom bullets of similar weight and caliber. The few cents per bullet difference can make the difference between success and failure on a hunting trip costing many thousands. They are available from most gunshops that carry handloaders' bullets and reloading supplies.

Quick-expanding bullets. The hunter of deer in open country, antelope, sheep, goat, and light African plains animals needs a bullet that quickly expands inside these relatively small, light-skinned critters. Ideal examples of these bullets are the Winchester-Western Power Point series and Remington's Hi-Speed Pointed Soft Point Core-Lokt series. This type of Core-Lokt is of different construction than the heavier-base Express Core-Lokt discussed above.

Winchester-Western Power Points range from the 100-grain (Soft Point) .243 Win. to the 270 grain Power Point .375 H&H Magnum. The Power Point/Soft Point is essentially an enclosed hollowpoint. A small forward section of the jacket encloses a hollow space. Some notable Power Point bullets are the 140-grain .264 Win. Magnum, 150-grain .270 Win., 150- and 175-grain 7mm Rem. Magnum (the author prefers 175-grain Rem. Core-Lokt or Nosler), 150- and 180-grain .30–06 Springfield. Remington's Hi-Speed Pointed Soft Point Core-Lokt offers fast expanding action.

Winchester .30–06 riflemen can use Silvertip or Power Point (Soft Point) 150 grain, 180 grain, and 220 grain.

Varmint bullets

These range from the 25-grain .17 Rem. to the 90-grain .244 Rem. and a few heavier bullets. Varmint bullets, which are often used in the vicinity of small villages, farmhouses, and out-buildings and in cattle-inhabited pastures, must be incapable of ricocheting. The high-velocity bullets are designed to shatter on impact. Varmint bullets are either pointed or hollowpoint. Most Winchester varmint bullets are designated Pointed Soft Point (PSP) or Open Point Expanding (OPE). Remington's are Hi-Speed Hollow Point or Hi-Speed Soft Point.

The .22 centerfire cartridges are strictly for varmints or benchrest shooting. Dual-purpose cartridges like the .243 Win., .244 Rem., 6mm Rem., and .257 Roberts can be used on varmints or deer-class game. The lighter bullets like the 80-grain .243 Win. bullet are designed for varmints only. The 100-grain bullet with its heavier jacket is for use on deer-class game. The 80 grain is inadequate for deer, and the 100 grain is not too heavy for varmints but its heavier jacket will not disintegrate the way a varmint bullet should. Varmint hunters wanting a heavier .243 or 6mm bullet can get 100- or 105-grain custom varmint bullets.

Benchrest bullets

These are super-accurate bullets—usually .22 caliber—used for benchrest shooting. Such bullets are either made by custom bullet makers like Hornady, Speer, and Sierra or are handmade by shooters themselves. There are some high-quality precision benchrest bullet makers who confine their sales to a small region. The best-known small-production but high-precision benchrest bullet maker was the late Crawford Hollidge, a Boston department store owner.

CHAPTER 11

AMERICAN CENTERFIRE RIFLE CARTRIDGES

Cartridge nomenclature is a confusing subject. The .300 Weatherby Magnum (WM), .300 Win. Magnum, .300 H&H Magnum, .30–30 Win., .30–40 Krag, .30–06 Springfield, .308 Win. (7.62mm NATO), .308 Norma Magnum, .300 Savage, and .30 Rem. all use bullets of the same diameter but the cartridge cases are not interchangeable.

Some British and American designations are identical, while others differ. The former U.S. service round, "Cartridge, Ball, Caliber .30 Model 1906 (designed for M1903 Springfield)" is commonly called .30–06 (often pronounced "thirty ought six") is in Great Britain the caliber .300 U.S.A. or .300-inch U.S.A. The .30–06, sometimes known as the .30 U.S.A., is not to be confused with the .30–40 Krag, also known as the .30 U.S. Army.

Some cartridges are identified by their manufacturer by groove diameter—that is, bore diameter measured from groove to opposite groove in the rifling. Other cartridges using the same-diameter bullet are identified by land diameter (a smaller measurement, since the lands are the portions between the rifling cuts, or grooves, in a barrel). The current trend is to use groove diameter because it gives a higher figure or implies a larger caliber. The .236 Lee Navy was identified by land diameter. The .243 Winchester, using an identical-diameter bullet, is identified by groove diameter. The .244 Rem., .243 Win., and .240 Weatherby Magnum all use .236 bullets.

Some cartridges, like the century-old .44–40 Win., have more than 40 different designations. The caliber .45, Model of 1873 cartridge, also known as the .45 Government, is usually called the .45–70, though nearly a half-century has passed since cartridges have been loaded with 70 grains of black powder.

Black-powder cartridges were usually given three sets of figures, such as .45–70–500. The first figure denotes caliber in decimal fractions of an inch, and the second is the black-powder charge in grains. The final figure denotes bullet weight in grains. Early smokeless-propellant cartridges were usually given two sets of figures: .30–30 Win. The first figure is caliber, and the second figure is smokeless-propellant charge in grains. Today, we still have the .30–30 Win., but it may not be loaded with 30 grains of propellant.

Some black-powder cartridges were designated first by caliber (usually bullet diameter) and then by the length of the case. The British carried this system over into some smokeless cartridges for double rifles.

Early American cartridge calibers were designated by two digits (hundredths of an inch): .30, .45, .50, etc. The British almost invariably use three digits (thousandths of an inch): .303 British, .375 H&H Magnum.

The first American cartridge to use three figures was the .236 Lee Navy (1895). This was also the first American cartridge to use a metric designation. Thus we have the 6mm Navy. Cartridges stamped 6mm Lee Navy (or 6mm U.S.N.) are identical to those headstamped .236 Lee Navy (or .236 U.S.N.). There was a rimmed 6mm Lee Navy.

Other cartridges using the three-digit designation soon followed: .303 Savage, .405 Win., .351 Win. Most centerfire cartridges now use three figures. The .22 Hornet and .17 Rem. are among the few exceptions.

In the late 1930s, Winchester brought out two cartridges with a name attached: .218 Bee and .219 Zipper. Savage had introduced the deceased .22 Savage Hi-Power before World War I.

There are rimmed and rimless versions of the same basic cartridge. The M1894 Winchester designed by John Moses Browning was chambered for several cartridges, including the famed .30–30 Win. (originally .30 Win.), .25–35 Win., and .32 Win. Special. When Remington brought out the M8 semiauto rifle, also designed by John Moses Browning, rimless versions of the Winchester cartridges were introduced (rimless cartridges function more reliably in semiautomatic actions). They were the .25 Rem. (rimless .25–35 Win.), .30 Rem. (rimless .30–30 Win.), and .32 Rem. (rimless .32 Win. Special). The rimless .35 Rem. had no Winchester counterpart.

The British occasionally use two sets of figures separated by a slash: .577/.450. The example indicates a .577 case necked to .45 caliber. In the United States there is a .25–06 Rem. According to British usage this would be a .25 Rem. case opened to .30 caliber, but we turned the British system around. The .25 indicates a .25 caliber bullet based on the .30–06 case.

The first American factory cartridge designated in this manner was the .22–250 Rem. This is a .250–3000 Savage case necked to .22 caliber. (Cartridge nomenclature is all the more confusing because of the many exceptions to its rules. The "3000" in the .250–3000 designation, for instance, was a clever advertising gimmick—a boast about the cartridge's 3000 f.p.s., a very high velocity for its time.)

In England the .300 H&H Magnum cartridge is Holland & Holland's "Super Thirty." The double-rifle version is called "flanged" instead of "rimmed."

A peculiar English custom is the proprietary cartridge. Kynoch (long ago it absorbed Eley Bros.), an Imperial Metals Co. Ltd. subsidiary, is England's only major sporting rifle cartridge manufacturer. When a gunmaker like Holland & Holland develops a new cartridge, say the .375 Magnum, Kynock sells those cartridges only to Holland & Holland. Winchester was able to bring out the M70 in calibers .300 H&H Magnum and .375 H&H Magnum because Holland & Holland released their proprietary rights.

Some British gunmakers have their own designation for continental metric cartridges. John Rigby barrels and chambers imported actions for the 7×57 (7mm Mauser). Barrels are marked and cartridges headstamped ".275 Rigby." British gunmakers call the 6.5mm Mannlicher the .256.

This book is devoted to current sporting arms, plus arms which have been discontinued very recently and may still be stocked by some dealers and wholesalers. The writer deliberately has not included "orphan" cartridges—those cartridges for which arms are no longer made.

Some orphans ultimately acquire new parents. No rifles or sixguns for the .44–40 Win. were made for nearly 40 years, but recently a foreign manufacturer began producing a Winchester M73 replica. *Quien sabe?*

The omission of obsolete or orphan cartridges eliminates many like the .218 Bee, .25–20 Win., .30 Rem., .303 Savage, .32 Rem., .32 Win. Special, .351 Win. S.L.R., .348 Win., and .38–40 Win.

Not included are the .22 Savage Hi-Power and .38–55 Win. These are no longer made in the U.S.A. but are produced by Canadian Industries, Ltd. (CIL—formerly Dominion Cartridge). CIL no longer exports these cartridges, or any cartridge, to the United States.

.17 Remington

Introduced 1971. Necked-down .222 Rem. case. Standard bullet weight: 25 grains. Standard bullet diameter: 0.176 inch. Small rifle primer.

Ultra-smallbore bullet and cartridge experimenters have been working for a quarter-century to produce an ultra-high-velocity smallbore cartridge. The .17 Rem. is the first commercial attempt. It has not been a notable success. The .17 Rem., with an alleged velocity of about 4000 f.p.s. for a 25-grain bullet, is overshadowed by the return of the .220 Swift bullet at about 4100 f.p.s. When Remington brought out its .17, no .220 Swift rifle had been available since the Winchester M70 was revamped in 1964.

The .17 Rem. is a 250-yard cartridge. The light bullet sheds velocity very rapidly. Chronograph tests made by several organizations, including the author's Firearms Information & Research Service, failed to produce velocities in excess of 3900 f.p.s. This is considerably less than the Swift and not much more than .22–250 Rem.

The .17 Rem. requires a special cleaning rod for the extremely small bore. Metal fouling accumulates more rapidly (high velocity is a factor) than in larger-bore rifles.

Remington should receive credit for offering a new-caliber cartridge—and how were the Bridgeport-Ilion boys to know that the .220 Swift would return to haunt them? Factory cartridges are available only in the Remington brand.

.22 Hornet

Introduced 1930. .22 Winchester Center Fire case. Standard bullet weights: 45, 46 grains. Standard bullet diameter: 0.224 inch.

The first bolt-action centerfire cartridge for varmint shooting was developed about 1929 by Al Woody, civilian engineer, U.S. Armory, Springfield, Mass., and his associates. He loaded the .22 Winchester Center Fire (.22 W.C.F.) cartridge case with 45-grain French Velo Dog revolver bullets. He fitted a centerfire bolt to the .22 Long Rifle M1922 Springfield (modified M1903 Springfield).

Winchester brought out ammunition before commercial rifles were available.

The .22 Hornet was chambered in many single-shot rifles like the Winchester M85 Single-Shot.

The Hornet is a fine cartridge if the object is varmint stalking rather than long-range shooting. It makes minimum noise. This is fine for shooting in settled areas.

The last and best .22 Hornet American magazine rifle, the Winchester pre-1964 M70, was discontinued in the late 1950s. You can buy actions chambered for the Hornet, but the only magazine .22 Hornet rifles known to the author in current production are the expensive Savage/Anschutz M1432 and Walther KKJ Sportsman.

The Hornet cartridge has long been popular in Europe, where it is designated the 5.6×52R (5.56mm×52mm rimmed).

Ruger chambers his Number Three single-shot for the .22 Hornet. He should also chamber his superb Number One single-shot Varmint Rifle (about 8.5 lbs.) for this cartridge.

.22–250 Remington

Introduced 1965. Necked-down .250 Savage case. Standard bullet diameter: 0.224 inch. Standard twist: 1–14.0 inches. This original version of the .220 Swift produces slightly less than Swift velocity with heavier bullets. It sheds velocity less rapidly than the Swift. Standard bullet weights: 50, 55 grains. An extremely accurate cartridge to 350 yards (when there's no wind).

Though developed in the mid-1930s, this remained a wildcat until the mid-1960s; it was long known as the Varminter or .22 Gebby Varminter. Most major manufacturers now chamber rifles for this cartridge.

Cartridges with similar ballistics are the .224 Weatherby Magnum and .225 Win. The .22–250 is at its best in a rifle weighing (without scope) 8.75 lbs. to 9.75 lbs. like the Ruger M77, Winchester M70, and Remington M700 varmint versions. Roy Weatherby's Varmintmaster (6.5 lbs. without scope) is a first-rate arm for varmint hunters who like to walk.

.220 Swift

Introduced 1935. Modified 6mm (.236) Lee Navy case. Standard bullet weights: 46, 56 grains. Standard bullet diameter: 0.2245 inch.

The .220 Swift is Winchester's version of the original .22–250. The cartridge was developed by the author's Weybridge, Vermont, neighbor Jerome Bushnell Smith (1894–1948), along with Captain Grosvenor Wotkyns and J. B. Sweaney.

When Winchester brought out its modification, the Smith-Wotkyns-Sweaney cartridge was called the .22 WOS ("Wotkyns Original Swift").

In the mid-1960s, Browning Arms brought out a bolt-action rifle for the .22 WOS but called it the .22–250. No factory ammunition was available, but Browning thought there were sufficient .22–250 admirers to warrant the risk. Remington soon brought out .22–250 ammunition.

The first factory rifle chambered for the .220 Swift was the Winchester M54 bolt-action (improved M1903 Springfield/Mauser 98 action). First rifles were made in April 1935 and were released for sale in August. Only a few M54 .220 Swifts were made as the M54 was soon replaced by the M70.

The pre-1964 M70 was chambered throughout its life (1937–63) for the .220. The .243 Winchester seemingly spelled *finis* for the .220. When Winchester discontinued the pre-1964 M70 the .220 was dropped.

Many riflemen and hunters check muzzle velocities only on manufacturer's ballistics charts. The .220 was made only with 26-inch barrels. The 48-grain .220 has a muzzle velocity of about 4100 f.p.s.; the .243 has a muzzle velocity of 3500 f.p.s. The real story for the varmint shooter was at 300 yards, where the .220's velocity is 2440 f.p.s. and the 80-grain .243's is 2410 f.p.s. With improved propellants Norma now offers two .220 bullet types (50 grain).

The 50-grain semi-pointed full metal-jacketed Norma .220 Swift, with a muzzle velocity identical to its 50-grain softpoint, has a 300-yard residual velocity of 2295 f.p.s.

Swift bullets are more susceptible to crosswinds than 75–80-grain .243 varmint bullets.

In 1973 Bill Ruger made a few 26-inch-barrel Swifts. There was no magazine advertising. Despite this handicap, enough were sold so that Ruger has put the Swift into regular production. In 1974, Savage brought out the .220 Swift in its Model 112V single-shot bolt-action varmint rifle.

.222 Remington

Introduced 1950. Original case. Standard bullet weight: 50 grains. Standard bullet diameter: 0.224 inch.

This was probably the most popular .22 caliber centerfire cartridge ever placed on the market. However, there were many more potential varmint shooters than when the .22 Hornet appeared 20 years earlier.

This is a short-range (200 yards) varmint caliber. Its light report is an asset in settled areas. It is easy to load. Cartridges are relatively inexpensive.

This extremely accurate cartridge is very popular with benchrest shooters. It has virtually no recoil. Cartridges like the .243 Win., .244 Rem., and 6mm Rem. slowed the .222's popularity. Many hunters who didn't know any better—but who should have—had disappointing results on deer. The cartridge is not designed for use on game larger than woodchucks.

.222 Remington Magnum

Introduced 1958. Elongated .222 Remington case. Standard bullet weight: 55 grains. Standard bullet diameter: .2245 inch.

This cartridge, despite a propellant capacity one-third greater than that of the .222 Rem., never approached the .222 Rem. in popularity.

This was due to the ballistically similar .223 Rem. Remington dropped the cartridge from its M700. It is still available in the 40-X special-order rifle.

.223 Remington (5.56mm)

Introduced 1960. Case midway in length between .222 Rem. and .222 Rem. Magnum. This cartridge, like the .222 Rem. Magnum, .222 Rem. Special, and .224 Win., was part of an Army Ordnance program to develop a high-velocity .22 cartridge for full-automatic shoulder arms.

Now available in a few rifles like Remington's M700 varmint version, the .223 will become popular for match shooting.

This cartridge and its shoot-alike twin the .222 Rem. Magnum extend maximum range (compared to .222 Rem.) for varmint shooting to 225–250 yards. (See the discussion of the 5.6mm cartridge in Chapter 12.)

.224 Weatherby Magnum

Introduced 1963. Rimless belted bottleneck case. Standard bullet weights: 50, 55 grains. Standard bullet diameter: .2245 inch (maximum).

Ballistically the .224 Weatherby Magnum is almost identical with the .22–250 Rem. and .225 Win. Ruger, Winchester, and Remington all make heavy-barrel varmint rifles chambered for the .22–250. Weatherby makes a lovely-to-look-at and light-to-handle sporter and thus provides .22–250 ballistics in a light rifle. With the advent of .22–250 Rem. ammunition, Weatherby chambered the Varmintmaster for the .22–250 Rem.

.225 Winchester

Introduced 1964. Rim bottleneck original case. Standard bullet weight: 55 grains. Standard bullet diameter: 0.2245 inch (maximum).

This small-capacity case was fitted with a rim to adapt it to rifles with a standard .30–06 Springfield bolt.

The .225 is practically identical with the .22–250 Rem. and .224 Weatherby Magnum. It is an excellent cartridge but never became popular. Within a year of its appearance, the 30-odd-year-old wildcat .22 Varminter became commercially available as the .22–250 Rem.

.240 Weatherby Magnum

Introduced 1965. Original bottleneck cartridge case design with belt. Standard bullet weights: 70, 90, and 100 grains. Standard bullet diameter: 0.2435 inch.

This is Roy Weatherby's magnum answer to the .243 Win. and 6mm Rem. The 100-grain bullet for deer-class game has a 300-yard residual velocity about 300 f.p.s. faster than the 100-grain .243 Win. or the 100-grain 6mm. The 300-yard residual velocity of the 90-grain .240 Weatherby Magnum is 2475 f.p.s., compared to 2230 f.p.s. for the .243 Win.

.243 Winchester

Introduced 1955. Necked-down .308 Win. case. Standard bullet weights: 75, 80, 90, 100 grains. Standard bullet diameter: 0.236 inch. Large rifle primer.

The .243 Win. is probably the most popular centerfire rifle cartridge above .22 caliber and of nonmilitary origin. Originally offered in lightweight jacketed bullets for varmints at a factory-stated velocity of 3500 f.p.s. (26.0-inch barrel) and a 100-grain medium-weight jacketed bullet at 3080 f.p.s. (26.0-inch barrel) for light game like deer and antelope.

Since 1975 Winchester lists the 80-grain at 3420 f.p.s. and the 100-grain at 2960 f.p.s. These figures do not indicate a reduced loading but are based on the 24.0-inch barrel of current M70 varmint rifles. Current M70 .243 Win. sporters, like most other sporters, have 22.0-inch barrels.

The change of figures in current Winchester ballistics charts may have resulted from an informative article in *American Rifleman*

("Should You Shorten Your .243 Barrel?", April 1972). Tests were conducted by M. D. Waite, technical editor, and Kenneth C. Rayner, assistant technical editor.

Waite and Rayner commenced recording velocities with a 28.0-inch .243 barrel. After each series was fired and chronograph data recorded, the barrel was reduced in 1.0-inch increments to an 18.0-inch minimum.

Results were surprising. Maximum muzzle velocity with a 26.0-inch barrel was 3300 f.p.s. instead of the factory's alleged 3500 f.p.s. The 24.0-inch barrel—now standard on all .243 varmint rifles except the 26.0-inch bolt-action single-shot Savage M112V and the 27.0-inch barrel of the Swedish Carl Gustav V/T (Varmint/Target rifle) —produced a muzzle velocity of 3255 f.p.s., or nearly 250 f.p.s. less than stated factor ballistics.

The 22.0-inch barrel—sporter standard— produced a muzzle velocity of 3190 f.p.s., or more than 300 f.p.s less than alleged factory standards.

Using *American Rifleman* standards, varmint shooters wishing to secure maximum velocity with 80-grain factory loads should use the Carl Gustav V/T, whose 27.0-inch barrel produces a muzzle velocity of 3325 f.p.s.

Where actual ballistics differ considerably from factory ballistics, unwary shooters or those too lazy to field-check find the bullet drop and trajectory charts unreliable. In varmint shooting a matter of 1 or 2 inches may mean the difference between a kill and a miss or unnecessary wounding.

Since the advent of the .243 in 1955, about 90 percent of the author's chuck shooting has been done with .243 varmint rifles. The remaining 10 percent is accounted for by testing cartridges like .244 Rem., 6mm Rem., .22–250 Rem., .225 Win., .224 Weatherby Magnum, and .17 Rem.

The author never attempts to take chucks with a .243 Win. at less than 200 yards. Shots are measured with a 100-foot surveyor's tape. It is impossible to accurately measure shots taken across a valley. His longest successful shot, made with a .243 M70 Target rifle, was 429 measured yards across a flat meadow.

Given but one choice of caliber for varmint shooting, the author would select the .243 Win. or 6mm Remington. These 6mm bullets are less subject to wind drift and retain their velocity at longer ranges. The .220 Swift has an initial muzzle velocity of 600 f.p.s. more than the 80-grain .243 Win., yet the 330-yard residual velocity of these bullets is almost identical.

Classic varmint rifles weigh 9.50 to 9.75 lbs.

(without scope and sling), but the current trend —as in other rifle types—is toward shorter barrels and lighter rifles. Varmint rifles should be fitted with scopes of 10× or 12×. Bipods are most useful for steadying the rifle under field conditions.

The .243 Win. is available in bolt-action single-shot and bolt-action magazine rifles. It is made in lever-action, slide-action, and semiautomatic rifles. It is also available in Ruger's Number One single shot.

.244 Remington

Introduced 1955. Necked-down .257 Roberts (7mm Mauser) case. Standard bullet weight: 90 grains. Standard bullet diameter: .2435 inch.

The .243 Win. and .244 Rem. both appeared in August, 1955. Of these almost identical twins the .243 Win. became one of the greatest commercial centerfire cartridges. The .244 Rem. had such poor sales that Remington .244 rifles were soon dropped. Only Norma now loads the .244.

Winchester visualized the .243 Win. as a dual-purpose cartridge for use on varmints and deer. The .243 Win. with its 1-in-10-inch twist handles 75-80-grain varmint bullets and 100-grain deer bullets with equal facility and accuracy.

The .244 Rem. was designed strictly for varmint shooters. Its original 1-in-12-inch twist was designed to handle a 90-grain jacketed varmint bullet. The Speer Company, Lewiston, Idaho, issued a 105-grain bullet designed for deer-class game, but .244 Rem.'s 12-inch twist would not stabilize the longer, heavier bullet.

.25–06 Remington

Introduced 1970. Necked-down .30–06 Springfield case. Standard bullet weights: 87, 100, 120 grains. Standard bullet diameter: 0.257 inch.

This cartridge, with an accuracy potential to 400 yards, dates back 40-odd years to experiments with .30–06 Springfield cases—not quite the same overall dimensions—and caliber .250 bullets. It has been a popular wildcat for many years.

The 100-grain bullet has a muzzle velocity (24.0-inch barrel) of 3200 f.p.s. and a 500-yard residual velocity of 1830 f.p.s. A fine cartridge for riflemen wishing to use the same cartridge— different bullet weights and constructions—on varmints and deer-class plains and mountain game.

Prime rifles for this cartridge currently include

Remington M700 (both standard and varmint versions), M70 Winchester, and Ruger M77 and Number One single shot.

Barrel lengths are 24.0 inches.

.250–3000 Savage

Introduced about 1914. Shortened and necked-down .30–06 Springfield case. Bullet weights: 87, 100 grains. Bullet diameter: 0.257 inch.

This was small-arms and ammunition designer Charles Newton's second commercially successful high-velocity (high for those days) cartridge. Until about 1921 the cartridge was loaded with the 87-grain bullet with a 3000 f.p.s. muzzle velocity. The cartridge and rifles chambered for it continued as the .250–3000 for many years.

Its popularity decline began with the advent of the .257 Roberts (1935) and further decreased when the .243 Win. appeared. By 1960 no American rifles were made in this caliber, but cartridge manufacture has been continuous. The .250 Savage—as it should properly be known since the appearance of the 100-grain bullet—is experiencing a mild revival. It is now available in the Ruger M77 bolt-action. Savage has revived it in the rifle for which it was first chambered, the M99 lever-action.

.257 Weatherby Magnum

Introduced about 1945. Shortened, necked-down .300 H&H Magnum case. Standard bullet weights: 87, 100, 117 grains. Standard bullet diameter: 0.257 inch.

This is the flattest and farthest-ranging caliber .25 cartridge. It is an excellent varmint cartridge where noise is not a factor, though barrel life is shorter than with other .25s. A varmint shooter may average more than 500 shots per season, while a medium-size-game hunter usually shoots no more than a box of 20 rounds (including preseason sighters). The varmint shooter's barrel may last a shorter time, though for as many total shots as the larger-game hunter's, but he is also getting more pleasure in a shorter time period.

The .257 Weatherby Magnum in its early years received considerable publicity—some of it adverse—because African game animals up to Cape buffalo were killed with it (these hunters were backed up by professional hunters armed with large-bore double rifles).

The author has used the .257 Weatherby Magnum with proper bullet weights on chucks, mule deer, and antelope.

.264 Winchester Magnum

Introduced 1960. Necked-down .338 Win. Magnum case. Standard bullet weights: 100, 140 grains. Standard bullet diameter: 0.2645 inch (maximum).

This is Winchester's answer—it took 15 years—to Roy Weatherby's .257 Magnum. Minimum and maximum .264 bullet weights are slightly heavier. This is a plains and mountain rifle. The 100-grain bullet has a light jacket for varmints. The heavier-jacketed 140-grain bullet is for game up through caribou. It has been used on elk, but a heavier bullet in a larger caliber should be used for that magnificent creature. Hornady's 160-grain softpoint roundnose is the heaviest .264 (6.5mm) bullet available.

Few cartridges approach the .264's long-range ballistics. The 140-grain bullet with a muzzle velocity of 3200 f.p.s. has a 500-yard residual velocity of 2100 f.p.s. Its 500-yard energy is 1370 ft.-lbs. The only bullets with substantially greater 500-yard energy are the 270-grain .375 H&H Magnum and several Weatherbys. The .264's ballistics are based on the 26-inch barrel of the pre-1964 M70 Winchester. Current 24-inch barrels give about 100 f.p.s. less muzzle velocity and slightly less energy.

The .264 Win. Magnum's popularity was impaired by the advent of the 7mm Rem. Magnum.

.270 Weatherby Magnum

Introduced 1945. Shortened and necked-down .300 H&H Magnum case. Standard bullet weights: 100, 130, 150 grains. Standard bullet diameter: 0.277 inch.

The .270 Weatherby Magnum gives .270 Win. weight bullets about 300 f.p.s. more muzzle velocity and about 100 f.p.s. more at 300 yards.

.270 Winchester

Introduced 1925. Necked-down .30–06 Springfield case. Standard bullet weights: 100, 130, 150, 180 grains. Standard bullet diameter: 0.277 inch.

This 50-odd-year-old cartridge was the first American commercial cartridge—except limited Newtons—to be chambered in a bolt-action rifle that can take all North American game.

First released in 1925 for the Winchester M54, the .270 Win. won acceptance in the West (it's never been popular in the East), where it supplanted the .30–06 Springfield. Barring the .300 H&H, the limited Newtons, and Hoffman Magnums, the .270 remained our premier plains and mountain cartridge until the flood of post-World War II magnums.

Jack O'Connor has probably harvested more North American and African light-skinned game with the .270 Win. than anyone else. It has been his favorite cartridge for 50 years.

The advent of 7mm and .30 caliber magnums has not sounded the death knell of the .270. Many riflemen, ultrasensitive to recoil, prefer the .270. With the great increase in riflemen since World War II it is possible that more .270s are sold today than before the onslaught of the magnums. All bolt-action-rifle makers known to the author chamber at least one model for the .270 Win.

Ignore the 110-grain bullet (poor sectional density) and use the 130-grain for the lighter deer-class game. The 160-grain is only available from dealers handling Canadian Industries, Ltd. (CIL-Dominion). This roundnose long bullet is capable of deep penetration. The 150-grain is probably the best all-around .270 bullet.

.280 Remington

Introduced 1957. .270 Win. case with shoulder moved forward 0.05 inch. Neck expanded 0.006 inch. Standard bullet weights: 100, 150, 165 grains. (100-grain no longer available). Standard bullet diameter: 0.2835-0.284 inch (7mm).

This cartridge was designed to provide .270 Win. ballistics in Remington's M740/M742 semi-auto Woodsmaster. At the time of its introduction no semiautomatic sporting rifle—except sporterized versions of Capt. Melvin Johnson's recoil-operated rotary-magazine semiautomatic —were chambered for the .270 Win. Remington then chambered M700 and M721 bolt-actions for the .280. Today, Remington chambers only the M742 for the .280 Rem. Bill Ruger made a few M77s for the .280 Rem.

This cartridge will not do anything that the .270 Win. cannot do.

.30 U.S. M1 Carbine

Introduced 1940. Modified .32 Winchester Self Loading Rifle case. Standard bullet (sporting) weight: 110 grains. Standard bullet diameter: 0.3075 inch (maximum—.0008 inch tolerance).

Even in its soft and hollowpoint versions this is by no stretch of the imagination a "sporting" cartridge. There is a serious ricochet danger when firing at varmints, and it is inadequate for deer.

During the Korean War, General S. L. A. Marshall conducted a thorough survey of weapons usage in Korea. Front-line Marines—and many soldiers—ditched their carbines and swapped or otherwise obtained submachine guns or M1 rifles.

The major reason for the carbine's popularity among rear-echelon troops and unknowledgeable hunters was its light weight and compact size. It is "handy" or "convenient" to tote.

.30–06 Springfield

Introduced 1906. Elongated 8mm Mauser case necked down, or elongated 7mm Mauser case necked up. Standard bullet weights: 110 to 220 grains. Standard bullet diameter: 0.308 inch. Large rifle primer.

For more than 50 years this was one of the three most widely used military cartridges in the world (others: .303 British and 7.92mm Mauser). It has been used in bolt-action, lever-action, semiautomatic, and full automatic rifles, light and heavy ground machine guns, aircraft machine-guns, and single-shot rifles.

For many of its 70-odd years the .30–06 has been, as it is now, the world's number-one all-around sporting cartridge. The .30–06 with bullets of proper weight and construction for the game at hand is capable of taking 95 percent of the world's big game.

The .30–06, known officially as "Cartridge, Ball, Caliber 30, M1906," in its first version was a cupronickel-jacketed 150-grain spitzer bullet. It was the forerunner of modern sporting cartridges.

The three most widely used weights are the 150-grain for long-range game like antelope, sheep, caribou, and the lighter African plains game; the 180-grain roundnose for use against all but the heaviest North American game (in the brush); and a 180-grain spitzer for open-country shooting. The slow-to-expand 220-grain bullet is capable of taking all North American game including the big Alaskan brown bears, though most experts prefer a heavier bullet like those from the .338 Win. Magnum, .375 H&H Magnum, or even .458 Win. Magnum.

Elephants have been taken with full metal-jacketed—solid—220-grain bullets, but experienced dangerous-game hunters prefer a bullet of sufficient weight, energy, and velocity to stop an elephant in his tracks.

Other bullet weights range from the 110-grain bullet for varmints (its sectional density is insufficient for stability at long ranges, and it sheds velocity rapidly) to a limited-production special-purpose (big Arctic game) 280-grain bullet. This latter bullet was for use by the military only. The 165-grain custom bullet is popular among those who seek a compromise between the flat-shooting 150-grain and the heavier 180-grain bullet. Custom 168-grain and 200-grain bullets are popular among match shooters.

The late Grancel Fitz was probably the first American to bag all recognized North American big-game species—many of them record-class—and he did it with one rifle. This was a Griffin & Howe .30–06 Springfield sporter. This rifle after more than a quarter century of hard use—not abuse—bore the honorable badge of scars and worn bluing.

Jack O'Connor, best known for his advocacy and expert use of the .270 Win., has probably used the .30–06 Springfield as much or more than any other contemporary North American big-game hunter. He has used it in Africa too.

The author prefers .35 caliber or better for elk and grizzly; his favorite is the .375 H&H Magnum, though the .30–06 is adequate for all but rear-end or raking shots.

The .270 Win. and a host of other rifles shoot slightly flatter over long ranges than the 150-grain .30–06, though most of the author's shots at game like caribou, sheep, and antelope could have been made just as successfully with a .30–06 as with a .300 H&H Magnum, .375 H&H Magnum, or .257 Weatherby Magnum. Very few shots in North America—even at sheep and caribou—are made at ranges over 275 yards. The pronghorn antelope is an exception only occasionally.

Every major American ammunition manufacturer offers a greater variety of loadings in .30–06 Springfield than in any other caliber. Even Roy Weatherby offers his justly famed Mark V action in one non-Weatherby caliber—the .30–06.

Most American-made .30–06 sporting rifles are currently offered with 22.0-inch barrels. Factory ballistics are based on 24.0-inch barrels. The author likes the 24.0-inch barrel, which is one reason he prefers the pre-1964 M70 Win. with its 24.0-inch barrel to the fine Ruger M77 with a 22.0-inch barrel only. This is strictly a personal matter. Many big-game hunters do very well with 22.0-inch barrel .30–06s—and that includes Jack O'Connor.

The author has had considerable experience with the .30–06 cartridge, over 40 years, for hunting, target, and military uses. He once test-fired for accuracy and functioning some 200

Lewis light machine guns. He has taken antelope, sheep, caribou, whitetail, bear, elk, and zebra with this 70-odd-year-old cartridge.

.30–30 Winchester

Introduced 1895. Necked-down rimmed .38–55 Win. case. Standard bullet weights (current): 150, 170 grains. Standard bullet diameter: 0.3085 inch (maximum).

The .30 W.C.F., as it was originally known, and the .25–35 Win., both released in the summer of 1895, were the first sporting smokeless centerfire rifle cartridges made in America. The M94 Winchester was the first American sporting rifle designed to handle smokeless-propellant cartridges.

During the past 40 years the author has known, met, or corresponded with hundreds of .30–30 Win. owners, most of them owners of M94 Winchesters. Practically all were convinced their "trusty thutty-thutty" was the deer cartridge supreme. Many other cartridges in the short-range deer-rifle class are superior: .35 Rem., .38–55, and .44 Magnum.

The .30–30 Win. mystique is difficult, if not impossible, to explain. .30 caliber seems the magic figure among most rifle-owning Americans, be it a .30–30 Winchester, .30–06 Springfield, .308 Win., or .300 Weatherby Magnum. The caliber .30 trend commenced after the adoption in 1892 of the .30–40 Krag as our standard Army cartridge. The .30 caliber trend intensified after the adoption of the M1906 caliber .30 (.30–06 Springfield) in the M1903 Springfield. Next came the .30 Rem. and .30 Newton. Several million Americans were introduced to bolt-action rifles and the .30–06 in World War I. Some veterans took to the bolt-action, but many took to various other .30 calibers. Next came the .300 Savage, and for a few the .300 H&H Magnum and .30 wildcats.

Many .30–30 Win. hunters are not well informed about rifles and rifle calibers other than their own. Extreme cases—and the author knows a number—think all .30 caliber rifles, whether .30–30 Win. or .30–06 Springfield, have similar characteristics, "and I'd rather have a handy M94 Winchester than a cumbersome, heavy, expensive bolt-action." Others believe .300 caliber rifles use a much bigger (wider in diameter) bullet than .30 caliber cartridges. All .30 caliber cartridges known to the author use a 0.308-inch-diameter bullet.

The most persistent myth among American hunters, especially .30–30 Win. owners, is that "the thirty-thirty was once the standard U.S. Army cartridge" or "the old (1903) Springfield was a .30–30." The .30–30 Winchester cartridge was *never* adopted or used by the United States Armed Forces. About 1900, some Savage M99 lever-actions were purchased by the New York State Militia. The U.S. Bureau of Prisons occasionally purchased .30–30 Winchesters. This was a waste of the taxpayers' money, because U.S. Ordnance depots had surplus M1903 Springfields and M1917 Enfields.

Millions of deer are harvested with the .30–30 Win., but how many millions have escaped only to die a lingering death because of the cartridge's inadequacy?

The .30–30 Win. is the cartridge of rural and small-town deer hunters. Few of them ever hunt outside their bailiwick. Few hunters who travel to other states for deer hunting use the .30–30 Win. The .30–30 Win. hunters are familiar with the area where they hunt year in and year out. They know the life style, including food sources and deer herd movements, in their region. And their shots are usually made at close range. They rarely switch to other calibers or to non-lever-action rifles. They are convinced they have the best tool for the task at hand.

The popularity of the handy, lightweight M94 Winchester carbine has had much to do with the popularity of the .30–30 Win. cartridge.

.30–40 Krag

Introduced 1892. Rim bottleneck case. Standard commercial bullet weights (current): 180, 220 grains. Standard bullet diameter: 0.307-inch minimum, 0.308-inch maximum. Standard twist: 1-in-10 inches.

As our first smokeless-propellant cartridge enters the last quarter of its first century, there is still sufficient demand for our major small-arms ammunition manufacturers to keep two bullet weights in production.

Fifty years passed in which no .30–40 Krag rifles were made. In July, 1973, Bill Ruger announced his Number Three Single Shot in .30–40 Krag. The .30–40 Krag cartridge may enter its second century, as have the .45–70 Gov't., .44–40 Win., and .45 Colt.

The .30–40 Krag, today, is a medium-range cartridge for all North American game except polar and brown bears.

There is a tendency among non-knowledgeable riflemen to confuse the .30–40 Krag with the .30–06 Springfield. Both have been officially referred to as Caliber .30. Headstamps like W.R.A. .30 and W.R.A.CO. .30 Army (both .30–40 Krag) contributed to the confusion. To most of us, it has always been the .30–40 Krag. Headstamps marked .30 U.S.A. are for the .30–06 Springfield.

.300 H&H Magnum

Introduced about 1924. Necked-down .375 H&H Magnum. Standard bullet weights: 150, 180, 220 grains. Standard bullet diameter: 0.3085 inch.

The .300 H&H Magnum—known in England as "Holland's Super Thirty"—was the final cartridge in that firm's series of great magnums (.244 H&H Magnum was not made in America). The .300 H&H was designed to handle heavier bullets than the .275 H&H Magnum at greater ranges. (The .275 H&H Magnum—an attempt to best the .280 Ross—was loaded by Western Cartridge Co., but no American factory rifles were regularly chambered for it even though its excellent long-range 169-grain bullet gained wide acceptance in England and Africa.)

The .300 H&H Magnum with Western's 180-grain Open Point Expanding bullet was the author's favorite long-range rifle load for plains and mountain game (1940–65). He held 5 inches high at 400 yards, on the nose at 300 yards, and 4 inches low at 175 yards. He rarely used the 220-grain bullet, inasmuch as he considers the .300 H&H a long-range open-country rifle.

The .300 Magnum ballistics tables are among the few that approximate reality. All .300 H&H rifles known to the author have—and should have—26.0-inch barrels. Ballistics table data is for 26.0-inch barrels.

During its first decade in America the .300 H&H was available only in expensive English versions or custom American rifles made up on the long Mauser action.

The keenly sought Wimbledon Trophy for 1000-yard shooting at Camp Perry was first won with a .300 H&H Magnum in 1935 by the author's late friend Ben Comfort. Ben used a custom-made .300 H&H rifle with ammunition specially loaded by his friends—the Olins—in East Alton, Ill.

The .300 H&H won all Wimbledon Cups for the next quarter century (there were no matches during World War II). Any rifle capable of putting its bullets into the 18-inch V-ring of a 36-inch bull at 1000 yards is not to be lightly dismissed.

.300 Savage

Introduced about 1920. Shortened .30–06 Springfield case. Standard bullet weights (current): 150, 180 grains. Standard bullet diameter: 0.3085 inch.

This was the first caliber .30 smokeless sporting cartridge designed to work through short-length actions like the Savage rotary magazine M99. It was introduced for the M99. The M99 is the only rifle currently chambered for the .300 Savage. This excellent cartridge was doomed by the superior .308 Win. (7.62mm NATO).

.300 Weatherby Magnum

Introduced 1946. Radial-shouldered .300 H&H Magnum case. Standard bullet weights: 150 to 220 grains. Standard bullet diameter: 0.308 inch.

This was the first Weatherby Magnum cartridge. For many years it was the most controversial big-game cartridge. The hunting world is divided into two camps. Elmer Keith's camp advocates heavy bullets of moderate velocity for big game. Weatherby's camp advocates high velocity. Neither extreme is as sound as a compromise.

Some Weatherby cartridge failures are due to inexperienced hunters using improperly constructed handloaded bullets against too large a game animal or at excessive range. There have been—and still are—hunters who swear that the .300 Weatherby Magnum is a sure killer at 1000 yards on deer and sheep!

When loaded with the proper bullets, preferably Noslers, the .300 Weatherby Magnum can and has taken all North American game. It has also taken much African game. Most of the author's experience with Weatherby Magnums has been with the .257 and .340. He has seen numerous kills made with the .300 Weatherby Magnum. There is no doubt the cartridge is capable of taking all but the largest game. Weatherby offers calibers above .300 Weatherby Magnum for the largest game but only because many African game laws are based on conservative British cartridges. (Nevertheless, it is fortunate that caliber restrictions exist. Otherwise more dudes might be killed.)

Outside of Roy Weatherby, the most experienced .300 Weatherby Magnum user is probably Californian Elgin Gates. He has taken about all the various wild sheep of the world plus most other big-game animals in North America, Asia, and Africa.

Weatherby Magnums had their radial-shoulder origin back in the 1930s with a cartridge series known as P.M.V.F. Ralph Baden Powell, a California gun enthusiast, and a man named Miller blew out cases usually based on the .300 H&H Magnum. This meant expanding the case to increase its powder capacity. The radial shoulder had a reverse curve. Rifles chambered for those cartridges were free-bored (hence "F" in P.M.V.F.).

Nosler partition bullets are optionally available in most Weatherby calibers. The 150-grain bullet is ideal for long-range hunting, as is the 180-grain. The only North American need for the 220-grain is for our biggest game like brown and polar bears. Some of these have been taken with 180-grain Noslers.

Probably 99 percent of all .300 Weatherby Magnums are chambered in the Weatherby Mark V. From time to time a manufacturer chambers one of his rifles for a Weatherby caliber. Such efforts are usually short-lived. Weatherby-cartridge *aficionados* seem to prefer Weatherby rifles.

It is not necessary to purchase a Mark V Weatherby rifle. The .300 Weatherby Magnum and .340 Weatherby Magnum require full-length magnum actions. This means you can have a pre-1964 Winchester M70 rifle chambered for the .300 H&H Magnum or .375 H&H Magnum. A .30–06 barrel can be rechambered for the .300 Weatherby Magnum. Such a rifle, however, will cost nearly as much as a new Mark V rifle. This is because of the high demand for the superb M70 Magnums.

If a man is not fussy about fancy stock work but wants a .300 Weatherby Magnum, his best bet is a M1917 Enfield, which can be bought for about $50. If the barrel is not in good condition a surplus barrel can be picked up for a few dollars. The barrel can be rechambered for the .300 Weatherby Magnum. The author suggests removing the upper handguard, filing off the sight ears, and cutting the barrel to 24.0 inches (not less, as muzzle blast is quite severe even with a 26.0- or 24.0-inch barrel). Add a recoil pad. The cost of the rifle, rechambering, and other basic gunsmithing should not exceed $150. The strong Enfield action can be readily opened for the .300 Weatherby Magnum cartridge.

.300 Winchester Magnum

Introduced 1963. .338 Winchester case necked down to caliber .30. Standard bullet weights: 150, 180, 220 grains.

This is the fourth cartridge in Winchester's short-belted magnum series: .458 Win. Magnum (1956), .338 Win. Magnum (1959), .264 Win. Magnum (1960), and .300 Win. Magnum (1963). All work through standard .30–06-length actions.

The .264 and .338 Win. Magnums have identical neck lengths, but the .300 Win. Magnum has a shorter neck. This seats heavier and longer bullets deeper in the case. The base of the 220-grain bullet projects into the case body.

The .300 Win. Magnum is superior to the .300 H&H Magnum, equal to the .308 Norma Magnum and will perform like the .300 Weatherby Magnum. To some riflemen the .300 Win. Magnum is superior—moneywise—to the Weatherby. A M77 Ruger costs far less than the Mark V Weatherby. Factory ammunition is less expensive, and bolt throw is shorter. The Weatherby, however, is well worth its cost.

The .300 Win. Magnum is a fine "all-round" cartridge for all but the largest North American and African game. It has taken all of the bigger game, though many riflemen—including the author—prefer a little more insurance when going against dangerous game. Some African countries do not allow the use of calibers below .375 or .400 on dangerous game.

.303 British

Introduced 1888. Standard (sporting) bullet weights: 130 (Norma), 180, 215 grains. Standard bullet diameter: 0.311–0.312 (maximum). British and foreign cases are usually Berdan-primed. American-Canadian/Swedish (Norma cases marked "Re" for "reloadable") sporting loads have easily reloadable Boxer primers.

".303 British" is American nomenclature indicating a difference between .303 British and .303 Savage. Remarks concerning the .30–40 Krag apply to the .303 British. The .303—like the .30–40 Krag—can be loaded to maximum pressures in a P-14 Enfield.

.308 Norma Magnum

Introduced 1960. Shortened .300 H&H Magnum. Standard bullet weight (current): 180 grains (110- and 190-grain loads discontinued). Standard bullet diameter: 0.308 inch.

This was the first commercial "short magnum" in caliber .30 to appear on the American market. There would have been no need for this excellent cartridge had the .300 Win. Magnum been available at the time. Factory .308 Norma Magnum

ammunition is limited to the 180-grain bullet. Norma .308-chambered rifles are relatively scarce. Norma .308 sales dropped after the appearance of the .300 Win. Magnum. The cartridges have similar ballistics.

.308 Winchester (7.62mm NATO)

Introduced 1952. Shortened .30–06 case. Standard bullet weights: 110, 125, 150, 180, 200 grains. Standard bullet diameter: 0.308 inch. Large rifle primer.

The .30–06 was the U.S. service cartridge of two world wars, the Mexican Punitive Expedition (1916–17), various "banana-republic" campaigns, and the Korean War. The United States was the only military force in World War II with a semiautomatic M1 Gerand. M1903 Springfields were Limited Standard in World War II during the early U.S. phase because there were insufficient M1s. After World War II, Ordnance searched for a new rifle and a new cartridge, wanting to remain with caliber .30 but changing to a shorter case. Winchester developed the cartridge—a shortened .30–06 Springfield. The sporting version of the cartridge is the .308 Win. The military version is the 7.62mm NATO.

The M14 rifle for which the 7.62mm NATO was designed was a failure. Conservative U.S. military arms designers rejected the straight-line stock—essential to reduce recoil in a lightweight caliber .30 rifle capable of full automatic fire. The M14 was largely replaced in Vietnam by the even lighter but virtually recoilless M16 in caliber 5.56mm (.223 Rem.).

The 7.62mm cartridge replaced the caliber .30–06 because it required less brass to manufacture; brass is always scarce in wartime, and a soldier could carry more rounds of the lighter cartridge. The shorter 7.62mm cartridge required a shorter—hence lighter—action.

The .308 Win. is a very popular sporting cartridge, even though it is not as powerful or as versatile as the .30–06 Springfield. It is an excellent long-range military match target cartridge up to 1000 yards.

The author cannot see any advantage of the .308 Win. in a bolt-action sporter over the .30–06. Rarely is the .308 chambered in a shorter action. The Ruger M77 short-stroke action and Sako are major exceptions. In most bolt-action rifles the standard-length (.30–06) action is used. The bolt stop is of a different length for other-length cartridges. Hence there is little weight saved. Bolt throw is rarely shorter. A bolt-action-minded man is better off with the .30–06

Springfield. The major advantage of the .308 Win. lies in lever-action, slide-action, and semi-automatic rifles.

.338 Winchester Magnum

Introduced 1959. Shortened and necked-down .375 H&H Magnum. Standard bullet weights: 200, 250, 300 grains. Standard bullet diameter: 0.338 inch.

For many years riflemen and hunters used .33 and .35 caliber cartridges: .33 Win. (M86), .35 Whelen, and .350 Griffin & Howe. Some riflemen imported the .333 Jeffries and .350 Rigby Magnums. Most of us could hunt big game throughout the world and not be too undergunned or overgunned with the .300 Win. Magnum and .375 H&H Magnum. The .338 Win. Magnum will do "almost" everything the .375 H&H Magnum can do. But it will be a long time before many African nations allow calibers below .375 H&H on dangerous game.

This cartridge in its heavier loadings is capable of handling all North American and most African game. One minor point: the .375 H&H Magnum ammunition is available throughout Africa's and India's big-game country. The .338 Win. Magnum ammunition is less widely distributed.

.340 Weatherby Magnum

Introduced 1963. Full-length .375 H&H case necked to .338 caliber. Standard bullet weights: 200, 210, 250 grains (275, 285, 300-grain custom bullets available). Standard bullet diameter: 0.338 inch.

This was Roy Weatherby's one-upmanship on Winchester's .338 Magnum. It is also a modification of the 40-year-old .334 OKH wildcat.

This cartridge will handle all North American game including big bears and probably all African game, provided 300-grain solids are available for use on the thick-skinned critters like rhino and elephant. (It is worth repeating here that some African countries prohibit calibers below .375 or .400 on dangerous species.)

The 250-grain semipointed expanding bullet has a muzzle velocity of 2850 f.p.s. (26.0-inch barrel). The 250-grain .338 Win. Magnum has a muzzle velocity of 2700 f.p.s. (24.0-inch barrel). The .340 Weatherby Magnum has a 300-yard velocity of 2049 f.p.s. The .338 Win. Magnum had only 109 f.p.s. less, and this with a 2-inch-shorter barrel.

No figures are available for the .340 Weatherby Magnum with 275- or 300-grain bullets but

the slightly greater propellant capacity of the .340 Weatherby Magnum probably gives it a slightly greater edge.

.35 Remington

Introduced about 1908. Standard bullet weights: 150, 200 grains. Standard bullet diameter: 0.356 inch.

This cartridge was designed for the Remington semiautomatic Woodsmaster M8 (1906–36) and its improved successor the M81 (1936–50), and for the slide-action Gamemaster Remington M14/M14½ (1912–35) and its improved successor the M141/M141½ (1935–50). It is still chambered in the lever-action M336 Marlin.

Forget the poor-sectional-density 150-grain bullet. The 200-grain bullet is far superior to the .30–30 Win. and .32 Win. Special or similar cartridges (.30 Rem., .32 Rem.) for deer and black bear. It is a short-range (150-yard) cartridge.

Brush and timber hunters whose target is the whitetail deer might consider the .35 Remington in the side-ejection M336 Marlin with a 2.5× Redfield Widefield scope.

.350 Remington Magnum

Introduced 1965. Shortened and necked-down .375 H&H Magnum case. Standard bullet weights: 200, 250 grains. Standard bullet diameter: 0.358 inch.

This cartridge was introduced in the 20-inch-barrel bolt-action M600 carbine (1965–67) and in the similar M660 bolt-action carbine (1968–69). It was briefly chambered in Ruger's M77.

The .350 Rem., a short-case magnum, was designed for use against all but the largest North American game. The handy 20-inch barrel produces a horrendous muzzle blast. Bench-testing riflemen can wear ear protectors, but hunters cannot. Some shooters were discomfited not only by the muzzle blast but by the sharp recoil of the .350 Magnum in the 6.5-lb. (without scope) M600/M660 carbine.

The 250-grain bullet has a muzzle velocity of 2410 f.p.s. The 300-yard velocity is 1870 f.p.s. Muzzle energy is a respectable 3320 ft.-lbs. The 300-yard energy is 1780 ft.-lbs.

.358 Norma Magnum

Introduced about 1959. Necked-down and shortened .375 H&H case. Standard bullet weight: 250 grains. Standard bullet diameter:

0.358 inch. Standard twist: 1-in-14 inches. Large Boxer rifle primer (reloadable).

Norma once loaded several bullet types—all 250 grains. The .358 was an excellent cartridge but doomed by the .338 Win. Magnum. It was further handicapped by being regularly available in only one rifle, an imported expensive one, and by limited ammunition availability.

The 250-grain softpoint semipointed bullet has a 2790 f.p.s. muzzle velocity. Its 300-yard velocity is 2001 f.p.s., or slightly higher than the .338 Win. Magnum and just under the .340 Weatherby Magnum. The difference is insignificant. The .338 Win. Magnum and .358 Norma Magnum provide residual velocities close to the .340 Weatherby Magnum without using a full-length .375/.300 H&H case or a full-length magnum action.

.375 H&H Magnum

Introduced 1912. Standard bullet weights: 235, 270, 300 grains. Standard bullet diameter: 0.366 inch.

The term ".375 H&H Magnum" is strictly American. However, since the Winchester M70 in this caliber is widely used in Africa, many white African hunters and other professionals use the American term. Many prefer American ammunition because current bullets have superior construction and the loads are somewhat more powerful than British loads.

The standard British designation for the .375 H&H is a mouth-filler: ".375 Belted Rimless Magnum Nitro-Express (Holland)." The rimmed .375 for use in double-barrel rifles is the ".375 Flanged Magnum Nitro-Express (Holland)."

This is one of the world's great cartridges. The author's acquaintance, the late John "Pondoro" Taylor, an Anglo-Irish remittance man turned Moslem and a professional African hunter for nearly a half-century, killed more than 5000 head of dangerous game with his three double-barrel and two magazine .375 H&H Magnums.

The .375, while not an elephant stopper, is perfectly capable of harvesting the great beast provided you can pick your target. Many professionals, particularly in non-British Africa (perhaps one should say "former" British Africa), use their .375s for all African big and dangerous game.

The .375 H&H Magnum has excessive punch for any North American game save big Alaskan bears. It is excellent for elk and moose. The .270-grain bullet has about the same trajectory as the excellent long-range 180-grain .30–06

spitzer. The .375 can serve as a long-range rifle on sheep, caribou, and African plains game.

If a world traveler could tote but one rifle and cartridge, the .375 would be difficult to surpass. During the 1920s and 1930s, gunmakers like Hoffman Arms and Griffin & Howe manufactured .375s using the expensive ($100) Magnum Mauser action or the far less expensive but excellent surplus M1917 Enfield action.

Thanks to the foresight of Winchester executive Ed Pugsley, Winchester chambered the M70—an improved M54/M1903 Springfield —for both the .300 H&H Magnum and the .375 H&H Magnum. The .375 M70 immediately caught on in Africa, where it became known for its accuracy and reliability. It cost about one-third as much as English (Mauser-action) rifles and German Mausers, some of which were inferior to the M70.

Some American riflemen and hunters were fascinated by the romance and deadliness of the multi-use cartridge and the reliability and accuracy of the rifle. Some, like the author, were also fascinated by that long (3.6-inch) gleaming cartridge.

The author was a 17-year-old Vermont country boy when the M70 .375 first appeared. The price was $61.95. He had absolutely no use for a .375 for Vermont deer and woodchucks. However, he has never been known for his practicality, so he ordered one. It was fitted with an American-made Noske 2½× scope fitted to Griffin & Howe side mounts. The serial number, as he remembers, was 0140.

The M70 .375 originally had a standard-weight 24.0-inch barrel. This was later changed to 25.0 inches. Post-1964 M70s have a 24.0-inch barrel, which the author believes is about right.

The 270-grain bullet is designed for use on game taken at ranges up to about 300 yards. For use in the woods against elk, moose, and big African plains game like the eland and kudu, the 300-grain softpoint types are better. There is a 300-grain solid for use against the big stuff. The author has examined various commercial solids, and every one has been deformed in its passage through buffalo, rhino, and elephant. Winchester should make a solid .375 jacket with the same strength and weight as its superb 500-grain solid .458 Win. Magnum jacket.

Fred Barnes, Durango, Colo., designed a superb 300-grain solid. Hornady, Grand Island, Nebr., also makes a fine solid.

Barnes' softpoint .375 bullets are properly made with two jacket thicknesses, the 0.032-inch jacket for use against North American big stuff and the 0.048-inch jacket for use against big African game.

.378 Weatherby Magnum

Introduced about 1952. .416 Rigby case with a belt added. Standard bullet weights: 270, 300 grains. Standard bullet diameter: 0.375 inch. Standard twist: 1-in-12 inches. Large rifle primer (Federal #215).

This cartridge—where African game regulations allow—is capable of handling with efficiency and dispatch the largest thick-skinned game. The 300-grain bullet has a 3000 f.p.s. muzzle velocity and a whopping muzzle energy of 5700 ft.-lbs. This is 700 more than the powerful .458 Win. Magnum. However, many hunters, including the author, prefer the heavier 500-grain .458 Win. Magnum despite lesser velocity and muzzle energy.

We believe this cartridge would be even more devastating if 350-grain Barnes bullets were used.

.44 S&W Magnum

Introduced 1956. Elongated .44 S&W Special case. Standard bullet weight: 240 grains. Standard bullet diameter: 0.429 inch.

It was inevitable that the world's most powerful factory handgun cartridge would ultimately be chambered in a rifle. This followed the century-old tradition of having a rifle and revolver using the same cartridges. Example: .32-20 Win., .38-40 Win., and .44-40 Win.

Some cartridges, like the Norma, are designed specifically for rifle use only. The factory recommends that rifle loads not be used in handguns. Because such superb revolvers as the Smith & Wesson M29 and Ruger's Single Action Superblackhawk are so well made, most handgunners use rifle and handgun loads interchangeably.

The .44 S&W Magnum, when used in rifles like Ruger's semiautomatic, is strictly a short-range brush cartridge for deer and black bear. Effective range is about 100 yards. Game as big as elk has been killed at several hundred yards with .44 S&W Magnum sixguns, but it takes an expert handgun hunter like Elmer Keith to bring off such a feat.

.44-40 Winchester

Introduced 1873. Rim/bottleneck case. Standard bullet weight (current): 200 grains. Standard bullet diameter: 0.425 inch. Standard twist:

1-in-20/1-in-36 inches. Large rifle primer. Original propellant: black powder.

This was the popular rifle-sixgun combination of the Winchester trio (the other two: .38-40 Win. and .32-30 Win.). Many frontiersmen liked the same ammunition for their Winchesters and Colts.

The .44-40 Win. is our oldest centerfire rifle and our first successful commercial centerfire cartridge.

Tens of thousands, possibly more, .44-40 carbines were sold south from the Rio Grande to Tierra del Fuego. South American rubber plantation owners purchased them for their plantation workers. Short-barrel (14-16-inch) carbines were extremely popular there.

The Winchester M73 has been revived by an Italian arms maker. There was a Spanish copy of the M92 called "El Tigre."

Buffalo Bill and his Wild West Show folk were partial to Winchester M73s and M92s. Bill, taking no chances, broke thousands of tossed glass balls with .44-40 Win., the cases loaded with No. 12 shot.

This is a good deer and bear cartridge, but today all fair-condition Winchester M73s and M92s are collectors' items.

It is unsafe to use present-day .44-40 Win. ammunition in M73 Winchester or in Colt Single Action Army revolvers with serial numbers below 160,000.

.444 Marlin

Introduced 1964. .30-40 Krag case necked out to 2.0 inches and rim trimmed. Standard bullet weight: 240 grains. Standard bullet diameter: 0.429 inch.

This is a far better short-range deer killer than the .30-30 Win. and a host of medium-power short-range .30 and .35 caliber cartridges. Ammunition is made only by Remington, and the one rifle is a Marlin. The .444 is more powerful and somewhat longer-ranged than the .44 Magnum cartridge when the latter is fired in a rifle like the Ruger semiautomatic. Ruger admirers would like the rifle chambered for the .444 Marlin.

.45 Government (.45-70)

Introduced 1873. Standard sporting bullet weights (current): 405 grains. Standard bullet diameter: 0.457 inch. Standard twist: 1-in-22 inches (Springfield). Large rifle primer. Original propellant: black powder.

The U.S. Army Ordnance Board made two major decisions in the early 1870s: to reduce service cartridge caliber from .50 to .45 but to retain the full 70-grain black-powder load of the .50–70 Gov't. cartridge.

The .45 Gov't. cartridge in the rifle and carbine decimated and subdued the plains Indians. The original .45 Gov't. loading for rifle and carbine was 70 grains of black powder and a 500-grain lead lubricated bullet. This load had excessive recoil in the cavalry carbine. The carbine load was reduced to a 405-grain lead bullet and 55 grains of black powder. The two loads were identified by a "C" headstamped on the .45–55 405-grain carbine load and an "R" on the .45–70 500-grain rifle load.

Despite variations of the original 70-grain black-powder load, the cartridge has always been called the .45–70. Many government loadings are of but passing historical notice. There were, for example, the .45–70–230 U.S. Government Short Range and the .45–20–230 U.S. Government Armory Practice.

Commercial loadings included, besides .45–50–500/.45–70–405/.45–55–405, the .45–70–350 W.C.F. (Winchester Center Fire), .45–70–330 W.C.F., and .45–70 Winchester High Velocity (300-grain bullet).

Early cases were inside-primed centerfire. To the uninitiated, these copper cases look like rimfire cases. They may be identified by a horizontal indentation just above the rim.

Original thin-wall copper cases caused trouble. On every fifth shot the cartridge would stick in the chamber. The thin copper walls heated too rapidly, thus swelling the case so it would not normally extract. The ejector would then tear through the thin copper rim. Removal required a broken-shell extractor. Some troopers died before they could chamber a sixth round. Some years later case walls were made of thicker copper. Copper (and later tinned copper), not brass, was standard for service-issue cartridge cases until almost the turn of the century.

With adequate loadings and bullets, the .45–70 has taken every species of North American game including big bears and bison.

The sole commercial load available today is inadequate, but heftier loads would be dangerous in the many trapdoor M1873 Springfields that are in use. These rifles were designed for black-powder loads not exceeding 15,000 p.s.i. A rifle like Bill Ruger's Number One Single Shot can handle pressures in excess of 50,000 p.s.i. Handloads are the only solution for new rifles. Black-

powder loads of 70 and 55 grains gave greater velocity and energy than the present factory load. You can safely approach 2000 f.p.s. with handloads. An excellent lead bullet is the 330-grain Gould bullet (Lyman mold #457122) for deer and bear.

Three rifles chambered for maximum .45–70 loads are now available: Ruger Number One Single Shot, Ruger Number Three Single Shot, and the tubular-magazine lever-action Marlin M95. The M95's side ejection makes it ideal for scope mounting.

Harrington & Richardson's replicas of the trapdoor Springfield should be used only with current factory .45–70 ammunition or black-powder handloads.

Many .45–70 Winchester M86 rifles and carbines are too valuable as collectors' items to be subjected to rough usage. Other collectors' .45–70s: Remington Rolling Block and Winchester's Hotchkiss bolt action.

It is a fitting tribute to this effective historic cartridge that it is undergoing a revival.

.458 Winchester Magnum

Introduced 1956. Straight rimless case derived from shortened .375 H&H Magnum. Bullet weights: 500, 510 grains. Standard bullet diameter: .457 inch. Standard twist: 1-in-14 inches. Large rifle primer. Annealed neck.

The 500-grain solid full-metal case or metal jacket is the best-constructed solid ever made, and the author is not forgetting those superb solids old John Rigby furnished for his .416 Rigby (bolt-action) and his double rifles. When you hit your elephant between the eyes (the best spot for a frontal shot) the bullet has to plow through 2–3 feet of honeycomb bone before striking the brain. The author has examined many 500-grain .458 bullets that reached their mark. All retained their original shape and their weight.

The 500-grain solid should be used only on rhino, Cape buffalo, and elephant.

Don't worry about recoil. You won't even notice it. Better to be a live hunter with a black-and-blue shoulder than a stomped-on hunter who used too light a bullet or a poorly constructed one.

The 500-grain solid, a masterpiece of design, has a 220-grain jacket. Several companies make .458 cartridges, but all the hunters and professional hunters the author knows or corresponds with use Winchester cartridges.

.460 Weatherby Magnum

Introduced 1960. .378 Weatherby Magnum case opened up for .457 bullets. Standard bullet weight: 500 grains. Standard bullet diameter: 0.457 inch. Standard twist: 1-1-14 inches. Large rifle primer (Federal #215).

This is the biggest round in the Winchester-Weatherby one-upmanship bout. The .460 Weatherby Magnum uses bullets of the same weight and diameter as the .458 Win. Magnum but at higher velocities. Many hunters, including the author, would prefer heavier and larger-caliber bullets using the .378/.460 Weatherby Magnum case at .458 Win. Magnum velocities over .458 Win. Magnum weight and diameter bullets at a higher velocity.

Most African professional hunters back up clients with a rifle capable of stopping an elephant.

Until the advent of the .458 Win. Magnum, most of them used a double .577 or .600 rifle costing $1000–$2500, a large medium-bore like the .416 Rigby or .425 Westley Richards, or big-bore magazine rifles like the .500 Mauser or .505 Gibbs. The high cost of double rifles plus an uncertain ammunition supply brought the .458 Win. Magnum very much into the picture. When it first appeared (1956) the .458 M70 Winchester African cost $250. Even today, this rifle or the Ruger M77 in the same caliber can be bought for a very reasonable price. The Weatherby, which costs considerably more (though nothing like the price of a double rifle), nonetheless has a strong appeal among sportsmen who are devoted to the Weatherby style in rifle design and in cartridge velocity. A hunter who can afford a safari — and the arms and equipment for it — doesn't necessarily worry much about the expense of such a rifle.

CHAPTER 12

METRIC CENTERFIRE RIFLE CARTRIDGES

Cartridges designated in millimeters rather than in decimal fractions of an inch may be placed in several categories.

1. Cartridges originally developed and manufactured in America. Examples: 6mm Lee Navy (.236 Lee Navy), 5.56mm (.223 Rem.), and 7.62mm NATO (.308 Win.). Here the metric nomenclature is that usually assigned to military loads while the other designation is usually applied by civilians to sporting loads.

2. Cartridges originally designed abroad which have been made here in sporting or military loads or both and for which American sporting rifles have been chambered. Examples: 7mm Mauser, 7.65 Argentine/Belgian Mauser, and 9mm Mauser.

3. Cartridges imported for rifles or for combination rifle-shotguns which have never been made in the United States. Examples: 10.75 Mauser, 8×57 Mannlicher-Schoenauer, and 7×57R.

4. Cartridges which have been made in the U.S. on military contract for allies but which have not been made in the U.S. in sporting loads. Example: 6.5mm Mannlicher-Carcano. Sporting loads may or may not have been available through importers.

5. Military cartridges and cases. Some importers—not knowledgeable or reputable ones—have imported full jacketed military cartridges. Military bullets are pulled and sporting type projectiles are substituted. Sometimes sporting bullets are the same weight as the military originals. However, bullets of an entirely different weight may be substituted for the military bullet but without changing the propellant charge. This is a dangerous practice. It is often impossible for the purchaser to determine whether the reload has the proper propellant charge. Avoid all cartridges where substitutions have been made. Many loads will be fired in rifles more than 75 years old. The rifle action may have been prop-

erly designed, but aging metal often deteriorates from fatigue and stress. Better to spend a few more cents for a commercial cartridge than lose your rifle and possibly your eyesight or receive a disabling wound.

6. Cartridge cases like the 7mm Weatherby Magnum which are made abroad (Norma) but which are loaded here in the States. (At one time Weatherby cartridges may have been loaded abroad as well.)

Some metric cartridges have more than one designation. The 8×57 Mauser (second figure denotes case length in millimeters) is known in America as the 8mm Mauser. The German military designation was 7.92mm.

The letter "R" attached as a suffix to the case length (example: 7×57R) indicates that the case is a rimmed version of the original rimless cartridge.

European manufacturers frequently designate a caliber by dual numbers. Norma headstamps 7mm Mauser cartridges "NORMA 7×57." United States manufacturers usually use the first number; thus "R-P 7mm." Western formerly marked its cases "7mm Mauser."

In the past, some European ammunition firms have assigned a number to each case. Deutch Waffen Munitionsfabriken (DWM) and G. Roth once designated cartridges in this manner. Sometimes bullets were designated by number.

The first American-designed and -manufactured cartridge to use the metric designation was probably the 6mm Lee Navy (1895), also known as the .236 Lee Navy. The last American cartridge to receive a metric designation was the 7mm Rem. Magnum. Others have included the 6mm Rem. and 7mm Weatherby Magnum. U.S. military designations have been previously noted.

Purchasers of obsolete military rifles for which sporting ammunition is available only through limited sources like Norma should buy an ample supply of cartridges before purchasing the rifle. These cartridges are subject to discontinuance of manufacture without prior notice.

6mm Remington

Introduced 1963. Necked-down .257 Roberts case. Standard bullet weights: 80, 100 grains. Standard bullet diameter: 0.2345 inch (maximum). Large rifle primer.

The 6mm Rem. and the .244 Rem. case are identical and are interchangeable. The only difference in the case is the headstamp.

The switch from the .244's original 1-in-12-inch twist for the 90-grain bullet to the 1-in-10-inch twist for the 80- and 100-grain bullets created confusion among riflemen. Remington solved the problem by changing the name from .244 Rem. Magnum (see Chapter 9) to 6mm Rem. for all rifles with the 1-in-10-inch twist.

The change to the faster twist and the offering of 80-grain lightweight jacketed bullets for varmints and the 100-grain heavier jacketed bullet for use on deer-class game places the 6mm Rem. on a par with the .243 Win. The .243, however, had such an enormous headstart in the popularity race that the 6mm has not caught up and never will. Nearly every manufacturer, American and foreign, of centerfire bolt-action rifles offers the .243 Win., but very few chamber these same rifles for the 6mm Rem. Some nitpicking handloaders—mostly varminters—prefer the 6mm Rem. to the .243 Win. because of the alleged superiority of the case neck angle.

6.5 JAP (6.5mm Japanese Army, Arisaka—DWM 481)

Semi-rim case. Standard bullet weights (Norma): 139, 156 grains. Standard bullet diameter: 0.263 inch. Standard twist: 1-in-7.5 inches. Large rifle (Boxer) primer.

Tens of thousands of GIs brought home Japanese Army rifles. Many were rechambered for American cartridges. The Arisaka—a very strong but clumsy-looking action—reached the high tide of its popularity in the years before 1950. Its popularity has been receding ever since.

Only a selected number of stores carry Norma ammunition, and an even smaller number carry the 6.5mm Japanese cartridge. A. F. Stoeger imported DWM sporting cartridges before World War II. The only real advantage of the Arisaka—despite its very strong action—was the low price of military surplus rifles. There is no advantage, today, in purchasing a 6.5mm Japanese rifle.

6.5mm Remington Magnum

Introduced 1966. Necked-down .350 Rem. Magnum case. Standard bullet weight range: 100 to 120 grains. Standard bullet diameter: 0.264 inch. Standard twist: 1-in-8 inches. Large rifle primer.

The 6.5mm Rem. Magnum, like the .350 Rem. Magnum, was chambered in the short-lived Remington M600 and M660 20-inch-barrel bolt-action carbines. Muzzle blast in the short barrel was severe. The cartridge, comparable to the .264 Win. Magnum, was also offered in the M700 for a couple of years.

The .25–06 Rem. will do anything the 6.5 Rem. Magnum will do and at less cost, with somewhat less noise, and with greater accuracy.

6.5 mm Mannlicher (6.5×54 Mannlicher-Schoenauer)

Introduced about 1900. Rimless bottleneck case. Standard Norma bullet weights: 77, 139, 156 grains. Standard bullet diameter: 0.263 inch. Standard twist (Steyr): 1-in-7.5 inches. Large rifle (Boxer) primer (Norma).

Shortly before leaving on his 1933 safari to British East Africa, Ernest Hemingway purchased from Abercrombie & Fitch a full-length Mannlicher-type-stock 6.5mm Mannlicher-Schoenauer for his wife. The same type of rifle figured in Hemingway's short story *The Short Happy Life of Francis Macomber*.

The 6.5mm Mannlicher cartridge in both its original and improved version by Gibbs of Bristol was also the favorite of the author's friend Dr. Vilhjalmur Stefansson (1879–1962). Anthropologist, geographer, historian, a leading Arctic explorer and one of the greatest Arctic authorities of all times, Stefansson used the 6.5mm exclusively on his three expeditions (1906–07, 1908–12, and 1913–18). "Steff" harvested hundreds of caribou, muskox, seal, and polar bear during his 10 Arctic years. Another advocate of the 6.5 Mannlicher was Charles Sheldon, big-game hunter, leading conservationist, and one of the most experienced Alaskan hunters. He took hundreds of Alaskan game animals, including the polar bear and big brown bears, with his 6.5mm Mannlicher. The long 156-grain bullet with its great sectional density was capable of driving into the vitals of the largest North American game animals.

Western Cartridge Company did not resume production of 6.5mm ammunition after World War II. The 7×57 Mauser will do anything the 6.5mm Mannlicher will do, and the 7mm Rem. or 7mm Weatherby Magnum will do it even better.

6.5×55 Swedish Mauser

Rimless bottleneck case. Standard (Norma) bullet weights: 77, 93, 139, 156 grains. Standard bullet diameter: 0.263 inch. Standard twist: 1-in-7.5 inches. Large (Boxer) rifle primer (Norma).

This cartridge, similar in performance to the 6.5mm Mannlicher-Schoenauer, has never been manufactured in the United States. It was the longtime service cartridge of Sweden and Norway. Tens of thousands of 6.5×55 surplus military rifles have been imported into the United States.

Carl Gustav rifles are currently imported in this caliber. This cartridge, chambered in a Carl Gustav target rifle, took top honors in the 1972 World Rifle Championship Matches in Tucson, Ariz.

7mm Remington Magnum

Introduced 1962. Belted bottleneck case, necked-up .264 Win. Magnum. Standard bullet weights: 110, 125, 150, 175 grains. Standard bullet diameter: 0.284 inch. Standard twist: 1-in-10 inches. Large rifle primer.

The first 7mm magnum appeared shortly before World War I. The .280 rimmed Ross became a popular long-range cartridge with British Army officers stationed in India, but its 140-grain copper tube bullet acquired a bad reputation in Africa, where it was used against heavy-boned, thin-skinned game like lion (a use for which it was never designed). Several fatalities resulted.

Following World War II, considerable publicity was given several wildcat 7mm magnums. Jack O'Connor sparked interest with an *Outdoor Life* article titled "The Big Sevens," while Warren Page repeatedly reported on his great successes with a wildcat 7mm Mashburn Magnum.

Remington arms and ammunition designer Mike Walker, a leading benchrest shooter—together with Les Bowman, the Cody, Wyo., guide, outfitter, and arms consultant—experimented with several 7mm magnums. The result was the 7mm Rem. Magnum.

This cartridge rapidly became the most popular of all belted magnums. The 150-grain bullet has a muzzle velocity of 3260 f.p.s. and muzzle energy is 3540 ft.-lbs. The 300-yard velocity is 2440 f.p.s., and residual energy is 1990 ft.-lbs. Midrange trajectory for 300 yards is 4.9 inches.

The 175-grain bullet originally was the typical 7mm roundnose type. Remington soon adopted a semi-pointed bullet with a resulting increase in velocity. Present 100-yard velocity is 3070 f.p.s. and energy is 3660 ft.-lbs. The 300-yard velocity is 2120 f.p.s., and energy is 1750 ft.-lbs.

The 125-grain and 110-grain bullets have a high initial velocity but because of their poor ballistic coefficient shed velocity too rapidly.

The classic all-round 7mm magnum bullet, the 160-grain, was thrust aside in favor of the 150-grain because the 150-grain gives a higher initial velocity and is therefore more impressive at least to novices. Handloaders, however, have a variety of 160-grain bullets to choose from. There are also the standard 7mm bullet weights like the 139-grain and 154-grain.

Many hunters, including the author, prefer the 7mm magnums to the "Big Thirty" magnums. The rifle can be somewhat lighter and the bullets have superior sectional density. The recoil is lighter in rifles of equal weight.

In factory loads the 150-grain is a superb long-range cartridge for sheep, goat, caribou, and African plains game. The 175-grain is adequate on all North American game with the possible exception of rear-end shots on moose and elk and the big Alaskan brown bears. It is adequate for all African plains game. The author would rather go up against the Big Five with a .375 H&H Magnum or a .458 Win. Magnum.

A 7mm magnum rifle with scope needs to weigh no more than 8.0 lbs. A 2.5–7× scope is an excellent all-round sight for the 7mm Rem. Magnum. A 4× scope would be the best all-round fixed-power scope.

7mm Weatherby Magnum

Introduced about 1945. Shortened and necked-down .300 H&H Magnum case. Standard bullet weights: 139, 154, 175 grains. Standard bullet diameter: .284 inch. Standard twist: 1-in-10 inches. Large rifle primer.

This cartridge, like other 7mm magnums, is an excellent long-range cartridge for lighter game like sheep and caribou. The 175-grain bullet is capable of taking all North American game with the possible exception of the big Alaskan brown bear.

7×57 (7mm Mauser)

Introduced 1892. Necked-down 8×57 Mauser case. Standard bullet weights: 110, 139, 150, 175 grains. Standard bullet diameter: 0.284 inch. Standard twist (military): 1-in-8.75 inches. Standard twist (usual custom/commercial): 1-in-10 inches. Large rifle primer.

The 7mm Mauser (along with the .30–06 Springfield and the .375 H&H Magnum) is one of the world's oldest and most popular sporting cartridges. Though it has never been extremely popular in the United States, it has nonetheless had a very devoted coterie of followers who purchase enough cartridges to keep it on the lists of ammunition manufacturers.

The original military round was a 172-grain full metal-jacketed roundnose bullet with a muzzle velocity of about 2300 f.p.s. in the standard 28–30-inch infantry rifle barrels.

The standard sporting bullet weight for many years was the 175-grain roundnose softpoint. The late Karamojo Bell, a wiry Scots elephant hunter, killed many of his 1000-plus elephants with a 7mm Mauser using "solid" bullets as the British call full metal-jacketed projectiles.

North Americans—unless they used imported German or British ammunition—were confined to the 175-grain roundnose bullet until the 1920s, when Western Cartridge Co. loaded some 139-grain spitzer bullets for a South American republic. An 139-grain Western Open Point Expanding bullet was soon released to hunters. The alleged 3000 f.p.s. in a 30.0-inch barrel yielded about 2850 f.p.s. in standard 24.0-inch sporting barrels.

This bullet, highly effective on deer, antelope, sheep, goat, caribou, and African plains game out to about 250–275 yards, resulted in a mild demand for 7mm sporting rifles.

Winchester responded with the M54 bolt-action magazine rifle and its grand successor the M70. Remington offered its M30—a sporter version of the M1917 Enfield—and Griffin & Howe made many sporters, either on the M1903 Springfield action or the superior commercial Mauser short action.

Despite its increase in popularity, the 7mm fared badly at the hands of the ammunition manufacturers. Western and then Remington dropped the 139-grain bullet shortly before World War II. Shooter demand brought a brief revival of the 139-grain Western O.P.E. load but it was not revived after World War II. Winchester also discontinued its excellent but little-known 150-grain bullet.

No American manufacturer resumed 7mm rifle production after World War II. In 1974 Ruger reintroduced the 7mm in the M77.

The M70 Winchester was listed as being available in that caliber, but orders were filled by fitting barrels made before World War II onto M70 actions. The last 7mm barrel was fitted to an M70 action for Jack O'Connor. He cut the barrel down to 22.0 inches, turned down the barrel to save weight, and had a custom stock fitted.

The 175-grain bullet—the only load regularly and conveniently available to American hunters—was kept alive for nearly 30 years following World War II by virtue of the large influx of imported surplus military Mausers.

The only American-made 7mm factory—as opposed to custom or imported—rifle currently available is the Ruger M77. A number of imports, including the FN Mauser Supreme, are chambered for the 7mm Mauser.

Today factory loadings range from the 110-grain Norma softpoint through the 175-grain roundnose. Other loadings include the 150-grain Norma and 139-grain Federal softpoint. The author considers the 110-grain softpoint to have too poor a sectional density for practical use.

Those who remain with factory loads might do well to use the 139-grain or 150-grain bullet for long-range shooting and confine the 175-grain to moose, elk, and big bear. This long 175-grain bullet is capable of deep penetration on large game.

Handloaders can use the 160-grain Nosler for an all-round load. The author prefers the H-type jacket of the Nosler partition bullet to the same weight Sierra or Speer bullets. There is also the excellent 154-grain Hornady bullet. Some handloaders like the 130-grain Sierra, which can be given about 3000 f.p.s. (24.0-inch barrel). The author has had no experience with the 145-grain Speer bullet, though many have reported excellent results on mule deer, antelope, sheep, and caribou.

Jack O'Connor's wife, Eleanor—one of this nation's finest big-game rifle shots—has had very fine results with her 7mm. On a 1962 Mozambique safari she took seventeen head of game with nineteen shots. Only one—kudu—of the seventeen head required more than one shot. Her bag includes black bear, Dall sheep, eland, elk, Grant's gazelle, impala, kudu, mule deer, reedbuck, roan antelope, Stone sheep, waterbuck, and zebra. In some instances she has taken several of one species.

A 160-grain Speer bullet backed by 52 grains of Dupont 4350 produces a velocity of about 2650 f.p.s. in her 22.0-inch-barrel rifle. The author uses the same load with a 160-grain Nosler partition bullet for a velocity of about 2700 f.p.s. in either a Winchester M70 or Ruger M77 (both have a 24.0-inch barrel).

The author's experience with the 7mm stretches over a 40-year span but it has not been extensive because he is always trying another caliber or using his .375 H&H Magnum on all sorts of game. Also, his favorite long-range rifle for thin-skinned game for a quarter-century was the .300 H&H Magnum. However, he would not be too badly handicapped if he had to use the 7mm against 95 percent of all the world's big game. He would even face an elephant—at a respectable distance of 50 yards and in the open—if he had a good 175-grain solid and was backed up by a white hunter with a .458 Win. Magnum.

His bag taken with a 7mm Mauser includes six whitetails, two mule deer, one antelope, one mountain goat, one bighorn, three caribou, four zebra, and three black bear.

Most of this game was taken before the advent of the 160-grain Nosler partition bullet, with 139-grain Western Open Point Expanding bullets with the 154-grain Hornady handloads.

There is no need for a 7mm Mauser rifle with sling and scope to weigh more than 7.5 lbs. That some factory rifles (with attached scope) weigh more is due solely to the fact that basic factory stocks are designed to fit a number of calibers. If you wish to have a light 7mm rifle but do not wish to spend the money required for turning down the barrel diameter (thus requiring custom or semi-custom stock), weight can be saved by "cheesecaking" (drilling holes) in the magazine sidewalls, shaving some thickness off the receiver—but not too much—routing out the bottom of the barrel channel, replacing a steel trigger guard with a lightweight alloy one, and thinning down the stock. None of these weight-saving techniques should be carried to excess.

Spanish M93 Mausers and the small-ring M95 Mexican/Chilean Mausers should be avoided when selecting a 7mm rifle or action. These one-locking-lug actions are not designed for loads in excess of 45,000 p.s.i. The M98 and M1909 Mauser actions, along with commercial Mauser actions and the Czech military VZ 24, can safely handle recommended maximum handloads. The Czech action and the G33/40 actions are longer than the short K actions but shorter than the standard M98 actions. These actions both have weight and have a shorter bolt throw.

Rifle maker John Rigby of Dublin and London once made 7mm Mauser rifles and offered proprietary cartridges under the designation .275 Rigby.

Many thousands of Remington rolling-block rifles were made in 7mm Mauser—mostly for export as military rifles—then purchased by war surplus dealers during the late 1940s and early 1950s and dumped on the American market. Headspace problems frequently developed. This once honorable but now ancient action should not be used with modern high-velocity 7mm loads. Hang your 7mm rolling-block on the wall; look at it but don't shoot it.

Beware of surplus military ammunition. Some years ago when the author was associated with the H. P. White Laboratory, one of the nation's largest importers of military arms and ammunition submitted some full metal-jacketed military ammunition made a few years before in Spain. Pressures exceeded 100,000 p.s.i. These cartridges could have detonated old military rifles designed for loads not in excess of 45,000 p.s.i. Even high-velocity contemporary loads don't range above 55,000. Those Spanish military cartridges would have wrecked even the finest of contemporary actions.

The shooter who is sensitive to recoil or who wants a light big-game rifle will have to search a long way to find a cartridge as efficient, as reliable, and as versatile as the old 7mm Mauser.

7×57R (7mm rimmed Mauser)

Introduced about 1900. Rimmed 7×57 Mauser case. This rimmed version of the 7×57 rimless Mauser was designed for combination rifle-shotguns. Ammunition has never been made in the United States and can be obtained only from European sources. The cartridge may be discontinued by the time this book is in print.

7×61 Sharpe & Hart

Introduced about 1952. Necked-down and shortened .300 H&H Magnum case. Standard bullet weight: 160 grains (all types). Standard bullet diameter: 0.284 inch. Standard twist: 1-in-10 inches. Large (Boxer) rifle primer (Norma). Available in Norma brand only.

This cartridge was developed by the author's friend the late Captain Philip Sharpe and Richard Hart. It was designed as an all-round rifle load for North American big game and African plains game. The cartridge was chambered in the fine Danish-made Schultz & Larsen rifle, which never became popular because the ammunition and rifle had such a high price and relatively small distribution.

7.62mm Russian

Introduced about 1891. Rimmed bottlenecked cartridge. Standard bullet weight (current): 172 grains (pointed softpoint boattail; Norma). Standard bullet diameter: 0.308–0.311 inch. Standard twist: 1-in-10 inches. Large (Boxer) rifle primer (Norma).

This cartridge, currently available only through Norma, may be discontinued by the time this book appears in print. Remington formerly made a 150-grain Bronze Point bullet.

The 7.62mm Russian (strictly American nomenclature) is also known as the 7.62×54R (R for rimmed). Official designation was 7.62mm Moisin-Nagant (after the rifle). DWM case number 378. It was the standard service cartridge of the Imperial Russian Army from 1891 to 1917 and of the Red Army from 1917 until World War II.

During World War I, Winchester made 293,816 M95 nondetachable-box-magazine lever-action rifles with bayonets for the Czar's army. Winchester also supplied 174,000,000 cartridges for the Russians. Remington, too, made millions of 7.62mm service cartridges.

Remington also made M1891 Moisin-Nagant rifles for the Russians. Alexander Kerensky's government repudiated all Czarist contracts. The U.S. government bailed Remington out by purchasing more than 600,000 rifles, which it shipped to Siberia, where they were successfully used by White Russians against Red Army Commander Leon Trotsky's troops.

Many of the M95 Winchesters shipped to Russia during World War I were used by Russian civilians against Hitler's invaders in World War II. Some of these rifles were captured and taken to Germany, where U.S. surplus dealers purchased them for resale in the United States. These rifles, along with all M95s, are now collectors' items. The M95 chambered for the 7.62 Russian cartridge was the only M95 caliber which had a slot for charge strip (clip) loading.

The 7.62mm Russian cartridge has ballistics similar to the .303 British and .30–40 Krag.

7.65mm Argentine/Belgian Mauser

Introduced about 1889. Necked-down 8mm (7.92mm) case. Standard bullet weights: 54 to 219 grains. Standard bullet diameter: 0.310 inch. Standard twist: 1-in-10 inches (Mauser). Large rifle primer. Service ammunition has Berdan primer. Norma has reloadable Boxer primer.

The world's second-oldest rimless military cartridge has had very limited popularity in the U.S., though both ammunition and rifle have been here. The cartridge is almost identical in performance to the .30–06 Springfield. The only currently available sporting load known to the author is the 150-grain Norma. Some foreign service ammunition — full metal-jacketed — is available in limited quantity.

Winchester manufactured the cartridge from 1900 to 1939. The final Winchester load had a 215-grain bullet. Remington also made a 216-grain softpoint bullet. The Winchester bolt-action M54 (1925–36) was chambered (1930–36) for the 7.65mm Argentine. The M70 Winchester during the first year of its existence (1937–38) was offered in 7.65mm Argentine Mauser. It is believed the M70 was fitted with M54 barrels and that when the barrels were sold out, no more M70s were chambered for the cartridge. A few Remington M30/M30Ss were also chambered for the 7.65mm. The very few M70s chambered for the 7.65mm Mauser, together with a few 9mm Mausers, are among the rarest M70s and are in great demand by M70 collectors.

Some 7.65mm Argentine military Mausers have been offered as surplus on the U.S. market. These rifles — among the earliest Mausers — had a straight-line 5-shot magazine which projected through the bottom of the stock.

Belgian models include the M1889/M1935. Similar but not identical Argentine Mausers included the M1891/M1909. These were M1890/M1893/M1903 Turkish Mausers.

The 7.65mm Mausers adopted after 1893 used the M98 GEW action with its 5-shot nondetachable staggered box magazine.

8×56 (8mm) Mannlicher-Schoenauer

Introduced into U.S. by Winchester, 1904. Rimless case based on 8×57 Mauser. Standard bullet weights: 170, 202 grains. Standard bullet diameter: 0.325 inch. Standard twist: 1-in-9.5 inches. Large rifle (Boxer) primer. Continental primers are Berdan.

This cartridge, while designed to cash in on the justifiable popularity of the 8×57 Mauser, has the performance characteristics of the .35 Rem. rather than of the 8×57 Mauser. Ammunition is made by DWM and RWS. Winchester ceased its manufacture shortly before World War II.

Cases may be headstamped "8mm M/S" or "8MANN."

8×57 (7.92mm) Mauser

Introduced 1888. Perhaps the first rimless-case military cartridge. Standard bullet weights: 150 to 236 grains. Standard bullet diameter: 0.318 inch (M1888 rifle and M98's through 1904), 0.323 inch (all M98s and sporter-based M98s after 1904).

This is the world's greatest military cartridge, in terms of influence. It has also spawned more sporting cartridges—including American—than any other military or sporting cartridge: the 7mm Mauser, 7.65mm Mauser, .30–06 Springfield, 7.62 NATO (.308 Win). The 9mm Mauser, a medium-bore sporting cartridge once made here in the U.S. (both rifles and ammo) is but a necked-up 8mm Mauser. Mannlicher—Mauser's lesser competitor—cashed in on the 8mm Mauser's fame by slightly revamping the case and calling it the 8mm Mannlicher-Schoenauer cartridge (also U.S. made before World War II).

Cartridges like the .243 Win., .244 Rem., 6mm Rem., .250 Savage, .257 Roberts, .270 Win. and .358 Win. are collateral descendants of the 8mm Mauser (all have the original 8mm head dimensions, but case lengths and neck width varies).

The 8mm Mauser was first chambered in the M1888 Mauser, a bastard Mauser/Mannlicher with Mauser action and Mannlicher detachable clip.

The 8mm Mauser (1888–1904) cartridge's 227-grain roundnose metal-jacketed bullet had a muzzle velocity of 2110 f.p.s. (30.0-inch barrel, infantry rifle). Bullet diameter was 0.318 inch. In 1905 the German army adopted a 154-grain spitzer bullet. Its diameter was 0.323 inch. Bullets with the 0.323-inch diameter were designated "S" for spitzer (sharp). The M1888 cases (8mm) when loaded with the .323 "S" bullet were designated 8×57 JS. "J" stands for "Jaeger" (infantry). The 8mm cases when loaded with the M1888 0.318-inch diameter bullet were designated 8×57 J. 8×57 J is designated 8×57 JR when rimmed. A rimmed version of the 8×57 JS is designated 8×57 JRS. German military nomenclature for the 8.57S is 7.92mm or sometimes just 7.9mm.

After World War I, rifles chambered for both the 8×57 J and 8×57 JS were brought home by returning soldiers. The 8×57 JS Mausers had been liberated from the Kaiser's finest. The 8×57 J Mausers—the army disposed of them after outfitting its troops—were probably liberated from German civilians who purchased them as pre-World War I surplus.

Some Austrian-made M1888s (8×57 J) made their way to the United States. Some were directly imported as sporters or surplus while others had been liberated in the Eastern Kingdom (Austria).

Austrian-made M1888s designed for sale within the Austro-Hungarian Empire were tagged with well-known Austrian arms names: Haenel-Mannlicher and Schilling-Mannlicher. The same Austrian-made arms when sold in Germany became Haenel-Mauser or Schilling-Mauser.

Some Austrian rifles were made in both 8×57 J and 8×57 JR diameters.

American ammunition manufacturers—and the shooting public—found the 8mm business confusing. Remington and Winchester offered the 236-grain softpoint 8mm Mauser-Mannlicher (8×57 J) cartridge with the information on the box that the cartridge was for Mauser, Sauer-Mauser, and Schilling-Mauser M1888 and Haenel-Mannlicher M1888. Winchester and Peters also made a 170-grain bullet.

The author micrometered 100 assorted Remington, Peters, and Winchester cartridges and the average was 0.318 inch.

Remington offered the 170-grain Mauser "Special" that is designed for chambers that are worn or oversized. These bullets miked 0.323 inch.

Remington headstamps for the 0.318-inch bullet (8×57 J) and for the 0.323-inch bullet (8×57 JS) were identical. Thus these bullets could be correctly identified only if they came from a new box. In loose lots they were indistinguishable. Western and Peters manufactured a 200-grain softpoint cartridge designed for the 8mm Mannlicher-Schoenauer. Headstamps were designated either "8mm MANN" or "8mm M/s." It would be possible to confuse the 8mm M/s headstamp with the "8mm Mauser Special."

There are other 8mm cartridges, including the 8mm Lebel (no longer made in the U.S.), 8×60, 8×63, and 8×64 Brennecke. Unless you can positively identify German army service 8mm ammunition either by the box, by measurements, or by reading the headstamp code, you'd better purchase factory ammunition.

One 8mm load (0.322-inch bullet) is currently manufactured by Remington-Peters. It is a 170-grain softpoint roundnose. CIL (Canadian Industries, Ltd.) makes a similar-weight bullet.

Notable 8×57 JS imports include 123-grain softpoint pointed, 159-grain softpoint roundnose, 196-grain softpoint roundnose, 198-grain hollowpoint, 198-grain full metal-jacketed boattail, 227-grain softpoint roundnose. They are, of course, all 0.322-inch-diameter bullets. These are all loaded by Norma.

Norma offers 8×57 J cartridges (0.318-inch bullet) in four types, ranging from the 159-grain softpoint roundnose through a 198-grain softpoint roundnose.

DWM and RWS imports may or may not be regularly available.

Many Americans with 8mm Mausers use them not at all or very little because they don't like the only available American loads and are unaware of the wide selection of imported 8mm loads.

The 8mm/06 is a popular wildcat for the economy-minded. This is a full-length .30–06 Springfield case opened up to 8mm. It is an inexpensive procedure to have a gunsmith extend the 8mm chamber to accommodate the longer .30–06 case.

8×57 JR Mauser

Introduced about 1900. 8mm Mauser case with rim. Standard bullet diameter: 0.318 inch. Standard bullet weight (current): 196 grains, softpoint roundnose. Standard twist, 1-in-8.5 inches. Large (Boxer) rifle primer (Norma).

The only arms chambered for the 8×57 JR that the author has seen are the special combination rifle-shotguns: one rifle barrel, one shotgun barrel; two shotgun barrels, one centerfire rifle barrel (this is famed *drilling* combination); and two shotgun barrels, one centerfire rifle barrel/one rimfire rifle barrel, sometimes known as the Rube Goldberg Special. (There may also be bolt or other actions for this cartridge.)

8×57 JRS Mauser

Introduced after 1905. Rimmed 8×57 Mauser case with "S" bullet. Standard bullet weight: 196 grains. Standard bullet diameter: 0.322 inch. Standard twist: 1-in-8.5 inches. Large (Boxer) rifle primer (Norma). This is the rimmed version of the 8×57 JS.

PART IV

RIMFIRE RIFLES

CHAPTER / 13

SINGLE-SHOT RIMFIRE RIFLES

There are two basic single-shot rifle types: purely single-shot actions like the Remington rolling block, Stevens Crack Shot and Little Scout; and single-shot versions of bolt-action magazine rifles.

There are two basic categories of single-shot bolt-action rifles: the inexpensive type designed primarily as a youngster's first rifle; and match rifles costing several hundred dollars.

The Remington rolling block was one of the first actions for .22 rimfire cartridges. The first version, known as the Sporting Rifle #1 Single Shot Rolling Block (1867–90), was succeeded by the Sporting Rifle #1½ Single Shot Rolling Block (1888–97). The #1 weighed 8.0–12.0 lbs. The #1½ was a lighter version, averaging 7.5 lbs. Another popular rimfire rifle was the Sporting Rifle #2 Single Shot Rolling Block (1873–1910). This was the author's second .22 rimfire rifle. It cost $1.25 secondhand in 1930.

A popular falling-block .22 rimfire target rifle was the Stevens Walnut Hill series — named after the Massachusetts rifle range — some of which were barreled by the famed Harry Pope.

The Stevens Little Scout and Crack Shot were inexpensive falling-block plinking rifles which were surprisingly accurate for their price and weight. The latter was recently revived by Savage Arms.

One of the first bolt-action match rifles was the Winchester M52 — originally a magazine rifle, but for some years available in a single-shot version.

The prices of bolt-action single-shot rifles have risen even more sharply than those of bolt-action centerfire magazine rifles. The author brought his first new single-shot bolt-action — a Winchester M67 — for $5 in 1935. Today, a similar rifle costs about $50.

The single-shot bolt-action, particularly one that has to be manually cocked (a cocking piece is pulled back after the bolt has been operated to feed a round into the chamber), is an ideally safe first rifle for youngsters.

GARCIA BRONCO RIFLE

Manufacturer: Rossi Arms, Brazil

Importer/distributor: Garcia Corp./Firearms International

Action type: swing-out

Safety: crossbolt

Barrel length: 20.0 inches

Stock: skeleton type; rust-resistant, crackle finish

Buttplate: crescent (rifle) type formed by stock; no buttplate

Overall length: 32.0 inches

Length of pull: 13.875 inches

Drop at comb: 1.75 inches

Drop at heel: 3.0 inches

Weight: 3.0 lbs.

Trigger pull: 4.5 lbs.

Sight, rear: slot in receiver bridge

Sight, front: bead

Scope adaptability: no provision

Caliber: .22 Short, .22 Long, .22 Long Rifle, .22 Long Rifle Shot

Comment: This is a special-purpose rifle for the boater or for the backpacker who may want an occasional shot for the pot.

HARRINGTON & RICHARDSON M750

Action type: bolt

Safety: side thumb lever

Barrel length: 22.0 inches; tapered

Stock: 1-piece uncheckered walnut-stained American hardwood; uncapped semi-pistol grip; fluted comb

Buttplate: shotgun type; plastic with white line spacer

Overall length: 39.0 inches

Length of pull: 13.5 inches

Drop at comb: 1.5 inches

Drop at Monte Carlo: 2.0 inches

Drop at heel: 2.5 inches

Weight: 5.0 lbs.

Trigger pull: 5.0 lbs.

Sight, rear: Rocky Mountain, crudely adjustable for elevation

Sight, front: dovetail blade

Scope adaptability: receiver grooved for tip-off mount

Caliber: .22 Short, .22 Long, .22 Long Rifle

Comment: A typical low-priced single-shot rifle suitable for beginners.

ITHACA M49 SADDLEGUN

Manufacturer: Erma Werke, West Germany

Importer/distributor: Ithacagun

Action type: lever; Martini type

Magazine: none, but dummy tubular magazine

Safety: rebounding hammer

Barrel length: 18.0 inches

Stock: 2-piece plain walnut, glossy finish; fore-end barrel band

Buttplate: Shotgun type; plastic

Overall length: 36.0 inches

Length of pull: standard/magnum, 14.0 inches; Youth, 12.0 inches

Drop at comb: 1.75 inches

Drop at heel: 2.5 inches

Weight: standard, 5.5 lbs.; Youth, 5.25 lbs.

Trigger pull: 5.0 lbs.

Sight, rear: Rocky Mountain, crudely adjustable for elevation

Sight, front: dovetail blade

Scope adaptability: receiver grooved for tip-off mount

Caliber: .22 Short, .22 Long, .22 Long Rifle, .22 Long Rifle Shot, .22 Win. Rimfire Magnum (magnum version of rifle only)

Comment: This inexpensive single-shot rifle with its dummy magazine has the appearance (more or less) of the Winchesters that "won the West." Good workmanship and materials.

REMINGTON M40-XR SERIES RIFLE

Action type: bolt; single-shot

Ejection: side

Safety: thumb, 2-position

Barrel length: 24.0 inches; heavy barrel, countersunk muzzle

Stock: American walnut; position style; thumb groove; front swivel block with guide rail; adjustable hand stop and sling swivel

Buttplate: 2-way adjustable

Overall length: 42.5 inches

Length of pull: 13.5 inches

Drop at comb: 0.0 inches

Drop at Monte Carlo: 0.0 inches

Drop at heel: adjustable

Weight: 10.125 lbs.

Trigger pull: 2.0–4.0 lbs., adjustable

Sight, rear: none furnished; optional at extra cost is Redfield Olympia micrometer, 1/4-minute clicks

Sight, front: none furnished; optional at extra cost is Redfield Olympia with 10 inserts

Scope adaptability: barrel drilled and tapped for target scope blocks

Caliber: .22 Long Rifle

Comment: This is Remington's top-of-the line smallbore target rifle. It was designed by Mike Walker. Only American competitor is the 57-year-old, but improved, Winchester M52. Both rifles have won many local, state, regional, national, and international matches. (The Winchester M52 has won many more because it has been around a third of a century longer than the M40 Remington.)

REMINGTON M540-XR/M540-XRJR SERIES RIFLE

Action type: bolt; single loader; target

Ejection: side

Safety: thumb, 2-position

Barrel length: 26.0 inches; medium-weight target, countersunk muzzle

Stock: 1-piece American walnut; position type; Monte Carlo comb; cheekpiece; full-length guide rail on fore-end for front swivel block (front swivel block, sling, and front swivel optional at extra cost)

Buttplate: 5-way adjustable; 3.75-inch adjustment (M540-XR); same range for shorter stock (M540-XRJR)

Overall length: adjustable; M540-XR, 43.50–46.75 inches; M540-XRJR, 41.75–45.0 inches

Length of pull: adjustable buttplate; M540-XR, 12.75–16.9 inches; M540-XRJR, 11.0–14.25 inches

Drop at comb: 0.0 inches

Drop at Monte Carlo: 0.0 inches

Drop at heel: adjustable

Weights: 8.85 lbs. without sights; 9.65 lbs. with receiver and front sight

Trigger pull: 1.0–2.0 lbs., adjustable

Sight, rear: none furnished; optional Redfield micrometer #75, ½-minute clicks

Sight, front: Redfield #63 Globe with 7 inserts

Scope adaptability: barrel drilled and tapped for target scope bases

Caliber: .22 Long Rifle

Comment: This is Remington's second-line match rimfire rifle. It, too, was designed by Mike Walker.

REMINGTON M580 SERIES RIFLE

Action type: bolt; single-shot

Ejection: side

Safety: thumb, 2-position

Barrel length: 24.0 inches

Stock: 1-piece walnut-stained hardwood; no checkering; uncapped pistol grip; Monte Carlo comb

Buttplate: shotgun type; plastic

Overall length: standard, 42.375 inches; Boy's, 41.375 inches

Length of pull: standard, 13.75 inches; Boy's, 12.75 inches

Drop at comb: 2.5 inches

Drop at Monte Carlo: 2.0 inches

REMINGTON M580 SERIES RIFLE (continued)

Drop at heel: 2.5 inches

Weight: standard, 4.75 lbs.; Boy's 4.6 lbs.

Trigger pull: 4.5 lbs.

Sight, rear: Rocky Mountain, crudely adjustable for windage

Sight, front: bead

Scope adaptability: receiver grooved for tip-off scope mount

Caliber: .22 Short, .22 Long, .22 Long Rifle; .22 Long Rifle Shot for M580 SB (smoothbore)

Comment: Better-than-average single-shot bolt-action rifle for beginning shooters. The Boy's rifle version is one of the few single-shots that have a suitable-length stock for younger shooters.

SAVAGE STEVENS M72 CRACKSHOT RIFLE

Action type: falling block; case-hardened frame

Safety: half-cock hammer

Barrel length: 22.0 inches; octagonal

Stock: 2-piece American walnut; straight grip; uncheckered; oil finish

Buttplate: Shotgun type; hard rubber

Overall length: 37.0 inches

Length of pull: 14.0 inches

Drop at comb: 1.75 inches

Drop at heel: 2.75 inches

Weight: 4.5 lbs.

Trigger pull: 5.0–6.0 lbs.

Sight, rear: Rocky Mountain, crudely adjustable for elevation

Sight, front: dovetail blade

Scope adaptability: no provision

Caliber: .22 Short, .22 Long, .22 Long Rifle, .22 Long Rifle Shot

Comment: The M72 is a revival of one of the most popular and, originally, inexpensive .22 rimfire rifles ever made. The author owned one when he was eight or nine years old. Many adults buy one of these delightful rifles just for nostalgia, but the Crackshot rifle can still shoot.

EXPLODED VIEW OF SAVAGE STEVENS MODELS 72 AND 74 SINGLE-SHOT RIFLE

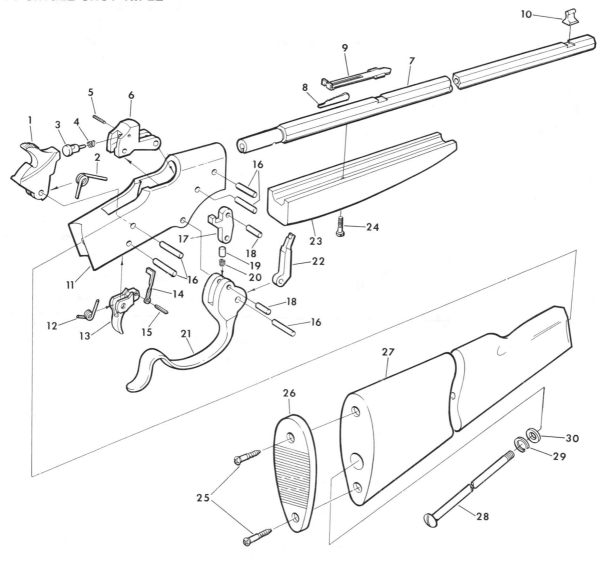

No.	Part Name	No.	Part Name	No.	Part Name
1	Hammer	11	Frame	21	Lever
2	Hammer Spring	12	Trigger Spring	22	Extractor
3	Firing Pin	13	Trigger	23	Forend
4	Firing Pin Spring	14	Hammer Block	24	Forend Screw
5	Firing Pin Securing Pin	15	Hammer Block Pin	25	Butt Plate Screws
6	Breech Block	16	Hammer Pin	26	Butt Plate
7	Barrel	17	Link	27	Stock
8	Rear Sight Step	18	Link Pin	28	Stock Bolt
9	Rear Sight	19	Detent Plunger	29	Stock Bolt Washer
10	Front Sight	20	Detent Plunger Spring	30	Stock Bolt Lock Washer

SAVAGE STEVENS M73/M73-Y RIFLES

Action type: bolt; alloy receiver; enclosed bolt

Safety: sliding; goes on automatically when bolt is worked

Barrel length: M73, 20.0 inches; M73-Y, 18.0 inches; both lengths free-floating

Stock: 1-piece walnut-stained hardwood; unchecked; uncapped semi-pistol grip

Buttplate: shotgun type; hard rubber

Overall length: M73, 38.5 inches; M73-Y, 35.0 inches

Length of pull: M73, 14.0 inches; M73-Y, 12.5 inches

Drop at comb: 1.5 inches

Drop at heel: 2.5 inches

Weight: M73, 4.75 lbs.; M73-Y, 4.5 lbs.

Trigger pull: 5.0–6.0 lbs.

Sight, rear: Rocky Mountain, crudely adjustable

Sight, front: dovetail bead

Scope adaptability: receiver grooved for tip-off mount

Caliber: .22 Short, .22 Long, .22 Long Rifle, .22 Long Rifle Shot

Comment: The smaller-size M73-Y Youth rifle is an excellent idea. About 90 percent of all .22 rifles are used by kids, yet most stocks are too big for younger shooters.

WALTHER KKM INTERNATIONAL MATCH RIFLE

Manufacturer: Carl Walther Waffenfabrik, West Germany

Importer/distributor: Interarms

Action type: single-shot; bolt

Safety: none

Barrel length: 28.0 inches

Stock: 1-piece heavy European walnut; hand-checkered pistol grip with thumb hole and hand-shelf; adjustable cheek rest; flat fore-end with adjustable weight and sliding rail holding palm rest

Buttplate: metal underarm hook type; adjustable for drop and length of pull

Overall length: 46.0 inches

Weight: 15.5 lbs.

Trigger pull: adjustable match type with basic pull of 7.0–21.0 oz. or 32.0–33.0 oz.

Sight, rear: fully adjustable micrometer aperture

Sight, front: Olympic-type tube with interchangeable post and aperture inserts

Scope adaptability: target-scope bases provided

Caliber: .22 Long Rifle

Data: Barrel is heavy tapered match type. Left-hand stock is available at extra cost.

Comment: One of the world's finest Olympic match rifles.

WALTHER U.I.T. MATCH RIFLE

Manufacturer: Carl Walther Waffenfabrik, West Germany

Importer/distributor: Interarms

Action type: single-shot; bolt

Safety: none

Barrel length: 25.5 inches

Stock: 1-piece European walnut; hand-checkered match-type pistol grip; flat fore-end with sliding rail for palm rest or sling

Buttplate: metal, adjustable for drop and length of pull

Overall length: 44.75 inches

Weight: 10.2 lbs.

Trigger pull: adjustable match type with basic pull of 7.0–21.0 oz. or 32.0–33.0 oz.

Sight, rear: fully adjustable micrometer aperture

Sight, front: tube with interchangeable post and aperture inserts

Caliber: .22 Long Rifle

Data: Left-hand stock available at extra cost on special order.

Comment: Finely crafted rifle designed for special matches and conforming to both U.I.T. (Union Internationale de Tir) and NRA match requirements.

WALTHER "PRONE 400" MATCH RIFLE

Manufacturer: Carl Walther Waffenfabrik, West Germany

Importer/distributor: Interarms

Action type: single-shot; bolt

Safety: none

Barrel length: 25.5 inches

Stock: 1-piece European walnut, split to allow Monte Carlo cheekpiece adjustment; hand-

WALTHER "PRONE 400" MATCH RIFLE (continued)

checkered match-type pistol grip; flat fore-end with sliding rail for palm rest or sling

Buttplate: metal with rubber recoil pad, adjustable for drop and length of pull

Overall length: 44.75 inches

Weight: 10.25 lbs.

Trigger pull: adjustable match type with basic pull of 7.0–21.0 oz. or 32.0–49.0 oz.

Sights: none provided as standard; purchaser can choose from wide variety of Walther or other match sights

Scope adaptability: target-scope bases provided

Caliber: .22 Long Rifle

Data: Left-hand stock available at extra cost.

Comment: Superbly designed and crafted target rifle for International Prone 400 competition.

WALTHER MOVING TARGET MATCH RIFLE

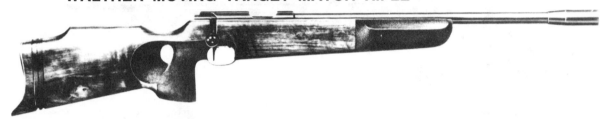

Manufacturer: Carl Walther Waffenfabrik, West Germany

Importer/distributor: Interarms

Action type: single-shot; bolt

Safety: none

Barrel length: 23.5 inches

Stock: 1-piece European walnut; thumb hole; hand checkering on oversized (match-style) pistol grip; comb adjustable for drop

Buttplate: metal with slight underarm hook; adjustable for drop and length of pull

Overall length: 42.0 inches

Weight: 8.3 lbs.

Trigger pull: match type with 18.0-oz. pull, which is standard for running-boar event

Sights: none provided as standard; purchaser can choose from variety of Walther or other fine sights

Scope adaptability: none, as rifle is intended for match in which scope is not used

Caliber: .22 Long Rifle

Data: Sliding barrel weight is provided. Left-hand stock available at extra cost.

Comment: A highly specialized rifle, designed just for the international running-boar target matches.

WINCHESTER M52D MATCH RIFLE

Action type: bolt

Safety: thumbpiece lever

Barrel length: 28.0 inches; free-floating

Stock: 1-piece American walnut; match type with no checkering; full uncapped pistol grip; accessory channel on bottom of fore-end; combined handstop and forward swivel

Buttplate: plastic with white plastic spacer

Overall length: 46.0 inches

Length of pull: 13.625 inches

Drop at comb: 0.25 inch (taken from bore centerline)

Drop at heel: none (taken from bore centerline)

Weight: 13.5 lbs.

Trigger pull: adjustable down to 16.0 oz.

Sight, rear: none; drilled and tapped for receiver sight

Sight, front: none; drilled and tapped for target sight

Scope adaptability: bases for target scope provided

Caliber: .22 Long Rifle only

Data: The M52 Winchester match rifle first appeared in 1919 when it was shown to shooters at Camp Caldwell, N.J. Sales began in the fall of 1920.

The original M52 had a standard-weight barrel of 9.5 to 10.0 lbs. The original stock resembled the M1903 Springfield N.R.A. Sporter type, with a forward barrel band. There are numerous variations and improvements. Three stock types are currently available.

M52s from 1919 to 1929 were fitted with what became known as the "slow lock." This term was not used until after the 1929 advent of the speed lock. The speed lock was redesigned in 1937.

M52A (1932–35). Receiver and locking lug were strengthened. This was probably due to the advent of high-velocity ammunition, though match shooters almost invariably use standard/match-velocity ammunition.

M52B (1935–47). A single-shot adaptor and adjustable sling swivel were added to the M52A.

M52C (1947–61). An easily adjustable vibration-free trigger system was installed.

M52D (1961–to date). Magazine and single-shot adaptor were replaced by a single-shot with loading platform. A free-floating barrel with adjustable bedding system replaced the previous fixed barrel. A handstop and adjustment channel were added to the new magazine-less stock.

M52 Sporting Rifle. See Chapter 17.

Comment: The M52 was the first successful .22 Long Rifle magazine match rifle. For nearly 40 years it was not challenged by any American as the king of the smallbore match rifles. Its chief competition today is the superb Remington 40-X series.

WINCHESTER M52D INTERNATIONAL MATCH RIFLE

Action type: bolt

Safety: thumbpiece lever

Barrel length: 28.0 inches; counter-bored muzzle lead-lapped

Stock: laminated international match style stock; thumb hole and full-hand pistol grip; aluminum combination handstop and forward sling swivel; long under-fore-end channel for accessories; adjustable palm-rest assembly meets International Shooting Union (ISU) specifications

Buttplate: aluminum; adjustable vertically and horizontally; underarm hook

Overall length: 44.5 inches to 46.5 inches

Length of pull: adjustable; 12.6 to 14.6 inches

Drop at comb: 0.0625 inch

WINCHESTER M52D INTERNATIONAL MATCH RIFLE
(continued)

Drop at Monte Carlo: 0.0625 inch

Drop at heel: 0.5625 inch

Trigger pull: adjustable nondrag trigger system; ISU trigger system or Kenyon trigger system available at extra cost

Sights: none supplied

Scope adaptability: scope blocks available at extra cost

Caliber: .22 Long Rifle only

Comment: This rifle, designed for international matches, is one of several such rifles, including Anschutz, Remington, and Walther. The M52D is as accurate as any. Price range $500 plus. Available on special order only.

WINCHESTER M52D INTERNATIONAL PRONE MATCH RIFLE

Action type: bolt; speed lock

Safety: thumbpiece lever

Barrel length: 28.0 inches; counter-bored muzzle

Stock: 1-piece walnut with high rollover comb; full pistol grip; uncheckered; accessory rail; combination handstop/front swivel

Buttplate: plastic with white line spacer

Overall length: 46.0 inches

Length of pull: 13.625 inches

Drop at center of cheekpiece: none

Drop at heel: 0.25 inch (taken from bore centerline)

Weight: 11.5 lbs.

Trigger pull: not specified

Sights: none

Scope adaptability: scope blocks furnished

Caliber: .22 Long Rifle only

Comment: This rifle, based on the M52D action, is designed for use in international prone matches. It is available on special order only.

CHAPTER / 14

LEVER-ACTION RIMFIRE RIFLES

The lever-action is the oldest rimfire magazine rifle. The first .22 rimfire lever-action was the Winchester M73 rifle designed specifically for the .22 Short and .22 Long cartridges. This model, introduced in 1884, was discontinued in 1904. There was one version for .22 Shorts and another version for the recently developed .22 Long. Cartridges were not interchangeable. Not quite 20,000 of these rifles were made. A few rifles were made on special order for the .22 Extra Long cartridge.

The M73 was an excellent rifle, but the M90 Winchester slide-action, designed by John Moses Browning, cut M73 sales. Most of that era's hunters preferred higher-powered rimfires like the .25 Stevens Long or .32 or .38 Stevens Long.

The most successful .22 rimfire lever-action rifle is the M39 Marlin, which has been around since 1891. It has been in continuous production, except during the two world wars, longer than any other American rifle, including the famed M94 Winchester.

For more than a half-century the Marlin M39 was the only lever-action rimfire rifle. Even Winchester, with which the term lever-action seems nearly synonymous, didn't have a rimfire lever-action on the market until a few years ago. After that, Browning and Ithaca brought out lever-actions. The Marlin, however, because of its fine reputation and lower price, will probably remain supreme. The Winchester M9422 presently costs more than the .30–30 M94.

The .22 rimfire lever-action has never been a very popular action. The slide-action, or pump, was the dominant .22 rimfire magazine rifle from the 1890s until the mid-1950s, when the semiautomatic took the lead.

All .22 rimfire lever-action rifles known to the author have exposed hammers and tubular magazines.

BROWNING BL-22 LEVER-ACTION RIFLE

Manufacturer: Miroku, Japan

Importer/distributor: Browning Arms

Action type: lever; exposed hammer

Magazine type: tubular; beneath barrel

Magazine capacity: .22 Short, 22-shot; .22 Long, 17-shot; .22 Long Rifle, 15-shot

BROWNING BL-22 LEVER-ACTION RIFLE (continued)

Ejection: side

Safety: half-cock hammer; disconnect system prevents firing during lever operating cycle; inertia firing pin prevents accidental firing due to blow on hammer

Barrel length: 20.0 inches; recessed muzzle

Stock: 2-piece walnut; no checkering on Grade I; checkered pistol grip and fore-end on Grade II

Buttplate: shotgun type; plastic

Overall length: 36.75 inches

Length of pull: 13.5 inches

Drop at comb: 1.625 inches

Drop at heel: 2.25 inches

Weight: 5.0 lbs.

Trigger pull: 5.0 lbs.

Sight, rear: folding leaf, crudely adjustable for elevation

Sight, front: bead

Scope adaptability: receiver grooved for tip-off mount

Caliber: .22 Short, .22 Long, .22 Long Rifle, .22 CB cap, .22 Long Rifle Shot

Data: Short-stroke lever (33°). Machined steel receiver.

Comment: This well-made lever-action carbine, like the Winchester M9422, is designed to resemble John M. Browning's M94. The designer was Val Browning.

ITHACA M72 SADDLEGUN

Manufacturer: Erma Werke, West Germany

Importer/distributor: Ithacagun

Action type: lever; exposed hammer

Magazine type: tubular; beneath barrel

Magazine capacity: 15-shot

Safety: rebound hammer

Barrel length: 18.5 inches

Stock: 2-piece walnut; uncheckered; barrel band on fore-end

Buttplate: shotgun type; plastic

Overall length: 35.125 inches

Length of pull: 13.5 inches

Drop at comb: 1.75 inches

Drop at heel: 2.5 inches

Weight: 5.5 lbs.

Trigger pull: 5.0 lbs.

Sight, rear: Rocky Mountain, crudely adjustable for windage and elevation

Sight, front: bead on ramp with removable sight protector

Scope adaptability: grooved for tip-off mount

Caliber: .22 Long Rifle (.22 Short and .22 Long will not function through action)

Comment: This is an excellent lever-action rimfire rifle. It compares in quality and price with the Winchester M9422.

MARLIN GOLDEN M39A/M39M LEVER-ACTION RIFLE/CARBINE

Marlin Model 39A

Marlin Model 39M

Action type: lever; exposed hammer

Magazine type: tubular; beneath barrel

Magazine capacity:

M39A: .22 Short, 26-shot; .22 Long, 21-shot; .22 Long Rifle, 19-shot

M39M: .22 Short, 21-shot; .22 Long, 16-shot; .22 Long Rifle, 15-shot

Ejection: side

Safety: half-cock hammer

Barrel length: M39A, 24.0 inches; M39M, 20.0 inches

Stock: 2-piece American walnut; uncheckered; plastic pistol-grip cap with white line spacer on M39A; straight grip on M39M; fluted comb on both

Buttplate: shotgun type; black plastic with white line spacer

Overall length: M39A, 40.0 inches; M39M, 36.0 inches

Length of pull: 13.625 inches

Drop at comb: 1.75 inches

Drop at heel: 2.6 inches

Weight: M39A, 6.75 lbs.; M39M, 6.1 lbs.

Trigger pull: 5.0 lbs.

Sight, rear: Rocky Mountain, crudely adjustable for elevation

Sight, front: bead on ramp; Wide-Scan (extra view) head

Scope adaptability: solid-top receiver drilled and tapped for scope mount (or receiver sight); scope adapter base; offset hammer is furnished for convenience when scope is attached

Caliber: .22 Short, .22 Long, .22 Long Rifle

Data: This is the most popular lever-action .22 rimfire rifle/carbine. Designed by John Marlin, it has been on the market longer than any other

MARLIN GOLDEN M39AF/M39M
LEVER-ACTION RIFLE/CARBINE (continued)

American centerfire or rimfire rifle. It is three years older than John M. Browning's famed M94. All other current lever-actions have been on the market for less than 10 years. Early models were solid frame, but the takedown version (U.S. Patent #584,177), designed by Lewis Hopburn, is dated June, 1897.

Comment: This is one of the best .22 rimfire rifle/carbines made to date. It is the only .22 lever-action designed to accommodate full-diameter (1.0-inch) scope rings as well as the smaller 0.875-inch mounts that are standard for .22 caliber.

WINCHESTER M9422/M9422M LEVER-ACTION CARBINE

Action type: lever; hammer

Magazine type: tubular; beneath barrel

Magazine capacity: .22 Short, 21-shot; .22 Long, 17-shot; .22 Long Rifle, 15-shot; .22 W.M.R. (M9422M only), 11-shot

Safety: half-cock hammer; 2-piece firing mechanism operates only when action is fully closed and locked

Barrel length: 20.5 inches

Stock: 2-piece American walnut; straight carbine stock; no checkering; barrel band near front of fore-end

Buttplate: shotgun type; plastic

Overall length: 37.125 inches

Length of pull: 13.5 inches

Drop at comb: 1.75 inches

Drop at heel: 2.5 inches

Weight: 6.25 lbs.

Trigger pull: not specified

Sight, rear: Rocky Mountain, crudely adjustable for elevation

Sight, front: white bead on ramp with detachable head

Scope adaptability: grooved for tip-off mount

Caliber: .22 Short, .22 Long, .22 Long Rifle; .22 W.M.R. in M9422M only

Data: This is a rimfire version of the famed M94 Winchester carbine. A major design variation is the solid top and side ejection, which makes for easy and conventional scope mounting. Forged steel receiver.

Comment: It is a wonder that Winchester, with the great popularity of the M94, waited for more than half a century before bringing out the M9422. The author prefers the M9422/M9422M over its competitors, but this personal view does not mean that the others are not well worth their cost.

CHAPTER 15

SLIDE-ACTION RIMFIRE RIFLES

The slide-action was the first .22 rimfire design of which two models both nearly approached the million mark in sales.

The first successful rimfire slide-action, or pump-action, rifle was designed by John Moses Browning and his brother Matthew. U.S. Patent #385,238 was issued to the Brownings on June 26, 1888. They assigned rights to Winchester for a payment taken partly in cash and partly in arms and ammunition for their store. First delivery to the warehouse of the "Winchester 22 Caliber Repeating Rifle Model 1890" was on December 1, 1890. When manufacture was discontinued on December 31, 1932, about 850,000 had been sold. There was sufficient stock on hand to advertise the rifle until 1941.

The M90, prototype of millions to come, had a tubular magazine beneath the 24.0-inch octagonal barrel. The first 15,500 rifles were solid-frame. The takedown was introduced in late 1892. The solid frame was discontinued shortly afterward. In those days .22 rimfire rifles did not chamber .22 Short, Long, and Long Rifle cartridges interchangeably. There was a Winchester M90 chambered for each of those cartridges plus the .22 Winchester Rimfire. The magazine and feed mechanism was designed for one specific chambering. The .22 W.R.F. cartridge—a super .22 Long Rifle—was specifically developed for the rifle. The .22 Long Rifle chambering was added in 1919.

The M90 was the most popular slide-action rifle ever made. The M90 and its sales were closely followed by the M06 slide-action (1906–32), which sold about a thousand less than the M90. The M06 used the M90 action. It was fitted with a 20.0-inch round barrel. Originally chambered for the .22 Short cartridge only, Winchester decided in 1908 to broaden its cartridge capacity and in that year it became the first .22 slide-action rifle to chamber interchangeably the .22 Short (15 cartridges), .22 Long (12 cartridges) and .22 Long Rifle (11 cartridges).

The M06 was replaced in 1932 by the M62. This used the M90 action, but the crescent rifle-type butt was changed to the flat shotgun-type. Magazine capacity was increased by lengthening the barrel to 23.0 inches. The rifling was changed to provide greater stability and accuracy for the interchangeable use of Short, Long, and Long Rifle cartridges. In 1940 the M62-A, incorporating several modifications to the action, was released. The M62/M62-A was discontinued in 1958 after more than 400,000 had been sold.

The biggest single source of M90, M06, and M62 sales was the thousands of shooting galleries. It is a testimonial to these rifles, which once sold for little more than $10, that many of them had more than 250,000 rounds poured through their barrels. Some fired more than 500,000 rounds. The M62, nearly 20 years after its discontinuance, is still found by the thousands in shooting galleries. Gallery owners prefer the exposed-hammer to hammerless models.

The first successful hammerless .22 rimfire slide-action rifle was designed by the noted firearms designer John Pedersen, born in Denmark but long a Wyoming resident. The M12 Remington (1909–36) was succeeded by the M121 Fieldmaster (1936–54). The M572 Fieldmaster, introduced in 1955, is still on the market.

Winchester, in response to demands created by its Remington competition, developed the hammerless slide-action M61 in 1932. It was discontinued in 1962 after slightly fewer than 350,000 had been made. The M61 was replaced in 1963 by the M270 hammerless slide-action, which was discontinued in 1974.

The hammerless slide-action was never as popular as the exposed-hammer version. Since the flooding of the .22 rimfire market with numerous semiautomatics, slide-action sales are down to such an extent that only three makes are currently on the market. One of these, Garcia's Rossi Gallery Model (made in Brazil), is a reproduction of the Winchester M90. The second is

High Standard's Flite-King, a pump not unlike the Remington. The third is the Remington M572 Fieldmaster itself, which still survives in its standard form plus a deluxe edition and a smoothbore version with the barrel choked for .22 Long Rifle shot cartridges.

GARCIA-ROSSI GALLERY MODEL RIFLE

Manufacturer: Rossi Arms, Brazil

Importer/distributor: Garcia Corp./Firearms International

Action type: slide; exposed hammer

Magazine type: tubular; beneath barrel

Magazine capacity: .22 Short, 20-shot; .22 Long, 16-shot; .22 Long Rifle, 13-shot; .22 W.R.M., 10-shot (in Magnum rifle only; cannot be used interchangeably in rifle chambered for standard .22 cartridges)

Ejection: side

Safety: half-cock hammer

Barrel length: 24.0 inches

Stock: 2-piece walnut; straight grip; ribbed classic fore-end

Buttplate: shotgun type; steel

Overall length: 42.0 inches

Length of pull: 13.125 inches

Drop at comb: 2.0 inches

Drop at heel: 2.125 inches

Weight: 5.25 lbs.

Trigger pull: 4.5 lbs.

Sight, rear: Rocky Mountain, crudely adjustable for windage and elevation

Sight, front: bead

Caliber: .22 Short, .22 Long, .22 Long Rifle, interchangeably; .22 W.R.M. in special chambering

Data: Unlike most of today's rifles, this is not a solid-frame model but a quick-takedown rifle.

Comment: This is a replica of the Winchester M90 slide-action rifle.

HIGH STANDARD M6006 FLITE-KING SLIDE-ACTION RIFLE

Action type: slide; hammerless

Magazine type: tubular

Magazine capacity: .22 Short, 24-shot; .22 Long, 19-shot; .22 Long Rifle, 17-shot

Ejection: side

Safety: crossbolt

Barrel length: 24.0 inches

Stock: 2-piece American walnut; impressed checkering on pistol grip; plastic pistol-grip cap with white line spacer; slight Monte Carlo; fluted comb; fore-end (slide handle) uncheckered but vertically grooved for finger traction

High Standard M6006 Flite-King

Buttplate: shotgun type; black plastic with white line spacer

Overall length: 41.75 inches

Length of pull: 14.0 inches

Drop at comb: 1.5 inches

Drop at Monte Carlo: 1.5 inches

Drop at heel: 2.8 inches

Weight: 5.5 lbs.

Trigger pull: 4.5 lbs.

Sight, rear: Rocky Mountain, crudely adjustable for windage

Sight, front: post

Scope adaptability: receiver grooved for tip-off mount

Caliber: .22 Short, .22 Long, .22 Long Rifle

Data: Only current .22 pump rifle with a "compromise" stock—a slight Monte Carlo comb elevation—to position the shooter's eye a little better when using a scope. The pump-handle fore-end is a bit fuller than those on competitors. In fact, it's advertised as "semi-beavertail." While that designation may smack of advertising exaggeration, for a shooter with man-sized hands the fore-end may be more comfortable than those on some rimfire rifles. The Flite-King also has a larger magazine capacity than other current slide .22s.

Comment: This High Standard is rather similar in appearance and operation to the Remington M572 and is in the same price bracket. Though the prices of rimfire rifles have soared in recent years, these are reasonable by comparison with many rimfire repeaters employing other types of actions.

REMINGTON M572 FIELDMASTER SLIDE-ACTION SERIES

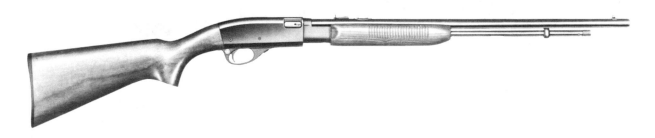

Action type: slide; hammerless

Magazine type: tubular

Magazine capacity: .22 Short, 20-shot; .22 Long, 17-shot; .22 Long Rifle, 14-shot; .22 Long Rifle Shot (smoothbore version), 14-shot

EXPLODED VIEW OF REMINGTON M572 FIELDMASTER SLIDE-ACTION RIFLE

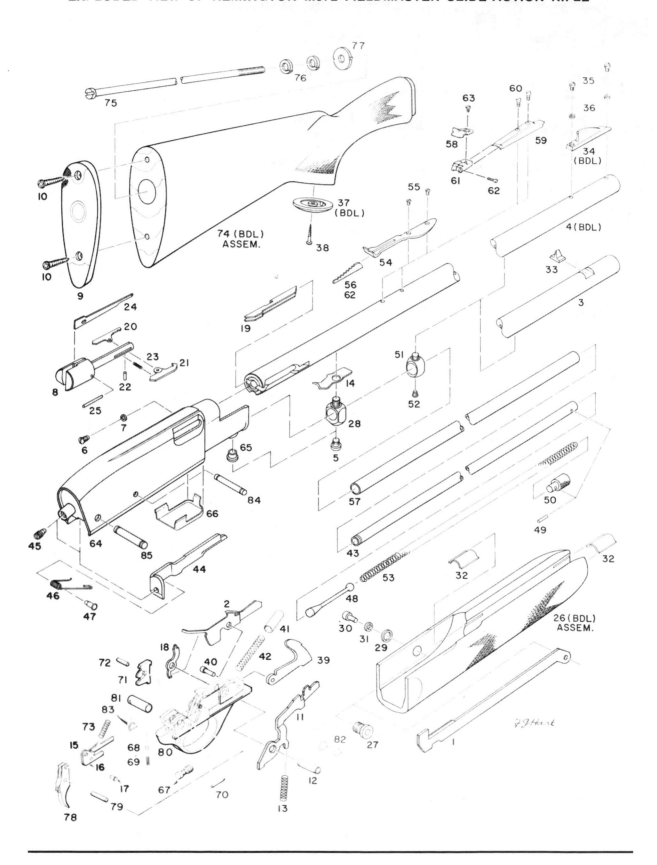

REMINGTON M572 FIELDMASTER (continued)

Ejection: side

Safety: crossbolt

Barrel length: 24.0 inches

Stock: 2-piece American walnut; uncheckered pistol-grip and fore-end on M572A; M572 BDL (DeLuxe) has checkered pistol grip and fore-end; sling swivels and sling available at extra cost

Buttplate: shotgun type; plastic

Overall length: 42.0 inches

Length of pull: 13.5 inches

Drop at comb: 1.5 inches

Drop at heel: 2.5 inches

Weight: 5.5 lbs.

Trigger pull: 4.5 lbs.

Sight, rear: Rocky Mountain, crudely adjustable for elevation

Sight, front: blade; M572 BDL has blade on ramp

Scope adaptability: receiver grooved for tip-off mount

Caliber: .22 Short, .22 Long, .22 Long Rifle, .22 Long Rifle Shot (smoothbore only)

Data: In addition to M572 Fieldmaster (standard) and M572 BDL (deluxe version, also described above in specifications), this Remington series includes the M572 SB. The "SB" stands for smoothbore—a special barrel choked for use with .22 LR shot cartridges. This version is sold at the same price as the M572 BDL.

Comment: An excellent rifle for those who like the slide-action for small-game hunting and plinking.

Parts List for Remington M572 Fieldmaster

No.	Part Name	No.	Part Name	No.	Part Name
1	Action Bar	29	Fore-end Nut	57	Outer Magazine Tube
2	Action Bar Lock	30	Fore-end Screw	58	Rear Sight Aperture, BDL Grade
3	Barrel	31	Fore-end Screw Lock Washer	59	Rear Sight Base. BDL Grade
4	Barrel, BDL Grade	32	Fore-end Support	60	Rear Sight Base Screw, BDL Grade
5	Barrel Lock Screw	33	Front Sight	61	Rear Sight Slide, BDL Grade
6	Barrel Dowel Screw	34	Front Sight, BDL Grade	62	Elevation Screw, BDL Grade
7	Barrel Dowel Screw Washer	35	Front Sight Screw	63	Windage Screw, BDL Grade
8	Bolt	36	Front Sight Washer	64	Receiver
9	Butt Plate	37	Grip Cap, BDL Grade	65	Receiver Bushing
10	Butt Plate Screw	38	Grip Cap Screw	66	Receiver Cover
11	Carrier	39	Hammer	67	Safety
12	Carrier Pivot Tube	40	Hammer Pin	68	Safety Detent Ball
13	Carrier Spring	41	Hammer Plunger	69	Safety Spring
14	Cartridge Ramp	42	Hammer Spring	70	Safety Spring Retaining Pin
15	Connector, Left	43	Inner Magazine Tube	71	Sear
16	Connector, Right	44	Locking Bar	72	Sear Pin
17	Connector Pin	45	Locking Bar Retaining Screw	73	Sear Spring
18	Disconnector	46	Locking Bar Spring	74	Stock Assembly, BDL Grade
19	Ejector	47	Locking Bar Spring Stud	75	Stock Bolt
20	Extractor, Left	48	Magazine Follower	76	Stock Bolt Lock Washer
21	Extractor, Right	49	Magazine Pin	77	Stock Bolt Washer
22	Extractor Pin	50	Magazine Plug	78	Trigger
23	Extractor Spring	51	Magazine Ring	79	Trigger Pin
24	Firing Pin	52	Magazine Screw	80	Trigger Plate, R. H.
25	Firing Pin Retaining Pin	53	Magazine Spring	81	Trigger Plate Pin Bushing, Rear
26	Fore-end Assembly, BDL Grade	54	Open Sight Leaf	82	Trigger Plate Pin Detent Spring, Front
27	Fore-end Escutcheon	55	Open Sight Screw	83	Trigger Plate Pin Detent Spring, Rear
28	Fore-end Hanger	56	Open Sight Step	84	Trigger Plate Pin, Front
				85	Trigger Plate Pin, Rear

CHAPTER 16

SEMIAUTOMATIC RIMFIRE RIFLES

The semiautomatic—a slow starter in terms of popularity—is today's favorite rimfire rifle action. There are more than twice as many semiautomatic rimfire rifles as there are of any one other action type.

The first rimfire semiautomatic was the Winchester M03 (1904–32). About 126,000 M03s were sold despite the handicap of being chambered for an oddball cartridge—the .22 Winchester Automatic Rimfire cartridge. The M03 was, like all other .22 rimfires, a straight blowback action. The rifle had a 20.0-inch round barrel. The tubular buttstock magazine held 10 cartridges. The rifle was designed by Thomas Crossley Johnson, a longtime Winchester designer.

The second rimfire semiautomatic was a John Moses Browning design. Patented in 1913, the rifle was made by Fabrique Nationale d'Armes de Guerre from 1914 to December 31, 1957. More than 200,000 were made. At that time, Remington having discontinued its American version of the Browning, FN continued making the rifle for sale in America and elsewhere. (The original FN model had not been sold in America, while the Remington version was made under license.)

The second rifle to appear on the American scene was the Remington Model C (1914–28). This rifle, chambered for a special .22 load, the .22 Remington Autoloading cartridge, was designed by a C. H. Barnes.

In 1922 Remington commenced manufacturing the Browning semiautomatic, designated the M24 (1922–34). It had a 19.0-inch barrel and was chambered for .22 Short, .22 Long, and .22 Long Rifle, interchangeably.

In 1934 Remington modified the M24 to handle both standard and Remington Hi-Speed cartridges. Barrel length was 24.0 inches. The new designation was M241 (1935–51).

In 1933 Winchester, in response to customer demand for a semiautomatic chambered for the .22 Long Rifle and other standard .22 rimfire cartridges, brought out the M63. This was a modified and improved M03. It was discontinued in 1958 after about 175,000 had been made.

During World War II, Harrington & Richardson developed the .22 semiautomatic "General." This was based in part on the M50 and M55 submachine gun, designed by Eugene Reising, that was chambered for the .45 ACP cartridge.

The General was soon retired. It was too heavy and too expensive for kids. Of excellent design and workmanship, it was ahead of its time.

In the late 1950s and early 1960s the rimfire market became inundated with .22 semiautomatic rifles. The ones currently available are described in this chapter.

Semiautomatic rimfires come in three magazine types: tubular magazine in stock, tubular magazine under barrel (this popular type was inherited from the beneath-the-barrel magazine of lever and pump rifles; it provides greater magazine capacity than does any other type), and detachable box magazine, better known as the "clip."

Semiautomatic rimfire rifles currently range in price from about $60 to more than $150.

BROWNING .22 AUTOLOADING RIFLE

Manufacturer: Fabrique Nationale, Belgium

Importer/distributor: Browning Arms

Action type: semiautomatic; locked breech

Magazine type: tubular; in stock

Magazine capacity: .22 Short, 16-shot; .22 Long Rifle, 11-shot

Ejection: bottom

Safety: crossbolt (right); left-hand optional at no extra charge

Barrel length: .22 Short, 22.0 inches; .22 Long Rifle, 19.25 inches

Stock: 2-piece walnut; checkered pistol grip and fore-end.

Buttplate: shotgun type; plastic

Overall length: 22.0-inch barrel, 40.0 inches; 19.25-inch barrel, 37.0 inches

Length of pull: 13.75 inches

Drop at comb: 1.1875 inches

Drop at heel: 1.625 inches

Weight: .22 Short, 4.75 lbs.; .22 Long Rifle, 4.92 lbs.

Trigger pull: 5.0 lbs.

Sight, rear: folding leaf, crudely adjustable

Sight, front: white bead

Scope adaptability: barrel drilled and tapped to accept special Browning barrel mount base or 2-base ring mounts

Caliber: .22 Short, .22 Long Rifle

Data: This rifle, designed by John Moses Browning, has been in continuous production longer than any other semiautomatic .22 rimfire rifle, and it may be the most popular. It is an unusual design in that most .22 semiautomatic rifles are of the blowback type with an unlocked breech. This rifle has a non-mechanically locked action in which recoil operates the breechblock.

Comment: The lightweight, sleek lines and reliability of this semiautomatic have combined to keep it in production for more than 60 years. No other semiautomatic .22 rimfire rifle has been in production for half as long. It is the only semiautomatic .22 rimfire rifle to achieve worldwide use.

Designer Browning's original working model is in the Utah National Guard's John M. Browning Armory, Ogden, Utah.

CHARTER ARMS AR-7 EXPLORER CARBINE

Action type: straight blowback; unlocked breech

Magazine type: detachable straight-line box

Magazine capacity: 8-shot

Safety: lever

Barrel length: 16.0 inches; alloy with steel liner

Stock: high-impact plastic, barrel readily unscrews from alloy receiver and stows in watertight flotation stock; hollow stock has full pistol grip

Buttplate: plastic trap door opens to allow stock insertion

Length of pull: 13.75 inches

Drop at comb: 2.0 inches

Drop at heel: 2.25 inches

Weight: 2.75 lbs.

Trigger pull: 6.0-7.0 lbs.

Sight, rear: U-slot

Sight, front: blade

Caliber: .22 Long Rifle

Comment: This ingenious survival rifle was designed by the Armalite Corporation, whose Eugene Stoner once designed the AR-15/M16 weapons series and another similar series for the Cadillac Gauge Corp. The unit floats and is accurate enough to take small game.

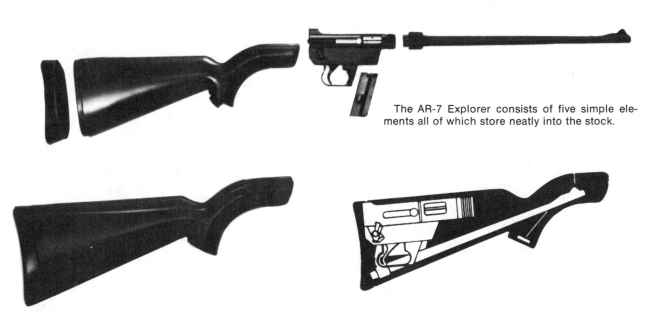

The AR-7 Explorer consists of five simple elements all of which store neatly into the stock.

The interior of the AR-7 Explorer stock stores the action, the magazine and barrel.

HECKLER & KOCH (HK) M300 SEMIAUTOMATIC .22 MAGNUM

Manufacturer: Heckler & Koch, West Germany

Importer/distributor: Security Arms Co.

Action type: semiauto; blowback

Magazine type: detachable straight-line box

Magazine capacity: 5-shot

Safety: sliding lever, left side of triggerbow

Barrel length: 19.7 inches

Stock: 1-piece European walnut; checkered (16 lines per inch) pistol grip and fore-end; Schnabel fore-tip; cheekpiece with European-style smallbore rifle comb; sling swivels

Buttplate: shotgun type; plastic with white line spacer

Overall length: 39.5 inches

Length of pull: 13.5 inches

Drop at comb: 1.75 inches

Drop at heel: 3.25 inches

Weight: 5.75 lbs.

Trigger pull: 3.5 lbs. (single-stage trigger)

Sight, rear: sporting, crudely adjustable for windage

Sight, front: bead on ramp

Scope adaptability: rifle fitted with base part of HK05 mount; scope part of clamp costs extra; standard American scope rings will also fit base mount

Caliber: .22 W.R.M.

Data: Part of trigger-guard and trigger assembly are plastic and sheet-metal stampings. The plastic is not as bad-looking as it sounds, but a rifle costing $200 plus (without scope bases) should have machined steel parts even though the price would have to go up.

Comment: A well-made rifle and quite accurate. The author fired 20 5-shot groups with average group of 1.35 inches. This rifle and the Marlin are the only two semiautomatic rifles chambered for the .22 W.M.R. At press time Security Arms had, at least for the present, discontinued importing the Heckler & Koch rifle.

HIGH STANDARD M6005 SPORT KING SEMIAUTOMATIC RIFLE

Action type: semiautomatic

Magazine type: tubular; beneath barrel

Magazine capacity: .22 Short, 21-shot; .22 Long, 17-shot; .22 Long Rifle, 15-shot

Ejection: side

Safety: thumb slide

Barrel length: 22.25 inches

Stock: 1-piece American walnut; impressed checkering on pistol grip; black plastic pistol-grip cap with white line spacer; slight Monte Carlo; fluted comb

Buttplate: shotgun type; black plastic with white line spacer

Overall length: 42.75 inches

Length of pull: 14.0 inches

Drop at comb: 1.5 inches

Drop at Monte Carlo: 1.5 inches

Drop at heel: 2.8 inches

Weight: 5.5 lbs.

Trigger pull: 4.5 lbs.

Sight, rear: Rocky Mountain, crudely adjustable for windage

Sight, front: post

Scope adaptability: receiver grooved for tip-off mount

Caliber: .22 Short, .22 Long, .22 Long Rifle

Comment: A good, reliable, low-priced rimfire semiauto.

MARLIN GLENFIELD M60 SEMIAUTOMATIC RIFLE

Action type: semiauto

Magazine type: tubular; beneath barrel

Magazine capacity: 18-shot

Ejection: side

Safety: crossbolt

Barrel length: 22.0 inches

Stock: 1-piece walnut-stained hardwood; impressed checkering; uncapped pistol grip

Buttplate: plastic

Overall length: 40.5 inches

Length of pull: 13.625 inches

Drop at comb: 1.75 inches

Drop at heel: 2.6 inches

Weight: 5.5 lbs.

Trigger pull: not specified

Sight, rear: Rocky Mountain, crudely adjustable for windage

Sight, front: white metal bead

Scope adaptability: nonglare receiver top grooved for tip-off mount

Caliber: .22 Long Rifle

Data: Chrome-plated trigger. Rustproof (alloy) receiver.

Comment: This is Marlin's economy version of the tubular-magazine semiautomatic Marlin M49.

MARLIN M49DL SEMIAUTOMATIC RIFLE

Action type: semiauto; blowback; bolt-hold-open mechanism

Magazine type: tubular; beneath barrel

Magazine capacity: 18-shot

Ejection: side

Safety: crossbolt

Barrel length: 22.0 inches; Micro-Groove (16 grooves)

Stock: 1-piece American walnut; checkered pistol grip and fore-end; plastic pistol-grip cap with white line spacer

Buttplate: shotgun type; plastic (curved) with white line spacer

Overall length: 40.5 inches

Length of pull: 13.625 inches

Drop at comb: 1.75 inches

Drop at heel: 2.6 inches

Weight: 5.5 lbs.

Trigger pull: 5.0 lbs.

Sight, rear: Rocky Mountain, crudely adjustable for elevation

Sight, front: blade

Scope adaptability: receiver grooved for tip-off mount

Caliber: .22 Long Rifle

Comment: Typical semiautomatic tubular-magazine rifle of good design and quality.

MARLIN M99C SEMIAUTOMATIC RIFLE

Action type: semiauto; blowback; bolt-hold-open mechanism

Magazine type: tubular; beneath barrel

Magazine capacity: 18-shot

Ejection: side

Safety: crossbolt

Barrel length: 22.0 inches; Micro-Groove

Stock: 1-piece American walnut; impressed checkering on uncapped pistol grip and fore-end; high-gloss finish

Buttplate: shotgun type; plastic (curved) with white line spacer

Overall length: 40.5 inches

Length of pull: 13.75 inches

Drop at comb: 1.75 inches

Drop at Monte Carlo: 1.75 inches

Drop at heel: 2.5 inches

Weight: 5.5 lbs.

Trigger pull: 5.0 lbs.

Sight, rear: Rocky Mountain, crudely adjustable for elevation

Sight, front: blade on ramp

Scope adaptability: receiver grooved for tip-off mount

Caliber: .22 Long Rifle

Comment: A medium-price semiautomatic rifle suitable for plinking or close-range small-game shooting. Marlin offers (at extra cost) its M300B 4× scope for this rifle.

Marlin 99M1

MARLIN M99M1 AUTOLOADER

Action type: semiauto; blowback; unlocked breech

Magazine type: tubular; inside fore-end

Magazine capacity: 9-shot

Safety: crossbolt

Barrel length: 18.0 inches; Micro-Groove

Stock: 1-piece American walnut; upper barrel guard; uncheckered; uncapped pistol grip; barrel band on fore-end; sling swivels

Buttplate: shotgun type; black plastic with white line spacer

Overall length: 37.0 inches

Length of pull: 13.75 inches

Drop at comb: 1.75 inches

Drop at Monte Carlo: 1.75 inches

Drop at heel: 2.5 inches

Weight: 4.5 lbs.

Trigger pull: 5.0 lbs.

Sight, rear: adjustable for elevation; removable for sight base placement

Sight, front: blade on ramp

Scope adaptability: receiver grooved for tip-off mount

Caliber: .22 Long Rifle

Comment: This copy of the U.S. Carbine, Cal. .30 M1, has a tubular magazine inside the stock. The magazine tube is loaded as are slide-action magazines, from the front. This is a light, fairly accurate rifle for plinking or rabbit shooting.

MARLIN M782 MAGNUM AUTOLOADER

Action type: semiauto; straight blowback; unlocked breech

Magazine type: detachable straight-line box

Magazine capacity: 7-shot

Safety: thumb slide

Barrel length: 22.0 inches; Micro-Groove

Stock: 1-piece American walnut; reverse checkering on pistol grip and fore-end; uncapped pistol grip; sling swivels; leather carrying strap; Mar-Shield finish

Buttplate: shotgun type; plastic with white line spacer

Overall length: 41.0 inches

Length of pull: 13.75 inches

Drop at comb: 1.5 inches

Drop at Monte Carlo: 2.0 inches

Drop at heel: 2.5 inches

Weight: 6.0 lbs.

Trigger pull: 5.0 lbs.

Sight, rear: folding semi-buckhorn, crudely adjustable for elevation

Sight, front: brass bead on ramp

Scope adaptability: receiver grooved for tip-off mount

Caliber: .22 W.R.M.

Comment: This is the only current American-made autoloader chambered for the .22 W.R.M. cartridge. Such a rifle has long been overdue.

The only other .22 W.R.M. autoloader known to the author is the very fine Heckler & Koch HK-M300. The latter costs three times as much as the Marlin. It is a superior rifle but the accuracy difference is not that great.

MARLIN M989M2 AUTOLOADER

Action type: semiauto; straight blowback; unlocked breech

Magazine type: detachable straight-line box

Magazine capacity: 7-shot

Safety: crossbolt

Barrel length: 18.0 inches; Micro-Groove

Stock: 1-piece American walnut with upper handguard; uncheckered; Monte Carlo comb; uncapped pistol grip; sling swivels

Buttplate: shotgun type; plastic with white line spacer

Overall length: 37.0 inches

Length of pull: 13.5 inches

Drop at comb: 1.5 inches

Drop at Monte Carlo: 2.0 inches

Drop at heel: 2.5 inches

Weight: 4.5 lbs.

Trigger pull: 5.0 lbs.

Sight, rear: removable sight, adjustable for windage and elevation

Sight, front: blade on ramp

Scope adaptability: receiver grooved for tip-off mount

Caliber: .22 Long Rifle

Comment: This carbine is identical to the Marlin M99M1 except for magazine type.

MOSSBERG M353 AUTO CARBINE

Action type: semiauto; straight blowback; unlocked breech

Magazine type: detachable straight-line box

Magazine capacity: 7-shot

Safety: crossbolt

Barrel length: 18.0 inches; AC-KRO-GRUV

Stock: 1-piece American walnut; reverse checkering on pistol grip and fore-end; extension fore-end of plastic (Tenite) flips down to serve as pistol grip or monopod; very slight Monte Carlo

Buttplate: shotgun type; plastic with white line spacer

Overall length: 38.0 inches

Length of pull: 14.0 inches

Drop at comb: 1.5 inches

Drop at heel: 2.5 inches

Weight: 5.0 lbs.

Trigger pull: not specified

Sight, rear: Rocky Mountain, crudely adjustable for elevation

Sight, front: bead on ramp

Scope adaptability: receiver grooved for tip-off mount

Caliber: .22 Long Rifle

Comment: An inexpensive .22 autoloader designed for plinking and hunting small game at moderate ranges.

REMINGTON NYLON M66 SERIES RIFLE

Action type: semiauto; blowback

Magazine type: tubular; in buttstock

Magazine capacity: .22 Long Rifle, 14-shot; .22 Short (Gallery Model), 15-shot

Ejection: side

Safety: slide (top tang)

Barrel length: 19.625 inches

Stock: 2-piece nylon (Dupont Zytel); plastic white diamond inlay both sides of fore-end; checkered pistol grip and fore-end; white line spacer with pistol-grip cap

Buttplate: shotgun type; plastic with white line spacer

Overall length: 38.5 inches

Length of pull: 13.625 inches

Drop at comb: 2.0 inches

Drop at heel: 2.25 inches

Weight: 4.0 lbs.

Trigger pull: 4.5 lbs.

Sight, rear: Rocky Mountain, crudely adjustable for elevation

Sight, front: blade

Scope adaptability: receiver grooved for tip-off mount

Caliber: .22 Long Rifle, .22 Short (Gallery Model)

Data: Zytel nylon is lighter than a walnut stock of identical dimensions. It is extremely durable and, unlike wood, will not warp. It doesn't look traditional but it is functional.

M66 nylon variations:

1. MB (Mohawk Brown) has a brown stock and blued barrel.

2. AB (Apache Black) has a black stock with chromed barrel and receiver.

3. GS (Gallery Special) fires .22 Shorts only.

Any of the above may be obtained with installed sling and sling swivel at extra cost. A 4× scope is available at extra cost for the MB model.

Comment: Nearly everyone familiar with this rifle knows the durability of the stock; its color does not fade and it does not crack or chip. What is not as well known is the reliability of the rifle. The M66 rifle established a world's record for breaking wooden blocks. No malfunctions occurred while 100,010 aerial targets (wooden blocks) were fired at. Only six blocks were missed—a total of 100,004 hits. This extremely rugged and reliable rifle is fine for kids—or for adults who frequently tote a rimfire rifle in a pickup truck or jeep or who take a rifle along on canoe voyages or horse-packing trips.

EXPLODED VIEW OF REMINGTON NYLON 22 CALIBER AUTOLOADER.

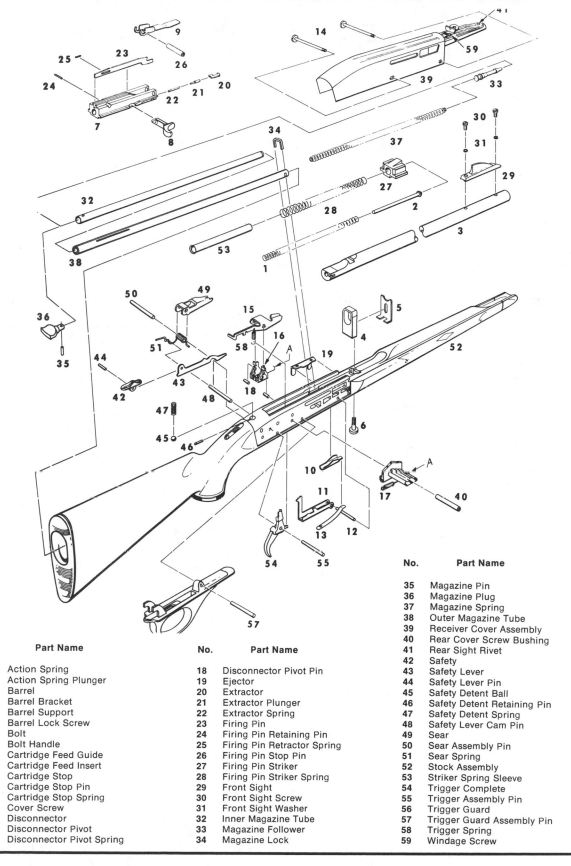

No.	Part Name
1	Action Spring
2	Action Spring Plunger
3	Barrel
4	Barrel Bracket
5	Barrel Support
6	Barrel Lock Screw
7	Bolt
8	Bolt Handle
9	Cartridge Feed Guide
10	Cartridge Feed Insert
11	Cartridge Stop
12	Cartridge Stop Pin
13	Cartridge Stop Spring
14	Cover Screw
15	Disconnector
16	Disconnector Pivot
17	Disconnector Pivot Spring

No.	Part Name
18	Disconnector Pivot Pin
19	Ejector
20	Extractor
21	Extractor Plunger
22	Extractor Spring
23	Firing Pin
24	Firing Pin Retaining Pin
25	Firing Pin Retractor Spring
26	Firing Pin Stop Pin
27	Firing Pin Striker
28	Firing Pin Striker Spring
29	Front Sight
30	Front Sight Screw
31	Front Sight Washer
32	Inner Magazine Tube
33	Magazine Follower
34	Magazine Lock

No.	Part Name
35	Magazine Pin
36	Magazine Plug
37	Magazine Spring
38	Outer Magazine Tube
39	Receiver Cover Assembly
40	Rear Cover Screw Bushing
41	Rear Sight Rivet
42	Safety
43	Safety Lever
44	Safety Lever Pin
45	Safety Detent Ball
46	Safety Detent Retaining Pin
47	Safety Detent Spring
48	Safety Lever Cam Pin
49	Sear
50	Sear Assembly Pin
51	Sear Spring
52	Stock Assembly
53	Striker Spring Sleeve
54	Trigger Complete
55	Trigger Assembly Pin
56	Trigger Guard
57	Trigger Guard Assembly Pin
58	Trigger Spring
59	Windage Screw

REMINGTON M552 SPEEDMASTER SERIES

Action type: semiauto; blowback

Magazine type: tubular; beneath barrel

Magazine capacity: .22 Short, 20-shot; .22 Long, 17-shot; .22 Long Rifle, 15-shot

Ejection: side

Safety: crossbolt

Barrel length: rifle, 23.0 inches; carbine, 21.0 inches

Stock: 1-piece American walnut with uncapped pistol grip; M552 BDL (DeLuxe) version has impressed checkering and high-gloss DuPont RK-W finish; sling and sling swivels available at extra cost

Buttplate: shotgun type; plastic

Overall length: rifle, 42.0 inches; carbine, 40.0 inches

Length of pull: 13.625 inches

Drop at comb: 1.625 inches

Drop at heel: 2.625 inches

Weight: rifle, 5.75 lbs.; carbine, 5.5 lbs.

Trigger pull: 4.5 lbs.

Sight, rear: Rocky Mountain, crudely adjustable for elevation

Sight, front: bead

Scope adaptability: receiver grooved for tip-off mount

Caliber: .22 Short, .22 Long, .22 Long Rifle

Data: M552 series variations:
1. M552A (rifle).
2. M552C (carbine).
3. M552 BDL (DeLuxe) rifle has checkered pistol grip and fore-end, DuPont RK-W high-gloss finish, blade ramp front sight, and windage adjustment screw for rear sight.
4. M552GS (Gallery Special) is chambered for .22 Short cartridges only.

Comment: This is a reliable rifle, sufficiently accurate for plinking and small-game shooting.

RUGER M10/22 RIFLE

Action type: semiauto

Magazine type: rotary (spool); detachable box

Magazine capacity: 10-shot

Ejection: side

Safety: crossbolt

Barrel length: 18.5 inches

Stock: American walnut with oil finish; carbine version has uncapped pistol grip and no checkering; DeLuxe Sporter has hand-checkered pistol grip and fore-end

Buttplate: shotgun type; plastic

Overall length: 37.0 inches

Length of pull: 13.75 inches

Drop at comb: 1.25 inches

Drop at heel: 1.75 inches

Weight: 5.0 lbs.

Trigger pull: 5.0-6.0 lbs.

Sight, rear: folding leaf, crudely adjustable for elevation

Sight, front: gold bead

Scope adaptability: drilled and tapped for scope bases or for tip-off mount; scope base adaptor furnished

Caliber: .22 Long Rifle

Data: This is the only current rifle known to the author which has a rotary (spool type) magazine combined with a detachable box. The rotary magazine, made famous by the Savage M99 and Mannlicher, is probably the most reliable magazine type, *i.e.* the least subject to jams. The magazine guides are made of steel. This material further decreases chance of malfunction. Magazine fits flush with stock. Spare magazines are available at extra cost.

Comment: This rifle, because of its unique magazine design, may well be the most reliable of all .22 rimfire rifles. Design and workmanship are up to Ruger's usual high standards. This rifle costs less than many inferior rifles. It costs about half as much as the excellent Weatherby Mark XXII, which is the most expensive .22 caliber rimfire rifle.

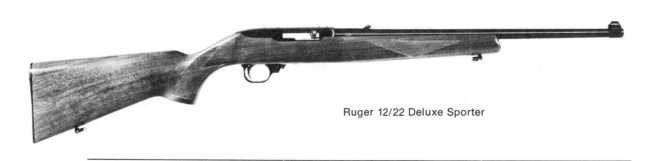

Ruger 12/22 Deluxe Sporter

WEATHERBY MARK XXII DELUXE SEMIAUTOMATIC RIFLE
(Detachable-box Magazine)

Manufacturer: Howa Machinery Co., Japan

Importer/distributor: Weatherby, Inc.

Action type: semiauto; blowback; unlocked breech

Magazine type: detachable straight-line box

Magazine capacity: 5-shot supplied with rifle; 10-shot available at extra cost

Safety: thumb slide

Barrel length: 24.0 inches

Stock: 1-piece walnut; hand-cut skip-line checkering panels on fore-end; checkered full-size pistol grip capped with rosewood tip at 45° angle; white plastic spacer; Monte Carlo comb; cheekpiece; nondetachable sling swivels (0.625 inch wide)

Buttplate: shotgun type; solid rubber recoil pad with black and white plastic spacers

Overall length: 42.74 inches

Length of pull: 13.75 inches

Drop at comb: 1.875 inches

Drop at Monte Carlo: 2.0 inches

Drop at heel: 2.625 inches

Weight: 6.35 lbs.

Trigger pull: not specified

Sight, rear: U-notch with fixed 50-yard leaf and folding leafs for 75 and 100 yards

Sight, front: gold bead on ramp

Scope adaptability: receiver grooved for tip-off mount

Caliber: .22 Long Rifle

Data: Aluminum-alloy receiver and triggerbow are black chrome. All steel parts have high-polish blue typical of Weatherby rifles. Stock has high-gloss finish also typical of Weatherby arms.

On the right side of the receiver is a selector switch and two positions marked AUTO and S.S. (for single-shot). With the selector switch on AUTO, the rifle fires every time the trigger is released and depressed in standard semiautomatic fashion. With the switch in the S.S. position the bolt remains open after each shot. To fire the next shot the selector switch must be moved forward to release the bolt and chamber a loaded round. This is an excellent safety feature for shooters having their first experience with a semiautomatic.

The bolt is engine-turned.

Disassembly for cleaning is easy: Remove magazine loading tube. Remove take-down pin at rear of receiver. Action will now clear the stock. Further disassembly should not be undertaken by owner (nor should it be normally necessary).

This rifle was originally made for Weatherby by Pietro Beretta. The author's Mark XXII was Italian-made. For several years the rifle has been made in Japan under the supervision of the Weatherby quality-control staff.

Comment: This is a superbly made, reliable, accurate, and handsome rifle. The author, who generally prefers a traditional stock rather than the Weatherby style, likes this one. So do most shooters.

The Ruger 10/22 and the Winchester M490 are probably as well made, but for a big man the full-size stock and longer barrel seem a better fit.

This rifle is as accurate as European rifles costing $300, or about twice as much as the Weatherby. Inasmuch as the superb old M52 Winchester Sporter is no longer available, this rifle is an excellent choice for adults interested in squirrel shooting.

The rifle is far more popular than its price tag might indicate. The author knows several gun-shops with long lists of back orders for the gun.

The optional Weatherby 4× scope is one of the best of its type; in fact it is as good as or better than any scope of comparable tube diameter and magnifying power.

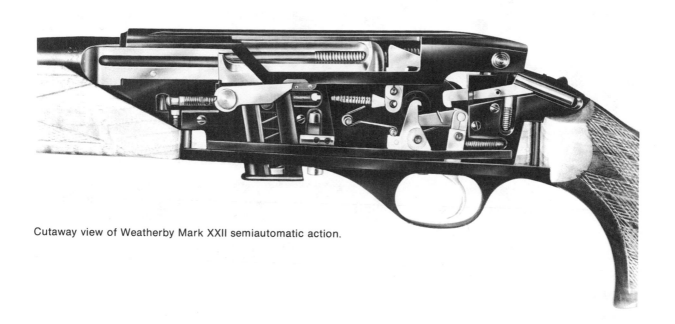

Cutaway view of Weatherby Mark XXII semiautomatic action.

WEATHERBY MARK XXII DELUXE SEMIAUTOMATIC (Tubular Magazine)

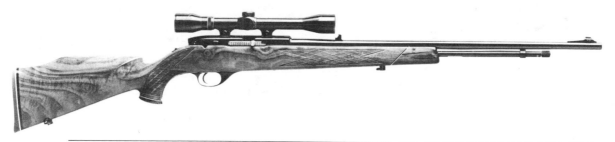

Manufacturer: Howa Machinery Co., Japan

Importer/distributor: Weatherby, Inc.

Action type: semiauto; blowback; unlocked breech

Magazine type: tubular; beneath barrel

Magazine capacity: 15-shot

Safety: thumb slide

Barrel length: 24.0 inches

Stock: 1-piece walnut; hand-cut skip-line checkering on pistol grip and fore-end; full-size pistol grip capped with rosewood and white plastic spacer; cheekpiece; Monte Carlo comb; nondetachable sling swivels (0.625 inch wide)

Buttplate: shotgun type; brown rubber recoil pad with white and black spacer

Overall length: 42.75 inches

Length of pull: 13.75 inches

Weatherby Mark XXII Deluxe Semiautomatic Sporter

Drop at comb: 1.875 inches

Drop at Monte Carlo: 2.0 inches

Drop at heel: 2.625 inches

Weight: 6.35 lbs.

Trigger pull: not specified

Sight, rear: U-notch rear with fixed 50-yard leaf and folding leafs for 75 and 100 yards

Sight, front: gold bead on ramp

Scope adaptability: receiver grooved for tip-off mount

Caliber: .22 Long Rifle

Data: For basic action description see Mark XXII detachable-box-magazine version.

Comment: For general comment see Mark XXII detachable-box-magazine version. The author prefers the detachable box (for rimfires but not centerfire rifles) to the tubular magazine. It is quicker to load, empty, and reload.

WINCHESTER M190/M290 SEMIAUTOMATIC RIFLE

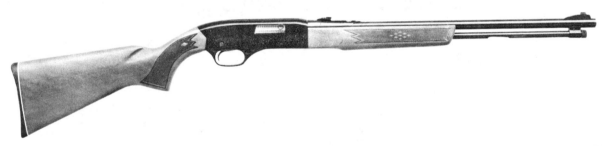

Action type: semiauto; blowback

Magazine type: tubular; beneath barrel

Magazine capacity: .22 Long, 17-shot; .22 Long Rifle, 15-shot

Safety: crossbolt

Barrel length: 22.5 inches; tapered

Stock: 2-piece walnut-stained hardwood; no checkering on M190; reverse checkering on M290 pistol grip and fore-end

Buttplate: shotgun type; plastic; white line spacer on M290

Overall length: 39.0 inches

Length of pull: 13.625 inches

Drop at comb: 1.75 inches

Drop at heel: 2.75 inches

Weight: 5.0 lbs.

Trigger pull: not specified

Sight, rear: Rocky Mountain, crudely adjustable for elevation

Sight, front: white bead on post

Scope adaptability: receiver grooved for tip-off mount

Caliber: .22 Long, .22 Long Rifle

Comment: An inexpensive reliable tubular magazine rimfire rifle.

WINCHESTER M490 SEMIAUTOMATIC RIFLE

Action type: semiauto; blowback

Magazine type: detachable straight-line box

Magazine capacity: standard, 5-shot; 10-shot and 15-shot available at extra cost

Safety: crossbolt

Barrel length: 22.0 inches; tapered

Stock: 1-piece American walnut with satin finish; impressed checkering on pistol grip and fore-end; plastic pistol-grip cap

Buttplate: shotgun type; plastic

Overall length: 42.0 inches

Length of pull: 13.625 inches

Drop at comb: 1.375 inches

Drop at heel: 2.5 inches

Weight: 6.0 lbs.

Trigger pull: not specified

Sight, rear: sporting leaf, adjustable for elevation

Sight, front: white bead on ramp with removable head

Scope adaptability: receiver grooved for tip-off mount

Caliber: .22 Long Rifle

Data: Steel receiver. Serrated trigger. Serrated cocking handle serves as open action lock.

Comment: The M490 and the Ruger are the handsomest and most reliable U.S.-made semiautomatic .22 caliber rifles that the author has extensively tested. The superb Japanese-made Weatherby Mark XXII is also handsome and reliable but costs approximately twice as much.

The M490, the Ruger, and the Weatherby Mark XXII are among the few adult-size .22 rimfire rifles.

CHAPTER 17

BOLT-ACTION MAGAZINE RIMFIRE RIFLES

Among rimfires, the bolt action was a late starter. The first major bolt-action rimfire magazine rifle was the U.S. Magazine Rifle (M1903 Springfield) M1922. This was the M1903 Springfield with a rimfire bolt and a .22 caliber magazine inserted into the regular magazine. Several modifications to this rifle were designated M2, M1922M1, M1922M2, and MII.

All models were converted to the later improvements. When these modifications were made the markings (stamped on the forward section of the receiver) were changed. The letter *A* was added after the serial number of the M1922M2 rifles. A *B* was added after the serial numbers of the MII and M1922MII rifles.

All M1922s were fitted with a Lyman #48 micrometer receiver sight. This version of the #48 had 10 graduations for each completed turn of the windage and elevation adjustment screws. The front sight was the blade type.

The M1922 weighed just under 9 pounds and was 43.75 inches long with the 24.0-inch barrel.

This is one of the most accurate .22 rimfire rifles the author has ever fired. His first experience with it was at Fort Devens in 1936 when he fired the 1000-inch range. That's right, the 1000-inch range. Sights and targets, as he remembers, were set up to make the 1000-inch range comparable to the 1000-yard range with the Caliber .30 M1903.

He acquired one of these through the National Rifle Association and used it for many years—fitted with a variety of hunting scopes—for small game.

There was one slight disadvantage to the M1922 Springfields: the bolt throw was somewhat longer than necessary for the .22 Long Rifle cartridge. However, the advantages of sufficient stock, accurate barrel, and bedding more than compensated for the long bolt throw.

The first high-quality commercial .22 rimfire sporter was the Winchester M52 Sporter. This splendid rifle used the M1927 speedlock and action of the M52 Winchester match rifle. The sporter with a 24.0-inch barrel weighed 7.25 lbs. During the first ten years or so of its existence it was generally fitted with a Lyman #48 micrometer sight and blade or bead front. During the last twenty years it was frequently fitted with scopes of 2.5–4×.

The sporter stock resembled that of the M54 and M70. It had a full pistol grip with a hard rubber cap. The fore tip was durable black plastic. Both the pistol grip and fore-end were checkered. It was fitted with quick-detachable sling swivels. The sling was a 1-inch leather military type.

This was the finest .22 rimfire bolt-action sporter ever made. No other American sporter has approached it, and no foreign rifle known to the author equals it. This superb sporting rifle was killed in 1958 for one reason. There are not enough adult Americans who require a .22 rimfire sporting rifle with the characteristics of the M52—at least not enough to pay the $150 that the rifle ultimately cost. However, old M52 sporters fetch up to $500 today and sometimes more.

Far too few adult American riflemen realize the grand sporting potential of a fine .22 rimfire rifle. To most Americans a .22 is a kid's rifle. Only in the deep South, where squirrel hunting is a fine art, do many adult riflemen use the .22 rimfire.

An accurate .22 fitted with a 2.5–4× scope is capable of dropping squirrels at ranges up to 100 yards. A man who can do this can be prouder than the brush shooter who accidentally stumbles onto a whitetail and drops it. Hunting, seeking, finding, and dropping a squirrel at 50 to 100 yards is both hunting and riflemanship.

There are some excellent imports like the Savage/Anschutz and Walther KKJ, but these have stocks which do not appeal to most American riflemen. The best American-made bolt-action sporter is probably Remington's M541-S.

The average bolt-action rimfire rifle is bought for a boy. It is more apt to have a tubular magazine than a detachable straight-line box. The capacity of 25 .22 Shorts is a powerful appeal to youngsters.

Winchester was first on the American scene with a bolt-action box-magazine inexpensive sporter. In August, 1926, two such rifle types were delivered to the Winchester warehouse in New Haven. The Winchester M57 was like the M56 except that it had a heavier barrel, a larger stock with sling swivels, and better sights. The M56 was discontinued in 1929 after only 8,200 had been sold. The M57—a superior rifle—was discontinued after about 18,600 had been sold.

The next box-magazine bolt-action repeater was the M69. This was a lower-priced rifle which Winchester hoped would sell better than the M56/M57. About 350,500 were sold between 1935 and 1963.

The finest .22 rimfire bolt-action detachable-magazine rifle that Winchester has ever made, other than the M52 Sporter, was the M75 (1938–58). It was available in both target and sporter versions. Many of the M75 Target rifles were purchased during World War II by the government. This medium-priced version of the M52 was very accurate. M75s bring a fairly high price today because no comparable rifle except the

Remington 540-S is on the market. It is ironic that Winchester, a pioneer in the field, no longer makes a .22 bolt-action repeater.

Remington began producing the bolt-action detachable-magazine sporting rimfire rather late. The first such Remington was the M511 Scoremaster, a low-priced rifle (1939–62).

The first Remington to compare with the Winchester M75 was the M513-S. This was the sporting version of the M513 Matchmaster. The next medium-priced Remington was the current M540-S. This is the sporting version of the M540 medium-priced match rifle.

The difference between a low-priced .22 bolt-action magazine rifle, a medium-priced one, and one in the $300 bracket is a matter of stocking and trigger mechanism.

One reason for the decline of the fine .22 caliber bolt-action magazine rifle is the increasing improvement in the semiautomatics. Three accurate, handsome, and well made semiautomatics are the Ruger 10/22, Winchester M490, and Weatherby Mark XXII. These rifles are relatively inexpensive and cost one-half to one-third as much as an imported first-line bolt-action. They are extremely accurate and make fine squirrel rifles.

HARRINGTON & RICHARDSON M865 PLAINSMAN RIFLE

Action type: bolt

Magazine type: detachable straight-line box

Magazine capacity: 5-shot

Safety: side thumb lever

Barrel length: 22.0 inches; tapered

Stock: 1-piece uncheckered walnut-stained hardwood; uncapped semi-pistol grip; Monte Carlo; fluted comb

Buttplate: shotgun type; plastic with white line spacer

Overall length: 39.0 inches

Length of pull: 13.5 inches

Drop at comb: 1.5 inches

Drop at Monte Carlo: 2.0 inches

Drop at heel: 2.5 inches

Weight: 5.1 lbs.

H & R M865 PLAINSMAN RIFLE (continued)

Trigger pull: 4.0 lbs.

Sight, rear: Rocky Mountain, crudely adjustable for elevation

Sight, front: dovetail blade

Scope adaptability: receiver grooved for tip-off mount

Caliber: .22 Short, .22 Long, .22 Long Rifle

Comment: A magazine version of the M750 single-shot rifle.

MARLIN-GLENFIELD M20 BOLT-ACTION RIFLE

Action type: bolt

Magazine type: detachable straight-line box

Magazine capacity: 7-shot

Safety: sliding thumb

Barrel length: 22.0 inches

Stock: 1-piece walnut-stained hardwood; reverse checkering on fore-end and pistol grip; uncapped semi-pistol grip

Buttplate: shotgun type; plastic

Overall length: 41.0 inches

Length of pull: 13.75 inches

Drop at comb: 1.5 inches

Drop at heel: 2.25 inches

Weight: 5.5 lbs.

Trigger pull: not specified

Sight, rear: Rocky Mountain, crudely adjustable for elevation

Sight, front: bead on ramp with Wide-Scan hood

Scope adaptability: receiver grooved for tip-off mount

Caliber: .22 Short, .22 Long, .22 Long Rifle

Comment: This is one of the least-expensive bolt-action rifles on the market. It is entirely adequate as a boy's rifle for plinking and small game.

Note: The Glenfield M200C is the M20 plus an inexpensive 4× scope.

MARLIN M780 BOLT-ACTION RIFLE

Action type: bolt

Magazine type: detachable straight-line box

Magazine capacity: 7-shot

Safety: sliding thumb

Barrel length: 22.0 inches; Micro-Groove

Stock: 1-piece American walnut; reverse checkering on pistol grip and fore-end; uncapped semi-pistol grip; Monte Carlo comb

Buttplate: shotgun type; plastic with white line spacer

Overall length: 41.0 inches

Length of pull: 13.75 inches

Drop at comb: 1.5 inches

Marlin Model 780 bolt action rifle

Drop at Monte Carlo: 1.375 inches

Drop at heel: 2.5 inches

Weight: 5.5 lbs.

Trigger pull: 5.0 lbs.

Sight, rear: Rocky Mountain, crudely adjustable for elevation

Sight, front: bead on ramp with Wide-Scan hood

Scope adaptability: receiver grooved for tip-off mount

Caliber: .22 Short, .22 Long, .22 Long Rifle

Comment: A rugged, medium-quality average-priced rifle.

MARLIN M781 BOLT-ACTION RIFLE

Action type: bolt

Magazine type: tubular; beneath barrel

Magazine capacity: .22 Short, 25-shot; .22 Long, 19-shot; .22 Long Rifle, 17-shot

Safety: sliding thumb

Barrel length: 22.0 inches; Micro-Groove

Stock: 1-piece American walnut; reverse checkering on pistol grip and fore-end; uncapped semi-pistol grip; Monte Carlo comb

Buttplate: shotgun type; plastic with white line spacer

Overall length: 41.0 inches

Length of pull: 13.75 inches

Drop at comb: 1.5 inches

Drop at Monte Carlo: 1.375 inches

Drop at heel: 2.5 inches

Weight: 6.0 lbs.

Trigger pull: 5.0 lbs.

Sight, rear: Rocky Mountain, crudely adjustable for elevation

Sight, front: bead on ramp with Wide-Scan hood

Scope adaptability: receiver grooved for tip-off mount

Caliber: .22 Short, .22 Long, .22 Long Rifle

Comment: A well-made, medium-priced bolt-action magazine rifle.

EXPLODED VIEW OF MARLIN M780 BOLT ACTION RIFLE.

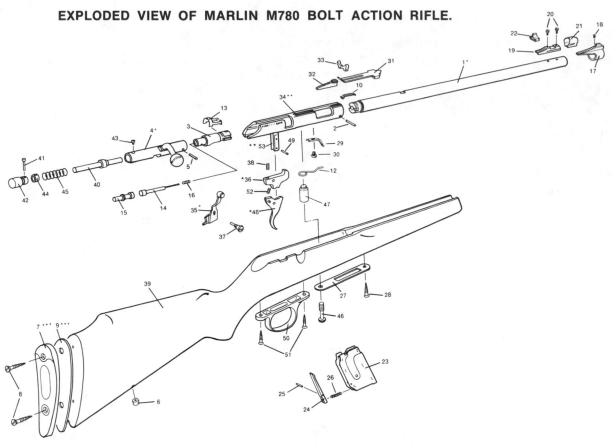

No.	Part Name	No.	Part Name	No.	Part Name
1	Barrel	19	Front Sight Ramp Base	35	Safety
2	Barrel Retaining Pin	20	Front Sight Ramp Base Screw (2)	36	Sear
	Breech Bolt (Complete)	21	Front Sight Ramp Hood	37	Sear & Safety Pivot Screw
3	Breech Bolt, Front	22	Front Sight Ramp Insert	38	Sear Spring
4	Breech Bolt, Rear	23	Magazine Complete (7 shot only)	39	Stock
5	Breech Bolt Retaining Pin	24	Magazine Catch	40	Striker
6	Bullseye	25	Magazine Catch Pin	41	Striker Cam Pin
7	Buttplate	26	Magazine Catch Spring	42	Striker Knob
8	Buttplate Screw (2)	27	Magazine Guard Plate	43	Striker Retaining Screw
9	Buttplate Spacer	28	Magazine Guard Plate Screw	44	Striker Sleeve
10	Cartridge Guide Spring	29	Magazine Receiver Catch	45	Striker Spring
11	N/A	30	Magazine Receiver Catch Screw	46	Takedown Screw
12	Ejector		Rear Sight (Old Style) (Not Shown)	47	Takedown Screw Stud
13	Extractor		Rear Sight Elevator (Old Style) (Not Shown)	48	Trigger, Gold
14	Firing Pin, Front		Rear Sight Complete (New Style) Consisting of:	49	Trigger Pin
15	Firing Pin, Rear	31	Rear Sight Base	50	Trigger Guard
16	Firing Pin Spring	32	Rear Sight Elevator	51	Trigger Guard Screw (2)
17	Front Sight Assembly (Old Style)	33	Rear Sight Folding Leaf	52	Trigger Spring
18	Front Sight Binding Screw (Old Style)	34	Receiver	53	Trigger Stud
	Front Sight (Complete) Consisting of:				

MARLIN M783 MAGNUM

Action type: bolt

Magazine type: tubular; beneath barrel

Magazine capacity: 12-shot

Safety: thumb slide

Barrel length: 22.0 inches; Micro-Groove

Stock: 1-piece American walnut; reverse checkering on pistol grip and fore-end; uncapped pistol grip; Monte Carlo comb; sling swivels with leather carrying strap; Mar-Shield finish

Buttplate: shotgun type; plastic with white line spacer

Overall length: 41.0 inches

Length of pull: 13.75 inches

Drop at comb: 1.5 inches

Drop at Monte Carlo: 2.0 inches

Drop at heel: 2.5 inches

Weight: 6.0 lbs.

Trigger pull: 5.0 lbs.

Sight, rear: Rocky Mountain, crudely adjustable for elevation

Sight, front: bead on ramp with Wide-Scan hood

Scope adaptability: receiver grooved for tip-off mount

Caliber: .22 W.R.M.

Comment: A sturdy, medium-priced bolt-action rifle.

MOSSBERG M144 SUPER TARGET

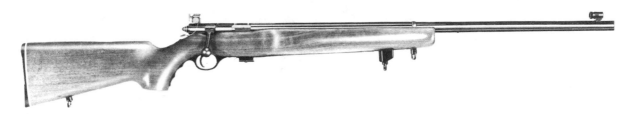

Action type: bolt

Magazine type: detachable straight-line box

Magazine capacity: 7-shot

Safety: thumb slide

Barrel length: 26.0 inches; medium heavy; crowned muzzle

Stock: 1-piece American walnut with finger grooves in pistol grip; uncheckered; beavertail fore-end; black plastic adjustable handstop on underside of fore-end; high comb for target-type scope; cheekpiece; target-type sling swivels

Buttplate: shotgun type; serrated plastic

Overall length: 44.5 inches

Length of pull: 14.0 inches

Drop at comb: 1.5 inches

Drop at heel: 1.625 inches

Weight: 8.0 lbs.

Trigger pull: not specified

Sight, rear: Mossberg S-331 (micrometer)

Sight, front: Lyman 17A target sight with inserts

Scope adaptability: receiver grooved for tip-off mount

Caliber: .22 Short, .22 Long, .22 Long Rifle

Comment: This inexpensive target rifle is designed for young marksmen. Any match rifle should have blocks for a target scope. A good rifle for the tyro shooter. First-rate .22 rimfire match rifles cost $350–500 or more. This one costs about $100. It is comparable to the late Winchester M75 but is not up to the Remington M540 at about $150 (with iron sights). Spare magazines are available.

MOSSBERG M340B BOLT ACTION

Action type: bolt

Magazine type: detachable straight-line box

Magazine capacity: 7-shot ("Magic 3-Way" magazine adjusts for .22 Short, .22 Long and .22 Long Rifle)

Safety: sliding thumb

Barrel length: 24.0 inches; AC-KRO-GRUV; crowned muzzle

Stock: 1-piece walnut-stained hardwood; uncheckered; finger grooves in uncapped semi-pistol grip; Monte Carlo comb; sling swivels

Buttplate: shotgun type; plastic with white line spacer

Overall length: 43.5 inches

Length of pull: 14.0 inches

Drop at comb: 1.5 inches

Drop at Monte Carlo: 2.5 inches

Drop at heel: 2.5 inches

Weight: 6.5 lbs.

Trigger pull: not specified

Sight, rear: S-330 micrometer, adjustable for windage and elevation in ¼-minute clicks

Sight, front: S-320 bead on ramp with removable hood

Scope adaptability: receiver grooved for tip-off mount

Caliber: .22 Short, .22 Long, .22 Long Rifle

Comment: An inexpensive bolt-action rifle. Costs were pared by using walnut-stained hardwood in lieu of black walnut for stock. Suitable for plinking and small game. Spare magazines are available.

MOSSBERG M341 SPORTER

Action type: bolt

Magazine type: detachable straight-line box

Magazine capacity: 7-shot ("Magic 3-Way" magazine adjusts for .22 Short, .22 Long and .22 Long Rifle)

Safety: sliding thumb

Barrel length: 24.0 inches; AC-KRO-GRUV

Stock: 1-piece American walnut; Monte Carlo comb and cheekpiece; checkered pistol grip and fore-end; sling swivels

Buttplate: shotgun type; plastic with white line spacer

Overall length: 43.5 inches

Length of pull: 14.0 inches

Drop at comb: 1.5 inches

Drop at Monte Carlo: 2.0 inches

Drop at heel: 2.5 inches

Weight: 6.5 lbs.

Trigger pull: not specified

Sight, rear: sporting-type U-notch, crudely adjustable for windage and elevation; receiver drilled and tapped for receiver sight

Sight, front: bead on ramp

Scope adaptability: receiver grooved for tip-off mount

Caliber: .22 Short, .22 Long, .22 Long Rifle

Comment: This is an accurate, well-made rifle. With a scope it will take squirrels at 50 yards, or better if you can hold. Spare magazines are available. Appearance and carrying ease would be improved if the magazine were a 5-shot box, flush with stock bottom.

MOSSBERG M640K CHUCKSTER

Action type: bolt

Magazine type: detachable straight-line box

Magazine capacity: 5-shot

Safety: sliding thumb

Barrel length: 24.0 inches; AC-KRO-GRUV

Stock: 1-piece American walnut; checkered pistol grip and fore-end; slight Monte Carlo comb; plastic capped full pistol grip; sling swivels

Buttplate: shotgun type; plastic with white line spacer

Overall length: 44.75 inches

Length of pull: 14.0 inches

Drop at comb: 1.5 inches

Drop at Monte Carlo: 2.0 inches

Drop at heel: 2.5 inches

Weight: 6.0 lbs.

Trigger pull: not specified

Sight, rear: U-notch, crudely adjustable for windage and elevation

Sight, front: bead on ramp

Scope adaptability: receiver grooved for tip-off mount

Caliber: .22 W.R.M.

Comment: This is one of the finest .22 W.R.M. rifles on the market—and at a modest price.

EXPLODED VIEW OF REMINGTON MODELS 580, 581, AND 582.

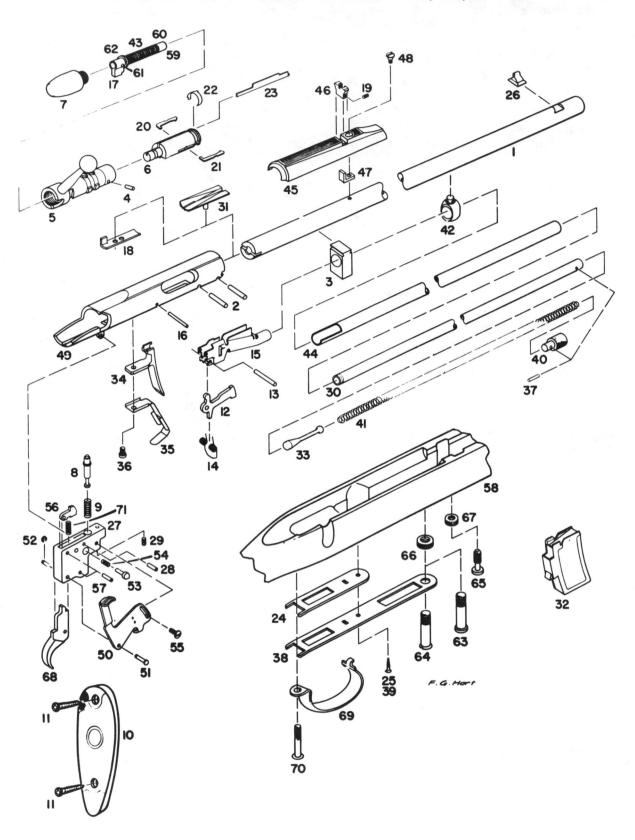

F.G.Hart

REMINGTON M581 SERIES BOLT-ACTION RIFLE

Action type: bolt

Magazine type: detachable straight-line box

Magazine capacity: 5-shot; 10-shot available at extra cost

Ejection: side

Safety: thumb

Barrel length: 24.0 inches

Stock: 1-piece walnut-stained hardwood; no checkering; uncapped pistol grip; sling and swivels available at extra cost

Buttplate: plastic

Overall length: 42.375 inches

Length of pull: 14.0 inches

Drop at comb: 1.75 inches

Drop at Monte Carlo: 1.75 inches

Drop at heel: 3.0 inches

Weight: 4.375 lbs.

Trigger pull: 4.5 lbs.

Sight, rear: Rocky Mountain, crudely adjustable for windage

Sight, front: bead

Scope adaptability: receiver grooved for tip-off mount

Caliber: .22 Short, .22 Long, .22 Long Rifle

Data: This is a takedown model. Disassembly is fast and simple, involving a single screw. Rifle can be had with left-hand action at slight extra cost.

Comment: A durable, medium-priced rifle for younger shooters.

Parts List of Remington Models 580, 581 and 582.

No.	Part Name	No.	Part Name	No.	Part Name
1	Barrel (582)	26	Front Sight	50	Safety
2	Barrel Assembly Pin	27	Housing (See Trigger Housing Sub Assembly)	51	Safety Pivot Pin
3	Barrel Bracket (582)	28	Housing Pin	52	Safety Pivot Pin Retaining Washer
4	Bolt Assembly Pin	29	Housing Lock Screw	53	Safety Detent
5	Bolt Body Assembly	30	Inner Magazine Tube (582)	54	Safety Detent Spring
6	Bolt Head	31	Loading Platform (580)	55	Safety Retainer Pin
7	Bolt Plug	31a	Loading Platform Screw	56	Safety Retainer Pin Retaining Washer
8	Bolt Stop	32	Magazine Assembly (581)	57	Sear
9	Bolt Stop Spring	33	Magazine Follower (582)	58	Sear Pin
10	Butt Plate	34	Magazine Guide (581)	59	Stock Assembly (582)
11	Butt Plate Screw	35	Magazine Latch (581)	60	Striker Assembly
12	Carrier (582)	36	Magazine Latch Screw (581)	61	Striker
13	Carrier Pin (582)	37	Magazine Pin (582)	62	Striker Cross Pin
14	Carrier Spring (582)	38	Magazine Plate (581)	63	Striker Washer
15	Cartridge Feed Insert (582)	39	Magazine Plate Screw (581)	64	Takedown Screw (580)
16	Cartridge Feed Insert Pin (582)	40	Magazine Plug (582)	65	Takedown Screw (581)
17	Cocking Piece	41	Magazine Spring (582)	66	Takedown Screw (582)
18	Ejector (580)	42	Magazine Ring (582)	67	Takedown Screw Escutcheon (580)
19	Elevation Screw	43	Main Spring	68	Takedown Screw Escutcheon (582)
20	Extractor, L. H.	44	Outer Magazine Tube (582)	69	Trigger
21	Extractor, R. H.	45	Rear Sight Base	70	Trigger Guard
22	Extractor Spring	46	Rear Sight Eyepiece	71	Trigger Guard Screw
23	Firing Pin	47	Rear Sight Leaf	72	Trigger Pin
24	Floor Plate (580-582)	48	Rear Sight Screw	73	Trigger Spring
25	Floor Plate Screw (580-582)	49	Receiver Assembly (582)		

REMINGTON M582 SERIES RIFLE

Action type: bolt

Magazine type: tubular; beneath barrel

Magazine capacity: .22 Short, 20-shot; .22 Long, 15-shot; .22 Long Rifle, 14-shot

Ejection: side

Safety: thumb

Barrel length: 24.0 inches

Stock: 1-piece walnut-stained hardwood; no checkering; uncapped pistol grip; Monte Carlo comb

Buttplate: plastic

Overall length: 42.375 inches

Length of pull: 14.0 inches

Drop at comb: 1.75 inches

Drop at Monte Carlo: 1.75 inches

Drop at heel: 3.0 inches

Weight: 5.0 lbs.

Trigger pull: 4.5 lbs.

Sight, rear: Rocky Mountain, crudely adjustable for elevation

Sight, front: bead

Scope adaptability: receiver grooved for tip-off mount

Caliber: .22 Short, .22 Long, .22 Long Rifle

Data: Remington M582 is a one-screw takedown model, basically the same as the M581 but with a tubular magazine.

Comment: Rugged, medium-priced tubular-magazine rifle for young hunters and plinkers.

REMINGTON M541-S "CUSTOM" SPORTER BOLT-ACTION MAGAZINE RIFLE

Action type: bolt

Magazine type: detachable straight-line box

Magazine capacity: 5-shot; 10-shot available at extra cost

Ejection: side

Safety: thumb type (lever)

Barrel length: 24.0 inches

Stock: 1-piece American walnut; checkered pistol grip and fore-end; design similar to Remington M700 centerfire bolt-action; rosewood-stained fore-end tip and pistol-grip cap; white line spacers; sling and swivels available at extra cost

Buttplate: shotgun type; plastic with white line spacer

Overall length: 42.625 inches

Length of pull: 13.75 inches

Drop at comb: 0.875 inch

Drop at heel: 0.875 inch

Weight: 5.5 lbs.

Trigger pull: 4.5 lbs.

Sight, rear: none

Sight, front: none

Scope adaptability: receiver drilled and tapped for scope bases or receiver sight; receiver grooved for tip-off mount

Caliber: .22 Short, .22 Long, .22 Long Rifle

Data: Bolt has six locking lugs and twin extractors. Adjustable trigger pull.

Comment: Among standard factory models, the M541-S sporter is the only American bolt-action .22 rimfire currently made for serious sporting use by adults.

SAVAGE M65-M MAGNUM

Action type: bolt; recessed head; twin extractors

Magazine type: detachable straight-line box

Magazine capacity: 5-shot

Safety: thumb slide

Barrel length: 20.0 inches

Stock: 1-piece walnut-stained hardwood; reverse checkering; uncapped semi-pistol grip; Monte Carlo fluted comb; flat-bottom fore-end with semi-slab sides

Buttplate: shotgun type; hard rubber

Overall length: 39.0 inches

Length of pull: 14.0 inches

Drop at comb: 1.5 inches

Drop at Monte Carlo: 1.625 inches

Drop at heel: 2.5 inches

Weight: 5.5 lbs.

Trigger pull: 5.0–6.0 lbs.

Sight, rear: Rocky Mountain, crudely adjustable for elevation

Sight, front: bead

Scope adaptability: receiver grooved for tip-off mount

Caliber: .22 W.R.M.

Comment: A well-made rimfire rifle with steel receiver.

EXPLODED VIEW OF SAVAGE M65-M MAGNUM

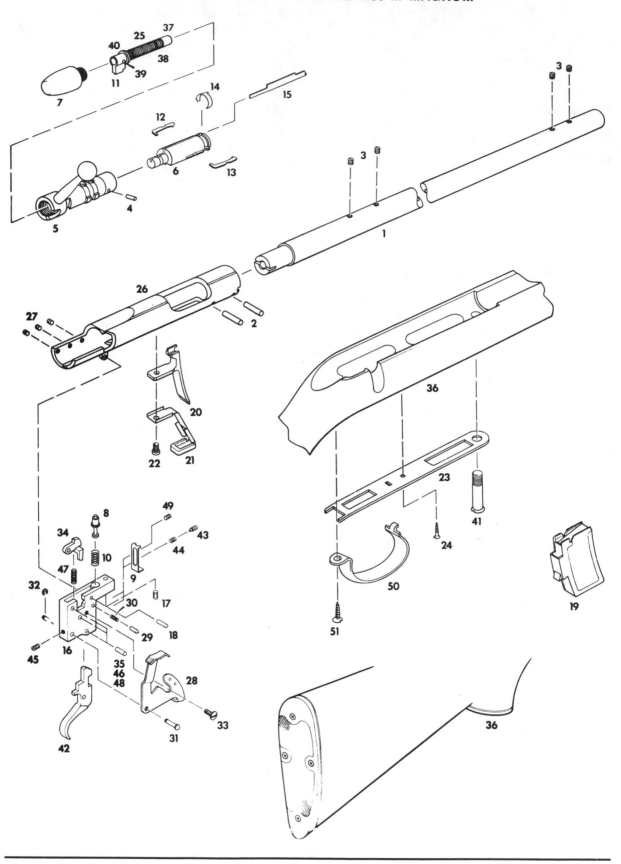

SAVAGE ANSCHUTZ M54/M54-M SPORTERS

Manufacturer: Anschutz, West Germany

Importer/distributor: Savage

Action type: bolt; steel receiver; shrouded bolt

Magazine type: detachable straight-line box

Magazine capacity: 5-shot

Safety: wing

Barrel length: 24.0 inches

Stock: French walnut; skip-line hand checkering; Monte Carlo comb; rollover cheekpiece; plastic pistol-grip cap with white line spacer; Schnabel fore-end tip; quick-detachable sling swivel studs

Buttplate: shotgun type; hard rubber with white line spacer

Overall length: 42.0 inches

Length of pull: 14.0 inches

Drop at comb: 1.25 inches

Drop at Monte Carlo: 1.25 inches

Drop at heel: 2.0 inches

Weight: 6.25 lbs.

Savage Anschutz M54 Sporter

Parts list of Savage M65-M Magnum.

No.	Part Name	No.	Part Name	No.	Part Name
1	Barrel	18	Housing Pin	35	Sear Pin
2	Barrel Assembly Pin	19	Magazine Assembly	36	Stock Assembly
3	Barrel Plug Screw	20	Magazine Guide	37	Striker Assembly
4	Bolt Assembly Pin	21	Magazine Latch Assembly	38	Striker
5	Bolt Body Assembly	22	Magazine Latch Screw	39	Striker Cross Pin
6	Bolt Head	23	Magazine Plate	40	Striker Washer
7	Bolt Plug	24	Magazine Plate Screw	41	Takedown Screw
8	Bolt Stop	25	Mainspring	42	Trigger
9	Bolt Stop Release	26	Receiver Assembly	43	Trigger Adjusting Screw
10	Bolt Stop Spring	27	Receiver Plug Screw	44	Trigger Adjusting Spring
11	Cocking Piece	28	Safety	45	Trigger Engagement Screw
12	Extractor, L. H.	29	Safety Detent	46	Trigger Pin
13	Extractor, R. H.	30	Safety Detent Spring	47	Trigger Spring
14	Extractor Spring	31	Safety Pivot Pin	48	Trigger Spring Retaining Pin
15	Firing Pin	32	Safety Pivot Pin Washer	49	Trigger Stop Screw
16	Housing	33	Safety Retainer Screw	50	Trigger Guard
17	Housing Lock Screw	34	Sear	51	Trigger Guard Screw

SAVAGE ANSCHUTZ M54/54-M SPORTERS (continued)

Trigger pull: adjustable; minimum, 3.0 lbs.

Sight, rear: folding leaf

Sight, front: bead on ramp with removable sight protector

Scope adaptability: receiver drilled and tapped for standard scope bases

Caliber: .22 Short, .22 Long, .22 Long Rifle, .22 W.R.M. (M54-M only)

Comment: This is a relatively expensive rifle that compares in accuracy to the fine old Winchester M52 Sporter. It is capable of 1-inch—or slightly better—5-shot groups at 100 yards. It is unfortunate that its looks are marred by the unnecessary rollover cheekpiece, but that is strictly a personal opinion.

SAVAGE/ANSCHUTZ M164/M164-M RIFLES

Manufacturer: Anschutz, West Germany

Importer/distributor: Savage

Action type: bolt; steel receiver; shrouded bolt

Magazine type: detachable straight-line box

Magazine capacity: 5-shot

Safety: side slide

Barrel length: 24.0 inches

Stock: 1-piece European walnut; checkered full pistol grip; Schnabel fore-end tip; Monte Carlo fluted comb; full cheekpiece

Buttplate: shotgun type; hard rubber with white line spacer

Overall length: 40.25 inches

Length of pull: 14.0 inches

Drop at comb: 1.5 inches

Drop at Monte Carlo: 1.5 inches

Drop at heel: 2.25 inches

Weight: 6.0 lbs.

Trigger pull: adjustable; minimum, 3.0 lbs.

Sight, rear: folding leaf

Sight, front: bead on ramp with removable sight protector

Scope adaptability: receiver grooved for tip-off mount

Caliber: .22 Short, .22 Long, .22 Long Rifle, .22 W.R.M. (M164-M only)

Comment: This is a high-quality rimfire bolt-action rifle. It is entirely suitable for adults who enjoy precision potting of squirrels and other small game.

SAVAGE STEVENS M34 RIFLE

Action type: bolt; recessed bolt face; double extractors; steel receiver

Magazine type: detachable straight-line box

Magazine capacity: 5-shot; 10-shot available at extra cost

Safety: thumb slide

Barrel length: 20.0 inches

Stock: 1-piece walnut-stained American hardwood; reverse checkering; uncapped semi-pistol grip; Monte Carlo; fluted comb

Buttplate: shotgun type; hard rubber

Overall length: 39.0 inches

Length of pull: 14.0 inches

Drop at comb: 1.5 inches

Drop at Monte Carlo: 1.625 inches

Drop at heel: 2.5 inches

Weight: 5.5 lbs.

Trigger pull: 5.0–6.0 lbs.

Sight, rear: Rocky Mountain, crudely adjustable for windage

Sight, front: dovetail bead

Scope adaptability: receiver grooved for tip-off mount

Caliber: .22 Short, .22 Long, .22 Long Rifle

Comment: A moderately priced, well-made .22 rimfire rifle.

WALTHER KKJ SPORTSMAN RIFLE

Manufacturer: Carl Walther Waffenfabriken, West Germany

Importer/distributor: Firearms International

Action type: bolt

Magazine type: detachable straight-line box

Magazine capacity: flush, 5-shot; extension, 8-shot

Safety: thumb slide

Barrel length: 22.5 inches

Stock: European walnut; hand checkered pistol grip and fore-end; cheekpiece; plastic-capped pistol grip; sling swivels

Buttplate: shotgun type; hard rubber

Overall length: 40.5 inches

Length of pull: 13.75 inches

Drop at comb: 2.0 inches

Drop at heel: 2.9 inches

Weight: 5.5 lbs.

Trigger pull: not specified; double set trigger available

Sight, rear: military type with folding leaf marked in meters

Sight, front: bead on ramp with removable hood

WALTHER KKJ SPORTSMAN RIFLE (continued)

Scope adaptability: receiver dovetailed for scope mounts

Caliber: .22 Short, .22 Long, .22 Long Rifle; .22 W.R.M. chambering is also available

Comment: This may well be the finest .22 caliber rimfire sporting rifle available. It is capable of 1-inch 5-shot groups at 100 yards from a rest. The KKJ is expensive, and its cheekpiece is far too small, but this .22 sporter is about the best we have today.

It is not a kid's rifle. It is designed for the serious small-game hunter who wants an accurate and dependable rifle, and should be fitted with a standard 1-inch-diameter scope, not one of the inexpensive .22 scopes.

CHAPTER 18

RIFLE AND HANDGUN RIMFIRE CARTRIDGES

The rimfire is our oldest and most popular metallic cartridge. Of the dozens of calibers once available only the .22 rimfire and 5mm Rem. are still made, but the survivors include the world's most widely used cartridges: .22 Short and .22 Long Rifle. Today's generation thinks of the rimfire cartridge as being strictly .22 caliber, but in the past rimfires have made up to at least .58 caliber.

The last of the medium-large rimfires to go was the .41 Swiss Vetterli. This used a 300-grain lead bullet and as late as 1939 cost $1.05 a box. Production of the .44 Henry Flat, .25 Stevens Short, .25 Stevens Long, .32 Short, .32 Long, and .38 Short was not resumed after World War II. The last big rimfire handgun cartridge discontinued was the .41 Short for the Remington derringer.

The rimfire was still a strong, if losing, contender in cartridge lists at the turn of the century. There were the .22 Extra Long, .32 and .38 Extra Long, .44 Colt and Win. (not to be confused with the .44–40 Win.), .44 Extra Long Howard, .56–46 Spencer Rifle, .56–50 Spencer Carbine, .56–52 Spencer Rifle, and .56–56 Spencer Carbine.

Rimfire case material

Copper was the uniform rimfire case material from the introduction of the .22 rimfire in 1854 until Remington introduced the stronger brass case for its .22 Hi-Speed loads in 1930. Brass is now the standard case material.

Western and later Winchester-Western used nickel-plated brass cases for the Super-X and Super-Speed loadings. (Today Remington's .22 Short Gallery loads can be had with standard brass cases or nickel-plated brass so that shooters can easily keep their gallery loads separate.) During World War II, when there was a brass shortage, steel was used for some .22 Long Rifle cases.

Bullet coatings

Until the advent of high-velocity loads, almost all rimfire bullets were outside-lubricated. This was, and is, the most effective method of lubricating lead bullets. However, many .22 hunters and plinkers carry ammunition loose in their pockets. Lubricants picked up tobacco crumbs, lint, and other foreign matter that accumulates in a man's pockets. Various platings have been applied, usually to the high-velocity loads.

Western and later Winchester-Western used Lubaloy, an American version of the British Nobeloy. Remington used a cadmium plating called Silvadry. No plating is as effective a lubricant as the original grease. Today all high-velocity loadings known to the author are plated. This reduces barrel life, but .22 rimfire barrels have such an extraordinarily long life in terms of rounds fired that for practical purposes the shorter life is of no importance.

.22 B.B. Cap (Bullet Breech Cap)

This was the smallest .22 rimfire cartridge. It is no longer made in this country. The B.B. Cap used a 20-grain bullet about as wide as it was long. It was designed for use in the Flobert rifle but was later used for informal living-room or basement target shooting. The B.B. Caps remembered by the author had a sharp wadcutter shoulder to cut clean holes in the paper.

Muzzle velocity in a 6-inch-barrel revolver was 750 f.p.s., and about 875 f.p.s. in a 20-inch-barrel rifle.

.22 C.B. Cap (Conical Ball Cap)

This uses a 29-grain bullet in the same size case as the B.B. Cap. It makes more noise than the B.B. but is no more accurate. It does not cut such a clean hole.

Muzzle velocity is about 750 f.p.s. in a 6-inch-barrel revolver and 975 f.p.s. in a 20-inch-barrel rifle. Cascade recently revived the C.B. Cap.

.22 Short (standard)

Developed in 1854 for Smith & Wesson, this is our oldest and one of our most popular cartridges. It was introduced as a handgun load but for many years its greatest popularity has been for rifle shooting. Its chief use is in shooting galleries and by economy-minded kids. A few international pistol (semiauto) matches require the .22 Short. Only a very few target handguns are made for the .22 Short.

Shorts are the least expensive of the three standard .22 rimfire load (Short, Long, and Long Rifle).

The Short is ideal for tin-can and other plinking but is not an adequate small-game cartridge, though it works well at short range in the hollowpoint version on rats.

The .22 Short was loaded into the 1930s with black powder, though both semi-smokeless and smokeless propellants had been available for many years. Back in the Depression era the author bought Shorts for twelve cents a box. High-velocity .22 Shorts were not as popular because of their much higher price: fifteen cents.

The standard short lead bullet weighs 29 or 30 grains. Its muzzle velocity in a rifle is about 1045 f.p.s. In handguns, depending on barrel length, velocity averages about 925 f.p.s. The .22 Short for nearly a century used copper cases in the standard loading. In the 1950s most companies shifted to brass cases for both standard and high-velocity loads.

.22 Short (high velocity)

In 1930 Remington introduced the first American high-velocity .22 rimfire cartridge. The trade designation was "Hi-Speed." All Remington Hi-Speed cases were and still are brass, as are those cases of other manufacturers that the author is familiar with. Western soon followed with a "Super-X" high velocity and Winchester with its "Super-Speed" version. Lesser competitors did likewise.

The muzzle velocity of the .22 Short high-velocity load is about 1095 f.p.s. from the average rifle muzzle. Handgun velocity runs 150 f.p.s. or so less.

.22 Short Hollowpoint

The 27-grain bullet has a rifle muzzle velocity of about 1120 f.p.s. and about 150 f.p.s. less in the average handgun barrel. This hollowpoint is deadly on game no larger than rats.

.22 Short Gallery (disintegrating)

These are standard-velocity loads, but the bullet pulverizes on the target to prevent ricochets. Both Remington and Winchester-Western make two bullet weights. Remington offers a 29-grain bullet with an average rifle muzzle velocity of 1045 f.p.s. and a 15-grain bullet with an average rifle muzzle velocity of about 1700 f.p.s. Winchester offers a 27-grain bullet and a 15-grain bullet with similar velocities.

Remington dubs its disintegrating bullets ".22 Short Gallery" loads. Winchester-Western calls the 27-grain bullet the ".22 Short Gallery" and the 15-grain bullet the ".22 Short Super Gallery." Previous Winchester-Western terminology has been "Kant Splash" and "Spatter Proof."

These bullets should not be used on game.

The gallery bullet led to the World War II development of the Caliber .30, Cartridge, Frangible Ball (T-44). This 108-grain bullet, developed at Duke University, was composed of equal parts Bakelite and powdered lead. The exposed portion of the bullet was waterproofed. This bullet type was developed so that training gunners could fire directly at aircraft rather than at a sleeve tow target. The bullet disintegrated on the aircraft's skin.

.22 Short Match (pistol)

The only .22 Short pistol match ammunition known to the author that is currently available in the United States is the British-made Eley Short Pistol Match cartridge.

Pistol match ammunition usually has a velocity just below that of standard-velocity loads. Both rifle and pistol match ammunition also has selected cases, at least in theory. Cases and bullets are machine-miked, and cases which do not have a narrower tolerance range than standard loadings are rejected for match ammunition.

Eley Short Pistol ammunition has won many international rapid-fire matches. Matches using the .22 Short cartridge are more popular in England and on the Continent than in North America. Many top American pistoleers of the past 50 years have never shot a .22 Short match unless they were in international competition.

.22 Short Blank

These are used for starter guns in sporting events, in theatrical affairs, and in the training of hunting dogs. They are charged with black powder and have a waterproofed flat wad. These blanks will not normally operate the action of a semiautomatic arm. Arms which have fired blank cartridges should be thoroughly cleaned after use. Some blanks contain mercuric primers, and others—not American—use corrosive primers. Blank cases known to the author are copper.

.22 Long

This halfbreed cartridge has a .22 Long Rifle case and a .22 Short bullet. It is neither as efficient nor as accurate as the Short or Long Rifle.

Remington makes the .22 Long in the standard-velocity version with the "Target" designation. Winchester-Western makes the .22 Long in Super-X. The Long is not made in hollowpoint or match versions. It is too inaccurate for the latter.

.22 Long Rifle (standard velocity)

This cartridge was developed about 1888 for the J. Stevens Arms & Tool Company by Union Metallic Cartridge Company (U.M.C.). One of the most widely used cartridges in the world, it is far more popular in revolvers than the .22 Short and it is almost universal in semiautomatic arms and match rifles.

The man who designed this cartridge was William Morgan Thomas, better known as U.M.C. Thomas because he designed so many successful bullets and cartridges for U.M.C. and then for Remington U.M.C.

The .22 Long Rifle, like other .22 rimfires dating back to the nineteenth century, has been made with black, semi-smokeless, and smokeless propellants. Millions of dollars have been spent to bring this cartridge to its present high state of development.

The standard-velocity version is excellent for long-range plinking or basic target practice. It is not very efficient on game. The .22 Long Rifle high-velocity hollowpoint is the ticket for squirrels and rabbits.

The standard-velocity .22 Long Rifle is more accurate than the high-velocity version. This doesn't mean that the high-velocity loading is inaccurate but that the standard-velocity is better when it comes to counting up the scores on target paper. Velocity of the 40-grain lead bullet is about 1150 f.p.s. from the average rifle muzzle.

.22 Long Rifle (high velocity)

The high-velocity .22 Long Rifle was introduced by Remington in 1930 along with the several other .22 rimfire high-velocity loadings. Rifle muzzle velocity averages about 1250 f.p.s.

The author sees little need for this load except in the hollowpoint version. The standard velocity is better for target practice and for long-range plinking. The .22 Long Rifle high-velocity hollowpoint is better for small game.

.22 Long Rifle Hollowpoint (high velocity)

The 36-grain (Rem.) or 37-grain (W-W) hollowpoint bullet is an excellent killer on game like squirrels and rabbits.

.22 Long Rifle Match (pistol)

For a good many years, pistol and revolver shooters used the same .22 Long Rifle match ammunition in both rifle and handgun. During the past few years, pistol ammunition has developed. Match pistol ammunition is subject to the same exacting specifications as match rifle ammunition. There may be other differences, but the only difference obvious to the author is the bullet shape. There seems to be smoother feeding from magazine into chamber with the pistol match bullet than with the rifle match bullet. Virtually all .22 rifle matches use single-shot rifles, so there is no feeding problem.

For many years there were more .22 revolvers like the Colt Officer's Match and the S&W K-22 than there were semiautomatics. Today most matches are shot with semiautomatics: .22 Long Rifle, .38 Special, and .45 ACP. The trend toward .22 autos led to the development of the specially shaped bullet for pistol ammunition.

Eley makes two .22 Long Rifle "Match" ammunition types. Eley .22 L.R. Pistol is a standard-velocity ammunition in the same accuracy category as Remington's "Target" and W-W's T-22 cartridges. Eley's match load is Eley Pistol Match.

Remington's Pistol Match is that firm's only load specifically designed for match use and is comparable with Eley's Pistol Match.

Winchester-Western's pistol match ammunition is .22 Long Rifle Super-Match Mark IV (rifle match ammunition is Mark III).

.22 Long Rifle Match (rifle)

The terms "match" and "target" cartridges are misleading. Today, Remington calls its standard-velocity .22 Long Rifle cartridge "Target .22 Long Rifle." Winchester-Western dubs its standard-velocity cartridges "T-22" (T implying target). Because of the cost factor many rifle and handgun competitors use standard-velocity loads for daily practice, saving special match ammunition for final practice and matches. Eley's standard-velocity loads are Match Long Rifle.

Remington's .22 Long Rifle match (rifle) cartridges are termed "Rifle Match .22 Long Rifle."

Winchester-Western offers .22 Long Rifle Super-Match III (plain lead bullet) and .22 Long Rifle Super Match Gold (plated bullet). Eley's top match load is Eley Tenex (for ten X's). Savage—Eley importers—noted that at the 1972 Munich Olympics more than 90 percent of .22 caliber competitors—including Americans—used Eley Tenex. In the prone match 97 percent used Tenex.

.22 Long Rifle Shot cartridge

There are two basic types: a shotshell with a crimp of the rose or star shape; and a transparent hollow plastic bullet-shaped container replacing the standard 40-grain bullet. Shot size is usually #11 or #12. Shot charge weight is about 0.125 oz. Shot cartridges are most effective when fired in a smoothbore rifle—which with a smoothbore barrel ceases to be a rifle and becomes a smallbore shotgun. Some manufacturer—as the author remembers it was Mossberg—once developed a miniature skeet game called Mo-skeet-o.

Shot cartridges can be used in rifled long arms or handguns. The more worn the bore is the more effective the shot is. Shot cartridges, preferably in a cartridge like a .44 Magnum, .44–44 Win., or .45 Colt, are useful against poisonous snakes like Florida rattlers. Long-rifle shot cartridges use high-velocity loads.

.22 Long Rifle stud driver loads

These blank-type loads are identified by the wad color. They are designed to operate stud driver guns only; under no conditions whatever should they be fired in rifles or handguns.

.22 Winchester Autoloading

The only known rifle chambered for this cartridge was the M03 Winchester Autoloading Rifle (1903–32). About 126,000 were made. The Colt Officer's Model Revolver was once chambered for this cartridge.

.22 Winchester Rimfire Magnum

This cartridge was introduced about 1959 and is chambered in rifles and revolvers. The .22 W.R.M. is much more effective than the .22 Long Rifle, but ammunition is considerably more expensive and cannot be used interchangeably in a rifle or handgun chambered for Shorts, Longs, and Long Rifles.

A 40-grain jacketed hollowpoint has a muzzle velocity of about 1900 f.p.s. The 40-grain full metal-jacketed bullet has the same muzzle velocity. This cartridge can take woodchucks up to about 100 yards.

.22 W.R.F. (Remington Special)

The only rifle known to the author that was chambered for this cartridge was the Remington M16 Autoloader (1914–28). No rifles have apparently been made for this cartridge in nearly 50 years. With a 45-grain lead bullet at a muzzle velocity of 1320 f.p.s., it was far superior to the .22 Winchester (M03) Autoloading cartridges.

5mm Remington Magnum

This cartridge, slightly smaller than .224 inch (the diameter of .22 bullets), was designed to compete with the .22 W.R.M. It was introduced in 1970. (As a measure of its popularity Remington ceased producing a rifle for it.) It was an effective and accurate cartridge, but was probably doomed because it was made only in a bolt-action rifle. No semiautomatic—today's most popular type—was chambered for the round.

PART V

SHOTGUNS

CHAPTER / 19

SINGLE-SHOT SHOTGUNS

Single-barrel single-shot shotguns have two basic categories:

1. Inexpensive shotguns designed for kids or for economy-minded farmers and other rural dwellers who occasionally pot a bird or a chicken-stealing varmint. The inexpensive single-barrel single-shot shotgun may well be our most popular type of arm. Tens of thousands are shipped annually to rubber and other plantations in the far corners of the earth. They are used by the workers for protection against snakes and other critters. Single-barrel single-shot shotguns are occasionally toted by big-game hunters in the northwestern United States and Canada for bagging an occasional grouse for the camp pot.

2. Trap guns ranging from about $350 to $5000 (you can pay more for custom arms). For a century or more the single-barrel was the only trap gun. In recent years the trap game allows double-barrel side-by-side and over/under and multi-shot semiautomatic and slide-action guns.

The typical inexpensive single-shot has two basic characteristics: exposed hammer, and, except in some youth models, full choke. They may or may not have checkering.

The full choke dates back to the black-powder era when most guns were full-choked. The full choke is a handicap for about 90 percent of scattergunning. Most upland-bird and decoyed-waterfowl shots are made at ranges not exceeding 35–40 yards. Rare exceptions are the occasional long shot on pheasant or nondecoyed waterfowl. For someone who occasionally needs a full choke, one solution is a multi-choke device like the Poly-Choke. Such a device, however, increases the gun's cost by at least 50 percent.

There are quite a few single-shot gunners who ultimately switch to the bolt-action magazine scattergun, which costs little more than a good single-shot. After a spot of practice the single-barrel shotgunner can, by holding a spare shot cartridge in his left hand, fire two shots about as rapidly as the cumbersome, slow, bolt-actions. Most bolt-actions have full-choke borings. Mossberg offers a multi-choke device on its bolt-actions.

The single-shot is a very reliable and durable arm. There is little that can go wrong with one. The author owned three. His first shotgun, acquired at age 11, was a secondhand 16-bore Iver Johnson Champion with a worked-over nail in lieu of the factory firing pin. He used this from 1930 to 1936, when he acquired a new Winchester M37 in 16-bore. Later a M37 in .410-bore was purchased. With these three guns the author took rabbits, squirrels, grouse, pheasant, crows, ducks, and hawks.

The single-barrel trap gun has one notable feature. There is no safety. None is required because the trap shooter doesn't load his gun until he is on the line and ready to fire.

The Monte Carlo comb, now popular not only

on trap guns but on rifles, originated at Monte Carlo, scene of many live-bird shoots. The raised comb was designed to minimize recoil. (On a rifle, it also positions the shooter's eye for scope sighting; and on a trap shotgun it lines his master eye up on the barrel rib.)

Trap barrels were traditionally 34 inches long. Now, the 32-inch barrel is usually optional, and 30 inches is common. Choke was always full, but modified is now offered as an option with many models. A dense pattern is needed to break clay birds consistently, and this becomes all the more important as a trap shooter gains skill enough to move back from the 16-yard line (the standard distance from the trap house out of which the targets hurtle)—that is, when the shooter increases the distance and fires from a handicap yardage. The full choke was crucial for achieving dense patterns until the advent in recent years of improved shotshells featuring plastic collars or pouches enclosing the shot charge. The protective collar greatly reduces the deformation of shot pellets as they travel through the bore, and an important effect is to produce denser, more uniform patterns. With this achieved, the full choke is not so important. It may, in fact, keep the pattern too tight for the shooter who tends to "get on" his targets fast enough so that the pellet pattern doesn't open up much before overtaking the bird. Thus a full choke can lose an occasional clay bird for some shooters, and these shooters prefer a trap gun with modified choke (or a special choke constriction somewhere between full and modified).

Incidentally, a $5000 trap gun won't shoot any better or last any longer than a $500 gun, but the expensive affairs are truly things of great beauty, and beauty is always something we need more of.

BROWNING MBT-99 TRAP

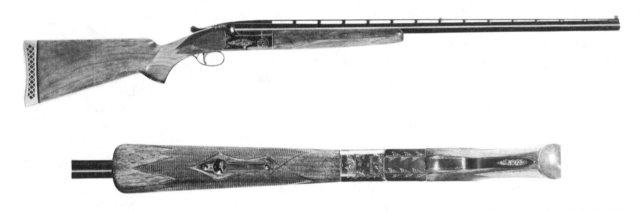

Manufacturer: Miroku, Japan

Importer/distributor: Browning Arms

Action type: break-top; hammerless

Ejection: automatic

Safety: none

Barrel length & choke: 32.0 or 34.0 inches, full, improved modified, or modified

Rib: floating ventilated, 0.9675 inch wide

Stock: 2-piece French walnut; hand-checkered (20 lines per inch); hand-rubbed semi-gloss finish; full uncapped pistol grip

Buttplate: contoured ventilated recoil pad with white line spacer

Overall length: 32.0-inch barrel, 49.375 inches; 34.0-inch barrel, 51.375 inches

Length of pull: 14.375 inches

Drop at comb: 1.9175 inches

Drop at heel: 1.625 inches

Weight: 32.0-inch barrel, 8.0 lbs.; 34.0-inch barrel, 8.125 lbs.

Sights: ivory front and center beads

Bore: 12, 2.75-inch case

Comment: This well-made, tightly fitted single-barrel trap gun replaces the former Broadway. The Broadway tag is now applied to the trap version of the Browning Superposed (over/under).

EXPLODED VIEW OF BROWNING MODEL BT99 TRAP GUN.

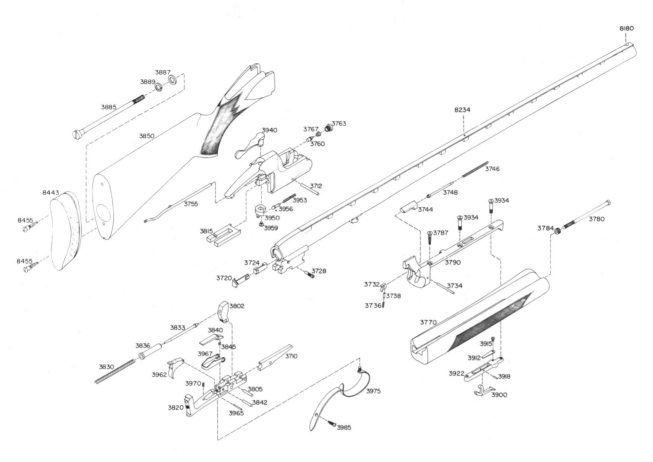

No.	Part Name	No.	Part Name	No.	Part Name
3710	Cocking Lever	3784	Forearm Bolt Escutcheon	3912	Take Down Lever Spring
3712	Cocking Lever Pin	3787	Forearm Screw	3915	Take Down Lever Spring Screw
3720	Ejector	3790	Forearm Bracket	3918	Take Down Lever Pin
3724	Ejector Extension	3802	Hammer	3922	Take Down Lever Bracket
3728	Ejector Stop Screw	3805	Hammer Pin	3934	Take Down Lever Bracket Screw
3732	Ejector Sear	3815	Locking Bolt	3940	Top Lever
3734	Ejector Sear Pin	3820	Tang Piece	3950	Top Lever Dog
3736	Ejector Sear Spring	3830	Mainspring	3953	Top Lever Dog Spring
3738	Ejector Sear Spring Follower	3833	Mainspring Guide	3956	Top Lever Dog Spring Guide
3744	Ejector Hammer	3836	Mainspring Sleeve	3959	Top Lever Screw
3746	Ejector Hammer Spring	3840	Sear	3962	Trigger
3748	Ejector Hammer Spring Guide	3842	Sear Pin	3965	Trigger Pin
3755	Ejector Trip Rod	3845	Sear Spring	3967	Trigger Safety
3760	Firing Pin	3850	Stock Trap W/Pad	3970	Trigger Spring
3763	Firing Pin Bushing	3885	Stock Bolt	3975	Trigger Guard
3767	Firing Pin Spring	3887	Stock Bolt Washer	3985	Trigger Guard Screw
3770	Forearm Beavertail Type	3889	Stock Bolt Lock Washer	8180	Bradley Type White Ivory Front Sight
3780	Forearm Bolt	3900	Take Down Lever	8234	White Ivory Center Sight

BERETTA MARK II TRAP GUN

Manufacturer: Pietro Beretta, Italy

Importer/distributor: Beretta Arms Co.

Action type: break-top; hammerless; underbolt

Ejection: automatic

Safety: none

Barrel length & choke: 32.0 or 34.0 inches, full

Rib: ventilated and matted

Stock: European walnut; hand-checkered pistol grip and extra-long beavertail fore-end

Buttplate: ventilated recoil pad

Overall length: 32.0-inch barrel, 49.375 inches; 34.0-inch barrel, 51.375 inches

Length of pull: 14.375 inches

Drop at comb: 1.375 inches

Drop at Monte Carlo: 1.375 inches

Drop at heel: 1.75 inches

Weight: 32.0-inch barrel, 8.35 lbs.; 34.0-inch barrel, 8.5 lbs.

Bore: 12, 2.75-inch case

Data: The Mark II is decorated with modest machine etching; more expensive grades are available.

Comment: This is one of the better lower-priced single-barrel trap guns. It has an excellent action and a well-designed stock.

GARCIA BRONCO .410

Manufacturer: Rossi Arms, Brazil

Importer/distributor: Garcia Corp./Firearms International

Action type: swing-out; hammerless

Ejection: nonautomatic

Safety: crossbolt

Barrel length & choke: 18.5 inches, full

Rib: none

Stock: skeleton metal with rust-resistant crackle finish

Buttplate: contoured; no separate buttplate

Overall length: 32.0 inches

Length of pull: 13.75 inches

Drop at comb: 1.75 inches

Drop at heel: 2.5 inches

Weight: 3.5 lbs.

Bore: .410, 3-inch case

Data: This is a takedown model. It disassembles in seconds and has a taken-down length of 21.75 inches.

Comment: This is the least expensive .410 shotgun known to the author. It could be used for backpacking or as a boat gun.

HARRINGTON & RICHARDSON M158 TOPPER

Action type: break-top; exposed hammer

Ejection: nonautomatic

Safety: half-cock hammer; rebounding hammer

Barrel length & choke:

12-bore: 28.0 inches, full or modified; 30.0 inches, 32.0 inches or 36.0 inches, full

16-bore: 28.0 inches, modified

20-bore: 28.0 inches, full or modified

.410-bore: 28.0 inches, full

Rib: none

Stock: 2-piece walnut-stained uncheckered hardwood; uncapped semi-pistol grip

Buttplate: red rubber ventilated recoil pad with white line spacer

Overall length: 26.0-inch barrel, 43.5 inches; 28.0-inch barrel, 45.5 inches; 30.0-inch barrel, 47.5 inches; 32.0-inch barrel, 49.5 inches; 36.0-inch barrel, 53.5 inches

Length of pull: 14.0 inches

Drop at comb: 2.0 inches

Drop at heel: 3.0 inches

Weight: 5.5–6.25 lbs.

Sights: brass bead front

Bore: 12, 16, 2.75-inch case; 20, .410, 3.0-inch case

Comment: An inexpensive single-barrel gun that has been around for many years, and probably will be for many more.

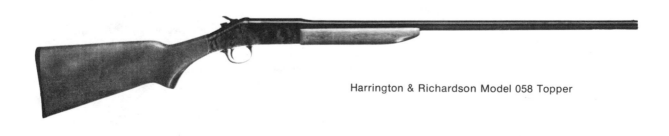

Harrington & Richardson Model 058 Topper

HARRINGTON & RICHARDSON M162 TOPPER BUCK GUN

Action type: break-top; exposed hammer

Ejection: nonautomatic

Safety: half-cock hammer; rebounding hammer

Barrel length & choke: 24.0 inches, cylinder (slug)

Rib: none

Stock: 2-piece walnut-stained uncheckered hardwood; uncapped semi-pistol grip

Buttplate: red ventilated recoil pad with white plastic spacer

Overall length: 40.0 inches

Length of pull: 14.0 inches

Drop at comb: 2.0 inches

Drop at heel: 3.0 inches

Weight: 6.0 lbs.

Sights: rear, folding leaf; front, blade

Bore: 12, 3.0-inch case

Comment: This is the only American-made single-shot scattergun specifically designed for slug shooting. Its barrel is shortened (to rifle length) and cylinder-bored for slugs, and it has crude but adequate rifle-style sights.

HARRINGTON & RICHARDSON M198 TOPPER

Action type: break-top; exposed hammer

Ejection: nonautomatic

Safety: half-cock hammer; rebounding hammer

Barrel length & choke: 28.0 inches; 20-bore, modified; .410-bore, full

Rib: none

Stock: 2-piece ebony-stained uncheckered hardwood; uncapped semi-pistol grip

Buttplate: black ventilated recoil pad with white line spacer

Overall length: 43.0 inches

Length of pull: 12.25 inches

Drop at comb: 2.0 inches

Drop at heel: 3.0 inches

Weight: 5.5 lbs.

Bore: 20, 2.75-inch case; .410, 3.0-inch case

Data: Ebony-stained wood and chrome frame. Action identical to M158 and M490.

Comment: Same as for M158 and M490

HARRINGTON & RICHARDSON M490 TOPPER YOUTH GUN

Action type: break-top; exposed hammer

Ejection: nonautomatic

Safety: half-cock hammer; rebounding hammer

Barrel length & choke: 26.0 inches; 20-bore, modified; .410-bore, full

Rib: none

Stock: 2-piece walnut-stained uncheckered hardwood; uncapped semi-pistol grip; semi-beavertail fore-end

Buttplate: red ventilated recoil pad with white line spacer

Overall length: 40.5 inches

Length of pull: 12.25 inches

Drop at comb: 2.0 inches

Drop at heel: 3.0 inches

Sights: front, brass bead

Bore: 20, .410, 3.0-inch case

Data: Short-stocked youth version of M158.

Comment: Durable, reliable single-barrel shotgun in sizes suitable for kids.

ITHACA CENTURY SKB SINGLE-BARREL TRAP GUN

Manufacturer: SKB, Japan

Importer/distributor: Ithacagun

Action type: break-top; hammerless

Ejection: automatic

Safety: none

Barrel length & choke: 32.0 or 34.0 inches, full

Rib: matted, semi-ventilated

Stock: 2-piece French walnut; hand-checkered; with straight comb; Century Trap MC version has Monte Carlo comb; full pistol grip with rounded natural cap; full beavertail fore-end; satin finish

Buttplate: contoured ventilated recoil pad

Overall length: 32.0-inch barrel, 49.5 inches; 34.0-inch barrel, 51.5 inches

Length of pull: 14.5 inches

Drop at comb: 1.5 inches

Drop at Monte Carlo (if applicable): 1.5 inches

Drop at heel: 2.0 inches

Weight: 32.0-inch barrel, 7.08 lbs.; 34.0-inch barrel, 8.0 lbs.

Sights: Bradley front; mid-rib bead

Bore: 12, 2.75-inch case

Data: Ithaca for many years has been noted as America's foremost producer of fine trap guns. This one, made to Ithaca design and specifications and under Ithaca quality control, is hand-fitted both with metal-to-metal and wood-to-metal. The gun is balanced 0.625 inch forward of the hingepin.

The trigger bow is engraved and there is fine-quality scroll engraving on the receiver. The bore is chromed and the outside of the barrel is black-chrome finished.

Comment: There are more expensive trap guns, because of their engraving and gold inlay, but the author doubts if there is a more reliable one or one with more handsome basic lines.

ITHACA E SERIES TRAP GUN

Action type: break-top; hammerless

Ejection: automatic

Safety: none

Barrel length & choke: 30.0, 32.0, or 34.0 inches, full

Rib: ventilated matted rib

Stock (4E): top-grade American walnut; hand-checkered (22 lines per inch) pistol grip and full beavertail fore-end; straight classic stock

Stock (5E): for another $1000, probably the finest figured American walnut, checkered 24 lines per inch; otherwise same as 4E

Buttplate: contoured rubber recoil pad

Overall length: 30.0-inch barrel, 47.375 inches; 32.0-inch barrel, 49.375 inches; 34.0-inch barrel, 51.375 inches

Length of pull: 14.375 inches

Drop at comb: 1.375 inches

Drop at heel: 1.375 inches

Weight: 30.0-inch barrel, 8.0 lbs.; 32.0-inch barrel, 8.25 lbs.; 34.0-inch barrel, 8.5 lbs.

Sights: Bradley front; mid-rib bead

Bore: 12, 2.75-inch case

Data: Receiver of the M4E is engraved with a trap-shooting scene on one side and American Indian scene on the other. M5E is more elaborately engraved, with a gold woodcock inlaid on the right side of the frame and a pheasant on the left. An American eagle is engraved on the triggerbow.

ITHACA PERAZZI COMPETITION I TRAP GUN

Manufacturer: Manifattura Armi Perazzi, Italy

Importer/distributor: Ithacagun

Action type: break-top; hammerless; underbolt

Ejection: automatic

Safety: none

Barrel length & choke: 32.0 or 34.0 inches, choked to customer's order

Rib: ventilated, concave and matted

Stock: 1-piece or 2-piece European walnut; hand-fitted and hand-checkered; beavertail fore-end; full pistol grip; semi-satin finish

Buttplate: contoured ventilated recoil pad

Overall length: 32.0-inch barrel, 49.0 to 49.5 inches (depending on pull length); 34.0-inch barrel, 51.0 to 51.5 inches (depending on pull length)

Stock dimensions: Perazzi Competition Number I Trap Gun offers 8 different stock dimensions; interchangeable stocks are available for those who wish different stock dimensions for different matches

Stock Code #1

Length of pull: 14.5 inches

Drop at comb: 1.375 inches

Drop at Monte Carlo: 1.375 inches

Drop at heel: 2.125 inches

Stock Code #4

Length of pull: 14.5 inches

Drop at comb: 1.5 inches

Drop at Monte Carlo: 1.5 inches

Drop at heel: 2.125 inches

Stock Code #6

Length of pull: 14.5 inches

Drop at comb: 1.5625 inches

Drop at Monte Carlo: 1.5625 inches

Drop at heel: 2.0 inches

Stock Code #12

Length of pull: 14.5 inches

Drop at comb: 1.375 inches

Drop at heel: 1.375 inches

Stock Code #13

Length of pull: 14.5 inches

Drop at comb: 1.5 inches

Drop at heel: 1.5 inches

Stock Code #14

Length of pull: 14.5 inches

Drop at comb: 1.5 inches

Drop at heel: 1.875 inches

Stock Code #15

Length of pull: 14.0 inches

Drop at comb: 1.5 inches

Drop at heel: 2.375 inches

Stock Code #16

Length of pull: 14.5 inches

Drop at comb: 1.375 inches

Drop at heel: 1.875 inches

Weight: 32.0-inch barrel, 8.35 lbs.; 34.0-inch barrel, 8.5 lbs.

Sights: Bradley bead front; mid-rib brass bead

Bore: 12, 2.75-inch case

Data: At Perazzi, each engraver has his price (or prices). The cost to the purchaser depends in part on the engraver and type of engraving chosen. For this model, the highest-quality engraving is called Lusso TM-0; second grade is Lusso TM-4 and third grade is Lusso TM-3. The price of a Perazzi shotgun, be it field, trap, or skeet, is also affected by the stock one selects. It is high.

Comment: This trap gun ranks among the world's finest. It has won a gold Olympic medal and the 1973 Grand American plus many other international and national shoots.

SAVAGE STEVENS M94-C/M94-Y SINGLE-SHOT

Action type: break-top; exposed hammer

Safety: half-cock hammer

Barrel length & choke:

12-bore: 28.0, 30.0, 32.0, or 36.0 inches, full

16-bore: 28.0 inches, full

20-bore: 28.0 inches, full; 26.0 inches (Youth Model), modified

.410-bore: 26.0 inches, full

Stock: 2-piece walnut-stained hardwood; reverse checkering on uncapped pistol grip; semi-beavertail fore-end

Buttplate: hard rubber

Overall length: 26.0-inch barrel, 42.0 inches; 26.0-inch barrel Youth Model, 40.5 inches; 28.0-inch barrel, 44.0 inches; 30.0-inch barrel, 46.0 inches; 32.0-inch barrel, 48.0 inches; 36.0-inch barrel, 52.0 inches

Length of pull: 14.0 inches

Drop at comb: 1.5 inches

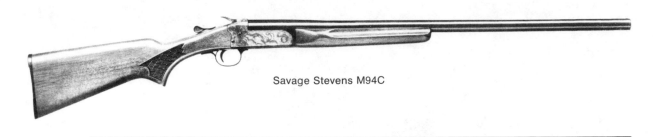

Savage Stevens M94C

Drop at heel: 2.5 inches

Weight range: 5.5 lbs. (Youth Model) to 6.5 lbs., depending on barrel length

Sight: gold bead front

Bore: 12, 20, .410, 3.0-inch case; 16, 2.75-inch case

Comment: This reliable, relatively inexpensive shotgun has been around for more than 40 years. It is not as well finished as the Winchester M37A, but is as rugged.

UNIVERSAL BAIKAL IJ-18 SINGLE-SHOT

Manufacturer: Russian State Firearms Factory, U.S.S.R.

Importer/distributor: Universal Sporting Goods

Action type: break-top; under-lever release

Safety: crossbolt in trigger guard

Barrel length & choke:

12-bore: 28.0 inches, modified; 30.0 inches, full

20-bore: 26.0 inches, modified

Stock: 2-piece walnut; machine-checkered pistol grip and fore-end

Buttplate: plastic with white line spacer

Length of pull: 14.25 inches

Drop at comb: 1.5 inches

Drop at heel: 2.5 inches

Weight:

12-bore: 28.0-inch barrel, 6.2 lbs.; 30.0-inch barrel, 6.4 lbs.

20-bore: 5.7 lbs.

Sights: metal bead front

Bore: 12, 20

Comment: Well-built single-barrel scattergun, priced competitively with comparable low-cost American-made models.

EXPLODED VIEW OF SAVAGE-STEVENS MODEL 94 C AND Y, AND SERIES K-107.

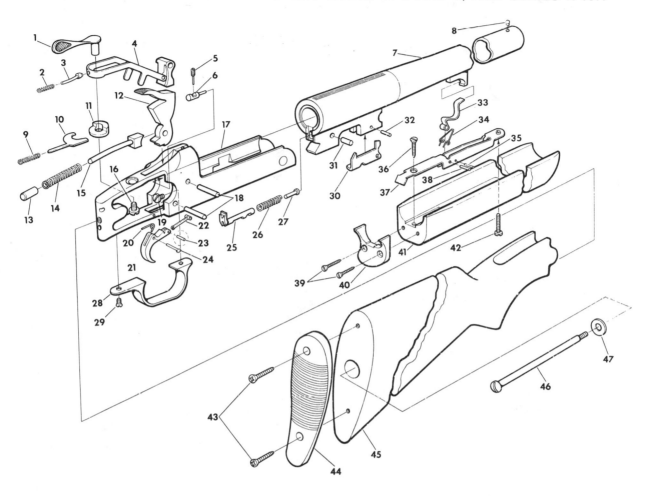

No.	Part Name	No.	Part Name	No.	Part Name
1	Top Snap	17	Frame	34	Fore-end Spring Spring
2	Locking Bolt Plunger Spring	18	Locking Bolt, Hammer Pin	35	Fore-end Spring Spring Pin
3	Locking Bolt Plunger	19	Trigger Guard Screw	36	Fore-end Spring Housing Screw
4	Locking Bolt Assembly	20	Trigger Spring	37	Fore-end Spring Housing
5	Firing Pin Screw	21	Trigger		Fore-end Spring Housing
	(Specify Gauge)	22	Hammer Stop Link Assembly		Assembly
6	Firing Pin		(Series K)	38	Fore-end Spring Pin
7	Barrel (Specify Gauge and	23	Link Pin (Series K)	39	Fore-end Iron Head Screw
	Length)	24	Trigger Pin	40	Fore-end Iron Head
8	Front Sight	25	Extractor	41	Fore-end Wood (Specify Gauge)
9	Top Snap Plunger Spring	26	Ejector Spring		Fore-end Assembly
10	Top Snap Plunger	27	Ejector Starter Pin		(Specify Gauge)
11	Top Snap Sleeve	28	Trigger Guard	42	Fore-end Screw
12	Hammer	29	Trigger Guard Screw	43	Butt Plate Screw
13	Mainspring Plunger Seat	30	Ejector Hook	44	Butt Plate
14	Mainspring	31	Extractor Stop Pin	45	Stock (CHECKERED)
15	Mainspring Plunger Assembly	32	Extractor Lever Pin	46	Stock Bolt
16	Top Snap Screw	33	Fore-end Spring	47	Stock Bolt Washer

WINCHESTER M37/M37A SINGLE-SHOT

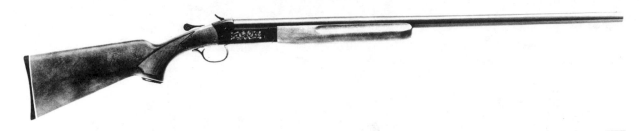

Action type: break-top; exposed hammer

Safety: half-cock hammer

Barrel length & choke:

12-bore: 30.0, 32.0, or 36.0 inches, full

16-bore: 30.0 inches, full

20-bore: 28.0 inches, full; 26.0 inches (Youth Model), modified

28-bore: 28.0 inches, full

.410-bore: 26.0 inches, full

Stock: 2-piece walnut-stained hardwood; machine-checkered pistol grip and bottom of fore-end; fluted semi-beavertail fore-end; full pistol grip with plastic cap and white line spacer

Buttplate: plastic with white line spacer; recoil pad on Youth Model

Overall length: 26.0-inch barrel (Youth Model), 40.75 inches; 26.0-inch barrel, 42.25 inches; 28.0-inch barrel, 44.25 inches; 30.0-inch barrel, 46.25 inches; 32.0-inch barrel, 48.25 inches; 36.0-inch barrel, 52.25 inches

Length of pull: 14.0 inches; 12.5 inches on Youth Model

Drop at comb: 1.375 inches

Drop at heel: 2.375 inches

Weight:

12-bore: 30.0-inch barrel, 5.75 lbs.; 32.0-inch barrel, 6.0 lbs.; 36.0-inch barrel, 6.25 lbs.

16-bore: 30.0-inch barrel, 6.25 lbs.

20-bore: 28.0-inch barrel, 6.0 lbs.

28-bore: 28.0-inch barrel, 6.25 lbs.

.410-bore: 26.0-inch barrel, 5.5 lbs.

20-bore Youth Model: 26.0-inch barrel, 5.75 lbs.

.410-bore Youth Model: 26.0-inch barrel, 5.25 lbs.

Sights: gold bead front

Bore: 12, 20, .410, 3.0-inch case; 16, 28, 2.75-inch case

Data: Winchester took the M37 Steelbuilt (1936–63), added a gold trigger, automatic ejection, and machine checkering, fluted the fore-end, grooved the hammer spur, and came up with the M37A. The original M37 sold more than 1,000,000 in 26 years.

Comment: The author has pleasant memories of the original M37. He owned two, a 16-bore and a .410-bore. The .410 was used on rabbits exclusively but the 16-bore accounted for untold pheasants, ruffed grouse, foxes, and ducks.

The M37A, though it no longer has a walnut stock, is an improvement over its predecessor. The automatic ejector is essential on a single-shot shotgun if one wants to get in a fast second shot.

It is unfortunate that Winchester adheres to the ancient American tradition of providing full choke as standard on single-barrel shotguns including—until recently—slide-actions and semi-automatics.

The old M37 was available in a greater choice of barrel lengths.

This is the best single-shot scattergun known to the author, excluding trap guns.

CHAPTER / 20

OVER/UNDER SHOTGUNS

The over/under shotgun is the most popular multiple-shot nonrepeating shotgun on the market today. Though a good over/under costs more to manufacture than a side-by-side double of comparable quality, the former is outselling the latter by at least ten to one.

The first commercially successful over/under shotgun was John Moses Browning's "Superposed." The Browning firm has always designated its top-of-the-line over/under as "Superposed" rather than "over/under."

Browning filed for his "Superposed" patents on October 14, 1923, and September 29, 1924. U.S. Patents 1,578,638-39 were granted on March 30, 1926. The Superposed, one of Browning's greatest achievements, was his last. He died on November 26, 1926, in Belgium, while awaiting production of the first Superposed by Fabrique Nationale.

Save for a brief hiatus during World War II, when the Nazis operated the FN plant, the Superposed has been in constant production since its 1927 introduction. It has long been the standard by which all other production boxlock over/under shotguns are judged.

The Superposed was available in 12-bore only when it was first sold in the United States in 1928. The very popular 20-bore was later designed—it has a lighter and smaller receiver—by Val A. Browning, John Moses Browning's son. It is also available in 28-bore and .410. It has never been produced for the United States in 16-bore.

The original version had double triggers. These are preferred by most Europeans on both side-by-side and over/under doubles. During the early 1930s, Val A. Browning designed the unique "twin-single" trigger. This was done to satisfy both those who preferred double triggers and those who liked the single trigger. With the twin single, first one barrel and then the second barrel could be fired by depressing either trigger, once for the first shot and once for the second

shot. Or one shot could be fired by pressing either the front or rear trigger and the second shot could be fired by pressing the other trigger.

This complicated system was ultimately replaced in the late 1930s by the selective single trigger. In this system, as with side-by-side doubles, either barrel may be fired first by moving the thumb safety selector.

Only five over/under shotguns known to the author have been made in the United States. Only the Remington M3200, successor to the pre-World War II M32, is manufactured in the U.S. today. Marlin and Savage once made inexpensive over/unders. A few hundred were made by a small Rhode Island firm shortly after World War II. Bill Ruger, arms designer and president of Sturm, Ruger Co., Inc., has designed an over/under that will be made in America. Like his other arms, it is extremely well designed, and it shows the same high quality of workmanship always associated with Ruger. It's scheduled for delivery to dealers in late 1976.

Major over/under-producing countries today are Japan and Italy. Belgium, Spain, West Germany, and the Soviet Union produce limited quantities. Some companies import over/unders designed in the country of manufacture. The Belgian-made Browning Superposed was designed by an American. Winchester designed the Model 101, made in Japan. The less expensive Browning over/under is Japanese-made.

Some critics, usually side-by-side devotees, claim it takes longer to eject empties and to reload an over/under than it does a side-by-side double. They also claim the over/under is more subject to wind pressure because of the greater surface presented. These claims have very little if any practical justification.

Guns like the fine Browning Superposed and the Winchester M101 have the two barrels brazed or otherwise joined together. Many European over/unders, including the Winchester M101 designed for the European market, utilize the lighter yet very rugged monobloc construction. Here two barrels are united by being fitted into a single block of steel.

The ventilated rib is more or less standard on over/unders. It was originally designed for trap guns that may be fired several hundred times in the course of a day's shoot. The added weight is insignificant.

Shotguns designed primarily for wildfowling would be better off with a solid rib; it is very difficult to dry out the perforations of a ventilated rib after a day's shoot on the marsh. Salt water is particularly corrosive. It would be better if wildfowl guns fitted with ventilated ribs were given a hard black chrome finish outside. All shotguns, and probably rifles, too, are rust-resistant if the barrel interiors are chromed. (It must be admitted, however, that some gunsmiths object to chromed bores because the chrome makes any barrel alteration far more difficult.)

Most over/unders made in America, like the Remington M3200, or designed for American shooters usually have a semi-beavertail fore-end. This is much more desirable than the slivers sometimes fitted to European guns.

Actions

Box lock. Most over/under guns utilize the Anson & Deeley type box lock. Examples: Browning Superposed, Winchester Model 101 and Remington M3200. The box lock, though not as easy to reach for thorough cleaning or drying, is sturdier than the side lock.

Side lock. This action type usually is found on more expensive English guns like the Woodward (made by Purdey), the Beretta SO series, and some Spanish guns. The side lock, as its name implies, has removable side plates which give ready access to the action for cleaning and drying. The two disadvantages of the side lock are cost and a weakening of the small of the stock. Today over/unders are so well designed and crafted that the advantages of side locks are no longer as important as formerly.

Locking systems

Underbolt. This system, used on the Browning Superposed, Winchester M101, and most other over/unders, consists of an underbolt—sometimes two underbolts—locking the barrels to the action.

Crossbolt. A few guns utilize the doll's-head extension—an extension of the barrel which fits into the receiver—plus a Greener crossbolt. This bolt fits through a hole in the doll's-head exten-

sion. The purpose of the bolting system is to keep barrels and action from separating during firing or at any other time.

Trigger systems

Double or twin triggers. This classic system was inherited from the side-by-side double-trigger gun. It is the simplest to design and manufacture. It is still the most reliable system. No mechanical selector system is required. You select the choke you need and pull the trigger for that particular barrel. Usually, as with side-by-side doubles, the front trigger fires the more open barrel.

The twin-trigger system is at its best when the front trigger is hinged. This allows more rapid access to the rear trigger when a follow-up shot is immediately required.

Most European gunners still prefer double triggers on their over/under guns. Nearly all over/unders designed for sale in the United States are currently fitted with selective single triggers. Beretta in the fine SO series offers the option of a single selective or double-trigger system.

Selective single trigger. A few European-made over/unders designed largely for American sale were available shortly before World War II. It has only been in the last 20 years that the over/under with selective single trigger has become popular in America.

Many early European manufacturers, including some of the finest, had considerable difficulty in designing trouble-free selective single-trigger systems. Today such systems as found in the Browning Superposed, the Winchester M101, and the Beretta SO series are probably as reliable as the old twin-trigger systems.

The combination sliding tang safety and barrel selector is almost universal on currently produced over/under guns. The slide, easily worked with the thumb, functions as a conventional safety. When it's pushed forward, the action can be fired. Whether manually operated or automatically actuated as the gun is opened (and the action thus cocked), the safety is on when in the rear position. The slide also moves to the left or right, and this sets the mechanism to fire one barrel or the other first. Normally the lower barrel—or the right barrel on a side-by-side—has the least choke and is fired first, while the tighter bore is reserved for the follow-up shot which is apt to be at longer range as a bird or clay target moves away. The firing order remains set until the shooter changes it—which he can do instantly by moving the slide if, for example, he has a chance for just one long shot and wants to fire the tight barrel rather than the more open one. When the first barrel has been fired the second barrel is automatically set to fire. It is not necessary to move the barrel selector for the second shot.

Some guns employ a separate selector slide or button—not integral with the safety—and a few use a behind-the-trigger safety/selector button.

Nonselective single trigger. This is usually found on a few less expensive guns. This system is not such a handicap as it might seem, because most first shots are from the more open barrel. There is no necessity for selective triggers on guns whose barrels have identical choke, like full and full or skeet and skeet.

Firing systems

Inertial. Here the recoil upon firing the first barrel cocks the trigger of the second barrel. This is the system used by the Browning Superposed, Winchester Pigeon Grade, Winchester Xpert, and others. Normally this system will fail only if the first cartridge misfires, which rarely happens with factory ammunition. It may occur with faulty reloads or very old shot shells in which the primer ingredients have deteriorated.

During a period of nearly 40 years the writer fired more than 200,000 rounds through a Browning Superposed fitted with twin-single triggers and utilizing the inertia system. He had less than 20 misfires, and these were caused by using World War I era ammunition—all that was immediately at hand.

Mechanical. Here both firing pins are mechanically cocked when the action is opened (or, in a few models, when it is closed). In theory this is the more reliable system in that the second barrel can be fired if the cartridge in the first barrel fails to fire.

Ejection systems

Selective automatic ejectors. This system, the same as with side-by-side double guns, automatically ejects an empty case while retaining a loaded case—if one remains—in the chamber. The empty is ejected over the shoulder when the gun is broken open. The merits of auto ejection are obvious.

Some gunners, notably trap and skeet shooters and other reloaders, modify the ejection system by removing springs so the cases can be manually extracted. This way one doesn't have to hunt on the ground for fired cases and they are less subject to damage.

All but the cheapest over/unders (and custom guns built for handloaders who want no ejectors) are now regularly fitted with selective automatic ejectors.

Safeties

The sliding tang safety combined with the barrel selector is almost universal, but at least one over/under utilizes a crossbolt behind the trigger-bow. There is no real advantage in this unless reduced cost is a factor.

The nonautomatic safety is to be preferred, and most good guns are so fitted. A nonautomatic safety means that when the gun is closed the safety must be manually pushed into the safe position. The letter S or word "SAFE" usually appears when the safety is in that position. Many shots have been lost with automatic safeties. A gunner who has expended his two cartridges and is trying to reload quickly for following shots must manually move the safety slide to the rear. This takes critical time.

Many trap guns have no safety. This is because the gun is only loaded just before firing from a designated station of the trap range.

BROWNING CITORI OVER/UNDER FIELD GUN

Manufacturer: Miroku Firearms, Japan

Importer/distributor: Browning Arms

Action type: box lock; break-top

Ignition system: mechanical

Trigger: single selective; tang selector

Locking system: underbolt

Ejection: selective automatic

Safety: manual; sliding tang selector

Barrel length & choke:

12-bore: 30.0 inches, full & full or full & modified; 28.0 or 26.0 inches, modified & full or improved cylinder & modified

20-bore: 28.0 or 26.0 inches, modified & full or improved cylinder & modified

Stock: 2-piece walnut; machine-checkered; full pistol grip; fluted modified beavertail fore-end; high-gloss finish

Buttplate: 12-bore, ventilated rubber recoil pad; 20-bore; black plastic

Length of pull: 14.25 inches

Drop at comb: 12-bore, 1.625 inches; 20-bore, 1.5 inches

Drop at heel: 12-bore, 2.5 inches; 20-bore, 2.375 inches

Weight:

12-bore: 26.0-inch barrels, 7.5 lbs.; 28.0-inch barrels, 7.65 lbs.; 30.0-inch barrels, 7.75 lbs.

20-bore: 26.0-inch barrels, 6.65 lbs.; 28.0-inch barrels, 6.75 lbs.

Sights: ivory bead on ventilated rib

Bore: 12, 20, 3.0-inch case

Comment: This is one of the better over/under shotguns in the below-$500 price range. It is an excellent buy.

BROWNING CITORI OVER/UNDER SKEET GUN

Manufacturer: Miroku Firearms, Japan

Importer/distributor: Browning Arms

Action type: box lock; break-top

Ignition system: mechanical

Trigger: single nonselective

Locking system: underbolt

Ejection: nonautomatic

Safety: nonautomatic; sliding tang

Barrel length & choke: 26.0 or 28.0 inches, skeet & skeet

Stock: 2-piece walnut; machine-checkered; full pistol grip; fluted beavertail fore-end; high-gloss finish

Buttplate: ventilated recoil pad

Length of pull: 14.375 inches

Drop at comb: 1.5 inches

Drop at heel: 2.0 inches

Weight:

12-bore: 26.0-inch barrels, 7.5 lbs.; 28.0-inch barrels, 7.7 lbs.

20-bore: 26.0-inch barrels, 6.7 lbs.; 28.0-inch barrels, 6.8 lbs.

Sights: front and mid-rib ivory bead; ventilated rib width 0.4 inch on 12-bore and 0.3125 inch on 20-bore

Bore: 12, 20, 2.75-inch case

Data: Notable feature is nonselective trigger. Lower barrel fires first. Nonautomatic ejection is not a handicap on a skeet field. For those who reload, as most skeet and trap shooters do today, it is an advantage.

Comment: A reliable, fast-handling, and good-looking lower-priced over/under.

BROWNING CITORI OVER/UNDER TRAP GUN

Manufacturer: Miroku Firearms, Japan

Importer/distributor: Browning Arms

Action type: box lock; break-top

Ignition system: mechanical

Trigger: single nonselective

Locking system: underbolt

Ejection: nonautomatic

Safety: no safety

Barrel length & choke: 30 inches, full & full, improved modified & full, or modified & full

Stock: 2-piece walnut; Monte Carlo; machine-checkered; semi-pistol grip; fluted semi-beavertail fore-end

Buttplate: ventilated rubber recoil pad

Length of pull: 14.375 inches

Drop at comb: 1.375 inches

Drop at Monte Carlo: 1.375 inches

Drop at heel: 2.0 inches

Weight: 8.625 lbs.

Sights: ivory bead front on 0.375-inch-wide ventilated rib

Bore: 12, 2.75-inch case

Data: The nonselective trigger fires the lower (more open) barrel first.

Comment: A medium-priced trap gun that is well made and is entirely suitable for any trap shooter.

BROWNING SUPERPOSED LIGHTNING 12-BORE OVER/UNDER

Manufacturer: Fabrique Nationale, Belgium

Importer/distributor: Browning Arms

Action type: box lock; break-top

Ignition system: inertial

Trigger: single selective; sliding tang selector

Locking system: underbolt

Ejection: automatic selective

Safety: nonautomatic; sliding tang selector

Barrel length & choke: 26.5 or 28.0 inches, full & improved modified, modified & improved cylinder, or skeet & cylinder

Stock: 2-piece walnut; hand-checkered; semi-pistol grip; semi-beavertail fore-end; high-gloss finish

Buttplate: black plastic

Length of pull: 14.24 inches

Drop at comb: 1.625 inches

BROWNING SUPERPOSED LIGHTNING 12-BORE OVER/
UNDER (continued)

Drop at heel: 2.5 inches

Weight: 26.5-inch barrels, 7.35 lbs.; 28.0-inch barrels, 7.5 lbs.

Sights: ivory bead front on 0.3125-inch-wide ventilated rib

Grades available: Grade I (standard), Diana, Midas, and Custom; Custom grade offers engraving and checkering to suit purchaser's taste and pocketbook

Bore: 12, 2.75-inch case

Data: This Superposed—like all Superposed variations—has, according to Browning, "22 different types of steel . . . 794 precision operations on the 84 parts . . . 67 parts have different heat treatments . . . 1,490 instruments and gauges check the parts . . . parts are subject to 2,310 different checks and measurements . . . skilled craftsmen perform 155 hand operations . . . All parts are handfitted . . . functional tests include proof firing and pattern checking and rigid final inspection by experienced gunsmith inspectors."

The above statement is not a mere advertising blurb. The author has seen these steps during a visit to the Fabrique Nationale plant in Belgium.

The Superposed was formerly offered in two weights, Standard and Lightning. The Standard weight is now available in only the 12-bore Magnum gun.

Superposed variations are offered in three basic grades:
1. Grade I (standard)—light engraving.
2. Diana Grade—fine engraving on silver steel plus denser wood with fancier pattern. Finer checkering.
3. Midas Grade—18-karat gold bas-relief birds. Finer and denser wood with finer checkering than Diana Grade. Each gun has a different design.

Custom checkering and engraving is also available. A side-plate extension can be added to provide more room for engraving and bas-relief figures.

Comment: The Browning Superposed has long been the standard by which all other box-lock over/under shotguns are judged. The basic Grade I variation is as fine a box-lock over/under as made anywhere in the world. No over/under has finer materials or superior workmanship. No mechanical improvements are probably possible at this stage of gunmaking technology. More expensive guns are more expensive only because of wood, checkering and engraving, and bas-relief figures.

Most non-monobloc over/unders are patterned after the Superposed. The single selective trigger mechanism has established the standard.

Double triggers and straight stocks, available to the European market, can be obtained by Americans on special order.

Inflation has affected prices throughout the world. The Superposed is no exception. The author purchased his first Superposed in the late 1930s. Cost new was $85. The same gun today costs more than a dozen times as much. However, the Superposed is an excellent investment. No matter what you pay today, it will cost more next year. Your secondhand Superposed will also be worth more. A Superposed that cost about $100 before World War II now fetches $500 or more.

The Superposed is one of the few over/under guns that can be obtained with one or more sets of extra barrels. A shooter who already owns a Superposed can also obtain extra sets of barrels for it. To ensure a perfect fit, the gun must be returned to the factory for fitting. The time required is 6–9 months.

There is but one feature—and it's a small one—that the author doesn't like about the Superposed: Each extra set of barrels must have its own fore-end.

BROWNING SUPERPOSED LIGHTNING SMALL BORE OVER/UNDER

Manufacturer: Fabrique Nationale, Belgium

Importer/distributor: Browning Arms

Action type: box lock; break-top

Ignition system: inertial

Trigger: single selective; tang selector

Locking system: underbolt

Ejection: automatic selective

Safety: nonautomatic; tang slide

Barrel length & choke: 26.5 or 28.0 inches, full & full, full & improved modified, modified & improved cylinder, skeet & cylinder

Stock: 2-piece walnut; hand-checkered; pistol grip; semi-beavertail fore-end; high-gloss finish.

Buttplate: black plastic

Length of pull: 14.25 inches

Drop at comb: 1.5 inches

Drop at heel: 2.375 inches

Weight:

  20-bore: 26.5-inch barrels, 6.25 lbs.; 28.0-inch barrels, 6.5 lbs.

28-bore: 26.5-inch barrels, 6.45 lbs.; 28.0-inch barrels, 6.625 lbs.

.410-bore: 26.5-inch barrels, 6.625 lbs.; 28.0-inch barrels, 6.875 lbs.

Grades available: Grade I (standard), Diana, and Midas; custom checkering and engraving to purchaser's taste

Sights: ivory bead front on 0.25-inch-wide ventilated rib

Bore: 20, .410, 3.0-inch case; 28, 2.75-inch case

Data: Same basic data as for 12-bore except smaller and lighter receiver, bore, and weights.

Comment: One of the finest smallbore box-lock over/under shotguns.

BROWNING SUPERPOSED LIGHTNING SKEET OVER/UNDER

Manufacturer: Fabrique Nationale, Belgium

Importer/distributor: Browning Arms

Action type: box lock; break-top

Ignition system: inertial

Trigger: single selective; tang selector

Locking system: underbolt

Ejection: automatic selective

Safety: nonautomatic; tang slide

Barrel length & choke: 26.5 or 28.0 inches, skeet & skeet

Stock: 2-piece walnut; hand-checkered; pistol grip; semi-beavertail fore-end; high-gloss finish

Buttplate: ventilated rubber recoil pad

Length of pull: 14.375 inches

Drop at comb: 1.5 inches

Drop at heel: 2.0 inches

Weight:

  12-bore: 26.5-inch barrels, 7.5 lbs.; 28.0-inch barrels, 7.75 lbs.

20-bore: 26.5-inch barrels, 6.5 lbs.; 28.0-inch barrels, 6.75 lbs.

28-bore: 26.5-inch barrels, 6.7 lbs.; 28.0-inch barrels, 6.85 lbs.

.410-bore: 26.5-inch barrels, 6.5 lbs.; 28.0-inch barrels, 6.7 lbs.

Sights: ivory bead front and steel mid-rib bead; ventilated rib width 0.6125 inch

Grades available: Grade I (standard), Diana, Midas; custom work on special order

Bore: 28, 20, 12, 2.75-inch case; .410, 2.5-inch case

Data: Similar to basic model.

Comment: One of the finest skeet guns made. An All-Gauge Skeet Set (one gun with four matched sets of barrels) is also available in either the 26.5-inch or 28.0-inch barrel length. The set is built on a 12-bore receiver, and the interchangeable barrels are so designed that the gun has the same weight regardless of whether the 12-bore or .410 barrels are in place.

BROWNING SUPERPOSED LIGHTNING TRAP OVER/UNDER

Manufacturer: Fabrique Nationale, Belgium

Importer/distributor: Browning Arms

Action type: box lock; break-top

Ignition system: inertial

Trigger: single selective; tang selector

Locking system: underbolt

Ejection: automatic selective

Safety: none

Barrel length & choke: 30.0 inches, full & full, full & improved modified, or modified & full

Stock: 2-piece black walnut; hand checkering; pistol grip; high-gloss finish

Buttplate: red ventilated rubber recoil pad

Length of pull: 14.375 inches

Drop at comb: 1.435 inches

Drop at heel: 1.625 inches

Weight: 7.75 lbs.

Sights: ivory bead front and mid-rib steel bead; ventilated rib width 0.3125 inch

Grades available: Grade I (standard), Diana, Midas; custom to order available

Bore: 12, 2.75-inch case

Data: Same as for basic model.

Comment: A fine trap gun.

BROWNING SUPERPOSED BROADWAY TRAP OVER/UNDER

Manufacturer: Fabrique Nationale, Belgium

Importer/distributor: Browning Arms

Action type: box lock; break-top

Ignition system: inertial

Trigger: single selective; tang selector

Locking system: underbolt

Ejection: automatic selective

Safety: nonautomatic; tang slide

Barrel length & choke: 30.0 or 32.0 inches, full & full, improved modified & full, or modified & full

Stock: 2-piece European walnut; hand-checkered; pistol grip; high-gloss finish

Buttplate: ventilated recoil pad

Length of pull: 14.375 inches

Drop at comb: 1.45 inches

Drop at heel: 1.625 inches

Weight: 30.0-inch barrels, 7.875 lbs.; 32.0-inch barrels, 8.0 lbs.

Sights: ivory bead front and metal mid-rib bead; ventilated rib width 0.625 inch

Bore: 12, 2.75-inch case

Data: Same as basic data for Superposed Field Grade 12-bore. Broadway's main distinguishing feature is extra-wide rib of 0.625 inch. Broadway is only Superposed fitted with 32.0-inch barrels (optional with 30.0-inch).

Comment: One of the better trap guns. Available in Grade I (standard), Diana, and Midas grades.

BROWNING SUPERPOSED MAGNUM OVER/UNDER

Manufacturer: Fabrique Nationale, Belgium

Importer/distributor: Browning Arms

Action type: box lock; break-top

Ignition system: inertial

Trigger: single selective; tang selector

Locking system: underbolt

Ejection: selective automatic

Safety: nonautomatic; tang slide

Barrel length & choke: 28.0 or 30.0 inches, full & full (any standard choke combination can be ordered and usually without extra charge)

Stock: 2-piece black walnut; hand-checkered; full pistol grip; semi-beavertail fore-end; high-gloss finish; fancier wood and finer checkering on Diana and Midas grades

Buttplate: ventilated rubber recoil pad

Length of pull: 14.25 inches

Drop at comb: 1.625 inches

Drop at heel: 2.5 inches

Weight: 28.0-inch barrels, 7.9375 lbs.; 30.0-inch barrels, 8.0625 lbs.

Sights: raised steel bead on ventilated rib; rib width 0.3125 inch

Bore: 12, 3.0-inch case

Data: Same as for basic Superposed except for recoil pad and chambering.

Comment: This is one of the finest over/under 12-bore 3.0-inch Magnums made today. As noted elsewhere, solid ribs are preferable on shotguns designed solely for wildfowl. However, anyone who can afford the least expensive grade can afford to have a custom solid rib fitted or have the barrels black-chromed.

Engraving and checkering details of Midas grade Browning Superposed shotgun.

BROWNING SUPERPOSED SUPERLIGHT OVER/UNDER

Manufacturer: Fabrique Nationale, Belgium

Importer/distributor: Browning Arms

Action type: box lock; break-top

Ignition system: inertial

Trigger: single selective; tang selector

Locking system: underbolt

Ejection: automatic selective

Safety: nonautomatic; tang slide

Barrel length & choke: 26.5 inches, full & improved modified, modified & improved cylinder, or skeet & cylinder

Stock: 2-piece walnut; hand-checkered; straight grip; high-gloss finish

Length of pull: 14.25 inches

Drop at comb: 12-bore, 1.625 inches; 20-bore, 1.5 inches

Drop at heel: 12-bore, 2.5 inches; 20-bore, 2.375 inches

Weight: 12-bore, 6.5 lbs.; 20-bore, 6.0 lbs.

Sights: ivory bead; solid rib; 12-bore rib width 0.3125 inch, 20-bore rib width 0.25 inch

Grades available: Grade I (standard), Diana, and Midas. Custom checkering and engraving available to suit purchaser.

Bore: 12, 2.75-inch case; 20, 3.0-inch case

Data: Except for straight grip and solid rib, this is same as basic Superposed.

Comment: This is one of the finest and lightest over/unders.

CHARLES DALY SUPERIOR GRADE FIELD OVER/UNDER

Manufacturer: Miroku Firearms, Japan

Importer/distributor: Charles Daly, Inc.

Action type: box lock; break-top

Ignition system: inertial

Trigger: single selective; tang selector

Locking system: monobloc

Ejection: automatic selective

Safety: automatic; tang slide

Barrel length & choke: 28.0 inches, full & modified; 26.0 inches, modified & improved cylinder

Stock: 2-piece walnut; machine-checkered; full pistol grip with black plastic cap and white line spacer; fluted beavertail fore-end; polyurethane finish

Buttplate: black plastic

Length of pull: 14.0 inches

Drop at comb: 1.5 inches

Drop at heel: 2.5 inches

Weight:

12-bore: 26.0-inch barrel, 7.25 lbs.; 28.0-inch barrel, 7.5 lbs.

20-bore: 26.0-inch barrel, 6.25 lbs.; 28.0-inch barrel, 6.5 lbs.

Sights: metal bead front on ventilated rib

Bore: 12, 2.75-inch case; 20, 3.0-inch case

Data: Medium bright-blue barrels. Light engraving or etching on receiver.

Comment: A good low-priced over/under field gun. Checkering is fairly well executed. Good fit of wood to metal.

CHARLES DALY SUPERIOR GRADE OVER/UNDER MAGNUM

Manufacturer: Miroku Firearms, Japan

Importer/distributor: Charles Daly, Inc.

Action type: box lock; break-top

Ignition system: inertial

Trigger: single selective; tang selector

Locking system: monobloc

Ejection: automatic selective

Safety: automatic; tang slide

Barrel length & choke: 30.0 inches, full & modified

Stock: 2-piece walnut; machine checkering; fluted beavertail fore-end; full pistol grip with black plastic cap and white line spacer; polyurethane finish

Buttplate: ventilated rubber recoil pad

Length of pull: 14.0 inches

Drop at comb: 1.5 inches

Drop at heel: 2.5 inches

Weight: 7.75 lbs.

Sights: metal bead front on ventilated rib

Bore: 12, 3.0-inch case

Data: Similar to Superior Grade Field version except for barrel length, weight, and recoil pad.

Comment: Similar to Superior Grade Field version comment. All 12-bore Magnums should weigh at least 8.0 lbs., and 8.25 lbs. is even better.

CHARLES DALY SUPERIOR GRADE OVER/UNDER SKEET

Manufacturer: Miroku Firearms, Japan

Importer/distributor: Charles Daly, Inc.

Action type: box lock; break-top

Ignition system: inertial

Trigger: single selective; tang selector

Locking system: monobloc

Ejection: automatic selective

Safety: automatic; tang slide

Barrel length & choke: 12-bore, 26.0 inches, skeet & skeet; 20-bore, 28.0 or 26.0 inches, skeet & skeet

Stock: 2-piece walnut; machine-checkered; fluted beavertail fore-end; full pistol grip with black plastic cap and white line spacer; polyurethane finish

Buttplate: black plastic

Length of pull: 14.0 inches

Drop at comb: 1.5 inches

Drop at heel: 2.5 inches

Weight:

12-bore: 7.25 lbs.

20-bore: 26.0-inch barrels, 6.25 lbs.; 28.0-inch barrels, 6.5 lbs.

Sights: metal bead front and mid-rib on ventilated rib

Bore: 12, 2.75-inch case; 20, 3.0-inch case

Data: Same as for Superior Grade Field except for chokes.

Comment: Same as for Superior Grade Field. A sturdy, inexpensive skeet gun.

CHARLES DALY SUPERIOR GRADE OVER/UNDER TRAP

Manufacturer: Miroku Firearms, Japan

Importer/distributor: Charles Daly, Inc.

Action type: box lock; break-top

Ignition system: inertial

Trigger: single selective; tang selector

Locking system: monobloc

Ejection: automatic selective

Safety: nonautomatic; tang slide

Barrel length & choke: 32.0 inches, full & improved modified; 30.0 inches, full & improved modified or full & modified

Stock: 2-piece walnut; machine-checkered; fluted beavertail fore-end; full pistol grip with black plastic cap and white line spacer; polyurethane finish

Buttplate: ventilated rubber recoil pad

Length of pull: 14.375 inches

Drop at comb: 1.5 inches

Drop at heel: 2.5 inches

Weight: 30.0-inch barrels, 8.0 lbs.; 32.0-inch barrels, 8.25 lbs.

Sights: metal bead front and mid-rib on ventilated rib

Bore: 12, 2.75-inch case

Data: Same as for Superior Grade Field except for barrel lengths, chokes, and recoil pad.

Comment: An excellent medium-priced trap gun.

CHARLES DALY SUPERIOR GRADE OVER/UNDER MONTE CARLO TRAP

Manufacturer: Miroku Firearms, Japan

Importer/distributor: Charles Daly, Inc.

Action type: box lock; break-top

Ignition system: inertial

Trigger: single selective; tang selector

Locking system: monobloc

Ejection: automatic selective

Safety: nonautomatic; tang slide

Barrel length & choke: 32.0 or 30.0 inches, full & improved modified

Stock: 2-piece walnut; checkered; fluted beavertail fore-end; full pistol grip with black plastic cap and white line spacer; Monte Carlo comb

Buttplate: ventilated recoil pad

Length of pull: 14.0 inches

Drop at comb: 1.5 inches

Drop at Monte Carlo: 1.5 inches

Drop at heel: 2.5 inches

Weight: 30.0-inch barrels, 7.75 lbs.; 32.0-inch barrels, 8.0 lbs.

Sights: front and mid-rib metal bead on ventilated rib

Bore: 12, 2.75-inch case

Comment: A well-designed, well-crafted, relatively inexpensive trap gun.

CHARLES DALY DIAMOND GRADE FIELD GUN

Manufacturer: Miroku Firearms, Japan

Importer/distributor: Charles Daly, Inc.

Action type: box lock; break-top

Ignition system: inertial

Trigger: single selective; tang selector

Locking system: monobloc

Ejection: automatic selective; can be switched to extraction only

Safety: nonautomatic; tang slide

Barrel length & choke: 28.0 inches, full & modified; 26.0 inches, modified & improved cylinder

Stock: 2-piece French walnut; hand-checkered; full pistol grip with black plastic cap and white line spacer; fluted beavertail fore-end; polyurethane finish

Buttplate: black plastic

Length of pull: 14.0 inches

Drop at comb: 1.5 inches

Drop at heel: 2.5 inches

Weight: 26.0-inch barrels, 7.25 lbs.; 28.0-inch barrels, 7.5 lbs.

Sights: metal bead front on ventilated rib

Bore: 12, 2.75-inch case

Data: Silver-gray etched or engraved receiver. Gold-plated trigger. This gun employs "Selexor" ejection system, which permits shooter to switch from automatic ejection to merely extraction whenever he wishes.

Comment: A well-designed and well-crafted field-grade over/under for its price class ($600 in 1976).

CHARLES DALY DIAMOND GRADE INTERNATIONAL TRAP

Manufacturer: Miroku Firearms, Japan

Importer/distributor: Charles Daly, Inc.

Action type: box lock; break-top

Ignition system: inertial

Trigger: single selective; tang selector

Locking system: monobloc

Ejection: automatic selective; can be switched to extraction only

Safety: nonautomatic; tang slide

Barrel length & choke: 32.0 inches, full & improved modified; 30.0 inches, full & full, full & modified, or full & improved modified

Stock: 2-piece French walnut; hand-checkered; Monte Carlo; fluted beavertail fore-end; semi-gloss polyurethane finish

Buttplate: Pachmayr ventilated rubber recoil pad

Length of pull: 14.375 inches

Drop at comb: 1.5 inches

Drop at Monte Carlo: 1.5 inches

Drop at heel: 2.5 inches

Weight: 30.0-inch barrels, 8.0 lbs.; 32.0-inch barrels, 8.25 lbs.

Sights: metal bead front and mid-rib on ventilated rib

Bore: 12, 2.75-inch case

Data: Same as for Diamond Grade Field Gun except barrel lengths, borings, and Monte Carlo stock.

Comment: A well-designed and well-executed trap gun.

CHARLES DALY DIAMOND GRADE SKEET

Manufacturer: Miroku Firearms, Japan

Importer/distributor: Charles Daly, Inc.

Action type: box lock; break-top

Ignition system: inertial

Trigger: single selective; tang selector

Locking system: monobloc

Ejection: automatic selective; can be switched to extraction only

Safety: nonautomatic; tang slide

Barrel length & choke: 26.0 inches, skeet & skeet

Stock: 2-piece French walnut; hand-checkered; fluted beavertail fore-end; full pistol grip with black plastic cap; polyurethane finish

Buttplate: black plastic

Length of pull: 14.0 inches

Drop at comb: 1.5 inches

Drop at heel: 2.5 inches

Weight: 7.5 lbs.

Sights: metal bead front and mid-rib on ventilated rib

Bore: 12, 2.75-inch case

Data: Same as for Diamond Grade Field Gun except for chokes.

Comment: A good skeet gun.

CHARLES DALY OVER/UNDER FLAT TOP DIAMOND GRADE INTERNATIONAL TRAP

Manufacturer: Miroku Firearms, Japan

Importer/distributor: Charles Daly, Inc.

Action type: box lock; break-top

Ignition system: inertial

Trigger: single selective; tang selector

Locking system: monobloc

Ejection: automatic selective; can be switched to extraction only

Safety: nonautomatic; tang slide

Barrel length & choke: 32.0 or 30.0 inches, full & improved modified

Stock: 2-piece French walnut; hand-checkered; fluted beavertail fore-end; full pistol grip with black plastic cap and white line spacer; polyurethane finish

Buttplate: Pachmayr ventilated rubber recoil pad

Length of pull: 14.375 inches

Drop at comb: 1.5 inches

Drop at Monte Carlo: 1.5 inches

Drop at heel: 2.5 inches

Weight: 30.0-inch barrels, 8.0 lbs.; 32.0-inch barrels, 8.25 lbs.

Sights: metal bead front and mid-rib on flat-top ventilated rib

Bore: 12, 2.75-inch case

Data: Same as regular trap, but with flat-top rib.

Comment: Same as for regular trap.

FRANCHI FIELD GRADE FALCONET OVER/UNDER

Manufacturer: Luigi Franchi, Italy

Importer/distributor: Stoeger Arms Corp.

Action type: box lock; break-top

Ignition system: mechanical

Trigger: single selective; tang selector

Locking system: monobloc

Ejection: automatic selective

Safety: automatic; behind trigger

Barrel length & choke:

12-bore: 30.0 or 28.0 inches, modified & full; 26.0 inches, improved cylinder & modified; 24.0 inches, cylinder & improved cylinder

20-bore: 28.0 inches, modified & full; 26.0 inches, improved cylinder & modified; 24.0 inches, cylinder & improved cylinder

Stock: 2-piece Italian walnut; hand-checkered; pistol grip; high-gloss (epoxy) finish

Buttplate: black plastic

Length of pull: 14.5 inches

Drop at comb: 1.5 inches

Drop at heel: 2.5 inches

Weight:

12-bore: 24.0-inch barrels, 6.0 lbs.; 26.0-inch barrels, 6.25 lbs.; 28.0-inch barrels, 6.35 lbs.; 30.0-inch barrels, 6.5 lbs.

20-bore: 24.0-inch barrels, 6.0 lbs.; 26.0-inch barrels, 6.15 lbs.; 28.0-inch barrels, 6.25 lbs.

Sights: metal bead front on ventilated rib

Bore: 12, 2.75-inch case; 20, 3.0-inch case

Data: The extremely light weight of this arm, notably in the 12-bore, is achieved through the use of a light but strong metal alloy. The selective single trigger has overhead sears.

There are two versions of this least expensive Falconet. Both have lightly engraved bird scenes. The receiver of the "Buckskin" has a silvery-type finish. The "Ebony" has a dark finish.

Comment: This ultra-lightweight over/under is well made and is a good buy. The 12-bore would be easier to shoot if fitted with a ventilated recoil pad. This, of course, can be installed by a gunsmith for the purchaser. The 20-bore is a delight to handle.

FRANCHI SILVER FALCONET OVER/UNDER

Manufacturer: Luigi Franchi, Italy

Importer/distributor: Stoeger Arms Corp.

Action type: box lock; break-top

Ignition system: mechanical

Trigger: single selective; tang selector

Locking system: monobloc

Ejection: automatic selective

Safety: automatic; tang slide

Barrel length & choke: 30.0 or 28.0 inches, modified & full; 26.0 inches, improved cylinder & modified; 24.0 inches, cylinder & improved cylinder

Stock: 2-piece Italian walnut; hand-checkered; pistol grip; high-gloss (epoxy) finish

Buttplate: black plastic

Length of pull: 14.25 inches

Drop at comb: 1.5 inches

Drop at heel: 2.25 inches

Weight: 24.0-inch barrels, 6.875 lbs.; 26.0-inch barrels, 7.0 lbs.; 28.0-inch barrels, 7.125 lbs.; 30.0-inch barrels, 7.25 lbs.

FRANCHI SILVER FALCONET
OVER/UNDER (continued)

Sights: metal bead front on ventilated rib

Bore: 12, 2.75-inch case

Data: Interiors of barrels are chromed. Pickled silver receiver with light engraving (English-type scroll).

Comment: A well-made, low-priced over/under.

FRANCHI PEREGRINE M400 OVER/UNDER FIELD GRADE

Manufacturer: Luigi Franchi, Italy

Importer/distributor: Stoeger Arms Corp.

Action type: box lock; break-top

Ignition system: mechanical

Trigger: single selective; selector button on trigger

Locking system: monobloc

Ejection: automatic selective

Safety: automatic; tang slide

Barrel length & choke: 28.0 inches, full & modified; 26.5 inches, full & modified, modified & improved cylinder, or improved cylinder & cylinder

Stock: 2-piece Italian walnut; hand-checkered; beavertail fore-end; pistol grip with black plastic cap; polyurethane finish

Buttplate: black plastic

Length of pull: 14.5 inches

Drop at comb: 1.5 inches

Drop at heel: 2.25 inches

Weight: 26.5-inch barrels, 7.0 lbs.; 28.0-inch barrels, 7.125 lbs.

Sights: metal bead front on ventilated rib

Bore: 12, 2.75-inch case

Data: Same as for M451 except for all-steel receiver, which accounts for additional weight.

Comment: Save for weight, same as for M451.

FRANCHI PEREGRINE M451 OVER/UNDER FIELD GRADE

Manufacturer: Luigi Franchi, Italy

Importer/distributor: Stoeger Arms Corp.

Action type: box lock; break-top

Ignition system: mechanical

Trigger: single selective; selector button on trigger

Locking system: monobloc

Ejection: automatic selective

Safety: automatic; tang slide

Barrel length & choke: 28.0 inches, full & modified; 26.5 inches, full & modified, improved cylinder & cylinder, or modified & improved cylinder

Stock: 2-piece Italian walnut; hand checkering; full pistol grip with black plastic cap; beavertail fore-end; polyurethane finish

Buttplate: black plastic

Length of pull: 14.5 inches

Drop at comb: 1.5 inches

Drop at heel: 2.25 inches

Weight: 26.5-inch barrels, 6.0625 lbs.; 28.0-inch barrels, 6.25 lbs.

Sights: metal bead on ventilated rib

Bore: 12, 2.75-inch case

Data: Receiver weight is saved by utilizing a lightweight alloy. Blued barrels and chrome-plated bores.

Comment: This is probably the lightest 12-bore made. As noted above, considerable weight is saved through an alloy receiver. This ultra-lightweight 12-bore should be fitted with a recoil pad.

This is one of a very few with 26.5-inch barrels choked full & modified. The improved cylinder & cylinder bore is practically a skeet-bored gun. It is the least expensive in Franchi's Falconet line.

FRANCHI PEREGRINE M3003 OVER/UNDER SKEET

Manufacturer: Luigi Franchi, Italy

Importer/distributor: Stoeger Arms Corp.

Action type: box lock; break-top

Ignition system: mechanical

Trigger: single selective; selector button on trigger

Locking system: monobloc

Ejection: automatic selective

Safety: automatic; tang slide

Barrel length & choke: 26.5 inches, skeet 1 & skeet 2

Stock: 2-piece Italian walnut; hand checkering; beavertail fore-end; full pistol grip; satin finish

Buttplate: ventilated rubber recoil pad

Length of pull: 14.375 inches

Drop at comb: 1.5 inches

Drop at heel: 2.25 inches

Weight: 7.5 lbs.

Sights: metal bead front on ventilated rib

Bore: 12, 2.75-inch case

Data: This is Franchi's $2000 skeet gun (prices effective in 1976). It features a steel receiver and true hand-cut checkering rather than so-called hand checkering that is done with a high-speed hand-operated electric cutter. Nicely engraved receiver.

Comment: A fine skeet gun for those who can afford it.

FRANCHI PEREGRINE M3003 OVER/UNDER TRAP

Manufacturer: Luigi Franchi, Italy

Importer/distributor: Stoeger Arms Corp.

Action type: box lock; break-top

Ignition system: mechanical

Trigger: single selective; selector button on trigger

Locking system: monobloc

Safety: nonautomatic; tang slide

Barrel length & choke: 30.0, 29.0, or 28.0 inches, full & modified

Stock: 2-piece European walnut; hand-checkered; full pistol grip; beavertail fore-end; satin finish

FRANCHI PEREGRINE M3003 OVER/UNDER TRAP
(continued)

Buttplate: ventilated rubber recoil pad

Length of pull: 14.375 inches

Drop at comb: 1.5 inches

Drop at heel: 2.0 inches

Weight: 7.75 lbs., all barrel lengths

Sights: metal bead front and mid-rib on ventilated rib

Bore: 12, 2.75-inch case

Data: Save for barrel lengths, chokes, and stock dimensions, same as for M3003 Skeet.

Comment: A good $2000 trap gun.

BERETTA BL-2/S OVER/UNDER FIELD GRADE

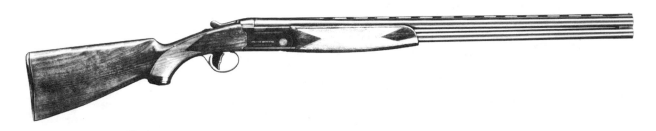

Manufacturer: Pietro Beretta, Italy

Importer/distributor: Beretta Arms Co.

Action type: box lock; break-top

Ignition system: mechanical

Trigger: selective Speed-Trigger (see data below)

Locking system: monobloc

Ejection: automatic selective

Safety: automatic; tang slide

Barrel length & choke: 28.0 inches, full & modified; 26.0 inches, modified & improved cylinder

Stock: 2-piece Italian walnut; hand-checkered; beavertail fore-end; full pistol grip; polyurethane finish

Buttplate: black plastic

Length of pull: 14.125 inches

Drop at comb: 1.5 inches

Drop at heel: 2.5 inches

Weight: 26.0-inch barrels, 7.25 lbs.; 28.0-inch barrels, 7.5 lbs.

Sights: metal bead front on ventilated rib

Bore: 12, 2.75-inch case

Data: This latest Beretta entry — and the least expensive of them all — introduces a new trigger mechanism. The trigger itself is the barrel selector. Press the upper half of the trigger to fire the open-choke barrel and the lower half to fire the tighter-choke barrel.

Comment: The Speed-Trigger selector may well be one of the best trigger developments since the single trigger was introduced. I wonder if a gloved hand might foul up the operation. Gloves, however, are worn by only a small minority of gunners — usually cold-weather wildfowlers or hare hunters.

Though this over/under is at the bottom of Beretta's over/under price line, it has the craftsmanship associated with much more expensive Beretta arms.

Close-up photo of the Beretta BL-2/S trigger. The upper half is pressed to fire the open-choke barrel; press the lower half to fire the tighter-choke barrel.

BERETTA BL-2S OVER/UNDER MAGNUM

Manufacturer: Pietro Beretta, Italy

Importer/distributor: Beretta Arms Co.

Action type: box lock; break-top

Ignition system: inertial

Trigger: selective Speed-Trigger (see data for Field Grade)

Locking system: monobloc

Ejection: automatic selective

Safety: automatic; tang slide

Barrel length & choke: 30.0 inches, full & modified

Stock: 2-piece Italian walnut; hand-checkered; beavertail fore-end with wrap-around hand checkering; full pistol grip; polyurethane finish

Buttplate: ventilated rubber recoil pad

Length of pull: 14.125 inches

Drop at comb: 1.5 inches

Drop at heel: 2.5 inches

Weight: 7.75 lbs.

Sights: metal bead front

Bore: 12, 3.0-inch case

Data: Same as for Field Grade except magnum chambering and recoil pad.

Comment: Same as for Field Grade. As noted elsewhere, 12-bore Magnums should weigh at least 8.0 lbs. or even slightly more.

BERETTA BL-3 FIELD GRADE 12-BORE OVER/UNDER

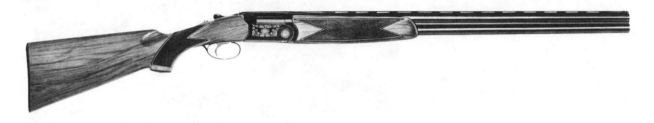

Manufacturer: Pietro Beretta, Italy

Importer/distributor: Beretta Arms Co.

Action type: over/under; box lock; monobloc

Ignition system: mechanical

Trigger: single selective; tang selector

Locking system: dual locking lugs projecting from breech face fit into corresponding slots in monobloc assembly

Ejection: manual; extractors only

Safety: automatic; tang slide; not integral with barrel selector

Barrel length & choke: 28.0 inches, modified & full; 26.0 inches, improved cylinder & modified

Stock: 2-piece hand-checkered European walnut; capped pistol grip

Buttplate: black plastic

Length of pull: 14.125 inches

Drop at comb: 1.5 inches

Drop at heel: 2.5 inches

Weight: 26.0-inch barrels, 7.15 lbs.; 28.0-inch barrels, 7.25 lbs.

Sights: metal bead front on ventilated rib

Bore: 12, 2.75-inch case

Data: Barrels are drilled and reamed; monobloc is machined; barrels are then machined to fit interior of monobloc. Monobloc is heated and barrels are inserted while cold. Cooling monobloc shrinks to fit barrels. This is considered a better method than brazing monobloc unit to barrels or vice versa.

A notable feature on all BL series is the gas-escape channel in event of primer failure.

Comment: Other BL series features include engine-turned side of monobloc unit, spring-loaded firing pins that retract into breech, and main springs of Swedish coil steel (this type of spring is superior to flat springs). Even the BL-3, least expensive in the BL series, shows considerable hand work.

BERETTA BL-3 MAGNUM OVER/UNDER

Manufacturer: Pietro Beretta, Italy

Importer/distributor: Beretta Arms Co.

Action type: over/under; box lock; monobloc

Ignition system: mechanical

Trigger: single selective; tang selector

Locking system: dual locking lugs projecting from breech face fit into corresponding slots in monobloc assembly

Ejection: manual; extractors only

Safety: automatic; tang slide; not integral with barrel selector switch

Barrel length & choke: 30.0 inches, modified & full

Stock: 2-piece hand-checkered European walnut; capped pistol grip

Buttplate: ventilated rubber recoil pad

Length of pull: 14.125 inches

Drop at comb: 1.5 inches

Drop at heel: 2.5 inches

Weight: 7.5 lbs.

Sights: metal bead front on ventilated rib

Bore: 12, 3.0-inch case

Data: Same as for BL-3 field grade save for recoil pad.

Comment: Same as for field grade BL-3. Any 12-bore magnum, as noted elsewhere, should weigh at least 8 lbs. Arms designed for wildfowling should have a solid rib. Barrels should be bright-chromed inside with black-chromed exterior. Nonautomatic safety is preferable to automatic safety.

BERETTA BL-3 12-BORE SKEET WIDE-RIB OVER/UNDER

Manufacturer: Pietro Beretta, Italy

Importer/distributor: Beretta Arms Co.

Action type: over/under; box lock; monobloc

Ignition system: mechanical

Trigger: single selective; tang selector

Locking system: dual locking lugs projecting from breech face fit into corresponding slots in monobloc assembly

Ejection: manual; extractors only

Safety: nonautomatic; tang slide not integral with barrel selector

Barrel length & choke: 26.0 inches, skeet & skeet

Stock: 2-piece hand-checkered European walnut; capped pistol grip

Buttplate: black plastic

Length of pull: 14.125 inches

Drop at comb: 1.5 inches

Drop at heel: 2.5 inches

Weight: 7.25 lbs.

Sights: metal bead front; mid-rib bead; ventilated rib

Bore: 12, 2.75-inch case

Data: Except for choke and sights, same as 12-bore BL-3 field grade.

Comment: Same as for BL-3 field grade.

BERETTA BL-3 SMALLBORE FIELD GRADE SKEET OVER/UNDER

Manufacturer: Pietro Beretta, Italy

Importer/distributor: Beretta Arms Co.

Action type: over/under; box lock; monobloc

Ignition system: mechanical

Trigger: selective single; tang selector

Locking system: dual locking lugs projecting from breech face fit into corresponding slots in monobloc assembly

Ejection: manual; extractors only

Safety: automatic on smallbore field grade; nonautomatic on smallbore skeet; tang slide not integral with barrel selector

Barrel length & choke: 28.0 inches, modified & full; 26.0 inches, improved cylinder & modified or skeet & skeet

Stock: 2-piece hand-checkered European walnut; capped pistol grip

Buttplate: black plastic

Length of pull: 14.125 inches

Drop at comb: 1.5 inches

Drop at heel: 2.5 inches

Weight: 26.0-inch barrels, 6.0 lbs.; 28.0-inch barrels, 6.25 lbs.

Sights: metal bead front on field grade; metal bead front and mid-rib on smallbore skeet gun; ventilated rib on all BL-3s

Bore: 20, 3.0-inch case

Data: Same as for BL-3 field grade 12-bore.

Comment: A well-made lower-priced over/under smallbore and/or skeet gun. For general comment on BL-3 series see BL-3 field grade 12-bore.

BERETTA BL-3 WIDE-RIB TRAP OVER/UNDER

Manufacturer: Pietro Beretta, Italy

Importer/distributor: Beretta Arms Co.

Action type: over/under; box lock; monobloc

Ignition system: mechanical

Trigger: single selective; tang selector

Locking system: dual locking lugs projecting from breech face fit into corresponding slots in monobloc assembly

Ejection: manual; extractors only

Safety: nonautomatic; tang slide not integral with barrel selector

Barrel length & choke: 30.0 inches, improved modified & full

Stock: 2-piece hand-checkered European walnut; Monte Carlo; capped pistol grip

Buttplate: ventilated recoil pad

Length of pull: 14.375 inches

Drop at comb: 1.375 inches

Drop at Monte Carlo: 1.375 inches

Drop at heel: 1.75 inches

Weight: 7.5 lbs.

Sights: metal bead front and mid-rib bead; ventilated rib

Bore: 12, 2.75-inch case

Data: Same as for BL-3 field grade except for stock dimensions, wider ventilated rib, and ventilated recoil pad.

Comment: Same as for BL-3 field grade. Trap shooters who desire a choke other than the standard combination available will have to select another arm.

BERETTA BL-4/12-BORE MAGNUM OVER/UNDER

Manufacturer: Pietro Beretta, Italy

Importer/distributor: Beretta Arms Co.

Action type: over/under; box lock; monobloc

Ignition system: mechanical

Trigger: selective single; tang selector

Locking system: dual locking lugs projecting from breech face fit into corresponding slots in monobloc assembly

Ejection: automatic; selective

Safety: automatic; tang slide not integral with barrel selector

Barrel length & choke: 30.0 inches, full & full

Stock: 2-piece European walnut; hand-checkered; capped pistol grip; hand-rubbed satin finish

Buttplate: ventilated recoil pad

Length of pull: 14.125 inches

Drop at comb: 1.5 inches

Drop at heel: 2.5 inches

Weight: 7.5 lbs.

Sights: ivory bead on ventilated rib

Bore: 12, 3.0-inch case

Comment: See BL-4 field grade for general comment. The author's personal taste is for a minimum of 8 lbs. for a 12-bore Magnum.

BERETTA BL-4 FIELD GRADE OVER/UNDER

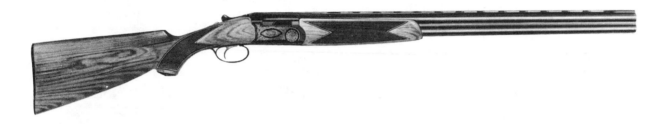

Manufacturer: Pietro Beretta, Italy

Importer/distributor: Beretta Arms Co.

Action type: over/under; box lock; monobloc

Ignition system: mechanical

Trigger: single selective; tang selector

Locking system: dual locking lugs projecting from breech face fit into corresponding slots in monobloc assembly

Ejection: automatic selective

Safety: automatic; tang slide not integral with barrel selector switch

Barrel length & choke: 30.0 or 28.0 inches, modified & full; 26.0 inches, improved cylinder & modified

Stock: 2-piece European walnut; capped pistol grip; hand-checkered; satin hand-rubbed finish

Buttplate: black plastic

Length of pull: 14.125 inches

Drop at comb: 1.5 inches

Drop at heel: 2.5 inches

Weight: 26.0-inch barrels, 7.25 lbs.; 28.0-inch barrels, 7.35 lbs.; 30.0-inch barrels, 7.5 lbs.

Sights: ivory bead on ventilated rib

Bore: 12, 2.75-inch case

Comment: This is a well-designed and well-made, moderate-priced over/under. The monobloc construction makes it somewhat lighter than similar non-monobloc over/unders.

The automatic safety can readily be converted to nonautomatic. The Swedish coil mainsprings are far more desirable than flat springs.

The BL-4 shows evidence of considerable and painstaking fitting.

BERETTA BL-4 SMALLBORE OVER/UNDER

Manufacturer: Pietro Beretta, Italy

Importer/distributor: Beretta Arms Co.

Action type: over/under, box lock; monobloc

Ignition system: mechanical

BERETTA BL-4 SMALLBORE OVER/UNDER (continued

Trigger: selective single; tang selector

Locking system: dual locking lugs projecting from breech face fit into corresponding slots in monobloc assembly

Ejection: automatic; selective

Safety: automatic; tang slide not integral with barrel selector

Barrel length & choke: 28.0 inches, modified & full; 26.0 inches, improved cylinder & modified

Stock: 2-piece European walnut; hand-checkered; capped pistol grip; hand-rubbed satin finish

Buttplate: black plastic

Length of pull: 14.125 inches

Drop at comb: 1.5 inches

Drop at heel: 2.5 inches

Weight: 26.0-inch barrels, 5.85 lbs.; 28.0-inch barrels, 6.0 lbs.

Sights: ivory bead on ventilated rib

Bore: 20, 3.0-inch case

Comment: The BL-4 smallbore saves weight over the 12-bore by using a small receiver. Weight is also saved by the monobloc construction.

BERETTA BL-4 SKEET OVER/UNDER SMALL BORE

Manufacturer: Pietro Beretta, Italy

Importer/distributor: Beretta Arms Co.

Action type: box lock; break-top

Ignition system: mechanical

Trigger: single selective; tang selector

Locking system: monobloc

Ejection: automatic selective

Safety: nonautomatic; tang slide not integral with barrel selector

Barrel length & choke: 26.0 inches, skeet & skeet

Stock: 2-piece European walnut; hand-checkered; capped pistol grip; hand-rubbed satin finish

Buttplate: black plastic

Length of pull: 14.125 inches

Drop at comb: 1.5 inches

Drop at heel: 2.5 inches

Weight: 6.0 lbs.

Sights: ivory bead front and metal bead mid-rib; ventilated rib

Bore: 20, 3.0-inch case; 28, 2.75-inch case

Comment: Same as for BL-4 12-bore skeet gun. One of the lightest smallbore skeet guns available. This is partly due to monobloc construction.

BERETTA BL-4 WIDE RIB SKEET OVER/UNDER

Manufacturer: Pietro Beretta, Italy

Importer/distributor: Beretta Arms Co.

Action type: box lock; break-top

Ignition system: mechanical

Trigger: single selective; tang selector

Locking system: monobloc

Ejection: automatic selective

Safety: nonautomatic; tang slide not integral with barrel selector

Barrel length & choke: 26.0 inches, skeet & skeet

Stock: 2-piece European walnut; hand-checkered; capped pistol grip; hand-rubbed satin finish

Buttplate: black plastic

Length of pull: 14.125 inches

Drop at comb: 1.5 inches

Drop at heel: 2.5 inches

Weight: 7.25 lbs.

Sights: ivory bead front; metal bead mid-rib; 0.375-inch-wide rib

Bore: 12, 2.75-inch case

Comment: A well-designed and well-crafted skeet gun of moderate price.

BERETTA BL-4 WIDE RIB TRAP OVER/UNDER

Manufacturer: Pietro Beretta, Italy

Importer/distributor: Beretta Arms Co.

Action type: box lock; break-top

Ignition system: mechanical

Trigger: single selective; tang selector

Locking system: monobloc

Ejection: automatic selective

Safety: nonautomatic; tang slide not integral with barrel selector

Barrel length & choke: 30.0 inches, modified & full

Stock: 2-piece European walnut; hand-checkered; capped pistol grip; hand-rubbed satin finish

Buttplate: ventilated rubber recoil pad

Length of pull: 14.375 inches

Drop at comb: 1.125 inches

Drop at Monte Carlo: 1.125 inches

Drop at heel: 1.375 inches

Weight: 7.5 lbs.

Sights: front and mid-rib metal bead on ventilated rib

Bore: 12, 2.75-inch case

Data: Same as for basic Field Grade except for stock dimensions and recoil pad.

Comment: A well-made, moderately priced trap gun.

BERETTA BL-6 FIELD GRADE OVER/UNDER 12-BORE

Manufacturer: Pietro Beretta, Italy

Importer/distributor: Beretta Arms Co.

Action type: box lock with dummy side plates; break-top

Ignition system: mechanical

Trigger: single selective; tang selector

Locking system: monobloc

Ejection: automatic selective

BERETTA BL-6 FIELD GRADE OVER/UNDER 12-BORE
(continued)

Safety: automatic; tang slide not integral with barrel selector

Barrel length & choke: 28.0 inches, modified & full; 26.0 inches, improved cylinder & modified

Stock: 2-piece European walnut; hand-checkered; capped full pistol grip; hand-rubbed satin finish

Buttplate: black plastic

Length of pull: 14.125 inches

Drop at comb: 1.25 inches

Drop at heel: 2.5 inches

Weight: 26.0-inch barrels, 7.25 lbs.; 28.0-inch barrels, 7.5 lbs.

Sights: white metal bead front on ventilated rib

Bore: 12, 2.75-inch case

Data: This has the same basic action as the Beretta BL-4 series. A major difference is the dummy side plate. This provides a greater area for engraving. The side plate has no practical function as it does in the sidelock action.

Comment: This is Beretta's top-of-the-line box-lock action. It is a fine over/under.

BERETTA BL-6 MAGNUM OVER/UNDER

Manufacturer: Pietro Beretta, Italy

Importer/distributor: Beretta Arms Co.

Action type: box lock with dummy side plates; break-top

Ignition system: mechanical

Trigger: single selective; tang selector

Locking system: monobloc

Ejection: automatic selective

Safety: automatic; tang slide not integral with barrel selector

Barrel length & choke: 30.0 inches, modified & full

Stock: 2-piece European walnut; hand-checkered; capped pistol grip; hand-rubbed satin finish

Buttplate: ventilated rubber recoil pad

Length of pull: 14.125 inches

Drop at comb: 1.5 inches

Drop at heel: 2.5 inches

Weight: 7.5 lbs.

Sights: metal bead front on ventilated rib

Bore: 12, 3.0-inch case

Data: Same as for Field Grade.

Comment: An excellent 12-bore Magnum. However, no 12-bore Magnum should weigh less than 8.0 lbs. The author prefers full and modified chokes for his 12-bore duck gun, but every 12-bore Magnum should be available in full & full for those who want these borings.

BERETTA BL-6 SKEET OVER/UNDER 20-BORE

Manufacturer: Pietro Beretta, Italy

Importer/distributor: Beretta Arms Co.

Action type: box lock with dummy side plates; break-top

Ignition system: mechanical

Trigger: single selective; tang selector

Locking system: monobloc

Ejection: automatic selective

Safety: automatic; tang slide not integral with barrel selector

Barrel length & choke: 28.0 inches, modified & full; 26.0 inches, improved cylinder & modified or skeet & skeet

Stock: 2-piece European walnut; hand-checkered; capped pistol grip; hand-rubbed satin finish

Buttplate: black plastic

Length of pull: 14.125 inches

Drop at comb: 1.5 inches

Drop at heel: 2.5 inches

Weight: 26.0-inch barrels, 6.0 lbs.; 28.0-inch barrels, 6.25 lbs.

Sights: metal bead front and mid-rib

Bore: 20, 3.0-inch case

Data: See Field Grade 12-bore.

Comment: This is identical to 12-bore Field Grade save for bore and weight. The 20-bore uses a smaller receiver than the 12-bore.

BERETTA BL-6 WIDE RIB SKEET OVER/UNDER

Manufacturer: Pietro Beretta, Italy

Importer/distributor: Beretta Arms Co.

Action type: box lock with dummy side plates; break-top

Ignition system: mechanical

Trigger: single selective; tang selector

Locking system: monobloc

Ejection: automatic selective

Safety: automatic; tang slide not integral with barrel selector

Barrel length & choke: 26.0 inches, skeet & skeet

Stock: 2-piece European walnut; hand-checkered; capped pistol grip; hand-rubbed satin finish

Buttplate: black plastic

Length of pull: 14.125 inches

Drop at comb: 1.5 inches

Drop at heel: 2.5 inches

Weight: 7.25 lbs.

Sights: metal bead front and mid-rib

Bore: 12, 3.0-inch case

Data: Same as for Field Grade except for skeet boring and wide rib.

Comment: Same as for Field Grade 12-bore.

BERETTA BL-6 OVER/UNDER TRAP GUN

Manufacturer: Pietro Beretta, Italy

Importer/distributor: Beretta Arms Co.

Action type: box lock with dummy side plates; break-top

Ignition system: inertial

Trigger: single selective; tang selector

Locking system: u-shaped receiver bolt arms engage holes alongside barrels

Ejection: automatic selective

Safety: nonautomatic; tang slide not integral with barrel selector

Barrel length & choke: 32.0 inches, full & full; 30.0 inches, modified & full

Stock: 2-piece European walnut; hand-checkered (24 lines per inch); Wundhammer swell along pistol grip (right side)

Buttplate: ventilated recoil pad

BERETTA BL-6 OVER/UNDER TRAP GUN (continued)

Length of pull: 14.375 inches

Drop at comb: 1.375 inches

Drop at Monte Carlo: 1.375 inches

Drop at heel: 1.75 inches

Weight: 30.0-inch barrels, 7.75 lbs.; 32.0-inch barrels, 7.9 lbs.

Sights: metal bead front and mid-rib

Bore: 12, 2.75-inch case

Data: Monobloc breech is permanently united with barrels by heating and shrinking process.

Comment: This BL-6 replaced former BL-5 as top of the line in the BL series. Notable and desirable feature is shallow depth of action (2.48 inches high).

The arm is very well finished and well made. Its barrels are high-luster blue. Floral engraving on dummy sideplates is well executed.

Handling qualities are excellent. It performs well on the trap field.

BERETTA BL-6 WIDE RIB TRAP OVER/UNDER

Manufacturer: Pietro Beretta, Italy

Importer/distributor: Beretta Arms Co.

Action type: box lock with dummy side plates; break-top

Ignition system: mechanical

Trigger: single selective; tang selector

Locking system: monobloc

Ejection: selective automatic

Safety: nonautomatic; tang slide not integral with barrel selector

Barrel length & choke: 30.0 inches, full & full or improved modified & full

Stock: 2-piece European walnut; hand-checkered; Monte Carlo buttstock; capped pistol grip

Buttplate: ventilated recoil pad

Length of pull: 14.375 inches

Drop at comb: 1.375 inches

Drop at Monte Carlo: 1.375 inches

Drop at heel: 1.75 inches

Weight: 7.5 lbs.

Sights: metal bead front and mid-rib

Bore: 12, 2.75-inch case

Data: Same as for basic Field Grade save stock dimensions and recoil pad.

Comment: One of the better medium-priced over/under trap guns.

BERETTA SIDELOCK SO SERIES OVER/UNDERS

Manufacturer: Pietro Beretta, Italy

Importer/distributor: Beretta Arms Co.

Action type: sidelock; break-top

Ignition system: mechanical

Trigger: selective single or double

Locking system: dual lugs either side of upper barrel lock into concealed slots in breech via modified Greener crossbolt

Ejection: automatic selective

Safety: automatic except on skeet and trap versions (nonautomatic safety supplied on request for field models)

Barrel length & choke: 28.0 inches, modified & pull; 26.0 inches, improved cylinder & modified (on special order, available in any length from 26 to 30 inches, full, modified, improved cylinder, improved modified, cylinder, skeet #1, or skeet #2)

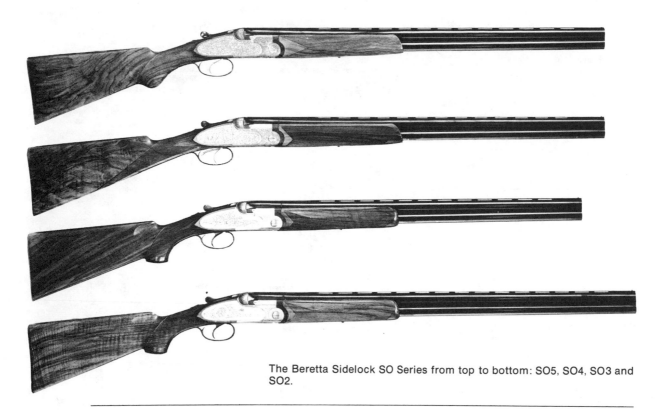

The Beretta Sidelock SO Series from top to bottom: SO5, SO4, SO3 and SO2.

Stock: figured European walnut; straight or various modifications of pistol grips; checkering is fine, ranging upward from SO-2 to SO-5

Buttplate: SO-2, checkered buttplate; SO-3, SO-4, SO-5 have hand-checkered butts; ventilated recoil pad furnished on request

Length of pull: 14.125 inches

Drop at comb: 1.5 inches

Drop at heel: 2.5 inches

Weight: 7.0 to 7.25 lbs., depending on barrel length

Sights: all versions except SO-5 have medium bead steel front sight; SO-5 has ivory bead front; trap and skeet models have metal mid-rib bead

Bore: 12, 2.75-inch case

Data: Sidelock action has only five parts plus three pivot pins and one screw. Double internal safety mechanism prevents discharge if gun is dropped. Chrome-lined barrels are furnished on request. Each barrel is cut and reamed individually. Lead lapped and polished.

Ventilated rib is matted to eliminate or reduce glare. Triggers on SO-2, SO-3, and SO-4 are checkered blue steel. SO-5 trigger or triggers are gold-plated.

Buttstocks and fore-ends are cut from same piece of wood to ensure perfect match. Wood figure and grain increase in beauty in ascending grades. (SO-5 is top grade.) Standard finish is a dozen or more hand-rubbed coats. Semi-gloss or high-gloss finish is available on order. The checkering is of highest quality.

Comment: The SO series is as fine a sidelock over/under as made anywhere in the world. It is to be regretted that this sidelock is not available in 20-bore.

ITHACA SKB M500 OVER/UNDER FIELD GRADE

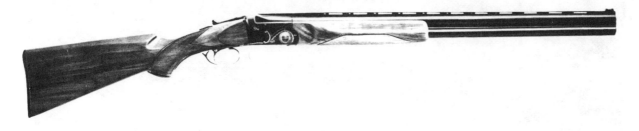

Manufacturer: SKB, Japan

Importer/distributor: Ithacagun

Action type: box lock; break-top

Trigger: single selective; triggerbow selector

Locking system: monobloc

Ejection: automatic selective

Safety: automatic; tang slide

Barrel length & choke:

12-bore: 30.0 or 28.0 inches, full & modified; 26.0 inches, modified & improved cylinder

20-bore: 28.0 inches, full & modified; 26.0 inches, modified & improved cylinder

Stock: 2-piece walnut; hand-checkered fore-end and full pistol grip; semi-beavertail fluted fore-end; pistol grip with black plastic cap and white line spacer; semi-gloss (satin) finish

Buttplate: black plastic

Length of pull: 14.0 inches

Drop at comb: 1.5 inches

Drop at heel: 2.625 inches

Weight:

12-bore: 26.0-inch barrels, 7.0 lbs.; 28.0-inch barrels, 7.25 lbs.; 30.0-inch barrels, 7.5 lbs.

20-bore: 26.0-inch barrels, 6.25 lbs.; 28.0-inch barrels, 6.5 lbs.

Sights: Raybar (translucent front) on ventilated rib

Bore: 12, 2.75-inch case; 20, 3.0-inch case

Comment: This is the least expensive of the SKB over/under series. M500 is a medium-priced over/under. The M700 includes only skeet and trap arms. M600 and M700 offer progressively fancier grades of French walnut, finer hand checkering, and somewhat more detailed engraving.

All grades have barrels chromed inside and outside.

The M600 and M700 have gold-plated triggers and pickled (silver-color) receivers.

The Series 500 is probably the best over/under in its price range. The author prefers a sliding barrel selector on the tang to a button in the trigger bow. However, if all your guns have the same barrel selector location, then the trigger-bow location is good.

ITHACA SKB M500 FIELD GRADE MAGNUM

Manufacturer: SKB, Japan

Importer/distributor: Ithacagun

Action type: box lock; break-top

Ignition system: inertial

Trigger: single selective; triggerbow selector

Locking system: monobloc

Ejection: automatic selective

Safety: nonautomatic; tang slide

Barrel length & choke: 30.0 inches, full & improved modified

Stock: 2-piece walnut; hand checkering; semi-beavertail fore-end; full pistol grip with black plastic cap and white line spacer; semi-gloss (satin) finish

Buttplate: ventilated rubber recoil pad

Length of pull: 14.0 inches

Drop at comb: 1.5 inches

Drop at heel: 2.625 inches

Weight: 8.0 lbs.

Sights: Raybar front

Bore: 12, 3.0-inch case

Data: Same action and basic features as M500 Field Grade.

Comment: Despite its reasonable price, for weight and anti-rust qualities this is one of the best 12-bore Magnum over/under guns on the market. Barrels bright-chromed inside and dark-chromed outside, like the M500's, should be a must on all scatterguns for waterfowl use.

Too many — and some are far more expensive — 12-bore Magnums weigh far too little. Eight pounds should be the minimum weight.

ITHACA SKB M600 OVER/UNDER FIELD GRADE

Manufacturer: SKB, Japan

Importer/distributor: Ithacagun

Action type: box lock; break-top

Ignition system: inertial

Trigger: single selective; triggerbow selector

Locking system: monobloc

Ejection: automatic selective

Safety: nonautomatic; tang slide

Barrel length & choke:

12-bore: 30.0 or 28.0 inches, full & modified; 26.0 inches, modified & improved cylinder

20-bore: 28.0 inches, full & modified; 26.0 inches, modified & improved cylinder

Stock: 2-piece French walnut (finer grade than M500); hand checkering; pistol grip with black plastic cap and white line spacer; fluted fore-end; semi-gloss (satin) finish

Buttplate: black plastic with white spacer

Length of pull: 14.0 inches

Drop at comb: 1.5 inches

Drop at heel: 2.625 inches

Weight:

12-bore: 26.0-inch barrels, 7.0 lbs.; 28.0-inch barrels, 7.25 lbs.; 30.0-inch barrels, 7.5 lbs.

20-bore: 26.0-inch barrels, 6.25 lbs.; 28.0-inch barrels, 6.5 lbs.

Sights: Raybar front

Bore: 12, 2.75-inch case; 20, 3.0-inch case

Data: Same mechanical data as for M500. Superior wood, checkering and engraving.

Comment: Same basic comment as for 500 Series.

ITHACA SKB M600 OVER/UNDER SKEET

Manufacturer: SKB, Japan

Importer/distributor: Ithacagun

Action type: box lock; break-top

Ignition system: inertial

Trigger: single selective; triggerbow selector

Locking system: monobloc

Ejection: automatic selective

Safety: nonautomatic; tang slide

Barrel length & choke: 28.0 or 26.0 inches, skeet & skeet

Stock: 2-piece French walnut; hand-checkered; pistol grip and semi-beavertail fore-end; pistol grip with black plastic cap and white line spacer; semi-gloss (satin) finish

Buttplate: ventilated rubber recoil pad with white line spacer

Length of pull: 14.0 inches

Drop at comb: 1.5 inches

Drop at heel: 2.25 inches

Weight:

12-bore: 26.0-inch barrels, 7.5 lbs.; 28.0-inch barrels, 7.75 lbs.

20-bore: 26.0-inch barrels, 7.0 lbs.; 28.0-inch barrels, 7.25 lbs.

Sights: Bradley-type front and metal mid-rib bead

Bore: 12, 20, 2.75-inch case

Data: Same as for Field Grade M600 except chokes and less drop at heel.

Comment: A well-crafted medium-priced skeet gun.

ITHACA SKB M600 OVER/UNDER SMALLBORE SKEET — 28/.410 BORES

Manufacturer: SKB, Japan

Importer/distributor: Ithacagun

Action type: box lock; break-top

Ignition system: inertial

Trigger: single selective; triggerbow selector

Locking system: monobloc

Ejection: automatic selective

Safety: automatic; tang slide

Barrel length & choke: 28.0 inches, skeet & skeet

Stock: 2-piece French walnut; hand-checkered; pistol grip and semi-beavertail fore-end; pistol grip with black plastic cap and white line spacer; semi-gloss (satin) finish

Buttplate: ventilated recoil pad with white line spacer

Length of pull: 14.0 inches

Drop at comb: 1.5 inches

Drop at heel: 2.5 inches

Weight: 7.25 lbs.

Sights: Bradley-type front and metal mid-rib bead

Bore: 28, 2.75-inch case; .410, 2.5-inch case

Comment: Basic data same as M600 Field Grade. A Combination skeet set can also be purchased — one frame, three sets of interchangeable 28.0-inch barrels in 20-, 28- and .410-bore. This version weighs 7.25 lbs., regardless of which set of barrels is in place. It comes with a fitted black case.

ITHACA SKB M600 OVER/UNDER TRAP GUN

Manufacturer: SKB, Japan

Importer/distributor: Ithacagun

Action type: box lock; break-top

Ignition system: inertial

Trigger: single selective; triggerbow selector

Locking system: monobloc

Ejection: automatic selective

Safety: automatic; tang slide

Barrel length & choke: 32.0 or 30.0 inches, full & improved modified

Stock: 2-piece French walnut; hand-checkered; full pistol grip with black plastic cap and white line spacer

Buttplate: ventilated rubber recoil pad

Length of pull: 14.5 inches

Drop at comb: 1.5 inches

Drop at Monte Carlo (if applicable): 1.5 inches

Drop at heel: 2.0 inches

Weight: 30.0-inch barrels, 8.0 lbs.; 32.0-inch barrels, 8.25 lbs.

Sights: Bradley-type front and metal mid-rib head

Bore: 12, 2.75-inch case

Data: Same basic data, save for stock dimensions and barrel lengths, as M600 Field Grade. Buyer has choice of straight stock or Monte Carlo comb.

Comment: Same basic comment as for M600 Field Grade. A good trap gun.

ITHACA SKB M600 OVER/UNDER TRAP DOUBLES

Manufacturer: SKB, Japan

Importer/distributor: Ithacagun

Action type: box lock; break-top

Ignition system: inertial

Trigger: single selective; triggerbow selector

Locking system: monobloc

Ejection: automatic selective

Safety: nonautomatic; tang slide

Barrel length & choke: 32.0 or 30.0 inches, special boring (see data below)

Stock: 2-piece French walnut; hand checkering; pistol grip; pistol grip with black plastic cap and white line spacer; semi-gloss (satin) finish

Buttplate: ventilated rubber recoil pad

Length of pull: 14.5 inches

Drop at comb: 1.5 inches

Drop at Monte Carlo (if applicable): 1.5 inches

Drop at heel: standard, 1.875 inches; Monte Carlo, 2.0 inches

Weight: 30.0-inch barrels, 8.0 lbs.; 32.0-inch barrels, 8.25 lbs.

Sights: Bradley-type front and mid-rib metal bead

Bore: 12, 2.75-inch case

Data: Same as regular trap gun except special boring, designed for shooting doubles and International trap. Choked for 21 yards on the first target and 30 yards for the second target. It's available with straight or Monte Carlo stock.

Comment: Said to be the only over/under choked in this manner. A well-designed, well-crafted, and well-stocked gun.

ITHACA SKB M680 OVER/UNDER

Manufacturer: SKB, Japan

Importer/distributor: Ithacagun

Action type: box lock; break-top

Ignition system: inertial

Trigger: single selective; triggerbox selector

Locking system: monobloc

Ejection: automatic selective

Safety: nonautomatic; tang slide

Barrel length & choke:

12-bore: 28.0 inches, full & modified; 26.0 inches, modified & improved cylinder

20-bore: 28.0 inches, full & modified; 26.0 inches, modified & improved cylinder

Stock: same as 600 Series except straight stock (no pistol grip)

Buttplate: black plastic with white line spacer

Length of pull: 14.0 inches

Drop at comb: 1.5 inches

Drop at heel: 2.625 inches

Weight:

12-bore: 26.0-inch barrels, 7.25 lbs.; 28.0-inch barrels, 7.5 lbs.

20-bore: 26.0-inch barrels, 6.25 lbs.; 28.0-inch barrels, 6.5 lbs.

Sights: Raybar front and middle bead on ventilated rib

Bore: 12, 2.75-inch case; 20, 3.0-inch case

Data: Except for straight stock and wrap-around checkering, identical to 600 Series.

Comment: This is one of the few straight-stock over/under guns.

ITHACA M700 OVER/UNDER SKEET

Manufacturer: SKB, Japan

Importer/distributor: Ithacagun

Action type: box lock; break-top

Ignition system: inertial

Trigger: single selective; triggerbow selector

Locking system: monobloc

Ejection: automatic selective

Safety: nonautomatic; tang slide

Barrel length & choke: 28.0 or 26.0 inches, skeet & skeet

Stock: 2-piece French walnut; hand-checkered; full pistol grip with black plastic cap and white line spacer; semi-gloss (satin) finish

Buttplate: ventilated rubber recoil pad with white line spacer

Length of pull: 14.0 inches

Drop at comb: 1.5 inches

Drop at heel: 2.25 inches

Weight:

12-bore: 26.0-inch barrels, 7.75 lbs.; 28.0-inch barrels, 8.0 lbs.

20-bore: 26.0-inch barrels, 7.0 lbs.; 28.0-inch barrels, 7.25 lbs.

Sights: Bradley-type front and metal mid-rib bead

Bore: 12, 20, 2.75-inch case

Data: Same basic action as M500 and M600. Fancier wood and scrollwork. Finer checkering. Silver-color frame. Stock finish resembles oil but is more water-resistant.

Comment: A fine skeet gun. Same basic comment as for M500 and M600.

ITHACA SKB SERIES 700 OVER/UNDER TRAP

Manufacturer: SKB, Japan

Importer/distributor: Ithacagun

Action type: box lock; break-top

Ignition system: inertial

Trigger: single selective; triggerbow selector

Locking system: monobloc

Ejection: automatic selective

Safety: nonautomatic; tang slide

Barrel length & choke: 32.0 or 30.0 inches, full & improved modified

Stock: 2-piece French walnut; hand-checkered, full pistol grip with black plastic cap and white line spacer

Buttplate: ventilated rubber recoil pad with white line spacer

Length of pull: 14.5 inches

Drop at comb: 1.5 inches

Drop at Monte Carlo (if applicable): 1.5 inches

Drop at heel: standard, 1.875 inches; Monte Carlo, 2.0 inches

Weight: 30.0-inch barrels, 8.0 lbs.; 32.0-inch barrels, 8.1 lbs.

Sights: Bradley-type front and mid-rib metal bead on ventilated rib

Bore: 12, 2.75-inch case

Data: See above and general 700 Series comment under M700 Skeet.

Comment: Same basic comment as for M700 Skeet. Choice of straight comb or Monte Carlo.

ITHACA SKB M700 OVER/UNDER (TRAP) DOUBLES

Manufacturer: SKB, Japan

Importer/distributor: Ithacagun

Action type: box lock; break-top

Ignition system: inertial

Trigger: single selective; triggerbow selector

Locking system: monobloc

Ejection: automatic selective

Safety: nonautomatic; tang slide

Barrel length & choke: 32.0 or 30.0 inches, special boring (see data below)

Stock: 2-piece French walnut; hand-checkered; full pistol grip with black plastic cap and white line spacer; straight comb or Monte Carlo

Buttplate: ventilated rubber recoil pad with white line spacer

Length of pull: 14.5 inches

Drop at comb: 1.5 inches

Drop at Monte Carlo (if applicable): 1.5 inches

Drop at heel: standard, 1.875 inches; Monte Carlo, 2.0 inches

Weight: 30.0-inch barrels, 8.0 lbs.; 32.0-inch barrels, 8.25 lbs.

Sights: Bradley-type front and mid-rib metal bead

Bore: 12, 2.75-inch case

Data: Same as for M700 trap gun except for special International boring. This is designed to hit first target at 21 yards and second at 30 yards.

Comment: Same as for basic M700 trap gun.

KRIEGHOFF OVER/UNDER M32 SERIES

Manufacturer: Krieghoff, West Germany

Importer/distributor: Krieghoff Guns Co.

Action type: box lock; break-top

Ignition system: mechanical

Trigger: single selective; triggerbow selector

Locking system: Krieghoff patented multi-bolt system

Ejection: automatic selective

Safety: nonautomatic; tang slide

Barrel length & choke: 28.0 inches, all skeet bores; various lengths and chokes—your order—for trap

Stock: finest-grade French walnut; hand-cut checkering (lines per inch depend on grade); several designs available (a trapshooter, for instance, can use interchangeable stocks for various events)

Buttplate: ventilated recoil pad is standard

Weight: depends on barrel lengths and stock types

Sights: plastic or metal bead front and mid-rib

Bore: 12, 20, 28, 2.75-inch case; .410, 2.5-inch case

Data: Krieghoff guns range from a little old cheap $1800 Standard Grade to a Super Crown Grade in versions ranging from $7000 to $15,000. At the latter price they include three extra sets of barrels.

Comment: This is one of the finest over/unders in existence. The metalwork, both interior and exterior, is of the highest quality. The French walnut is absolutely top drawer, and its epoxy finish is excellent. The author has seen Purdeys that had no finer workmanship.

Gold-inletted figures cost a minimum of $8,000. (On the $6,500 arm you only get silver inlays.)

Spare barrels—price depends on grade—commence at a low of $700 and range upward. Grades, in ascending order, are Standard, San Remo, Monte Carlo, Crown, and Super Crown.

The Krieghoff Gun Company, P.O. Box 48-1367, Miami, Fla. 33148, will provide full details.

MANUFRANCE FALCOR OVER/UNDER FIELD MODEL

Manufacturer: Manufacture Française, France

Importer/distributor: Interarms

Action type: box lock

Ignition system: inertial

Trigger: single selective; tang selector

Locking system: monobloc plus two underlogs

Ejection: automatic selective

Safety: nonautomatic; tang slide

Barrel length & choke: 27.5 inches, modified & full; 26.0 inches, modified & improved cylinder or skeet & skeet

Stock: 2-piece European walnut; hand checkering (18 lines per inch); pistol grip; fluted fore-end; polyurethane semi-gloss finish

Buttplate: black plastic fitted to steel plate

Length of pull: 13.875 inches

Drop at comb: 1.3125 inches

Drop at heel: 2.25 inches

Weight: 26.0-inch barrels, 7.0 lbs.; 27.5-inch barrels, 7.25 lbs.

Sights: metal bead front on ventilated rib

Bore: 12, 2.75-inch case

Comment: A handsome, well-designed and well-crafted over/under in the $600-or-so price range. The use of small underlugs on the barrel makes for an attractively shallow receiver (2.52 inches in height).

An interesting feature is the interchangeable buttplate. It is available in several thicknesses, thus providing a variety of lengths of pull.

MIIDA M612 OVER/UNDER FIELD GRADE

Manufacturer: Olin-Kodensha, Japan

Importer/distributor: Marubeni America Corp.

Action type: box lock; break-top

Ignition system: inertial

Trigger: single selective; tang selector

Locking system: underbolt

Ejection: automatic selective

Safety: automatic; tang slide

Barrel length & choke: 28.0 inches, full & modified

Stock: 2-piece walnut; hand-checkered (20 lines per inch); full pistol grip with black plastic cap and white line spacer; white plastic diamond inlay in grip cap; semi-gloss polyurethane finish

Buttplate: black plastic

Length of pull: 13.75 inches or (optional) 14.0 inches

Drop at comb: 1.5 inches

Drop at heel: 2.5 inches

Weight: 6.925 lbs.

Sights: brass bead front on ventilated rib

Bore: 12, 2.75-inch case

Data: This grade has a silver-gray trigger and blued receiver.

Comment: This is a fast-handling, easy-to-point, well-designed, inexpensive field gun.

MIIDA M2100 OVER/UNDER SKEET

Manufacturer: Olin-Kodensha, Japan

Importer/distributor: Marubeni America Corp.

Action type: box lock; break-top

Ignition system: inertial

Trigger: single selective; tang selector

Locking system: underbolt

Ejection: automatic selective

Safety: automatic; tang slide

Barrel length & choke: 27.0 inches, skeet & skeet

Stock: 2-piece walnut; hand-checkered (20 lines per inch); beavertail fore-end; full pistol grip with black plastic cap and white line spacer; white diamond inlay in cap; semi-gloss polyurethane finish

Buttplate: black plastic

Length of pull: 13.75 inches or (optional) 14.0 inches

Drop at comb: 1.5 inches

Drop at heel: 2.5 inches

Weight: 7.75 lbs.

Sights: bead front and mid-rib

Bore: 12, 2.75-inch case

Data: Silver-gray trigger. Modest scrollwork on silver-gray receiver.

Comment: The French walnut stock on this model, as on all Miida over/unders, has a handsome reddish-brown color. An excellent low-priced skeet gun. It is the least expensive of the three Miida skeet guns.

MIIDA M2200 OVER/UNDER SKEET

Manufacturer: Olin-Kodensha, Japan

Importer/distributor: Marubeni America Corp.

Action type: box lock; break-top

Ignition system: inertial

Trigger: single selective; tang selector

Locking system: underbolt

Ejection: automatic selective

Safety: automatic; tang slide

Barrel length & choke: 27.0 inches, skeet & skeet

Stock: 2-piece French walnut; hand-checkered (20 lines per inch); beavertail fore-end, full pistol grip with black plastic cap and white line spacer; semi-gloss polyurethane finish

Buttplate: black plastic

Length of pull: 13.75 inches or (optional) 14.0 inches

Drop at comb: 1.5 inches

Drop at heel: 2.5 inches

Weight: 7.75 lbs.

Sights: metal bead front and mid-rib

Bore: 12, 2.75-inch case

Data: Silver-gray receiver. Gold-plated trigger.

Comment: Similar to M2100 Skeet.

MIIDA M2200 OVER/UNDER TRAP

Manufacturer: Olin-Kodensha, Japan

Importer/distributor: Marubeni America Corp.

Action type: box lock; break-top

Ignition system: inertial

Trigger: single selective; tang selector

Locking system: underbolt

Ejection: automatic selective

Safety: automatic; tang slide

Barrel length & choke: 29.75 inches, full & improved modified

Stock: 2-piece French walnut; hand-checkered (20 lines per inch); beavertail fore-end; full pistol grip with black plastic cap and white line spacer; semi-gloss polyurethane finish

Buttplate: Pachmayr ventilated rubber recoil pad

Length of pull: 14.0 inches

Drop at comb: 1.375 inches

Drop at heel: 1.75 inches

Weight: 7.75 lbs.

Sights: metal bead front and mid-rib; 0.45-inch-wide ventilated rib

Bore: 12, 2.75-inch case

Data: Similar to M2200 Skeet save for barrel length, choke, and recoil pad. Gold-plated trigger. Silver-gray receiver.

Comment: Miida's lowest-priced trap gun. An excellent buy.

MIIDA M2300 OVER/UNDER SKEET

Manufacturer: Olin-Kodensha, Japan

Importer/distributor: Marubeni America Corp.

Action type: box lock; break-top

Ignition system: inertial

Trigger: single selective; tang selector

Locking system: underbolt

Ejection: automatic selective

Safety: automatic; tang slide

Barrel length & choke: 27.0 inches, skeet & skeet

Stock: 2-piece French walnut; hand-checkered (20 lines per inch); beavertail fore-end; full pistol grip with black plastic cap and white line spacer; white plastic diamond inlay in cap; semi-gloss polyurethane finish

Buttplate: black plastic

Length of pull: 13.75 inches

Drop at comb: 1.5 inches

Drop at heel: 2.5 inches

Weight: 7.75 lbs.

Sights: bead front and mid-rib; 0.32-inch-wide ventilated rib

Bore: 12, 2.75-inch case

Data: Silver-gray receiver. Gold-plated trigger.

Comment: A well-designed, inexpensive skeet gun.

MIIDA M2300 OVER/UNDER TRAP

Manufacturer: Olin-Kodensha, Japan

Importer/distributor: Marubeni America Corp.

Action type: box lock; break-top

Ignition system: inertial

Trigger: single selective; tang selector

Locking system: underbolt

Ejection: automatic selective

Safety: nonautomatic; tang slide

Barrel length & choke: 29.75 inches, improved modified & full

Stock: 2-piece walnut; hand-checkered; full pistol grip with black plastic cap and white line spacer; white plastic diamond inlay in cap; semi-gloss polyurethane finish

Buttplate: red rubber ventilated recoil pad with white line spacer

Length of pull: 14.0 inches

Drop at comb: 1.375 inches

Drop at heel: 1.875 inches

Weight: 7.6 lbs.

Sights: white plastic front and metal mid-rib bead

Bore: 12, 2.75-inch case

Data: Attractive walnut stock has thick comb, which is considered desirable for trap shooting. Light floral engraving or etching. Bores and chambers are hard-chrome-plated. Hand-filling fore-end.

Comment: A well-designed and well-crafted medium-priced trap gun. Excellent handling qualities.

MIIDA OVER/UNDER GRANDEE SKEET

Manufacturer: Olin-Kodensha, Japan

Importer/distributor: Marubeni America Corp.

Action type: box lock with dummy side plates; break-top

Ignition system: inertial

Trigger: single selective; tang selector

Locking system: underbolt

Ejection: automatic selective

Safety: nonautomatic; tang slide

Barrel length & choke: 26.0 inches, skeet & skeet

MIIDA OVER/UNDER GRANDEE SKEET (continued)

Stock: 2-piece top-quality French walnut; hand-checkered; beavertail fore-end; white ivory cap on full pistol grip; hand-rubbed polyurethane finish

Buttplate: white ivory

Length of pull: 14.0 inches

Drop at comb: 1.5 inches

Drop at heel: 2.5 inches

Weight: 7.75 lbs.

Sights: silver front and mid-rib bead

Bore: 12, 2.75-inch case

Data: All working parts are hand-honed. Dummy side plates and receiver are engraved. Gold inlays. Outer breechblock, ejectors, and locking levers are engine-turned. Gold-plated trigger.

Comment: This skeet gun and comparable Grandee Trap are Miida's top-of-the-line over/unders. Price range is around $2000 (1976). This and the trap version are fine pieces of the gunmaker's art.

MIIDA OVER/UNDER GRANDEE MODEL TRAP

Manufacturer: Olin-Kodensha, Japan

Importer/distributor: Marubeni America Corp.

Action type: box lock; break-top

Ignition system: mechanical

Trigger: single selective; tang selector

Locking system: underbolt

Ejection: automatic selective

Safety: nonautomatic; tang slide

Barrel length & choke: 29.0 inches, full & full

Stock: 2-piece French walnut; hand-cut checkering; fluted beavertail fore-end; full pistol grip; semi-gloss finish

Buttplate: ventilated recoil pad

Length of pull: 14.0 inches

Drop at comb: 1.3125 inches

Drop at heel: 2.125 inches

Weight: 7.875 lbs.

Sights: metal bead front and mid-rib

Bore: 12, 2.75-inch case

Data: Same as basic Miida trap guns save for finer engraving and checkering.

Comment: One of the better—and expensive—trap guns.

NIKKO M5000-II OVER/UNDER FIELD

Manufacturer: Nikko Firearms, Japan

Importer/distributor: Kanematsu-Gosho U.S.A., Inc.

Action type: box lock; break-top

Ignition system: mechanical

Trigger: selective single; tang selector

Locking system: underbolt

Ejection: selective automatic

Safety: nonautomatic; tang slide

Barrel length & choke:

12-bore: 30.0 inches, modified & full; 28.0 inches, modified & improved cylinder or modified & full; 26.0 inches, improved cylinder & modified

20-bore: 28.0 inches, modified & improved cylinder or modified & full; 26.0 inches, improved cylinder & modified

Stock: 2-piece French walnut; hand-checkered (22 lines per inch); pistol grip; high-gloss finish

Buttplate: checkered black plastic

Length of pull: 13.875 inches

Drop at comb: 1.5625 inches

Drop at heel: 2.25 inches

Weight:

12-bore: 26.0-inch barrels, 6.75 lbs.; 28.0-inch barrels, 6.9 lbs.; 30.0-inch barrels, 7.1 lbs.

20-bore: 26.0-inch barrels, 6.5 lbs.; 28.0-inch barrels, 6.65 lbs.

Sights: metal bead front on ventilated rib

Bore: 12, 2.75-inch case; 20, 3.0-inch case

Comment: This is a well-made over/under with barrels bright blue. Frame, bottom plate, and triggerbow are polished bright with hand-engraved floral patterns. Overall workmanship is excellent. One of the better over/under field guns.

NIKKO M5000-I OVER/UNDER TRAP

Manufacturer: Nikko Firearms, Japan

Importer/distributor: Kanematsu-Gosho U.S.A., Inc.

Action type: box lock; break-top

Ignition system: mechanical

Trigger: single selective; tang selector

Locking system: underbolt

Ejection: automatic selective; spring-loaded

Safety: nonautomatic; tang slide

Barrel length & choke: 30.0 inches, improved modified & full

Stock: 2-piece dark French walnut; hand-checkered (22 lines per inch); pistol grip; high-gloss finish

Buttplate: ventilated rubber recoil pad with white line spacer

Length of pull: 14.3125 inches

Drop at comb: 1.375 inches

Drop at heel: 1.75 inches

Weight: 7.75 lbs.

Sights: metal bead front and mid-rib; ventilated rib width 0.43 inch, with narrow center groove to help guide shooter's eye

Bore: 12, 2.75-inch case

Comment: A well-made trap gun showing excellent workmanship, and it's in the lower price range of over/under trap guns.

PERAZZI MIRAGE LIVE-BIRD OVER/UNDER

Manufacturer: Manifattura Armi Perazzi, Italy

Importer/distributor: Ithacagun

Action type: box lock; break-top

Ignition system: mechanical

Trigger: single; under barrel fires first (optionally available: upper barrel fires first, or double triggers)

Locking system: monobloc

Ejection: automatic selective

Safety: nonautomatic; tang slide

Barrel length & choke: 28.0 inches, full & modified

Stock: 2-piece European walnut; hand-checkered, full pistol grip; beavertail fore-end; semi-gloss finish

Buttplate: ventilated recoil pad

Stock dimensions: eight stock-dimension combinations available; stocks readily interchangeable

Weight: 8.0 lbs.

Sights: metal bead front and mid-rib

Bore: 12, 2.75-inch case

Data: Same basic data as for other Perazzi competition models. Hand-honed chokes. Open spaces between barrels to dissipate heat and reduce wind resistance.

Comment: Unfortunately, live-bird (pigeon) shooting is illegal in most states. This is not to say that it is not sometimes practiced. Mexico is the nearest place for live-bird shooting. The author had some great live-bird shooting in Havana in the pre-Castro era. Monte Carlo, Monaco, has seen some lively bird shoots. Many live-bird competitors use a Monte Carlo stock, but note that the barrels, though choked modified and full, are shorter than those of most trap guns. A good live-pigeon gun seems to be a kind of compromise between a trap gun and a field gun.

PERAZZI MIRAGE SKEET OVER/UNDER

Manufacturer: Manifatturi Armi Perazzi, Italy

Importer/distributor: Ithacagun

Action type: box lock; break-top

Ignition system: mechanical

Trigger: single; under barrel fires first (optionally available: upper barrel fires first, or double triggers; trigger systems readily interchangeable)

Locking system: monobloc

Ejection: automatic selective

Safety: nonautomatic; tang slide

Barrel length & choke: 28.0 inches, skeet & skeet

Stock: 2-piece European walnut; hand-checkered; full pistol grip; beavertail fore-end; semi-gloss finish

Buttplate: ventilated recoil pad

Stock dimensions: eight stock-dimension combinations available; readily interchangeable stocks

Weight: 8.0 lbs.

Sights: metal bead front and mid-rib; tapered ventilated rib

Bore: 12, 2.75-inch case

Data: See MX-8 Trap.

PERAZZI MIRAGE TRAP OVER/UNDER

Manufacturer: Manifatturi Armi Perazzi, Italy

Importer/distributor: Ithacagun

Action type: box lock; break-top

Ignition system: mechanical

Trigger: single; under barrel fires first (optionally available: upper barrel fires first, or double triggers; trigger systems readily interchangeable)

Locking system: monobloc

Ejection: automatic selective

Safety: nonautomatic; tang slide (can be ordered without safety)

Barrel length & choke: 32.0 or 30.0 inches, full & improved modified

Stock: 2-piece European walnut; hand-checkered; full pistol grip; beavertail fore-end

Buttplate: ventilated rubber recoil pad

Stock dimensions: choice of 8 different stocks, each with varying dimensions; stocks readily interchangeable.

Weight: 30.0-inch barrels, 8.25 lbs.; 32.0-inch barrels, 8.5 lbs.

Sights: metal bead front

Bore: 12, 2.75-inch case

Data: Same as MX-8 Trap save for standard-height ventilated rib. The rib is tapered.

PERAZZI MX-8 OVER/UNDER TRAP

Manufacturer: Manifatturi Armi Perazzi, Italy

Importer/distributor: Ithacagun

Action type: break-top

Ignition system: mechanical

Trigger: single; under barrel fires first (optionally available: upper barrel fires first, or double triggers; trigger systems readily interchangeable)

Locking system: monobloc

Ejection: automatic selective

Safety: nonautomatic; tang slide (can be ordered without safety)

Barrel length & choke: 32.0 or 30.0 inches, full & improved

Stock: 2-piece fancy European walnut; full pistol grip; oil-type finish

Buttplate: ventilated rubber recoil pad

Stock dimensions: eight stock-dimension combinations available for any competition Perazzi; all Perazzi competition-model stocks are readily interchangeable

Weight: 8.5 lbs.

Sights: metal bead front and mid-rib

Bore: 12, 2.75-inch case

PERAZZI MX-8 OVER/UNDER TRAP GUN (continued)

Data: This trap model was designed expressly for Italian trap shot Ennio Mattarelli, who won the 1968 Olympic Gold Medal in trapshooting.

Note (see illustration) open space between upper and lower barrels is ribbed, but not in conventional manner. Vents allow better barrel cooling when long-shot strings are fired. Perazzi considers that ribs hold barrels together better than with entire open space as on the old Remington M32, new M3200, or early Browning Superposed guns. The vented middle rib is a logical compromise.

Air spaces between barrels reduce wind resistance to a minimum. How much this is an actual factor has not been determined.

Comment: Perazzi competition guns are in the $2000-and-up bracket. The only improvement one could make is on fancier engraving and gold or platinum inlays. Mechanically, it would be difficult to improve on Perazzi craftsmanship and design.

REMINGTON M3200 FIELD GRADE OVER/UNDER

Action type: box lock; break-top

Ignition system: mechanical

Trigger: single selective; tang selector

Locking system: twin side bolts; sliding top lock

Ejection: automatic selective

Safety: nonautomatic; tang slide

Barrel length & choke: 28.0 or 30.0 inches, modified & full; 26.0 inches, improved cylinder & modified

Stock: 2-piece American walnut; machine-checkered (20 lines per inch); fluted semi-beavertail fore-end; full pistol grip with rosewood cap; DuPont RK-W bowling-alley high-gloss finish

Buttplate: checkered rosewood

Length of pull: 14.0 inches

Drop at comb: 1.5 inches

Drop at heel: 2.5 inches

Weight: 26.0-inch barrels, 7.75 lbs.; 28.0-inch barrels, 8.0 lbs.; 30.0-inch barrels, 8.25 lbs.

Sights: metal bead front

Bore: 12, 2.75-inch or 3.0-inch case

Data: The M3200, like its Remington predecessor the M32, has an open space between the barrels. This is designed to reduce barrel heating on guns from which long shot strings are fired, as in trap or skeet. It also reduces weight a trifle. Another unusual design feature is the combination safety/barrel selector. On most guns that combine the safety and selector, the slide moves forward or back as a safety, left or right as a barrel selector. The Remington's device, however, pivots to the right to select the top barrel for the first shot, to the left to select the bottom barrel, and in its central position—without sliding it backward—puts the action on safety.

Comment: One of the best guns in its price class.

REMINGTON M3200 MAGNUM

Action type: box lock; break-top

Ignition system: mechanical

Trigger: single selective; tang selector

Locking system: twin side bolts; sliding top lock

Ejection: automatic selective

Safety: nonautomatic; tang slide

Barrel length & choke: 30.0 inches, full & full or modified & full

Stock: 2-piece American walnut; machine-checkered (20 lines per inch); full pistol grip with rosewood cap; fluted semi-beavertail fore-end; DuPont RK-W bowling-alley high-gloss finish

Buttplate: ventilated rubber recoil pad

Length of pull: 14.0 inches

Drop at comb: 1.5 inches

Drop at heel: 2.5 inches

Weight: 8.25 lbs.

Sights: ventilated rib

Bore: 12, 3.0-inch case

Data: Similar to Field Grade M3200.

Comment: A well-designed and well-crafted shotgun, but it could weigh another 8–12 oz.

REMINGTON M3200 OVER/UNDER SKEET GUN

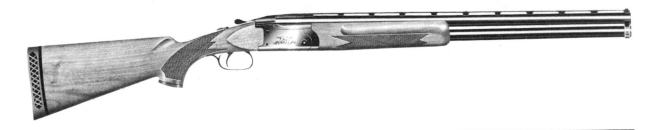

Action type: box lock; break-top

Ignition system: mechanical

Trigger: single selective; tang selector

Locking system: twin side bolts; sliding top lock

Ejection: automatic selective

Safety: nonautomatic; tang slide

Barrel length & choke: 26.0 or 28.0 inches, skeet & skeet

Stock: 2-piece American walnut; machine-checkered; fluted beavertail fore-end; full pistol grip with rosewood cap; DuPont RK-W bowling-alley high-gloss finish

Buttplate: ventilated rubber recoil pad

Length of pull: 14.0 inches

Drop at comb: 1.5 inches

Drop at heel: 2.5 inches

Weight: 26.0-inch barrels, 7.75 lbs.; 28.0-inch barrels, 8.0 lbs.

Sights: ivory bead front; metal bead mid-rib

Bore: 12, 2.75-inch case

Data: Similar to Model 3200 Field Grade except for chokes and recoil pad.

Comment: One of the better over/under skeet models.

REMINGTON M3200 OVER/UNDER TRAP GUN

Action type: box lock; break-top

Ignition system: mechanical

Trigger: single selective; tang selector

Locking system: twin side bolts; sliding top lock

Ejection: automatic selective

Safety: nonautomatic; tang slide

Barrel length & choke: 30.0 or 32.0 inches, full & improved modified

Stock: 2-piece selected American walnut; machine-checkered; full pistol grip with rosewood cap; fluted beavertail fore-end

Buttplate: ventilated rubber recoil pad

Drop at comb: 1.5 inches

Drop at Monte Carlo (if applicable): 1.5 inches

Drop at heel: standard, 1.5 inches; Monte Carlo, 2.0 inches

Weight: 30.0-inch barrels, 8.25 lbs.; 32.0-inch barrels, 8.5 lbs.

Sights: ivory bead front; metal bead mid-rib

Bore: 12, 2.75-inch case

Data: Basic data same as for Field Grade M3200. Available with either standard or Monte Carlo stock.

Comment: A well-designed and fast-handling trap gun.

SAVAGE M333 OVER/UNDER FIELD GRADE

Manufacturer: Valmet, Finland

Importer/distributor: Savage Arms

Action type: box lock; break-top

Ignition system: mechanical

Trigger: single selective; triggerbow selector

Locking system: twin bolts in breech fit into corresponding slot in barrel assembly

Ejection: automatic selective

Safety: automatic; tang slide

Barrel length & choke:

12-bore: 28.0 or 30.0 inches, full & modified; 26.0 inches, modified & improved cylinder or skeet & skeet

20-bore: 28.0 inches, full & modified; 26.0 inches, modified & improved cylinder or skeet & skeet

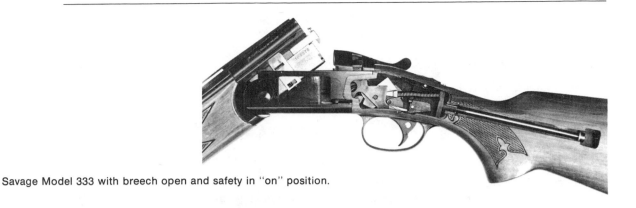

Savage Model 333 with breech open and safety in "on" position.

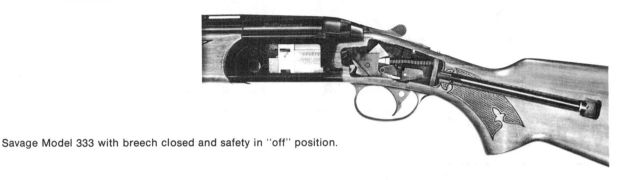

Savage Model 333 with breech closed and safety in "off" position.

Stock: 2-piece walnut; impressed checkering; semi-pistol grip; high-gloss finish

Buttplate: black hard rubber

Length of pull: 14.0 inches

Drop at comb: 1.5 inches

Drop at heel: 2.5 inches

Weight:

12-bore: 26.0-inch barrels, 6.75 lbs.; 28.0-inch barrels, 7.0 lbs.; 30.0-inch barrels, 7.25 lbs.

20-bore: 26.0-inch barrels, 6.25 lbs.; 28.0-inch barrels, 6.5 lbs.

Sights: metal bead front and mid-rib

Bore: 12, 2.75-inch case; 20, 3.0-inch case

Comment: Similar to the least expensive Savage M330 except for ventilated rib and automatic selective ejection.

SAVAGE M330 OVER/UNDER FIELD GRADE

Manufacturer: Valmet, Finland

Importer/distributor: Savage Arms

Action type: box lock; break-top

Ignition system: mechanical

SAVAGE M330 OVER/UNDER FIELD GRADE
(continued)

Trigger: single selective; triggerbow selector

Locking system: monobloc

Ejection: manual

Safety: automatic; tang slide

Barrel length & choke:

  12-bore: 30.0 or 28.0 inches, full & modified; 26.0 inches, modified & improved cylinder

  20-bore: 28.0 inches, full & modified; 26.0 inches, modified & improved cylinder

Stock: 2-piece walnut; impressed checkering; uncapped semi-pistol grip; high-gloss waterproof finish

Buttplate: black hard rubber

Length of pull: 14.0 inches

Drop at comb: 1.5 inches

Drop at heel: 2.5 inches

Weight:

  12-bore: 26.0-inch barrels, 6.75 lbs.; 28.0-inch barrels, 7.0 lbs.; 30.0-inch barrels, 7.25 lbs.

  20-bore: 26.0-inch barrels, 6.25 lbs.; 28.0-inch barrels, 6.5 lbs.

Sights: brass bead front on unribbed barrel

Bore: 12, 2.75-inch case; 20, 3.0-inch case

Data: Etched designs on blued receiver.

Comment: This is one of the least-expensive over/unders. It has sturdy construction. It is an excellent buy for the man who wants an over/under but who cannot afford to spend much money.

SAVAGE M333 OVER/UNDER SKEET

Manufacturer: Valmet, Finland

Importer/distributor: Savage Arms

Action type: box lock; break-top

Ignition system: mechanical

Trigger: single selective; triggerbow selector

Locking system: monobloc

Ejection: automatic selective

Safety: automatic; tang slide

Barrel length & choke: 26.0 inches, skeet & skeet

Stock: 2-piece walnut; reverse checkering; uncapped semi-pistol grip; high-gloss finish

Buttplate: black hard rubber

Length of pull: 14.0 inches

Drop at comb: 1.5 inches

Drop at heel: 2.5 inches

Weight: 12-bore, 7.0 lbs.; 20-bore, 6.25 lbs.

Sights: metal bead front and mid-rib

Bore: 12, 2.75-inch case; 20, 3.0-inch case

Comment: Same as for M333 Field Grade save for skeet boring. This is just about the least expensive over/under skeet model.

SAVAGE M333-T OVER/UNDER TRAP

Manufacturer: Valmet, Finland

Importer/distributor: Savage Arms

Action type: box lock; break-top

Ignition system: mechanical

Trigger: single selective; triggerbow selector

Locking system: monobloc

Ejection: manual

Safety: nonautomatic; tang slide

Barrel length & choke: 30.0 inches, full & improved modified

Stock: 2-piece walnut; impressed checkering; Monte Carlo comb; uncapped semi-pistol grip; high-gloss finish

Buttplate: ventilated rubber recoil pad

Length of pull: 14.5 inches

Drop at comb: 1.5 inches

Drop at Monte Carlo: 1.5 inches

Drop at heel: 2.5 inches

Weight: 7.75 lbs.

Sights: metal bead front and mid-rib on ventilated rib

Bore: 12, 2.75-inch case

Data: Same as for M333 Field Grade except for Monte Carlo stock, recoil pad, and choke.

Comment: A sturdy, reliable, but unfancy trap gun. It is just about the least expensive trap gun on today's (1976) market. This is ideal for the embryo trapshooter who has a minimal amount to spend.

UNIVERSAL-BAIKAL MODEL IJ-27E OVER/UNDER

Manufacturer: Soviet State Arms Plant, USSR

Importer/distributor: Universal Sporting Goods, Inc.

Action type: box lock; break-top

Ignition system: mechanical

Trigger: double triggers

Locking system: underbolt

Ejection: automatic selective (manual optional at slightly reduced price)

Safety: nonautomatic; tang slide

EXPLODED VIEW OF THE SAVAGE MODEL 333T OVER/UNDER 12 GAUGE

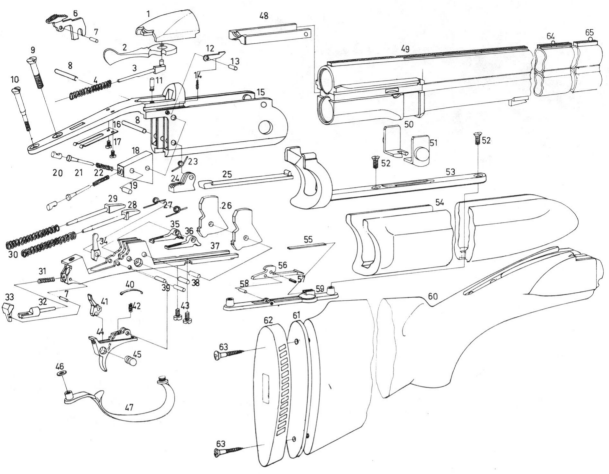

No.	Part Name	No.	Part Name	No.	Part Name
1	Locking Bolt	23	Cocking Lever Spring	45	Selector Button
2	Trap Snap	24	Cocking Crank	46	Trigger Guard Washer
3	Top Snap Plunger	25	Cocking Slide	47	Trigger Guard
4	Top Snap Spring	26	Hammer	48	Extractor
6	Safety Button	27	Sear Spring	49	Barrels
7	Safety Detent, Inertia Block Pin	28	Mainspring Plunger (Right)	50	Barrel Pivot Pin (Left)
8	Firing Pin Block, Cocking Crack Pin	29	Mainspring Plunger (Left)	51	Barrel Pivot Pin (Right)
9	Top Tang Screw (Front)	30	Mainspring	52	Fore-end Snap Housing Screw
10	Top Tang Screw (Rear)	31	Inertia Block Spring	53	Forend Iron
11	Top Snap Pin	32	Inertia Block Plunger	54	Forend Wood
12	Top Slide Trip	33	Inertia Block	55	Forend Snap Spring
13	Top Slide Trip Pin	34	Safety Level	56	Forend Snap
14	Top Slide Trip Spring	35	Sear (Left)	57	Forend Snap Stop Pin
15	Frame **PRICE ON APPLICATION**	36	Sear (Right)	58	Forend Snap Pin
16	Safety Spring	37	Trigger Plate	59	Forend Snap Housing
17	Safety Spring Screw	38	Sear Pin, Hammer Pin	60	Stock Complete
18	Firing Pin Block	39	Trigger Pin, Safety Lever Pin	61	Butt Plate Liner
19	Striker Pin	40	Selector Spring	62	Recoil Pad
20	Striker	41	Selector Lever	63	Recoil Pad Screw
21	Firing Pin	42	Trigger Spring	64	Rear Sight
22	Firing Pin Spring	43	Trigger Plate Screws	65	Front Sight
		44	Trigger		

UNIVERSAL-BAIKAL MODEL IJ-27E OVER/UNDER (continued)

Barrel length & choke: 28.0 inches, full & modified; 26.0 inches, modified & improved cylinder

Stock: 2-piece walnut; machine-checkered (19 lines per inch); Monte Carlo comb; full pistol grip; brown plastic pistol grip cap with white plastic spacer; barrels attached to fore-end with Deeley (of Anson & Deeley) type latch; high-gloss finish

Buttplate: brown rubber ventilated recoil pad

Length of pull: 15.125 inches

Drop at comb: 1.375 inches

Drop at Monte Carlo: 1.25 inches

Drop at heel: 2.625 inches

Weight: 26.0-inch barrels, 7.0 lbs.; 28.0-inch barrels, 7.25 lbs.

Sights: brass bead front on ventilated rib

Bore: 12, 2.75-inch case

Data: Front trigger fires lower (more open) barrel. Throughbolt attaches stock to frame. Animal scenes on either side of receiver. European grouse on triggerbow.

Comment: The author test-fired 500 rounds with one sample gun. Loads ranged from light skeet loads through standard upland-game loads to 2.75-inch magnum loads. Recoil with latter was fairly severe.

Ejector problems included no ejection or ejection of loaded case with retention of fired case. Trigger pulls tested at an excessively high poundage. One trigger tested at 11.0 lbs. and the other at about 8.0 lbs.

Test patterns fired at 40 yards (10 rounds each barrel) gave approximate full-choke pattern with full-choke barrel and improved-cylinder patterns with modified-choke barrels. This spread all too often happens with many more expensive guns. Such deviation is a good reason for the owner of every shotgun to test-pattern his gun.

Fortunately, the arm has a one-year warranty.

This is one of the lowest-priced over/unders on the market and is one of a very few on the U.S. market fitted with double triggers.

The difficulties encountered should have been detected by the factory inspection. Most problems were corrected by a local gunsmith.

WEATHERBY REGENCY OVER/UNDER FIELD GRADE

Manufacturer: Howa Machinery Co., Japan

Importer/distributor: Weatherby, Inc.

Action type: box lock with dummy sideplates; break-top

Ignition system: mechanical

Trigger: single selective; triggerbow selector

Locking system: includes Greener crossbolt

Ejection: automatic selective

Safety: nonautomatic; tang slide

Barrel length & choke:

12-bore: 30.0 inches, full & modified; 28.0 inches, full & modified or modified & improved cylinder; 26.0 inches, modified & improved cylinder

20-bore: 28.0 or 26.0 inches, full & modified or modified & improved cylinder

Stock: 2-piece French walnut; hand-checkered; flared full pistol grip with rosewood cap and white line spacer; fluted fore-end; high-gloss finish

Buttplate: red ventilated rubber recoil pad

Length of pull: 14.25 inches

Drop at comb: 1.5 inches

Drop at heel: 2.5 inches

Weight:

12-bore: 26.0-inch barrels, 7.25 lbs.; 28.0-inch barrels, 7.375 lbs.; 30.0-inch barrels, 7.5 lbs.

20-bore: 26.0-inch barrels, 6.7 lbs.; 28.0-inch barrels, 6.875 lbs.

WEATHERBY REGENCY OVER/UNDER FIELD GRADE (continued)

Sights: metal bead front

Bore: 12, 2.75-inch case; 20, 3.0-inch case

Data: Typical high-gloss Weatherby bluing. Floral engraving on action, dummy sideplates and bottom of trigger bow. Simulated gold-plated trigger.

Comment: This is an excellent over/under shotgun. It pleases those who like Weatherby's rifle styling, but it is not offensive to many lovers of classic-design shotguns. The author would prefer about 4 ounces less weight in the 20-bore.

WEATHERBY REGENCY OVER/UNDER SKEET MODEL

Manufacturer: Howa Machinery Co., Japan

Importer/distributor: Weatherby, Inc.

Action type: box lock with dummy sideplates; break-top

Ignition system: mechanical

Trigger: single selective; in front of trigger

Locking system: includes Greener crossbolt

Ejection: automatic selective

Safety: nonautomatic; tang slide

Barrel length & choke: 26.0 or 28.0 inches, skeet & skeet

Stock: 2-piece fancy American walnut; hand-checkered; flared full pistol grip with rosewood cap and white line spacer; fluted fore-end; high-gloss finish

Buttplate: ventilated red rubber recoil pad

Length of pull: 14.25 inches

Drop at comb: 1.5 inches

Drop at heel: 2.5 inches

Weight:

12-bore: 26.0-inch barrels, 7.25 lbs.; 28.0-inch barrels, 7.375 lbs.

20-bore: 26.0-inch barrels, 6.7 lbs.; 28.0-inch barrels, 6.875 lbs.

Sights: metal bead front

Bore: 12, 2.75-inch case; 20, 3.0-inch case

Data: Same as for Field Grade save for skeet & skeet choke.

Comment: Same as for Field Grade. An excellent skeet gun.

WEATHERBY REGENCY OVER/UNDER TRAP MODEL

Manufacturer: Howa Machinery Co., Japan

Importer/distributor: Weatherby, Inc.

Action type: box lock with dummy sideplates; break-top

Ignition system: mechanical

Trigger: single selective; triggerbow selector

Locking system: includes Greener crossbolt

Ejection: automatic selective

Safety: nonautomatic; tang slide

Barrel length & choke: 30.0 or 32.0 inches, full & full, full & improved modified, or full & modified

Stock: 2-piece fancy American walnut; hand-checkered; flared full pistol grip with rosewood cap and white line spacer; fluted fore-end; high-gloss finish

Buttplate: red ventilated recoil pad

Length of pull: 14.375 inches

Drop at comb: 1.375 inches

Drop at heel: 1.875 inches

Weight: 30.0-inch barrels, 7.75 lbs.; 32-0-inch barrels, 8.0 lbs.

Sights: metal bead front and mid-rib

Bore: 12, 2.75-inch case

Data: Same as for Field Grade except for borings, barrel lengths, and stock dimensions.

Comment: Same as for Field Grade. A good trap gun.

WINCHESTER M101 FIELD GRADE—12-BORE

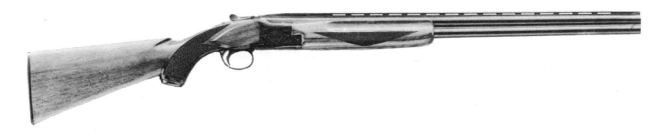

Manufacturer: Olin-Kodensha, Japan

Importer/distributor: Winchester-Western

Action type: box lock; break-top

Ignition system: mechanical

Trigger: single selective; tang selector

Locking system: underbolt

Ejection: automatic selective

Safety: nonautomatic; tang slide

Barrel length & choke: 28.0 or 30.0 inches, modified & full; 26.0 inches, modified & improved cylinder

Stock: 2-piece French walnut; hand-checkered; full pistol grip with black plastic cap; fluted fore-end; high gloss polyurethane finish

Buttplate: black plastic

Length of pull: 14.0 inches

Drop at comb: 1.5 inches

Drop at heel: 2.5 inches

Weight: 26.0-inch barrels, 7.25 lbs.; 28.0-inch barrels, 7.5 lbs.; 30.0-inch barrels, 7.75 lbs.

Sights: metal bead front

Bore: 12, 3.0-inch case

Data: Jeweled action and barrel lugs. Light engraving. Ventilated rib. Hand-checkered pistol grip and some checkering on fore-end. Inside of barrel is chromed.

Comment: This over/under was designed by Winchester-Western engineers. It is made in the Japanese plant of Olin-Kodensha. Olin Industries, Winchester's parent corporation, owns 50 percent of Olin-Kodensha stock.

Fine walnut is used for buttstock and fore-end of the M101. Each stock is given five coats of polyurethane lacquer. The finish is sprayed on the stock. Each coat is dried and hand-rubbed. After the fifth and final coat, stocks designed for the U.S. market are polished to a high gloss. Those for the non-U.S. market—mostly European—are not polished after the final coat. This gives European-bound M101s the classic dull finish. Its water-resistant capabilities are superior to the traditional oil finish.

Stocks designed for the U.S. market are checkered after all lacquer has been applied. Once the checkering has been completed, oil is hand-rubbed into checkered areas.

Non-U.S.-market stocks are checkered before applying lacquer. Most stocks are checkered by women at home. "Hand" checkering is done with a hand-operated high-speed checkering tool that cuts one line at a time. Checkering is about 22 lines per inch.

The M101s for the European market use a monobloc construction. This makes for lighter construction. Europeans like light guns and use light loads.

The light "engraving" is done with an electric tool.

From a mechanical standpoint this is as fine a box-lock/mechanical trigger over/under as the author has used. Shotguns of this type which cost more money have the added cost in fine borderless checkering and costly engraving and gold figure inlaying.

WINCHESTER M101 OVER/UNDER FIELD GRADE—SMALLBORE

Manufacturer: Olin-Kodensha, Japan

Importer/distributor: Winchester-Western

Action type: box lock; break-top

Ignition system: mechanical

Trigger: single selective; tang selector

Locking system: underbolt

Ejection: automatic selective

Safety: nonautomatic; tang slide

Barrel length & choke: 26.5 inches, modified & improved cylinder; 28.0 inches, modified & full

Stock: 2-piece French walnut; hand-checkered; capped full pistol grip; fluted fore-end; high-gloss polyurethane finish

Buttplate: black plastic

Length of pull: 14.0 inches

Drop at comb: 1.5 inches

Drop at heel: 2.5 inches

Weight:

  20-bore: 28.0-inch barrels, 6.5 lbs.; 26.5-inch barrels, 6.25 lbs.

  28-bore: 28.0-inch barrels, 6.375 lbs.; 26.5-inch barrels, 6.25 lbs.

  .410-bore: 28.0-inch barrels, 6.5 lbs.; 26.5-inch barrels, 6.25 lbs.

Sights: metal bead front

Bore: 20, .410, 3.0-inch case; 28, 2.75-inch case

Data: Same as for 12-bore Field Grade except for lighter action.

Comment: Same as for 12-bore Field Grade.

WINCHESTER M101 OVER/UNDER MAGNUM

Manufacturer: Olin-Kodensha, Japan

Importer/distributor: Winchester-Western

Action type: box lock; break-top

Ignition System: mechanical

Trigger: single selective; tang selector

Locking system: underbolt

Ejection: selective automatic

Safety: nonautomatic; tang slide

Barrel length & choke: 30.0 inches, full & full or modified & full

Stock: 2-piece French walnut; hand-checkered; pistol grip with black plastic cap; semi-beavertail fore-end with finger groove; high-gloss finish

Buttplate: ventilated recoil pad

Length of pull: 14.0 inches

Drop at comb: 1.5 inches

Drop at heel: 2.5 inches

Weight: 7.75 lbs.

Sights: metal bead front

Bore: 12, 3.0-inch case

Data: Same as for Field Grade except chokes and barrel length.

Comment: This is a very good though light 12-bore Magnum.

WINCHESTER M101 OVER/UNDER SKEET

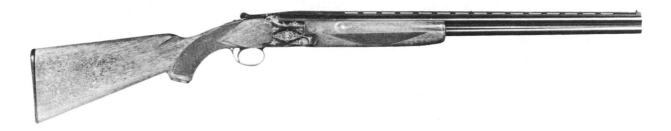

Manufacturer: Olin-Kodensha, Japan

Importer/distributor: Winchester-Western

Action type: box lock; break-top

Ignition system: mechanical

Trigger: single selective; tang selector

Locking system: underbolt

Ejection: automatic selective

Safety: nonautomatic; tang slide

Barrel length & choke:

12-bore & 20-bore: 26.5 inches, skeet 1 & skeet 2

28-bore & .410-bore: 28.0 inches, skeet 1 & skeet 2

Stock: 2-piece French walnut; hand-checkered; full pistol grip with black plastic cap; finger-grooved semi-beavertail fore-end; high-gloss finish

Buttplate: black hard rubber

Length of pull: 14.0 inches

Drop at comb: 1.5 inches

Drop at heel: 2.5 inches

Weight: 12-bore, 7.25 lbs.; 20-bore, 6.5 lbs.; 28-bore & .410 bore, 6.375 lbs.

Sights: metal bead, front and middle

Bore: 12, 28, 2.75-inch case; 20, .410, 3.0-inch case

Data: Same as for Field Grade save barrel lengths and chokes. Wood is slightly fancier than Field Grade.

Comment: A fine skeet gun.

WINCHESTER PIGEON GRADE OVER/UNDER FIELD GUN

Manufacturer: Olin-Kodensha, Japan

Importer/distributor: Winchester-Western

Action type: box lock; break-top

Ignition system: inertial

Trigger: single selective; tang selector

Locking system: underbolt

Ejection: automatic selective

Safety: nonautomatic; tang slide

Barrel length & choke: 26.0 inches, improved cylinder & modified; 28.0 inches, modified & full

WINCHESTER PIGEON GRADE OVER/UNDER FIELD GUN
(continued)

Stock: 2-piece French walnut; hand-checkered; full uncapped pistol grip; fluted fore-end; high-gloss finish

Buttplate: black ventilated rubber recoil pad with white line spacer

Length of pull: 14.0 inches

Drop at comb: 1.5 inches

Drop at heel: 2.5 inches

Weight:

12-bore: 26.0-inch barrels, 7.25 lbs.; 28.0-inch barrels, 7.5 lbs.

20-bore: 26.0-inch barrels, 6.25 lbs.; 28.0-inch barrels, 6.5 lbs.

Sights: metal bead front and mid-rib

Bore: 12, 2.75-inch case; 20, 3.0-inch case

Data: Silver-gray "satin-finish" frame, checkered trigger.

Comment: The Pigeon Grade is Winchester's top-of-the-line over/under shotgun.

WINCHESTER PIGEON GRADE OVER/UNDER SKEET GUN

Manufacturer: Olin-Kodensha, Japan

Importer/distributor: Winchester-Western

Action type: box lock; break-top

Ignition system inertial

Trigger: single selective; tang selector

Locking system: underbolt

Ejection: automatic selective

Safety: nonautomatic; tang slide

Barrel length & choke: 27.0 inches, skeet & skeet

Stock: 2-piece French walnut; hand-checkered; fluted fore-end; high-gloss finish

Buttplate: ventilated black rubber recoil pad with white line spacer

Length of pull: 14.0 inches

Drop at comb: 1.5 inches

Drop at heel: 2.5 inches

Weight: 7.25 lbs.

Sights: metal bead front and mid-rib; ventilated rib

Bore: 12, 20, 2.75-inch case

Data: See Pigeon Grade Field Gun.

Comment: This and the other Pigeon Grade M101s have an inertial firing system rather than the mechanical system of the less expensive M101s. Other features include finer hand checkering and fancier wood.

The receiver is silver-gray and is hand-engraved, as is the trigger guard.

WINCHESTER PIGEON GRADE OVER/UNDER TRAP GUN

Manufacturer: Olin-Kodensha, Japan

Importer/distributor: Winchester-Western

Action type: box lock; break-top

Ignition system: inertial

Trigger: selective single; tang selector

Locking system: underbolt

Ejection: automatic selective

Safety: nonautomatic; tang slide

Barrel length & choke: 30.0 or 32.0 inches, full & full or modified & full

Stock: 2-piece French walnut; hand-checkered; capped pistol grip; finger grooves on semi-beavertail fore-end; high-gloss finish

Buttplate: black ventilated rubber recoil pad with white line spacer

Length of pull: 14.375 inches

Drop at comb: 1.375 inches

Drop at Monte Carlo (if applicable): 1.875 inches

Drop at heel: 2.5 inches

Weight: 30.0-inch barrels, 8.0 lbs.; 32.0-inch barrels, 8.25 lbs.

Sights: white bead front and mid-rib

Bore: 12, 2.75-inch case

Data: This over/under trap gun replaces the single-barrel trap (1967–73). Unlike the standard M101, it uses the inertia-activated trigger rather than the mechanical trigger.

WINCHESTER XPERT FIELD GRADE OVER/UNDER SHOTGUN

Manufacturer: Olin-Kodensha, Japan

Importer/distributor: Winchester-Western

Action type: box lock; break-top

Ignition system: mechanical

Trigger: single selective; tang selector

Locking system: underbolt

Ejection: automatic selective

Safety: nonautomatic; tang slide

Barrel length & choke:

12-bore: 30.0 inches, full & full; 28.0 inches, full & modified; 26.0 inches, improved cylinder & modified

20-bore: 28.0 inches, full & modified; 26.0 inches, improved cylinder & modified

Stock: 2-piece walnut; machine-checkered; uncapped pistol grip; fluted fore-end; high-gloss finish

Buttplate: black plastic

Length of pull: 14.0 inches

Drop at comb: 1.5 inches

Drop at heel: 2.5 inches

Weight:

12-bore: 26.0-inch barrels, 7.25 lbs.; 28.0-inch barrels, 7.5 lbs.; 30.0-inch barrels, 7.75 lbs.

20-bore: 26.0-inch barrels, 6.25 lbs.; 28.0-inch barrels, 6.5 lbs.

Sights: metal bead front on ventilated rib

Bore: 12, 2.75-inch or 3.0-inch case; 20, 3.0-inch case

Comment: Soaring production costs prompted Winchester to issue this over/under for about $100 less than the M101 and about $200 less than the Pigeon Grade over/under. The wood is not as finely figured, the checkering is machine-cut, and there is no engraving. It is, however, a very good over/under shotgun. It may well be the best buy in its price category.

WINCHESTER XPERT OVER/UNDER SKEET GUN

Manufacturer: Olin-Kodensha, Japan

Importer/distributor: Winchester-Western

Action type: box lock; break-top

Ignition system: mechanical

Trigger: single selective; tang selector

Locking system: underbolt

Ejection: automatic selective

Safety: nonautomatic; tang slide

Barrel length & choke: 26.0 inches, skeet & skeet

Stock: 2-piece walnut; machine-checkered; un-capped pistol grip; fluted fore-end; high-gloss finish

Buttplate: black plastic

Length of pull: 14.0 inches

Drop at comb: 1.5 inches

Drop at heel: 2.5 inches

Weight: 20-bore, 6.5 lbs., 12 bore, 7.5 lbs.

Sights: metal bead front and mid-rib; ventilated rib

Bore: 12, 20, 2.75-inch case

Comment: This is one of the better low-priced skeet over/under guns.

WINCHESTER XPERT OVER/UNDER TRAP GUN

Manufacturer: Olin-Kodensha, Japan

Importer/distributor: Winchester-Western

Action type: box lock; break-top

Ignition system: mechanical

Trigger: single selective; tang selector

Locking system: underbolt

Ejection: automatic selective

Safety: nonautomatic; tang slide

Barrel length & choke: 30.0 inches, full & full

Stock: 2-piece walnut; machine-checkered; fluted fore-end; full pistol grip with black plastic cap; high-gloss finish

Buttplate: black ventilated recoil pad

Length of pull: 14.0 inches

Drop at comb: 1.5 inches

Drop at Monte Carlo (if applicable): 1.5 inches

Drop at heel: 2.5 inches

Weight: 8.25 lbs.

Sights: metal bead front and mid-rib

Bore: 12, 2.75-inch case

Comment: Without engraving and fancy wood, this is nonetheless one of the best of the relatively inexpensive trap guns.

CHAPTER 21

SIDE-BY-SIDE DOUBLE-BARREL SHOTGUNS

The side-by-side double-barrel shotgun, largely written off by Americans in the two decades following World War II, is making a modest comeback.

Today, only Savage's Stevens-Fox line of inexpensive side-by-side doubles and the Winchester M21—by custom order only at $3000 plus—are regularly made in America.

Most doubles on the American market are made in Italy, Japan, and Spain. Inflation in those countries is slowly forcing the prices ever upward.

Oddly enough, the over/under, which is more expensive to manufacture, is outselling the double by a probable 10-to-1 margin. In part the reason may be that many Americans raised on the rifle prefer a single sighting plane. A fine over/under can be fully as beautiful—at least to this author—as a side-by-side double.

The Purdey, long the side-by-side twin-tube by which all others are judged, may soon fade from the scene along with other elegant anachronisms like the Holland & Holland and Westley Richards.

The British have long been proud, and justly so, of their fine shotguns. Most of these guns are hand-made by a few workers. Today machine tools can perform at least 90 percent of the work done by a hand craftsman. The remaining 10 percent can be finished by hand.

It is too late for fine British gunmakers to switch to machine production, with the final touches being supplied by hand craftsmen. The British who can afford fine shotguns—or double rifles—already have them. About 100,000 shotguns are imported annually. Most of these are from the Continent.

Several of the author's British shooting friends who own one or several fine doubles with sidelocks often take along an inexpensive box-lock double when they head for Africa or other far parts.

Fine English double guns rarely get knocked about as much as do American doubles. The British, who like to order their doubles in pairs, use these guns for estate shooting at driven birds.

Actions

More than 95 percent of current production side-by-side shotguns—it's been about the same ratio for a century—use the Anson & Deeley box lock. It is the sturdiest of twin-tube actions.

The side lock—it has removable sideplates—like those of the Purdey and Holland & Holland has long been considered the finest shotgun action. Some sidelocks require a screwdriver to remove or replace sideplates. Others use the Holland & Holland levers, which are instantly removable or replaceable without a screwdriver.

The major mechanical advantage of the sideplate is the accessibility of the action for cleaning and repair. The major disadvantage is that the action location weakens the stock at its most vulnerable location—the small.

The sideplate provides additional space for engraving and inlays. This also raises the price because of the cost of the extra artwork.

Today, the advantage of the sidelock—except as a surface for additional decoration—is far less than in the past. Improved metallurgy, rigorous factory inspection, and quality design and workmanship on better box-lock twin-tube guns has lessened the need for the sidelock.

Barrels

The information about over/under barrels and chokes in Chapter 20 is also applicable to side-by-side double guns.

Side-by-side aficionados stoutly maintain that their favorite is less subject to wind pressure than the over/under barrels, which present a broader surface to the wind. Those of us with extensive experience with both side-by-side and over/under guns fail to detect an appreciable difference.

Felt recoil is slightly less in the over/under than in the side-by-side double.

There may well be a slight advantage to the single sighting plane of the over/under, though the advent of the raised ventilated rib has eliminated some of the over/under's edge.

Chromed bores are an advantage, in that they are free from rust problems and probably protect the bores from being excessively battered by hundreds of thousands—or even millions—of individual pellets passing through the tubes.

Bright blued barrels such as found on Weatherby arms are beautiful to behold. For those of us who like bright blue, the dull finish of black chrome barrel exteriors takes a bit of getting used to. The author likes bright blue on his upland guns and appreciates the anti-rust qualities of black chrome on his waterfowl guns. Owners of waterfowl guns with regular blued barrels and ventilated ribs should take care to wipe dry the areas between the posts—and the posts themselves—after a day in the blind. A light coat of oil should be given those areas.

Safeties

The classic safety location for many years has been the tang. The usual location for the barrel selector has also been the tang. Some arms, like Ithaca's SKB, have a sliding tang safety and a separate barrel selector inside the triggerbow. This is probably all right, but many of us who own several side-by-side and/or over/under guns prefer to have the same type of safety and barrel selector in the same location on all arms.

For many years only trap guns had manual (nonautomatic) safeties. Today, an increasing number of double guns—particularly in the middle and upper price brackets—of all types are fitted with a manual safety. This can possibly save a split second in getting off a shot, and it is—in the opinion of some, including the author—a "safer" safe method. One is much more aware of the safety if he has to consciously put the selector in the safe position.

Some trap guns, to the horror of ignorant safety devotees, have no safety at all. The arm is used only on the line at the trap field. The arm when loaded is always pointed at the target area. The shot cartridges are inserted just before the traps are pulled.

Triggers

Comments made on over/under trigger systems apply with about equal validity to side-by-side trigger systems.

The so-called "gold plating" on triggers—the author doesn't particularly care for the stuff—does provide some rust protection.

Few shotgun triggers—and not enough handgun and rifle triggers—are checkered or serrated. A firmer grip, particularly on waterfowl gun triggers, would be ensured if the triggers were checkered or serrated.

Locking/bolting systems

Most of these systems are the same as those used on over/unders. Most over/unders use bolting systems which are directly derived from the double-barrel shotgun or double-barrel rifle.

Few double-barrel side-by-side shotguns are currently made in America, but dozens of manufacturers have produced them in the past. Almost all, regardless of manufacturer, used a single or double underbolt. The major American exception was the late and oft-lamented L. C. Smith double with the rotary bolt.

Twin-tube arms which employ other systems usually feature the underbolt or bolts in addition to their sometimes patented system. Few of the numerous patented systems were substantial safety improvements. They were—and still are—produced with the primary object of selling the idea to potential purchasers that a specific maker's bolting system is superior to those of other makers.

A system widely used on the Continent and in England is the Greener crossbolt. The original patent granted to designer W. W. Greener has long since expired.

This round crossbolt—there are square or off-round versions—is used in conjunction with a barrel extension which projects rearward from between the twin tubes. When the gun is closed and cocked, the bolt slides through a hole in the extension. This provides a second or third lock between barrels and receiver.

Some arms, like the Krieghoff, use dual extensions and crossbolts. The author, over the past 40-odd years, has used a large number of arms with various locking systems. He has never had any problems with a well-designed and well-crafted arm. The only scatterguns that opened at the time of firing were two cheap single-shot, single-barrel arms costing no more than $5 when originally manufactured, which was at least 50 years earlier.

Stocks

The basic stocks for side-by-side doubles are the same as for those of the over/under scattergun: (1) straight (no pistol grip) stock, which is usually termed "English classic" or vice versa; (2) full pistol grip, which is usually capped with plastic, hard rubber, and sometimes with ivory, horn, or steel; and (3) semi-pistol grip, which may or may not be capped.

The straight stock should be confined to those arms in which only light or moderate field loads are used. Many shooters of twin-trigger guns prefer a straight stock because they alter their hold slightly—sliding the shooting hand back a fraction of an inch—to pull the rear trigger. The full pistol grip helps keep the arm in position and gives the hand a good hold on the stock. In the author's opinion, it should always be fitted to scatterguns used with full or magnum loads. As for the semi-pistol grip, its only real advantage is in the eyes of some beholders.

French or Circassian walnut is the finest classic wood.

The dull, hand-rubbed oil finish has been the classic finish for fine stocks for many years. It has taken time for many of us to become accustomed to the high-gloss polyurethane finish. This finish, however, provides far better "waterproofing" than oil. Some stocks, like those on Ithaca's SKB Series, have several coats of polyurethane applied, but the last coat is not rubbed to a high-gloss finish. Those who prefer the dull finish thus can have it and waterproofing too.

Many best double guns have no buttplate (this doesn't apply to arms designed for magnum loads, which are properly fitted with quality ventilated recoil pads) but have the wood of the butt checkered. Some shooters, including this one, prefer a more durable buttplate like hard rubber. Checkered steel is rarely used for buttplates, though there is no reason it cannot be used on arms designed for light loads.

Trap guns are invariably fitted with ventilated recoil pads. This is because several hundred rounds may be fired in the course of a shooting day. Some skeet double guns are fitted with recoil pads, and some are not. The author prefers recoil pads on his skeet guns.

BERNADELLI BRESCIA EXTERNAL HAMMER DOUBLE

Manufacturer: Vincenzo Bernadelli, Italy

Importer/distributor: Sloan's Sporting Goods, Inc.

Action type: Anson & Deeley box lock; break-top; external hammers

Ignition system: mechanical

Trigger: double (single nonselective available on special order at extra cost)

Locking system: Purdey underbolts and Greener crossbolt

Ejection: manual

Safety: half-cock external hammers

Barrel length & choke:

12-bore: 29.5 inches or 27.5 inches, full & modified; 25.5 inches, modified & improved cylinder

20-bore: 27.5 inches, full & modified; 25.5 inches, modified & improved cylinder

Stock: 2-piece European walnut (fancy grade at extra cost); hand-cut checkering; classic English field (splinter) fore-end (beavertail available at extra cost); full pistol grip (straight stock available at extra cost); semi-gloss finish

Buttplate: black hard rubber (Pachmayr ventilated rubber recoil pad available at extra cost)

Length of pull: 14.325 inches

Drop at comb: 1.5 inches

Drop at heel: 2.375 inches

Weight:

12-bore: 25.5-inch barrels, 6.75 lbs.; 27.5-inch barrels, 7.0 lbs.; 29.5-inch barrels, 7.25 lbs.

20-bore: 25.5-inch barrels, 6.0 lbs.; 27.5-inch barrels, 6.2 lbs.

BERNADELLI BRESCIA EXTERNAL
HAMMER DOUBLE (continued)

Sights: metal bead front on raised matted rib (hollow rib available at extra cost)

Bore: 12, 2.75-inch case; 20, 3.0-inch case (16, 2.75-inch case available on special order)

Data: Case-hardened receiver and dummy sideplate. Light engraving. Custom dimensions and fancier engraving at extra cost.

Comment: A quality double gun for the man who wants an external-hammer gun.

BERNADELLI ELIO DOUBLE

Manufacturer: Vincenzo Bernadelli, Italy

Importer/distributor: Sloan's Sporting Goods, Inc.

Action type: Anson & Deeley box lock; break-top; internal hammers

Ignition system: mechanical

Trigger: double, front trigger hinged (single nonselective trigger available at extra cost)

Locking system: Purdey-type underbolts (Greener crossbolt available at extra cost)

Ejection: automatic selective

Safety: nonautomatic; tang slide (automatic available at extra cost)

Barrel length & choke: 27.5 inches, full & modified; 25.5 inches, modified & improved cylinder

Stock: 2-piece European walnut (fancy figured wood available at extra cost); hand-cut checkering; English field (splinter) fore-end (beavertail available at extra cost); right-hand or left-hand cheekpiece available at extra cost; straight or pistol grip; semi-gloss finish

Buttplate: black hard rubber (Pachmayr ventilated rubber recoil pad available at extra cost)

Length of pull: 14.375 inches

Drop at comb: 1.575 inches

Drop at heel: 2.375 inches

Weight: 25.5-inch barrels, 6.0 lbs.; 27.5-inch barrels, 6.15 lbs.

Sights: metal bead on customer's specifications

Bore: 12, 2.75-inch case

Data: Silver-gray receiver. Fine scroll engraving on receiver and bottom of triggerbow. Custom dimensions available at extra cost.

Comment: This is the lightest 12-bore gun on the current market. The author would not recommend continual firing—without recoil pad—of heavy field or 2.75-inch magnum loads.

This is a fine shotgun in the upper medium price range.

BERNADELLI ITALIA EXTERNAL HAMMER DOUBLE

Manufacturer: Vincenzo Bernadelli, Italy

Importer/distributor: Sloan's Sporting Goods, Inc.

Action type: Anson & Deeley box lock; break-top; external hammers

Ignition system: mechanical

Trigger: double (nonselective single available at extra cost)

Locking system: Purdey-type underbolts and Greener crossbolt

Ejection: manual

Safety: half-cock external hammers

Barrel length & choke:

12-bore: 29.5 or 27.5 inches, full & modified; 25.5 inches, modified & improved cylinder

20-bore: 27.5 inches, full & modified; 25.5 inches, modified & improved cylinder

Stock: 2-piece European walnut (fancy grade available at extra cost); hand-cut checkering; classic English field (splinter) fore-end (beavertail available at extra cost); straight English-type stock (pistol grip available at extra cost); semi-gloss finish

Buttplate: black hard rubber (Pachmayr ventilated rubber recoil pad available at extra cost)

Length of pull: 14.325 inches

Drop at comb: 1.5 inches

Drop at heel: 2.375 inches

Weight:

12-bore: 25.5-inch barrels, 6.75 lbs.; 27.5-inch barrels, 7.0 lbs.; 29.5-inch barrels, 7.25 lbs.

20-bore: 25.5-inch barrels, 6.0 lbs.; 27.5-inch barrels, 6.2 lbs.

Sights: metal bead front on raised matted rib (hollow rib available at extra cost)

Bore: 12, 2.75-inch case; 20, 3.0-inch case (16, 2.75-inch case available on special order)

Data: Custom dimensions available at extra cost.

Comment: Same as Brescia Grade but with full scroll engraving.

BERNADELLI ROMA 6 DOUBLE

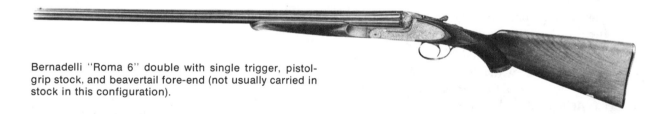

Bernadelli "Roma 6" double with single trigger, pistol-grip stock, and beavertail fore-end (not usually carried in stock in this configuration).

Manufacturer: Vincenzo Bernadelli, Italy

Importer/distributor: Sloan's Sporting Goods, Inc.

Action type: Anson & Deeley box lock with dummy sideplates; break-top; internal hammers

Trigger: double triggers, front trigger hinged (nonselective single available at extra cost)

Ignition system: mechanical

Locking system: Purdey-type underbolts (Greener crossbolt available at extra cost)

Ejection: automatic selective

Safety: nonautomatic; tang slide (automatic available at extra cost)

Barrel length & choke:

12-bore: 29.5 inches, full & modified (not always in stock but available on special order at extra cost); 27.5 inches, full & modified; 25.5 inches, modified & improved cylinder

20-bore: 27.5 inches, full & modified; 25.5 inches, modified & improved cylinder

Stock: 2-piece fancy European walnut; hand-cut checkering; straight grip (pistol grip to order at extra cost; extra fancy wood to order at extra cost); classic English field (splinter) fore-end (beavertail fore-end available at extra cost); semi-gloss finish

Buttplate: horizontal serrations on black hard-rubber buttplate (standard or Pachmayr ven-

BERNADELLI ROMA 6 DOUBLE (continued)

tilated rubber recoil pad available at extra cost)

Length of pull: 14.2 inches

Drop at comb: 1.5625 inches

Drop at heel: 2.375 inches

Weight:

12-bore: 25.5-inch barrels, 6.75 lbs.; 27.5-inch barrels, 7.0 lbs.; 29.5-inch barrels, 7.25 lbs.

20-bore: 25.5-inch barrels, 5.875 lbs.; 27.5-inch barrels, 6.125 lbs.

Sights: metal bead front on raised matted rib (hollow rib available at extra cost)

Bore: 12, 2.75-inch case; 20, 3.0-inch case·

Data: Action and sideplates finished in silver-gray. Fully engraved scroll on action and sideplates.

Comment: This is a more expensive version (over $1000 in 1976) of the Premier Grade Gamecock. It is a well-designed and well-executed double.

BERNADELLI V. B. HOLLAND DELUXE

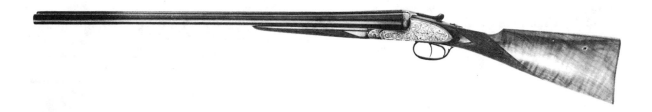

Manufacturer: Vincenzo Bernadelli, Italy

Importer/distributor: Sloan's Sporting Goods, Inc.

Action type: sidelock Holland & Holland hammerless type with double safety sears; screw-type sideplates (Holland & Holland has detachable sideplates at extra cost)

Ignition system: mechanical

Trigger: double triggers, front trigger hinged (single available at extra cost)

Locking system: underbolt

Ejection: automatic selective

Safety: nonautomatic tang slide (automatic available at extra cost)

Barrel length & choke: many customer options

Stock: 2-piece European walnut; hand-cut checkering; straight or pistol grip and beavertail or English field (splinter) styles at customer order

Buttplate: to customer order

Stock dimensions: to customer order

Sights: to customer order on raised matted rib

Bore: 12, 2.75-inch case

Data: As noted, many specifications are at the customer's order. The gun normally has fine scroll engraving, but custom designs, including game scenes, are available at extra cost. Extra barrels are available. These spare barrels cost less if ordered with the gun than if ordered afterward, when the arm must be returned to the factory for special fitting.

Comment: Bernadelli's best quality shotgun is, at nearly $5000 (1976), the firm's most expensive double gun. Because Italian labor is less costly than British labor, this arm would cost nearly $10,000 if made in England. It is a very fine double gun.

BROWNING MODEL B-B/S DOUBLE

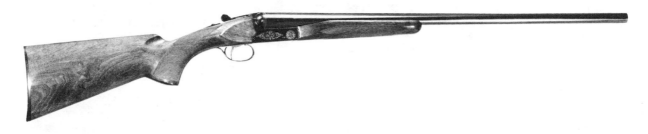

Manufacturer: Miroku Firearms, Japan

Importer/distributor: Browning Arms

Action type: box lock; break-top; hammerless

Ignition system: inertial

Trigger: single nonselective

Locking system: underbolt

Ejection: automatic selective

Safety: automatic; tang slide

Barrel length & choke:

  12-bore: 30.0 inches, full & full or full & modified; 28.0 inches, full & modified; 26.0 inches, modified & improved cylinder

  20-bore: 28.0 inches, full & modified; 26.0 inches, modified & improved cylinder

Stock: 2-piece; hand-checkered (20 lines per inch); full uncapped pistol grip; full beavertail fore-end; satin (semi-gloss) finish

Buttplate: black plastic

Length of pull: 14.25 inches

Drop at comb: 12-bore, 1.625 inches; 20-bore, 1.5 inches

Drop at heel: 12-bore, 2.5 inches; 20-bore, 2.375 inches

Weight:

  12-bore: 26.0-inch barrels, 7.2 lbs.; 28.0-inch barrels, 7.35 lbs.; 30.0-inch barrels, 7.5 lbs.

  20-bore: 26.0-inch barrels, 6.875 lbs.; 28.0-inch barrels, 7.0 lbs.

Sights: German nickel-silver bead on raised matted rib

Bore: 12, 20, 3.0-inch case (12, 2.75-inch case on early production models)

Comment: This is one of the best lower-priced side-by-side double-barrel shotguns. The design and workmanship are up to usual Browning standards. The fit of metal to wood is excellent. The checkering is well executed.

If the author were going to purchase a side-by-side shotgun in this price range, this would be his choice. The Ithaca SKB—with a smaller range of barrel/choke options—is also an excellent side-by-side, but he prefers the sliding tang safety/barrel selector.

DAVIDSON M63B DOUBLE-BARREL SHOTGUN

Manufacturer: Fabrica Armes ILJA, Spain

Importer/distributor: Davidson

Action type: Anson & Deeley box lock; break-top; hammerless

Ignition system: mechanical

Trigger: double

Locking system: Greener-type crossbolt, except underbolts on 28-bore and .410-bore

Ejection: manual

Safety: automatic; tang slide

DAVIDSON M63B DOUBLE-BARREL SHOTGUN
(continued)

Barrel length & choke:

12-bore: 30.0 or 28.0 inches, full & modified; 26.0 inches, modified & improved cylinder

16-bore, 20-bore, 28-bore: 28.0 inches, full & modified; 26.0 inches, modified & improved cylinder

.410-bore: 25.0 inches, full & full

Stock: 2-piece European walnut; machine-checkered; full pistol grip with black plastic cap and white line spacer; English (splinter) type fore-end; synthetic finish

Buttplate: black plastic with white line spacer

Length of pull: 14.0 inches

Drop at comb: 1.5 inches

Drop at heel: 1.5 inches

Weight:

12-bore: 26.0-inch barrels, 6.75 lbs.; 28.0-inch barrels, 7.0 lbs.; 30.0-inch barrels, 7.25 lbs.

16-bore: 26.0-inch barrels, 6.5 lbs.; 28.0-inch barrels, 6.75 lbs.

20-bore: 26.0-inch barrels, 6.25 lbs.; 28.0-inch barrels, 6.45 lbs.

28-bore: 26.0-inch barrels, 6.25 lbs.; 28.0-inch barrels, 6.5 lbs.

.410-bore: 5.75 lbs.

Sights: metal bead front on matted rib; rib tapers from 0.375 inch at breech end to 0.025 inch at muzzle

Bore: 12, 16, 20, 28, 2.75-inch case; .410, 3.0-inch case

Comment: One of the least-expensive double-barrel shotguns on the American market. It is worth its price.

DAVIDSON M63B MAGNUM DOUBLE BARREL

Manufacturer: Fabrica Armes ILJA, Spain

Importer/distributor: Davidson

Action type: Anson & Deeley box lock; break-top; hammerless

Ignition system: mechanical

Trigger: double

Locking system: Greener crossbolt

Ejection: manual

Safety: automatic; tang slide

Barrel length & choke:

10-bore: 32.0 inches, full & full

12-bore: 30.0 inches, full & modified

20-bore: 28.0 inches, full & modified

Stock: 2-piece European walnut; machine-checkered; full pistol grip with black plastic cap and white line spacer; semi-beavertail fore-end; synthetic finish

Buttplate: ventilated rubber recoil pad

Length of pull: 14.0 inches

Drop at comb: 1.5 inches

Drop at heel: 2.5 inches

Weight: 20-bore, 6.75 lbs.; 12-bore, 7.5 lbs.; 10-bore, 10.625 lbs.

Sights: metal bead front on raised matted rib; tapered rib is 0.375 inch wide at breech and 0.25 inch at muzzle

Bore: 10, 3.5-inch case; 12, 20, 3.0-inch case

Comment: One of the relatively few double-barrel 10-bore Magnums. In the author's opinion, no 10-bore Magnum double should weigh less than 12.0 lbs.

ITHACA SKB M100 FIELD GRADE DOUBLE

Manufacturer: SKB, Japan

Importer/distributor: Ithacagun

Action type: Anson & Deeley box lock; break-top; hammerless

Ignition system: inertial

Trigger: single selective; triggerbow selector

Locking system: underbolt

Ejection: manual

Safety: automatic; tang slide

Barrel length & choke:

12-bore: 30.0 or 28.0 inches, full & modified; 26.0 inches, modified & improved cylinder

20-bore: 28.0 inches, full & modified; 25.0 inches, modified & improved cylinder

Stock: 2-piece walnut; hand-checkered; English (splinter) fore-end; full pistol grip; oil-type polyurethane finish

Buttplate: black plastic

Length of pull: 14.0 inches

Drop at comb: 1.5 inches

Drop at heel: 2.625 inches

Weight:

12-bore: 26.0-inch barrels, 6.85 lbs.; 28.0-inch barrels, 7.0 lbs.; 30.0-inch barrels, 7.2 lbs.

20-bore: 25.0-inch barrels, 6.0 lbs.; 28.0-inch barrels, 6.75 lbs.

Sights: Raybar front on matted rib

Bore: 12, 20, 3.0-inch case

Data: Scrollwork on receiver. Chromed bores. Imitation gold-plated trigger.

Comment: One of the best inexpensive doubles for those who do not require ventilated rib, nonautomatic safety, or automatic selective ejection.

ITHACA SKB M150 FIELD GRADE DOUBLE

Manufacturer: SKB, Japan

Importer/distributor: Ithacagun

Action type: Anson & Deeley box lock; break-top; hammerless

Ignition system: inertial

Trigger: single selective; triggerbow selector

Locking system: underbolt

Ejection: manual

Safety: automatic; tang slide

Barrel length & choke:

12-bore: 30.0 or 28.0 inches, full & modified; 26.0 inches, modified & improved cylinder

20-bore: 28.0 inches, full & modified; 25.0 inches, modified & improved cylinder

Stock: 2-piece unfigured French walnut; hand-checkered; full pistol grip; beavertail fore-end with wrap-around checkering; oil-type polyurethane finish

Buttplate: black plastic

Length of pull: 14.0 inches

Drop at comb: 1.5 inches

Drop at heel: 2.25 inches

Weight:

12-bore: 26.0-inch or 28.0-inch barrels, 7.0 lbs.; 30.0-inch barrels, 7.2 lbs.

20-bore: 25.0-inch barrels, 6.0 lbs.; 28.0-inch barrels, 6.25 lbs.

Sights: Raybar front on matted rib

Bore: 12, 2.75-inch case; 20, 3.0-inch case

ITHACA SKB M150 FIELD GRADE DOUBLE (continued)

Data: Same as for M100 except for beavertail fore-end.

Comment: Same as for M100, except this author prefers wrap-around checkering and the full beavertail fore-end.

ITHACA SKB M200E FIELD GRADE DOUBLE

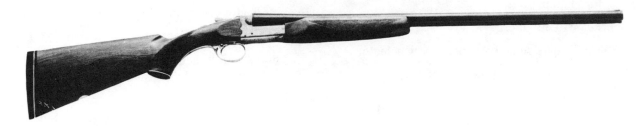

Manufacturer: SKB, Japan

Importer/distributor: Ithacagun

Action type: Anson & Deeley box lock; break-top; hammerless

Ignition system: inertial

Trigger: single selective; triggerbow selector

Locking system: underbolt

Ejection: automatic selective

Safety: nonautomatic; tang slide

Barrel length & choke:

12-bore: 30.0 or 28.0 inches, full & modified; 26.0 inches, modified & improved cylinder

20-bore: 28.0 inches, full & modified; 25.0 inches, modified & improved cylinder

Stock: 2-piece French walnut; hand-checkered; pistol grip with black plastic cap and white line spacer; oil-type polyurethane finish

Buttplate: black plastic with white line spacer

Length of pull: 14.0 inches

Drop at comb: 1.5 inches

Drop at heel: 2.625 inches

Weight:

12-bore: 26.0-inch barrels, 6.75 lbs.; 28.0-inch barrels, 7.0 lbs.; 30.0-inch barrels, 7.25 lbs.

20-bore: 25.0-inch barrels, 6.0 lbs.; 28.0-inch barrels, 6.25 lbs.

Sights: Raybar front

Bore: 12, 2.75-inch case; 20, 3.0-inch case

Data: Scroll engraving. Barrels have bright chrome interior and black chrome exterior.

Comment: This is a higher-grade version of the M100.

ITHACA SKB M200E SKEET DOUBLE

Manufacturer: SKB, Japan

Importer/distributor: Ithacagun

Action type: Anson & Deeley box lock; break-top; hammerless

Ignition system: inertial

Trigger: single selective

Locking system: underbolt

Ejection: automatic selective

Safety: nonautomatic; tang slide

Barrel length & choke: 26.0 inches, skeet & skeet

Stock: 2-piece French walnut; hand-checkered; beavertail fore-end with wrap-around hand checkering; pistol grip with black plastic cap and white line spacer; oil-type polyurethane finish

Buttplate: ventilated rubber recoil pad with white line spacer

Length of pull: 14.0 inches

Drop at comb: 1.5 inches

Drop at heel: 2.5 inches

Weight: 12-bore, 7.25 lbs.; 20-bore, 6.25 lbs.

Sights: Bradley-type front on matted rib and metal bead mid-rib

Bore: 12, 2.75-inch case; 20, 3.0-inch case

Data: Same as for M200E Field Grade except boring, recoil pad, and 0.25 inch less drop at heel.

Comment: Same basic comment as for M200E Field Grade. One of the best low-priced skeet guns on the market.

SAVAGE-FOX MODEL B DOUBLE

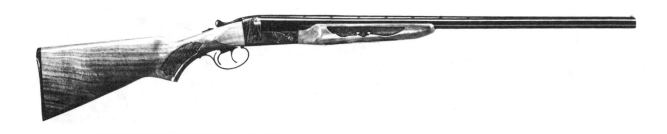

Action type: Anson & Deeley box lock; internal hammers

Ignition system: mechanical

Trigger: double

Locking system: underbolt

Ejection: manual

Safety: automatic; tang slide

Barrel length & choke:

12-bore: 30.0 or 28.0 inches, full & modified; 26.0 or 24.0 inches, modified & improved cylinder

20-bore: 28.0 inches, full & modified; 26.0 or 24.0 inches, modified & improved cylinder

.410 bore: 26.0 inches, full & full

Stock: 2-piece American walnut; impressed checkering; uncapped semi-pistol grip; beavertail fore-end; polyurethane finish

Buttplate: black plastic

Length of pull: 14.0 inches

Drop at comb: 1.5 inches

Drop at heel: 2.5 inches

Weight:

12-bore: 24.0-inch barrels, 6.75 lbs.; 26.0-inch barrels, 7.0 lbs.; 28.0-inch barrels, 7.5 lbs.; 30.0-inch barrels, 7.75 lbs.

20-bore: 24.0-inch barrels, 6.75 lbs.; 26.0-inch barrels, 7.0 lbs.; 28.0-inch barrels, 7.25 lbs.

.410 bore: 6.75 lbs.

Sights: metal bead front and mid-rib

Bore: 12, 20, .410, 3.0-inch case

Comment: This is a twin-trigger and hence less-expensive version of the Savage-Fox Model B-SE.

EXPLODED VIEW OF SAVAGE FOX–MODELS BST, B-C, B-D-B-E, AND B SERIES F SHOTGUN

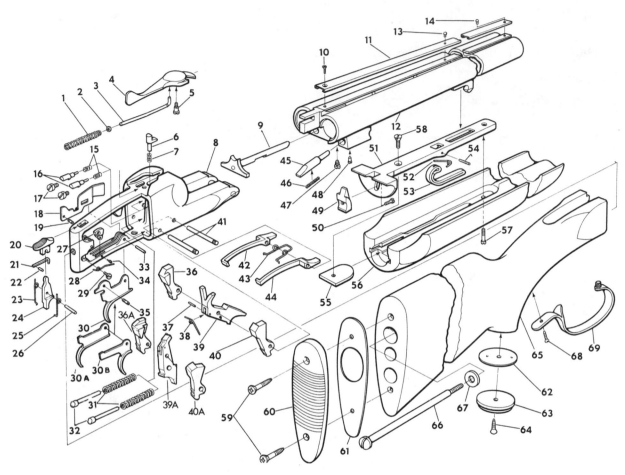

No.	Part Name
1	Top Snap Plunger Spring
2	Top Snap Plunger Collar
3	Top Snap Plunger
4	Top Snap
5	Top Snap Screw
6	Top Snap Trip
7	Top Snap Trip Spring
8	Frame
9	Extractor (Specify Gauge)
10	Top Rib Lock Screw
11	Top Rib
12	Barrel
13	Rear Sight
14	Front Sight
15	Firing Pin Spring
16	Firing Pin
17	Firing Pin Retaining Screw
20	Safety Button
21	Safety Spring
22	Safety Plunger
24	Safety Lever
	Trigger Spring (right)
	Trigger Spring (left)
26	Safety Lever Pin
30A	Trigger (right)
30B	Trigger (left)
31	Mainspring
32	Mainspring Plunger

No.	Part Name
33	Trigger Pin
36	Hammer (left)
37	Cocking Lever Spring Pin
38	Cocking Lever Spring
39	Cocking Lever
40	Hammer (right)
41	Sear, Socking Lever and Hammer Pin
42	Sear (left)
43	Sear Spring
44	Sear (right)
45	Cocking Plunger
46	Cocking Plunger Spring
47	Extractor Screw
48	Cocking Plunger Retaining Screw
49	Ejector
50	Ejector Screw
51	Forend Iron
	Forend Iron Assembly
52	Forend Spring Spring
53	Forend Spring
54	Forend Spring Pin
55	Forend Insert
56	Forend Wood (Specify Gauge)
	Forend Assembly (Specify Gauge)
57	Forend Screw

No.	Part Name
58	Forend Screw
59	Butt Plate Screw
60	Butt Plate
61	Butt Plate Liner
62	Pistol Grip Cap Liner
63	Pistol Grip Cap
64	Pistol Grip Cap Screw
65	Stock
66	Stock Bolt
67	Stock Bolt Washer
68	Trigger Guard Screw
69	Trigger Guard

PARTS FOR MODEL BST ONLY

No.	Part Name
18	Slide
19	Stud
23	Slide Spring
	Safety Lever
25	Trigger Spring
27	Inertia Block
28	Inertia Block Spring
29	Inertia Block Spring Screw
30	Trigger
34	Inertia Block Screw
35	Trigger Stud

SAVAGE-FOX MODEL B-SE DOUBLE

Action type: Anson & Deeley box lock; break-top; hammerless

Ignition system: mechanical

Trigger: single nonselective

Locking system: underbolt

Ejection: automatic selective

Safety: automatic; tang slide

Barrel length & choke:

  12-bore: 30.0 or 28.0 inches, full & modified; 26.0 inches, modified & improved cylinder

  20-bore: 28.0 inches, full & modified; 26.0 inches, modified & improved cylinder

  .410-bore: 26.0 inches, full & full

Stock: 2-piece American walnut; impressed checkering; uncapped semi-pistol grip; beavertail fore-end; polyurethane finish

Buttplate: black plastic

Length of pull: 14.0 inches

Drop at comb: 1.5 inches

Drop at heel: 2.5 inches

Weight:

  12-bore: 26.0-inch barrels, 7.25 lbs.; 28.0-inch barrels, 7.5 lbs.; 30.0-inch barrels, 7.75 lbs.

  20-bore: 26.0-inch barrels, 7.0 lbs.; 28.0-inch barrels, 7.25 lbs.

  .410-bore: 6.75 lbs.

Sights: metal bead front and mid-rib on ventilated rib

Bore: 12, 20, .410, 3.0-inch case

Data: Case-hardened frame.

Comment: This is the fanciest version of the least expensive double-barrel shotgun (Savage Stevens M311).

SAVAGE-STEVENS M311

Action type: Anson & Deeley box lock; internal hammers

Ignition system: mechanical

Trigger: double

Locking system: underbolt

Ejection: manual

SAVAGE-STEVENS M311 (continued)

Safety: automatic; tang slide

Barrel length & choke:

12-bore: 30.0 inches, full & full; 28.0 inches, full & modified; 26.0 inches, modified & improved cylinder

16-bore: 28.0 inches, full & modified

20-bore: 28.0 inches, full & modified; 26.0 inches, modified & improved cylinder

.410-bore: 26.0 inches, full & full

Stock: 2-piece walnut-stained hardwood; impressed checkering; uncapped semi-pistol grip; beavertail fore-end

Buttplate: black plastic with white line spacer

Length of pull: 14.0 inches

Drop at comb: 1.5 inches

Drop at heel: 2.5 inches

Weight:

12-bore: 26.0-inch barrels, 7.25 lbs.; 28.0-inch barrels, 7.5 lbs.; 30.0-inch barrels, 7.75 lbs.

16-bore: 7.5 lbs.

20-bore: 26.0-inch barrels, 7.0 lbs.; 28.0-inch barrels, 7.25 lbs.

.410 bore: 6.75 lbs.

Sights: metal bead front on solid rib

Bore: 12, 20, .410, 3.0-inch case; 16, 2.75-inch case

Data: Case-hardened receiver.

Comment: This is the least expensive double-barrel shotgun known to the author. He used a secondhand one nearly 40 years ago. A friend bought it and still uses the gun for upland birds and waterfowl.

This is not a fancy shotgun, but it is very sturdily made. There is little that can go wrong with its simple box-lock mechanism.

STAR GAUGE DOUBLE BARREL 12-BORE

Manufacturer: Armas Erbi, Spain

Importer/distributor: Interarms

Action type: Anson & Deeley box lock; break-top; hammerless

Ignition system: mechanical

Trigger: double

Locking system: underbolt

Ejection: manual

Safety: automatic; tang slide

Barrel length & choke: 28.0 inches, full & modified; 26.0 inches, modified & improved cylinder

Stock: 2-piece Spanish walnut; machine-checkered; beavertail fore-end; uncapped pistol grip; semi-gloss finish

Buttplate: ventilated rubber recoil pad

Length of pull: 13.5 inches

Drop at comb: 1.375 inches

Drop at heel: 2.56125 inches

Weight: 26.0-inch barrels, 7.125 lbs.; 28.0-inch barrels, 7.25 lbs.

Sights: brass bead front

Bore: 12, 2.75-inch case

Data: Case-hardened frame.

Comment: This is an excellent inexpensive shotgun for those who do not mind the absence of a ventilated rib, pistol-grip cap, and automatic selective ejectors. After all, these items are niceties and not essential. The automatic safety can readily be converted to nonautomatic by any competent gunsmith.

STAR GAUGE DOUBLE BARREL SMALLBORE

Manufacturer: Armas Erbi, Spain

Importer/distributor: Interarms

Action type: Anson & Deeley box lock; break-top; hammerless

Ignition system: mechanical

Trigger: double

Locking system: underbolt

Ejection: manual

Safety: automatic; tang slide

Barrel length & choke:

20-bore: 28.0 inches, full & modified; 26.0 inches, modified & improved cylinder

.410-bore: 26.0 inches, full & full or modified & improved cylinder

Stock: 2-piece Spanish walnut; machine-checkered; beavertail fore-end; uncapped pistol grip; semi-gloss finish

Buttplate: ventilated rubber recoil pad

Length of pull: 13.5 inches

Drop at comb: 1.5 inches

Drop at heel: 2.25 inches

Weight:

20-bore: 26.0-inch barrels, 6.25 lbs.; 28.0-inch barrels, 6.5 lbs.

.410-bore: 5.75 lbs.

Sights: brass bead front

Bore: 20, .410, 3.0-inch case

Data: Same as for Star Gauge 12-bore except for smaller receiver, bore, and chokes. Case-hardened receiver.

Comment: A well-made, inexpensive small-bore double-barrel shotgun for those who can forego a ventilated rib, automatic selective ejection, and superior checkering.

WEBLEY & SCOTT M720 DOUBLE BARREL

Manufacturer: Webley & Scott, England

Importer/distributor: Harrington & Richardson

Action type: Anson & Deeley box lock; break-top; hammerless

Ignition system: mechanical

Trigger: double

Locking system: underbolt

Ejection: automatic selective

Safety: nonautomatic; tang slide

Barrel length & choke: 26.0 inches, improved modified & improved cylinder

Stock: 2-piece French walnut; straight grip; hand checkering; English (splinter) fore-end; oil-type finish

Buttplate: hand-checkered

Length of pull: 13.75 inches

Drop at comb: 1.5 inches

WEBLEY & SCOTT M720 DOUBLE BARREL (continued)

Drop at heel: 2.25 inches

Weight: 6.0 lbs.

Sights: metal bead front

Bore: 20, 3.0-inch case

Data: Engine-turned flat rib. Good engraving.

Comment: A finely crafted, well-designed upland-game gun. It might sell better in America if the fore-end were semi-beavertail.

WEBLEY & SCOTT M728 DOUBLE BARREL

Manufacturer: Webley & Scott, England

Importer/distributor: Harrington & Richardson

Action type: Anson & Deeley box lock; break-top; hammerless

Ignition system: mechanical

Trigger: double

Locking system: underbolt

Ejection: automatic selective

Safety: automatic; tang slide

Barrel length & choke: 25.0 inches, improved modified & improved cylinder

Stock: 2-piece French walnut; straight grip; hand checkering; English (splinter) fore-end; oil-type finish

Buttplate: hand-checkered

Length of pull: 13.75 inches

Drop at comb: 1.5 inches

Drop at heel: 2.25 inches

Weight: 5.5 lbs.

Sights: metal bead front

Bore: 28, 2.75-inch case

Data: Same as for M720 save for weight, barrel length, and bore. Smooth concave rib.

Comment: Same as for M720.

WINCHESTER M21 CUSTOM DOUBLE BARREL

Action type: box lock; break-top; hammerless

Ignition system: mechanical

Trigger: single selective

Locking system: underbolt

Ejection: automatic selective (plain extractors or selective automatic extractors were optional until 1942)

Safety: standard originally fitted with automatic safety; Duck, Skeet, and Trap versions fitted with nonautomatic safety; today most custom M21s are fitted with nonautomatic safety; automatic safety is optional

Barrel length & choke: 26.0, 28.0, 30.0, or 32.0 inches (32.0 inches on 12-bore only); choked to order with any standard combination

Stock (standard): 2-piece select American walnut; hand checkering; straight or pistol grip optional at no extra cost; fore-end standard or beavertail

Buttplate: hard rubber, except hand-checkered butt on skeet gun and ventilated rubber recoil pad on trap gun

Weight: 6.25 lbs. to 8.0 lbs., depending on bore, barrel length, stock dimensions and style, wood density

Bores: 12-bore, 2.75- or 3.0-inch case; 16-bore, 2.75-inch case; 20-bore, 2.75- or 3.0-inch case; 28-bore, 2.75-inch case; .410-bore, 2.5- or 3.0-inch case

Comment: The M21, even in its least expensive grade and at its lowest price—about $75 in the early 1930s—is probably the finest double-barrel shotgun, in terms of mechanism, that has ever been produced in the United States. Its fancier grades during its line production days (particularly pre-World War II) made it one of the best quality guns ever produced in the United States. Following World War II, in an effort to reduce production costs without substantially elevating prices, the quality of checkering and wood fitting to metal deteriorated slightly.

The few guns made up annually are undoubtedly made from stock on hand when the production arm was discontinued in 1959. About a year later the M21 was offered—as it still is—in custom grades only.

CHAPTER 22

SLIDE-ACTION SHOTGUNS

The slide, pump, or trombone action is almost exclusively an American product.

There are two basic slide-action types: the exposed-hammer type, as represented by the Winchester M93 and M97, and the internal-hammer type, which is the only kind made today. John Moses Browning designed both the first successful exposed-hammer and the first successful concealed-hammer slide-action shotgun.

Before the Winchester M93, introduced in April 1894, there had been several attempts at slide-action shotgun designs. None were commercially successful. The M93 was designed by Browning in 1890. Patent #441,390 was granted November 25, 1890. Browning assigned patent rights to Winchester.

Browning and his brother Matthew were master trap shots. During the 1890s they were members of the famed "Four B's" trap team. The other members were Augustus "Gus" Becker and A. F. Bigelow. Browning's favorite trap gun—a M93—hangs in the John Moses Browning Museum in the National Guard Armory, Ogden, Utah.

All M93s had a solid frame and were chambered for the 2.625-inch-long 12-bore shot cartridge. Current standard 12-bore shot cartridges are 2.75 inches long. Model M93s, designed for black powder, are not safe with smokeless loads. Consider your M93 a collector's item. Hang it on the wall.

The advent of smokeless propellants lead to a redesign of the M93. Winchester records show that about 34,000 M93s were manufactured. The improved M93 was introduced in 1897. This famed M97 was made until 1958. About 1,240,000 M93s and M97s were made. M97 serial numbers include M93 serial numbers.

The M97 was available in solid frame only until October 1898, when a takedown version was introduced. All M97 12-bores were chambered for the 2.75-inch case. The M97 was introduced in 16-bore in February 1900. It was available only in the takedown version.

M97 variations include: (1) Field Gun (1897–1958); (2) Trap Gun (1897–1931); (3) Special Trap Gun; (4) Pigeon Grade Trap Gun (1897–1939); (5) Brush Gun (1897–1931); (6) Solid Frame Riot Gun (1898–1935); (7) Takedown Riot Gun (1912–35); (8) Trench Gun, commercial version (1920–35); (9) Tournament Grade Trap Gun (1910–31); and (10) Standard Trap Gun (1931–39).

Today's slide-action shotgun, save for the internal hammer, differs but little from the M97. Metallurgy has improved, stocks are straighter, the ventilated rib has been introduced, but the basic arm is the same.

The author knows of no poorly made slide-action shotgun. Most of them are about the same. Some manufacturers offer fancy wood and better-than-average checkering, but the $1000 shotgun is no better mechanically than the slide-action shotgun costing less than $200. The chances are that any new slide-action purchased today will last half a century or more. The author knows several M97s that have seen hard annual use for 50 to 75 years.

No exposed-hammer shotguns are made today. The exposed-hammer M97 Winchester survived by 50 years the advent of the internal-hammer slide-action. The M97 was less expensive and it had a great reputation for durability and reliability. Many shotgunners still prefer the exposed hammer because they can tell at a glance whether or not the arm is cocked.

The first successful internal-hammer shotgun, as already noted, was also designed by John Moses Browning. He filed for it on July 10, 1903. Patent #781,765 was granted on February 7, 1905. Originally known as the Hammerless Pump Action Shotgun Model 1903, it was first marketed in early 1904 as the Stevens M520. Savage Arms continued production of the M520 after the firm took over J. T. Stevens. The shotgun—the patent has long since expired—was the granddaddy of the current-production Savage M30.

John D. Pederson created Remington's first internal-hammer slide-action. The M10 (1907–29) was a typical slide-action, with bottom ejection. It was an excellent gun—well designed and well made.

Remington's next internal-hammer shotgun, designed by John Moses Browning, was the M17. Browning filed for the patent on his final slide-action shotgun on November 26, 1913. U.S. patent #1,143,170 was granted on June 15, 1915. Wartime operations and reconversion problems held up production until 1921. After the patent expired, this lightweight gun—it weighed about 5.5 lbs.—was taken over by Ithaca. This is Ithaca's current-production Featherlight. It has been in production longer than any other current-production internal-hammer slide-action. It, too, has bottom ejection, a feature preferred by some lefthanded shooters who don't like to have ejected shells fly across their line of vision as the cases do when they come out of a port on the right side of the receiver.

HIGH STANDARD FLITE-KING SERIES SLIDE ACTION

Action type: slide; internal hammer

Magazine type: tubular

Magazine capacity: 5-shot (2-shot plus 1 in chamber when fitted with wildfowl plug)

Safety: crossbolt

Barrel length & choke:

12-bore: 30.0 inches, full; 28.0 inches, full or modified; 26.0 inches, improved cylinder; 27.0 inches with adjustable choke device

20-bore: 28.0 inches, full or modified; 26.0 inches, improved cylinder; 27.0 inches with adjustable choke device

.410-bore: 26.0 inches, full

Stock: 2-piece American walnut; impressed checkering; pistol grip with black plastic cap; finger-grooved fore-end

Buttplate: ventilated rubber recoil pad with white line spacer

Overall length: 30.0-inch barrel, 49.75 inches; 28.0-inch barrel, 47.75 inches; 26.0-inch barrel, 45.75 inches

Length of pull: 14.0 inches

Drop at comb: 1.5 inches

Drop at heel: 2.5 inches

Weight:

12-bore: 30.0-inch barrel, 7.5 lbs.; 28.0-inch barrel, 7.25 lbs.; 26.0-inch barrel, 7.0 lbs.

20-bore: 28.0-inch barrel, 6.25 lbs.; 26.0-inch barrel, 6.0 lbs.

.410 bore: 6.0 lbs.

Sights: brass bead front

Bore: 12, 20, 2.75-inch case; .410, 3.0-inch case

Data: These are fixed-barrel guns except for the 12-bore, which has a takedown barrel that can be interchanged with other High Standard 12-bore barrels to switch barrel length and choke.

Comment: At press time High Standard had suspended production temporarily in order to concentrate on meeting demand for military and police shotguns. However, plans were to resume production, offering both plain barrels and ventilated ribs, and both field guns and trap and skeet versions.

ITHACA FEATHERLIGHT M37 SLIDE ACTION

Action type: slide; internal hammer

Magazine type: tubular

Magazine capacity: 5-shot (2-shot plus 1 in chamber when fitted with wildfowl plug)

Safety: crossbolt

Barrel length & choke:

12-bore: 30.0 inches, full; 28.0 inches, modified; 26.0 inches, improved cylinder

16-bore: 28.0 inches, full or modified; 26.0 inches, improved cylinder or full

20-bore: 28.0 inches, full or modified; 26.0 inches, improved cylinder

Stock: 2-piece American walnut; pistol grip with plastic cap and white line spacer; amount and type of checkering varies with grade; Supreme Grade has checkering; Monte Carlo available at extra cost

Buttplate: recoil pad on Supreme Grade at no extra cost; standard buttplate is black plastic with white line spacer

Overall length: 30.0-inch barrel, 50.0 inches; 28.0-inch barrel, 48.0 inches; 26.0-inch barrel, 46.0 inches

Length of pull: 14.0 inches

Drop at comb: 1.625 inches

Drop at heel: 2.625 inches

Weight (plain barrel):

12-bore: 26.0-inch barrel, 6.25 lbs.; 28.0-inch barrel, 6.5 lbs.; 30.0-inch barrel, 6.75 lbs.

16-bore: 26.0-inch barrel, 5.75 lbs.; 28.0-inch barrel, modified 6.0 lbs., full 6.25 lbs.

20-bore: 26.0-inch barrel, 5.25 lbs.; 28.0-inch barrel, modified 5.75 lbs., full 6.0 lbs.

Sights: Ithaca translucent Raybar; all versions except Standard Grade and Deerslayer fitted with ventilated rib

Bore: 12, 16, 20, 2.75-inch case

Data: This shotgun is unusual in that it uses the same bottom of the receiver port for both loading and ejection. It is the lightest slide-action shotgun on the market.

Comment: This well-made shotgun handles fast and points beautifully. It is particularly light in the 26.0-inch-barrel 20-bore version.

ITHACA M37 FEATHERLIGHT DEERSLAYER SLIDE ACTION

Action type: slide; internal hammer

Magazine type: tubular

Magazine capacity: 5-shot (2-shot plus 1 in chamber when fitted with wildfowl plug)

Safety: crossbolt

Barrel length & choke: 26.0 or 20.0 inches, special slug choke

Stock: 2-piece American walnut; machine-checkered; pistol grip with black plastic cap and white line spacer; Super DeLuxe Deerslayer has better wood and checkering

Buttplate: rubber recoil pad with white line spacer

Overall length: 26.0-inch barrel, 45.0 inches; 20.0-inch barrel, 39.0 inches

Length of pull: 14.0 inches

Drop at comb: 1.625 inches

Drop at heel: 2.625 inches

Weight:

12-bore: 20.0-inch barrel, 6.0 lbs.; 26.0-inch barrel, 6.5 lbs.

16-bore: 20.0-inch barrel, 5.75 lbs.; 26.0-inch barrel, 6.25 lbs.

20-bore: 20.0-inch barrel, 5.5 lbs.; 26.0-inch barrel, 6.0 lbs.

Sights: bead front; Rocky Mountain rear; receiver grooved for tip-off mount

Bore: 12, 16, 20, 2.75-inch case

Data: Same basic data as for standard M37.

Comment: A good slug gun for those who must by law or by preference use rifled slugs on deer.

MARLIN M120 MAGNUM SLIDE ACTION

Action type: slide; internal hammer

Magazine type: tubular

Magazine capacity: 3.0-inch case, 4-shot (2-shot plus 1 in chamber when fitted with wildfowl plug); 2.75-inch case, 5-shot

Safety: crossbolt

Barrel length & choke: 30.0 inches, full; 28.0 inches, modified; 26.0 inches, improved cylinder

Stock: 2-piece; impressed checkering; pistol grip with plastic cap; high-gloss finish

Buttplate: recoil pad

Overall length: 30.0-inch barrel, 49.9375 inches; 28.0-inch barrel, 47.9375 inches; 26.0-inch barrel, 45.9375 inches

Length of pull: 14.0 inches

Drop at comb: 1.625 inches

Drop at heel: 2.5625 inches

Weight: 26.0-inch barrel, 8.0 lbs.; 28.0-inch barrel, 8.25 lbs.; 30.0-inch barrel, 8.5 lbs.

Sights: metal bead front and mid-rib

Bore: 12, 3.0-inch case

Data: The receiver is machined from a steel block. Barrel and all other parts, except brass bead sights, are steel. Barrels are readily interchangeable without tools. The breechblock system is strong and reliable.

Comment: This is one of a very few 12-bore Magnums available with 26-inch improved-cylinder barrels. This means the same gun can be used to shoot skeet or waterfowl over decoys. For long-range ducks and geese the 30-inch barrel is best. Skeet shooters or decoy gunners can purchase the extra 26-inch barrel.

The author fired 10 boxes of 3.0-inch Magnum shotshells. There were no malfunctions with the 250 rounds of Magnum loads, nor with 250 rounds—fired at one visit to the range—of skeet loads.

The ventilated rib has a dull finish to reduce glare. The stock is well designed and looks good except for the impressed checkering. The extra-large safety button can readily be located with gloved fingers. Simple instructions make it easy to reverse the safety for southpaws.

MARLIN M120 SLUG GUN

Action type: slide; internal hammer

Magazine type: tubular

Magazine capacity: 5-shot (2-shot plus 1 in chamber with wildfowl plug installed — slug guns not normally used on wildfowl)

Safety: crossbolt

Barrel length & choke: 26.0 inches, special slug choke

Stock: 2-piece American walnut; impressed checkering; pistol grip with black plastic cap and white line spacer

Buttplate: ventilated recoil pad with white line spacer

Overall length: 45.9375 inches

Length of pull: 14.0 inches

Drop at comb: 1.625 inches

Drop at heel: 2.5625 inches

Weight: 8.0 lbs.

Sights: rifle bead front with detachable ramp; Rocky Mountain rear

Bore: 12, 2.75-inch case

Data: Same as for Standard M120 except for sights and choke.

Comment: A good deer-slug gun but barrel might be shorter.

MARLIN M120 TRAP GUN

Action type: slide; internal hammer

Magazine type: tubular

Magazine capacity: 5-shot (2-shot plus 1 in chamber when fitted with wildfowl plug)

Safety: crossbolt

Barrel length & choke: 30.0 inches, full

Stock: 2-piece American walnut; hand-checkered; pistol grip with black plastic cap and white line spacer; Monte Carlo comb; high-gloss finish

Buttplate: black ventilated recoil pad with white line spacer

Overall length: 50.5 inches

Length of pull: 14.25 inches

Drop at comb: 1.25 inches

Drop at Monte Carlo: 1.25 inches

Drop at heel: 1.75 inches

Weight: 7.75 lbs.

Sights: metal bead front and middle

Bore: 12, 2.75-inch Magnum case

Data: Same as for Standard M120.

Comment: A well-constructed, reliable trap gun.

MARLIN MXR 120 MAGNUM GOOSE GUN

Action type: slide; internal hammer

Magazine type: tubular

Magazine capacity: 4-shot (2-shot plus 1 in chamber when fitted with wildfowl plug)

Safety: crossbolt

Barrel length & choke: 40.0 inches, full

Stock: 2-piece American walnut; impressed checkering; pistol grip with black plastic cap and white line spacer

Buttplate: ventilated recoil pad with white line spacer

Overall length: 59.9375 inches

Length of pull: 14.0 inches

Drop at comb: 1.625 inches

Drop at heel: 2.5625 inches

Weight: 9.0 lbs.

Sights: metal bead front

Bore: 12, 3.0-inch case

Data: This is identical to the M120 Magnum except for the 40.0-inch barrel.

Comment: This 5-foot-long scattergun is the heaviest 12-bore Magnum on the market. This weight is its sole advantage over any other 12-bore Magnum. The additional weight, however, doesn't compensate for the clumsiness, nor does the alleged superiority of the extra-long sighting plain.

More than 95 percent of geese — and this is a goose gun — are taken with barrels of no more than 30 inches. The remainder are taken with barrels of miscellaneous lengths, and more are probably below 30 inches than over.

MOSSBERG M500 SERIES SLIDE ACTION

Action type: slide; internal hammer

Magazine type: tubular

Magazine capacity: 4-shot (2-shot plus 1 in chamber when fitted with wildfowl plug)

Safety: top tang

Barrel length & choke:

12-bore: 30.0 inches, full; 28.0 inches, modified; 26.0 inches, improved cylinder

20-bore: 28.0 inches, modified; 26.0 inches, improved cylinder

.410-bore: 26.0 inches, full or improved cylinder

Stock: 2-piece American walnut; impressed checkering; pistol grip with black plastic cap and white line spacer

Buttplate: ventilated recoil pad with white line spacer

Overall length: 30.0-inch barrel, 49.5 inches; 28.0-inch barrel, 47.5 inches; 26.0-inch barrel, 45.5 inches

Length of pull: 14.0 inches

Drop at comb: 1.5 inches

Drop at heel: 1.375 inches

Weight:

12-bore: 30.0-inch barrel, 7.25 lbs.; 28.0-inch barrel, 7.0 lbs.; 26.0-inch barrel, 6.75 lbs.

20-bore: 28.0-inch barrel, 6.5 lbs.; 26.0-inch barrel, 6.25 lbs.

.410-bore: 6.0 lbs.; add about 4 oz. for ventilated rib

Sights: front metal bead

Bore: 12, 20, 2.75-inch or 3.0-inch case; .410, 3.0 inch case

Data: Aluminum-alloy receiver with twin action guides. Bolt and carrier are chromed machine steel. Double extractors. Barrel is machined from bar stock.

Comment: This is a reliable shotgun in a price range somewhat lower than the Remington and Winchester standards. Like the Savage, it is a good buy for economy-minded shooters. The M500 can be bought with or without a ventilated rib and with or without C-LECT-CHOKE (Mossberg's variable-choke device).

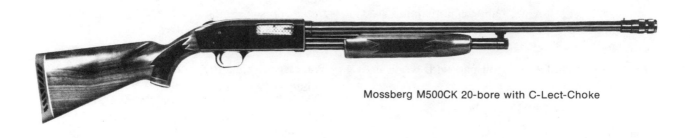

Mossberg M500CK 20-bore with C-Lect-Choke

MOSSBERG M500 SERIES SLIDE ACTION (continued)

Series 500 letter codes
  A: 12-bore
  C: 20-bore
  E: .410-bore

K: when added to any one or combination of above symbols indicates C-LECT-CHOKE variable choke.
M: Magnum
R: when added to above symbols indicates a ventilated rib.

MOSSBERG M500 SERIES SLUGSTER SLIDE ACTION

Action type: slide; internal hammer

Magazine type: tubular

Magazine capacity: 4-shot (plus 1 in chamber)

Safety: top tang

Barrel length & choke: 24.0 inches, special slug choke

Stock: 2-piece American walnut, impressed checkering; pistol grip with plastic cap and white line spacer

Buttplate: ventilated recoil pad

Overall length: 43.75 inches

Length of pull: 14.0 inches

Drop at comb: 1.5 inches

Drop at heel: 2.5 inches

Weight: 12-bore, 6.5 lbs.; 20-bore, 6.0 lbs.

Sights: metal bead front; Rocky Mountain rear, crudely adjustable for elevation

Bore: 12, 20, 3.0-inch case

Data: Same as for standard M500 except for barrel length.

Comment: A well-designed and well-constructed deer-slug gun.

REMINGTON M870 WINGMASTER SLIDE ACTION

Action type: slide; internal hammer

Magazine type: tubular

Magazine capacity: 4-shot (2-shot plus 1 in chamber when fitted with wildfowl plug)

Safety: crossbolt

Barrel length & choke:

12-bore: 30.0 inches, full; 28.0 inches, full or modified; 26.0 inches, improved cylinder

16-bore: 28.0 inches, full or modified; 26.0 inches, improved cylinder

20-bore: 28.0 inches, full or modified; 26.0 inches, improved cylinder

Stock: 2-piece American walnut; machine-checkered; pistol grip with plastic cap; fancy hand-checkered wood available on special orders

Buttplate: black plastic

Overall length: 26.0-inch barrel, 45.5 inches; 28.0-inch barrel, 47.5 inches; 30.0-inch barrel, 49.5 inches

Length of pull: 14.0 inches

Drop at comb: 1.625 inches

Drop at heel: 2.5 inches

Weight (plain barrel): 12-bore, 28.0-inch barrel, 7.0 lbs.; 16-bore, 28.0-inch barrel, 6.75 lbs.; 20-bore, 28.0-inch barrel, 6.5 lbs.; add 4.0 oz. for ventilated rib; add or subtract 4.0 oz. for longer or shorter barrel

Sights: ivory bead front

Bore: 12, 16, 20, all 2.75-inch case

Data: This all-steel shotgun is available in several versions, all described herein—Skeet, Trap, Lightweight 20, Magnum, Deer Slug, standard-weight Wingmaster and Small Bore 28 and .410. Expensive fancy-wood hand-checkered versions are available on special order. All barrels are available with plain or ventilated rib.

Comment: Along with the venerable Winchester M12, this is one of the best on the market. It is available in more bores and barrel/choke variations than any other slide-action. It is also available in a left-handed version, with the crossbolt safety reversed and ejection on the left side.

REMINGTON M870 LIGHTWEIGHT

Action type: slide; concealed hammer

Magazine type: tubular

Magazine capacity: 4-shot (2-shot plus 1 in chamber when fitted with wildfowl plug)

Safety: crossbolt

Barrel length & choke: 26.0 inches, improved cylinder; 28.0 inches, modified or full

Stock: 2-piece American walnut; machine-checkered (formerly impressed); pistol grip with plastic cap and white line spacer

Buttplate: black ventilated recoil pad

Overall length: 26.0-inch barrel, 45.5 inches; 28.0-inch barrel, 47.5 inches

Length of pull: 14.0 inches (including recoil pad)

Drop at comb: 1.625 inches

Drop at heel: 2.5 inches

Weight: 26.0-inch barrel, 5.5 lbs.; 28.0-inch barrel, 5.75 lbs.; add 2.0–4.0 oz. for ventilated rib; 28.0-inch barrel in 3.0-inch Magnum, 6.0 lbs.

Sights: bead

Bore: 20, 2.75- or 3.0-inch case

Data: Same as for standard weight versions. Steel receiver. Barrels interchange within same bore and case length. Available with plain barrel or ventilated rib.

Comment: One of the lightest, handiest and best-made slide-actions.

EXPLODED VIEW OF REMINGTON M870 WINGMASTER SLIDE-ACTION SHOTGUN

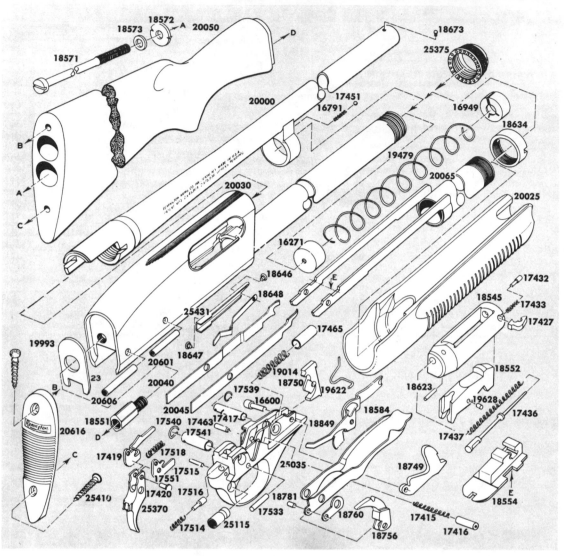

No.	Part Name	No.	Part Name	No.	Part Name
16271	Magazine Follower, 12 Ga.	**18551**	Receiver Stud		Magazine Cap Detent, Magazine Cap Detent Spring)
16600	Hammer Pin	**18554**	Slide		
16791	Magazine Cap Detent Spring	**18571**	Stock Bolt	**20025**	Fore-end, AP GRADE, (wood only), 12 Ga.
16949	Magazine Spring Retainer	**18572**	Stock Bolt Lock Washer		
17415	Carrier Dog Follower Spring	**18573**	Stock Bolt Washer	**20030**	Receiver Assembly, 12 Ga. (includes Receiver, Ejector, Ejector Rivet, Front; Ejector Rivet, Rear; Ejector Spring, Magazine Tube, Barrel Support, Shell Latch, Left; Shell Latch, Right)
17416	Carrier Dog Follower	**18584**	Carrier, 12–16 Ga.		
17417	Carrier Pivot Tube	**18623**	Firing Pin Retaining Pin		
17419	Connector, Left	**18634**	Fore-end Tube Nut		
17420	Connector Pin	**18646**	Ejector Rivet, Front		
17427	Extractor	**18647**	Ejector Rivet, Rear		
17432	Extractor Plunger	**18648**	Ejector Spring		
17436	Firing Pin	**18673**	Front Sight (Plain Barrel)	**20040**	Shell Latch, Left, 12 Ga.
17437	Firing Pin Retractor Spring	**18749**	Hammer	**20045**	Shell Latch, Right, 12 Ga.
17451	Magazine Cap Detent	**18750**	Sear	**20050**	Stock Assembly, AP GRADE (includes Stock, Butt Plate, Butt Plate Screws (2))
17463	Sear Pin	**18756**	Carrier Dog		
17465	Hammer Plunger	**18760**	Carrier Dog Washer		
17514	Safety Spring	**18781**	Carrier Dog Pin	**20065**	Fore-end Tube Assembly (includes Action Bar, Left; Action Bar, Right; Fore-end Tube)
17515	Safety Spring Retaining Pin	**18849**	Action Bar Lock		
17516	Safety Plunger	**19014**	Hammer Spring		
17518	Sear Spring	**19479**	Magazine Spring		
17533	Trigger Pin	**19622**	Action Bar Lock Spring	**20601**	Trigger Plate Pin, Front
17539	Trigger Plate Pin Detent Spring, Front	**19628**	Locking Block Stud	**20606**	Trigger Plate Pin, Rear
		19993	Stock Bearing Plate	**20616**	Butt Plate
17540	Trigger Plate Pin Detent Spring, Rear	**20000**	Barrel Assembly, PLAIN, 12 Ga. (26″, 28″, 30″) (includes Barrel, Barrel Guide Ring, Barrel Guide Pin, Steel Front Sight,	**25035**	Trigger Plate, R.H.
				25115	Safety
17541	Trigger Plate Pin Bushing			**25370**	Trigger
17551	Connector, Right			**25375**	Magazine Cap
18545	Breech Bolt, 12 Ga.			**25410**	Butt Plate Screw

REMINGTON M870 SMALLBORE SLIDE ACTION

Action type: slide; concealed hammer

Magazine type: tubular

Magazine capacity: 28-bore, 4-shot (2-shot plus 1 in chamber when fitted with wildfowl plug); .410-bore 3.0-inch case, 3-shot (2-shot plus 1 in chamber when fitted with wildfowl plug)

Safety: crossbolt

Barrel length & choke: 25.0 inches, improved cylinder, modified, or full

Stock: 2-piece American walnut; machine-checkered (formerly impressed); pistol grip with plastic cap and white line spacer

Buttplate: black plastic

Overall length: 44.5 inches

Length of pull: 13.875 inches

Drop at comb: 1.5 inches

Drop at heel: 2.5 inches

Weight: 28-bore, plain barrel 5.5 lbs.; ventilated rib 6.0 lbs.; .410-bore, plain barrel 6.0 lbs., ventilated rib 6.25 lbs.

Sights: front metal bead

Bore: 28, 2.5-inch case; .410, handles 2.5-inch or 3.0-inch case

Data: Same as for M870 save for weight and barrel length and choke combinations. Either plain barrel or ventilated rib available.

Comment: One of the few better slide-actions chambered for the 28 and .410.

REMINGTON M870 BRUSHMASTER (DEER GUN) SLIDE ACTION

Action type: slide; concealed hammer

Magazine type: tubular

Magazine capacity: 4-shot (2-shot plus 1 in chamber when fitted with wildfowl plug)

Safety: crossbolt

Barrel length & choke: 20.0 inches, improved cylinder

Stock: 2-piece American walnut; machine-checkering (formerly impressed); pistol grip with plastic cap

Buttplate: plastic

Overall length: 39.5 inches

Length of pull: 14.0 inches

Drop at comb: 1.625 inches

Drop at heel: 2.5 inches

Weight: 12-bore, 6.75 lbs.; 20-bore, 6.5 lbs.

Sights: bead front; Rocky Mountain rear, crudely adjustable for elevation

Bore: 12, 20, 2.75-inch case

Data: Same as for basic M870.

Comment: A well-made slug gun for deer.

REMINGTON M870 MAGNUM SLIDE ACTION

Action type: slide; concealed hammer

Magazine type: tubular

Magazine capacity: 4-shot (2-shot plus 1 in chamber when fitted with wildfowl plug)

Safety: crossbolt

Barrel length & choke: 12-bore, 30.0 inches, full or modified; 20-bore, 28.0 inches, full or modified

Stock: 2-piece; machine-checkered (formerly impressed); pistol grip with plastic cap and white line spacer

Buttplate: ventilated recoil pad

Overall length: 28.0-inch barrel, 47.5 inches; 30.0-inch barrel, 49.5 inches

Length of pull: 14.0 inches

Drop at comb: 1.625 inches

Drop at heel: 2.5 inches

Weight: 12-bore, 30.0-inch plain barrel, 7.25 lbs.; 20-bore, 28.0-inch plain barrel, 6.75 lbs.; add 4.0 oz. for ventilated rib

Sights: metal bead front

Bore: 12, 20, 3.0-inch case

Data: Same as for basic M870 except weights and barrel specifications.

Comment: One of the better Magnum slide-action shotguns.

REMINGTON M870 SKEET SLIDE ACTION

Action type: slide; internal hammer

Magazine type: tubular

Magazine capacity: 4-shot (plus 1 in chamber)

Safety: crossbolt

Barrel length & choke: 12-bore, 26.0 inches, skeet or Cutts Compensator; 20-bore, 26.0 inches, skeet; 28-bore, 25.0 inches, skeet; .410-bore, 25.0 inches, skeet choke

Stock: 2-piece American walnut; machine-checkered; full pistol grip capped with plastic; fancy wood and hand checkering on more expensive grades

Buttplate: ventilated recoil pad on 12-bore

Overall length: 26.0-inch barrel, 45.0 inches; 25.0-inch barrel, 44.5 inches

Length of pull: 14.0 inches

Drop at comb: 1.625 inches

Drop at heel: 2.5 inches

Weight: 12-bore, 7.0 lbs.; 20-bore, 6.75 lbs.; 28-bore, 6.5 lbs.; .410-bore, 6.0 lbs.; skeet cap for smaller bores adds up to 12.0 oz. for those who wish all skeet bores to weigh same

Sights: ivory bead front; metal mid-rib bead

Bore: 12, 20, 2.75-inch case; 28, .410, 2.5-inch case

Data: Same basic data as for standard-weight M870. Tournament and Premier Grades—special order only—have hand-polished action, fancier wood.

Comment: An excellent skeet gun for those who like slide-actions.

REMINGTON M870 TRAP MODEL

Action type: slide; concealed hammer

Magazine type: tubular

Magazine capacity: 4-shot (plus 1 in chamber)

Safety: crossbolt

Barrel length & choke: 30.0 inches, full or modified trap

Stock: 2-piece American walnut; machine checkering; pistol grip with plastic cap; Monte Carlo available

Buttplate: red ventilated recoil pad

Overall length: 47.375 inches

Length of pull: 14.375 inches

Drop at comb: 1.5 inches

Drop at Monte Carlo (if applicable): 1.5 inches

Drop at heel: standard, 1.75 inches; Monte Carlo, 2.0 inches

Weight: 8.25 lbs.

Sights: ivory bead front; metal mid-rib bead

Bore: 12, 2.75-inch case

Data: Same basic data as for standard M870. Trap barrels are interchangeable with Standard barrels in same chambering and bore. Tournament and Premier Grades have special woods, hand checkering, and hand-polished action parts. The All-American Trap, the least expensive grade, has a plain barrel and is available only in a standard righthand version.

Comment: One of the most popular—and justly so—slide-action trap guns.

SAVAGE M30D/M30 FIELD GRADE SLIDE ACTION

Action type: slide; concealed hammer

Magazine type: tubular

Magazine capacity: 4-shot (2-shot plus 1 in chamber when fitted with wildfowl plug)

Safety: top tang

Barrel length & choke:

12-bore: 26.0 inches, improved cylinder; 28.0 inches, modified or full; 30.0 inches, full

20-bore: 26.0 inches, improved cylinder; 28.0 inches, modified or full

.410-bore: 26.0 inches, full

Stock: 2-piece American walnut; impressed checkering; semi-pistol grip

Buttplate: red ventilated recoil pad on 30D; black hard rubber on 30FG

SAVAGE M30D/M30 FIELD GRADE SLIDE ACTION
(continued)

Overall length: 26.0-inch barrel, 45.5 inches; 28.0-inch barrel, 47.5 inches; 30.0-inch barrel, 49.5 inches

Length of pull: 14.0 inches

Drop at comb: 1.5 inches

Drop at heel: 2.5 inches

Weight (add 2.0–4.0 oz. to M30D for ventilated rib):

12-bore: 26.0-inch barrel, 7.0 lbs.; 28.0-inch barrel, 7.25 lbs.; 30.0-inch barrel, 7.25 lbs.

20-bore: 26.0-inch barrel, 6.75 lbs.; 28.0-inch barrel, 7.0 lbs.

.410-bore: 26.0-inch barrel, 6.75 lbs.

Sights: front and mid-plane bead on M30D; front bead on M30

Bore: 12, 20, .410, 3.0-inch case

Data: Machined steel receiver and polished steel bolt. Barrel lengths and chokes are interchangeable with same bore.

Comment: This is a very rugged inexpensive shotgun. For the shooter who has to be careful with his dollars it's an excellent buy. M30D is the "Deluxe" version. It has a ventilated rib, ventilated recoil pad, and machine-"engraved" decoration on the receiver. M30 is the field grade —plain barrel, plain receiver, hard rubber buttplate. Savage also offers the M30D Combination—same as M30D but with an interchangeable 22.0-inch slug barrel for deer hunting.

SAVAGE M30 SLUG SLIDE ACTION

Action type: slide; concealed hammer

Magazine type: tubular

Magazine capacity: 4-shot (2-shot plus 1 in chamber when fitted with wildfowl plug); 1 shot less when 3.0-inch 12 or 20 Magnum or 3.0-inch .410 cases are used

Safety: top tang

Barrel length & choke: 22.0 inches, special slug

Stock: 2-piece American walnut; impressed checkering; semi-pistol grip

Buttplate: black hard rubber

Overall length: 41.5 inches

Length of pull: 14.0 inches

Drop at comb: 1.5 inches

Drop at heel: 2.5 inches

Weight: 7.5 lbs.

Sights: bead front; Rocky Mountain rear

Bore: 12, 3.0-inch case

Data: Except for barrel and sights, same as for M30 Field Grade.

Comment: A well-constructed slug gun for the economy-minded deer hunter. Because this shotgun costs less than most of its contemporaries doesn't mean it is poorly built. It is mass-produced and has few frills.

WEATHERBY PATRICIAN SLIDE ACTION

Manufacturer: Howa Machinery Corp., Japan

Importer/distributor: Weatherby, Inc.

Action type: slide; internal hammer; short stroke

Magazine type: tubular

Magazine capacity: 4-shot (2 plus 1 in chamber when fitted with wildfowl plug)

Safety: crossbolt

Barrel length & choke: 30.0 inches, full; 28.0 inches, full or modified; 26.0 inches, improved cylinder, skeet, or modified

Stock: 2-piece dark American walnut; machine-cut checkering (20 lines per inch); fluted fore-end; full pistol grip with white line spacer, rosewood cap, and white plastic diamond inlay; very high gloss finish

Buttplate: red rubber ventilated recoil pad with white line spacer

Overall length: 30.0-inch barrel, 50.125 inches; 28.0-inch barrel, 48.125 inches; 26.0-inch barrel, 46.125 inches

Length of pull: 14.375 inches

Drop at comb: 1.5625 inches

Drop at heel: 2.375 inches

Weight: 30.0-inch barrel, 7.75 lbs.; 28.0-inch barrel, 7.5 lbs.; 26.0-inch barrel, 7.25 lbs.

Sights: metal bead front

Bore: 12, 2.75-inch case

Data: Aluminum-alloy receiver and triggerbow with hard anodized black finish. Barrel has typical Weatherby high-gloss blue. Breechblock moves rearward by action transmitted through dual action bars. Rearward-moving breechbolt carrier cams carrier locking block down and out of engagement with the barrel extension locking shoulder. Designed by Fred Jennie.

Comment: Many gunners dislike the usual exposed forward portion of the tubular magazine in front of the slide. Weatherby eliminated this eyesore with a longer slide. Front end of fore-end is counterbored to conceal the sides of the magazine cap. This is, in the author's view, one of the most handsome slide-action scatterguns. The action is very strong, the wood is beautiful, the metal parts are finely finished. It is to be regretted that this fine shotgun—and it is not as expensive as many others—is not available in 20-bore. It has excellent handling qualities on skeet and trap layouts, in the duck blind, and in the uplands.

WINCHESTER M12 TRAP SLIDE ACTION

Action type: slide; internal hammer

Magazine type: tubular

Magazine capacity: 5-shot (2-shot plus 1 in chamber when fitted with wildfowl plug)

Safety: crossbolt

Barrel length & choke: 30.0 inches, full

Stock: 2-piece select American walnut; full pistol grip with black plastic cap

Buttplate: ventilated recoil pad

Overall length: 49.75 inches

Length of pull: 14.375 inches

Drop at comb: 1.375 inches

Drop at Monte Carlo (if applicable): 1.5 inches

Drop at heel: standard, 1.875 inches; Monte Carlo, 2.125 inches

Weight: 8.25 lbs.

Sights: metal bead front

Bore: 12, 2.75-inch case

Data: For many years the Winchester M12 was the most popular of all pump shotguns, and it may still be the most famous. It was also one of the earliest internal-hammer slide-action shotguns. Designed by Thomas Crossley Johnson, it was introduced in 1913, just a decade after John Moses Browning applied for a patent on the first such gun—the direct forebear of the Savage M30.

A trap version of the M12 appeared in 1914, and the currently produced M12 Trap is the fifth variation of that original model. Differences include the shape and size of the slide, stock shape and dimensions, barrel lengths, and ribs. Winchester makes a claim that is probably quite accurate regarding the performance of the M12 in competition—namely, that it has won more championship trap matches than any other gun.

The trap grade is only one of several M12s that have won adherents over the years. Bores have included the standard 12 gauge and 3-inch 12 Magnum, 16, 20, and 28. They were made in field grade, skeet, and a beautiful Pigeon Grade. For half a century various M12s were produced, always to rigid quality standards both in the ma-

WINCHESTER M12 TRAP SLIDE-ACTION (continued)

terials used and in the workmanship, despite rising production costs. Finally, in 1963, the M12 was relegated to special-order status. By then, 1,968,307 M12s had been made. (The two-million mark has now been passed.) For the next decade the M12 remained a custom gun. Then it was returned to regular—or almost regular—production and once again a field or skeet M12 could be obtained. But in 1975 the Winchester catalog omitted all but one survivor, the M12 Trap.

The price of the M12 had risen to nearly thrice the cost of the Winchester M1200 and other competitors made by Mossberg, Remington, Savage, etc. A dedicated trap shooter is willing to pay the price of the M12 (especially since it's lower than the price of many over/under and side-by-side trap guns). But the average buyer of a slide-action shotgun can get something much less expensive for hunting and even for skeet. The demise of all the M12s but the trap version is mourned by shotgunners who appreciate quality and tradition.

Comment: The surviving trap version upholds the M12's rank as the best-selling slide-action shotgun and the one that has been in production longer than any other. It is extremely reliable, smooth-handling and smooth-functioning, well balanced, good-looking, certainly one of the best ever made.

The Winchester Model 12 Field Grade with ventilated rib. Since 1972, only the trap version is available.

Parts List for Weatherby Patrician Pump Shotgun

No.	Part Name	No.	Part Name	No.	Name
1	Cap—Fore-end	26	Follower—Dog	51	Sear Pin
2	Barrel Assembly	27	Spring—Dog Follower	52	Retainer—Magazine Spring
3	Bead—Barrel	28	Spring—Detent	53	Plug—Magazine
4	Screw—Detent	29	Pivot Tube—Hammer	54	Follower—Magazine
5	Spring—Detent	30	Lockshaft Assembly	55	Spring—Magazine
6	Plunger—Detent	31	Hammer	56	Magazine
7	Forearm	32	Plunger—Hammer	57	Retainer—Latch Pin
8	Slide Assembly	33	Spring—Hammer Plunger	58	Latch Pin
9	Nut—Fore-end Tube	34	Spring—Detent	59	Spring—Latch
10	Bolt	35	Cam	60	Latch—Feed
11	Pin—Retaining	36	Plunger—Cam	61	Blocker
12	Firing Pin	37	Spring—Cam Plunger	62	Retainer—Ejector
13	Spring—Firing Pin	38	Pin—Trigger	63	Ejector
14	Extractor	39	Pin—Disconnector	64	Spring—Ejector
15	Plunger—Extractor	40	Disconnector	65	Insert—Housing Factory Installation only
16	Spring—Extractor	41	Pin—Trigger Spring		
17	Locking Block	42	Spring—Trigger	66	Adaptor—Stockbolt
18	Carrier	43	Trigger	67	Buffer
19	Pin-Front Trigger Frame	44	Screw—Retainer	68	Housing
20	Lever—Fore-end Release	45	Spring—Safety	69	Screw—Wood
21	Ring—Retaining	46	Plunger—Safety	70	Recoil Pad
22	Pivot—Lifter	47	Safety Button	71	Stockbolt
23	Pin—Lifter Dog	48	Frame—Trigger	72	Lockwasher
24	Lifter	49	Spring—Sear	73	Washer—Buttstock
25	Dog—Lifter	50	Sear	74	Buttstock Sub-Assembly

EXPLODED VIEW OF WEATHERBY PATRICIAN PUMP SHOTGUN

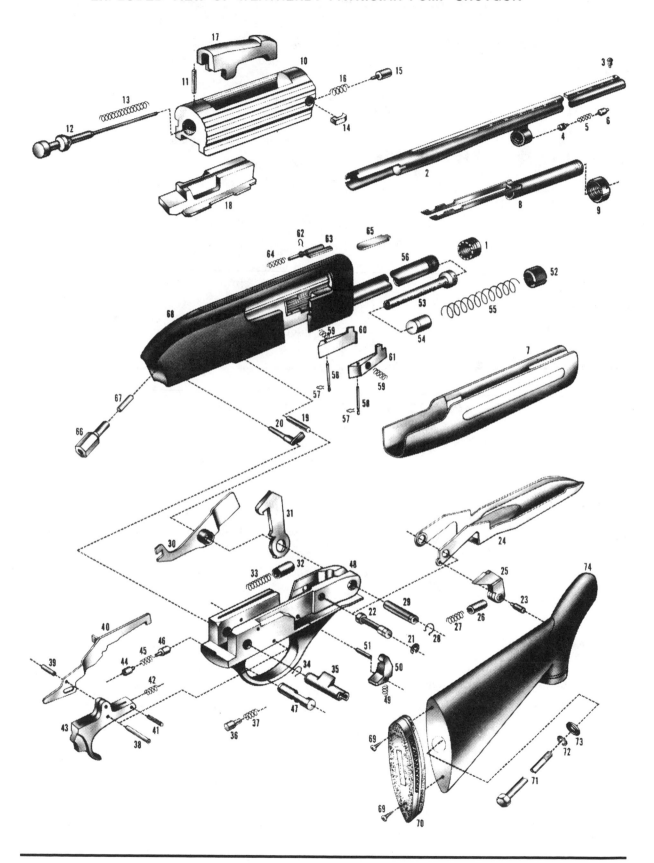

WINCHESTER M1200 WINCHOKE SLIDE ACTION

Action type: slide; internal hammer

Magazine type: tubular

Magazine capacity: 4-shot (2-shot plus 1 in chamber when fitted with wildfowl plug)

Safety: crossbolt

Barrel length & choke: 28.0 inches, Winchoke only (three separate tubes, one for each choke desired: full, modified, or improved cylinder; spanner supplied)

Stock: 2-piece American walnut; machine-checkered; pistol grip with black plastic cap; gloss finish

Buttplate: black plastic

Overall length: 48.625 inches

Length of pull: 14.0 inches

Drop at comb: plain barrel, 1.375 inches; ventilated rib, 1.5 inches

Drop at heel: plain barrel, 2.375 inches; ventilated rib, 2.5 inches

Weight: 12-bore, 7.0 lbs.; 20-bore, 6.5 lbs.; add 4.0 oz. for ventilated rib

Sights: metal bead front

Bore: 12, 20, 2.75-inch case

Data: Action data same as for standard M1200.

Comment: This is an excellent choice for a gunner who wants multi-chokes but doesn't want to purchase extra barrels. The 28-inch barrel is a good compromise between 26-inch and 30-inch lengths. It can be had with or without a ventilated rib.

WINCHESTER M1200 MAGNUM SLIDE ACTION

Action type: slide; internal hammer

Magazine type: tubular

Magazine capacity: 4-shot (2 plus 1 in chamber when fitted with wildfowl plug)

Safety: crossbolt

Barrel length & choke: 12-bore, 30.0 inches, full; 20-bore, 28.0 inches, full

Stock: 2-piece American walnut; machine-checkered; pistol grip with plastic cap

Buttplate: ventilated rubber recoil pad

Overall length: 30.0-inch barrel, 50.625 inches; 28.0-inch barrel, 48.625 inches

Length of pull: 14.0 inches

Drop at comb: plain barrel, 1.375 inches; ventilated rib, 1.5 inches

Drop at heel: plain barrel, 2.375 inches; ventilated rib, 2.5 inches

Weight: 30.0-inch barrel, 7.675 lbs.; 28.0-inch barrel, 7.325 lbs.

Sights: metal bead front

Bore: 12, 20, 3.0-inch case

Data: Same as for standard M1200 except for weight, 3.0-inch chamber, barrel length, and choke.

Comment: Any 12-bore Magnum should weigh at least 8 lbs., and 8.5 lbs. is even better.

WINCHESTER M1200 SLIDE ACTION

Action type: slide; internal hammer

Magazine type: tubular

Magazine capacity: 4-shot (2-shot plus 1 in chamber when fitted with wildfowl plug)

Safety: crossbolt

Barrel length & choke:

12-bore: 30.0 inches, full; 28.0 inches, modified; 26.0 inches, improved cylinder

20-bore: 28.0 inches, full or modified; 26.0 inches, improved cylinder

Stock: 2-piece American walnut; machine checkering; pistol grip with plastic cap

Buttplate: ventilated rubber recoil pad

Overall length: 30.0-inch barrel, 50.625 inches; 28.0-inch barrel, 48.625 inches; 26.0-inch barrel, 46.625 inches

Length of pull: 14.0 inches

Drop at comb: plain barrel, 1.375 inches, ventilated rib, 1.5 inches

Drop at heel: plain barrel, 2.375 inches; ventilated rib, 2.5 inches

Weight:

12-bore: plain barrel, 6.75 to 7.0 lbs.; ventilated rib, 7.0 to 7.25 lbs.

20-bore: plain barrel, 6.5 to 6.75 lbs.; ventilated rib, 6.75 to 7.0 lbs.

Sights: metal bead front

Bore: 12, 20, 2.75-inch case

Data: This shotgun, like its semiautomatic counterpart, the M1400, is an entirely new design. The bolt head, like that of a bolt action, has a breech-locking, rotating 4-lug bolt. This substantially reduces stress on the receiver during firing. Many M1200 components, including the bolt, are interchangeable with those of the M1400. This facilitates manufacturing and reduces costs.

Comment: The most advanced slide-action shotgun design.

CHAPTER 23

SEMIAUTOMATIC SHOTGUNS

The semiautomatic, or autoloading, shotgun, both recoil- and gas-operated, was an American invention. Semiautomatics made in Europe and Japan are either American-designed or copies of American designs. Their market is essentially the United States.

The basic types of semiautomatic action are: long recoil, short recoil, and gas-operated.

Long recoil

All shotguns—with one exception, a Winchester flop—made up to 1939 used John and Matthew Browning's long-recoil system. You name it—Browning, Breda, Beretta, Franchi, Remington, or Savage—it used Browning patents. Winchester's one pre-1939 attempt, the Model 1911, was a failure. To have been successful it would have infringed Browning's patents.

The long-recoil system, like that used on the Browning-designed Remington M8/M81 semiautomatic rifle, operates on recoil created by the force of expanding gases on a recoil spring. In long-recoil arms like the Browning rifle and shotgun, the barrel recoils within an outer barrel jacket.

Short recoil

This system was utilized by Winchester on its never-too-popular semiautomatic M40 and M59 shotguns. The system, however, is an improvement over the long-recoil system. The fixed-position barrel has a floating chamber (designed by the late Marshal David "Carbine" Williams). The floating chamber only moves about 0.1 inch when the gun is fired. The bolt moves rearward under its own momentum. While the bolt travels rearward the empty case is extracted and ejected. The loaded cartridge pops into line and is pushed into the chamber by the forward-moving bolt. Once the cartridge is fully chambered the action is closed and locked.

Gas-operated

The semiautomatic shotgun had been on the market for more than 50 years before High Standard Manufacturing Corp. brought out the first successful gas-operated shotgun. Here expanding gas is forced through a port. This gas forces the bolt to the rear, thus unlocking the bolt and extracting and ejecting the fired case. As the bullet or shot charge leaves the barrel, pressure drops and the bolt slides forward, pushing a loaded cartridge into the chamber and simultaneously closing and locking the action. This is a simpler, lighter, and less complicated system. Even Browning, which originated the long-recoil system, now builds a gas-operated shotgun (M2000) besides its long-recoil-operated Auto-5. The Auto-5 is the only long-recoil-operated shotgun made today.

The Brownings and Winchester

By 1903 John Moses Browning had been associated with the Winchester Repeating Arms Company for nearly 20 years, and every Winchester rifle and shotgun designed since 1885 had been Browning-designed.

The Browning-designed M93 and its improved successor the M97 (1897–1958), with sales of 1,000,000 plus, were the most successful exposed-hammer slide-action shotguns ever made. After designing his semiautomatic shotgun, John Moses and his brother Matthew worked closely with Winchester's patent attorneys in drawing up a patent which was so airtight that it would be impossible for anyone to legitimately make a long-recoil rifle or shotgun without infringing the patent.

The brainchildren of John and Matthew Browning earned—and are still earning—millions of dollars for Winchester. Winchester had paid the Brownings only about $100,000 for 44 patents. Browning got the patents and then assigned all rights to Winchester. Winchester, in turn, paid Browning a pittance—part in cash and part in trade goods—for the rights.

Old John may have been a Mormon country boy from Utah, but over the years he had seen Winchester prosper on his idea. He knew he had a winner in the semiautomatic shotgun design. After receiving his patent he told Winchester President Thomas Gray Bennett that he would negotiate only on a royalty basis. Bennett—a pompous fellow who got his job by virtue of being the son-in-law of Winchester founder and longtime president Oliver Prince Winchester—said it was against Winchester's policy to pay royalties.

After considerable dickering, John and Matthew said they'd go elsewhere. Somewhere along the line Bennett or a henchman indicated that the plant was tooled up for M97 production and that the semiautomatic might not sell and if it did it would cut M97 sales.

The brothers Browning immediately made an appointment with Remington Arms President Marcellus Hartley. York State farm boy Hartley had been a co-founder of America's largest sporting goods firm, Schuyler, Graham and Hartley. He took over the financially decrepit E. Remington & Sons and converted it into Remington Arms Co. in 1888. (In 1867 Hartley and his partners Schuyler and Graham had founded Union Metallic Cartridge. Remington and U.M.C. were combined into one corporation in 1912.)

John and Matthew Browning went to Hartley's office at 315 Broadway. It was January 8, 1902. They waited for their appointment with Hartley. An agitated man shot out of the office, saying Hartley had just died of heart failure.

John and Matthew packed their bags and went to Liège, Belgium, to visit Fabrique Nationale. They arranged for the manufacture and sale of their shotgun in all countries outside the United States. It is still made there today. Browning Arms later became a Fabrique Nationale stockholder. The Belgian government was—and possibly still is—an FN stockholder. Mauser Werke, Oberndorf, was a stockholder before World War I.

On their way back to Ogden, Utah, John and Matthew visited Remington's new president, grandson of Marcellus Hartley. Marcellus Hartley Dodge was interested in acquiring American manufacturing rights to the new semiautomatic.

The Brownings signed a contract that netted them more than $1,000,000 in the first ten years, proving that Thomas G. Bennett had been a poor prophet.

Winchester, noting the popularity of the Browning semiautomatic both abroad and at home, had employee Thomas Crossley Johnson design a recoil-operated shotgun. Johnson, who had helped John Browning draw up the patent specifications for the Browning semiautomatic, saw to his dismay that it would be extremely difficult, if not impossible, to develop a recoil-operated gun that did not infringe Browning patents.

The Winchester M11 was Winchester's first hammerless semiautomatic shotgun. It was not a success. Only 82,000 were sold before it was discontinued in 1925.

Winchester waited 15 years before attempting to produce another semiautomatic shotgun. This, too, was not a success. The long-recoil-operated arm was discontinued in 1941 after only 12,000 had been sold. Winchester's next attempt—the M50, a short-recoil-operated arm—was somewhat more popular. It sold about 200,000 before its discontinuance in 1961.

The M50 was replaced in 1960 by the M59 short-recoil nonrecoiling-barrel shotgun. This was dropped from the line in 1965 after only five years of production.

The M59 had one unusual feature. The barrel consisted of 500 miles of glass fibers wound about a very thin barrel tube. The outer glass was dyed deep blue. The barrel was lighter than a conventional shotgun barrel, yet quite strong and reliable. Some shooters felt that it made the M59 muzzle-light and therefore hard to swing smoothly, with good control, on birds or clay targets. But there were plenty of other shooters who applauded this lightness; it gave them a light, fast-handling semiauto for such uses as grouse and woodcock hunting.

The shotgun was discontinued not because the barrel was unsuccessful but because the gas-operated shotgun was replacing both short-recoil and long-recoil mechanisms. In the previous year (1964) Winchester offered its first gas-operated semiautomatic shotgun, the M1400. Many M1400 parts, including the bolt, were interchangeable with the M1200 slide-action shotgun.

HOW A MODERN PUMP SHOTGUN WORKS (REMINGTON MODEL 870)

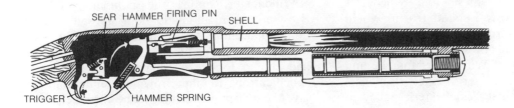

1. Starting with the gun loaded and cocked, pulling the trigger trips the sear, releasing the hammer to strike the firing pin and fire the shell.

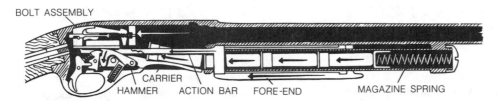

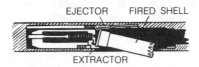

2. Pulling the fore-end rearward moves the action bar and bolt assembly toward the rear, ejecting the fired shell (see also top-view detail of ejection) pressing the hammer down into cocked position, and moving the new shell onto the carrier.

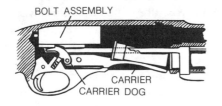

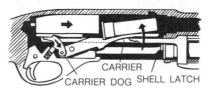

3. Detail of the carrier mechanism (left) shows how the bolt assembly at its rearmost position engages the carrier dog. As the bolt assembly moves forward (right), it moves the carrier dog downward, pivoting the carrier and new shell up into loading position. At the same time the shell latch moves to the right to hold the remaining shells in the magazine.

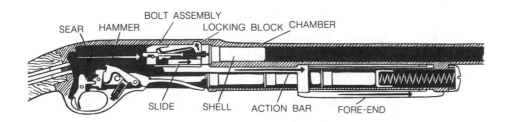

4. As the fore-end action bar and bolt assembly continue to move forward, the new shell is pushed into the chamber, and the sear engages the hammer, locking it. At the final movement of the fore-end, the slide continues forward, pushing the locking block up to lock the action for firing.

HOW A GAS OPERATED SHOTGUN WORKS (REMINGTON MODEL 58)

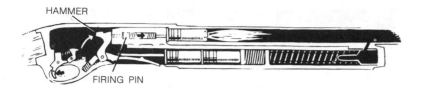

HAMMER

FIRING PIN

1. Starting with the gun cocked and loaded, squeezing the trigger releases the hammer, which strikes the firing pin and fires the shell.

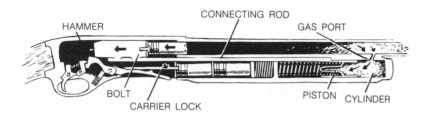

CONNECTING ROD

HAMMER

GAS PORT

BOLT

CARRIER LOCK

PISTON   CYLINDER

2. The gas generated by the fired shell is metered down through the gas port in the barrel into the cylinder. The pressure of the gas in the cylinder pushes the piston and connecting rod rearward, moving the bolt from the chamber. As the bolt travels rearward it recocks the hammer and opens the carrier lock.

FIRED SHELL

SHELL   MAGAZINE SPRING

CARRIER

3. Further rearward travel of the bolt ejects the spent shell through the side opening, and the magazine spring pushes a fresh shell onto the carrier.

BOLT   PISTON SPRING

CARRIER

PISTON   PORT

4. The piston spring starts the piston forward, moving the bolt forward, and pivoting the carrier to bring the new shell into loading position. As bolt moves all the way forward, it loads the new shell into the chamber. The spent gas escapes through the port.

BROWNING AUTO-5

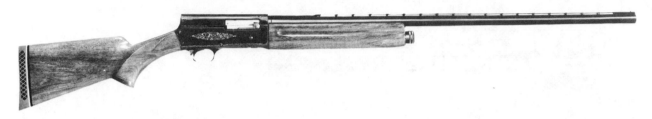

Manufacturer: Fabrique Nationale, Belgium

Importer/distributor: Browning Arms

Action type: semiautomatic; long recoil

Magazine type: tubular

Magazine capacity: 5-shot (2-shot plus 1 in chamber when fitted with wildfowl plug)

Safety: crossbolt; large button to enable shooter to use with gloves

Barrel length & choke:

12-bore 3.0-inch Magnum: 32.0 and 30.0 inches, full; 28.0 inches, full or modified

12-bore 2.75-inch (Light 12): 30.0 inches, full; 28.0 inches, full or modified; 26.0 inches, improved cylinder or cylinder

16-bore 2.75-inch (Sweet 16): 28.0 inches, full or modified; 26.0 inches, modified, improved cylinder, or cylinder

20-bore 3.0-inch Magnum: 28.0 inches, full or modified; 26.0 inches, full, modified, or improved cylinder

20-bore 2.75-inch: 28.0 inches, full or modified; 26.0 inches, modified, improved cylinder, or cylinder

Note: Above barrel lengths and chokes are all available with plain or ventilated-rib barrels. Any choke may be obtained in any standard barrel length with a slight charge for reboring. Not included in above are skeet and slug borings.

Stock: 2-piece French walnut; checkered pistol grip and fore-end; full uncapped pistol grip; semi-gloss finish

Buttplate: hard rubber; ventilated recoil pad on 12-bore 3.0-inch Magnum

Overall length: 32.0-inch barrel, 50.125 inches; 30.0-inch barrel, 48.125 inches; 28.0-inch barrel, 46.125 inches; 26.0-inch barrel, 44.125 inches

Length of pull: 14.25 inches

Drop at comb: 1.625 inches

Drop at heel: 2.5 inches

Weight (add about 4 oz. for ventilated rib):

12-bore 3.0-inch Magnum: 32.0-inch barrel, 8.75 lbs.; 30.0-inch barrel, 8.625 lbs.; 28.0-inch barrel, 8.5 lbs.

12-bore 2.75-inch: 30.0-inch barrel, 7.375 lbs.; 28.0-inch barrel, 7.35 lbs.; 26.0-inch barrel, 7.2 lbs.

16-bore 2.75-inch: 28.0-inch barrel, 6.75 lbs.; 26.0-inch barrel, 6.625 lbs.

20-bore 3.0-inch: 28.0-inch barrel, 7.125 lbs.; 26.0-inch barrel, 7.0625 lbs.

20-bore 2.75-inch: 28.0-inch barrel, 6.35 lbs.; 26.0-inch barrel, 6.25 lbs.

Sights: bead front

Bore: 12, 2.75-inch or 3.0-inch case; 16, 2.75-inch case; 20, 2.75-inch or 3.0-inch case

Data: This was the first semiautomatic shotgun and for the first 54 years of its existence it was the only semiautomatic shotgun type (long recoil). All successful semiautomatic shotguns made during that era were either legitimately licensed or pirated versions of the Browning. More than 2,000,000 Brownings plus hundreds of thousands of copies have been sold.

All chokes and barrel lengths are available with either plain barrel or ventilated-rib barrel; all plain barrels except the 12 Magnum have matted top surfaces to reduce glare.

EXPLODED VIEW OF BROWNING AUTO 5 SHOTGUN, STANDARD, LIGHT AND MAGNUM MODELS—12, 16, AND 20 GAUGE

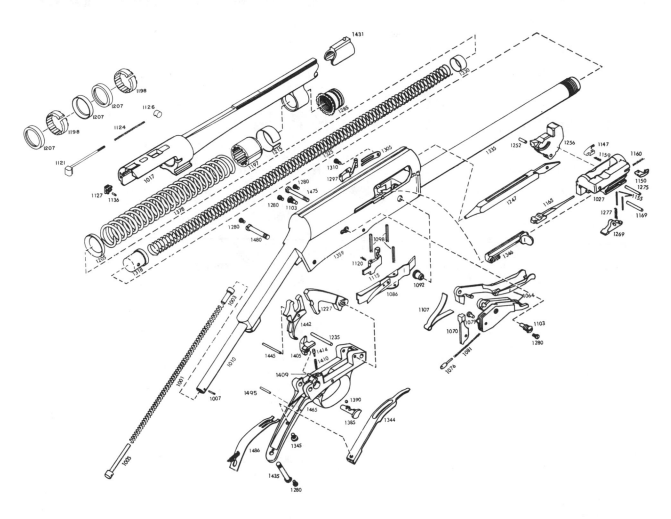

No.	Part Name	No.	Part Name	No.	Part Name
1001	Action Spring	1136	Ejector Rivet	1287	Mag. Cap-W/O Swivel Eyelet
1007	Action Spring Plug Pin	1147	Extractor Left	1305	Magazine Cutoff Spring
1010	Action Spring Tube	1150	Extractor Right	1310	Magazine Cutoff Spring Screw
1017	Barrel Extension	1155	Extractor Pin Left & Right	1318	Magazine Follower
1027	Breech Block	1159	Extractor Spring Left	1325	Magazine Spring
1064	Carrier Assembly 2 Piece	1160	Extractor Spring Right Hand	1330	Magazine Spring Retainer
1070	Carrier Dog	1165	Firing Pin	1335	Magazine Tube 5-Shot
1076	Carrier Dog Follower	1169	Firing Pin Stop Pin	1344	Mainspring
1079	Carrier Dog Pin	1198	Friction Piece Bronze Magnum	1345	Mainspring Screw
1081	Carrier Dog Spring	1207	Friction Ring	1346	Operating Handle
1086	Carrier Latch Assembly	1215	Friction Spring	1359	Receiver
1092	Carrier Latch Button	1227	Hammer Assembly-Standard	1378	Recoil Spring
1098	Cartridge Stop Pin	1235	Hammer Pin	1410	Safety Sear Spring
1103	Carrier Screw	1247	Link	1414	Safety Sear Spring Follower
1107	Carrier Spring Trigger Plate Type	1269	Locking Block Latch 2-Piece Carrier	1431	Sight Bead Plain & Vent
1115	Carrier Stop	1275	Locking Block Latch Pin	1435	Tang Screw for Pistol Grip Stock
1120	Cartridge Stop Spring	1277	Locking Block Latch Spring	1442	Trigger For Crossbolt Safety
1121	Ejector & Ejector Rod Magnum	1280	Lock Screw	1445	Trigger Pin
1126	Ejector Spring Retainer Magnum	1285	Mag. Cap-W/O Swivel Eyelet	1475	Trigger Plate Screw-Front
1127	Ejector			1480	Trigger Plate Screw-Rear
				1486	Trigger Spring-Pin Retained
				1495	Trigger Spring Retaining Pin

BROWNING AUTO-5 (continued)

Comment: There are two schools of thought about the Browning. (1) Those who dislike the square receiver. Before World War II Abercrombie & Fitch offered a rounded-shoulder conversion of the arm. This conversion was also carried out by several independent gunsmiths. (2) Those who believe—and there may be truth to it—that the big receiver bridge helps in fast pointing.

In 1973 Browning produced its first gas-operated semiautomatic shotgun, the Browning M2000. The old recoil-operated Browning may be around for a considerable time.

BROWNING AUTOMATIC 5 HUNTING/SKEET MODEL

Manufacturer: Fabrique Nationale, Belgium

Importer/distributor: Browning Arms

Action type: semiautomatic; long recoil

Magazine type: tubular

Magazine capacity: 4-shot (2-shot plus 1 in chamber when fitted with wildfowl plug)

Safety: crossbolt

Barrel length & choke: 28.0 inches, improved or modified; 26.0 inches, improved, modified, or skeet

Stock: 2-piece French walnut; checkered uncapped pistol grip and fore-end

Buttplate: plastic

Overall length: 28.0-inch barrel, 46.125 inches; 26.0-inch barrel, 44.125 inches

Length of pull: 14.25 inches

Drop at comb: 1.375 inches

Drop at heel: 2.5 inches

Weight (add about 4 oz. for ventilated rib):

12-bore, 28.0-inch barrel: 7.35 lbs.

12-bore, 26.0-inch barrel: 7.175 lbs.

20-bore, 28.0-inch barrel: 6.35 lbs.

20-bore, 26.0-inch barrel: 6.25 lbs.

Sights: bead front

Bore: 12, 20, 2.75-inch case

Data: This gun is available with a ventilated rib or a plain barrel featuring a matted top. Trigger is gold-plated.

Comment: This has long been a popular skeet semiautomatic, if only because it is so well known and has been made for nearly 50 years in the skeet version. It is designated hunting/skeet because many shooters find the skeet choke deadly on upland game and waterfowl up to 35 yards.

BROWNING M2000 SEMIAUTOMATIC SHOTGUN

Manufacturer: Fabrique Nationale, Belgium

Importer/distributor: Browning Arms

Action type: semiautomatic; gas-operated

Magazine type: tubular

Magazine capacity: 2.75-inch case, 4-shot; 3.0-inch case, 3-shot (2-shot when fitted with wildfowl plug)

Safety: crossbolt in triggerguard, reversible for left-handed shooters.

Barrel length & choke: 32.0 inches, full (3.0-inch case only); 30.0 inches, full; 28.0 inches, modified; 26.0 inches, improved cylinder (2.75-inch case only)

Stock: 2-piece French walnut; 20 line-per-inch checkering on pistol grip and fore-end; finger-grooved fore-end; high-gloss polyurethane finish

Buttplate: black plastic

Overall length: 32.0-inch barrel, 51.375-inches; 30.0-inch barrel, 49.375-inches; 28.0-inch barrel, 47.375-inches; 26.0-inch barrel, 45.375 inches.

Length of pull: 14.25 inches

Drop at comb: 1.625 inches

Drop at heel: 2.5 inches

Weight: 32.0-inch barrel, 7.5 lbs; 30.0-inch barrel, 7.375 lbs; 28.0-inch barrel, 7.25 lbs; 26.0-inch barrel, 7.225 lbs. (add 4 oz. for ventilated rib)

Sight: metal bead front

Bore: 12-bore, 2.75-inch case or 3.0-inch case.

Data: Cold-forged machined steel receiver with brazed inserts. Loading port is on left side of receiver. Shot cartridge on carrier ready for loading is visible through loading port slot. Ejection is through right side of receiver.

Comment: This is the first Browning gas-operated autoloading shotgun. It has a square-backed receiver like that of the old long-recoil Browning. Location of its loading port is unusual. Most semiautomatics have bottom-of-receiver loading ports. The two lengths of shot cartridges are not interchangeable with one barrel. A separate barrel is required for each case length. This fine shotgun should be fitted with a ventilated recoil pad. The wood is finely figured and handsome. The arm handles easily.

FRANCHI M520 SEMIAUTOMATIC

Manufacturer: Armi Franchi, Italy

Importer/distributor: Stoeger Arms Corp.

Action type: semiautomatic; gas-operated

Magazine type: tubular

Magazine capacity: 4-shot (2-shot when fitted with wildfowl plug)

Safety: crossbolt in trigger guard

Barrel length & choke: 28.0-inch barrel, full, improved modified, or modified; 26.0-inch barrel, modified, improved modified, or cylinder

Stock: 2-piece European walnut; machine-checkered; full uncapped pistol grip; high-gloss finish

Buttplate: black plastic

Overall length: 28.0-inch barrel, 47.875 inches; 26.0-inch barrel, 45.875 inches

Length of pull: 13.875 inches

Drop at comb: 1.5 inches

Drop at heel: 2.35 inches

Weight: 7.0 lbs.

Sight: metal bead front

Bore: 12, 2.75-inch case

Data: Chromed bore and alloy receiver. Unusual features of the new Franchi semiautomatic shotgun include: (1) magazine isolated from gas-operated piston to eliminate malfunctions created by carbon deposits; (2) loading made easier because cartridge carrier doesn't have to be unlocked to fill magazine; (3) gas expelled through two ports located in the forward portion

FRANCHI M520 SEMIAUTOMATIC (continued)
of the fore-end; (4) precisely machined gas-tight piston, eliminating need for plastic or rubber seal.

Comment: This well-designed lightweight 12-bore semiautomatic shotgun meets the usual high Franchi manufacturing and performance standards.

FRANCHI STANDARD AUTOMATIC SHOTGUN

Manufacturer: Armi Franchi, Italy

Importer/distributor: Stoeger Arms Corp.

Action type: semiautomatic; recoil-operated

Magazine type: tubular

Magazine capacity: 4-shot (2-shot when fitted with wildfowl plug)

Safety: crossbolt in trigger guard

Barrel length & choke: 30.0-inch barrel, full (12-bore only); 28.0-inch barrel, full or modified; 26.0-inch barrel, skeet (ventilated rib only), modified or 24.0-inch barrel, modified or improved cylinder

Stock: 2-piece European walnut; machine-checkered; finger-grooved fore-end; full uncapped pistol grip; semi-gloss finish

Buttplate: black plastic (rubber recoil pad available at extra cost)

Overall length: 30.0-inch barrel, 49.5 inches; 28.0-inch barrel, 47.5 inches; 26.0-inch barrel, 45.5 inches; 24.0-inch barrel, 43.5 inches

Length of pull: 14.0 inches

Drop at comb: 1.5 inches

Drop at heel: 2.25 inches

Weight:

12-bore: 30.0-inch barrel, 6.375 lbs.; 28.0-inch barrel, 6.25 lbs.; 26.0-inch barrel, 6.125 lbs.; 24.0-inch barrel, 6.0 lbs.

20-bore: 28.0-inch barrel, 5.250 lbs.; 26.0-inch barrel, 5.125 lbs.; 24.0-inch barrel, 5.0 lbs.

Sight: metal bead front

Bore: 12, 20, 2.75-inch case

Data: In addition to the 12- and 20-bores, Stoeger imports a limited number in 28-bore (2.75-inch case; same specifications as for 20-bore). Gun's design is based on Browning long-recoil patents. Most chokes and barrel lengths are available with a plain or ventilated-rib barrel. Skeet borings are available with ventilated rib only.

Comment: Probably the world's lightest semiautomatic shotgun. Very well crafted. Chromed bore.

FRANCHI MAGNUM AUTOMATIC SHOTGUN

Manufacturer: Armi Franchi, Italy

Importer/distributor: Stoeger Arms Corp.

Action type: semiautomatic; recoil-operated

Magazine type: tubular

Magazine capacity: 4-shot (2-shot with waterfowl plug installed)

Safety: crossbolt in trigger guard

Barrel length & choke: 32.0 (12-bore only) or 30.0 inches, full

Stock: 2-piece European walnut; machine-checkered; finger-grooved fore-end; full uncapped pistol grip; semi-gloss finish

Buttplate: ventilated rubber recoil pad

Overall length: 32.0-inch barrel, 51.5 inches; 30.0-inch barrel, 49.5 inches; 28.0-inch barrel, 47.5 inches

Length of pull: 14.0 inches

Drop at comb: 1.5 inches

Drop at heel: 2.25 inches

Weight:

12-bore: 32.0-inch barrel, 8.25 lbs.; 30.0-inch barrel, 8.0 lbs.

20-bore: 6.0 lbs.

Sights: metal bead front

Bore: 12 or 20, 3.0-inch case

Comment: Same as for Standard Automatic model.

FRANCHI SLUG GUN

Manufacturer: Armi Franchi, Italy

Importer/distributor: Stoeger Arms Corp.

Action type: semiautomatic; recoil-operated

Magazine type: tubular

Magazine capacity: 4-shot

Safety: crossbolt in trigger guard

Barrel length & choke: 24.0 inches, cylinder

Stock: 2-piece European walnut; finger-grooved fore-end; full uncapped pistol grip; semi-gloss finish

Buttplate: black plastic

Overall length: 43.5 inches

Length of pull: 14.0 inches

Drop at comb: 1.5 inches

Drop at heel: 2.25 inches

Weight: 12-bore, 6.0 lbs.; 20-bore, 5.5 lbs.

Sight, rear: adjustable for elevation and windage

Sight, front: metal bead on ramp

Comment: Chromed bore. One of the lightest semiautomatic slug guns. Well crafted.

HIGH STANDARD SUPERMATIC SEMIAUTOMATIC

Action type: semiautomatic; gas-operated

Magazine type: tubular

Magazine capacity: 12-bore, 5-shot (2-shot plus 1 in chamber when fitted with wildfowl plug); 20-bore, 3-shot

Safety: crossbolt

Barrel length & choke:

12-bore: 30.0 inches, full; 28.0 inches, modified; 27.0 inches with adjustable choke device

20-bore: 28.0 inches, full or modified; 26.0 inches, improved cylinder; 27.0 inches with adjustable choke device

Stock: 2-piece American walnut; impressed checkering; pistol grip with black plastic cap

Buttplate: ventilated rubber recoil pad with white line spacer

Overall length: 30.0-inch barrel, 49.75 inches; 28.0-inch barrel, 47.75 inches; 26.0-inch barrel, 45.75 inches

Length of pull: 14.0 inches

Drop at comb: 1.5 inches

Drop at heel: 2.5 inches

Weight:

12-bore: 30.0-inch barrel, 7.75 lbs.; 28.0-inch barrel, 7.5 lbs.

20-bore: 28.0-inch barrel, 7.25 lbs.; 26.0-inch barrel, 7.0 lbs.

Sights: brass bead front

Bore: 12, 20, 2.75-inch case

Data: Available with plain barrel or ventilated rib. Trap and skeet versions are also offered.

Comment: At press time, production was temporarily suspended so that High Standard could concentrate on turning out police and military shotguns. However, plans were to resume production in the near future.

INTERARMS MANUFRANCE SEMIAUTOMATIC SHOTGUN

Manufacturer: Manufacture Française d'Armes et Cycles de St. Etienne, France

Importer/distributor: Interarms

Action type: semiautomatic; gas-operated

Magazine type: tubular

Magazine capacity: 2-shot

Safety: crossbolt in trigger guard

Barrel length & choke: 30.0 inches, full; 28.0 inches, modified; 26.0 inches, improved cylinder

Stock: 2-piece European walnut with impressed checkering on pistol grip and fore-end; semi-gloss finish

Buttplate: black plastic

Overall length: 30.0-inch barrel, 50.875 inches; 28.0-inch barrel, 48.875 inches; 26.0-inch barrel, 46.875 inches

Length of pull: 14.332 inches

Drop at comb: 1.5 inches

Drop at heel: 2.2 inches

Weight: 30-inch barrel, 6.75 lbs.; 28.0-inch barrel, 6.625 lbs.; 26.0-inch barrel, 6.5 lbs.; add about 4.0 oz. for ventilated rib

Sight: metal bead front

Bore: 12, 2.75-inch case

Comment: This simply designed autoloader functions reliably with a variety of loads.

ITHACA MAG 10 SEMIAUTOMATIC

Action type: semiautomatic; gas-operated

Magazine type: tubular

Magazine capacity: 2-shot plus 1 in chamber (maximum allowed for waterfowl)

Safety: crossbolt

Barrel length & choke: 32.0 inches, full

Stock: 2-piece select American walnut; hand checkering; capped full pistol grip

Buttplate: ventilated rubber recoil pad with white line spacer

Overall length: 54.25 inches

Length of pull: 14.125 inches

Drop at comb: 1.5 inches

Drop at heel: 2.375 inches

Weight: 11.75 lbs.; about 12.25 lbs. loaded

Sights: metal bead front

Bore: 10, 3.5-inch Magnum case

Data: This is currently the world's only semiautomatic 10-bore 3.5-inch Magnum. It is the first multi-shot 10-bore Magnum made in the United States since Ithaca, which made the first 10-bore 3.5-inch Magnum in 1932, did not resume double magnum production after World War II.

All gas-system components are stainless steel. The receiver is machined from a block of solid steel.

The gas system is unusual. The piston is stationary but the cylinder moves. When the gun is fired, powder gas enters the sole gas port. The expanding gas forces the operating slide, cylinder, and action bar about 0.625 inch rearward. The rearward-moving cylinder cams the breechblock's after end downward. This motion disengages the barrel extension from the locking lug. The breechblock unit—operating slide and link group—compresses the action spring recessed in the buttstock. During the movement the empty case is ejected. A plastic buffer prevents metal-to-metal contact.

Some trigger-system components are steel stampings. The trigger housing is aluminum alloy. The carrier and some allied components are investment castings. The piston, gas cylinder, operating handle, carrier, release, and trigger are stainless steel. The barrel has a ventilated rib.

Comment: The actual recoil of about 44 lbs. seems less than in a double 10-bore Magnum because of the gas-operated action. Actual recoil is, of course, the same in either a double or semiautomatic of equal weight.

This slow-to-handle arm is handicapped by the low pattern density. The only factory load is 2.0 oz. of No. 2 shot. When fired from a full-choke arm like the Mag10, there seem to be about twice as many shot within an inner 15.0-inch circle than there are in the entire 30.0-inch circle at 40 yards.

The 10-bore Magnum would be more useful and far more effective if loaded with No. 4 shot. Performance can be improved with handloads or by opening up the choke very slightly with a Poly-Choke-type device.

ITHACA M51 DEERSLAYER SEMIAUTOMATIC

Action type: semiautomatic; gas-operated

Magazine type: tubular

Magazine capacity: 2-shot

Safety: crossbolt in trigger guard

Barrel length & choke: 24.0 inches; special slug choke

Stock: 2-piece American walnut; reverse checkering; black plastic pistol grip cap with white line spacer; high-gloss finish

Buttplate: black plastic

Overall length: 43.5 inches

Length of pull: 14.0 inches

Drop at comb: 1.5 inches

Drop at heel: 2.25 inches

Weight: 7.5 lbs.

Sight, rear: crudely adjustable for windage and elevation

Sight, front: red bead on ramp

Scope adaptability: sight base grooved for scope mount

Bore: 12, 2.75-inch case

Comment: A reliable, good-looking shotgun for deer hunters.

ITHACA M51 DELUXE SKEET SEMIAUTOMATIC

Action type: semiautomatic; gas-operated

Magazine type: tubular

Magazine capacity: 2-shot

Safety: crossbolt in trigger guard

Barrel length & choke: 26.0 inches, skeet

Stock: 2-piece fancy grade American walnut;

ITHACA M51 DELUXE SKEET SEMIAUTOMATIC
(continued)

machine-checkered; black plastic pistol-grip cap; finger-grooved fore-end; semi-gloss finish

Buttplate: black plastic

Overall length: 45.5 inches

Length of pull: 14 inches

Drop at comb: 1.5 inches

Drop at heel: 2.25 inches

Weight: 8.0 lbs.

Sight: metal bead front

Bore: 12, 20, 2.75-inch case

Comment: An excellent skeet gun.

ITHACA M51 DELUXE TRAP GRADE SEMIAUTOMATIC

Action type: semiautomatic; gas-operated

Magazine type: tubular

Magazine capacity: 2-shot

Safety: crossbolt in trigger guard

Barrel length & choke: 30.0 inches, full

Stock: 2-piece fancy grade American walnut; machine-checkered; black plastic pistol-grip cap; finger-grooved fore-end; semi-gloss finish; available with Monte Carlo comb

Buttplate: red rubber ventilated recoil pad

Overall length: 49.5 inches

Length of pull: 14 inches

Drop at comb: 1.325 inches; Monte Carlo, 1.5 inches

Drop at Monte Carlo (if applicable): 1.5 inches

Drop at heel: 1.425 inches; Monte Carlo, 2.0 inches

Weight: 8.0 lbs.

Sight: Bradley-type front

Bore: 12, 2.75-inch case

Comment: A well designed and crafted trap gun at a reasonable price.

ITHACA M51 STANDARD AND MAGNUM SEMIAUTOMATICS

Action type: semiautomatic; gas-operated

Magazine type: tubular

Magazine capacity: 2-shot

Safety: crossbolt in trigger guard

Barrel length & choke: 30.0 inches, full (12-bore only); 28.0 inches, full or modified; 26.0 inches, improved cylinder

Stock: 2-piece American walnut; reverse checkering on pistol grip and fore-end; black plastic pistol-grip cap with white line spacer; high-gloss finish

Buttplate: black plastic

Overall length: 30.0-inch barrel, 49.5 inches

Length of pull: 14.0 inches

Drop at comb: 1.5 inches

Drop at heel: 2.25 inches

Weight: 12-bore, 7.5 lbs (Magnum, 7.75 lbs.); 20-bore, 7.25 lbs. (Magnum, 7.5 lbs.); add about 4.0 oz. for ventilated rib

Sight: Ithaca Raybar (plastic bar which transmits light)

Weight: 12, 20, 2.75-inch or 3.0-inch case

Comment: A well designed and crafted semiautomatic shotgun.

ITHACA SKB MODEL XL300

Manufacturer: SKB, Japan

Importer/distributor: Ithacagun

Action type: semiautomatic; gas-operated

Magazine type: tubular

Magazine capacity: 4-shot (2-shot when fitted with wildfowl plug)

Safety: crossbolt in trigger guard

Barrel length & choke: 30.0 inches, full (12-bore only); 28.0 inches, full or modified; 26.0 inches, improved cylinder

Stock: 2-piece walnut; machine-checkered; pistol grip with black plastic cap and white line spacer; oil-type finish

Buttplate: black plastic with white line spacer

Overall length: 30.0-inch barrel, 49.5 inches; 28.0-inch barrel, 47.5 inches; 26.0-inch barrel, 45.5 inches

Length of pull: 14.0 inches

Drop at comb: 1.5 inches

Drop at heel: 2.5 inches

Weight (add about 4.0 oz. for ventilated rib):

12-bore: 30-inch barrel, 7.25 lbs.; 28.0-inch barrel, 7.125 lbs.; 26.0-inch barrel, 7.0 lbs.

20-bore: 28.0-inch barrel, 6.25 lbs.; 26.0-inch barrel, 6.0 lbs.

Sight: brass bead front on plain barrel; Raybar front on ventilated rib

Weight: 12, 2.75-inch case; 20, 3.0-inch case.

Comment: One of the world's lightest shotguns in 20-bore, this is as mechanically fine a semiautomatic as obtainable.

ITHACA SKB MODEL XL900

Manufacturer: SKB, Japan

Importer/distributor: Ithacagun

Action type: semiautomatic; gas-operated

Magazine type: tubular

Magazine capacity: 4-shot (2-shot when fitted with wildfowl plug)

Safety: crossbolt in trigger guard

Barrel length & choke: 30.0 inches, full (12-bore only); 28.0 inches, full or modified; 26.0 inches, improved cylinder

Stock: 2-piece walnut; machine-checkered; pistol grip with black plastic cap and white line spacer; oil-type finish

ITHACA SKB MODEL XL900 (continued)

Buttplate: black plastic with white line insert

Overall length: 30.0-inch barrel, 49.5 inches; 28.0-inch barrel, 47.5 inches; 26.0-inch barrel, 45.5 inches

Length of pull: 14.0 inches

Drop at comb: 1.5 inches

Drop at heel: 2.5 inches

Weight:

12-bore: 30.0-inch barrel, 7.5 lbs.; 28.0-inch barrel, 7.375 lbs.; 26.0-inch barrel, 7.25 lbs.

20-bore: 28.0-inch barrel, 6.25 lbs.; 26.0-inch barrel, 6.25 lbs.

Sight: Raybar front on ventilated rib

Bore: 12, 2.75-inch case; 20, 3.0-inch case

Comment: Same as for Model XL 300; the XL 900 has fancier engraving and better checkering.

ITHACA SKB MODEL XL900 SKEET

Manufacturer: SKB, Japan

Importer/distributor: Ithacagun

Action type: semiautomatic; gas-operated

Magazine type: tubular

Magazine capacity: 4-shot (2-shot when fitted with wildfowl plug)

Safety: crossbolt in trigger guard

Barrel length & choke: 26.0 inches, skeet

Stock: 2-piece walnut; machine-checkered; pistol grip with black plastic cap and white line spacer; oil-type finish

Buttplate: ventilated rubber recoil pad

Overall length: 47.5 inches

Length of pull: 14.0 inches

Drop at comb: 1.5 inches

Drop at heel: 2.25 inches

Weight: 12-bore, 7.5 lbs.; 20-bore, 7.0 lbs.

Sights: Bradley type front and middle bead on ventilated rib

Bore: 12, 20, 2.75-inch case

Comment: A fine medium-priced skeet gun.

ITHACA SKB MODEL XL900 SLUG GUN

Manufacturer: SKB, Japan

Importer/distributor: Ithacagun

Action type: semiautomatic; gas-operated

Magazine type: tubular

Magazine capacity: 4-shot

Safety: crossbolt in trigger guard

Barrel length & choke: 24.0 inches; special slug boring

Stock: 2-piece walnut; machine-checkered; pistol grip with black plastic cap and white line spacer; oil-type finish

Buttplate: black plastic with white plastic spacer

Overall length: 43.5 inches

Length of pull: 14.0 inches

Drop at comb: 1.5 inches

Drop at heel: 2.5 inches

Weight: 12-bore, 7.0 lbs.; 20-bore, 6.5 lbs.

Sight, rear: open, crudely adjustable for windage and elevation

Sight, front: blade on ramp

Scope adaptability: rear sight base grooved for long eye relief scope mount

Bore: 12, 2.75-inch case; 20, 3.0-inch case

Comment: A good slug gun.

ITHACA SKB MODEL XL900 TRAP

Manufacturer: SKB, Japan

Importer/distributor: Ithacagun

Action type: semiautomatic; gas-operated

Magazine type: tubular

Magazine capacity: 4-shot

Safety: crossbolt in trigger guard

Barrel length & choke: 30.0 inches, full or improved modified

Stock: 2-piece walnut; machine-checkered; pistol grip with black plastic cap and white line spacer; straight (standard) or Monte Carlo; oil-type finish

Buttplate: ventilated rubber recoil pad

Overall length: 49.5 inches

Length of pull: 14.5 inches

Drop at comb: 1.5 inches

Drop at Monte Carlo (if applicable): 1.5 inches

Drop at heel: 1.875 inches; Monte Carlo, 2.0 inches

Weight: 7.75 lbs.

Sights: Bradley front and middle bead on ventilated rib

Bore: 12, 2.75-inch case

Comment: A good trap gun.

REMINGTON M1100 FIELD GRADE

Action type: semiautomatic; gas-operated; short-stroke piston

Magazine type: tubular

Magazine capacity: 4-shot (2-shot plus 1 in chamber when fitted with wildfowl plug)

Safety: crossbolt

Barrel length & choke:

12-bore: 30.0 inches, full; 28.0 inches, full or modified; 26.0 inches, improved cylinder

16-bore & 20-bore: 28.0 inches, full or modified; 26.0 inches, improved cylinder

Stock: 2-piece American walnut; reverse checkering on full pistol grip and fore-end; black plastic pistol-grip cap and white line spacer

Buttplate: black plastic with white line spacer

Overall length: 30.0-inch barrel, 50.0 inches; 28.0-inch barrel, 48.0 inches; 26.0-inch barrel, 46.0 inches

Length of pull: 14.0 inches

Drop at comb: 1.5 inches

Drop at heel: 2.5 inches

Weight:

12-bore: 26.0-inch barrel, 7.25 lbs.; 28.0-inch barrel, 7.5 lbs.; 30.0-inch barrel, 7.75 lbs.

16-bore: 26.0-inch barrel, 7.125 lbs.; 28.0-inch barrel, 7.375 lbs.

20-bore: 26.0-inch barrel, 7.0 lbs.; 28.0-inch barrel, 7.25 lbs.

REMINGTON M1100 FIELD GRADE (continued)

Sights: metal bead front

Bore: 12, 16, 20, 2.75-inch case

Data: Matted-top steel receiver. Chromed bolt. Acid-etched scrollwork on receiver. Aluminum-alloy triggerbow. Plain barrel or ventilated rib.

The M1100 uses the gas metering system now popular on semiautomatic shotguns. This system is described under the Weatherby Centurion semiautomatic shotgun.

Comment: A well-designed and well-crafted medium-priced semiautomatic shotgun. Left-hand action (ejection and safety) were introduced in 1972 (12-bore and 20-bore only).

REMINGTON M1100 SKEET GUN

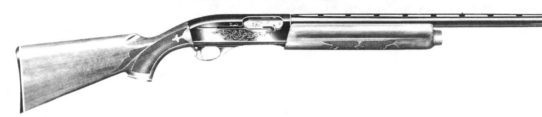

Action type: gas-operated; semiautomatic; short-stroke piston

Magazine type: tubular

Magazine capacity: 4-shot

Safety: crossbolt

Barrel length & choke: 26.0 inches, skeet or Cutts Compensator; 25.0 inches, skeet, available on 28-bore and .410 only

Stock: 2-piece American walnut; checkered full pistol grip and fore-end; M1100SB skeet has fancy-grade walnut and finer checkering; full pistol grip with plastic cap and white line spacer

Buttplate: plastic with white line spacer

Overall length: 26.0-inch barrel, 46.5 inches; 25.0-inch barrel, 45.5 inches

Length of pull: 14.0 inches

Drop at comb: 1.5 inches

Drop at heel: 2.5 inches

Weight: 12-bore, 7.5 lbs.; 20-bore, 7.25 lbs.; 28-bore, 6.75 lbs.; .410-bore, 7.25 lbs.; an adjustable weight can add up to 12.0 oz. on 28- and .410-bores

Sights: ivory bead front; mid-rib metal bead

Bore: 12, 20, 28, 2.75-inch case; .410, 2.5-inch case

Data: The M1100SB costs slightly more and has a better grade of walnut. Either version has a ventilated rib. By using the adjustable weights, which screw on at the front of the magazine tube, a shooter can use guns of identical weight, feel, and handling qualities in all skeet events, from 12-bore matches to .410.

Comment: One of the most popular—and deservedly so—skeet semiautomatics.

REMINGTON M1100 TRAP GUN

Action type: semiautomatic; gas operated; short-stroke piston

Magazine type: tubular

Magazine capacity: 4-shot

Safety: crossbolt (reversible for southpaws)

Barrel length & choke: 30.0 inches, full or modified trap

Stock: 2-piece select American walnut; impressed checkering; pistol grip with black plastic cap and white line spacer

Buttplate: ventilated red rubber recoil pad

Overall length: 50.5 inches

Length of pull: 14.375 inches

Drop at comb: 1.375 inches

Drop at Monte Carlo (if applicable): 1.375 inches

Drop at heel: standard, 1.75 inches; Monte Carlo, 1.875 inches

Weight: 8.5 lbs.

Sights: ivory bead front, metal bead mid-rib

Bore: 12, 2.75-inch case

Data: See M1100 Field Grade.

Comment: For general comments see M1100 Field Grade. This is a popular trap gun among those who prefer semiautomatics to slide or double-barrel types.

REMINGTON M1100 DEER GUN

Action type: semiautomatic; gas-operated; short-stroke piston

Magazine type: tubular

Magazine capacity: 4-shot (2-shot plus 1 in chamber when fitted with wildfowl plug)

Barrel length & choke: 22.0 inches, special slug

Safety: crossbolt

Stock: 2-piece American walnut; reverse checkered full pistol grip and fore-end; plastic pistol grip cap with white line spacer; DuPont RK-W high-gloss finish

Buttplate: plastic with white line spacer

Overall length: 42.35 inches

Length of pull: 14.0 inches

Drop at comb: 1.5 inches

Drop at heel: 2.5 inches

Weight: 12-bore, 7.0 lbs.; 20-bore, 6.75 lbs.

Sight, front: blade on ramp

Sight, rear: Rocky Mountain, crudely adjustable for windage and elevation

Bore: 12, 20, 2.75-inch case

Comment: An excellent slug gun for deer.

REMINGTON M1100 SMALL GAUGE

Action type: semiautomatic; gas-operated; short-stroke piston

Magazine type: tubular

Magazine capacity: 4-shot (2-shot plus 1 in chamber when fitted with wildfowl plug)

Safety: crossbolt

Barrel length & choke: 25.0 inches, full, modified, and improved cylinder

Stock: 2-piece American walnut; reverse checkering; pistol grip with black plastic cap and white line spacer

Buttplate: black plastic with white line spacer

Overall length: 45.5 inches

Length of pull: 14.0 inches

Drop at comb: 1.5 inches

Drop at heel: 2.5 inches

EXPLODED VIEW OF REMINGTON M1100, 20 GAUGE.

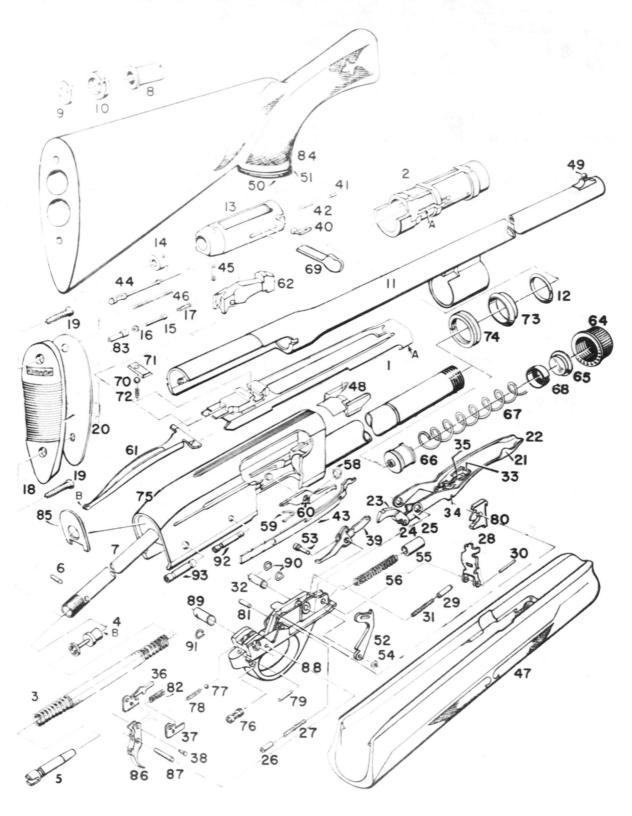

REMINGTON M1100 SMALL GAUGE (continued)

Weight: 28-bore ventilated rib, 6.5 lbs.; 28-bore plain, 6.25 lbs.; .410-bore ventilated rib, 7.0 lbs.; .410-bore plain, 6.57 lbs.

Sights: metal bead front

Bore: 28, 2.75-inch case; .410, 3.0-inch case

Data: See general information on M1100 Field Grade.

Comment: This is one of the few semiautomatics to offer a variety of chokes in 28 and .410-bores.

REMINGTON M1100 MAGNUM

Action type: semiautomatic; gas-operated; short-stroke piston

Magazine type: tubular

Magazine capacity: 4-shot (2-shot plus 1 in chamber when fitted with wildfowl plug)

Safety: crossbolt

Barrel length & choke:

12-bore: 30.0 inches, full or modified

20-bore: 28.0 inches, full or modified

Stock: 2-piece American walnut; reverse checkering; pistol grip with black plastic cap and white line spacer

Buttplate: red ventilated recoil pad with white line spacer

Overall length: 30.0-inch barrel, 50.125 inches; 28.0-inch barrel, 48.125 inches

Length of pull: 14.0 inches

Drop at comb: 1.5 inches

Drop at heel: 2.5 inches

Weight: 30.0-inch barrel, 7.75 lbs.; 28.0-inch barrel, 7.25 lbs.

Sights: metal bead front

Bore: 12, 20, 3.0-inch case

Data: See M1100 Field Grade.

Comment: No 12-bore Magnum should weigh less than 8.5 lbs. Recoil in a too-light Magnum 12 exceeds that of a 12-lb. 10-bore Magnum.

Parts List for Remington M1100, 20 Gauge

No.	Part Name	No.	Part Name	No.	Part Name
1	Action Bar Assembly	32	Carrier Pivot Tube	64	Magazine Cap
2	Action Bar Sleeve	33	Carrier Release	65	Magazine Cap Plug
3	Action Spring	34	Carrier Release Pin	66	Magazine Follower
4	Action Spring Follower	35	Carrier Release Spring	67	Magazine Spring
5	Action Spring Plug	36	Connector, Left	68	Magazine Spring Retainer
6	Action Spring Plug Pin	37	Connector, Right	69	Operating Handle
7	Action Spring Tube	38	Connector Pin	70	Operating Handle Plunger
8	Action Spring Tube Nut	39	Disconnector	71	Operating Handle Plunger Retainer
9	Action Spring Tube Nut Washer	40	Extractor	72	Operating Handle Spring
10	Action Spring Tube Nut Lock Washer	41	Extractor Plunger	73	Piston
11	Barrel Assembly	42	Extractor Spring	74	Piston Seal
12	Barrel Seal	43	Feed Latch	75	Receiver Assembly
13	Breech Bolt	44	Firing Pin	76	Safety
14	Breech Bolt Buffer	45	Firing Pin Retaining Pin	77	Safety Detent Ball
15	Breech Bolt Return Plunger	46	Firing Pin Retractor Spring	78	Safety Spring
16	Breech Bolt Return Plunger Retaining Ring	47	Fore-end Assembly	79	Safety Spring Retaining Pin
		48	Fore-end Support Assembly	80	Sear
17	Breech Bolt Return Plunger Spring	49	Front Sight—for VENT RIB use No. 18796	81	Sear Pin
18	Butt Plate			82	Sear Spring
19	Butt Plate Screw	50	Grip Cap	83	Slide Block Buffer
20	Butt Plate Spacer	51	Grip Cap Spacer	84	Sock Assembly
21	Carrier	52	Hammer	85	Stock Bearing Plate
22	Carrier Assembly	53	Hammer Pin	86	Trigger
23	Carrier Dog	54	Hammer Pin Washer	87	Trigger Pin
24	Carrier Dog Pin	55	Hammer Plunger	88	Trigger Plate, R.H. Safety
25	Carrier Dog Washer	56	Hammer Spring	89	Trigger Plate Pin Bushing
26	Carrier Dog Follower	58	Interceptor Latch Retainer	90	Trigger Plate Pin Detent Spring, Front (Need 2)
27	Carrier Dog Follower Spring	59	Interceptor Latch Spring		
28	Carrier Latch	60	Interceptor Latch	91	Trigger Plate Pin Detent Spring, Rear
29	Carrier Latch Follower	61	Link	92	Trigger Plate Pin, Front
30	Carrier Latch Pin	62	Locking Block Assembly	93	Trigger Plate Pin, Rear
31	Carrier Latch Spring				

REMINGTON M1100 LIGHTWEIGHT 20/20 MAGNUM

Action type: semiautomatic; gas operated; short-stroke piston

Magazine type: tubular

Magazine capacity: 4-shot (2-shot plus 1 in chamber when fitted with wildfowl plug)

Safety: crossbolt

Barrel length & choke: 28.0 inches, full or modified; 26.0 inches, improved cylinder

Stock: 2-piece mahogany; reverse checkering; pistol grip with black plastic cap; DuPont RK-W finish

Buttplate: 2.75-inch chamber, plastic; 3.0-inch chamber, red rubber recoil pad

Overall length: 28.0-inch barrel, 48.125 inches; 26.0-inch barrel, 46.125 inches

Length of pull: 14.0 inches

Drop at comb: 1.5625 inches

Drop at heel: 2.625 inches

Weight: 28.0-inch barrel, 6.5 lbs.; 26.0-inch barrel, 6.35 lbs.; add about 4 oz. for ventilated rib

Sight: metal bead front

Bore: 20, 2.75-inch or 3.0-inch case

Data: See M1100 Field Grade for general data. This 20-bore lightweight differs from the Field Grade 20-bore in several ways: the receiver (machined steel) is smaller and the fore-end support has been omitted; the barrel extension is shorter; the lightweight barrel is identified by the marking "Lt. Wt."; and the buttstock and fore-end are mahogany rather than the heavier walnut used on other versions.

The author, who prefers side-by-sides or over/unders, has owned a 20-bore 2.75-inch-chamber Lightweight since 1971. Despite a slight tendency to shoot low, this is a well-made, good-looking, fast-handling arm. With the 26-inch improved-cylinder barrel it is a fine little skeet or upland game gun. Recoil with skeet or light field loads is virtually unnoticeable.

SMITH & WESSON M1000

Manufacturer: Howa Machinery Co., Ltd., Japan

Importer/distributor: Smith & Wesson

Action type: semiautomatic; gas-operated; short-stroke piston

Magazine type: tubular

Magazine capacity: 3-shot (2-shot plus 1 in chamber when fitted with wildfowl plug)

Safety: crossbolt

Barrel length & choke: 30.0 inches, full; 28.0 inches, modified; 26.0 inches, improved cylinder or skeet

Stock: 2-piece American walnut; checkering (20 lines per inch); pistol grip with black plastic cap and white line spacer; silver-colored S&W monogram inlaid in pistol-grip cap; high-gloss finish

Buttplate: black plastic with white line spacer

Overall length: 30.0-inch barrel, 50.5625 inches; 28.0-inch barrel, 48.5625 inches; 26.0-inch barrel, 46.5625 inches

Length of pull: 14.0 inches

Drop at comb: 1.5625 inches

Drop at heel: 2.5 inches

Weight: 26.0-inch barrel, 6.625 lbs.; 28.0-inch barrel, 6.75 lbs.; 30.0-inch barrel, 6.875 lbs.

Sights: metal bead front and mid-rib

Bore: 12, 2.75-inch case

Data: This shotgun uses the short-stroke floating-piston system of the M14 series rifle. Many semiautomatics of the past and some today have problems—or manual adjustment is required—in compensating for the varying pressures created by widely different loads, say between a light field load and a heavy Magnum load. The M1000 has a pressure-compensator valve unit which stabilizes gas-port pressure variations. The compensating components are in the fore section of the gas cylinder. The valve unit is a piece of resilient plastic between two metal components. Expanding gas pressure compresses the plastic piece as required to work the action properly with a given load.

The hollow piston has one part which aligns with two barrel ports. Powder gas, immediately upon entering the piston, forces the piston port into nonalignment with the barrel gas ports. No gas can now enter the piston. The gas inside the piston expands to drive the piston and action bar unit and breechblock rearward. After about 0.375 inch of travel, the breechbolt face cams downward, its lock thus disengaging the barrel extension.

Exhausted gas is forced upward through two fore-end top slots. While the piston and connector ring's rearward movement is halted after 1.85 inches of travel, the unlocked breechbolt and action bar unit continue their rearward track until the fired case has been extracted and ejected from the arm. Meanwhile the rearward-traveling breechbolt has compressed the action spring and cocked the hammer. The bottom of the breechbolt, in moving forward, pushes a cartridge from the top of the magazine well into the chamber.

Aluminum-alloy receiver and triggerbow are black anodized. Trigger, breechbolt unit, and carrier are bright chrome-plated. Barrel is a high-luster blue with a ventilated rib.

Comment: This fast-handling, well-designed firearm unfortunately tends to shoot somewhat low—about 5 inches—at 40 yards. This might have been a fault only in the shotgun the author tested, since performance varies slightly from gun to gun in mass-produced arms. However, another M1000 tested by the NRA displayed a similar tendency. Two barrels tested by the author indicated a somewhat more open pattern than the indicated choke standard. Patterns with both barrels were somewhat irregular.

Recoil is rather severe with Magnum loads. A shotgun this light is primarily a fast-handling upland game gun, to be used with field loads. Extra barrels are available and are readily interchangeable.

WEATHERBY CENTURION SEMIAUTOMATIC SHOTGUN

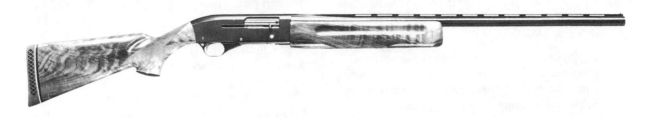

Manufacturer: Howa Machinery Co., Japan

Importer/distributor: Weatherby, Inc.

Action type: semiautomatic; gas-operated

Magazine type: tubular

Magazine capacity: 3-shot (2-shot plus 1 in chamber when fitted with waterfowl plug)

Safety: crossbolt

Barrel length & choke: 30.0 inches, full; 28.0 inches, full or modified; 26.0 inches, modified, improved cylinder, or skeet

Stock: 2-piece American walnut; hand checkering (20 lines per inch); pistol grip with rosewood cap and white line spacer; white plastic diamond inlay in cap; fluted fore-end; high-gloss finish

Buttplate: red rubber recoil pad with white line spacer

Overall length: 30.0-inch barrel, 50.25 inches; 28.0-inch barrel, 48.25 inches; 26.0-inch barrel, 46.25 inches

Length of pull: 14.25 inches

Drop at comb: 1.5625 inches

Drop at heel: 2.5625 inches

Weight: 30.0-inch barrel, 7.875 lbs.; 28.0-inch barrel, 7.75 lbs.; 26.0-inch barrel, 7.5 lbs.

Sights: metal bead front

Bore: 12, 2.75-inch case

Data: The Centurion, designed by Fred Jennie of Weatherby, operates via a floating, hollow, short-stroke piston that is guided by the magazine forward tubular extension. Immediately after ignition, expanding gas enters the cylinder through two ports. The gas pushes rearward both piston and slide assembly. After moving about 0.3125 inch the slide carrier cams the breechbolt's locking block down, thus disengaging the barrel extension. The piston halts after 0.5625 inch of travel.

Slide unit and unlocked breechbolt continue their rearward travel until the empty case is extracted from the chamber and ejected.

This is the only contemporary semiautomatic shotgun known to the author in which the front end of the magazine tube doesn't extend beyond the fore-end. This enhances the arm's handsome appearance. The barrel has a ventilated rib and, of course, the typical Weatherby high-gloss bluing.

Cross-shaped slots on the magazine cap have two functions: (1) Most powder gas, after entering the piston tube, escapes forward through these slots and thus away from the shooter. Only a small amount escapes through two fore-end grooves. This is an excellent feature. (2) A pin insert in the slots unscrews the magazine cap.

The receiver and trigger housing are black anodized aluminum alloy. Piston is stainless steel. Trigger has a gold-color finish. Other components are steel.

Comment: This is a well-designed arm. Both finish and workmanship are top-drawer. It would make a handsome and reliable addition to any shooting man's battery.

The author fired 350 rounds without malfunction. The firing included 2.75-inch Magnums, express loads, field loads, trap loads, skeet loads, and reloads. The 26.0-inch improved-cylinder barrel gave 55 percent patterns in a 30-inch circle at 40 yards. This conforms to standards. Pattern distribution was quite uniform.

This is one of the better semiautomatic arms that the author has fired during the past 40 years.

WINCHESTER M1400 MARK II—WINCHOKE

Action type: semiautomatic; gas-operated

Magazine type: tubular

Magazine capacity: 2-shot plus 1 in chamber

Barrel length & choke: 28.0 inches, choke supplied by three screw-in inserts (full, modified, and improved cylinder); these chokes are flush with muzzle

Safety: crossbolt

Stock: 2-piece American walnut; reverse checkering; full uncapped pistol grip and fore-end

Buttplate: ventilated rubber recoil pad

Overall length: 45.625 inches

Length of pull: 14.0 inches

Drop at comb: plain barrel, 1.375 inches; ventilated rib, 1.5 inches

Drop at heel: plain barrel, 2.375 inches; ventilated rib, 2.5 inches

Weight: 12-bore, 7.0 lbs.; 20-bore, 6.5 lbs.; add 4.0 oz. for ventilated rib

Sights: metal bead front

Bore: 12, 20, 2.75-inch case

Data: This was originally introduced as the M1400 but with minor modifications is now the M1400 Mark II and is only available with Winchoke. The introduction of Winchoke eliminated the need for separate skeet and trap models. There was also a slug model.

Many parts of the M1200 slide-action shotgun including bolts are interchangeable with the semiautomatic M1400. This reduces manufacturing operations and cuts production costs. The receiver is light alloy. The gun can be bought with a plain barrel or a ventilated rib.

Comment: This is a good buy for the economy-minded shooter who cannot afford a double-barrel gun or several barrels for a semiautomatic or slide-action shotgun. It means that one gun can serve for waterfowling and upland game.

The author wonders if a light alloy receiver can withstand the batterings of tens of thousands of trap rounds.

WINCHESTER SUPER-X MODEL 1

Action type: semiautomatic; gas-operated

Magazine type: tubular

Magazine capacity: 5-shot (2-shot plus 1 in chamber when fitted with wildfowl plug)

Safety: crossbolt

WINCHESTER SUPER-X MODEL 1 (continued)

Barrel length & choke: 30.0 inches, full; 28.0 inches, modified; 26.0 inches, improved cylinder

Stock: 2-piece American walnut with machine-cut checkering on full pistol grip and fore-end

Buttplate: ventilated rubber recoil pad

Overall length: 30.0-inch barrel, 50.0 inches; 28.0-inch barrel, 48.0 inches; 26.0-inch barrel, 46.0 inches

Length of pull: 14.0 inches

Drop at comb: 1.5 inches

Drop at heel: 2.5 inches

Weight: 30.0-inch barrel, 7.5 lbs.; 28.0-inch barrel, 7.44 lbs.; 26.0-inch barrel, 7.38 lbs.; add 4.0 oz. for ventilated rib

Sights: metal bead front and mid-rib

Bore: 12, 2.75-inch case

Data: Chrome molybdenum receiver, barrel and barrel extensions, and all other metal components. The short stroke—a machined steel rod rather than the usual stamped action bar—requires no adjustment for various-powered loads. The carrier system is machined steel. There's a choice of plain barrel or ventilated rib.

Comment: This is probably the best semiautomatic shotgun that Winchester has produced. It is one of the best-designed and best-crafted semiautomatic arms on the market. In view of the current growing popularity of the 20-bore, particularly in the 3.0-inch Magnum version, it is to be hoped that this excellent shotgun will soon be made in that bore.

WINCHESTER SUPER-X MODEL 1 SKEET GUN

Action type: semiautomatic; gas-operated

Magazine type: tubular

Magazine capacity: 4-shot plus 1 in chamber

Safety: crossbolt

Barrel length & choke: 26.0 inches, skeet

Stock: 2-piece American walnut; machine checkered full pistol grip and fore-end

Buttplate: black rubber recoil pad with white line spacer

Overall length: 46.25 inches

Length of pull: 14.25 inches

Drop at comb: 1.5 inches

Drop at heel: 2.0 inches

Weight: 7.75 lbs.

Sights: metal bead front and mid-rib

Bore: 12, 2.75-inch case

Data: See Super-X Model 1 for basic action data. This skeet version comes only with a ventilated rib.

Comment: A first-rate skeet gun for those who prefer semiautomatics.

WINCHESTER SUPER-X MODEL 1 SLUG GUN

Action type: semiautomatic; gas-operated

Magazine type: tubular

Magazine capacity: 4-shot plus 1 in chamber

Barrel length & choke: 22.0 inches, special slug

Safety: crossbolt

Stock: 2-piece American walnut; machine-checkered full pistol grip and fore-end

Buttplate: ventilated rubber recoil pad

Overall length: 42.0 inches

Length of pull: 14.375 inches

Drop at comb: 1.625 inches

Drop at heel: 2.625 inches

Weight: 7.0 lbs.

Sights: Rocky Mountain rear, crudely adjustable for elevation; bead front

Bore: 12, 2.75-inch case

Comment: This is as good a semiautomatic slug gun as one can find. It should be fitted with quick-detachable sling swivels but this minor matter can readily be corrected.

WINCHESTER SUPER-X MODEL 1 TRAP MODEL

Action type: semiautomatic; gas-operated

Magazine type: tubular

Magazine capacity: 4-shot plus 1 in chamber (2-shot plus 1 in chamber when fitted with wildfowl plug)

Safety: crossbolt

Barrel length & choke: 30.0 inches, modified or full

Stock: 2-piece American walnut; machine-checkered full pistol grip and fore-end; straight or Monte Carlo comb

Buttplate: ventilated rubber recoil pad with white line spacer

Overall length: 50.375 inches

Length of pull: 14.375 inches

Drop at comb: 1.375 inches

Drop at Monte Carlo (if applicable): 1.375 inches

Drop at heel: standard, 1.875 inches; Monte Carlo, 2.125 inches

Weight: 8.25 lbs.

Sights: metal bead front and mid-rib

Bore: 12, 2.75-inch case

Data: See Super-X Model 1 for basic action data. The trap version comes only with ventilated rib.

Comment: This shotgun, despite its youth, is doing very well under the rugged grind of tournament trap competition.

CHAPTER 24

BOLT-ACTION SHOTGUNS

The bolt-action magazine shotgun is deservedly the least popular kind of repeater. In a slug-barrel version it's an acceptable arm for deer hunting where the law requires that shotguns be used. Since it's inexpensive and rugged, it vies with the single-shot models as a "barn gun" for use on pest species around a farm, though for reasons given below the author sees no advantage in the bolt-action magazine scattergun over the break-top single-shot design. It would serve all right as a camp gun — again because of its low cost and ruggedness — except that it's big and cumbersome in most versions. Here the instant-takedown design of the break-top single-shot is a big advantage. There are a few wildfowlers (particularly those brought up on long-barreled, low-cost guns for pass-shooting at geese) who feel most comfortable with a bolt-action "Long Tom" but in the author's opinion the best excuse these people have is that they're set in their ways. Most shotgunners agree that the only shooter who needs this action is the shooter who feels he must have a repeater and can't afford any other kind.

It does cost only one-half to one-third as much as a field-grade slide-action. But the shooter would be better served with the ancient "corn-sheller" M97 Winchester — one of our most popular and reliable shotguns — than with a new bolt-action shotgun.

The bolt action is the slowest of all manually operated actions. A man with a single-barrel single-shot shotgun carrying one spare cartridge between the fingers of his left hand can get off two shots faster than a bolt-action man.

Bolt-action shotguns in the 3.0-inch 12-bore chambering should weigh 1 to 2 pounds more than any current model.

The sheer ugliness of this arm should put most people off, but thousands of shotgunners are perfectly content with their bolt-action shotguns — and contentment is a rare virtue these days.

MARLIN M55 GOOSE GUN

Action type: turnbolt

Magazine type: detachable straight-line box

Magazine capacity: 2-shot

Safety: sliding thumb

Barrel length & choke: 36.0 inches, full

Stock: 1-piece American walnut with semi-pistol grip; uncheckered; sling swivels and leather carrying strap

Buttplate: ventilated black recoil pad with white line spacer

Overall length: 57.0 inches

Length of pull: 14.25 inches

Drop at comb: 1.5 inches

Drop at heel: 2.5 inches

Weight: 7.25 lbs.

Sights: bead front

Bore: 12, 3.0-inch case

Data: M55 has a gold-plated trigger. A removable adaptor in the detachable magazine permits the use of standard or "short magnum" loads when 3.0-inch shells aren't necessary.

Comment: Irrespective of the advantages or disadvantages of a bolt-action shotgun, there is no reason for the long, ungainly 36-inch barrel. Its sole purpose is to lure buyers. The difference in velocity between 36-inch barrel and 30-inch barrel is barely perceptible. The shorter barrel will get more waterfowl because it is easier to handle and swing.

Such guns are a nuisance in a duck blind, car, or boat. They rarely fit into an upright gun cabinet. This arm is at least 1 lb. too light.

EXPLODED VIEW OF MOSSBERG MODELS 395K AND 395S

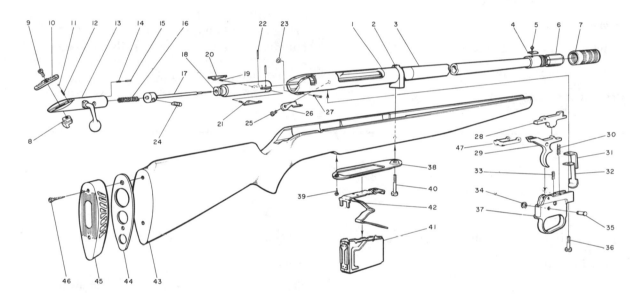

No.	Part Name	No.	Part Name	No.	Part Name
1	Receiver	16	Striker Spring	31	Angle Bar
2	Recoil Plate, Model 395K	17	Firing Pin	32	Magazine Latch
	Recoil Plate, Model 395S	18	Bolt Head	33	Trigger Spring
3	Barrel	19	Extractor Spring	34	Trigger Retaining Ring
4	Choke Index Plate,	20	Left Extractor	35	Trigger Pin
	Model 395K	21	Right Extractor	36	Trigger Housing Screw
5	Front Sight, Model 395K	22	Extractor Pin	37	Trigger Housing Complete
6	Choke Tube	23	Sear & Trigger Housing	38	Stock Plate
7	Choke Adjusting Sleeve		Retaining Ring	39	Stock Plate Screw & Nut
8	Safety Lock	24	Sear Pin	40	Take Down Screw
9	Safety Button Screw	25	Ejector Screw	41	Magazine
10	Safety Button w/6297 Plate	26	Ejector	42	Magazine Spring Assembly
11	Safety Click Ball	27	Sear & Trigger Housing	43	Stock complete
12	Safety Click Ball Spring		Retaining Pin	44	Recoil Pad Spacer
13	Bolt complete	28	Sear	45	Recoil Pad
	Bolt & Lever	29	Trigger	46	Recoil Pad Screw
14	Bolt Index Plunger Spring	30	Sear Spring	47	Safety Adapter
15	Bolt Index Plunger				

MARLIN M55S BOLT-ACTION SLUG GUN

Action type: turnbolt

Magazine type: detachable straight-line box

Magazine capacity: 2-shot

Safety: sliding thumb

Barrel length & choke: 24.0 inches, slug

Stock: 1-piece American walnut with uncapped semi-pistol grip; uncheckered; sling swivels with leather carrying strap; Mar-Shield finish

Buttplate: ventilated rubber recoil pad with white plastic spacer

Overall length: 45.0 inches

Length of pull: 14.25 inches

Drop at comb: 1.5 inches

Drop at heel: 2.5 inches

Weight: 7.5 lbs.

Sight, rear: Rocky Mountain, crudely adjustable for elevation

Sight, front: bead on ramp with Wide-Scan hood

Scope adaptability: receiver drilled and tapped for standard bases

Bore: 12, 3.0-inch case

Data: See M55 Goose Gun for basic action data.

Comment: This shotgun is at least 1.5 lbs. too light for long Magnum loads. The standard minimum weight for a 3.0-inch 12-bore Magnum is 8.5 lbs. The 24.0-inch barrel on this deer gun would take more geese than the 36.0-inch-barrel Goose Gun because it is much easier to handle.

MOSSBERG M395S SLUGSTER

Action type: turnbolt

Magazine type: detachable straight-line box

Magazine capacity: 3-shot

Safety: sliding thumb

Barrel length & choke: 24.0 inches, slug

Stock: 1-piece walnut-stained hardwood with uncapped semi-pistol grip; Monte Carlo comb; uncheckered; sling supplied

Buttplate: ventilated rubber recoil pad with white line spacer

Overall length: 45.0 inches

Length of pull: 14.0 inches

Drop at comb: 1.5 inches

Drop at Monte Carlo: 2.0 inches

Drop at heel: 2.5 inches

Weight: 6.75 lbs.

Sight, rear: folding leaf, crudely adjustable for elevation

Sight, front: partridge type on ramp

Scope adaptability: receiver can be drilled and tapped for scope mounts

Bore: 12, 3.0-inch case

Data: Plastic triggerbow.

Comment: An inexpensive shotgun design for slug use on deer.

MOSSBERG K SERIES C-LECT-CHOKE BOLT ACTION SHOTGUNS

Action type: turnbolt

Magazine type: detachable straight-line box (.410-bore is nondetachable)

Magazine capacity: 3-shot

Barrel length & choke: 28.0 inches (12-bore); 26.0 inches (20-bore); 25.0 inches (.410-bore); C-LECT-CHOKE (variable choke; instant selection is secured by twisting choke dial to full, modified, or improved cylinder)

Safety: sliding thumb

Stock: 1-piece walnut-stained uncheckered hardwood with uncapped semi-pistol grip; Monte Carlo comb

Buttplate: ventilated rubber recoil pad with white line spacer

Overall length: 28.0-inch barrel, 47.5 inches; 26.0-inch barrel, 45.5 inches; 25.0-inch barrel, 44.5 inches

Length of pull: 14.0 inches

Drop at comb: 1.5 inches

Drop at Monte Carlo: 2.0 inches

Drop at heel: 2.5 inches

Weight: 12-bore, 6.75 lbs.; 20-bore, 6.25 lbs.; .410-bore, 5.5 lbs.

Sights: bead on C-LECT-CHOKE

Bore: 12, 20, .410, 3.0-inch case

Comment: Most bolt-action and single-shot shotguns have full choke, the least useful of all chokes, but these shotguns have the great advantage of selective choke.

SAVAGE STEVENS M58 BOLT-ACTION SHOTGUN

Action type: turnbolt

Magazine type: detachable straight-line box

Magazine capacity: 3-shot

Safety: sliding thumb

Barrel length & choke: 24.0 inches, full

Stock: 1-piece walnut-stained hardwood; uncapped semi-pistol grip; reverse checkering on pistol grip

Buttplate: hard rubber

Overall length: 43.0 inches

Length of pull: 14.0 inches

Drop at comb: 1.5 inches

Drop at heel: 2.5 inches

Weight: 5.5 lbs.

Sights: bead

Bore: .410, 3.0-inch case

Data: Steel receiver and twin extractors.

Comment: An inexpensive magazine shotgun in a bore that ought to be used solely by experts, none of whom would use a bolt-action shotgun. Some people choose a .410 as a first gun for their youngsters, but this is a mistake. Even a youngster is not apt to be bothered by the recoil of a 20-bore gun with a properly proportioned stock, a recoil pad, sufficient weight, and reasonably light loads. A beginner often gets discouraged firing the pencil-thin .410 loads because it's so hard to hit with them that misses mount up unnecessarily. Moreover, in the author's opinion a beginning shotgunner ought to have the benefit of a shotgun that handles and looks like the guns he will use later—not a bolt-action model.

CHAPTER 25

COMBINATION RIFLE/SHOTGUNS

The full potential of the combination rifle/shotgun has never been realized by North American hunters. The combination rifle/shotgun reaches maximum use on the Continent, notably in Germany. The basic types are:

1. *One rifle barrel (rim- or centerfire)/one smoothbore barrel.* This is the only type regularly manufactured in the United States. Typical combinations: .22 Long Rifle/.410-bore shot cartridge; .222 Rem./20-bore Magnum shot cartridge; .222 Rem./12-bore shot cartridge. Savage Arms is the only regular manufacturer of this type of arm.

Savage now imports from Finland two combination arms: .308 Win./12-bore and .222 Rem./12-bore.

2. *Cape rifle/shotgun.* The above rifle/shotgun combination arms are the over/under type. The Cape rifle/shotgun combination—no longer made except possibly on special order—has side-by-side barrels. One barrel is usually chambered for a military (British) rifle cartridge and the other for a 16-bore (a few 12-bores were made).

The true Cape gun was rarely used by sportsmen on African safari or in India. These men used double rifles and shotguns.

The Cape, as its name indicates, found great favor among thrifty Boer settlers in the vast country north of Cape Town. They could not afford expensive British doubles and shotguns, so the Cape provided them with an arm for game ranging from the tiny dik-dik to the elephant, as well as birds for the pot. Impecunious British junior officers liked their versatility and low price.

Early Cape guns used the under lever rather than the more popular top lever of later years. All Cape guns observed or fired by the author had external hammers. The Cape's heyday ranged from the 1870s through 1925. Second-hand Capes were in demand to about World War II. Today, they are still useful in those calibers for which cartridges are available, but are be-coming collector's items. The author owned two Capes: a Westley-Richards .577–.450 Martini-Henry/12-bore and a Jeffrey .303/16-bore. Early rifles designed for black powder should be used only with black-powder cartridges.

3. *Two smoothbore barrels and one rifle barrel (usually centerfire).* The Germans designate this three-barrel combination as a *Drilling*. Shot-cartridge barrels are usually 16-bore. German *Drillings* are usually chambered for a rimmed cartridge of German/Austrian origin, though the author once owned a *Drilling* for the .25–35 Win. The .30–30 Win. was also a popular *Drilling* cartridge, as was—and still is—the .22 Hornet. The 7×57 Mauser (7mm) with a rim was a popular cartridge. The .243 Win. and .30–06 Springfield are currently popular among those who can afford the stiff price tag (well over $1000).

4. *Two rifle barrels (usually one centerfire and one rimfire) and two shot cartridge barrels.* The Germans call this four-barrel combination a *Vierling*.

5. *Two separate interchangeable barrels, one rifle and one shot cartridge barrel.* Either barrel can be used with the break-top frame. A typical combination is a .30–30 Win./12-bore barrel.

American rifle/shotguns

Savage once made a takedown version of the M99 that was optionally available with a .410-bore (2.5-inch chamber).

Before World War II, Marble Arms, Gladstone, Mich., manufactured the "Game Getter." This was an over/under long-barreled pistol. One barrel was chambered for the .22 Long Rifle. The other barrel accepted a .410 (2.5-inch chamber) shot cartridge. This barrel also accepted the .44–40 Win. rifle/handgun cartridge. The .44–40 Win. barrel chambered the regular .44–40 cartridge or a special "Marble's Game Getter" cartridge that was a .410 round ball (slug) loaded into the .44–40 case. This handy—or cumbersome—affair was fitted with a detachable skeleton stock. Manufacture ceased when the arm became illegal under the 1934 Federal Firearms Act (detachable stocks were outlawed). It was made with 12-, 15-, and 18-inch barrels.

The author used a Game Getter on his trapline for several years. He discarded it in favor of a .22 Colt Officer's Model sixgun.

The various Savage M24 Series arms with a .22 Long Rifle or .22 W.R.M. barrel in combination with a shot cartridge barrel are handy camp guns, good for rabbits, squirrel, or grouse. A Weaver 1X or even a 2.5X scope makes the arm more useful.

In states like Florida where the turkey, quail, and deer seasons commence about the same time, a shotshell barrel and rifle barrel are handy. The author used a *Drilling* chambered for the 16-bore shot cartridge and .22 Hornet. He loaded one barrel with No. 7½ shot for birds (other than turkey) and the second barrel with a rifle slug for deer. The .22 Hornet was handy to have for hunting turkey and small game. It was an excellent and practical combination.

COLT SAUER DRILLING

Manufacturer: J. P. Sauer & Sohn, West Germany

Importer/distributor: Colt Industries

Action type: break-top; top lever opening; two shotgun/one rifle; Greener type

Barrel selector: tang slide

Locking system: underbolt/Greener crossbolt

Safety: side tang

Barrel length & choke: 24.0 inches, modified & full

Stock: 2-piece European walnut; hand checkering (16 lines per inch); oil finish; pistol grip with plastic cap

Buttplate: recoil pad

Overall length: 41.75 inches

Length of pull: 14.25 inches (from front trigger)

Drop at comb: 1.5 inches

Drop at heel: 2.0 inches

Takedown length: 24.0 inches

Weight: 8.0 lbs.

Trigger system: two triggers (rifle trigger is set type)

Sight, rear: folding leaf, crudely adjustable for elevation

Sight, front: brass bead

Scope adaptability: no provision, but rib can be drilled and tapped for scope mount

Caliber/bore: .30–06/12-bore, 2.75-inch case; .243 Win./12-bore, 2.75-inch case

Comment: This is one of the finest contemporary *Drillings*. As of 1975 it was priced in the vicinity of $1500, so not too many will be sold.

The author has two criticisms: the arm should be available in a wider array of calibers and bores, and a man who appreciates such a firearm and who has the money to purchase one will probably want much finer checkering than the coarse 16-lines-per-inch type.

GARCIA BRONCO COMBINATION .22/.410

Manufacturer: Rossi, Brazil

Importer/distributor: Garcia Corp.

Action type: single shot, swing-out; under-lever release

Barrel selector: button on frame

Barrel length & choke: 18.5 inches, full

Safety: crossbolt

Stock: skeleton type; rust resistant, crackle finish

Overall length: 32 inches

Length of pull: 13.875 inches

Drop at comb: 1.75 inches

Drop at heel: 3 inches

Weight: 3.5 lbs.

Sight, rear: leaf on receiver bridge

Sight, front: bead

Scope adaptability: no provision

Caliber/bore: .22 rimfire/.410 bore

Data: This combination firearm features simple, quick takedown for pack or camp use.

Comment: An inexpensive smoothbore with a rifle that will handle the Short, Long, or Long Rifle cartridge.

ITHACA TURKEY GUN 12 GAUGE/.222

Manufacturer: Tikka, Finland

Importer/distributor: Ithaca Gun Co.

Action type: break-top; top lever opening

Barrel selector: button on frame

Safety: exposed hammer with half-cock safe position

Barrel length & choke: 24.5 inches, full

Stock: 2-piece European walnut; skip-line hand checkering; full pistol grip and fore-end; forward-sloping Monte Carlo comb; detachable sling swivels

Overall length: 45 inches

Length of pull: 14 inches

Drop at front of Monte Carlo: 1.875 inches

Drop at rear of Monte Carlo: 1.625 inches

Drop at heel: 2.25 inches

Weight: 7.5 lbs.

Sight, rear: folding leaf

Sight, front: bead on ramp

Scope adaptability: Receiver grooved for scope mount

Caliber/bore: .222/12 bore

Data: Supplied with 12-gauge full choke and .222 Rem. rifle barrel.

Comment: An excellent firearm for turkey and fox hunting. It would also serve well for a number of small-game and varmint species.

CUT-AWAY DRAWING OF THE ITHACA TURKEY GUN 12 GAUGE/.222 CALIBER

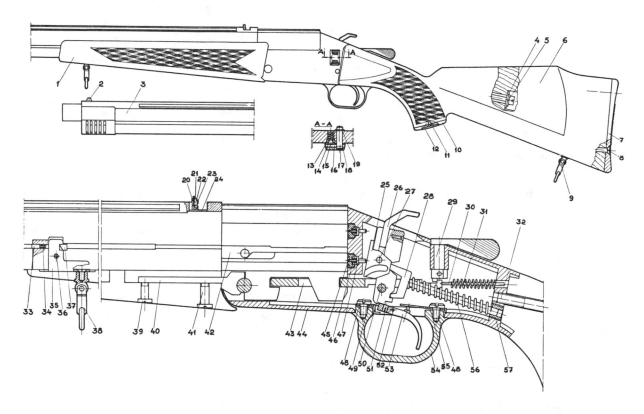

No.	Part Name	No.	Part Name	No.	Part Name
1	Wood, forend (screw mounted)	17	Pin, selector	39	Screw, forend front
1A	Wood, forend (nylon clip mounted)	18	Selector	40	Iron, forend
		19	Lockring	41	Screw, forend rear
2	Sight, front	20	Sight, rear	42	Extractor (12ga./.222 cal.)
3	Barrel set (see service page)	21	Blade, sight elevation	42A	Extractor (for guns with clip mounted forends)
4	Washer, stock bolt lock	22	Pin, sight blade		
5	Washer, stock bolt plain	23	Screw, sight blade	43	Bolt, action locking
6	Stock assembly (right hand)	24	Spring, rear sight	44	Frame (see service page)
6A	Stock assembly (left hand)	25	Plate, selector	45	Retainer, firing pin
6B	Stock assembly (right hand) for guns with clip mounted forends	26	Hammer	46	Spring, firing pin
		27	Pin, selector plate	47	Pin, firing
		28	Guide, mainspring	48	Screw, trigger guard
7	Plate, butt	29	Lever, top	49	Stop, trigger
8	Screw, butt plate	30	Guide, action bolt spring	50	Pin, hammer
9	Swivel, rear	31	Spring, action bolt	51	Screw, trigger adjusting
10	Cap, pistol grip	32	Bolt, stock	52	Pin, trigger
11	Screw, pistol grip cap	33	Guide, forend lock spring	53	Trigger
12	Plate, pistol grip cap screw	34	Spring, forend locking	54	Guard, trigger
13	Housing, restriction ball	35	Holder, forend	55	Spring, trigger
14	Spring, restriction ball	36	Screw, forend holder	56	Mainspring
15	Ball, restriction	37	Lock, forend	57	Screw, mainspring adjusting
16	Pin, locking	38	Swivel, front		

SAVAGE 24-C CAMPERS' MODEL

Action type: break-top; top lever opening; over/under rifle-shotgun; exposed hammer

Barrel selector: on hammer spur

Safety: rebounding hammer

Barrel length & choke: 20.0 inches, cylinder

Stock: 2-piece walnut-stained hardwood; straight grip; no checkering; finger groove on fore-end

Overall length: 36.0 inches

Length of pull: 13.5 inches

Drop at comb: 1.75 inches

Drop at heel: 2.75 inches

Weight: 5.75 lbs.

Sight, rear: crudely adjustable for elevation

Sight, front: ramp

Scope adaptability: grooved for tip-off mount

Caliber/bore: .22 Long Rifle/20-bore, 3.0-inch case

Data: This lightweight version in the M24 Series has a color-case-hardened frame and blued barrel, and it comes with a canvas carrying case.

Comment: A useful combination for youngsters or campers. Handy camp-meat gun on a big-game expedition.

SAVAGE M24-D (DELUXE) RIFLE/SHOTGUN

Action type: break-top; top lever opening; over/under rifle-shotgun; exposed hammer

Barrel selector: on hammer spur

Safety: rebounding hammer

Barrel length & choke: 24.0 inches, full

Stock: 2-piece American walnut; impressed checkering on pistol grip and fore-end; black plastic pistol grip cap with white line spacer

Buttplate: black plastic with white line spacer

Overall length: 40.0 inches

Length of pull: 14.0 inches

Drop at comb: 2.0 inches

Drop at Monte Carlo: 1.75 inches

Drop at heel: 2.625 inches

Weight: 6.75-7.5 lbs.

Sight, rear: Rocky Mountain, crudely adjustable for elevation

Sight, front: ramp

Scope adaptability: grooved for tip-off mount

Caliber/bore: .22 Long Rifle/.410-bore, 3.0-inch

case; .22 Long Rifle/20-bore, 3.0-inch case; .22 Magnum/20-bore 3.0-inch case

Data: Early M24 combinations had the barrel selector on the frame. Locating it on the hammer spur facilitates fast switching.

Comment: The .410-bore chambering should be ignored. The 20-bore in combination with the .22 Long Rifle (and scope) is good small game/bird combination.

SAVAGE M24 FIELD GRADE (F.G.) RIFLE/SHOTGUN

Action type: break-top; top lever opening; over/under rifle-shotgun; exposed hammer

Barrel selector: on hammer spur

Safety: rebounding hammer

Barrel length & choke: 24.0 inches, full

Stock: 2-piece walnut-stained hardwood; no checkering; uncapped semi-pistol grip

Overall length: 40.0 inches

Length of pull: 14.0 inches

Drop at comb: 1.75 inches

Drop at heel: 2.75 inches

Takedown length: 24.0 inches

Weight: 7.5 lbs.

Sight, rear: Rocky Mountain, crudely adjustable for elevation

Sight, front: ramp

Scope adaptability: grooved for tip-off mount

Caliber/bore: .22 Long Rifle/.410-bore, 3.0-inch case; .22 Long Rifle/20-bore, 3.0-inch case; .22 W.R.M./20-bore, 3.0-inch case

Comment: Similar to M24-D except stained hardwood stock is substituted for walnut stock; also without checkering and pistol-grip cap of slightly more expensive M24-D.

Early M24 series models did not have split barrel. The M24 Field Grade was given split barrels in 1972.

SAVAGE M24-V RIFLE/SHOTGUN

Action type: break-top; over/under rifle-shotgun; external hammer

Barrel selector: on hammer spur

Safety: half-cock; rebounding hammer

Barrel length & choke: 24.0 inches, full

Stock: 2-piece American walnut; impressed checkering; Monte Carlo comb; pistol grip with plastic cap and white line spacer

Buttplate: black plastic with white line spacer

Overall length: 40.0 inches

Length of pull: 14.0 inches

Drop at comb: 2.0 inches

Drop at Monte Carlo: 1.75 inches

Drop at heel: 2.625 inches

Takedown length: 24.0 inches

SAVAGE M24-V RIFLE/SHOTGUN (continued)

Weight: .222 Rem./20-bore, 6.75 lbs.; .30–30 Win./20-bore, 7.5 lbs.

Sight, rear: folding leaf, adjustable for elevation

Sight, front: ramp

Scope adaptability: drilled and tapped for scope bases

Caliber/bore: .30–30 Win./20-bore, 3.0-inch case; .222 Rem./20-bore, 3.0-inch case

Comment: This is an excellent low-priced combination. It is handy for the turkey and bird hunter in the .222 Rem./20-bore combination and for the deer and bird hunter in the .30–30 Win./20-bore combination.

SAVAGE M2400 RIFLE/SHOTGUN

Manufacturer: Valmet, Finland

Importer/distributor: Savage Arms

Action type: break-top; top lever opening; over/under rifle-shotgun; internal hammer

Barrel selector: button on trigger

Locking system: monobloc locking rails engaged by lock shield that slides forward when arm is closed

Safety: sliding tang

Barrel length & choke: 23.5 inches, improved modified

Stock: 2-piece walnut; machine checkering; uncapped pistol grip; Monte Carlo comb; finger-grooved fore-end

Buttplate: black recoil pad with white line spacer

Overall length: 40.5 inches

Length of pull: 14.0 inches

Drop at comb: 1.5 inches

Drop at Monte Carlo: 1.75 inches

Drop at heel: 2.5 inches

Takedown length: 23.5 inches

Weight: 7.5 lbs.

Sight, rear: folding leaf, crudely adjustable for elevation

Sight, front: blade

Caliber/bore: .308 Win. (7.62mm NATO)/12-bore, 2.75-inch case; .222 Rem./12-bore, 2.75-inch case

Data: Blued finish. Design elements similar to Savage M330 over/under shotgun; barrel selector on trigger. Top barrel is smoothbore; bottom barrel is rifled.

Comment: This is a very well-designed and well-crafted over/under shotgun/rifle combination. Some shooters may dislike the wide-open space between upper and lower barrel.

EXPLODED VIEW OF SAVAGE MODELS 24, 24C, 24D

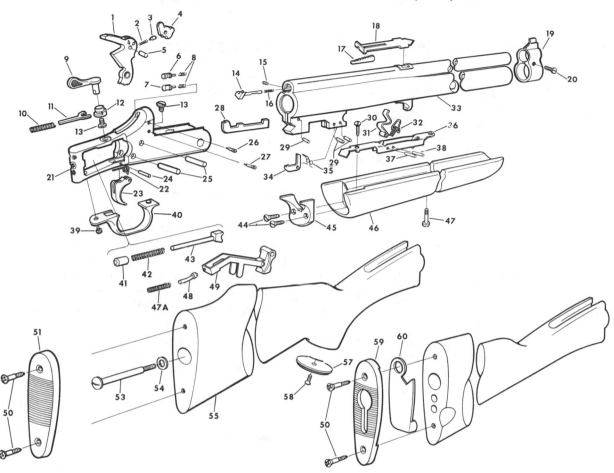

No.	Part Name	No.	Part Name	No.	Part Name
1	Hammer Assembly	23	Trigger	41	Mainspring Plunger Seat Trigger Guard
2	Selector Plunger Spring	24	Trigger Pin	42	Mainspring
3	Selector Plunger	25	Hammer, Locking Bolt Pin	43	Mainspring Plunger Assembly
4	Selector	26	Firing Pin Screw (Shotgun)	44	Fore-end Iron Head Screw
5	Selector Pin	27	Firing Pin Screw (Rifle)	45	Fore-end Pivot Plate
6	Firing Pin (Rifle)	28	Extractor	46	Fore-end Wood
7	Firing Pin (Shotgun)	29	Extractor Lever, Lever Spring and Stop Pin	47	Fore-end Screw
8	Firing Pin Spring	30	Fore-end Spring Housing Screw	47A	Locking Bolt Spring
9	Top Snap	31	Fore-end Spring	48	Locking Bolt Plunger
10	Top Snap Spring	32	Fore-end Spring Spring	49	Locking Bolt Assembly
11	Top Snap Plunger	33	Barrel	50	Butt Plate Screw
12	Top Snap Sleeve	34	Extractor Lever	51	Butt Plate
13	Top Snap, Trigger Guard Screw	35	Extractor Lever Spring	53	Stock Bolt
14	Extractor	36	Fore-end Spring Housing	54	Stock Bolt Washer
15	Extractor Screw		Fore-end Spring Housing Assembly	55	Stock
16	Extractor Spring	37	Fore-end Spring Pin	57	Pistol Grip Cap
17	Rear Sight Step	38	Fore-end Spring Spring Pin	58	Pistol Grip Cap Screw
18	Rear Sight	39	Trigger Guard Screw	59	Butt Plate
19	Barrel Band and Front Sight	40	Trigger Guard	60	Trap Cover
20	Barrel Band Screw				
21	Frame				
22	Trigger Spring				

CHAPTER 26

SHOTGUN CHOKES, BARREL LENGTHS, AND CARTRIDGE DESIGNS

The rifled barrel has been with us barely more than two centuries. The smoothbore has been with us since the first firearm was made. The American revolution and even the Civil War were fought largely with smoothbore muskets using slugs or balls rather than shot.

For many years the degree of choke has been theoretically standardized. The basic borings today are full, modified, and improved cylinder. The cylinder bore, still with us, is largely used for deer guns firing slugs or for short-barrel police guns.

Chokes

Until the late 1860s, shotgun or smoothbore barrels had no choke. Today, we designate such a barrel as "cylinder bore." In the true cylinder bore the barrel's interior has the same diameter all the way to the muzzle.

"Choke" means constricting the muzzle slightly (by a few hundredths of an inch) so that a degree of control is exercised over the shot pattern.

Choke was apparently "invented" by two Americans, each unknown to the other, and by an Englishman, unknown to either of the Americans. Fred Kimble, a market gunner, and a chap named Roper were the Americans. The Englishman was William R. Pape.

There is considerable variation between the chokes of some manufacturers. Today's chokes are more open than those of yesteryear, when the black-powder influence was still with us. The effect of choke is measured in terms of pattern density—that is, the average percentage of pellets in a shot charge that will strike within a 30-inch circle at 40 yards.

Full choke. About 70 percent pattern density is all one can expect today. (However an occa-sional gun delivers nearly 20 percent more with today's plastic shot-pouch wad columns, which protect the pellets as they travel through the bore and produce a tighter shot string.) Some tight chokes of yesterday ran to nearly 90 percent. One reason for the more open full choke is the tremendous improvement in shot cartridges. These improvements include the plastic shot pouches mentioned above.

The full choke is vastly overrated for most shooting. The average upland game and water-fowl decoy gunner is handicapping himself if his shotgun is full-choked.

Single-barrel gunners should use a variable-choke device.

Modified choke. This patterns at about 60 per-cent. It is a very useful choke and is about the maximum for most gunners, except long-range goose and pheasant shooters. The modified might be called the "pivot" or "swing" choke. On double-barrel guns—except those for goose shooting—it is usually in partnership with a full choke, or an improved-cylinder choke.

Improved cylinder. This is an ideal choke for most upland game and for decoyed ducks up to about 35 yards. The ideal upland-bird and de-coyed-waterfowl chokes are one barrel improved cylinder and the other modified. The man with a single-barrel slide-action or semiautomatic will not be severely handicapping himself if he uses improved cylinder. Pattern is about 50 percent.

Skeet choke. This type, too, varies somewhat depending on manufacturer but it is essentially another name for improved cylinder. Even those twin-barrel guns with chokes labeled Skeet 1 and Skeet 2 have improved-cylinder choke (more or less) in both barrels.

Cylinder. This often gives a variable pattern—depending on load and shot size—but the density rarely exceeds 40 percent at 40 yards. Its basic use is for short-barreled short-range "police-type" shotguns, though many gunners might benefit from its use in hunting certain upland birds such as woodcock.

Slug choke. This is a general description and may range from cylinder to improved cylinder. Some slug-gun manufacturers use the term "slug choke," while others simply call it by its right name.

Trap choke. For many years trap guns were almost invariably bored full choke (or even extra-full). Today, however, modified or modified-full may be offered as an option.

There is also the improved modified which is another compromise. In the past the term "half-choke" was applied to what now approximates modified. Quarter-choke approximated improved cylinder.

The classic myth about determining full choke: If a dime won't pass through the muzzle of a 12-bore the barrel is full choke. Dimes, as the author knows from miking many, are far from uniform diameter, especially worn dimes.

Shotshell case material

Brass. Probably the oldest and still the most durable material. It is commonplace to reload a brass case at least 100 times. All present brass cases are imported. When brass cases are loaded, wads must be cut to a slightly greater diameter than for a standard case because the brass case is thinner than the plastic one.

Cardboard with a paper wrapper. This type was with us from the late nineteenth century until after World War II. This case when subjected to humidity or moisture frequently swelled to such an extent that it could not function through a magazine or chamber in a barrel. This was but an inconvenience to civilian scattergunners, but it was a far different situation when American troops armed with "trench" or "riot" shotguns moved into the many caves of the Pacific Islands to clean out the enemy. A rush order was sent stateside for brass cartridges. They were produced and shipped to the Pacific, where they served our troops reliably.

Corrugated cardboard. These appeared shortly after World War II and were an improvement over the old cardboard/paper tubes.

Plastic. In the 1960s the cardboard and cardboard/paper shells were replaced by waterproof —or water repellent, at least—plastic. Plastic cases have improved over the years to the extent that nearly 100 percent of current shot cartridge case production is plastic. The folded, or star, crimp works best as a closure for the mouth of the plastic shell. It has replaced the old roll-crimp and top-wad closure. Plastic shells are easy to reload and they provide excellent shooting performances.

Aluminum. Winchester-Western during World War II supplied the Army Air Force—and possibly other services—with aluminum cases in .410-bore for use in survival kits. This is an excellent but expensive material. Various alloys have been used by European shotshell manufacturers, but to date no alloy case has offered significant competition for the very durable plastic case.

Case design

For many years there were two basic brass shot cartridge heads. The "low" brass case was used for field loads like Winchester REPEATER or XPERT loads, while express and/or magnum loads had a much higher brass head. Brand names are Super-X, Super Speed or Nitro Express, familiar to many Americans of both yesteryear and today.

Today, many cases are compression-formed plastic. The brass head merely serves to hold the primer and its battery cup. Some shot cartridges —more will probably follow—are entirely plastic except for the primer and its battery cup.

A major phenomenon among scattergunners has been the development of handloading shotshells. Today's skeet or trap shooter, unless he is very well off, must reload his empty cases or load new cases. Frequently clubs purchase a mechanical loader that can load up to 1800 shot cartridges per hour.

The author handloads trap loads, but for hunting purposes uses factory loads. The shooting season—particularly with the low waterfowl limits—doesn't offer that much shooting.

Barrel length

Barrel length, despite the great myth that "longer barrels shoot harder," has little effect on velocity. The trend for the past few years has been toward shorter barrels.

The standard length of 12-bore full-choke barrels is about 30 inches, though there are still some 32-inch barrels left. The 32-inch barrels— in the case of twin tubes—are usually bored full and full. The 20-gauge full-and-full barrels are usually 30 inches. There are relatively few full-and-full 20-gauge barrels.

Most twin-tube improved cylinder and modified combinations are 26 inches or 26.5 inches; the 0.5-inch difference seems pointless.

Barrel length, it will be noted, has a definite relationship to choke.

The full-and-full double-barrel is used largely for waterfowl. The flight pattern of ducks and geese is such that a longer sighting plain and a slow swing are required. Quail and woodcock, both usually shot at short range, require a more open choke. As already noted, the short, easy-to-swing 26-inch improved cylinder and modified chokes can also be deadly on decoyed waterfowl.

Much of the myth about long barrels comes from the black-powder days when considerable barrel length—they even had 40-inch barrels—was required to generate adequate velocity for long shots. With modern progressive-burning propellants the long barrel is no longer needed.

The trap-gun barrel still averages 30 to 34 inches. A long sighting plane and a slow-to-stop swing are required. The 32-inch barrel is entirely adequate, but sometimes tall men—including the author, who is 6 feet 7—like the 34-inch barrel.

A 26-inch-barrel slide-action or semiautomatic scattergun is about as long overall as a 30-inch-barrel break-top single-shot, or twin-tube side-by-side or over/under, which have no long receiver. This overall length is often a consideration in selection of a barrel length. Custom-made arms can be made in almost any barrel length or choke.

Variable-choke devices

Single-barrel guns like the single-shot, semi-auto, and slide actions have the inherent disadvantage of no choke selectivity. Over the years this condition has been remedied by several variable-choke devices. There are two basic types:

Permanently installed. These units can be adjusted through several degrees of choke, usually from improved cylinder through modified to full. Some devices have stops between the major ones. Examples: Poly-Choke and Mossberg C-LECT-CHOKE. The latter is usually factory-installed on the gun. Poly-Chokes are usually installed by your friendly, and one hopes competent, gunsmith. There are two types of Poly-Chokes: the original, in which the proper choke was selected manually; and an automatic version. Close shots are usually first shots, so the choke can be set at cylinder bore. After the first shot the choke selector automatically moves to the next degree of choke tightness.

Removable. The first or among the first variable-choke devices was the Cutts Compensator invented in the mid-1920s by Colonel Richard Cutts. He was probably better known for his Cutts Compensator of M1928AL Thompson Submachine guns than for the Cutts choke device (which also acted as a recoil device).

The Cutts is a 5- to 6-inch-long tube of slightly greater diameter than the exterior of the barrel. It is necessary to install a separate Cutts device for each desired choke pattern. Thus if you want an improved-cylinder choke, you remove the Cutts device already in the barrel and replace it with the desired choke.

Gas escaping through the slots (or gas escape ports) force the barrel down, thus reducing muzzle jump and recoil.

The Cutts, though effective, is an ungainly affair, and many users of lovely-lined doubles have thanked the stars—or something—that their guns were not so damnably encumbered.

Most Cutts users have several inches of the forward portion of their barrel removed so that the arm is not excessively long.

Several years ago Winchester brought forth a similar device in that only one choke pattern at a time could be installed. The device, now available only on the M144 Mark II semiautomatic shotgun, is the least offensive-looking of all variable-choke devices and it is as effective. It is not as efficient as the Poly-Choke because only one choke insert can be used at a time. The device is almost entirely inside the barrel. Unlike the Cutts, it doesn't seem to increase muzzle heaviness.

The author has fired a great many types of shotguns and experimented with several variable-choke devices, and solved the problem to his satisfaction by switching to the over/under.

PART VI

CENTERFIRE HANDGUNS

CHAPTER / 27

SINGLE-SHOT CENTERFIRE PISTOLS

The single-shot centerfire pistol, since the advent of Colt's Revolving Pistol, is the least popular handgun type. Except for target pistols, single-shot handguns suffered a long, steady decline. It remained for Remington with its XP-100 and Thompson/Center with its Contender to revive the single-shot as a sport/hunting arm. Today's highly accurate single-shots are frequently used with a scope sight specifically designed for handgun use.

The United States Army, except for its adoption of the Thompson submachine gun, M1 (Garand), and 5.56mm M16 automatic rifle, has been — and still is — conservative about arms. The service handgun from the Mexican War (1848–49) through the Civil War (1861–65) was either the cap-and-ball Colt's Revolving Pistol or a copy thereof. But shortly after Appomattox, the Army took a 30-year backward step and issued single-shot pistols to the cavalry. Fortunately the Army soon adopted the Model P (M1873) Colt Single Action Revolver.

The single-shot centerfire pistol adopted by the Army was designed and manufactured by Remington. All models, including U.S. Pistol, Model 1871, Caliber .50 Centerfire, used the rolling-block rifle action.

These pistols were, or could be, very accurate. The author's friend Douglas "Webby" Howe consistently hit a 1-foot-diameter target at the Arlington, Mass., Rifle Club's 100-yard range. He used black-powder handloads.

There was very little activity in the centerfire single-shot pistol field until 1965, when Bill Ruger designed the Hawkeye single-shot pistol for the now nearly defunct .256 Win. pistol cartridge. The Hawkeye ingeniously used the Blackhawk Single-Shot frame but with a swinging block in lieu of the usual cylinder. The pistol was not a commercial success.

Among modern hunting arms, the first successful centerfire single-shot pistols were the Remington XP-100, introduced in 1963, and the Thompson/Center Contender, introduced four years later. The Contender was designed by Warren Center, a fine arms designer formerly with the Iver Johnson Arms & Cycle Works. Center joined the Thompson investment-casting company in Rochester, N.H. Thompson/Center produces the Thompson/Center Contender single-shot pistol, which is available in both rimfire and centerfire calibers and employs interchangeable barrels.

Remington manufactures the XP-100, a unique bolt-action centerfire pistol with a molded plastic stock that extends almost to the muzzle and is contoured to provide a rest for the heel of the hand and a guide for the thumb and trigger finger. It's chambered only for the .221 Rem. Fireball cartridge, which means it is essentially a long-range varmint pistol. It functions like a miniature bolt-action single-shot rifle.

Many hunters have rechambered the XP-100 for heftier cartridges. Either of these handguns in the proper caliber is capable of taking game from woodchucks through deer at ranges not exceeding 100 yards. Their effectiveness is enhanced by specially designed scopes. The author uses scopes for bench-testing pistols but prefers the handier single- or double-action revolver with open micrometer sights adjustable for elevation and windage and with a cylinder of six cartridges. Perhaps this is because he is not confident of getting his game with one shot.

NAVY ARMS REMINGTON ROLLING BLOCK PISTOL REPLICA

Manufacturer: Navy Arms

Action type: rolling block

Magazine: none/single-shot

Safety: half-cock

Barrel length: 9.5 inches

Weight: 42.0 oz.

Height: 6.5 inches

Overall length: 14.0 inches

Trigger pull: 4.5 lbs.

Sight, rear: Rocky Mt. rear crudely adjustable for elevation

Sight, front: blade

Scope adaptability: yes

Finish: case hardened

Caliber: .22 L.R., .22 W.R.M., 22 Hornet, 5mm Rem. Mag., 357 Mag.

Comment: A well made reproduction of the Remington pistol.

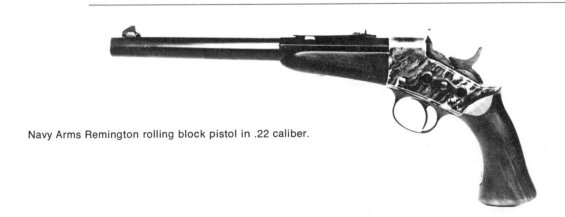

Navy Arms Remington rolling block pistol in .22 caliber.

REMINGTON XP-100 BOLT-ACTION SINGLE-SHOT PISTOL

Action type: bolt; short rifle action

Safety: sliding thumb

Barrel length: 10.5 inches (ventilated rib)

Stock: 1-piece DuPont "Zytel" Universal grip, molded to fit either right or left hand; black plastic fore-end tip

Overall length: 16.75 inches

Weight: 60.0 oz.

Trigger pull: not specified

Sight, rear: Rocky Mountain, crudely adjustable for elevation

Sight, front: blade

Scope adaptability: receiver drilled and tapped for mounts

Caliber: .221 Rem. Fireball

Comment: This pistol reminds some viewers of the late Buck Rogers' 24th-century rocket pistol with which he zapped Killer Kane. Its grip is surprisingly comfortable. This pistol, based on a short Remington rifle action, should be used with a pistol scope. It is one of the most accurate centerfire pistols the author has ever fired. The designer was Mike Walker.

Care should be exercised when firing so that a finger doesn't get in the way of the muzzle. This is easier to do than it sounds. Those of us used to scopes on a rifle always slide the left hand along the extended fore-end. One can easily forget this pistol doesn't have an extended fore-end—and there goes the tip of a finger. This happened to the late Stuart "the Great" Lathrop, one of the most experienced shooters known to the author.

Accessories: A zippered gun case is supplied with the pistol.

THOMPSON/CENTER CONTENDER SINGLE-SHOT PISTOL

Action type: single-shot; single action; break-top; underlever release formed by trigger guard

Safety: automatically functions when pistol is opened for loading; remains on safe until trigger is pulled; safety interlock prevents firing if barrel is not fully closed and locked

Barrel length: 8.75 or 10.0 inches

Stock: 2-piece American walnut; hand checkering

Overall length: 8.75-inch barrel, 12.25 inches; 10.0-inch barrel (with or without choke device), 13.5 inches

Thompson/Center Contender single-shot pistol.

THOMPSON/CENTER CONTENDER SINGLE-SHOT PISTOL (continued)

Weight: 8.75-inch barrel, 41.0 oz.; 10.0-inch barrel (with or without choke device), 43.0 oz.

Trigger pull: 4.5 lbs.; adjustable

Sight, rear: Rocky Mountain, adjustable for windage and elevation

Sight, front: ramp

Scope adaptability: drilled and tapped for mounts

Caliber:

Standard barrel: .22 Hornet, .22 Rem. Jet, .218 Bee, .221 Rem. Fireball, .222 Rem., .256 Win. Magnum, .25–35 Win., .30 M1 Carbine, .30–30 Win., .38 Super (.38 ACP), .38 Special, .357 Magnum, .45 ACP, .45 Colt, .44 Magnum, 9mm (Luger) Parabellum

10.0-inch bull barrel: .30 Herrett

10.0-inch barrel with choke: .357 Magnum, .44 Magnum, .45 Colt

Data: Serrated, wide target-type hammer spur, with adjustable position for selecting rimfire or centerfire. (For rimfire specifications and calibers, see Chapter 32.) Serrated, wide target-type trigger with adjustable trigger stop.

All barrels except .30 Herrett bull barrel are octagonal. Button rifling is used. Barrel lug is welded to barrel with electron beam. Each Contender frame accepts both centerfire and rimfire barrels. Dual firing pin is adjustable for either cartridge type.

Comment: This excellent pistol, designed by Warren Center, has achieved a just popularity. It is very accurate even with the factory rear sight, which is adjustable for windage and elevation. Nevertheless, maximum accuracy and effectiveness require a telescopic sight.

It is necessary to buy only one basic arm in order to take advantage of the array of calibers offered, because barrels in other calibers, both rimfire and centerfire, may be purchased separately.

Shot cartridges are becoming available in a growing number of pistol calibers. These handgun shot loads are often used to shoot small pest species, including venomous snakes, and to pot occasional small game during a big-game expedition or other wilderness trip. The rifled barrel of a conventional pistol is not conducive to top shot-load performance. Such performance is significantly improved by the T/C 10-inch barrel with choke, now offered in several calibers.

CHAPTER 28

SINGLE-ACTION CENTERFIRE REVOLVERS

Thanks to the old Saturday-afternoon horse operas and the pulp Western magazines and to today's TV westerns, certain arms are weapons of romance to millions of Americans who have never fired a shot. The Sharps buffalo rifle and lever-action Winchesters are examples. But one arm stands out above all others—the Colt single-action revolver with its traditional "hogleg" butt.

This is the real arm of romance. During his early youth the author whittled Colt replicas from orange-crate ends and centers (Winchesters were made from the side slats) and with a discarded sewing spool for a cylinder killed thousands of Indians, cattle rustlers, bank and stagecoach robbers, assorted outlaws, and just plain ornery human critters. Those orange-crate Peacemakers carried more notches than were sported by all the gunfighters of the Old West. His Winchesters were studded with brass carpet tacks, each representing a badman in Boot Hill.

The first commercial single-action was probably Sam Colt's triggerbowless 1836 Paterson Colt. It was named after its Paterson, N.J., plant. The venture failed, but only momentarily. A Paterson fell into the hands of a knowledgeable Texas Ranger named Samuel Walker.

Walker realized the six-shot revolving pistol would revolutionize horseback combat. Heretofore, a man fired one shot from each of his two or four single-shot pistols or sometimes four shots from two double-barrel pistols. When his muzzleloading pistols were empty the rider closed in with lance or saber. (Yes, once there was a lancer outfit in the United States Army. It was Reid's 22nd Pennsylvania Lancers in the Union Army.)

Indians and Mexicans were originally appalled at six-shooter firepower. A man often carried two sixguns, and with spare loaded cylinders.

Walker came North for a pow-wow with Colonel Sam'l. He told Colt a bigger caliber was needed. The Paterson was only a .36 caliber (the Colt-Walker was a .44) and a far more rugged arm was needed. The resulting arm was the heaviest American sixgun of the nineteenth century. It weighed 4.5 lbs. Not until the third quarter of the twentieth century would so heavy an arm appear, and it was a reproduction of the Colt-Walker.

The basic action of the M1873—and of 1975 single-actions—is similar to the 1836 Paterson, but the M1860 Army established the size and general handling qualities of the M1873 and today's successors.

The M1873—officially the Model P—was the M1860 with a topstrap over the cylinder. The cylinder was bored through for metallic cartridges—originally the .45 (Long) Colt—and the rammer (bullet seater) was transformed into an ejector. A loading gate was added.

The M1873 in caliber .45 Colt was designed for the United States Army. The Cavalry Model had a 7.5-inch barrel. The Infantry and Artillery Models had a 5.5-inch barrel. Colt sold a "civilian" model with a 4.75-inch barrel.

The M1873 was made in at least 16 different calibers, but the .45 Colt was the most popular for many years. The Colt .45 was not only the Army's number-one handgun during the Indian Wars but it was the favorite of gunfighting peace officers like Bat Masterson, Bear River Tom Smith, Bill Tilghman, Charlie Bassett, Pat Garrett, and others. Cowboys and outlaws liked it too.

City and town marshals and many sheriffs used the .45 Colt, but some U.S. deputy marshals, deputy sheriffs, and others who spent time on the range preferred the .44–40 Win. M73 rifle and the same cartridge in their sixgun. There were also outlaws who preferred it. One of Frank James's favorite guns was a .44–40 Remington revolver.

Dime novelist and vaudeville promoter E. Z. C. Judson, better known as Ned Buntline, presented 12-inch-barrel .45 Colts to several famous Western lawmen. These monstrous Buntline Specials were so muzzle-heavy and unwieldy that they were impossible to hold steady without resting them on a fence rail or some such support. There is no evidence that any of the lawmen who got them ever fired one for serious purposes, but the Buntlines did make reasonably good hammers as well as great conversation pieces—and there is some evidence that one lawman did use his as a club to "buffalo" an argumentative acquaintance.

Some two-gunmen were said to carry a short 4.75-inch-barrel Colt on the right hip for a faster draw. On the left hip rode a 7.5-inch Cavalry Model for use on the range.

The grand old Peacemaker was a durable arm, but parts were subject to breakage, including most of the trigger mechanism. Its major redeeming feature was the fact that it could be fired without a trigger and other parts.

Cowboys really didn't know much about guns. They killed rattlesnakes, shot up saloons, and "hurrahed" cowtowns. Their sixgun irreligiously drove staples into fence posts and removed the same. It was a general tool. Gunfighters, lawmen, and troopers were about the only .45 Colt users who kept their guns clean and in good repair.

The Colt has its competitors, but none achieved the century-long fame or usage of the M1873. One competitor was the S&W Schofield.

Shortly after the Army gave its initial order for Colts it purchased several thousand break-top Smith & Wesson Schofields. The Schofield (designed by a Cavalry officer named George Wheeler Schofield) had one advantage over the Colt. In the latter, cartridges are single-loaded through the loading gate. Empties are ejected one by one while the hammer is held at half cock and the cylinder revolved. The break-top Schofield ejected cartridges simultaneously. Loading was faster. The cartridge—a miserable puny thing—was the .45 S&W, a sawed-off .45 Colt case with only 29 grains of black powder (40 grains in the Colt). The shorter case was necessitated by the Schofield's design and construction. Although .45 S&W cartridges were issued for the .45 Colt revolver throughout much of its military career, some soldiers were reported to have purchased .45 Colt cartridges from local stores and trading posts. Very few knowledgeable civilians used the .45 S&W cartridge, though Jesse James and Cole Younger both used Schofield sixguns (among other revolvers).

There was also the Remington M1875 Army Revolver. It was an excellent weapon but was never very popular on the frontier. The Remington, including civilian sales, sold 25,000 (1875–89). The M1873 Colt during its first 22 years sold 160,000. The Remington weighed about 10 oz. more than the Colt. Some gunfighters preferred a heavier weapon because it was more accurate, partially because of lesser recoil, but most frontiersmen stayed with the M1873.

The Colt and Remington, like most handguns of that era, were available with a blued or nickeled finish.

The Army, once the Indian Wars were over, replaced the .45-caliber single-action Colt with the puny .38 Long Colt cartridge in the M1892 Colt (and successors). The Philippine Insurrection proved the inadequacy of the .38 Long Colt. Government arsenals hurriedly dug out stored single-actions and rushed them to the islands, where they were welcomed. The Army also shipped some double-action rod-ejection Colts. In 1908 the Army went back to caliber .45 Colt and in 1911 to the .45 ACP, which it still uses.

Colt continued production of the M1873, later known as the Single Action Army or the New Frontier, until 1942. The last original-production M1873s were shipped to England, where it was hoped that the sixgun could help repel the anticipated Nazi invasion. Total production (1873–1942) was about 359,000.

The spirit of the M1873 was kept alive during World War II by newspaper photographs of General Patton, wearing his M1873 .45 Colt and a .357 S&W Magnum with a 3.5-inch barrel. Patton wore these only for publicity purposes. When a newsman asked Patton if he wore his "pearl-handled" pistols in combat, the general replied, "Hell, son, only New Orleans whorehouse pimps wear pearl-handled pistols. These are ivory-handled."

After World War II there was a great demand for the M1873, but Colt had scrapped all M73 tools and machinery and did not intend to resume production. Prices skyrocketed. When Colt stopped production the standard list price was $37.50, and many were sold for less. The author bought a new M1873 for $27.50 in 1940.

As prices for secondhand Colts zoomed, it was inevitable that somebody would make replicas. Most of them were poorly done, with inferior materials or poor workmanship or both. Colt patents had expired many years before, so anybody could join the Peacemaker parade.

In 1954 arms designer and manufacturer Bill Ruger introduced his superb .357 Ruger Magnum Blackhawk. It incorporated all the improvements that sixgun experts like Elmer Keith had been trying to get Colt to add for nearly 30 years. Keith advocated replacing the easy-to-break flat springs with coil springs and replacing the curved top strap with a wide, flat top strap. Other improvements were made. All Ruger Blackhawks and Super Blackhawks (.44 Magnums) have been—and still are—fitted with a wide ramp front sight and a micrometer rear sight adjustable for windage and elevation.

It is difficult to make a flat statement about women or guns, but the author puts himself on record as saying that the single-action Ruger Blackhawk and Super Blackhawk are the best single-action revolvers ever made. There has been no compromise with quality, and prices—low at the start—have risen less than for any corresponding firearm. Today, the Ruger costs about half what a revived Colt single-action sells for.

Colt, after nearly 25 years of no M1873 production, tooled up to make the single-action in the 1960s. There were no improvements in the Colt. Except for a cylinder adapted to smokeless powder, introduced in the 1890s at serial #160,000, it was identical with the original. Later Colt brought out a single-action with a ramp front sight and micrometer rear. Called the Colt New Frontier Single Action Army, it has a flat-top frame and smooth walnut grips rather than the hard rubber used on the standard version. The action remains the same, however. Colt sells very few centerfire single-actions. The only people who buy the Colt in preference to the Ruger are those who enjoy the romance of owning a history-making Colt, or those who don't give a damn or don't know about the superiority of the single-action Rugers.

Imports appear occasionally, but most are more expensive than the Ruger and none have the Ruger's refinements, workmanship, or overall quality.

The Colt and other single-actions are frequently referred to as "six-shooters." Until 1973, this term was misleading. Knowledgeable six-shooter toters carried five loaded cartridges in the chamber. The hammer rested on an empty case or empty chamber. An accidental shooting could occur if the hammer accidentally struck the firing pin behind a loaded cartridge.

In July, 1973, Ruger introduced the New Model Blackhawk Single Action. This was the first single-action that could be safely carried with all six chambers loaded. Shortly thereafter a foreign import offered an inferior safety device.

Today's typical best-quality single-action centerfire revolver features a solid top strap and rod ejection. Calibers range from .30 Caliber U.S. M1 Carbine and .357 Magnum (which will safely chamber .38 Short Colt, .38 Long Colt, and .38 Special cartridges) to .41 Magnum, .44 Magnum (which will safely chamber .44 Russian and .44 S&W Special), and .45 Colt. The Ruger Blackhawk in caliber .357 Magnum can be converted to 9mm (Luger) Parabellum by substituting a cylinder of the latter caliber. The .45 Colt cylinder interchanges with the .45 ACP in the Ruger Blackhawk. Standard barrel lengths range from 4.75 inches to 7.5 inches. Colt offers a "hog wallow" sighted 12.0-inch barrel .45 Colt Buntline Special.

For sporting purposes, the major disadvantage of the single-action as compared to the modern double-action is the slowness of reloading. This is not much of a disadvantage. No game animal is apt to wait around while you miss six times, so you don't have to load up again in a big hurry.

The double-action can be fired faster than the single-action, but very few double-action toters can fire double-action (without cocking the hammer) effectively and accurately. A major factor is trigger pull. A single-action or a double-action fired as a single-action—with the hammer manually cocked for each shot—has a trigger pull that is about one-third that of a double-action fired without cocking the hammer. If you fire a double-action handgun without first thumbing the hammer back, the initial stage of the trigger pull cocks the hammer. The trigger pull is therefore not only heavy but long. And the gun tends to waver during this long, heavy pull. About the only practical purpose of double-action firing is speed for defense or police shooting—that is, at an assailant at short range. Trigger creep is another factor affecting accuracy. The more trigger creep, the less accurate a gun may be. It is probably better to have no creep and a heavy pull than a light pull with creep. The Ruger, for instance, has no trigger creep in either the Blackhawk Single Action or the Security-Six and Speed-Six double-actions. Trigger creep results from poor design or workmanship.

A single-action usually gets off the first shot before a double-action. A single-action like the Ruger Blackhawk will last a shooter's lifetime. It is accurate, the grip handles heavy recoil very well, and then it is also a weapon of excitement and romance.

COLT SINGLE ACTION ARMY REVOLVER

Action type: single-action revolver

Cylinder capacity: 6-shot

Safety: half-cock (hammer notch); must be loaded with only 5 shots so hammer rests on empty chamber

Barrel length (historical): 3.0 inches (Sheriff's/ Storekeeper's); 4.75 inches (Civilian); 5.5 inches (Artillery/Infantry); 7.5 inches (Cavalry); almost any barrel length was available on special order

Barrel length (current): 4.75, 5.5, or 7.5 inches

Weight:

.357 **Magnum:** 4.75-inch barrel, 40.5 oz.; 5.5-inch barrel, 41.5 oz.; 7.5-inch barrel, 43.0 oz.

.45 **Colt:** 4.75-inch barrel, 36.0 oz.; 5.5-inch barrel, 37.0 oz.; 7.5-inch barrel, 39.0 oz.

Stock (historical): 2-piece plain walnut succeeded by black composite rubber with rampant colt; plain or carved ivory available on special order; also plain pearl and sometimes stag; other materials to special order

Stock (current): black composite rubber with eagle and shield

Overall length: 4.75-inch barrel, 10.125 inches; 5.5-inch barrel, 10.875 inches; 7.5-inch barrel, 12.875 inches

Trigger pull: 4.0 lbs. (great variation in original production models)

Sight radius: 4.75-inch barrel, 5.75 inches; 5.5-inch barrel, 6.375 inches; 7.5-inch barrel, 8.375 inches

Sight, rear: fixed square notch

Sight, front: blade

Caliber (historical): .32–20 Win., .357 Magnum, .38 Long Colt, .38 Short Colt, .38 Special, .38–40 Win., .41 Long Colt, .41 Short Colt, .44 Colt, .44 Special, .44–40 Win., .45 ACP, .45 (Long) Colt, .450 Boxer, .455 Colt

Caliber (current): .357 Magnum, .45 (Long) Colt

Data: The old Single Action Army had a case-hardened frame with blued barrel, grip frame, trigger bow, and ejector rod; this was later replaced by blued frame and parts throughout the exterior; nickel plate was also furnished. Today the gun is Colt Blue with color-case-hardened frame. It also comes in a polished nickel-plate version with plain walnut stocks.

Comment: This is virtually the same as the original M1873. The frame is color-case-hardened. The cylinder, as with the original version on all guns serially numbered above 160,000, is designed for smokeless propellants.

More M1873s have probably been ornamented than any other American handgun. Aside from the factory standard of nickel-plated or blued barrel, cylinder, frame, and grip frame, there are gold- or silver-plated Colts. Nickel plating, though still available from the factory, is far inferior to chrome plating. The author has seen combinations such as blued throughout except nickel-plated cylinder, gold- or silver-plated with blued cylinder, nickel- or chrome-plated except for blued cylinder.

An M1873 that may well have been one of a kind was a copper-plated .44–40 Win. It belongs to a friend of Elmer Keith's. He asked his friend what he paid for the gun. "Swapped my woman and gave $15 to boot" was the reply.

Many Colts have expensive gold and silver inlays and engraving. Cattle brands were and still are a favorite engraving subject.

COLT NEW FRONTIER SINGLE ACTION ARMY

Action type: single-action revolver

Cylinder capacity: 6-shot

Safety: half-cock (hammer notch); must be loaded with only 5 shots so hammer rests on empty chamber

Barrel length: 5.5 or 7.5 inches

Weight:

.357 **Magnum:** 5.5-inch barrel, 42.0 oz.; 7.5-inch barrel, 44.0 oz.

.45 **Colt:** 5.5-inch barrel, 38.0 oz.; 7.5-inch barrel, 39.5 oz.

Stock: 2-piece plain walnut

Finish: Colt Blue with color-case-hardened frame

Overall length: 5.5-inch barrel, 10.875 inches; 7.5-inch barrel, 12.875 inches

Trigger pull: 4.0 lbs.

Sight, rear: micrometer, adjustable for windage and elevation

Sight, front: ramp type

Caliber: .357 Magnum, .45 (Long) Colt

Comment: Except for adjustable rear sight and front ramp, flat-top frame and walnut stocks, this is identical to the Single Action Army.

COLT BUNTLINE SPECIAL

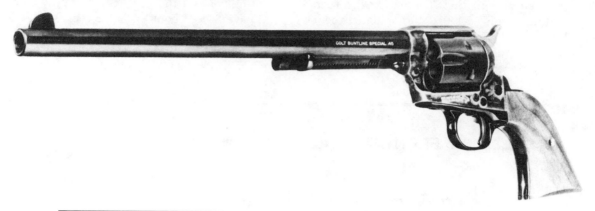

Action type: single-action revolver

Cylinder capacity: 6-shot

Safety: half-cock (hammer notch); must be loaded with only 5 shots so hammer rests on empty chamber

Barrel length: 12.0 inches

Weight: 42.0 oz.

Stock: 2-piece plain oiled walnut

Finish: blued with color-case-hardened frame

Trigger pull: 4.0 lbs.

Sight, rear: square notch fixed

Sight, front: blade

Caliber: .45 (Long) Colt

Comment: Except for barrel length, this is identical to the Single Action Army. This is a long-range revolver but its effectiveness and accuracy is considerably diminished by the lack of micrometer adjustable rear sight and a better front sight. The best front sight ever designed for long-range shooting was Elmer Keith's three-gold-bar sight. This high front sight had three gold bars for ranges of 100, 200, and 300 yards.

"Buntline" is derived from Ned Buntline, the pen name of dime novelist Edward Zane Carroll Judson. Buntline, as a publicity gimmick, gave Buntline Specials to Wyatt Earp, Bill Tilghman, Charlie Bassett, Neal Brown, and Bat Masterson. Each Buntline Special was fitted with a detachable walnut stock for long-range shooting. The sighting equipment is unknown—no record at Colt's—but Colt did make some long-barrel Peacemakers fitted with an adjustable back sight equipped with a leaf like those used on M1873 Springfields. None of the five recipients is ever known to have used the stocks. The walnut butt-stock had "Ned" carved into the wood. A holster accompanied each sixgun.

"There was a lot of talk in Dodge about the Specials slowing us on the draw," Earp told his biographer, Stuart N. Lake. "Bat and Bill Tilghman cut off the barrels to make them standard length [probably 7.5 inches, although in the summer of 1885 Masterson ordered a pair of 4.75-inch-barrel Colts direct from the Hartford factory]. Mine was my favorite over any other gun. I could jerk it as fast as my old one and I carried it on my right hip throughout my career as marshal. With it I did most of the sixgun work I had to do. My second gun, which I carried on my left hip, was the standard Colt's . . . with the seven-and-one-half inch barrel, the gun we called the 'Peacemaker.'" Much of what Earp told his biographer has been discredited, but there is evidence that he actually wore his Buntline and used it at least once—to hit Tom McLaury on the head. McLaury was a member of the Clanton faction, the victims of the Earp brothers and Doc Holliday at the O.K. Corral. So much for the romance of the Old West as personified by Wyatt Earp. In any event, the incident shows that the Buntline had practical uses even without the detachable shoulder stock.

HAMMERLI VIRGINIAN SINGLE ACTION REVOLVER

Manufacturer: Hammerli, Switzerland

Importer/distributor: Interarms

Action type: single-action revolver

Cylinder capacity: 6-shot

Safety: manually operated; to operate, the cylinder pin is pushed rearward so that cylinder cannot rotate; to fire pin is pulled forward

Barrel length: 4.625, 5.5, or 7.5 inches

Weight (average):

.357 Magnum: 4.625-inch barrel, 37.0 oz.; 5.5-inch barrel, 38.0 oz.; 7.5-inch barrel, 40.0 oz.

.45 Colt: 4.625-inch barrel, 36.0 oz.; 5.5-inch barrel, 37.0 oz.; 7.5-inch barrel, 39.0 oz.

Stock: 1-piece smooth European walnut

Overall length: 4.625-inch barrel, 9.25 inches; 5.5-inch barrel, 10.0 inches; 7.5-inch barrel, 12.0 inches

Trigger pull: not specified

Sight, rear: fixed square notch

Sight, front: blade

Caliber: .357 Magnum (also chambers .38 Long Colt, .38 Short Colt and .38 Special), .45 (Long) Colt (also chambers .45 S&W)

Data: This sixgun has a case-hardened frame; chrome triggerbow and backstrap; bright blued barrel and ejector rod housing.

Comment: The basic action, except for the safety feature, is almost an exact copy of the Colt Single Action Army, also known as the M1873 or Model P and sometimes the Frontier.

This is a very well-made sixgun. It is unfortunate that its maker—one of the finest match handgun makers—did not fit the arm with a ramp front and micrometer rear adjustable for windage and elevation. Such sights are available and can be readily installed by a knowledgeable pistolsmith.

The one-piece stock is superior to the two-piece stock. The safety feature is admirable, although that of the Ruger New Model Blackhawk is even better.

NAVY ARMS M1875 REMINGTON REPLICA

Manufacturer: Armi Uberti, Italy

Importer/distributor: Navy Arms

Action type: single-action revolver

Cylinder capacity: 6-shot

Barrel length: 7.5 inches

Weight: 34.0 oz.

Stock: plain walnut with oil finish (as original)

Overall length: 12.0 inches

NAVY ARMS M1875 REMINGTON REPLICA (continued)

Trigger pull: ?? lbs.

Sight, rear: groove; can be fitted with micrometer sight from independent sources

Sight, front: blade/bead (original sight was German-silver blade)

Calibers (original): .44 Rem., .44–40 Win., .45 Colt (also chambers .45 S&W)

Calibers (replica): .357 Magnum, .44–40 Win., .45 Long Colt (also chambers .45 S&W)

Data: The United States Army purchased a small number of these revolvers. Among Army purchases were nickel-plated ones for issue to Indian scouts, who preferred the bright nickel to the standard-issue blued/case-hardened M1875s.

The M1875 was discontinued in 1889 after 25,000 had been manufactured and sold.

The replica, introduced in 1974, has a large, all-steel frame and a checkered hammer spur. It lacks the lanyard swivel of the original. The standard version of this replica has a color-case-hardened frame, and the rest of the exterior metal is blued. A nickel-plated Indian Scout Model is also available.

Comment: The M1875 Remington Army revolver was just as good as the M1873 Colt. It was unfortunate for Remington that the company was two years behind Colt in issuing what was essentially a metallic-cartridge version of the Remington M1861 Army revolver (percussion/cap-and-ball).

Some Westerners, particularly peace officers who "buffaloed" their culprits, believed—and rightly so—that the webbing beneath the ejection rod made the arm somewhat more rugged than the M1873 Colt Peacemaker. Many peace officers like Wyatt Earp hit their arrestees over the head with the sixgun barrels instead of shooting them.

This replica is a well-made arm. It is even stronger than the original, which was made with relatively primitive steels and designed for black powder. The replica, made of modern steels, is entirely safe for smokeless loads. It is the only contemporary revolver known to the author that is currently chambered for the famed .44–40 Win. cartridge.

RUGER NEW MODEL BLACKHAWK, .357 MAGNUM

Action type: single-action revolver

Cylinder capacity: 6-shot

Transfer-bar safe-carrying feature: revolvers generally employ no safety slide (and need none); in New Model Rugers, transfer bar comes between hammer and pin when hammer is down—an automatic safety feature that blocks hammer and prevents accidental discharge so that gun can be carried with all six chambers loaded.

Barrel length: .357 and .41 Magnums, 4.625 or 6.5 inches; .30 M1 Carbine, 7.5 inches

Weight: 4.625-inch barrel, 40.0 oz.; 6.5-inch barrel, 42.0 oz.; 7.5-inch barrel, 44.0 oz.

Stock: 2-piece plain oiled walnut with Ruger medallion

Overall length: 4.625-inch barrel, 10.375 inches; 6.5-inch barrel, 12.25 inches; 7.5-inch barrel, 13.125 inches

Trigger pull: 3.5–4.0 lbs.; no creep

Sight, rear: micrometer adjustable for windage and elevation; protected by rib integral with frame

Sight, front: sloping partridge-type on ramp

Sight radius: 4.625-inch barrel, 5.625 inches; 6.5-inch barrel, 7.5 inches

Caliber: .30 M1 Carbine, .357 Magnum (also chambers .38 Special, .38 Long Colt, .38 Short Colt), .41 Magnum

Data: The original Ruger Blackhawk appeared in 1954. This improved version was introduced in 1973. It has a blued steel barrel, cylinder and frame, with a black anodized grip frame and trigger bow. In the .357 Magnum chambering, a stainless steel version is available. Everything is stainless steel, inside and out, except for the front and rear sights, which are blued. There will be no rust problems with this gun. The .30 M1 Carbine version, unlike the .357 and .41 Magnums, has a fluted cylinder. The safety mechanism incorporated into the New Model Blackhawk in 1973 means that these sixguns can be carried fully loaded without worrying that the hammer may be inadvertently slammed against the firing pin and thus cause an accidental discharge.

Comment: The author has gone on record as being less than enamored of the .30 M1 Carbine cartridge as a hunting load. However, in any of the three calibers that Ruger offers, this is a superbly designed and crafted single-action revolver. The lack of creep in the trigger pull is a boon to accuracy.

RUGER NEW MODEL BLACKHAWK CONVERTIBLE, .357 MAGNUM/9MM

Action type: single-action revolver

Cylinder capacity: 6-shot

Transfer-bar safe-carrying feature: revolvers generally employ no safety slide (and need none); in New Model Rugers, transfer bar comes between hammer and pin when hammer is down—an automatic safety feature that blocks hammer and prevents accidental discharge so that gun can be carried with all six chambers loaded.

Barrel length: 4.625 or 6.5 inches

Weight: 4.625-inch barrel, 40.0 oz.; 6.5-inch barrel, 42.0 oz.

Stock: 2-piece plain oiled walnut with Ruger medallion

Overall length: 4.625-inch barrel, 10.375 inches; 6.5-inch barrel, 12.25 inches

Trigger pull: 3.5–4.0 lbs.; no creep

Sight, rear: micrometer adjustable for windage and elevation; protected by rib integral with frame

Sight, front: sloping partridge type on ramp

Sight radius: 4.625-inch barrel, 5.625 inches; 6.5-inch barrel, 7.5 inches

Caliber: furnished with two cylinders for .357 Magnum (also chambers .38 Special, .38 Long Colt, .38 Short Colt) and for 9mm (Luger) Parabellum

RUGER NEW MODEL BLACKHAWK CONVERTIBLE,
.357 MAGNUM/9MM (continued)

Data: Blued steel barrel, cylinder, cylinder frame; black anodized alloy grip frame and triggerbow. The .357 Magnum/9mm Convertible must be ordered by a dealer through the factory. Owners of Blackhawk .357 Magnums who want the 9mm Parabellum cylinder must send their gun to the factory for initial installation. Once this has been done, it is a simple matter to swap the interchangeable cylinders.

Comment: Like the basic New Model Blackhawk, the Convertible is a superior firearm. And of course the two cylinders provide unusual versatility. Here is a single gun that can handle 9mm Parabellum cartridges in one cylinder and, in the other, .357 Magnums or any of three varieties of .38s.

RUGER NEW MODEL BLACKHAWK CONVERTIBLE, .45 COLT/.45 ACP

Action type: single-action revolver

Cylinder capacity: 6-shot

Transfer-bar safe-carrying feature: revolvers generally employ no safety slide (and need none); in New Model Rugers, transfer bar comes between hammer and pin when hammer is down—an automatic safety feature that blocks hammer and prevents accidental discharge so that gun can be carried with all six chambers loaded.

Barrel length: 4.625 or 7.5 inches

Weight: 4.625-inch barrel, 38.0 oz.; 7.5-inch barrel, 40.0 oz.

Stock: 2-piece oiled plain walnut with Ruger medallion

Overall length: 4.625-inch barrel, 10.125 inches; 7.5-inch barrel, 13.125 inches

Trigger pull: 3.5–4.0 lbs.; no creep

Sight, rear: micrometer adjustable for windage and elevation; protected by rib integral with frame

Sight, front: sloping partridge type on ramp

Sight radius: 4.625-inch barrel, 5.625 inches; 7.5-inch barrel, 8.375 inches

Caliber: .45 (Long) Colt (also chambers .45 S&W); .45 ACP

Data: Blued steel barrel, cylinder and cylinder frame; black anodized alloy grip frame and triggerbow. The .45 Colt/.45 ACP Convertible must be ordered by a dealer through the factory. Owners of .45 Colt New Model Blackhawks who want the .45 ACP cylinder must send their arm to the factory for installation. Once this has been done it is a simple matter to swap the interchangeable cylinders.

Comment: Owners using .45 Colt lead bullets will find the barrel of the New Model Blackhawk —or any other arm—will last for at least ten times as many rounds as when using metal-jacketed .45 ACP's. Lead bullets can be loaded into .45 ACP cases. However, even a handgun using full metal-jacketed bullets will last about 5000 rounds.

RUGER NEW MODEL SUPER BLACKHAWK, .44 MAGNUM

Action type: single-action revolver

Cylinder capacity: 6-shot

Transfer-bar safe-carrying feature: revolvers generally employ no safety slide (and need none); in New Model Rugers, transfer bar comes between hammer and pin when hammer is down—an automatic safety feature that blocks hammer and prevents accidental discharge so that gun can be carried with all six chambers loaded.

Barrel length: 7.5 inches

Weight: 48.0 oz.

Stock: 2-piece oiled walnut

Overall length: 13.375 inches

Trigger pull: 3.5–4.0 lbs.; no creep

Sight, rear: micrometer adjustable for windage and elevation; protected by ribs

Sight, front: blade on ramp

Caliber: .44 Magnum (also chambers .44 Special and .44 Russian)

Data: Wide target-type hammer spur; firing pin located in all-steel frame—largest single-action frame made. The bluing is dark and highly polished. The first Ruger chambered for the .44 Magnum was introduced in 1956. This was a few weeks after S&W introduced the first double-action sixgun chambered for the .44 Magnum cartridge. Ruger's single-action development paralleled the development of the S&W M29 .44 Magnum; it did not follow it.

The original Blackhawk Magnum was available with a 6.5-inch, 7.5-inch, or 10.0-inch barrel. The current Super Blackhawk is made with a 7.5-inch barrel only.

The Super Blackhawk introduced in 1959 is identical to the New Model Super Blackhawk except for the safety feature. The original Super Blackhawk was discontinued in 1973 when the New Model with its safety feature was introduced. The original is every bit as good as the New Model, but only five cartridges can be safely carried in the chambers.

This latter comment applies to all Blackhawks and Super-Single-Sixes made prior to the introduction of the New Model and its safety feature.

The New Model Super Blackhawk has the largest frame ever used on a commercially available single-action sixgun. The entire arm was built around the powerful .44 Magnum—the most powerful sixgun cartridge ever manufactured commercially.

Comment: This sixgun is capable of taking large game. Robert Petersen, publisher of *Guns & Ammo,* killed an Alaskan brown bear with the .44 Magnum Super Blackhawk. Elmer Keith and many other skilled sixgunners have used it to take game like elk.

CHAPTER 29

DOUBLE-ACTION CENTERFIRE REVOLVERS

The title of this chapter might read "Double/Single-Action Revolvers," because all the arms covered herein can be fired either double or single action. Current guns capable of double-action fire only are limited to so-called pocket-type revolvers. None of these known to the author is suitable for target or hunting purposes.

During World War II the British used some Webley-designed Enfield revolvers chambered for the .380 (.38 S&W) cartridge which had the hammer spur removed so that this holster arm had to be fired double action. Why this was done with a holster weapon is not exactly clear. It deprived the firer of his option to shoot single action when the occasion allowed. A shooter is always more accurate when he fires single action. Smith & Wesson produces one police-type revolver with a hammer shroud but the exposed hammer and option of single-action firing have become standard.

Contemporary double-action centerfire revolvers are of the solid-frame, swing-out cylinder, simultaneous-ejection type. Most break-top centerfire revolvers have been cheap affairs, usually chambered for the .32 S&W (short) or the .38 S&W. S&W made a few good break-top revolvers in caliber .45 S&W, .44 American, and .44 Russian during the last quarter of the nineteenth century. They were never as rugged as the solid-frame type. The British Webley service revolvers, ugly as they were, were the strongest of the break-top revolvers.

The break-top frame provided faster ejection and loading than rod ejection. Once the solid-frame swing-out cylinder simultaneous-ejection type was marketed, the break-top was on its way to obsolescence.

The double/single-action revolver appeared in England some years before it appeared in America. The Adams & Tranter was an early English double-action cap-and-ball sixgun. The author once owned an American-made double-action Starr cap-and-ball sixgun designed for the Union Army. During the Civil War, Colt was never able to keep up with the demand for its M1860 Army, caliber .44, and Navy, caliber .36. A disastrous fire which swept the Hartford plant stimulated other manufacturers.

The double-action revolver was never popular during the "winning of the West" (1866–90) or for some years afterward. Even today many Westerners prefer the single-action. One of the few Western gunmen (as opposed to gunfighters) to use a double-action revolver was William "Billy the Kid" Bonney. He used a double-action Colt Lightning Model, caliber .41 Colt.

The U.S. Navy took cognizance of the double-action in 1889 by adopting a Colt double-action revolver. The U.S. Army followed in 1892, and later regretted the drop from .45 Colt to .38 Long Colt caliber. There were later modifications of the M1889 and M1892 revolvers.

In 1897 Colt introduced the first top-quality solid-frame double-action revolver. This superb sixgun had the largest frame of any American revolver until S&W introduced its M29 caliber .44 Magnum (1956).

The New Service Colt was made in .38–40 Win., .44 Russian, .44–40 Win., .44 Special, .45 Colt, .45 ACP, .455 Colt and .476 Eley. It was not until the 1930s that Colt—because of potential customer demand—made a few .38 Specials and .357 Magnums.

There was a New Service Target Model, and in the early 1930s Colt introduced the Shooting Master. This was usually furnished with the rounded rather than the square butt.

The U.S. Army adopted the New Service Colt as the M1909. About the same time it was adopted by the Navy and Marine Corps. It was gradually replaced by the M1911 Colt semiautomatic pistol. During World War I the New Service, as noted elsewhere, was chambered for the .45 ACP cartridge. Both the M1917 Colt and its

S&W counterpart were Parkerized—dull finish—instead of the fine Colt or S&W blue.

Standard New Service barrel lengths were 4.5, 5.5, and 7.5 inches. The New Service target had a 7.5-inch barrel, while the Shooting Master had a 6.0-inch barrel. Other lengths were available on special order.

Military models of the New Service—except the U.S.M.C. version—had plain walnut grip panels with a square butt. The U.S.M.C. New Service had some checkering and a rounded butt. Colt blue was the standard finish, but nickel plating was available. Parkerizing was standard finish on the M1917, but the earlier M1909 series had Colt bluing. Military versions were marked U.S. PROPERTY.

Most pre-World War I commercial New Service Colts were fitted with hard black rubber grip panels. About 1920, hand-checkered—later machine-checkered—grip panels were adopted.

S&W had no arm comparable to the New Service in either size of frame or number of calibers. The fine S&W Triple Lock was generally available in .44 Special only.

S&W's top sixguns have one notable feature lacking in the New Service and all other pre-World War II Colt double-actions—the encased ejector rod. The rod encasing was omitted from the M1917 S&W because military authorities believed mud or other foreign matter might collect behind the rod, thus interfering with ejection.

Colt did not adopt the encased ejector rod until the late 1950s, when the firm brought out the Python, a fitting successor to the New Service but unfortunately not available in powerful calibers.

While ejector-rod encasing is desirable, the author, who has owned and fired more than a score of New Service revolvers, never damaged an ejector rod. He has also owned numerous encased-rod S&Ws, a Colt Python, and a Diamondback (.22 Long Rifle) and has never had the rod impeded by mud or other material, though he has deliberately fouled the encased rod.

In the caliber .38 Special category of target revolvers, the Colt Officer's Model Target revolver reigned supreme between the two world wars. This 34.0-oz. 6.0-inch-barrel revolver, except for the Colt Shooting Master, was the only major .38 Special revolver deemed suitable by the nation's top target .38 Special handgunners.

After World War II the S&W K-38 gained wide popularity. In the late 1950s the semiautomatic chambered for the .38 Special cartridge began to replace the sixgun on target ranges. Difficulties with a rimmed cartridge have largely been overcome. The Army Marksmanship Unit, Fort Benning, Ga., used a special rimless version of the .38 Special known as the .38 AMU, until cartridge-feed difficulties were overcome.

Since World War II, Smith & Wesson has replaced Colt as the number-one manufacturer of double-action revolvers. Ruger entered the field with the excellent Speed-Six, Security-Six, and Service-Six. Dan Wesson Arms has a small but excellent line of sixguns.

Spanish revolvers imported before World War II were of cheap materials and poor workmanship and design. Today several excellent Spanish-made revolvers, including the Astra, are sold here. These sixguns have nothing that is not provided by American arms.

S&W offers sixgun purchasers—in many models—the option of wide-spur target hammers, wider-than-standard target triggers, and extrasize stocks. Purchasers of these arms should seriously consider these options. Shooters with small hands will probably bypass target stocks.

Barrel lengths

Today's double-action sixgun barrel lengths—for sporting and hunting purposes—range from 4.0 to 8.375 inches. The latter length, found on S&W's .357, .41, and .44 Magnums, is rarely encountered. It is too long and cumbersome.

The 4.0-inch barrel is the most convenient and, though the shorter barrel produces slightly less velocity and energy than the 5.5- or 6.5-inch barrel, it is an extremely handy arm to carry.

The 5.5- to 6.5-inch barrels have a longer sighting plane and provide somewhat greater velocity and energy. These are good lengths for arms intended for target or hunting purposes.

Sights

For all shooting purposes save target work, the sloping serrated ramp is the best front-sight choice for most purposes, including hunting, plinking, and self-defense. Current sights of this type usually have a red insert. This is a mistake. The red bead under adverse lighting conditions—and sometimes under good conditions—looks black. A gold bead shows up much better against nearly all targets.

The rear sight should be of the micrometer type fully adjustable for windage and elevation. For added visibility the square notch of the rear sight should have a white outline insert as provided with many S&W rear sights.

REVOLVER VS. THE SEMIAUTOMATIC PISTOL

Advantages

1. Except among military personnel, the revolver is a more familiar arm than the semiautomatic pistol.

2. For the tyro shooter—including those who want a self-defense arm—the revolver is a safer gun.

3. In the event of a misfire the sixgunner merely pulls the trigger or cocks the hammer to bring another cartridge into the firing position.

4. The revolver, particularly when fired single action, usually has a superior trigger pull.

5. Sixguns will fire old ammunition whose reduced velocities might create malfunction in a semiautomatic pistol.

6. Expended cartridges are readily at hand for removal from the cylinder; semiautomatic pistols throw the expended cases some distance away.

Disadvantages

1. The sixgun is slower to load.

2. The sixgun is bulkier than the semiautomatic pistol.

3. The grip—single-action Colt-type grips excepted—is not as natural or as easy to hold as a semiautomatic's.

4. The sixgun is more difficult to disassemble for thorough cleaning. (However, Ruger's double-action sixguns—except for barrel removal from the frame—can be taken down in a minute or less with no tool but a coin.)

5. Barrel removal of a sixgun is a chore.

6. Worn or poorly made sixguns may have poor cylinder-barrel alignment, thus shaving bullets and reducing accuracy.

COLT DIAMONDBACK REVOLVER

Action type: double-action revolver

Cylinder capacity: 6-shot

Safety: rebounding hammer; safety bar blocks hammer

Barrel length: 4.0 inches (2.5-inch barrel not for sportsmen)

Weight: 28.0 oz.

Stock: checkered walnut, target type

Overall length: 9.0 inches

Trigger pull: single action, 4.0 lbs.; double action, 8.0–10.0 lbs.

Sight, rear: micrometer, adjustable for windage and elevation; ventilated rib

Sight, front: sloping ramp

Caliber: .38 Special

Data: The Diamondback employs a medium frame, all steel. The finish is Colt (bright) blue.

Comment: This is a scaled-down version of the Colt Python. It is one of the two best double-action sixguns made by Colt. The author, because he prefers big guns (he has hamlike hands), favors the Python even for the .38 Special cartridge. Small hands will find the Diamondback more comfortable, but it is not available in the far more effective .357 Magnum.

EXPLODED VIEW OF COLT DIAMONDBACK REVOLVER

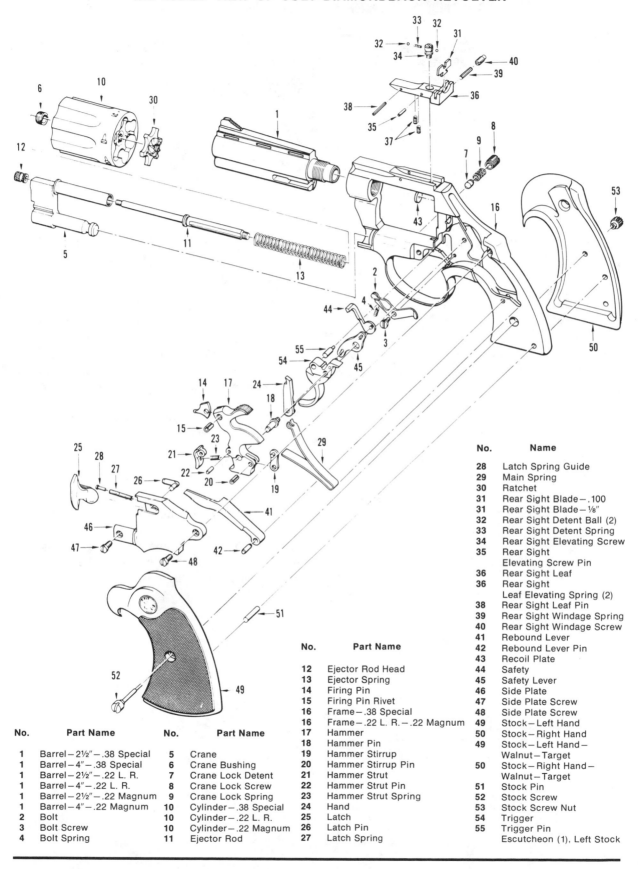

No.	Name
28	Latch Spring Guide
29	Main Spring
30	Ratchet
31	Rear Sight Blade—.100
31	Rear Sight Blade—⅛"
32	Rear Sight Detent Ball (2)
33	Rear Sight Detent Spring
34	Rear Sight Elevating Screw
35	Rear Sight Elevating Screw Pin
36	Rear Sight Leaf
36	Rear Sight Leaf Elevating Spring (2)
38	Rear Sight Leaf Pin
39	Rear Sight Windage Spring
40	Rear Sight Windage Screw
41	Rebound Lever
42	Rebound Lever Pin
43	Recoil Plate
44	Safety
45	Safety Lever
46	Side Plate
47	Side Plate Screw
48	Side Plate Screw
49	Stock—Left Hand
50	Stock—Right Hand
49	Stock—Left Hand—Walnut—Target
50	Stock—Right Hand—Walnut—Target
51	Stock Pin
52	Stock Screw
53	Stock Screw Nut
54	Trigger
55	Trigger Pin
	Escutcheon (1), Left Stock

No.	Part Name
12	Ejector Rod Head
13	Ejector Spring
14	Firing Pin
15	Firing Pin Rivet
16	Frame—.38 Special
16	Frame—.22 L. R.—.22 Magnum
17	Hammer
18	Hammer Pin
19	Hammer Stirrup
20	Hammer Stirrup Pin
21	Hammer Strut
22	Hammer Strut Pin
23	Hammer Strut Spring
24	Hand
25	Latch
26	Latch Pin
27	Latch Spring

No.	Part Name	No.	Part Name
1	Barrel—2½"—.38 Special	5	Crane
1	Barrel—4"—.38 Special	6	Crane Bushing
1	Barrel—2½"—.22 L. R.	7	Crane Lock Detent
1	Barrel—4"—.22 L. R.	8	Crane Lock Screw
1	Barrel—2½"—.22 Magnum	9	Crane Lock Spring
1	Barrel—4"—.22 Magnum	10	Cylinder—.38 Special
2	Bolt	10	Cylinder—.22 L. R.
3	Bolt Screw	10	Cylinder—.22 Magnum
4	Bolt Spring	11	Ejector Rod

COLT PYTHON REVOLVER

Action type: double-action revolver

Cylinder capacity: 6-shot

Safety: safety bar blocks hammer

Barrel length: 4.0 or 6.0 inches (2.5-inch barrel is not for sportsmen)

Weight: 4.0-inch barrel, 38.0 oz.; 6.0-inch barrel, 43.5 oz.

Stock: checkered walnut; target type

Overall length: 4.0-inch barrel, 9.25 inches; 6.0-inch barrel, 11.25 inches

Trigger pull: single action, 4.0 lbs.; double action, 8.0–10.0 lbs.

Sight, rear: micrometer, adjustable for windage and elevation

Sight, front: ramp

Sight radius: 4.0-inch barrel, 5.625 inches; 6.0-inch barrel, 7.625 inches

Caliber: .357 Magnum (will chamber .38 Special, .38 Long Colt, .38 Short Colt)

Data: Colt Royal (very bright) Blue finish or at extra cost polished nickel plate.

Comment: This is Colt's finest double-action revolver. It is the largest centerfire caliber in a Colt double-action. Along with S&W's top-of-the-line .357, .41 Magnum, and .44 Magnum revolvers, this is one of the finest double-action sixguns made.

Colt, which once manufactured the largest-frame American sixgun, the New Service and New Service Target, in calibers ranging from .38 Special to .476 Eley, did not return to big-frame double-action manufacture after World War II. Today, a shooter wanting a double-action .41 Magnum or .44 Magnum must go to S&W.

There are two schools of thought concerning handgun balance. Some shooters prefer the weight in the hand, while others like a muzzle-heavy balance like the Python's.

COLT TROOPER MK III REVOLVER

Action type: double-action revolver

Cylinder capacity: 6-shot

Safety: safety bar interposed between hammer and firing pin

Barrel length: 4.0 or 6.0 inches

Weight: 4.0-inch barrel, 39.0 oz.; 6.0-inch barrel, 42.0 oz.

Stock: checkered walnut; target type

Overall length: 4.0-inch barrel, 9.5 inches; 6.0-inch barrel, 11.5 inches

Trigger pull (nominal): single action, 4.0 lbs.; double action, 8.0–10.0 lbs.

Sight, rear: micrometer, adjustable for windage and elevation

Sight, front: ramp

Sight radius: 4.0-inch barrel, 5.5 inches; 6.0-inch barrel, 7.5 inches

Caliber: .357 Magnum

Data: The Trooper has a medium, all steel frame. The finish is bright blue or (at extra cost) nickel plating.

Comment: This is an excellent double-action sixgun for lawmen, who should never use a cartridge with less punch than the .357 Magnum, nor should they use a fixed-sight sidearm.

DAN WESSON M15-2 REVOLVER

Action type: double-action revolver

Cylinder capacity: 6-shot

Barrel length: 4.0 inches, 6.0 inches, or 8.0 inches (interchangeable); 2.5-inch barrel unsuitable for sporting use

Weight:

standard barrel: 4.0-inch barrel, 36.0 oz.; 6.0-inch barrel, 40.0 oz.; 8.0-inch barrel, 44.0 oz.; with vent-rib barrel shroud, deduct 1.0 oz. in any barrel length

with heavy barrel shroud: 4.0-inch barrel, 38.0 oz.; 6.0-inch barrel, 43.0 oz.; 8.0-inch barrel, 48.0 oz.; with vent-rib heavy barrel shroud, deduct 1.0 oz. in any barrel length

Stock: 1-piece walnut; checkered or unchecked; plain walnut stock blank also available for custom fitting

Overall length: 4.0-inch barrel, 9.25 inches; 6.0-inch barrel, 11.25 inches; 8.0-inch barrel, 13.25 inches

DAN WESSON M15-2 REVOLVER (continued)

Trigger pull: double action, 10.0 lbs.; single action, 3.5–4.0 lbs.

Sight, rear: micrometer adjustable for windage and elevation

Sight, front: ramp with field-interchangeable red, white, or yellow insert

Caliber: .357 Magnum

Data: This arm has a firing-pin disconnector; this feature, while not original, is certainly useful. Other features include a wide trigger with adjustable overtravel stop; wide-spur hammer with short double-action travel; all-steel medium frame; matte-finished hammer, topstrap, and shroud, with remainder of metal highly polished and blued.

Comment: Barrels of various lengths are readily interchangeable by means of a supplied accessory tool, making this an unusually versatile gun for the shooter who likes a longer barrel for one kind of hunting or another—or for target practice with lighter .38 Special wadcutter loads. Each barrel is fixed in a barrel shroud which also comes in several versions—standard; standard with ventilated rib which cuts weight slightly; heavy; or heavy with ventilated rib that makes it not quite so heavy. Naturally, the gun must be resighted whenever barrels are interchanged.

S&W M12/.38 COMBAT MASTERPIECE

Action type: double-action revolver

Cylinder capacity: 6-shot

Barrel length: 4.0 inches

Weight: 34.0 oz.

Stock: Magna type; checkered walnut

Overall length: 9.25 inches

Trigger pull: single action, 4.0 lbs.; double action, 8.0–10.0 lbs.

Sight, rear: micrometer, adjustable for windage and elevation

Sight, front: 0.125-inch-wide Baughman quick-draw ramp

Caliber: .38 Special

Data: The M12 has an all-steel medium frame, the same size as the K-38 Target Series.

Comment: While the .38 Special cartridge is inadequate for police officers and for most hunting, it is adequate for small game and excellent for target shooting.

As with other S&W sixguns this arm is more efficient when fitted with extra-cost target hammer and trigger and white outline for rear sight. Big men may prefer oversize target stocks.

S&W M14/K-38 MASTERPIECE

Action type: double-action revolver

Cylinder capacity: 6-shot

Barrel length: 6.0 or 8.375 inches

Weight: 6.0-inch barrel, 38.5 oz.; 8.375-inch barrel, 42.5 oz.

Stock: Magna type; checkered walnut

Overall length: 6.0-inch barrel, 11.125 inches; 8.375-inch barrel, 13.5 inches

Trigger pull: single action, 4.0 lbs.; double action, 8.0–10.0 lbs.

Sight, rear: micrometer, adjustable for windage and elevation

Sight, front: 0.125-inch-wide plain partridge

Caliber: .38 Special

Data: The M14 has a wide, grooved trigger (target type) and a wide, checkered hammer (also target type).

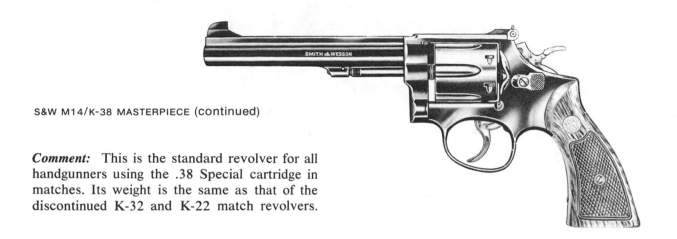

S&W M14/K-38 MASTERPIECE (continued)

Comment: This is the standard revolver for all handgunners using the .38 Special cartridge in matches. Its weight is the same as that of the discontinued K-32 and K-22 match revolvers.

S&W M19 "COMBAT" MAGNUM

Action type: double-action revolver

Cylinder capacity: 6-shot

Barrel length: 4.0 or 6.0 inches

Weight: 35.0 oz.

Stock: checkered Goncala Alves target type

Overall length: 4.0-inch barrel, 9.5 inches; 6.0-inch barrel, 11.5 inches

Trigger pull: single action, 4.0 lbs.; double action, 8.0–10.0 lbs.

Sight, rear: micrometer, adjustable for windage and elevation

Sight, front: 0.125-inch-wide Baughman quick-draw on ramp; 0.125-inch-wide partridge on 6.0-inch barrel

Caliber: .357 Magnum (also chambers .38 Special, .38 Long Colt, .38 Short Colt)

Data: All-steel medium frame. Choice of finish —bright blue or nickel.

Comment: This sixgun is built on a lighter frame for those who prefer this type. The arm's effectiveness is improved with extra-cost items like white outline for rear square notch, wide target hammer, and grooved target trigger.

EXPLODED VIEW OF S&W 14/K-38 MASTERPIECE

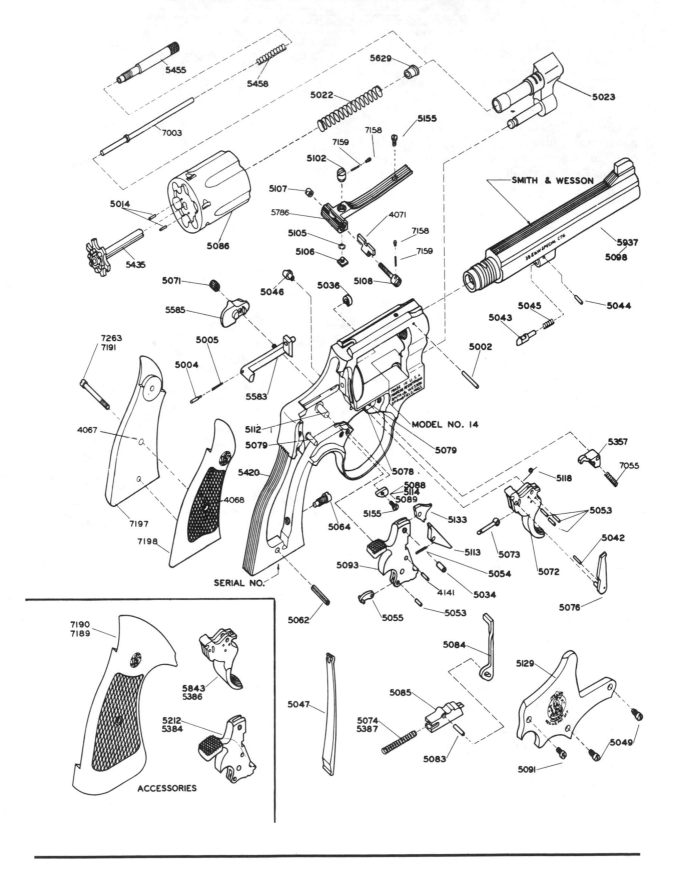

SMITH & WESSON

MODEL NO. 14

SERIAL NO.

ACCESSORIES

S&W M23

Action type: double-action revolver

Cylinder capacity: 6-shot

Barrel length: 6.5 inches

Weight: 41.75 oz.

Stock: Magna type checkered walnut

Overall length: 11.75 inches

Trigger pull: single action, 4.5 lbs.; double action, 9.0–11.0 lbs.

Sight, rear: micrometer, adjustable for windage and elevation

Sight, front: 0.125-inch-wide plain partridge

Caliber: .38 Special

Comment: This is a micrometer-sighted version of the famed .38/.44 Heavy Duty (M20). The M23 uses the large frame of the M24 .44 Special frame. This is one of the two finest sixguns designed for .38 Special use only (not .357 Magnum). The other is Colt's Diamondback.

Anyone ordering this arm should secure the extra-cost target-type wide hammer and grooved trigger. A white outline should be ordered for the rear sight's square notch. Target stocks are available at extra cost.

Parts List for S&W 14/K-38 Masterpiece

No.	Part Name	No.	Part Name	No.	Part Name
4067	Escutcheon	5072	Trigger	5155	Trigger Stop Screw
4068	Escutcheon Nut	5073	Trigger Lever	5212	Hammer, wide spur Target
4071	Rear Sight Slide 6" & 8⅜" Bbl.	5074	Rebound Slide Spring	5357	Cylinder Stop
4081	Rear Sight Assy. 6" & 8⅜" Bbl.	5076	Hand	5384	Hammer S.A.
4141	Sear Pin	5078	Trigger Stud	5386	Trigger S.A.
5002	Barrel Pin	5079	Cylinder Stop Stud	5387	Rebound Slide Spring
5004	Bolt Plunger	5079	Rebound Slide Stud	5420*	Frame, with studs, bushing & lug
5005	Bolt Plunger Spring	5083	Rebound Slide Pin	5435*	Extractor
5014	Extractor Pin	5084	Hammer Block	5455	Extractor Rod
5022	Extractor Spring	5085	Rebound Slide	5458	Center Pin Spring
5023	Yoke	5086	Cylinder, with extractor, pins & gas ring	5583	Bolt
5034	Hammer Nose Rivet	5088	Trigger Stop .500	5585	Thumbpiece
5036	Hammer Nose Bushing	5089	Trigger Stop S.A.	5629	Extractor Rod Collar
5042	Hand Pin	5091	Plate Screw, flat head	5786	Rear Sight Leaf
5043	Locking Bolt	5093	Hammer	5843	Trigger, wide Target type
5044	Locking Bolt Pin	5098	Barrel, 6"	5937	Barrel, 8⅜"
5045	Locking Bolt Spring	5102	Rear Sight Elevation Nut	7003	Center Pin
5046	Frame Lug	5105	Rear Sight Spring Clip	7055	Cylinder Stop Spring Single Action Kit
5047	Mainspring	5106	Rear Sight Elevation Stud		
5049	Plate Screw, crowned	5107	Rear Sight Windage Nut	7158	Rear Sight Plunger
5053	Hand Spring Pin	5108	Rear Sight Windage Screw	7159	Rear Sight Plunger Spring
5053	Hand Torsion Spring Pin	5112	Hammer Stud	7189	Stock, oversize Target, left
5053	Stirrup Pin	5113	Sear	7190	Stock, oversize Target, right
5053	Trigger Lever Pin	5114	Trigger Stop	7191	Stock Screw Square Butt
5054	Sear Spring	5118	Hand Torsion Spring	7197	Stock, left Square
5055	Stirrup	5129*	Side Plate	7198	Stock, right Square
5062	Stock Pin	5133	Hammer Nose	7263	Stock Screw Target
5064	Strain Screw	5155	Rear Sight Leaf Screw		
5071	Thumbpiece Nut				

S&W M24 TARGET

Action type: double-action revolver

Cylinder capacity: 6-shot

Barrel length: 6.0 inches

Weight: 45.0 oz.

Stock: checkered walnut; oversize target type

Overall length: 9.25 inches

Trigger pull: single action, 4.0 lbs.; double action, 8.0–10.0 lbs.

Sight, rear: micrometer, adjustable for windage and elevation

Sight, front: 0.125-inch-wide plain partridge

Caliber: .45 ACP

Data: The M24 has a wide, checkered target-type hammer, a wide, grooved target trigger, and of course a large all-steel frame.

Comment: This is a highly refined target version of the S&W M1917 double-action revolver. An extremely accurate sixgun, it is the only current double-action revolver in caliber .45 Colt ACP. It is an excellent hunting arm. It uses the .45 ACP cartridge with half-moon clips or the .45 Auto Rim cartridge. Regardless of which type is used, lead bullets or softpoint bullets should be used.

S&W M27 MAGNUM

Action type: double-action revolver

Cylinder capacity: 6-shot

Barrel length: 3.5, 5.0, 6.0, 6.5, or 8.375 inches

Weight: 3.5-inch barrel, 41.0 oz.; 5.0-inch barrel, 42.5 oz.; 6.0-inch barrel, 44.0 oz.; 6.5-inch barrel, 44.5 oz.; 8.375-inch barrel, 47.0 oz.

Stock: Magna type; checkered

Overall length: 3.5-inch barrel, 8.875 inches; 5.0-inch barrel, 10.375 inches; 6.0-inch barrel, 11.375 inches; 6.5-inch barrel, 11.875 inches; 8.375-inch barrel, 13.75 inches

Trigger pull: single action, 4.5 lbs.; double action, 8.0–10.0 lbs.

Sight, rear: micrometer, adjustable for windage and elevation; white-outlined square notch

Sight, front: choice of any S&W target sight

Caliber: .357 Magnum

Data: This large-frame revolver comes with a choice of finish—blued or nickeled.

Comment: Peace officers and hunters should select the 0.125-inch-wide Baughman quick-draw ramp front sight with red insert (gold would be better if it were available).

This handgun should always be ordered with target-type wide serrated hammer and with grooved target trigger. Men with big hands should get the oversize target stock. These three optional items are worth the extra cost.

The author would like to see this handgun with a 4.0-inch rather than a 3.5-inch minimum barrel length. The extra length slightly reduces the severe muzzle blast so noticeable with the shortest barrel.

The 8.375-inch barrel—and this applies to the same length in any caliber—is too clumsy and ill balanced for any use except target shooting.

S&W M28 HIGHWAY PATROLMAN

Action type: double-action revolver

Cylinder capacity: 6-shot

Barrel length: 4.0 or 6.0 inches

Weight: 4.0-inch barrel, 41.75 oz.; 6.0-inch barrel, 44.0 oz.

Stock: Magna type; checkered walnut

Overall length: 4.0-inch barrel, 9.25 inches; 6.0-inch barrel, 11.25 inches

Hammer: standard

Trigger pull: single action, 5.0 lbs.; double action, 9.0–11.0 lbs.

Sight, rear: micrometer, adjustable for windage and elevation

Sight, front: 0.125-inch-wide Baughman quick-draw front on ramp

Caliber: .357 Magnum

Comment: This sixgun uses the same frame as the M27 but the finish is not as highly blued. Though somewhat less expensive than the M27, the interior is as well finished and it has the advantage of a 4.0-inch barrel. This revolver should be ordered with target-type wide spur hammer and wide grooved trigger. Oversize target stocks should be ordered by men with big hands.

S&W M29/.44 MAGNUM

Action type: double-action revolver

Cylinder capacity: 6-shot

Barrel length: 4.0, 6.5, or 8.375 inches

Weight: 4.0-inch barrel, 43.0 oz.; 6.5-inch barrel, 47.0 oz.; 8.375-inch barrel, 51.5 oz.

Stock: oversize target type; checkered Goncalo Alves wood

Overall length: 4.0-inch barrel, 9.375 inches; 6.5-inch barrel, 11.875 inches; 8.375-inch barrel, 13.75 inches

S&W M29/.44 MAGNUM (continued)

Trigger pull: single action, 4.0 lbs.; double action, 8.0–10.0 lbs.

Sight, rear: micrometer, adjustable for windage and elevation; white-outlined square notch

Sight, front: serrated 0.125-inch-wide ramp with red insert

Caliber: .44 Magnum

Data: The M29 is another of the large-frame S&W revolvers that give the purchaser a choice of blued or nickeled finish at no difference in cost. Features include a wide, checkered target-type hammer spur and a wide, grooved, target-type trigger.

Comment: This handgun, together with the S&W M57 .41 Magnum, is the finest large-frame double-action revolver made. Colt's .357 Python does not have as large a frame.

This revolver was designed by S&W at the suggestion of leading U.S. handgun authority Elmer Keith. The .44 Magnum cartridge was designed at Keith's suggestion by Remington Arms in conjunction with S&W engineers.

The design, workmanship, and quality of materials and finish are exceeded by no other big-frame sixgun and equaled only by the M57 .41 Magnum. The sole difference between the two models is the caliber.

For details of the caliber .44 Magnum cartridge, see Chapter 31. The author would like to see this handgun chambered for the .45 Colt revolver cartridge.

The front sight should have a gold bead, which would stand out better against dark backgrounds. The red bead looks black in poor light.

Some .44 Magnum shooters prefer a smooth stock to a checkered one. They maintain that the severe recoil makes checkered stocks hurt their palms. A plain stock is available from S&W on special order.

Parts List for S&W M29/.44 Magnum

No.	Part Name	No.	Part Name	No.	Part Name
4067	Escutcheon	5074	Rebound Slide Spring	5456	Extractor Rod
4068	Escutcheon Nut	5078	Trigger Stud	5457	Center Pin Spring
4078	Rear Sight Slide 8⅜" bbl.	5079	Cylinder Stop Stud	5461	Frame, with studs, bushing & lug
4096	Rear Sight Assembly 4" & 6½" bbl.	5079	Rebound Slide Stud	5500	Yoke
4098	Rear Sight Assembly 8⅜" bbl.	5083	Rebound Slide Pin	5584	Bolt
4141	Sear Pin	5091	Plate Screw, flat head	5585	Thumbpiece
4165	Rebound Slide	5102	Rear Sight Elevation Nut	5750	Hammer Nose Spring
5005	Bolt Plunger Spring	5105	Rear Sight Spring Clip	5810	Barrel Pin
5014	Extractor Pin	5106	Rear Sight Elevation Stud	5843	Trigger, wide Target type
5021	Extractor Rod Collar	5107	Rear Sight Windage Nut	5856	Cylinder, with extractor, pins & gas ring
5022	Extractor Spring	5108	Rear Sight Windage Screw		
5034	Hammer Nose Rivet	5112	Hammer Stud	5857	Barrel, 6½"
5036	Hammer Nose Bushing	5113	Sear	5859	Gas Ring
5042	Hand Pin	5118	Hand Spring	5900	Rear Sight Slide 4" & 6½" bbl.
5045	Locking Bolt Spring	5155	Rear Sight Leaf Screw	5901	Barrel, 4"
5047	Mainspring	5219	Rear Sight Leaf	5912	Stock, checked Goncalo Alves Target, right
5049	Plate Screw, Crowned	5306	Trigger Stop Rod		
5053	Hand Spring Pin	5357	Cylinder Stop	5913	Stock, checked Goncalo Alves Target, left
5053	Hand Spring Torsion Pin	5389	Bolt Plunger		
5053	Stirrup Pin	5418	Hammer Nose	5930	Frame Lug
5053	Trigger Lever Pin	5421	Hammer, wide Target type	5941	Barrel, 8⅜"
5054	Sear Spring	5423	Hammer Block	7055	Cylinder Stop Spring
5055	Stirrup	5426	Hand	7158	Rear Sight Plunger
5062	Stock Pin	5429	Locking Bolt	7159	Rear Sight Plunger Spring
5064	Strain Screw	5430	Side Plate	7271	Center Pin
5071	Thumbpiece Nut	5431	Locking Bolt Pin	7263	Stock Screw
5073	Trigger Lever	5448	Extractor	7275	Center Pin

EXPLODED VIEW OF S&W M29/.44 MAGNUM

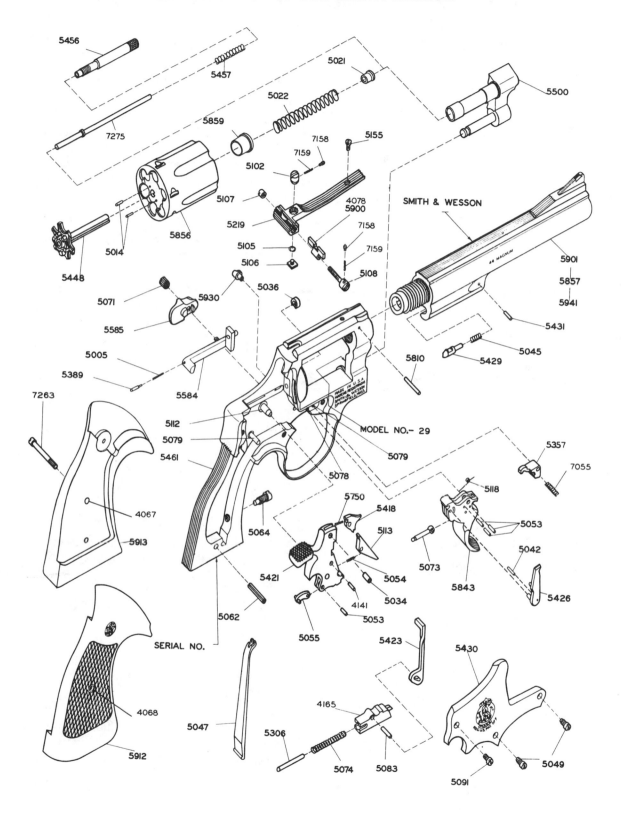

S&W M53

Action type: double-action revolver

Cylinder capacity: 6-shot

Barrel length: 4.0, 6.0, or 8.375 inches

Weight: 4.0-inch barrel, 37.5 oz.; 6.0-inch barrel, 40.0 oz.; 8.375-inch barrel, 43.5 oz.

Stock: Magna type; checkered walnut

Overall length: 4.0-inch barrel, 9.25 inches; 6.0-inch barrel, 11.25 inches; 8.375-inch barrel, 13.875 inches

Trigger pull: single action, 4.5 lbs.; double action, 8.0–10.0 lbs.

Sight, rear: micrometer, adjustable for windage and elevation

Sight, front: 0.125-inch-wide Baughman quick-draw

Caliber: .22 Rem. Jet (centerfire); .22 Long Rifle with individual chamber inserts

Comment: A very accurate medium-frame hunting/target-type sixgun. Individual chambers for the .22 Long Rifle cartridge can be inserted in .22 Jet chambers. Firing pin is adjustable for rim- or centerfire cartridges. Should be fitted with extra-cost white outline for rear sight notch, with target-type hammer and trigger.

S&W M57

Action type: double-action revolver

Cylinder capacity: 6-shot

Barrel length: 4.0, 6.5, or 8.375 inches

Weight: 4.0-inch barrel, 44.0 oz.; 6.5-inch barrel, 48.0 oz.; 8.375-inch barrel, 52.0 oz.

Stock: oversize target type; checkered Goncalo Alves wood

Overall length: 4.0-inch barrel, 9.375 inches; 6.5-inch barrel, 11.875 inches; 8.375-inch barrel, 13.75 inches

Trigger pull: single action, 4.0 lbs.; double action, 8.0–10.0 lbs.

Sight, rear: micrometer, adjustable for windage and elevation; white-outlined square notch

Sight, front: serrated 0.125-inch-wide ramp with red insert

Caliber: .41 Magnum

Data: The M57 has a Type-N (large) all-steel frame, a wide, checkered target-type hammer and wide, grooved target-type trigger. Choice of bright bluing or nickel plating.

Comment: This handgun is identical to the M29 .44 Magnum in all respects except caliber. It is slightly heavier because of the smaller-caliber barrel and cylinder (exterior dimensions identical to M29). This revolver and caliber were the result of Elmer Keith's request for a sixgun with slightly less power than the .44 Magnum.

CHAPTER 30

SEMIAUTOMATIC CENTERFIRE PISTOLS

The semiautomatic pistol, often called "automatic" or "autoloading," is the latest, though not necessarily the last, type of handgun action to appear on the market.

There are three basic semiautomatic actions, but here we are concerned only with the large-caliber (9mm and up) recoil-operated semiautomatic.

The semiautomatic pistol is not a good choice for big-game hunting. The full metal-jacketed "solid" big-bore rifle bullet is designed for use on thick-skinned game like Cape buffalo, rhino, and elephant; with that exception, the full metal-jacketed bullet is not a good choice for game. It slips into or through the game without adequate expansion. This is not to say that the .45 ACP 230-grain bullet won't kill game. It will, but properly designed lead or softpoint revolver bullets are much more effective.

The basic role of the semiautomatic pistol in the sporting world is that of target matches or plinking.

This chapter is not concerned with the so-called pocket automatics in calibers like .25 ACP (6.35mm), .32 ACP (7.65mm) or .380 ACP (9mm Short). In the United States these are strictly self-defense weapons, though the 7.65mm and 9mm Short (Kurz or Corto) are standard holster weapons for many European uniformed peace officers.

The first successful semiautomatic pistol used for military and some sporting purposes was the famed "broom-handle" M1896 Mauser, caliber 7.63mm (a few were made in 9mm Mauser—not 9mm Parabellum—caliber). This pistol, though never adopted as an official military sidearm by any nation, at least in the memory of Mauser Werke officials, was widely used as a personal sidearm by many officers in Czarist Russia, China, and other countries.

The original version used a 10-shot stripper clip. Later versions used detachable 10- and 20-shot magazines. There was also a full automatic version. Some M1896 pistols and successor models had detachable shoulder stocks. Some stocks were stiff leather holsters, while other stocks were hollow wooden holsters.

In U.S. Ordnance trials in Newport, R.I., in the early 1890s there was a semiautomatic pistol designed by German-born Hugo Borchardt, who had designed or improved several existing arms, including the Borchardt-Sharps. Borchardt returned to Germany, where he secured the backing of Georg Luger. The pistol was redesigned and was marketed by DWM as the 9mm Parabellum. This is the prized collector's arm known to Americans as the Luger. The term "Luger" is almost exclusively American. Elsewhere it is the "Parabellum," which means "for war."

In 1908 the German army adopted the pistol. Its official nomenclature was, and still is, Pistol '08 (1908). It was the standard sidearm for the Wehrmacht in World War I and was the limited standard in World War II.

The P-08 was made by many companies, including DWM, Mauser Werke, Simson of Stuhl, Vickers in England, and in Switzerland.

The 1919 Treaty of Versailles prohibited the manufacture in Germany of sidearms chambered for the 9mm Parabellum. P-08 manufacture was allowed only in caliber 7.65mm (known in the U.S.A. as caliber .30 Luger). This cartridge employed a necked-down 9mm case. German arms designers developed the new cartridge and arm so that the pistols could be readily converted to 9mm Parabellum by switching barrels and magazines.

In 1911 the United States Army adopted an improved version of the M1905 Colt (1900 patent) designed by John Moses Browning. This famed semiauto pistol—with slight exterior modifications (M1911A1)—is still the standard U.S. Army and U.S. Marine Corps sidearm.

The pistol was supplied to most of our allies

during World War II, the Korean Conflict and the ensuing brushfire wars, and the Vietnam War. The Norwegian government used it for about 40 years as the standard service pistol. During World War II it was produced in Norway for use by German troops. It was made in Pusan, Korea, during the early 1950s.

Unlicensed, and hence unpaid-for, copies have been and still are being made in Spain and Argentina. It was made in China during the regime of Chiang Kai-shek.

In caliber .45 matches, customized .45 Colts have reigned supreme for more than a half-century.

The 9mm Parabellum cartridge is more accurate at extended ranges, but the cartridge lacks the heavy punch of the 230-grain metal-case ACP bullet.

In 1938 another pistol entered the military and later the civilian arena—the Pistole 1938, better known as the P-38 Walther. This was the first double-action semiautomatic pistol adopted by any major power. It was the standard service arm of the World War II Wehrmacht and remains the same for the West German Republic's army. Most P-38s are in caliber 9mm Parabellum, though the same gun is now available in .30 Luger and .22 Long Rifle. A few experimental pistols were made in .38 Super Colt and .45 ACP.

P-38 usage will never reach that of the P-08, M1911/M1911A1 or the M1935 Browning Hi-Power. This is not because the pistol is not an excellent one but because the U.S. spread the M1911/M1911A1 throughout much of the world and because NATO powers except the United States and Germany use the M1935 Browning Hi-Power.

The Browning, though it lacks the double-action feature of the P-38, has a 13-shot magazine, a feature considered desirable by many military people.

Until World War II, the M1935 was made only in Belgium by FN. When the Nazis overran Belgium and took over wartime M1935 production for themselves, the British army, which had adopted the arm, generated production elsewhere. In Canada the John Inglis Co. produced more than a million M1935s for the Chinese Nationalist Army. Many of these, along with U.S.-supplied M1911/M1911A1s, ended up with Mao's millions.

It is interesting to note that of the three great military pistols, the Parabellum, the M1911/M1911A1, and the M1935, two were designed by John Moses Browning.

Today, the Parabellum is made by Mauser Werke, Colt makes an improved M1911/M1911A1, and FN continues M1935 production. These arms designs range from 50 to 75 years in age (the M1935 was designed several years before it went into production). The P-38 is approaching its 40th birthday.

Some arms described in this chapter are not fitted with micrometer sights adjustable for windage. However, existing micrometer sights can be modified to fit. You should do this to secure maximum effectiveness from your handgun.

The arms described in this chapter are locked-breech, recoil-operated, and air-cooled.

The unlocked-breech blowback system is designed for low-powered .22 caliber rimfires or pocket automatics like the .25 ACP, .32 ACP, and .380 ACP.

SEMIAUTOMATIC PISTOL VS. THE REVOLVER

Advantages

1. The semiautomatic is faster to load and reload than the revolver.
2. The semiauto is easier to clean thoroughly.
3. The semiauto has greater rapidity of fire.
4. The semiauto design allows no gas leakage or bullet shaving.
5. It is easier to replace semiauto parts, including barrel.
6. The semiauto usually has a better grip than the revolver.
7. The semiauto has greater magazine capacity than the revolver (in some arms more than twice the capacity).
8. The semiauto is more compact than the revolver.

Disadvantages

1. The semiauto requires perfect ammunition; defective ammunition jams it.
2. Clips must be in perfect condition or feeding jams result.
3. The semiautomatic is not as safe for tyros to handle as the revolver.
4. All other factors being equal, metal-jacketed bullets are not as effective as softpoint or lead bullets.
5. Empty cases which are thrown from the semiauto are sometimes dented during the ejection process and are more difficult to recover.
6. Fired cases sometimes eject in the shooter's face.
7. Normally, blanks or reduced loads cannot be used because the action will not function with them.
8. The magazine spring may deteriorate after being left loaded for an extended period. This can create functioning difficulties for those who keep a pistol for self-defense purposes and rarely use it.

BROWNING M1935 HI-POWER PISTOL

Manufacturer: Fabrique Nationale, Belgium

Importer/distributor: Browning Arms

Action type: semiautomatic; recoil-operated; locked breech; exposed hammer; air-cooled

Magazine type: detachable staggered box

Magazine capacity: 13-shot (10-shot on Belgian Army model; 15-shot on original inventor's model)

Safety: thumb safety (left side); cannot be activated unless hammer is cocked and slide is at rearmost position; pistol cannot be fired unless magazine is in position

Barrel length: 4.75 inches

Weight: 34.0 oz.

Stock: 2-piece checkered walnut

Overall length: 7.75 inches

Trigger pull: 5.0–8.0 lbs. (closer to 5.0 lbs. on most current commercial models)

Finish: Parkerized on most military models; medium-gloss blue on current civilian models

Sight, rear: fixed square notch or optional tangent leaf adjustable for 500 meters

Sight, front: barleycorn (half-moon) on current commercial models

Caliber: 9mm (Luger) Parabellum

Data: In 1923 the French Ministry of War asked John Moses Browning to submit prototypes of a semiautomatic pistol with an extra-large magazine capacity and chambered for the 9mm (Luger) Parabellum cartridge.

Browning submitted two distinctly different models. One, never patented, was a simple blowback. The second model resembles the present M1935 Hi-Power. It had a 15-shot magazine. The French ultimately adopted an inferior pistol and inferior cartridge.

In 1926 Browning applied for a U.S. patent covering the pistol's operating principles and mechanism. Patent No. 1,276,716 was issued August 27, 1927, several months after Browning's death. This was his last patent.

The M1935, also known as the Browning Hi-Power, was issued with a 13-shot magazine, which it currently retains. Its original manufacturer, Fabrique Nationale, continues to produce the M1935. Belgium was the first nation to adopt it as a standard service arm.

After the organization of NATO, all members except the United States (M1911/M1911A1 pistol) and West Germany (P-38 Walther) adopted the M1935. The current supply for the Canadian Armed Forces comes from World War II stocks. Some surplus has been sold in the U.S.A.

Standard military-issue stocks are usually black plastic. The Canadians used some M1896 Mauser-type holster-stocks (hollowed-out wood), which were fitted to a grip cut in the pistol. This type of holster-stock attached to the user's belt with a spring clip. A few Parabellum (Luger) type flat-board stocks were also issued. This stock type could not be used as a holster.

There were variations in extractor and ejector design and tolerances. Some interchange with other M1935s.

The standard service rear sight was the fixed square notch. Canadian M1935s designed for use with stock-holster combinations or for shoulder stocks alone were fitted with a rear tangent sight leaf.

Unless a special permit is purchased from the Treasury Department's Bureau of Alcohol, Tobacco, and Firearms (BATF) unit, it is illegal in the United States to own both a shoulder stock and an M1935 which has provision for attaching a stock. It is legal to own a holster-stock or a stock and an M1935 from which the stock lug has been removed.

Comment: This is one of the finest semiautomatic pistols made. For those who prefer a double-action semiautomatic pistol, some pistolsmiths can convert the M1935 to a double-action mechanism.

EXPLODED VIEW OF BROWNING M1935 HI-POWER PISTOL

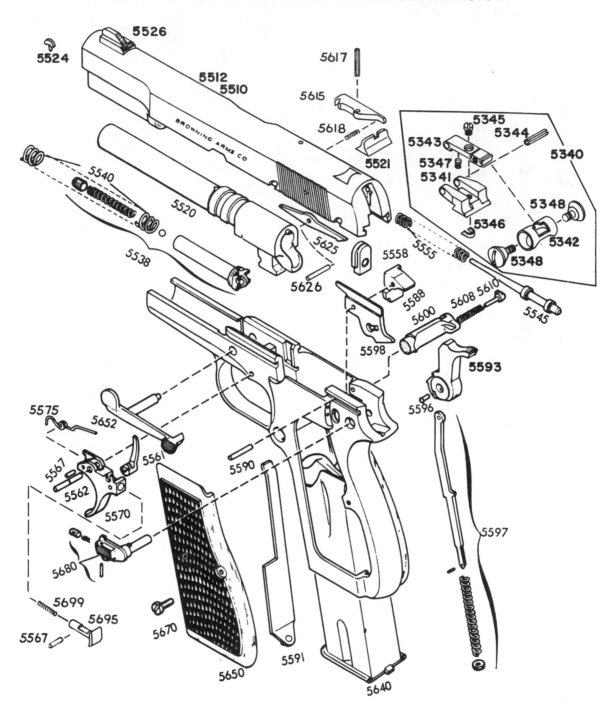

COLT COMBAT COMMANDER

Action type: semiautomatic; recoil-operated; locked breech; air-cooled; lanyard-type hammer

Magazine type: detachable straight-line box

Magazine capacity: .45 ACP, 7-shot; .38 Super and 9mm (Luger) Parabellum, 9-shot

Safety: thumb safety (left side); grip safety (backstrap)

Barrel length: 4.25 inches

Weight: .38 Super and 9mm (Luger) Parabellum, 36.5 oz.; .45 ACP, 35.0 oz.

Stock: 2-piece panel; sandblasted walnut

Overall length: 7.875 inches

Trigger pull: 5.0 lbs.

Sight, rear: square notch; micrometer adjustable for windage and elevation available

Sight, front: blade

Caliber: 9mm (Luger) Parabellum; .38 Super; .45 ACP

Data: All-steel frame, Colt Blue or satin nickel finish. 5.75-inch sight radius.

Comment: This is a heavier (all-steel) version of the alloy Lightweight Commander and a lighter compact version of the M1911/M1911A1.

Parts List for Browning M1935 Hi-Power Pistol

No.	Part Name	No.	Part Name	No.	Part Name
5520	Barrel	5604	Magazine Latch	5343	Sight Aperture Housing, Rear, Adjustable Sight Model
5598	Ejector	5608	Magazine Latch Spring		
5599	Ejector	5610	Magazine Latch Spring Guide	5344	Sight Aperture Housing Pin, Rear, Adjustable Sight Model
5615	Extractor	5614	Magazine Latch Spring Guide		
5616	Extractor	5695	Magazine Safety	5345	Sight Elevation Screw, Rear, Adjustable Sight Model
5617	Extractor Pin	5699	Magazine Safety Spring		
5618	Extractor Spring	5567	Magazine Safety Pin & Trigger Spring Pin	5346	Sight Elevation Screw Spring, Rear, Adjustable Sight Model
5620	Extractor Old Style				
5624	Extractor Old Style	5568	Magazine Safety Pin & Trigger Spring Pin	5347	Sight Elevation Spring, Rear, Adjustable Sight Model
5545	Firing Pin				
5555	Firing Pin Spring	5540	Recoil Spring	5348	Sight Windage Screw, Rear, Adjustable Sight Model
5558	Firing Pin Retaining Plate	5538	Recoil Spring Guide Assy. with Slide Stop Retaining Ball, Spring & Cap		
5559	Firing Pin Retaining Plate			5521	Sight—Rear
5650	Grip Plate—Left—French Walnut			5522	Sight—Rear
5654	Grip Plate—Left—Nacrolac Pearl	5680	Safety Assembly Complete	5524	Sight—Front
5660	Grip Plate—Right—French Walnut	5684	Safety Assembly Complete	5526	Sight—Front—Adjustable Sight Model
5664	Grip Plate—Right—Nacrolac Pearl	5588	Sear		
5670	Grip Plate Screw	5625	Sear Lever	5510	Slide—with Front Sight
5674	Grip Plate Screw	5626	Sear Lever Pin	5512	Slide—Adjustable Sight Model
5593	Hammer (New Type)	5627	Sear Lever Pivot Old Style	5514	Slide—with Front Sight
5594	Hammer	5628	Sear Lever Pivot Old Style	5652	Slide Stop
5595	Hammer (New Type)	5590	Sear Pin	5653	Slide Stop
5597	Hammer Strut Assembly with Mainspring, Mainspring Support Pin, & Nut	5591	Sear Spring with Button	5570	Trigger
		5340	Rear Sight Complete, Adjustable Sight Model	5574	Trigger—Gold Plated
				5561	Trigger Lever
5596	Hammer Strut Pin	5341	Rear Sight Base, Adjustable Sight Model	5562	Trigger Pin
5640	Magazine Complete			5563	Trigger Pin
5644	Magazine Complete	5342	Sight Aperture, Rear, Adjustable Sight Model	5575	Trigger Spring
5600	Magazine Latch				

COLT GOLD CUP NATIONAL MATCH MK IV/SERIES '70

Action type: semiautomatic; recoil-operated; locked breech; air-cooled; exposed hammer

Magazine type: detachable straight-line box

Magazine capacity: 7-shot

Safety: thumb safety (left side of frame); grip safety (backstrap)

Barrel length: 5.0 inches

Weight: 38.5 oz.

Stock: 2-piece checkered walnut

Overall length: 8.375 inches

Trigger pull: adjustable

Sight, rear: special Colt-Elliason, adjustable for windage and elevation

Sight, front: undercut blade

Caliber: .45 ACP

Data: Serrated trigger, all-steel frame (large), Colt Blue finish. This gun has a longer sight radius (6.75 inches) than the Colt Combat Commander.

Comment: This version of the Colt Gold Cup and customized/accurized other Colt .45 ACPs is the finest and most accurate .45 caliber target pistol made. The design by George Elliason, is a modification of the original John Moses Browning design. The author has been attending matches for more than 40 years and has never seen any target .45 that was not a basic Browning-designed Colt or Colt-licensed.

Features which a target Colt .45 ACP must have are a tight slide, tight barrel bushing, light trigger with no creep, and excellent sights.

Many old service M1911/M1911A1s have been converted to top match-winning pistols by gunsmiths like Jesse Harper.

COLT LIGHTWEIGHT COMMANDER

Action type: semiautomatic; recoil-operated; locked breech; air-cooled; lanyard-type hammer

Magazine type: detachable straight-line box

Magazine capacity: .45 ACP, 7-shot; .38 Super (ACP) and 9mm (Luger) Parabellum, 9-shot

Safety: thumb safety (left side); grip safety (on backstrap)

Barrel length: 4.25 inches

Weight: 27.0 oz.

Stock: 2 sandblasted walnut panels

Overall length: 7.875 inches

Trigger pull: 5.0 lbs.

Sight, rear: square notch; micrometer sight adjustable for windage and elevation available

COLT LIGHTWEIGHT COMMANDER (continued)

Sight, front: fixed blade

Caliber: .38 Super, .45 ACP, 9mm (Luger) Parabellum

Data: Alloy frame, Colt Blue finish.

Comment: This is lightweight version of the Combat Commander, which in turn is a light, compact version of the M1911/M1911A1. The author considers this too light for good accuracy.

COLT GOVERNMENT MODEL MK IV/SERIES 70

Action type: semiautomatic; recoil-operated; locked breech; single-action; exposed hammer; air-cooled

Magazine type: detachable straight-line box

Magazine capacity: .45 ACP, 7-shot; .38 Super and 9mm (Luger) Parabellum, 9-shot

Safety: thumb safety (left side); grip safety (on backstrap)

Barrel length: 5.0 inches

Weight: .38 Super and 9mm (Luger) Parabellum, 40.0 oz.; .45 ACP, 39.0 oz.

Stock: 2-piece sand-blasted walnut; checkered walnut discontinued; plastic checkered stocks used on some World War II guns

Overall length: 8.375 inches

Trigger pull: 5.0 lbs. current commercial; 5.5–6.5 lbs. new or repaired military

Sight, rear: square notch

Sight, front: blade

Caliber: .38 Super (.38 ACP), .45 ACP, 9mm (Luger) Parabellum

Data: All-steel frame, size 0. Colt Blue or optionally nickel plate; military versions usually Parkerized. This is a slightly modified version of the U.S. Pistol, Caliber .45 M1911 and its successor the M1911A1. The basic differences are the barrel and barrel bushing, which have been "accurized." Parts are interchangeable with M1911/M1911A1 or commercial version.

About 1905 the U.S. Army evinced an interest in adopting a semiautomatic pistol. John Moses Browning submitted two designs. The first was the .45 Caliber Military Model Hammerless Semi-Automatic Pistol. This model is similar to the M1905 Hammer Model; it is different in minor details and had no hammer. It was never

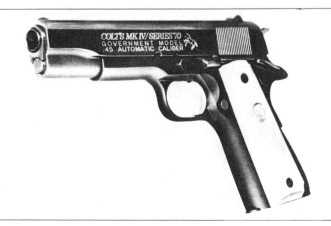

EXPLODED VIEW OF COLT GOVERNMENT MODEL MK IV/SERIES 70

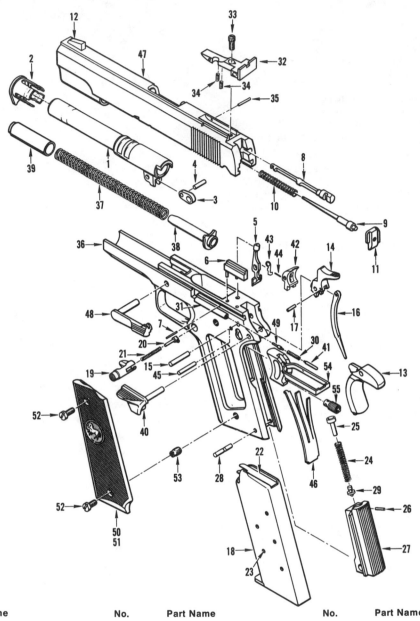

No.	Part Name	No.	Part Name	No.	Part Name
1	Barrel	20	Magazine Catch Lock	38	Recoil Spring Guide
2	Barrel Bushing	21	Magazine Catch Spring	39	Recoil Spring Plug
3	Barrel Link	22	Magazine Follower	40	Safety Lock
4	Barrel Link Pin	23	Magazine Spring	41	Safety Lock Plunger
5	Disconnector	24	Main Spring	42	Sear
6	Ejector	25	Main Spring Cap	43	Depressor
7	Ejector Pin	26	Main Spring Cap Pin	44	Depressor Spring
8	Extractor	27	Main Spring Housing—(Round)	45	Sear Pin
9	Firing Pin	27	Main Spring Housing—(Square)	46	Sear Spring
10	Firing Pin Spring	28	Main Spring Housing Pin	47	Slide
11	Firing Pin Stop	29	Main Spring Housing Pin Retainer	48	Slide Stop
12	Front Sight	30	Plunger Spring	49	Slide Stop Plunger
13	Grip Safety	31	Plunger Tube	50	Stock Assembly R.H.—Walnut
14	Hammer	32	Rear Sight Leaf	51	Stock Assembly L.H.—Walnut
15	Hammer Pin	33	Rear Sight Elevation Screw	52	Stock Screw—(4)
16	Hammer Strut	34	Rear Sight Elevation Spring—(2)	53	Stock Screw Bushing
17	Hammer Strut Pin	35	Rear Sight Leaf Pin	54	Trigger Detail Assembly
18	Magazine Tube Detail Assembly	36	Receiver	55	Trigger Stop
19	Magazine Catch	37	Recoil Spring		Elliason Sight—Not Shown

COLT GOVERNMENT MODEL MK IV/SERIES 70
(continued)

produced commercially. The second was the .45 Caliber Military Model 1905, with an exposed hammer. Several thousand were produced commercially.

In 1911 the U.S. Army, and later the Navy and Marine Corps, adopted a slightly modified version of the M1905 Military Hammer Model. This was the standard service pistol in World War I.

Patent No. 984,519, issued February 14, 1911, and Patent No. 1,070,582, issued April 23, 1913, applied to the M1911. The pistol was adopted March 29, 1911.

Most of the approximately 100,000 M1911s made between 1911 and April 1917 were manufactured by Colt. A few, now rare items, were made in Springfield Armory. U.S. entry into World War I generated a need for increased production. Colt, already in production, and Remington Arms were the only ones of ten contractors to produce effective quantities. Colt made nearly 500,000 and Remington made about 100,000. Most contractors never got into production.

After World War I most pistols were put into arsenal storage. The extensive experiences of the war led to minor external modifications. The modified pistol was designated M1911A1. Modifications included grip safety tang extended to better protect hand; clearance cut in receiver for trigger finger (easier for small fingers to reach trigger); trigger face cut back; trigger face knurled; mainspring housing arched to better conform with average hand; top of front sight widened.

During World War II both M1911 and M1911A1s were issued. Contracts were let to Colt (400,000), Ithaca (400,000), Remington-Rand (900,000), and Union Switch & Signal (50,000). These are approximate production figures.

The M1911/M1911A1 with slight or no modifications were adopted by numerous countries, including Norway (Germans continued production during occupation), Mexico, and Argentina. Pirated copies were made in Nationalist China. A Pusan, Korea, arsenal made M1911A1s during the Korean Police Action.

The original patents expired some years ago, but long before that, unlicensed copies were made in several countries. Mexico now uses a simplified M1911A1, the Obregon.

During World War I Colt furnished the M1911 in caliber .455 Self Loading Pistol to the Royal Navy. In World War II these same pistols were issued to the Royal Air Force. During and after World War II the United States furnished M1911/M1911A1 pistols to just about every Allied nation.

World War II M1911A1 production would have been greater except that the U.S. Navy and the U.S. Army Air Force adopted the Smith & Wesson Victory Model caliber .38 Special. Colt and S&W M1917 revolvers were used as Limited or Substitute Standard arms.

Comment: Most service personnel who used the .45 M1911/M1911A1 criticized its accuracy. This was because they were given inadequate training. The arm's effectiveness could also be improved by a rear sight adjustable for windage and elevation.

In the army before World War II the best rank-and-file pistol shots were U.S. Cavalrymen. In the infantry only officers and non-coms were generally issued sidearms. Field artillerymen were issued sidearms, but they rarely came into pistol contact with the enemy. The old horse cavalrymen—the author was one—knew how to use the pistol, both mounted and dismounted, and use it effectively.

The pistol, though capable of effective long-range work, is essentially a short-range self-defense arm. Civilian owners of M1911/M1911A1's should fit them with a micrometer rear sight. The trigger pull should be improved by an expert pistolsmith. The slide should be trued up, but not as much as in a match pistol or it will not function under adverse conditions of mud and dirt.

MAUSER (LUGER) P-08 PARABELLUM PISTOL

Manufacturer: Mauser Werke, West Germany

Importer/distributor: Interarms

Action type: semiautomatic, short recoil; locked toggle breech; fixed barrel; air-cooled

Magazine type: detachable straight-line box

Magazine capacity: 8-shot; 32-shot snail drum discontinued

Safety: thumb safety; extractor acts as loading indicator when elevated by chambered cartridge; the word LOADED also appears; when thumb safety is engaged the word SAFE appears on frame

Barrel length: 4.0 or 6.0 inches

Weight: 4.0-inch barrel, 32.0 oz.; 6.0-inch barrel, 35.0 oz.

Stock: 2-piece European walnut; sharply defined checkering (16 lines per inch)

Overall length: 4.0-inch barrel, 8.66 inches; 6.0-inch barrel, 10.66 inches

Trigger pull: 2.75 lbs., minimal creep

Sight, rear: fixed U-notch

Sight, front: tapered post, adjustable for windage

Caliber: 7.65mm (Luger) Parabellum (.30 Luger), 9mm (Luger) Parabellum

Data: Pistol has 8.6-inch sight radius with 4.0-inch barrel, 10.6-inch sight radius with 6.0-inch barrel. This slightly modified and improved version of the P-08 was designed by Hugo Borchardt and Georg Luger. Unlike the original P-08, this version has a grip safety. The front grip strap is curved. There are slight differences in the trigger shape, take-down lever, lock block, and safety lever.

Comment: The author prefers a curved forward strap, as it fits his hand better. Some hands, however, may be better adapted to the straight strap of the M-29 Parabellum. The 9mm Parabellum is not a good hunting cartridge, so perhaps it isn't important that this pistol's toggle-breech design doesn't accommodate scope mounting. The trend today is to use scoped pistols for hunting.

MAUSER (LUGER) M-29 (SWISS TYPE) PARABELLUM PISTOL

Manufacturer: Mauser Werke, West Germany

Importer/distributor: Interarms

Action type: semiautomatic; recoil-operated; fixed barrel; air-cooled

Magazine type: detachable straight-line box

Magazine capacity: 8-shot; 32-shot snail drum discontinued

Safety: thumb safety; grip safety; as with M1911/M1911A1 Colt, grip must be fully depressed before pistol will fire; extractor acts as loading indicator; when elevated by chambered cartridge; the word LOADED also appears; when thumb safety is engaged, the word SAFE appears on frame

Barrel length: 4.0 or 6.0 inches

Weight: 4.0-inch barrel, 32.0 oz.; 6.0-inch barrel,, 35.0 oz.

Stock: 2-piece oil-finished European walnut; clearly defined checkering (16 lines per inch)

Overall length: 4.0-inch barrel, 8.66 inches; 6.0-inch barrel, 10.66 inches

Trigger pull: 2.6 lbs.; minimal creep

Sight, rear: fixed U-notch

Sight, front: tapered post adjustable for windage

Sight radius: 4.0-inch barrel, 9.68 inches; 6.0-inch barrel, 11.68 inches

Caliber: 7.65mm (Luger) Parabellum (.30 Luger), 9mm (Luger) Parabellum

Data: This pistol resembles the M1929 Swiss Army model. The Swiss were the first to adopt the Luger pistol (M1901) in caliber 7.65mm Parabellum. An improved version, the M1904, was adopted by the Deutsch Kriegsmarine (German navy). This was chambered for the 9mm (Luger) Parabellum cartridge. In 1906 the original flat steel mainspring—easily broken as in the Colt Single Action Army revolver and others—was replaced by a coil spring.

The German army adopted the pistol in 1908, as noted earlier in this chapter. To facilitate wartime production, the grip safety was deleted. All commercial production prior to 1920 (German production ceased in November, 1918) was done by Deutsche Waffen und Munitionsfabriken (DWM). The firm's wartime production was implemented by Erfurt (German arsenal) manufacture.

About 1920 the Allies allowed Simson, GmbH, Stuhl, to manufacture the pistol for members of the 100,000-man German police force/army. Caliber was restricted to 7.65mm Parabellum.

During the 1930s, German arms production intensified. The P-'08 was made by Heinrich Krieghoff, maker of fine shotguns, for the ballooning Luftwaffe and by Mauser and Simson for the German army.

A. F. Stoeger imported Mauser-made P-08s, each stamped with the American eagle and the Mauser banner, for commercial use. These were probably the finest Lugers ever made.

Stoeger Lugers can be identified by the phrase (right side of frame): GENUINE LUGER—REGISTERED U.S. PATENT OFFICE. Above on the toggle: A. F. STOEGER, INC. NEW YORK. The American eagle was stamped on the top of the breechblock.

No arm today can bear the word "Luger" without permission of Stoeger Industries, successor to A. F. Stoeger, Inc. The term "Luger" was never employed in Germany, where the P-08 was and is called the Pistole (or P-08) Parabellum.

Stoeger offered 4.0-inch and 8.0-inch barrel lengths in caliber 9mm Parabellum. The 8.0-inch-barrel model had a folding-leaf sight mounted on the barrel just forward of the receiver. It is unfortunate that this sight is not fitted on current production models.

Between the two world wars the so-called Luger was made in England (by Vickers-Armstrong), in Holland and Switzerland. The pistol was adopted by Germany, Switzerland, Portugal, and Bulgaria. It was sold in substantial quantities in the USSR, Brazil, and Canada. It was widely used by many national police departments.

The present M29's frame, toggle, slide, and other major components are machined from forged steel. Investment steel castings are used for the safety arm, trigger, locking bolt, firing pin, and side plate.

The current M-29 has a straight front strap rather than the traditional curved strap of the P-08. The grip safety of the M1929 and pre-P-08 Parabellums is incorporated in the M-29. In the P-08 and all other Parabellums, except the M1929 and M-29, the trigger-lever well extends only partway to the top of the plate. In the M-29, as in the M1929, the well extends to the plate's top.

Basic field stripping can be readily accomplished without tools. However, the classic Parabellum tool (which includes a screwdriver) can be used to dismount the side grip (stock) panels and to remove the firing-pin container unit in the breech block.

The tool is helpful in pushing down the very stiff magazine spring while loading the magazine. Many experienced Parabellum users load the detachable box magazine with only seven instead of eight cartridges. This technique possibly prolongs the life of the magazine follower spring by not compressing it to its maximum.

Comment: This is a well-designed and well-made pistol. The muzzle is a bit light due to the exeedingly thin slender barrel. The gun could be improved by the addition of an adjustable rear sight and an improved front sight.

Some machining marks were noted on the two pistols test-fired by the author and on five others he examined in various gunshops. These marks would never have passed a prewar Mauser commercial inspector.

The American Eagle and Mauser banner are too shallowly etched to survive much handling.

The grip safety dug painfully into the author's hand during recoil. He easily removed it. This gouging occurred only with heavy 9mm military (German and Canadian) loads.

S&W M59 DOUBLE-ACTION PISTOL

Action type: semiautomatic; recoil-operated; double action; locked breech; external hammer

Magazine type: detachable staggered box

Magazine capacity: 14-shot

Safety: thumb safety (left side)

Barrel length: 4.108 inches

Weight: 30.0 oz.

Stock: 2-piece black nylon; checkered

Overall length: 7.5 inches

Trigger pull: 4.0 lbs.; minimal creep

Sight, rear: square notch; micrometer, adjustable for windage and elevation

Sight, front: 0.125-inch-wide serrated blade on ramp

Caliber: 9mm (Luger) Parabellum

Data: Aluminum alloy frame; steel slide and barrel. Magazine is all steel except cast-aluminum follower. Frame similar to but not identical with S&W M39. Many components, however, are interchangeable, including slide, barrel, extractor, and some internal components. Magazine, magazine catch, draw bar, and slide stop are wider because of greater—hence wider—magazine capacity. Black anodized frame and blued slide.

After the last shot is fired the slide remains open. The magazine disconnector makes it impossible to fire when magazine is removed.

This pistol can be fired by a long pull on the trigger or by cocking the hammer and then a short pull on the trigger. Standard smooth trigger with serrated spur.

Comment: The magazine of this pistol will accept 15 cartridges but this is not recommended. The extra cartridge places undue stress on the magazine spring. Many automatic pistol shooters, including the author, rarely if ever load any pistol magazine to its full capacity. Better one less round and a more reliably functioning magazine spring. If one deems it necessary, the one less cartridge in the magazine can be made up by placing one round in the chamber. Load the magazine to stated capacity and then slide one cartridge into the chamber.

This is a well-designed double-action semiautomatic pistol. It is made of fine materials, and workmanship is typically of the high quality expected of S&W sidearms.

Accuracy can be improved by having a custom pistolsmith straighten the slide. This straightening, however, should not be carried to an extreme, or the arm may not function under sandy or muddy conditions. This arm is obviously intended primarily for police and military markets. Semiautomatic pistols designed for such service must have greater tolerances than target arms of the same type.

The author fired 350 cartridges of various commercial and military makes without a single misfire or malfunction.

Despite the merits of this arm, the stopping power of the 9mm (Luger) cartridge is far less than that of the .45 ACP cartridges.

WALTHER PISTOLE 1938 (P-38) DOUBLE ACTION PISTOL

Manufacturer: Carl Walther Waffenfabriken, West Germany

Importer/distributor: Interarms

Action type: semiautomatic; recoil-operated; double-action, locked breech; air-cooled

Magazine type: detachable straight-line box

Magazine capacity: 8-shot

Safety: see data below

Barrel length: 4.925 inches standard; various lengths on experimentals and World War II special-purpose models; .22 Long Rifle version, 5.625 inches

Weight: original, 29.5 oz.; current P-38 alloy model, 28.0 oz.

Stock: original, hand-checkered walnut; military and current commercial, black plastic

Overall length: 8.5 inches

Sight, rear: fixed square notch; can be fitted with micrometer adjustable for windage and elevation

Sight, front: blade

Caliber: 7.65mm (.30 Luger) Parabellum, 9mm (Luger) Parabellum, .22 Long Rifle, .38 Super Colt (experimental only), .45 ACP (experimental only)

Data: In 1937, Waffenfabrik Walther (Carl Walther) issued a double-action pistol chambered for the 9mm (Luger) Parabellum cartridge. The workmanship, including hand-checkered stocks and fitting of components, made this pistol the equal in quality of any semiautomatic pistol ever produced, and it has the advantage of double action. The frame was steel and the finish was highest-quality bluing; current production has alloy frame and blue-black finish (matte black on military).

This pistol, designated "Heeres Pistole" (service pistol), is generally referred to as the Model HP (or H.P.). The HP was offered for sale in 1939 by A. F. Stoeger. The price was $75. It was designated the "Walther HP Army Pistol."

Stoeger noted that orders were being taken for the pistol in .38 Super and .45 ACP and that delivery could be expected by mid-1939. World War II intervened.

In 1938 the Wehrmacht adopted a slightly modified version of the Model HP. This was designated Pistole 1938 (P-38) for the year of adoption. Some changes were made in sear and safety design. These parts are not interchangeable with the HP.

World War II military-issue pistols carried a code rather than the manufacturer's trade name and trademark(s). P-38s marked "ac" were made in the Walther Zella-Mehlis plant. P-38s marked "byf" were made in the Mauser Werke, Oberndorf.

Sweden adopted the P-38 in 1939 as the standard army service pistol. The Swedish designation for the arm is P-39 (from year of adoption). The P-38 is now the standard service pistol of the West German Republic's army.

EXPLODED VIEW OF S&W M59 DOUBLE-ACTION PISTOL

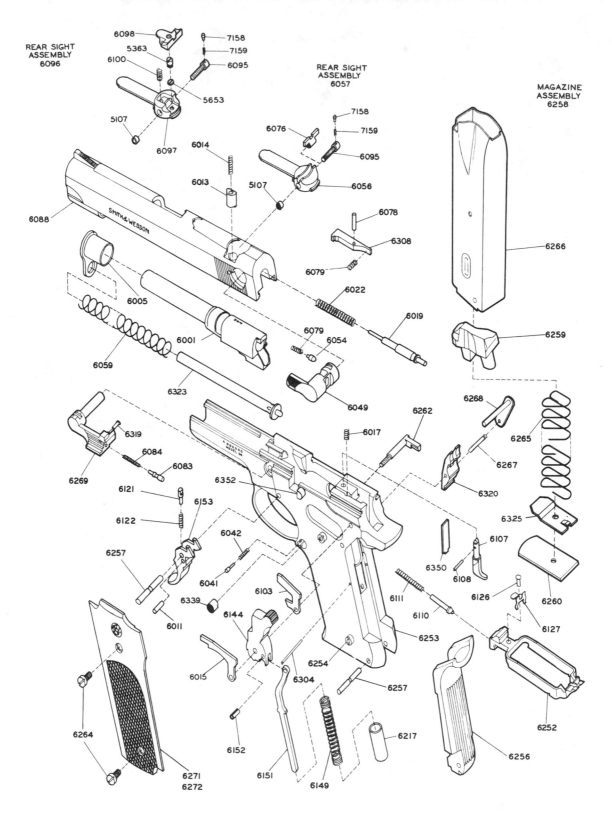

WALTHER PISTOLE 1938 (P-38) DOUBLE ACTION PISTOL (continued)

Until the advent of the P-38 all military semi-automatics had to be manually cocked. Walther adopted the double-action mechanism of the Walther PP (Polizeipistole) and the smaller PPK (Polizeipistole, Kriminal).

With the Walther double-actions it is just necessary to disengage the slide (thumb) safety and pull the trigger. The safety serves the double purpose of operating directly upon the firing pin and also uncocks the pistol. The hammer, which is automatically cocked after firing a shot, can be released by engaging the thumb safety.

The firing pin is always locked so that even when the safety is not engaged there is no possibility of accidentally firing.

The slide remains open after the last shot has been fired. Engage safety; insert loaded magazine; release safety. Cartridge slides forward into chamber and arm is ready to fire.

The P-38's breech-locking system resembles that of the military M1896 Mauser pistol. Upon firing, the rigid barrel interlocks with the bolt. The latter travels rearward until the bullet has left the muzzle. The bolt now disengages and permits the breech to return by itself.

Comment: This pistol was the number-one war trophy for European Theater GIs. Some wartime pistols were sabotaged by slave labor. Poor materials and poor workmanship characterized late wartime P-38s and most other Nazi weapons.

In some wartime pistols—identified by the round-headed firing pin—the safety performed only two functions. Competent pistolsmiths should check all wartime-production P-38s to ensure that they were properly assembled. It is possible for some pistols with broken or improperly fitted locking surfaces to fire accidentally as the slide goes forward. The P-38 should not be disassembled by any owner who does not know the proper assembly techniques.

The current production P-38s are well made and properly fitted. There are apt to be machining marks. The finish is not as fine as that of the prewar HP models. This doesn't detract from the fine design and general excellence of craftsmanship. The 1-piece hand-checkered stock is no longer available, but the discriminating owner can have a custom stock made.

Parts List for S&W M59 Double-Action Pistol

No.	Part Name	No.	Part Name	No.	Part Name
5107	Rear Sight Windage Nut	6088	Slide	6258	Magazine Assembly
6001	Barrel	6095	Rear Sight Windage Screw	6259	Magazine Follower
6005	Barrel Bushing	6103	Sear Release Lever	6260	Magazine Butt Plate
6011	Trigger Plunger Pin	6107	Disconnector	6262	Magazine Catch
6013	Ejector-depressor Plunger	6108	Disconnector Pin	6264	Stock Screw
6014	Ejector-depressor Plunger Spring	6110	Drawbar Plunger	6265	Magazine Spring
6015	Ejector Magazine Depressor	6111	Drawbar Plunger Spring	6266	Magazine Tube
6017	Ejector Spring	6121	Trigger Plunger	6267	Sear Pin
6019	Firing Pin	6122	Trigger Plunger Spring	6269	Slide Stop
6022	Firing Pin Spring	6126	Trigger Play Spring Rivet	6271	Stock, Left
6041	Magazine Catch Plunger	6127	Trigger Play Spring	6272	Stock, Right
6042	Mgazine Catch Plunger Spring	6144	Hammer	6288	Sideplate
6049	Manual Safety	6149	Mainspring	6304	Sear Spring Retaining Pin
6054	Manual Safety Plunger	6151	Stirrup	6308	Extractor
6056	Rear Sight Leaf	6152	Stirrup Pin	6319	Slide Stop Plunger Rivet
6057	Rear Sight Assembly	6153	Trigger	6320	Sear
6059	Recoil Spring	6217	Mainspring Plunger	6323	Recoil Spring Guide Assembly
6076	Rear Sight Slide	6252	Drawbar	6325	Magazine Butt Plate Catch
6078	Extractor Pin	6253	Frame (factory exchange only)	6339	Magazine Catch Nut
6079	Manual Safety Plunger Spring	6254	Frame Stud	6350	Sear Spring
6079	Extractor Spring	6256	Insert	6352	Slide Stop Button
6083	Slide Stop Plunger	6257	Insert Pin	7158	Rear Sight Windage Screw Plunger
6084	Slide Stop Plunger Spring	6257	Trigger Pin	7159	Rear Sight Windage Sc. Plg. Sprg.

CHAPTER 31

CENTERFIRE HANDGUN CARTRIDGES

Centerfire handgun ammunition has existed for more than a century. The oldest handgun cartridge—the .45 Colt (not to be confused with the .45 Automatic Colt Pistol cartridge)—was adopted in 1873 by the United States Army. The dual-purpose (rifle-handgun) .44–40 Win. also dates to 1873. This cartridge was an improved centerfire version of the .44 Henry Flat/.44 Henry Pointed rimfires.

Early centerfire handgun cartridge cases, like early centerfire rifle cartridge cases, were copper. Brass, however, has been the major centerfire case material for many years. Some brass cases have been nickel-plated. Steel was used by Germany in both world wars. Steel was used in some .45 ACP production during World War II but it is not as good as brass because of relatively poor obturation (i.e., it does not expand to fill the chamber as readily as brass).

Case head

There are three basic case-head types:

1. *Rimmed.* This is our oldest type because revolvers and single-shot pistols require a rim for extraction. Revolvers are older than semiautomatic pistols.

2. *Semi-rimless.* Cartridges so designated have a very slight, hardly noticeable rim. These are used in semiautomatic pistols like .25 (6.35mm) ACP, .32 (7.65mm) ACP, and .38 ACP. There is a very slight bearing of the rim against the rear of the chamber.

3. *Rimless.* This type is used in most semiautomatic pistols like the 9mm (Luger) Parabellum and .45 ACP. This type is much easier to load into box magazines than the rimmed type.

During World War I, Colt and other contractors could not supply sufficient quantities of the Caliber .45, Automatic Pistol, M1911. Smith & Wesson modified the Triple Lock Model to handle .45 ACP cases.

Two half-moon clips, each holding three cartridges, were used with the S&W M1917 and the Colt M1917 (modified New Service) revolvers. The clips held the rimless cases from sliding forward into the chambers so far that there would be no contact between firing pin and primer. The cases could not be extracted and ejected except one by one.

In late production arms, the shoulders were designed for the chambers. This allowed the .45 ACP to be fired without clips, but cases had to be punched out of the chambers one by one. After the war, Peters Cartridge Company (later absorbed by Remington) developed a .45 rimmed cartridge that could be fired in M1917 (and successor arms) without benefit of half-moon clips.

Case shape

Straight and/or slight tapered cases. This category includes all but two of the cases we are concerned with.

Bottleneck cases. The 7.65 (.30 Luger) Parabellum and .32–20 Win. are the only bottleneck cases that we are concerned with.

Bullet types

Lead. The oldest bullet type is still the most widely used revolver bullet.

Metal base or jacketed (softpoint). Sometimes lead bullets, particularly if the lead is quite soft, tend to expand excessively before adequate penetration has been made. The metal base holds together while its soft point expands. Softpoint bullets may or may not be hollowpointed.

Full metal-jacketed. The term is not quite correct because as in metal-jacketed rifle bullets the base is open. The full metal-jacketed bullet—required for military use by the Geneva Convention—has greater penetration than softpoints or lead bullets, but is not as effective. Barrel life with jacketed bullets is much shorter than with lead bullets.

Hollowpoint. These are usually softpoints that have been hollowpointed. These bullets when used at high velocity have a devastating effect upon animal tissue.

Blanks. These are used for sporting events, theatricals, the movies and TV shows, and training dogs.

Shot cartridges. Popular in the late black-powder and early smokeless era, this cartridge type is virtually nonexistent, save in the .44 Magnum shot cartridge designed for use in the Thompson/Center single-shot pistol. These are very useful in poisonous snake country.

During World War II the U.S. Army and U.S. Army Air Force used two shot cartridges designed for survival kits. Both types had to be single-loaded because they were too long for the .45 ACP magazines. Experiments have proved that the more worn—that is, the less rifled—a barrel is, the more effectively it handles shot.

Gas-check bullets. A gas check is a small metal cap which covers the base of a lead bullet. They have been generally used on revolver bullets where the velocity is above 1000 f.p.s. The first factory-loaded gas-check bullets known to the author are those for the .44 Magnum. The 250-grain bullet has initial velocity of nearly 1500 f.p.s. The bullet base would have been fused by the high temperatures had not a gas check been used.

Roundnose. This is one of the oldest and least effective bullet designs. A pointed bullet tends to glance off bone.

Slight flatnose. This is the most widely used revolver bullet type and is not much more effective than the roundnose.

Keith-type flatnose. This type, developed by Elmer Keith—this nation's most experienced handgunner—in the 1920s, is the most effective revolver bullet. For some reason ammunition makers have never gone whole hog and used the basic Keith bullet design. The .44 Magnum is a poorly modified version of the Keith design.

Primers

There are two basic sizes: large pistol and small pistol. At one time, .45 ACP primers and cases made at Frankfort Arsenal used a bastard-size primer. The usual dividing line is .38 caliber (.357), though .357 Magnum cases have been made with both large and small primers.

CARTRIDGES

The following section doesn't include pocket automatic pistol cartridges like the .25 ACP, .32 ACP, or .380 ACP, or such pocket revolver cartridges as the .32 S&W (Short). For the most part it covers only those cartridges used for match shooting or for small or big game. Most of these cartridges still have arms manufactured for them. The .32-20 Win. and .44-40 Win. are accepted because arms may once again be made for them. The .38 Long and Short Colt cartridges are included because they chamber in the .38 Special and .357 Magnum.

Automatic pistol cartridges or revolver cartridges with full metal jackets are usually poor game killers. The .45 ACP is a possible exception. Though this has long been a favorite of the author's he would not use it against big game provided he had an alternative like the .41 or .44 Magnum or handloads in the .45 Colt revolver.

.22 Remington Jet

Introduced 1962. Rimmed case. Bullet diameter: 0.221–0.223 inch. Standard weight: 40 grains (softpoint). This cartridge, the first factory-made .22 centerfire, is a dud. The only reason it has been listed for so many years is that S&W is using up barrels and cylinders already on hand.

Cases almost invariably set back, thus locking—or blocking—the cylinder so that it will not revolve to the next cartridge. Case setback can be reduced by removing all traces of lubricant from the chambers. Swab individual chambers with carbon tetrachloride. Caution must be exercised when using this fluid. It must not touch the skin, nor should its fumes, which can be fatal, be inhaled.

Smith & Wesson chambered the very fine—and accurate—K-Masterpiece series revolver for this cartridge. The revolver is fitted with dual firing pins. The centerfire pin is for the .22 Remington Jet cartridge (sometimes called the .22 Centerfire Magnum). The second firing pin is for the .22 Long Rifle rimfire cartridge. This cartridge can be used in the M53 S&W when each chamber is fitted with a .22 Jet case modified to act as an auxiliary .22 Long Rifle chamber.

The cartridge was advertised as having a muzzle velocity of about 2100 f.p.s. Neither the author with his Oegler T1440 Chronograph nor the H. P. White Laboratory has ever been able to obtain velocities exceeding 1827 f.p.s.

.221 Remington Fireball

Introduced 1963. Rimless case. Bullet diameter: 0.224 inch. Standard weight: 50 grains, semi-pointed softpoint.

Remington introduced the .221 Fireball—using a shortened .222 Rem. case—and with it the single-shot XP-100 bolt-action pistol, based on the Remington M760 bolt-action rifle series.

Both cartridge and pistol are extremely accurate. The pistol—the heaviest centerfire U.S. handgun—has a molded stock of DuPont Zytel (nylon). The XP-100 pistol weights 60.0 oz. and has a 10.5-inch barrel. Chronographed loads approximate factory ballistics: 2650 f.p.s. at the muzzle and 1825 f.p.s. at 200 yards.

The only other handgun known to the author, chambered for the .221 Fireball is another single-shot, the Thompson/Center Contender. Both the XP-100 and the Contender are extremely accurate. For maximum accuracy a handgun scope should be used for bench or varmint shooting.

.30 Caliber (7.65mm Parabellum) Luger

Introduced 1900. Rimless case. Standard bullet diameter: 0.308 inch. Standard bullet weight: 93 grains, metal case.

This cartridge is chambered in imported Parabellum (Luger) pistols. It is not a good game cartridge. It is very accurate when used in the longer-barreled Lugers.

.32–20 Winchester (.32 W.C.F.)

Introduced 1882. Rimmed case. Standard bullet diameter: 0.3125 inch (considerable variations will be found in older rifles and handguns). Standard bullet weights: 87–115 grains, lead and softpoint.

Handguns, including the M1873 Colt Single Action, were not chambered for the .32–20 until 1899. Both the rifle and the handgun were essentially designed for small game. The cartridge was capable of excellent accuracy in handguns like the Colt Single Action Target model.

No handguns known to the author have been chambered for the .32–20 since Colt halted single-action production at the beginning of World War II. We would like to see Ruger chamber his superb single-action Blackhawk for this fine cartridge. It is an infinitely superior cartridge to the Caliber .30 M1 Carbine cartridge, one of the cartridges for which the Blackhawk is now chambered.

The best load was the 115-grain softpoint bullet. This was perfectly capable of taking deer in the hands of a good handgun shot.

.32 S&W Long

Introduced 1896. Rimmed case. Standard bullet diameter: 0.313 inch (considerable varia-

tions will be found in older guns). Standard bullet weight: 85–101 grains. The 98-grain lead bullet is the only regularly available load today.

Since S&W discontinued (1973) the excellent K-32 Masterpiece for this cartridge, no comparable revolver is available. This is a very accurate target and small-game cartridge.

The .32 Colt New Police is identical except for the bullet shape. Cartridges for small-game hunting should always be the flatnose .32 Colt New Police rather than the roundnose .32 S&W Long.

.357 Magnum

Introduced 1935. Rimmed case. Standard bullet diameter: 0.357 inch. Standard bullet weight: 158 grains. Elmer Keith for many years advocated a high-velocity .44 Magnum. His friend Major Douglas B. Wesson, president of S&W, however, preferred a super .38 Special. His first step in that direction was the .38–44. This was a high-velocity loading for the .38 Special case. It was suitable for chambering only in heavy-frame .38 Specials like the .38 S&W Heavy Duty and .38–44 Outdoorsman.

A year after suggestions were made by Elmer Keith and Captain Philip B. Sharpe concerning the need for something heftier, S&W brought out the .357 Magnum. They added 0.1 inch to the .38 Special, to make sure the powerful load could not be used in existing .38 Special revolvers. They forgot the ancient .38 Long Colt. The author once blew up six M1892 Colt service revolvers on the first shot with .357 Magnum loads. (These test guns were fired, needless to say, by remote control.)

The .357 Magnum, at the time of its introduction, was with one exception the world's most powerful handgun cartridge. The exception was the Cabbot-Fairfax Mars cartridge.

The .357 Magnum cartridge was very controversial. Big-game handgunners like Keith still wanted a super .44 Special. They got it in 1956. Many police agencies, particularly in cities, maintained it was too powerful.

Today, the .357 Magnum is used by many state police forces and by game wardens. Since the advent of the more powerful .41 and .44 Magnums, some city departments have adopted the .357 Magnum. The author has used the .357 Magnum on small game up to coyotes since 1937. He used Keith's .44 Special handloads on bigger game until the advent of the .44 Magnum. Many hunters use the .357 Magnum on deer.

The .38 Special target loads (wadcutters) give excellent accuracy in the top-quality .357 Magnums fitted with micrometer sights adjustable for windage and elevation. The area of the bore forward of the front end (neck) of the .38 Special should be scrubbed occasionally to clean it out. Otherwise you may find it difficult to chamber the longer .357 Magnum cases.

The author's favorite top-quality .357 Magnum guns are the Ruger New Model Blackhawk, Colt Python, and Smith & Wesson Magnum. The handiest double-action barrel length is 4.0 inches. The 8.375-inch barrel of the S&W is too long; it has a poor balance. The 6.0-inch barrel of the double-action and the 6.5-inch barrel of the single-action are good for hunting, though the 4.0-inch barrel will often do the job. The .357 Magnum barrel should never be less than 4.0 inches. Otherwise there is excessive muzzle blast and velocity loss, and sometimes the bullet tends to keyhole.

.38 Long Colt

Introduced 1874. Rimmed case. Standard bullet diameter: 0.357 inch. Standard bullet weight: 190 grains. In 1889 the U.S. Navy adopted the .38 Long Colt cartridge. The Army made some changes in the load and adopted it in 1892. At that time the outside-lubricated bullet was replaced by an inside-lubricated bullet and the case was slightly lengthened. This cartridge became the .38 Long Colt, Inside Lubricated. This was the standard service cartridge until the Army adopted the .45 M1909 Colt revolver and cartridge.

The Army made a bad mistake—and like so many Army mistakes it cost lives—when the .45 Colt was abandoned for the .38 Long Colt.

During the Philippine Insurrection, fanatical Moros proved that the .38 Long Colt could not be depended on to stop a determined attack. A cry went up for the old manstopping .45 Colt. M1873 single-actions were taken out of storage and rushed to the Philippines.

The .38 Long Colt is mentioned here because the cartridge can be fired in any .38 Special or .357 Magnum handgun. It is not wise to fire high-velocity .38 Specials in those old .38 Long Colt service revolvers.

.38 Short Colt (short case); .38 Short Colt (long case)

Introduced 1874 (long case). Rimmed. Standard bullet diameter: 0.375 inch. Standard bullet weight: 125 grains.

This is not for game. It is mentioned here only because it will chamber—both versions—in arms chambered for the .38 Long Colt and therefore in

arms chambered for the .38 Special and .357 Magnum. The long case, originated in 1874, had a length of 0.733–0.78 inch. The .38 Short Colt (short case) originated with Remington or Peters about 1920. More than 50 years have passed since arms were chambered for this specific cartridge.

.38 Special

Introduced 1902. Rimmed case. Standard bullet diameter: 0.359 inch. Standard bullet weight: 158 grains (others range 110–149 grains).

Originally called the .38 S&W Special and later the .38 Colt Special, this cartridge was developed by Smith & Wesson for the S&W Military & Police Model revolver which appeared in 1902. It was intended to replace the unsatisfactory .38 Long Colt for service use, but eventually the military reverted to the .45 instead. The Colt version of the .38 Special cartridge came along in 1909. It differed only in the shape of the bullet, which was somewhat flattened instead of round-nosed.

The .38 Special is the world's most widely used centerfire revolver cartridge. It is standard for most police departments in the United States, though there is a trend among state police agencies, state highway patrols, and sheriff's offices to use the more powerful .357 Magnum.

This extremely accurate cartridge is one of the three used in handgun match competition. The others are the .22 Long Rifle and .45 ACP. For many years match shooters used .38 Special revolvers and .45 semiautomatic Colt pistols. The most widely used revolvers were the Colt Officer's Model and the S&W K-38 Masterpiece.

Today most match gunners use the .38 Special in the S&W or Colt semiautomatic pistol, even through rimmed cartridges are rarely used in semiautomatics because of feed problems. The difficulty, however, has been largely solved in the worked-over S&Ws and Colts.

The .38 Special, preferably with hollowpoint bullets, is fine for small game up through foxes but should not be used on deer or larger game.

The standard bullet weight is 158 grains. For many years the cartridge designated as the .38 S&W Special was loaded with a roundnose bullet, while the identical case loaded with a flatnose (not flat enough) bullet was the .38 Colt Special. Today the cartridge is simply the .38 Special, regardless of bullet type.

There is a wide variety of loads, ranging from the 95-grain semi-jacketed hollowpoint to the 200-grain lead bullet. The highest velocity is obtained with a maximum-load 158-grain lead bullet, having a muzzle velocity of 1090 f.p.s., which compares unfavorably with the 158-grain semi-jacketed hollowpoint .357 Magnum at 1550 f.p.s.

The standard target load is a 148-grain wadcutter.

.38 S&W

Introduced 1876. Rimmed case. Standard bullet diameter: 0.359 inch. Standard bullet weight: 146 grains (many others have been discontinued). This is essentially a pocket revolver cartridge and is not suitable for game. The best load was the 200-grain load introduced in the 1920s. The British went from caliber .455 to caliber .38 S&W, which they call a .380 — not to be confused with the .380 ACP (9mm Short). They used the 200-grain bullet as their standard service cartridge. Despite its low velocity it was a good killer up to 35 yards. This loading is no longer available in the United States.

.38 ACP (Colt Automatic Pistol)

Introduced 1900. Semi-rimless case. Standard bullet diameter: 0.359 inch. Standard bullet weight: 130 grains.

This is the oldest American semiautomatic pistol cartridge. It was originally made for the M1900 Colt Automatic Pistol, which was the first production semiautomatic pistol made in the United States.

In the 1930s Colt chambered its M1911A1 semiautomatic pistol for a souped-up or magnum version of the .38 ACP.

The new version, called the .38 Super ACP, should not be fired in the earlier Colts. In fact, all the earlier Colts are collector's items and should be treated as such.

Neither the standard nor the Super .38 Automatics are suitable game guns. The 130-grain bullets are either 1040 f.p.s. (.38 ACP) or 1280 f.p.s. (.38 Super ACP); neither has sufficient stopping power for anything but small game.

.41 Magnum

Introduced 1964. Rimmed case. Standard bullet diameter: 0.41 inch. Standard bullet weight: 210 grains.

Many shooters — including some who had looked forward to it — found the .44 Magnum just too much gun for them. They complained about the excessive recoil and the slowness in getting off a second shot because of the time required to pull the big gun down from recoil.

Elmer Keith and Gordon Boser had done considerable experimenting with the old .41 Long Colt. Keith persuaded S&W to bring out a .41 Magnum. The first ammunition was developed by Remington. There are two .41 Magnum factory loads. The first is a 210-grain softpoint bullet with a muzzle velocity of 1500 f.p.s. and muzzle energy of 1049 ft.-lbs. This is the load for lawmen and hunters. The second is a 210-grain lead bullet with a muzzle velocity of 1150 f.p.s. and muzzle energy of 550 ft.-lbs. This is a load for lawmen who are not permitted to use the more powerful load.

That more powerful load is suitable for all but our largest game. The two finest handguns chambered for the .41 Magnum are the S&W M57 double-action and the great Ruger New Model Blackhawk. The 4.0-inch-barrel S&W is ideal for lawmen or for those who tote a handgun much of the time.

.44 Magnum

Introduced 1956. Rimmed case. Standard bullet diameter: 0.427 inch. Standard bullet weight: 246 grains.

About 1926, Elmer Keith switched from the .45 Colt to the .44 Special. While the .44 and .45 cylinders were identical in exterior dimensions, the chamber walls of the .44 Special were slightly thicker because the .44 Special case is slightly smaller in diameter than the .45 Colt. This meant a greater safety margin for Keith's maximum loads.

Keith waged an almost singlehanded campaign for 30 years for a super .44 Special sixgun and load using his flatnose bullet. In 1956 S&W brought out the magnificent M29 sixgun and Remington developed the .44 Magnum cartridge.

The .44 Magnum was and still is the most powerful sixgun factory cartridge. However, the author once fired a revolver chambered for the .45–70 rifle cartridge. Who knows? One day we may have a handgun chambered for something more powerful. After all, there was once a .577 Howdah single-shot pistol.

The original Remington bullet was flatnose with a gas check to prevent hot gases from fusing the lead bullet base.

After Ruger brought out the handy semiautomatic carbine in .44 Magnum, Norma produced a softpoint (metal jacket with exposed lead upper half).

Sixgun experts like Keith and *Guns & Ammo* publisher Bob Petersen have taken elk and big Alaskan bear with the .44 Magnum. The author's best was only a deer.

The two finest handguns for which the .44 Magnum is chambered are the double-action Smith & Wesson M29 and the single-action Ruger New Model Super Blackhawk.

.44 Special

Introduced 1907. Rimmed case. Standard bullet diameter: 0.427 inches. Standard bullet weight: 240 grains.

The .44 Special is an elongated version of the obsolete .44 Russian. The latter, for many years, was one of our most accurate match cartridges. The .44 Russian cartridge has not been made since World War II. The .44 Special is superior to the .44 S&W Russian for hunting purposes.

Several very accurate .44 Special handguns were made by both S&W and Colt. Today, however, the Colts are collector's items. The Smith & Wesson M29 in caliber .44 Magnum when used with .44 Special loads is the most accurate .44 Special double-action revolver that the author has used. Likewise, the .44 Magnum Ruger Blackhawk is very accurate with .44 Specials.

.44–40 Winchester

Rifle version introduced 1873; sixgun version introduced 1878. Rimmed bottleneck case. Standard bullet diameter: 0.427 inch. Standard bullet weight: 200 grains, softpoint.

This is our oldest centerfire rifle cartridge, one of our oldest handgun cartridges, and our oldest rifle/sixgun cartridge. No .44–40 handgun has been available since Colt stopped production of its Single Action Colt and New Service sixguns in World War II. There are rumors that a Remington M1875 replica single-action revolver for the venerable cartridge may soon be introduced.

This is one of the most popular nonmilitary rifle cartridges of all time. For many years—until World War II—Winchester had one loading machine working five days a week producing nothing but .44–40 cartridges. This was and still is the most popular rifle cartridge in South America.

The .44–40 Win. has taken most North American big game. With proper handloads the .44–40 sixgun can take any game with the possible exception of Alaskan bears. The .44–40 Win. has the same bore specifications as the .44 Special and .44 Magnum.

.45 Automatic Colt Pistol (ACP)

Introduced 1905. Rimless case. Standard bullet diameter: 0.451 inch. Standard bullet weight: 230 grains.

The cartridge was originally chambered for the M1905 Colt Automatic Pistol. The original load was a 200-grain metal-case bullet. This load—never used in the service—was discontinued about 1925.

When the Army returned to .45 caliber and decided to adopt an automatic, this cartridge and the improved M1905 Colt, the M1911, were selected. The standard service and commercial bullet is a 230-grain metal-case.

The M1911 and its modification the M1911A1 have served the United States in two world wars, Korea, Vietnam, the 1916 Mexican Punitive Expedition, and lesser affairs in Latin America.

This cartridge, designed for use in a semiautomatic pistol, has seen worldwide use as a submachine-gun cartridge since the advent of the first commercial Thompson SMG in 1921. It has been used in other SMGs like the U.S. M3 and M3A1. It was and is used in revolvers and semiautomatic copies of the Thompson SMG. During World War II it was used in the so-called Liberator single-shot pistol, of which about 1,000,000 were made at a cost of less than $2 each.

No metal-case bullet is as good a killer as the same weight and caliber bullet of either lead or softpoint construction. The .45 ACP is most effective when used with one of those two bullet types. These types do not always function well through a semiautomatic pistol. The .45 ACP remains, however, a deadly short-range killer.

During World War II, two shot cartridges, the M12 and M15, were issued in Army Air Force Survival Kits. There have also been tracer or signal cartridges and various blanks and dummies for training or testing purposes.

.45 Auto Rim

Introduced 1920. Rimmed case. Bullet diameter: 0.454 inch. Standard bullet weight: 230 grains, metal case, roundnose (current).

After World War I, thousands of M1917 Colt and S&W revolvers (.45 ACP) were sold through the NRA and the Director of Civilian Marksmanship for less than $10 each. Many shooters, however, did not want to bother with half-moon clips. And many shooters prefer a lead bullet; it is more effective, and barrel life is far longer. Peters introduced a 230-grain roundnose bullet in 1922.

The best bullet type, alas no longer available, was a 250-grain flatnose lead bullet. This type was better than the above two types on all counts: heavier bullet; a flatnose is a better man or animal stopper; and the lead bullet is more effective than a full metal-cased bullet.

Handloaders, to secure maximum effectiveness, should also use the Keith bullet.

The original M1917 Colt, when in fine condition, is becoming a collector's item. The M1917 S&W is not so popular with collectors. There is, however, the M1955 S&W .45 ACP target revolver. Ruger offers a .45 Colt/.45 ACP outfit in which the same Blackhawk single-action can shoot either cartridge by changing cylinders.

.45 (Long) Colt

Introduced 1873. Rimmed case. Standard bullet diameter: 0.454 inch. Standard bullet weight: 250 grains.

For nearly three decades after Colt discontinued its Single Action Army (1941)—with minor exceptions—no American sixguns were chambered for this grand old cartridge. Each year now sees several new .45 Colt sixguns appear. Some soon disappear because of shoddy materials and workmanship.

The cartridge first appeared in 1873, but actual design commenced about 1871.

The U.S. Army used the M1873 Colt (1873–92), but contrary to horse operas, movies, and TV westerns, the .45 Colt cartridge was used by the Army only from 1873 to 1875. In that year the Army ordered several thousand break-top S&W Schofield revolvers chambered for the inferior .45 S&W cartridge (230-grain lead bullet and 29 grains of black powder). The .45 Colt used 40 grains of black powder and a 250-grain lead bullet.

The short S&W cartridge would fit in Colts chambered for the .45 Colt cartridge but not vice versa. The .45 S&W had to be used in the Schofield because of design considerations.

No one knows how many cavalry troopers died because they were armed with an inferior cartridge. It would have been better if the Army had recalled the few thousand Schofields and peddled them to civilians.

The Single Action Caliber .45 Colt was the favorite arm and cartridge of the cowboy and Western peace officer.

In 1909 after an untold number of American soldiers died because they were armed with the miserable .38 Long Colt cartridge, the Army, and soon afterward the Navy and Marine Corps, adopted the Colt New Service revolver in caliber .45 Colt.

The .45 Colt cartridge has a very narrow rim. A wide rim was not needed because of the rod ejection system of the M1873. Neither was it needed in the small number of so-called "Philippine" or "Alaskan" model double-action Colts which used rod ejection. The M1909, with its swing-out cylinder and simultaneous ejection, requires a wide rim for positive chambering and ejection. The M1909 cartridge is identical in all respects to the .45 Colt case except for its wider rim. When the M1909 cartridge is used in the single-action, only alternate chambers can be loaded.

Today's factory .45 Colt cartridges, like the factory-loaded .45–70s, are underloaded because arms nearly a century old are still fired. No smokeless propellant cartridges should be fired in M1873 Colts with a serial number below 160,000.

The .45 Colt with its original load of 40 grains of black powder is more powerful than current factory smokeless loads.

Handloaders should always use the Keith-type flatnose bullet with two wide grease grooves rather than factory bullets. The semi-pointed or roundnose factory bullet is far less effective. There are Keith-designed hollowpoint and hollowbase bullets. Lyman makes the molds.

The best single-action revolver ever made for the .45 Colt cartridge is the Ruger Blackhawk.

The .45 Colt, when handloaded with either black powder or a smokeless propellant and with a Keith bullet, is the most effective sixgun load available except the .41 and .44 Magnums.

PART VII

RIMFIRE HANDGUNS

CHAPTER / 32

SINGLE-SHOT RIMFIRE PISTOLS

The single-shot rimfire pistol capable of hunting and target accuracy is the narrowest of all handgun categories. The only single-shot hunting pistol capable of fine accuracy—it is designed for use with scopes—is the Thompson/Center Contender pistol.

Because of the development of highly accurate target revolvers and semiautomatic pistols, and with changing match rules, the single-shot target pistol is largely a relic.

Notable single-shot rimfire pistols of the past include the Colt Camp Perry model, the S&W Perfection, and Harrington & Richardson's single-shot U.S.R.A. model.

The Colt Camp Perry model used a double-action revolver frame. The 6-shot cylinder was replaced with a flat breech block that swung out, like a cylinder, for loading and extraction.

The H&R single-shot pistol used the frame of the famed H&R break-top Sportsman revolver.

The general description of rimfire single-shot pistols is similar to that of the centerfire single-shot pistols (Chapter 27). For several decades, single-shot .22 pistols were relatively common. The reason for their decline in more recent years is the availability of well-designed, well-built, reasonably priced, reliable rimfire repeaters. In this country the primary uses of a .22 rimfire handgun are hunting small game at short range, plinking, and target-shooting events in which the shooter can now use a revolver or a semiauto-

matic. Why buy a single-shot .22 when you can have a repeater?

There are, however, two exceptions to the rule that the advantages of a repeating rimfire handgun far outweigh those of the single-shot. The best-known exception is the previously mentioned Thompson/Center Contender .22. For one thing, it's more accurate than the average run of .22 handguns. For another, it offers the versatility of interchangeable barrels, not just for switching from one length to another but from one caliber to another—in other words, rimfire-centerfire interchangeability. If no centerfire barrels were available, it seems doubtful that the rimfire version could withstand the repeater competition on its own.

From time to time other single-shot rimfire pistols appear, and some are well-made but none, to the author's knowledge, has significantly wide distribution. Most of them don't remain on the market for many years. But this pertains to pistols of more or less traditional, easily recognized design and uses. Which brings up the second exception—the "free pistol." This is a very highly specialized match pistol whose sole use is in sophisticated and esoteric target events. It is the type of pistol used in a 50-meter pistol competition conducted under the auspices of the International Shooting Union. It is characterized by extreme precision of manufacture—including all tolerances—fast lock time, very light adjustable trigger pull, and fine match sights. But to the uninitiated it is probably characterized chiefly by its odd appearance. It has a long barrel but it certainly looks nothing like the old Buntline Special. The rear sight—a micrometer type adjustable for windage and elevation, of course—is apt to be mounted on a long adjustable base so that it can be moved forward or backward. This permits the shooter to move the sight back beyond the action so that it overhangs the stock and provides an extra-long sight radius. Stranger by far is the stock itself, which invariably has a large, sometimes adjustable thumb rest and usually a palm rest which may or may not be adjustable. A shooter can fit the stock to his hand almost as if it were an integral extension of that hand.

It, too, is an exception to the rule of what's advantageous since no other type of gun can substitute for it in the matches for which it is intended. Yet the free pistol is rarely found in the United States. In this context, incidentally, the word "free" means that such features as barrel length, trigger pull, and stock dimensions are not restricted by a national or international shooting organization.

There are no regularly scheduled free-pistol matches in the United States at present—a pity, perhaps, since competition of this kind fosters an attention to careful shooting *almost* analogous to benchrest-rifle competitions. A few (very few) American shooters compete in European free-pistol matches. But even in Europe, where the free-pistol competitions originated, not many shooters specialize (or compete) in free-pistol events.

In this country the best-known of these guns is probably the Hammerli free pistol—assuredly one of the best, and understandably expensive. Since it is currently available, it will be described in this chapter. Other such pistols are only occasionally—sporadically—available or can be obtained on special order through an American representative of one European maker or another, usually at a very high price.

HÄMMERLI MODEL 120 SINGLE-SHOT FREE PISTOL

Manufacturer: Hammerli, Switzerland

Importer/distributor: Gil Hebard Guns

Action type: single-shot, sliding bolt

Safety: none

Barrel length: 9.9999 inches (heavy barrel 120 HB, 5.7 inches)

Stock: 1-piece European walnut with right thumb rest. Grip angle to frame, 110 degrees. Model 120-2 has adjustable palm rest and is obtainable with right- or left-hand grip and thumb rest. Model 120 heavy barrel has right or left adjustable grip with palm rest.

Overall length: 9.9999-inch barrel, 14.75 inches long. With 5.70-inch barrel, 9.0 inches.

Weight: 44.0 oz. (Model 120-1), 41.0 oz. (Model 120 HB)

Trigger pull: Internally adjustable 1.80 oz.–12.0 oz. Length of pull is adjustable. Lock time is 0.0018 seconds. Basic length of travel, 0.27 inches.

Sight, rear: micrometer adjustable for windage and elevation. One click equals 0.60 inches at 50 meters.

Sight, front: Patridge type.

HAMMERLI MODEL 120 SINGLE-SHOT FREE PISTOL
(continued)

Finish: blue black.

Caliber: .22 Long Rifle

Comment: A well-made, inexpensive—$250 (1976)—free pistol.

HÄMMERLI M150 FREE PISTOL

Manufacturer: Hammerli Target Arms, Ltd., Switzerland and West Germany

Importer/distributor: Gil Hebard Guns

Action type: single-shot; sliding bolt; Martini-type action operated by side lever; straight-line hammerless ignition

Barrel length: 11.4 inches

Weight: 42.4 oz.; up to 49.4 oz. with weights

Stock: 1-piece oiled black walnut with thumb rest and adjustable palm rest; forestock under free-floating barrel holds extra weights

Overall length: 15.4 inches maximum (with rear sight moved back for longest possible sight radius)

Trigger pull: set trigger, adjustable to 2.0 oz. minimum

Sight, rear: micrometer match sight, adjustable for windage and elevation, and moveable to vary sight radius; leaf is canted slightly rearward to eliminate reflections; notch has flat bottom, slightly curved sides

Sight, front: interchangeable match blade, undercut to reduce reflections

Caliber: .22 Long Rifle

Data: Stock has an overhang which helps position the web of the shooter's hand, and rear sight can be slid back along this overhang to obtain maximum 15.4-inch sight radius. Barrel is free-floating, with 6-groove rifling. Ignition is vibration-free and very fast—0.0016 second, according to factory specifications. Barrel and some minor components are made in Lenzburg, Switzerland; other components are made in Tiengen, West Germany, where the pistol is assembled and tested.

Comment: Free pistols are made for a small elite of match specialists, not for casual shooters. Such guns are necessarily expensive. The Hammerli, at this writing, costs about $800, and the price may rise in the future. Its design and craftsmanship are exceptionally fine, making it worth the cost to marksmen competing in the International Shooting Union's 50-meter competition for which the gun is intended. Extra weights are optional but, as might be expected, standard accessories (at no additional cost) include a beautifully manufactured fitted case.

THOMPSON/CENTER CONTENDER SINGLE-SHOT PISTOL WITH RIMFIRE BARREL

Action type: single-shot; single action; break-top; underlever release formed by trigger guard

Safety: automatically functions when pistol is opened for loading; remains on safe until trigger is pulled; safety interlock prevents firing if barrel is not fully closed and locked

Barrel length: 8.75 or 10.0 inches

Weight: 8.75-inch barrel, 41.0 oz.; 10.0-inch barrel, 43.0 oz.

Stock: 2-piece American walnut; hand

Overall length: 8.75-inch barrel, 12.25 inches; 10.0-inch barrel, 13.5 inches

Trigger pull: 4.5 lbs.; adjustable

Sight, rear: Rocky Mountain, adjustable for windage and elevation

Sight, front: ramp

Scope adaptability: drilled and tapped for mounts

Caliber: .22 Long Rifle (barrel #301), .22 W.R.M. (barrel #302), 5mm Rem. (barrel #303)

Data: Similar to that of centerfire model (see Chapter 27). Hammer is serrated wide target type, adjustable for rimfire or centerfire cartridges. Trigger is also serrated wide target type, with adjustable trigger stop.

CHAPTER 33

SINGLE-ACTION RIMFIRE REVOLVERS

The rimfire version of the centerfire single-action revolver differs only in size, caliber, and minor details from its big brother, discussed in Chapter 28.

This chapter is not . concerned with the hundreds of cheap pocket-type .22 rimfire single-action revolvers but with arms capable of hunting and plinking accuracy. Most .22 rimfire single-action revolvers are scaled-down centerfire revolvers. The .22 caliber rimfire Colts are 7/8ths-scale Single Action Army revolvers. The Ruger Single-Six is a 7/8ths-scale Blackhawk.

Many years ago Colt made a full-scale Single Action Army (M1873) revolver chambered for the .22 Long Rifle cartridge. These sixguns are widely sought collector's items.

The single-action rimfire sixgun, like its centerfire counterpart, should always be fitted with a rear micrometer sight adjustable for windage and elevation if used in hunting situations.

COLT NEW FRONTIER .22/.22 MAGNUM

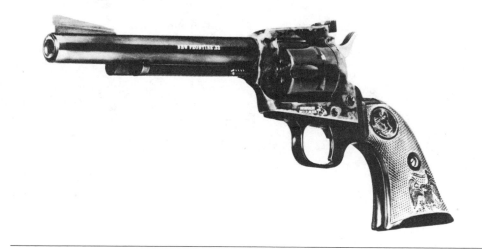

Action type: single action; rod ejection; coil spring

Cylinder capacity: 6-shot (5-shot for safety)

Barrel length: 4.375, 6.0, or 7.5 inches

Weight: 4.375-inch barrel, 29.5 oz.; 6.0-inch barrel, 31.0 oz.; 7.5-inch barrel, 33.0 oz.

Stock: 2-piece black composite rubber

Overall length: 4.375-inch barrel, 9.375 inches; 6.0-inch barrel, 11.25 inches; 7.5-inch barrel, 12.75 inches

Trigger pull: not specified

Sight, rear: micrometer, adjustable for windage and elevation

Sight, front: blade on ramp

COLT NEW FRONTIER .22/.22 MAGNUM (continued)

Caliber: .22 Long Rifle, .22 W.R.M.; furnished with interchangeable cylinders

Data: This is a 7/8ths-scale version of centerfire New Frontier; all steel frame. Standard trigger (smooth) and hammer (checkered spur). Color case hardened frame with blued cylinder, barrel, and ejection rod unit.

Comment: Same as .22 Colt Peacemaker except this has an adjustable rear sight.

COLT PEACEMAKER .22/.22 MAGNUM

Action type: single action; rod ejection; coil spring

Cylinder capacity: 6-shot (5-shot for safety)

Barrel length: 4.375, 6.0, or 7.5 inches

Weight: 4.375-inch barrel, 28.0 oz.; 6.0-inch barrel, 30.5 oz.; 7.5-inch barrel, 32.0 oz.

Stock: 2-piece black composite rubber

Overall length: 4.375-inch barrel, 9.628 inches; 6.0-inch barrel, 11.25 inches; 7.5-inch barrel, 12.75 inches

Trigger pull: not specified

Sight, rear: fixed square notch (micrometer adjustable for windage and elevation available from independent source)

Sight, front: blade

Caliber: .22 Long Rifle, .22 W.R.M.; furnished with interchangeable cylinders

Data: This is a 7/8ths-scale version of the centerfire Peacemaker. Steel frame, color case hardened with blued cylinder, barrel, and rod ejection unit. Standard trigger (smooth) and hammer (checkered spur).

Comment: This rimfire version of the standard Colt centerfire single-action Peacemaker (Single Action Army/New Frontier) has a coil spring which is far superior to the standard flat spring.

RUGER NEW MODEL SINGLE-SIX CONVERTIBLE

Action type: single action; rod ejection

Cylinder capacity: 6-shot

Transfer-bar safe-carrying feature: single-action revolvers employ no safety slide (and need none); in New Model Rugers, transfer bar comes between hammer and pin when hammer is down—an automatic safety feature that blocks hammer and prevents accidental discharge so that gun can be carried with all six chambers loaded

Barrel length: 4.875, 5.5, 6.5, or 9.5 inches

Weight: 4.875-inch barrel, 31.5 oz.; 5.5-inch barrel, 33.0 oz.; 6.5-inch barrel, 34.5 oz.; 9.5-inch barrel, 38.9 oz.

Stock: smooth walnut

Overall length: 4.875-inch barrel, 9.875 inches; 5.5-inch barrel, 10.825 inches; 6.5-inch barrel, 11.825 inches; 9.5-inch barrel, 14.825 inches

Trigger pull: 4.0 lbs.

Sight, rear: micrometer, adjustable for windage and elevation (protected by integral frame ribs)

Sight, front: sloping ramp

Caliber: .22 Long Rifle, with interchangeable .22 W.R.M. cylinder

Data: Serrated hammer. Cylinder frame, cylinder, trigger, transfer bar, barrel, and other components subject to stress made of hardened chrome molybdenum steel.

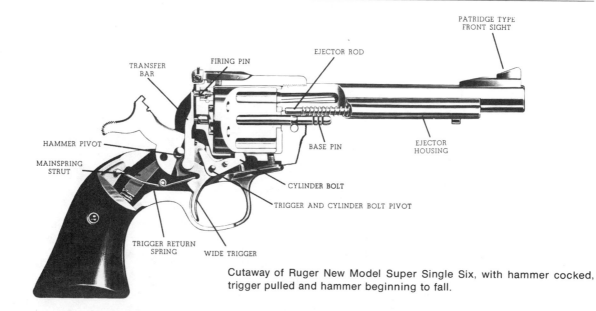

Cutaway of Ruger New Model Super Single Six, with hammer cocked, trigger pulled and hammer beginning to fall.

RUGER NEW MODEL SINGLE-SIX CONVERTIBLE
(continued)

This revolver, which has been on the market for more than 20 years, now has a safe-carrying feature which allows all six chambers to be loaded with live ammunition.

A flat surface in the end of the gate spindle allows a transfer bar to move down and up when the gate is closed. It locks transfer bar, trigger, and hammer when the gate is opened.

When opened, the loading gate depresses upper arm of gate detent spring. This in turn lowers cylinder latch. Cylinder can then be turned for loading. The hammer and trigger are immobilized by the gate interlock.

When the gate is closed, the gate detent spring arm turns to its upper position. This allows the cylinder latch to be engaged and disengaged by normal hammer operation.

Comment: This is probably the finest single-action rimfire revolver made. It is also the safest.

CHAPTER 34

DOUBLE-ACTION RIMFIRE REVOLVERS

The double-action rimfire revolver, like the single-action, is usually a rimfire version of a centerfire big brother.

The Diamondback—a scaled-down Python—is now the only Colt .22 rimfire revolver with target capabilities. Colt's .22 rimfire version of its Officer's Model was for many years the standard of all rimfire revolver match shooters.

The S&W K-22—also available in .22 W.R.M.—is the only match-quality .22 rimfire double-action revolver available today.

S&W's 4.0-inch-barrel K-22 Combat Masterpiece and Colt's 4.0-inch-barrel Diamondback are excellent sixguns for hunting. A few other double-action .22 sporting revolvers are available—and are listed in this chapter—but not many.

COLT DIAMONDBACK REVOLVER

Action type: double-action; swing-out cylinder

Cylinder capacity: 6-shot

Barrel length: 4.0 inches; 2.5-inch barrel unsuitable for sporting use

Weight: 28.5 oz.

Stock: 2-piece checkered walnut

Overall length: 9.0 inches

Trigger pull: double action, 9.0 lbs.; single action, 4.0 lbs.

Sight, rear: micrometer adjustable for windage and elevation

Sight, front: ramp on ventilated rib

Caliber: .22 Short, .22 Long, .22 Long Rifle

Data: This gun has a ventilated rib and a wide hammer spur. Finish is bright Colt bluing or, at extra cost, nickel plating.

Comment: Diamondback is a slightly smaller edition of the centerfire Colt Python. It has a crisp trigger pull and exhibits fine quality throughout.

HARRINGTON & RICHARDSON M940 ULTRA SIDEKICK REVOLVER

Action type: double-action; break-top

Cylinder capacity: 9-shot

Barrel length: 6.0 inches

Weight: 30.0 oz.

Stock: 2-piece checkered walnut

Overall length: 10.5 inches

Trigger pull: double action, 9.0 lbs.; single action, 4.0 lbs.

Sight, rear: notch, adjustable for windage

HARRINGTON & RICHARDSON M940 ULTRA SIDEKICK
REVOLVER (continued)

Sight, front: blade on ramp, adjustable for elevation; mounted on ventilated rib

Caliber: .22 Short, .22 Long, .22 Long Rifle

Data: Most of today's double-action revolvers employ swing-out cylinders, though High Standard offers some models with single-action-style loading gates. Harrington & Richardson also makes them both ways and, to the author's knowledge, is the only American maker still offering a third construction—the top-breaking action. This is not quite as strong as a solid frame, of course, but it has more than enough strength for a .22 rimfire revolver. When a break-top revolver of this sort is opened, an ejector mechanism (really an extractor) pushes the shells about halfway out of the cylinder. This isn't much faster than opening a swing-out cylinder and pushing the ejector rod, but it is faster than opening a loading gate and pushing the empties out one at a time.

Comment: A good moderate-priced .22 revolver for plinking or hunting small game at short range. The author would much prefer a micrometer rear sight. Like the High Standard line of double-action .22s, this H&R holds 9 shots instead of 6.

HARRINGTON & RICHARDSON M999 SPORTSMAN REVOLVER

Action type: double action; swing-out cylinder

Cylinder capacity: 9-shot

Barrel length: 6.0 inches

Weight: 33.0 oz.

Stock: 2-piece checkered walnut with thumb rest

Overall length: 10.75 inches

Trigger pull: double action, 9.0 lbs.; single action, 4.0 lbs.

Sight, rear: notch, adjustable for windage and elevation

Sight, front: ramp, mounted on ventilated rib

Caliber: .22 Short, .22 Long, .22 Long Rifle

Data: Gun comes with special lock and key so that it can't be fired by unauthorized persons. Features include trigger-guard extension and thumb rest on stock panels to provide steady hold. Barrel is slightly heavier than that on H&R M999 Sportsman, also to provide steadier hold for those who prefer a little extra weight in a revolver.

Comment: This is another good moderate-priced .22 revolver for plinking or short-range hunting of small game. It, too, is a nineshooter.

HIGH STANDARD HIGH SIERRA DELUXE REVOLVER

Action type: double action; interchangeable cylinders for standard or Magnum .22 rimfires

Cylinder capacity: 9-shot

Barrel length: 7.0 inches

Weight: 36.0 oz.

Stock: 2-piece uncheckered hand-rubbed walnut

Overall length: 12.5 inches

Trigger pull: double action, 9.0 lbs.; single action, 5.0 lbs.

Sight, rear: notch, adjustable for windage

Sight, front: blade

Caliber: .22 Short, .22 Long, .22 Long Rifle; interchangeable cylinder for .22 W.R.M.

Data: A double-action nineshooter with "Old West" styling. Octagonal barrel. Gold-plated backstrap and trigger guard; blued barrel and frame.

Comment: The author prefers better sights even for plinking or short-range small-game hunting, but all the High Standard handguns are first-rate moderate-priced firearms. This one is a fancier version of the Double-Nine and 9.5-inch-barreled Double-Nine Longhorn line. The interchangeable cylinders add Magnum versatility to a rimfire revolver.

HIGH STANDARD SENTINEL MARK IV REVOLVER

Action type: double action; swing-out cylinder

Cylinder capacity: 9-shot

Barrel length: 4.0 inches; 2.5-inch and 3.0-inch barrel lengths unsuitable for sporting use

Weight: 26.0 oz.

Stock: 2-piece smooth walnut wrap-around panels

Overall length: 9.0 inches

Trigger pull: double action, 9.0 lbs.; single action, 5.0 lbs.

Sight, rear: white-outlined notch, adjustable for windage and elevation

Sight, front: ramp with red insert

Caliber: .22 Short, .22 Long, .22 Long Rifle; or .22 W.R.M.

Data: Nicely blued; nickel-plated at extra cost.

Comment: This latest version of the Sentinel has better than average sights for a double-action .22, and it has a desirably smooth, no-creep trigger pull.

IVER JOHNSON T-526 TARGET MODEL REVOLVER

Action type: double action; loading gate

Cylinder capacity: 8-shot

Barrel length: 6.0 inches

Weight: 30.5 oz.

Stock: 1-piece Tenite; checkered; wrap-around with thumb rest

Overall length: 10.75 inches

Trigger pull: double action, 9.0 lbs.; single action, 4.0 lbs.

Sight, rear: notch, adjustable for windage

Sight, front: blade on ramp, adjustable for elevation

Caliber: .22 Short, .22 Long, .22 Long Rifle

Data: A rimfire eightshooter with better than average sights for a .22 double action at a very low price.

Comment: Its name notwithstanding, this is not a match-quality revolver, nor does it have the weight, trigger pull, sights, or configuration of a match .22. It is, however, a durably built gun and quite adequate for target *practice* as well as for plinking or small-game hunting at short range.

LLAMA MARTIAL .22 REVOLVER

Manufacturer: Llama Gabilondo, Spain

Importer/distributor: Stoeger Arms

Action type: double action; swing-out cylinder

Cylinder capacity: 6-shot

Barrel length: 6.0 inches

Weight: 40.0 oz.

Stock: 2-piece checkered walnut, Magna type

Overall length: 11.0 inches

Trigger pull: double action, 9.0 lbs.; single action, not specified

Sight, rear: white-outline micrometer adjustable for windage and elevation

Sight, front: blade on ramp, mounted on ventilated rib

Caliber: .22 Short, .22 Long, .22 Long Rifle

Data: Matte-finished rib and sight ramp; steel frame; serrated backstrap and frontstrap; floating firing pin; color case-hardened, grooved, wide trigger; color case-hardened, serrated, wide-spur hammer.

Comment: This import comes in a number of grades and styles. The description above covers the basic, no-fancy-options model, a medium-priced gun with good sights, solid weight, quality workmanship, good bluing, and features not often found on medium-priced .22 double-action revolvers. Various "Deluxe" versions are offered with engraving, "Satin" or gold-damascened finish, and—for those who care more about flamboyance than function or durability—"simulated pearl" stocks!

S&W M17 K-22 MASTERPIECE REVOLVER

Action type: double action; swing-out cylinder

Cylinder capacity: 6-shot

Barrel length: 6.0 or 8.375 inches

Weight: 6.0-inch barrel, 38.5 oz.; 8.375-inch barrel, 42.25 oz.

Stock: 2-piece checkered walnut Magna type (oversize target stocks available at slight extra cost)

Overall length: 6.0-inch barrel, 11.125 inches; 8.375-inch barrel, 13.5 inches

Trigger pull: single action, 3.5 lbs.; double action, 9.0 lbs.

Sight, rear: micrometer, adjustable for windage and elevation

Sight, front: 0.125-inch-wide partridge

Caliber: .22 Short, .22 Long, .22 Long Rifle

Data: Plain trigger (wide target type, grooved, available at slight extra cost). Standard hammer (wide checkered spur target type available at slight extra cost). Medium-size all-steel frame.

Comment: One of the most accurate .22 revolvers. Usually used in matches when .22 semiautomatic is not used.

S&W M18 COMBAT MASTERPIECE

Action type: double action; swing-out cylinder

Cylinder capacity: 6-shot

Barrel length: 4.0 inches

Weight: 35.0 oz.

Stock: 2-piece checkered walnut; Magna type (oversize checkered walnut target type available at slight extra cost); square butt

Overall length: 9.125 inches

Trigger pull: single action, 4.5 lbs.; double action, 9.0 lbs.

Sight, rear: micrometer, adjustable for windage and elevation

Sight, front: 0.125-inch-wide Baughman quick draw on ramp

Caliber: .22 Short, .22 Long, .22 Long Rifle

Data: Standard trigger (extra-wide grooved target type trigger available at slight extra cost). Standard hammer (wide spur target type available at slight extra cost). Medium-size all-steel frame (same as K-series).

Comment: This is identical to the K-22 Masterpiece with 4.0-inch barrel except for front sight. The 4.0-inch barrel is fine for short-range hunting and plinking. The .22 Combat Masterpiece with its Baughman quick-draw front sight is a better all-round choice than the 4.0-inch-barrel versions in the Kit Gun series.

S&W M34 9153 .22/32 KIT GUN

Action type: double action; swing-out cylinder

Cylinder capacity: 6-shot

Barrel length: 4.0 inches (2.0-inch barrel not for sporting use)

Weight: round butt, 22.5 oz.; square butt, 24.0 oz.

Stock: 2-piece checkered walnut; Magna type; round or square butt optional

Overall length: 8.0 inches

Trigger pull: single action, 2.5–3.5 lbs.; double action, 12.0 lbs.

Sight, rear: micrometer, adjustable for windage and elevation

Sight, front: 0.1-inch-wide serrated ramp

Caliber: .22 Long Rifle

Data: Standard (smooth) trigger and hammer; small-size all-steel frame.

Comment: This is one of the famed S&W Kit Gun series which has been around in one form or another for at least a half-century. It is designed for those—especially women—with small hands. Many fishermen carry one in their tackle box. While small in size, the Kit Gun has the typical high-quality S&W materials and craftsmanship. Men with large hands should select the square butt. Because of his big hands and general dislike of small handguns, the author prefers the 4.0-inch-barrel .22 Combat Magnum or Colt Python.

S&W M48 K-22 MASTERPIECE M.R.F.

Action type: double action; swing-out cylinder

Cylinder capacity: 6-shot

Barrel length: 4.0, 6.0, or 8.375 inches

Weight: 4.0-inch barrel, 37.0 oz.; 6.0-inch barrel, 39.0 oz.; 8.375-inch barrel, 41.5 oz.

Stock: 2-piece checkered walnut Magna type (oversize checkered walnut target stocks available at slight extra cost)

Overall length: 4.0-inch barrel, 9.25 inches; 6.0-inch barrel, 11.25 inches; 8.375-inch barrel, 13.5 inches

Trigger pull: single action, 3.5 lbs.; double action, 9.0 lbs.

Sight, rear: micrometer, adjustable for windage and elevation

Sight, front: 0.125-inch-wide partridge

Caliber: .22 W.R.M.

Data: Plain trigger (wide grooved target type available at slight extra cost). Standard hammer (extra-wide target type available at slight extra cost). Medium-size all-steel frame. Almost identical in weight and identical in size to other calibers in K-series.

Comment: A very accurate sixgun for hunting.

CHAPTER 35

SEMIAUTOMATIC RIMFIRE PISTOLS

The first successful .22 semiautomatic pistol, the Colt Woodsman, was, not surprisingly, designed by John Moses Browning. This Sports Model Woodsman, still available, was the sole arm of its type from its introduction in 1913 until the development of the High Standard semiautomatic sports pistol in the 1930s.

The Ruger Auto Pistol, which heralded the entrance of Sturm, Ruger on the shooting scene, is the most popular semiautomatic sports pistol currently available. The Ruger Auto Pistol sells more than all other makes of semiautomatic rimfire pistols combined.

The first match semiautomatic pistol was the Colt Target Woodsman, which is still made today. There are several excellent imports, including a target model by Walther.

Several .22 target pistols are chambered for the .22 Short cartridge. These pistols are designed for international match shooting. Rimfire matches within the United States normally use the .22 Long Rifle cartridge.

COLT (WOODSMAN) TARGETSMAN

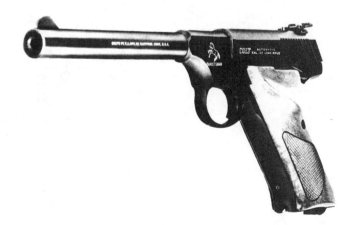

Action type: semiautomatic; blowback; hammerless; air-cooled

Magazine type: detachable straight-line box

Magazine capacity: 10-shot

Safety: thumb safety left side of frame; slide lock

Barrel length: 6.0 inches

Weight: 31.0 oz.

Stock: checkered walnut with thumb rest

Overall length: 10.875 inches

Trigger pull: 3.5–4.0 lbs.

Sight, rear: micrometer, adjustable for windage and elevation

Sight, front: blade

COLT (WOODSMAN) TARGETSMAN (continued)

Caliber: .22 Long Rifle

Data: S-type frame; Colt Blue finish.

Comment: A slightly less expensive version of the Woodsman Sport/Target model. This is not suitable for serious match shooting but is excellent as a hunting arm.

EXPLODED VIEW OF COLT (WOODSMAN) TARGETSMAN

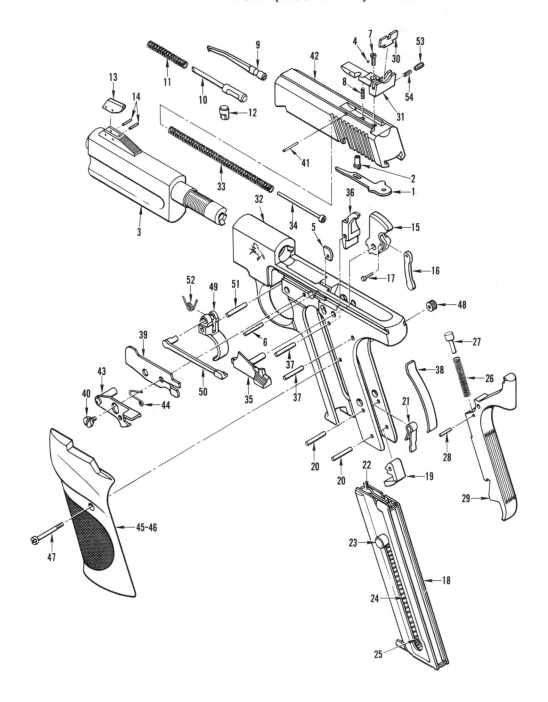

COLT WOODSMAN MATCH TARGET

Action type: semiautomatic; blowback; hammerless; air-cooled

Magazine type: detachable straight-line box

Magazine capacity: 10-shot

Safety: thumb safety on left side of frame; slide lock

Barrel length: 4.5 or 6.0 inches

Weight: 4.5-inch barrel, 34.5 oz.; 6.0-inch barrel, 39.0 oz.

Stock: checkered walnut panels with thumb rest

Overall length: 4.5-inch barrel, 10.5 inches; 6.0-inch barrel, 12.0 inches

Trigger pull: 3.0 lbs.

Sight, rear: Colt-Elliason; adjustable for windage and elevation

Sight, front: undercut ramp

Caliber: .22 Long Rifle

Data: S-type frame; Colt Blue finish.

Comment: The Colt Woodsman Match Target pistol has undergone many changes during the last 50 years. The original Woodsman design was by John Moses Browning, with some Match Target features suggested by George Elliason. The Woodsman Match Target was the only first-line rimfire American target pistol until about World War II, when some fine High Standard target pistols became available.

Parts List for Colt (Woodsman) Targetsman

No.	Part Name	No.	Part Name	No.	Part Name
1	Assembly Lock	18b	Magazine Base Lock		Retainer Pin — (2)
2	Assembly Lock Plunger	19	Magazine Catch	38	Sear Spring
3	Barrel Detail Assembly — 4½"	20	Magazine Catch Pin and	39	Side Plate
3	Barrel Detail Assembly — 6"		Main Spring Housing Lock Pin — (2)	40	Side Plate Screw
4	Rear Sight Detent Ball —	21	Magazine Catch Spring	41	Rear Sight Leaf Pin
	(2 Required)	22	Magazine Follower	42	Slide Detail Assembly
5	Ejector	23	Magazine Follower Stud	43	Slide Stop Detail Assembly
6	Ejector Pin	24	Magazine Spring	44	Slide Stop Spring
7	Rear Sight Elevating Screw	25	Magazine Spring Guide	45	Stock — Left Hand — Walnut
8	Rear Sight Elevating Spring	26	Main Spring		(With Thumb Rest)*
9	Extractor	27	Main Spring Cap	46	Stock — Right Hand — Walnut*
10	Firing Pin	28	Main Spring Cap Pin	47	Stock Screw
11	Firing Pin Spring	29	Main Spring Housing	48	Stock Screw Nut
12	Firing Pin Stop	30	Rear Sight — Blade ⅛"	49	Trigger
13	Front Sight — ⅛" Blade	30	Rear Sight Blade — .100	50	Trigger Bar
13	Front Sight Blade .100	31	Rear Sight Leaf Assembly	51	Trigger Pin
14	Front Sight Blade Pin — (2)	32	Receiver (Main Frame)	52	Trigger Spring
15	Hammer	33	Recoil Spring	53	Rear Sight Windage Screw
16	Hammer Strut	34	Recoil Spring Guide	54	Rear Sight Windage Spring
17	Hammer Strut Pin	35	Safety Lock Detail Assembly		Elliason Sight-Not Shown
18	Magazine Assembly	36	Sear	55	Rear Sight Detent Spring
18a	Magazine Base	37	Sear Pin and Main Spring		

COLT WOODSMAN SPORT/TARGET MODELS

Action type: semiautomatic; blowback; hammerless; air-cooled

Magazine type: detachable straight-line box

Magazine capacity: 10-shot

Safety: thumb safety on left side of frame; slide lock

Barrel length: Sport Woodsman, 4.0 inches; Target Woodsman, 6.0 inches

Weight: 4.0-inch barrel, 29.0 oz.; 6.0-inch barrel, 32.0 oz.

Stock: 2-piece checkered walnut panel with thumb rest

Overall length: 4.0-inch barrel, 9.0 inches; 6.0-inch barrel, 11.0 inches

Trigger pull: 4.0 lbs.

Sight, rear: micrometer, adjustable for windage and elevation

Sight, front: ramp type

Caliber: .22 Long Rifle

Data: S-type-frame; Colt Blue finish. This is the adjustable-sight version of the most famed .22 caliber rimfire semiautomatic pistol. More than 1,100,000 have been sold.

When Remington introduced the Hi-Speed .22 rimfire cartridge in the early 1930s all Woodsman models were fitted with an arched high-speed mainspring housing to handle the new cartridges. Owners of the old Woodsman with a flat housing should secure from Colt a high-speed housing.

Early Woodsman pistols were not fitted with adjustable rear sights. The Huntsman version of the Woodsman is still fitted with fixed sights. One should always purchase an adjustable-sighted Woodsman.

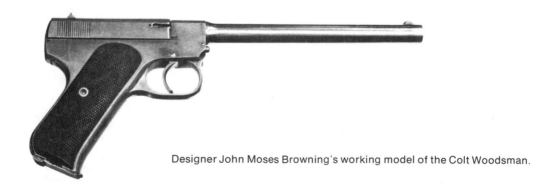

Designer John Moses Browning's working model of the Colt Woodsman.

HIGH STANDARD CITATION MATCH PISTOL

Action type: semiautomatic; blowback; internal hammer

Magazine type: detachable box

Magazine capacity: 10-shot

Safety: thumb slide

Barrel length: 5.5-inch bull barrel; 7.25-inch fluted barrel (military grip frame); 5.5 inches (standard grip frame) with bull barrel

Overall length: 5.5-inch barrel, 10.0 inches; 7.25-inch barrel, 11.5 inches

Weight: 44.5 oz. (both barrel lengths with military grip frame); 42.0-oz. with 5.5-inch barrel and standard grip frame

Stock: checkered walnut with thumb rest

Trigger pull: target type with built-in trigger stop. Pull adjustable 2.0–2.25 lbs.

Sight, rear: micrometer adjustable for windage and elevation

Sight, front: blade with flat face

Sight radius: 5.5-inch barrel, 8.75 inches; 7.25-inch barrel, 10.0 inches

Caliber: .22 Long Rifle

Comment: An excellent medium-priced match pistol. Also first rate for hunting and plinking.

HIGH STANDARD OLYMPIC ISU MATCH PISTOL

Action type: semiautomatic; blowback; internal hammer

Magazine type: detachable box

Magazine capacity: 10-shot

Safety: thumb slide

Barrel length: 6.75 inches

Weight: 40.0 oz.

Overall length: 11.25 inches

Stock: American walnut with thumb rest. Checkered. Stock designs available: military type (same angle as .45 Colt) or standard

Sight, rear: micrometer adjustable for windage and elevation

Sight, front: blade with flat back

Sight radius: 9.5 inches

Trigger pull: adjustable (for over-travel as well as weight); minimum not specified

Finish: blue

Caliber: .22 Short (designed for Olympic shooting and matches sponsored by International Shooting Union (ISU)

Comment: One of the finest .22 Short match pistols made in America. Compares favorably with many of the more expensive European imports.

HIGH STANDARD M9205 SHARPSHOOTING PISTOL

Action type: semiautomatic; blowback; hammerless; air-cooled

Magazine type: detachable straight-line box

Magazine capacity: 10-shot

Safety: thumb safety on left side of frame; slide lock

Barrel length: 5.5 inches

Weight: 44.5 oz.

Stock: checkered black plastic

Overall length: 10.0 inches

Trigger pull: 3.5 lbs. (no creep)

Sight, rear: micrometer, adjustable for windage and elevation

Sight, front: square undercut blade

Caliber: .22 Long Rifle

Data: Steel frame. Slide sides, barrel, and barrel release plunger are polished blue; frame is matte black. Bull barrel. Magazine follower has unique feature in that follow plate is extremely visible green plastic. One can tell at a glance whether magazine has any cartridges in it. Blued steel magazine has large thumb button to aid in depressing spring while loading. There is no magazine disconnector. Pistol can be fired while magazine is removed. Designed by James Reardon.

Comment: This pistol is billed as a medium-price target pistol. The author prefers to think of it as a "field .22." It makes an extremely accurate hunting and plinking pistol.

HIGH STANDARD TROPHY MATCH PISTOL

Action type: semiautomatic; blowback; internal hammer

Magazine type: detachable box

Magazine capacity: 10-shot

Safety: thumb slide

Barrel length: 5.50 inches and 7.25 inches

Overall length: 5.50-inch barrel, 9.75 inches; 7.25-inch barrel, 11.5 inches

Weight: 44.5 oz. for either barrel length. Weight variation is obtained by fluting 7.25-inch barrel

Stock: Checkered American walnut, with or without thumb rest

Trigger pull: adjustable from 2.0–2.25 lbs.

Sight, rear: micrometer adjustable for windage and elevation

Sight, front: blade with flat back

Sight radius: 5.5-inch barrel, 8.75 inches; 7.25-inch barrel, 10.0 inches

Caliber: .22 Long Rifle

Data: Stock is military type (same angle as .45 Colt).

Comment: An excellent pistol for NRA type matches.

HIGH STANDARD VICTOR (MILITARY) TARGET PISTOL

Action type: semiautomatic; blowback; internal hammer

Magazine type: detachable box

Magazine capacity: 10-shot

Safety: thumb slide with gold plated (for visibility) grooved thumb button

Barrel length: 5.5 inches or 4.5 inches (ventilated or solid rib)

Weight: 50-oz. (4.5-inch barrel has 2.0-oz. weight to make same as 5.5-inch barrel weight)

Overall length: 9.56125 inches

Stock: 2-piece American walnut grip panels. Sharply checkered. Waterproof finish. Right-hand thumb rest (left-hand thumb rest, optional)

Trigger pull: adjustable through stop in trigger guard. Maximum pull: 2.50 lbs.

Sight, rear: micrometer adjustable for windage and elevation. Square notch

Sight, front: 0.125-inch wide Patridge type

Sight radius: 8.56125 inches (5.5-inch barrel)

Caliber: .22 Long Rifle

Data: Deeply counterbored muzzle. Front sight is machined integrally with rib. Rear-sight adjustment screws designed for use with dime. Barrels, as with all High Standard .22 autos, are readily changeable by depressing barrel latch beneath barrel in forepart of frame.

Comment: The author considers this one of the finest .22 semiauto match pistols extant. Many match pistolmen who also shoot .45 caliber matches with the M1911 (and its match versions) prefer the feel-alike grip of this handgun.

In 1973 High Standard issued an Olympic Commemorative version of this superb pistol. This special issue, limited to 1000, had special inlays and engravings by noted Austrian-born engraver Walter Koluch.

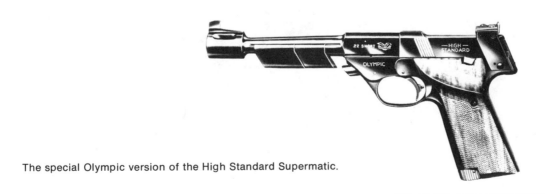

The special Olympic version of the High Standard Supermatic.

RUGER STANDARD MODEL .22 AUTOMATIC PISTOL

Action type: semiautomatic; blowback; internal hammer

Magazine type: detachable straight-line box

Magazine capacity: 9-shot

Safety: thumb slide on left side of frame

Barrel length: 4.75 or 6.0 inches

Weight: 4.75-inch barrel, 36.0 oz.; 6.0-inch barrel, 38.0 oz.

Stock: 2-piece hard rubber; sharp checkering; 2-piece walnut available at slight extra cost

Overall length: 4.75-inch barrel, 8.75 inches; 6.0-inch barrel, 10.0 inches

Trigger pull: 3.5 lbs.

Sight, rear: square notch, adjustable for windage only

Sight, front: partridge

Caliber: .22 Long Rifle

Data: Grooved and curved aluminum-alloy trigger, 2-stage pull, 0.375-inch-wide trigger. (Steel trigger available at extra cost; custom triggers available from some pistolsmith.) Polished and blued finish.

Comment: In 1949, arms designer William B. Ruger established a partnership with writer Alexander Sturm. The latter supplied most of the $50,000 initial capital. The first factory was in a small abandoned railroad station along Connecticut's Long Island Sound shore.

The initial advertisement was a one-inch ad in

Cut-away view of the Ruger Standard Automatic Model 22.

The American Rifleman. The look-alike sound-alike combination of Ruger with Luger undoubtedly attracted early attention. The pistol was an immediate success. Ever since its initial appearance it has always been on back order. It is the least expensive of any .22 semiautomatic sports pistol. Despite its low cost—partially due to Ruger design and manufacturing techniques—it is equal, and in some cases superior, to any semiautomatic .22 sports pistol.

The H. P. White Laboratory conducted independent tests for Ruger. One pistol—it then cost $37.50—was fired 41,000 rounds without a single malfunction. This is remarkable.

The pistol uses only coil springs. This established the Ruger-coil-spring system, which has been used in all Ruger revolvers. Fine-quality piano-wire coil springs are always superior to flat leaf springs.

This arm, though not fitted with a rear micrometer sight, is exceptionally accurate. A micrometer sight is available from Ruger or through independent sources. The author recommends that this pistol, unless it is to be used solely for plinking, be so equipped.

The author would also like to see a Baughman quick-draw front sight on a ramp, fitted with a gold bead insert. A gold bead shows up better against a variety of backgrounds than any other types of blade, bead, or insert.

RUGER MARK I TARGET/BULL BARREL MODELS

Action type: semiautomatic; blowback; internal hammer

Magazine type: detachable straight-line box

Magazine capacity: 9-shot

Safety: thumb slide on left side of frame

Barrel length: Mark I Target, 6.875 inches; Mark I Bull Barrel, 5.5 inches

Weight: 42.0 oz.

Stock: 2-piece hard rubber; sharp checkering (checkered walnut with thumb rests on left panel available at slight extra cost)

Overall length: 6.875-inch barrel, 10.875 inches; 5.5-inch barrel, 9.25 inches

Trigger pull: 3.5 lbs.

Sight, rear: micrometer, adjustable for windage and elevation

Sight, front: undercut 0.125-inch-wide partridge

Caliber: .22 Long Rifle

Data: Trigger grooved, 1-stage crisp pull. Polished and blued finish.

Comment: This pistol—the least expensive serious match arm—has won national competitions. Tens of thousands have been purchased by the Army and Navy for training purposes. A major feature contributing to this fine arm's accuracy is that the rear sight is always in one place. It does not move on the slide as do those of most .22 semiautomatic pistols.

The Mark I 5.25-inch barrel was discontinued along with a muzzle brake (optional) about the time the Bull Barrel version was introduced.

HAMMERLI/M208/211 INTERNATIONAL MATCH PISTOL

Manufacturer: Hammerli, Switzerland

Importer/distributor: Gil Hebard Guns

Action type: semiautomatic; blowback

Magazine type: detachable box

Magazine capacity: 8-shot

Barrel length: 5.9 inches

Weight: 38.0 oz. (35.0 oz. minus barrel weight)

Stock: (Model 208) 1-piece plain walnut with adjustable palm rest; (Model 211) 1-piece plain walnut with no palm rest

Overall length: 10.3 inches

Trigger pull: externally adjustable up to 2.25-3.0 lbs.

Sight, rear: micrometer adjustable for windage and elevation. 0.47 inch per click at 25 metres

Sight, front: 0.125-inch wide blade on ramp

Sight radius: 8.18 inches

Caliber: .22 Long Rifle

Comment: One of the finest international match pistols made.

HAMMERLI M230-1/M230-2 RAPID FIRE MATCH PISTOL

Manufacturer: Hammerli, Switzerland

Importer/distributor: Gil Hebard Guns

Action type: semiautomatic; blowback

Magazine type: detachable box

Magazine capacity: 5-shot

Barrel length: 6.3 inches

Weight: 44.0-oz. (with adjustable grips); Model 230-1, 44.0 oz. with nonadjustable grips

Stock: (Model 230-1) 1-piece nonadjustable grips; (Model 230-2) 1-piece adjustable grips with adjustable heelplate; European walnut

Overall length: 11.6 inches

Height: 5.7 inches

Width: 1.9 inches

Trigger pull: 5.25 oz.–10.5 oz.; adjustable for backlash and slack

Sight, rear: micrometer adjustable for windage and elevation; moves at 0.39-inch per click at 25 metres

Sight, front: 0.125-inch wide post

Sight radius: 9.96 inches

Caliber: .22 Short

Data: This arm is designed specifically for International Rapid Fire Competition. Finish is dull blue.

Comment: One of the finest arms of its type.

SMITH & WESSON M41 MATCH PISTOL

Action type: semiautomatic; blowback; internal hammer

Magazine type: detachable box

Magazine capacity: 10-shot

Safety: thumb slide

Barrel length: 5.0 inches (without muzzle brake), 7.375-inches (sans muzzle brake)

Overall length: 5.5-inch barrel, 9.625 inches (sans muzzle brake); 7.375-inch barrel, 12.0 inches (including muzzle brake)

Weight: 7.375-inch barrel, 43.5 oz.; 5.0-inch barrel, 44.5 oz.

Stock: 2-piece checkered walnut; modified thumb rest adaptable for right- and left-hand shooters

Trigger pull: 2.5 lbs.

Sight, rear: S&W micrometer adjustable for windage and elevation

Sight, front: target blade on ramp

Sight radius: 5.5-inch barrel, 8.0 inches; 7.375-inch barrel, 9.321 inches

Caliber: .22 Long Rifle (.22 Short version available for International Rapid Fire Course).

Comment: One of the best U.S. match pistols.

STOEGER LUGER .22

Action type: semiautomatic; blowback; toggle-joint breech; internal hammer; nonrecoiling barrel

Magazine type: detachable straight-line box

Magazine capacity: 11-shot

Safety: thumb slide, left side of frame; right-side safety for southpaws may be ordered at no extra cost

Barrel length: 4.5 inches

Weight: 30.25 oz.

Stock: early production models (1969–71) had resin-impregnated checkered wood; unpleasant resemblance to cheap plastic resulted in change to present unimpregnated plain walnut

Overall length: 9.0 inches

Stoeger Luger .22 with adjustable sight added at rear.

STOEGER LUGER .22 (continued)

Trigger pull: 3.0 lbs.

Sight, rear: fixed square notch

Sight, front: fixed blade, laterally adjustable

Caliber: .22 Long Rifle

Data: Standard trigger (smooth); internal hammer; aluminum-alloy frame; blued finish. This pistol, while differing in its actual action, resembles the Pistole '08 in exterior looks. The designer was Gary Wilhelm. The .22's weight is but 1.75 oz. lighter than the standard P-08, and the .22 barrel is about 0.5 inch longer than the standard P-08.

The frame is aluminum alloy. Some components are fabricated sheet steel or plastic. Barrel, breechbolt, and other components subject to substantial stress are steel.

A major feature of this pistol is the ease with which the firing mechanism may be removed for cleaning and/or repairs.

Comment: The pistol has the same handling qualities as the P-08. It is muzzle-light, but grip and natural pointing qualities have been retained.

This is an excellent plinking pistol. Hunters should purchase the target version, which is identical save for longer barrel and micrometer rear sights.

The arm is well made. It is the first regular-size P-08 type chambered for the .22 Long Rifle cartridge. Before World War II, Stoeger imported a special unit including .22 caliber barrel insert for converting the 7.65mm or 9mm Parabellum to .22 Long Rifle.

UNIQUE 69 D.E.S. MATCH PISTOL

Manufacturer: Manufacture d'Armes des Pyrénées Francaises, France

Importer/distributor: Connecticut Valley Arms

Action type: semiautomatic; blowback; internal hammer

Magazine type: detachable box

Magazine capacity: 10-shot

Safety: manual thumb slide (left side); slide catch (right side)

Barrel length: 5.875 inches

Overall length: 10.0 inches (with hand rest)

Weight: 36.0 oz.; barrel weights of 260 grams (included) and 350 grams (extra cost)

Stock: 2-piece French walnut with large thumb rest for right-handed shooters (left-handed shooters can have thumb rest at extra cost). Stock projects rearward to fully cover hand. Adjustable palm rest (Allen wrenches included)

Trigger pull: 2.2 lbs. (1000-grams or 1 kilogram). This meets international standards for basic pistol course

Sight, rear: micrometer adjustable for windage and elevation. Each click moves sight 8mm at 25 meters

Sight, front: blade with flat back

Calibers: .22 Long Rifle or .22 Short

Data: All steel parts. No alloys. Numerals on sheet steel magazine indicate "5" or "10" shots. Magazine floorplate is bright chrome plated.

Comment: This international match pistol, introduced in 1969, is of sophisticated design. The entire arm is well made and finely finished. It has won numerous international matches.

WALTHER GSP RIMFIRE MATCH PISTOL

Manufacturer: Carl Walther Waffenfabrik, West Germany

Importer/distributor: Interarms

Action type: semiautomatic; blowback

Magazine type: detachable box

Magazine capacity: 5-shot

Safety: thumb slide

Barrel length: 4.48 inches

Overall length: 11.8 inches

Height: 5.9 inches

Weight: 44.8 oz.

Stock: 1-piece match type with thumb rest and palm shelf

Trigger pull: two options; 1000 grams (2.2 lbs.) or 1360 grams (3.0 lbs.)

Sight, rear: micrometer adjustable for windage and elevation

Sight, front: blade with flat back

Sight radius: 10.14 inches

Finsih: dark blue

Caliber: .22 Long Rifle

Comment: One of the finest and most expensive .22 rimfire match semiautos available.

WALTHER MODEL OSP RAPID-FIRE RIMFIRE PISTOL

Manufacturer: Carl Walther Waffenfabrik, West Germany

Importer/distributor: Interarms

Action type: semiautomatic; blowback

Magazine type: detachable box

Magazine capacity: 5-shot

Safety: thumb slide

Barrel length: 4.48 inches

Overall length: 11.8 inches

Height: 5.9 inches

Trigger pull: 8.0–10.0 oz.

Stock: 1-piece European walnut with adjustable palm shelf

Sight, rear: micrometer adjustable for windage and elevation

Sight, front: blade with flat back

Sight radius: 8.58 inches

Finish: blue-black

Caliber: .22 Short

Comment: This pistol is essentially designed for rapid-fire international and Olympic competition.

WALTHER P-38 RIMFIRE DOUBLE ACTION PISTOL

Manufacturer: Carl Walther Waffenfabriken, West Germany

Importer/distributor: Interarms

Action type: semiautomatic; blowback; exposed hammer; air-cooled

Magazine type: detachable straight-line box

Magazine capacity: 8-shot

Safety: thumb slide, left side of frame

Barrel length: 5.825 inches

Weight: 28.0 oz.

Stock: checkered black plastic

Overall length: 8.5 inches

Trigger pull: 5.5 lbs.; creep noticeable but smooth

Sight, rear: U-notch; fixed

Sight, front: square blade

Caliber: .22 Long Rifle

Data: This arm resembles the P-38 9mm (Luger) Parabellum in appearance and size but is blowback-operated. The pin which projects above the loaded chamber of centerfire P-38s is absent, as is the internal locking block.

The frame is alloy, but the barrel and slide are steel. Frame is anodized black, slide and barrel are matte black.

The slide is skeletonized to reduce weight. Trigger and hammer are machined from solid steel blocks.

Comment: The pistol is well made, well designed, and reliable. It is easy to disassemble and reassemble.

It is accurate for an arm with fixed sights. Micrometer sights can be adapted to the P-38. Centerfire P-38 admirers might want a rimfire version for less expensive shooting.

PART VIII

GENERAL DATA

CHAPTER / 36

NOTES ON SPORTERIZATION, OPTICAL GEAR, AND ACCESSORIES

CUSTOMIZING AND SPORTERIZING

"Gunsmithing" and "custom gunsmithing" are widely abused and misunderstood terms. Sometimes the two terms are used interchangeably. There is no clear line of demarcation between the two. Not even gunsmiths agree.

Since we can't be definitive, let's be a bit arbitrary. Many, including the author, consider "gunsmithing" as the basic process of making repairs, replacing parts, fitting a recoil pad or quick-detachable sling swivels, and possibly altering the angle of a bolt handle to permit lower scope mounting. Fitting scope bases is another gunsmith chore.

"Custom gunsmithing" may include recontouring a barrel, modifying the exterior of an action, reshaping the triggerbow, fitting a quick-release floorplate, rebarreling, or rechambering.

A Vermont neighbor recently had his M1917 Enfield Caliber .30 (.30–06) "gunsmithed." This consisted in sawing off 2 inches from the 26-inch barrel and fitting scope blocks. The wooden fore-end was cut from near muzzle length to a length approximating a commercial sporter. The upper wooden handguard was removed. This work cost about $25.

Another friend also "sporterized" his M1917 Enfield. The military barrel was removed from the action. The Parkerized—dull—military finish was removed from the barrel and action. The whole unit was reblued. The rear sight "ears" were machined off. The magazine was shortened. (It originally held five rimmed .303 British cartridges. When chambered for the .30–06 cartridge it holds six of these rimless cartridges.)

My friend reduced triggerbow width. A floorplate release was installed inside the triggerbow. The M1917 has a massive action; it weighs more than other actions chambered for the .30–06 or similar cartridges. So he had the sheet-steel sides of the box magazine "Swiss-cheesed"—a series of holes were bored to remove excessive weight. Edges of the action were rounded off. This reduces weight and makes a more streamlined action.

A Redfield Sourdough front sight—it's unfortunately been discontinued but a few are still on some dealers' shelves—was installed on a ramp. A Williams' Guide Sight—one of the best open rear sights—was installed. A G&H quick-detachable double-lever side mount was installed. A custom trigger replaced the original two-stage military trigger.

Jim couldn't afford the $500 and up for a fine piece of French walnut custom-checkered. He bought a commercial semi-fitted American walnut stock for $125. Some decent 22-line-per-inch custom checkering cost him another $125. He purchased a ready-made checkered steel buttplate fitted with a trapdoor. The recess will hold the slide of his Lyman 48 micrometer sight when it is not in use. When the sight is in use the dummy slide will be toted in the trapdoor.

The rifle is fitted with quick-detachable sling swivels and a 0.875-inch-wide Whelen-type leather sling. Jim applied the several hand-rubbed coats of linseed oil — the so-called London-type oil finish — himself. The metalwork cost him about $250.

For $500 Jim has a far better rifle — in most ways — than any of the commercial sporters.

The M1917 action — it's far better than the M1903 Springfield — is obsolete in that, unlike most current production bolt-action rifles, it doesn't have a recessed bolt face. It does have the advantage of the Mauser-type extractor and ejector.

Today, a top-quality stock — usually French or Circassian walnut — with fine handwork and furniture — buttplate, swivels, pistol-grip cap holding spare front sights, etc. — done by a first-class stockmaker like Jerry Fisher, Kalispell, Montana, would cost $500–$600. Total costs depend on quality of wood, type of wood, amount of furniture and type, amount and lines per inch of checkering.

Borderless checkering is considered the best (borders often conceal slips of the checkering tool), and about 26 lines per inch is the practical maximum. More than 26 lines per inch means that diamonds are more easily damaged and the grip is not as secure.

Rifles whose calibers do not actually require solid — never ventilated — recoil pads can use one of three basic buttplate types: (1) solid plate with Neider-type checkering; (2) skeleton buttplate with hand-checkered wood (a metal framework outlines the buttstock's edges and prevents damage to the wood); or (3) checkered steel buttplate with trapdoor. The recess inside the trapdoor can be designed for a sight slide, thong and oiler cleaner, a spare cartridge, or a waterproof match safe. There is a European buttplate — rarely seen in this country — which is designed to hold a magazineful of cartridges. To prevent rattle, each cartridge is usually held within its own separate tube. Opening the trapdoor exposes all cartridge case heads.

Most shooters desiring finer details such as trapdoors for spare front sights and skeleton buttplates are shooters who also prefer the classic stock type as originally developed by British riflemakers. This stock has a dull oil finish — a dozen or more coats — and no Monte Carlo. It may or may not have a practical cheekpiece.

Many continental stocks have mere worthless slivers of cheekpieces.

The British introduced the fore-end cap. The best caps — they are not necessary — were originally made from the horn of the Cape buffalo. They can also be made of ebony but should never be made of Tenite or other plastic.

Fancy woods include bird's-eye maple, California mesquite — that's what Weatherby uses on its big .460 Weatherby Magnum — and myrtlewood. The author's only experience with the latter — and it was a good experience — was on a standard .340 Weatherby Magnum. A wood must not only look good — proper grain and fine figuring — but it must not crack or splinter under heavy recoil. Stocks on medium-bore rifles and big-bore rifles — bolt-action magazine ones — should have at least one and preferably two crossbolts.

Some eccentrics like zebra-striped wood. This effect is achieved by alternate laminations of light and dark wood. In the future laminated wood may ultimately replace one-piece stocks on factory but never on fine custom rifles.

Gunsmiths have been around since there were guns, but until shortly before World War I their prime function was repair. When the M1903 Springfield became available to civilian riflemen through the Director of Civilian Marksmanship via the National Rifle Association, "custom" gunsmithing entered our vocabulary.

President Theodore Roosevelt took a slightly modified M1903 to Africa on his 1909–10 safari. He was followed by the writer Stewart Edward White. After World War I — when several million Americans handled their first bolt-action rifles — prestigious Griffin & Howe entered the field. Between world wars and for some time afterward, their stocks and metalwork were superb.

Few individuals excel at both stockmaking and metalwork. Some great stockers: Louis Wundhammar, Robert Owen, Alvin Linden, and Thomas Shelhammer. Fine post-World War II stockers include Nate Bishop, Al Biesen, Leonard Brownell, and Jerry Fisher. A rising newcomer is Winston Churchill of Ludlow, Vt. Churchill is also a master engraver.

Noted barrel makers of the era included Adolph Neidner and Eric Johnson. One of the great metalworkers was the late August Pachmayr. This German-born craftsman could make a top-quality double-barrel shotgun with no tools but files.

In that era as now, few can afford top-quality gunsmithing or stocking. The appearance of the Krag, the M1903 Springfield, the M1917 Enfield, and the thousands of bolt action rifles brought home by American Expeditionary Force doughboys created a demand for "sporterized" military rifles. Examples of what could be done were mentioned above in connection with the M1917 Enfields. Basic sporterizing procedures will be detailed at the end of these comments on gunsmithing.

The demand for sporterization ascended sharply in the post-World War II and Korean War years. By the late 1960s the demand had plummeted. Federal legislation prohibited importation and sale of military arms from foreign sources. These included arms of American manufacture which had been shipped at one time to our allies or other customers.

For many years gunsmiths did a brisk business in rechambering arms — many of them of military origin — and sometimes rebarreling them for wildcat cartridges.

Many former wildcat cartridges became standard with rifles and ammunition made by regular arms makers. During the 1930s, wildcats like the .22 Hornet, .220 Swift, and .257 Roberts entered the list of standard cartridges. Following World War II the list soared: .22–250 Rem., .243 Win., .244 (6mm) Rem., .25–06 Rem., and others.

Cartridges based on experimentals and wildcats included .264 Win., .300 Win. Magnum, .338 Win., and .458 Win. Magnum. Then, too, there are Roy Weatherby's high-velocity cartridges.

Returning momentarily to the between-two-wars era, it was not until 1937 when Winchester brought out its greatly improved M54 as the M70 that American shooters and hunters were able to purchase at reasonable costs an American factory-made rifle for calibers like the .300 H&H Magnum and the .375 H&H Magnum.

Today there are virtually no basic requirements that are not filled by factory-chambered rifles and ammunition. There will always be wildcats but the demand will never be as great as in the past. Many gunsmiths — some of them alleged gunsmiths — have gone out of business because their prime stock in trade, wildcat conversions and military-rifle sporterization, is but a whisper of the past.

Not only has the source of military arms from abroad dried up, but here at home the armed services adopted the automatic M14 and M16. These arms cannot legitimately be purchased by civilian shooters unless they pay a $200 transfer tax in addition to the purchase price. Then, too, due to legislation sponsored by Senator Edward Kennedy, only replacement parts, no complete arms, can be sold to National Rifle Association members through the Director of Civilian Marksmanship.

The best available military action today, the M1898 Mauser, is obsolete in terms of currently available commercial rifle actions.

Many old bolt-actions will see decades more of use, but there is the question of age and metal fatigue. Most contemporary bolt-actions, with their boltface completely surrounding the cartridge head and vastly improved trigger mechanisms, are far superior to any military bolt-action. A man can spend more money for just the basic sporterization of a military rifle than for a factory rifle of fine design and workmanship.

One small source of income for gunsmiths is the desire of current factory-production rifle owners to improve their arms. Example: About 1960 the author purchased a new M70 Winchester in caliber .338 Win. Magnum. There was nothing wrong with the action, but he preferred a solid rubber recoil pad (ventilated pads despite their widespread use on rifles are for shotguns), and a knurled bolt handle, jewel-turned bolt, quick-detachable sling swivels, and Redfield Sourdough front sight. He also wanted a pistol-grip cap with a trap door for holding a spare front sight.

The author shipped the rifle to Griffin & Howe. Their bill for this work was about $160, or more than he paid for the rifle (at a discount house). About one-third of the cost was for the imported English trapdoor pistol-grip cap. In fitting the cap it was necessary to partially re-checker the grip.

Shooters who want changes on their current production rifles represent a minute minority of rifle purchasers.

Very few riflemen who wish to restock a rifle have a complete custom stock made. At least 95 percent use commercial stocks which are already shaped and partially inletted but uncheckered. Such precut blanks range from about $25 to $125. Most riflemen spending more money for a blank usually go whole hog and have a complete custom job.

Never have expensive work done by a gunsmith of unknown reputation. Ask to see examples of his work. It is unfortunate that gunsmiths do not have to pass examinations before hanging out their shingle. Anybody, competent or not, can set up shop.

If you plan extensive alterations, you are well advised to secure the services of a gunsmith who is at least known statewide, if not nationally. With some gunsmiths it is a case of *caveat emptor*.

BASIC SPORTERIZING PROCEDURES

This chapter opened with an account of how an Enfield M1917 was gunsmithed for a friend of the author's and how another Enfield M1917 was *custom* gunsmithed for another friend. The jobs done on both rifles certainly come under the heading of "sporterizing," although one involved a minimum of cost and alteration while the other involved extensive and elegant work, much of it for the sake of appearance rather than function. Obviously, there are almost infinite variations on the theme of sporterizing, but the term basically means nothing more than the modification of a military arm to make it suitable or more efficient for sporting use and to give it the handsomer appearance of a civilian arm.

It has been pointed out that sporterizing, once so popular it was almost a national fad among riflemen (and a thriving sub-industry among gunsmiths), has declined considerably. Good military surplus arms—especially those that lend themselves to sporterizing—have become harder to obtain and more expensive, while commercial sporters have multiplied.

Why, then, should anyone sporterize a military rifle or have one professionally sporterized? Some shooters do it because they happen to own or obtain a military rifle that has the potential to be transformed into a gem of a sporter. And many do it simply for the satisfaction of the creative urge—the pleasure of having a hand in designing and/or producing exactly the kind of sporter they consider ideal. There are some (not many) who have completely outfitted workshops and the skills necessary to do most or all of the work themselves. More commonly, they enlist the aid of a gunsmith, and if that gunsmith is not one of the more cantankerous breed he will listen to the sensible desires and suggestions of the client. This gives a rifleman the justified feeling that he has taken a hand in the design of his sporter.

Although a great many military arms can be successfully modified for civilian use, sporterization is most often an honor accorded to three eminently suitable rifles: the M98 Mauser (and its many variations), the M03 Springfield, and the M17 Enfield.

Occasionally, someone insists on sporterizing the U.S. Carbine, Caliber .30 M1. There is little one can really sporterize about the M1 Carbine beyond re-stocking it with good wood nicely contoured and checkered, fitting quick-detachable sling swivels, and installing sporting sights or scope blocks. The carbine cartridge is inadequate for deer (though some hunters refuse to be convinced by anything but sad experience). It is strictly a 75-yard cartridge for jack rabbits and the like—if one can find nothing better to point at a jack rabbit. And bear in mind that semiautomatic arms such as the M1 must have fairly loose chambers to ensure proper functioning.

If a hunter is enamored of the M1 Carbine's lightness, compactness, fast-handling qualities, and romantically martial appearance, why not buy an excellent civilian carbine such as the .44 Magnum Ruger, which has all those delights, looks rather like a sporterized M1 Carbine (though handsomer), chambers a useful cartridge, and can be purchased at an attractive price?

As for the three more suitable sporterization candidates mentioned above, there are fundamental gunsmithing operations that are generally agreed upon, regardless of additional refinements to suit the taste and bank account of the owner. These operations will be listed below.

M98 Mauser (and variations)

The M98 Mauser is the action from which at least 90 percent of the world's bolt-action rifles are derived. They include the M03 Springfield, M17 Enfield, Winchester M54 and M70, Ruger M77, Weatherby Mark V, etc. Depending on the original caliber and the primary uses for which the sporter is intended, sporterization may or may not include rechambering.

Many military Mausers have two distinct features: a straight bolt handle and a stepped barrel—that is, a barrel enlarged from muzzle to breech in a series of increments. One or both of these features may be altered. These and the other operations most commonly performed are as follows:

1. Reshape or replace bolt handle if necessary or if desired.

2. Replace barrel if desired. (A stepped barrel is obvious and unsightly only when a military fore-end is removed or a full-length military stock is cut back to sporter length. Sometimes a Mannlicher-style sporter stock is put on, and of course this reaches to the muzzle.)

3. If the original barrel is retained, it may be 30 inches long on an old infantry rifle, and it will then have to be shortened to desired length.

4. Drill and tap receiver for scope mounts (and/or micrometer sight) and replace military front sight with sporting type on a ramp (usually with a barrel band).

5. Install hinged magazine floorplate with triggerbow release catch.

6. If weight is excessive, reduce it slightly by "Swiss-cheesing" magazine walls. Triggerbow

may also be slimmed or replaced, thus enhancing appearance.

7. Remove military bluing and re-blue barrel and other parts.

8. Re-stock, if desired (usually with semi-custom inletted stock); bed, checker and finish stock.

9. Fit desired buttplate (such as checkered steel plate or solid rubber recoil pad).

10. Fit quick-detachable sling swivels and sporting sling.

U.S. Springfield M1903

The famed Springfield employed the M98 Mauser action with two minor "improvements" of dubious value—a two-part firing pin/cocking piece and a magazine cut-off. But the action is fundamentally similar. Again, rechambering may or may not be desired. Basic sporterization includes these steps:

1. If barrel is not replaced, remove folding-leaf rear sight.

2. Drill and tap receiver for scope mounts (and/or micrometer sight).

3. Remove military front sight; if "iron sights" rather than scope will be used, mount barrel band for flat-bead front on a ramp.

4. Replace the two-part cocking piece/firing pin unit with single-piece firing pin.

5. Inactivate magazine cut-off.

6. Alter angle of bolt handle if desired for appearance or if necessary for scope mounting.

7. File and polish barrel—removing military bluing or Parkerization—and reblue barrel and other parts.

8. Fit hinged magazine floorplate with trigger-bow release catch.

9. "Swiss-cheese" magazine walls and trim triggerbow width for lightness and good appearance.

10. Remove military stock; bed, checker, and finish semi-custom inletted stock.

11. Fit desired buttplate.

12. Fit quick-detachable sling swivels and sporting sling.

Note: If original stock is retained, remove upper handguard, cut fore-end back to about mid-barrel, checker, finish, and equip with furniture as outlined above for replacement stock.

Enfield M17 (U.S. Rifle Caliber .30, M1917)

The Enfield was one of the strongest and most reliable of all military bolt-actions. Its long magazine makes it an excellent candidate for rechambering. Of the three most-often-sporterized military weapons, it is the only one that can handle full-length magnum cartridges such as the .375 H&H Magnum or the .300 Weatherby Magnum without cutting into the receiver. Here are the basic sporterizing operations:

1. Reduce barrel (if original is retained) from original 26.0 inches to desired length.

2. Mill off rear sight "ears" and rear sight, and drill and tap for scope mounts (and/or micrometer sight).

3. Install barrel band for flat-bead front sight on a ramp base.

4. File and polish barrel, removing original bluing or Parkerization, and re-blue barrel and other parts.

5. Reduce magazine capacity to 5-shot so that floorplate can be installed flush with bottom of stock.

6. Fit hinged magazine floorplate with trigger-bow release catch.

7. "Swiss-cheese" magazine walls and trim triggerbow width for lightness and good appearance.

8. Remove military stock; bed, checker, and finish semi-custom inletted stock.

9. Fit desired buttplate.

10. Fit quick-detachable sling swivels and sporting sling.

Note: If original stock is retained, remove upper handguard, shorten fore-end to about mid-barrel, checker, finish, and equip with furniture as outlined for replacement stock.

Obviously, some of these steps with any of the three popular military rifles are for the sake of appearance only, not for functional purposes. They are optional refinements. One man's "junker" is another man's sporter.

RIFLE SCOPES

There are two basic kinds of rifle scopes: internal-adjustment and external-adjustment. Internal-adjustment scopes represent about 95 percent of all rifle scopes. They're used for hunting and varmint shooting. The hunting scope is installed in a top mount, side mount, or swing-off mount. About 95 percent of hunting scopes are top-mounted.

Top mounts may be one- or two-piece. The Weaver is typical of two-piece top mounts. Top mounts are the most secure, but they preclude the use of open sights.

The classic side mount is the Griffin & Howe Quick Detachable. This steel mount has two parts. The steel base, fitted on the left side of the receiver, requires a cut in the stock. The scope can be removed or replaced by operating two side levers. When put back in the mount, in its original position, the scope does not have to be sighted-in all over again; it does not lose its "zero."

During the 1930s many big-game hunters were reared on open and/or micrometer sights like the classic Lyman 48, and most Griffin & Howe Springfield Sporters were fitted with a G&H side mount plus a Lyman 48 and an open rear sight. In calibers not requiring a solid recoil pad, the Lyman 48 slide was often carried in a trapdoor buttplate. Sometimes a dummy slide was fitted into the sight. It did look better than an empty slide holder.

It has been alleged, and with a certain amount of theoretical truth, that the G&H side mount is not quite as rugged as a top mount. The author has used the G&H side mount for more than 40 years. Rifles carrying this mount have traveled hundreds of miles in saddle scabbards. Despite nasty spills, the mount has never given any trouble.

When traveling by air, a rifle must be cased and shipped in the cargo hold. Despite the cushioned rifle cases, a scope can get out of line. With the side mount you detach the scope and carry it in your hand baggage or in a shockproof case. Once you arrive at your take-off point for the wilderness you slide the scope into position and the rifle is ready to fire with the scope zeroed in. Should you be leery about carrying your scoped rifle in a saddle scabbard, you can carry the scope in a belt case where it is ready to slip into the side mount at a moment's notice.

The author does not recommend the Jaeger side mount. Made of aluminum, it lacks the strength of the G&H. Friends have suffered bent mounts when a horse rolled on a scabbard.

If you fit your side-mount rifle with a sight such as the Lyman 48—and in the author's opinion you should—get some practice with it at various ranges before leaving on your trek. Redfield makes a sight similar to the Lyman 48. Williams offers a rustproof micrometer sight known as the Foolproof. This is an excellent sight for big-bore magnums like the .458 Winchester Magnum. Both the Lyman and Redfield are superior for long-range shooting in that they have more precise adjustments.

Redfield and Pachmayr offer a unique swing-off mount. The scope is side-mounted on bearings. The scope may be instantly swung out of the way so that iron sights may be used.

The above mounts are for scopes with internal adjustments. Each scope has two separate dials, one for windage and one for elevation. They are graduated in clicks ranging from $\frac{1}{4}$-minute to 1-minute. With 1-minute adjustments, for every click of the dial the point of aim is moved 1 inch up, down, or sideways at 100 yards. The $\frac{1}{4}$-minute scopes move $\frac{1}{4}$-inch per click, obviously a finer adjustment; 1-minute or $\frac{1}{2}$-minute adjustments are normal for scopes on big-game rifles, while the $\frac{1}{4}$-minute click is preferred for varmint scopes.

Hunting scopes range from about $2\frac{1}{2}\times$ to about $9\times$. The basic hunting scope has a fixed power. In recent years the variable-power scope has gained popularity. A variable may range from $2\frac{1}{2}$-$5\times$ or from 3-$7\times$ or 3-$9\times$.

Too many hunters miss game because they leave the power dial at the highest or one of the higher powers. Most woods shots require a lower setting. Longer shots usually provide time for the shooter to dial his scope to a higher power.

The higher the power, the narrower the field of view. That is why lower powers are preferred for running shots. The higher powers should be reserved for game that is standing or lying still.

The author has hunted deer with scopes for more than 40 years and in many regions. Most deer hunters, at least those who hunt in the woods, are overpowered (though not excessively so) with a $4\times$ scope.

The $4\times$ usually provides enough magnification for huntsmen throughout the world. If additional power is required—varmint shooting excepted—it is probably better to purchase a variable-power scope like a 3-$7\times$. The latter scope provides adequate—is it ever really adequate?—width of field for woods or running game. The higher magnifications may prove useful for long shots at plains or mountain game.

Several years ago Redfield introduced the Widefield model, a scope with an almost rectangular eyepiece—shaped more or less like a TV screen. Weaver, Weatherby, and probably a few other companies have since introduced similar scopes. The wide, semi-rectangular eyepiece provides a slightly wider field of view than what is seen through a scope of equal power but with a conventional, round eyepiece. Some shooters feel that the difference is insignificant and that the wide eyepiece is a trifle cumbersome. Others, including the author, prefer this type to the round eyepiece on scopes used for running and/or big game.

In the late 1950s, Lyman—one of our first manufacturers of quality scopes—introduced the $10\times$ varmint scope. Prior to this, varmint shooters used target scopes with the external adjustments. Since then, similar scopes ranging from $8\times$ to $12\times$ have been introduced by most manufacturers. The author uses an 8× on his .22 Hornet and .22 Remingtons. He uses 10× or 12× on his longer-range .220 Swift, .22–250 Rem., and .243 Win.

It is possible to make finer adjustments with target scopes fitted with external adjustments — these are in the bases — but the internal-adjustment top-mounted varmint scope is more rugged. Few of us are capable of making field shots — using a sling or other rest — that utilize the full accuracy of the rifle and cartridge.

Target and benchrest shooters use scopes with magnifications up to about 30×. Higher powers are not always the best. Mirage and the slightest movement adversely affect accuracy.

Shooters will note that the 10× or 12× varmint scopes and higher-powered target-type scopes usually have figures marked in feet and yards. The shooter must estimate the range he is shooting at — unless on a target range where exact distance is known — and set the figures on the scope to that distance to ensure proper focus.

Reticles

Reticles, better known as graticules to the British, are now more or less standardized. There have been some strange reticles. There was the inverted post, for one.

The author has used many reticles. Nearly all his present scopes have medium crosshairs. Some woods hunters prefer a flat-top post. At its maximum efficiency, a horizontal crosshair complements the post. Pointed, or picket, posts should be avoided.

For obvious reasons, thick posts or crosshairs are a help in fast aiming — that is, the shooter's eye can find them and center them on the target almost instantly. But they blot out so much of the target area that shooters who try them often switch back to finer (medium) crosshairs that subtend less of the target.

Several years ago Leupold introduced a crosshair that offered the advantages of both thick and thin. The Leupold version is called the Duplex. It consists of a crosshair that is thick near the outside of the field of view (in other words, near the rim of the reticle) but quite thin at the center. The thick segments help the shooter align quickly and center the target, while the thin intersection provides an aiming point and an unobstructed view of a large part of the target (or all of the target, depending on its size and the range).

Lyman now offers a reticle of the same type, called the Center Range, and Redfield has one called the 4-Plex. In fact, many manufacturers and importers are marketing scopes with this kind of reticle. It has probably become the most popular of all hunting types, and with good reason. In some models, the thin segments of the crosshairs extend farther than in others. About half and half — half thick, half thin — seems ideal to the author.

The Lee Dot, designed by the late Thomas K. Lee, was popular with some benchrest and target shooters. There were various-size dots. Scopes fitted with the dot had no other reticle. They were (and are) fine for shooting at paper targets but many hunters, including the author, avoid them for hunting because they tend to obstruct game.

There have been various attempts to incorporate range-finding devices into reticles. The one devised by Bill Weaver is probably as good as or better than any other of its type. It can be useful particularly when one is using two bullet weights like the 150-grain and 180-grain caliber .30 or the 270-grain and 300-grain .375 H&H Magnum. It takes some experience to use this reticle so be sure to get in some practice shooting before you shove off for the outback.

Scope lenses should be given as much care as camera or binocular lenses. Use the cleaning procedures described in the binocular section.

Two types of cap are used to protect scope lenses. One is a "no-see-through" and the other is a "see-through" type. With the latter you can use the scope with the lens cap in place. The writer has ambivalent feelings about it. Why spend money to have fine lenses and then partially nullify the value of those lenses by using optically inferior transparent scope caps? There is no doubt that the latter are faster than the "no-see-throughs."

Where the temperatures are around zero or less it is better — if practical — to leave your scoped rifle outside the hunting lodge. If you must bring the scoped rifle inside (same for binoculars and camera lenses) then cover the lenses with transparent plastic wrap. This will help keep moisture from condensing on the lens.

BINOCULARS

A good binocular — or a monocular — is as almost essential in varmint, deer, and big-game hunting as the rifle or ammunition. It is a safety factor and can prevent you from shooting an illegal or undesirable trophy.

Since the end of World War II the 7×35 binocular has almost entirely replaced the 6×30 as the "all-round" glass. The "7" means 7 power and the second figure relates to the amount of light entering the binocular. A 7×50 glass has the same magnification as a 7×35 glass but the former admits more light.

The 7×35 is generally the best choice for the shooter/hunter who can afford but one glass. It is ideal for woods hunting, and for shots across woods clearings, pastures, or meadows. It provides a wide enough field of view and adequate magnification.

The 9×35 binocular is essentially the glass of the specialist who hunts the high, wide plains and mountain slopes of the Rocky Mountain West. It is also a good glass for the plains game of Africa.

The standard European glass is probably the 8×30. This is an excellent combination of power and light-gathering qualities. For the man who can afford but one glass the 8×30 is a good bet, though not quite as good as the 7×35.

Quality binoculars are usually offered with individual focus, meaning that each eyepiece can be individually adjusted to each eye; or with central focus, meaning that focus is secured by turning the wheel on the bridge between the two lens barrels.

Individual focus provides maximum adjustability for the vagaries of each eye. The major advantage of the central focus is speed in adjustment. It is supposed to be more dustproof. I've used both focus types and have never had trouble with either.

The coating of optics to reduce glare came in about World War II. For many years all first-rate binoculars, scopes, and camera lenses have been coated. Don't turn down a good deal in glasses — if it is a good deal — because they are not coated. Many manufacturers will coat uncoated glasses of their manufacture.

There is a lamentable tendency for manufacturers to provide soft or semi-soft leather or synthetic cases for their glasses. A good binocular, like a fine camera, requires maximum protection. Soft zippered cases do not provide the protection of the old hard cases.

Many binocular, rifle-scope, spotting-scope, and camera lenses have been scratched by the use of improper cleaning cloths or tissue. A common mistake is to use the cloths supplied by opticians for wiping eyeglass lenses. These cloths usually contain an abrasive which is harmful to fine lenses. There is no comparison between the quality of an eyeglass and that of a fine lens.

When cleaning off fingerprints, which contain grease, the author likes to use Kodak Lens Cleaning Tissue. Put a drop or two — or more — of Kodak Lens Cleaning Fluid on the tissue. Don't put the fluid directly on the lens surface. A lens may consist of 10 or more separate elements. These elements are put together in the factory.

Lens fluid should not but could loosen the cement and seep between the elements.

Never wipe dust from a lens. Use a small photographic lens blower and/or a small camel's-hair lens brush. The lens brush should always be kept in its case so that the hair will not accumulate dust.

Glasses should be protected from moisture and dust. If the glasses should be dunked or heavily rainsoaked don't take them apart. Send them immediately to the American manufacturer (if there are any left) or to the designated service station of the importer.

The handiest place for glasses is suspended from your neck. But it's annoying to have them banging about. The Banks Camera Harness helps solve this problem. A quick-release strap around your body holds them in position.

A monocular is half of a binocular, less the bridge — and a binocular that weighs 20 oz. will weigh about 8 oz. if only one lens barrel is used.

The author's monocular, a Carl Zeiss 8×30 weighs 8 oz. (plus 3 oz. more if the sturdy leather case is used). The monocular case fits handily into the pocket of a shirt or bush jacket. The monocular has an adapter so that it can be used as a 16-power telephoto lens on a Zeiss Icarex 35mm camera.

There are several "pocket" type binoculars on the market. None is as satisfactory as the Zeiss monocular.

SPOTTING SCOPES

The spotting scope is used by rifle and pistol target shooters, varmint shooters, trophy hunters, hunters of long-range, open-country game like antelope and caribou, and hunters of mountain game like sheep and goat. A spotting scope is also most useful for African plains game.

There are two basic modern types — the fixed power such as a 20×, and the zoom scope featuring adjustable magnification. Today, most fixed scopes offer one or more additional lenses — all interchangeable — in powers like 30× and 40×.

The zoom spotting scope is comparable to the variable-power rifle scope. The Weatherby 20×–45× is an excellent example of the fine zoom spotting scopes. Other manufacturers/importers include Bausch & Lomb, Bushnell, Redfield, Swift, and Unertl.

There are two common eyepiece types: right angle and 45° angle. The latter is generally considered more convenient. And there are two basic scope-stand types: tripod and bipod. The former are far more common. Most scopes have a socket that fits standard camera tripods.

GUN SHIPPING CASES

If you are about to embark on your first airplane flight accompanied by one or more rifles or shotguns, don't arrive at the airport expecting they can be stowed in pilot or stewardess compartments. Once, yes, but not since the rise of air piracy. Your rifle or shotgun must now be shipped in an appropriate and locked case carried in the cargo hold.

Since the nineteenth century baggage handlers have appropriately been called "baggage smashers." That is what they did and still do. Baggage smashers obviously resent people fortunate enough to take hunting holidays. Many baggage smashers are thieves. Gun cases are very conspicuous in appearance, especially the full-length rifle cases or the leg-of-mutton shotgun or double-rifle cases.

Federal law requires your case to be locked. Anyone can open one of these locks in a few seconds. The only real good of a lock is that it meets the federal requirements. Airlines make money selling cases to hunters who arrive at the airport without an approved gun case.

The standard case sold by major distributors appears to have been made by a single manufacturer. If not, the cases are almost identical. The case is made of a hard synthetic and has a foam lining. This material readily absorbs moisture, which it transmits to the firearm to produce rust. This can happen overnight. Each firearm carried in such a case should be thoroughly oiled (and that includes the bore unless it is chromed).

To be on the safe side, the author detaches the scope before shipping the rifle. This is where a side-mounted scope is of considerable value.

RIFLE SCABBARDS

The author has used scabbards since he undertook officer's training in the horse cavalry at Fort Ethan Allen, Vt., in 1937. Until the recent imposition of federal regulations for shipping rifles aboard aircraft, he used a custom rifle scabbard complete with detachable hood for carrying aboard planes.

Scabbards range from the open-ended skinny type for nonscoped rifles to more sophisticated and protective designs. Some have zipper closures. Shun them like the plague.

Since Roy Weatherby no longer sells his superb scabbard, the best available scabbard in the author's opinion is the Jack O'Connor scabbard made by the Lawrence Leather Co., Pendleton, Ore. Jack says he had nothing to do with the design but that it is a good scabbard. Other fine scabbards are made to order by individual saddlemakers.

The quality leather scabbard should be made of thick, heavy saddle leather. Seams should be sewn with heavy waxed linen thread. The hood should be quickly detachable. Stitches should be double-hooked. There should be a small drain hole in case water finds its way into the scabbard.

Location of the strap should allow the scabbard to be suspended from the saddle at different positions. The author's preference is on the forward left side of the saddle.

The interior of the scabbard should never be lined with real or imitation sheepskin or any other liner. Liners, despite advertising claims to the contrary, accumulate moisture.

CASES FOR TAKE-DOWN SHOTGUNS

The classic American case for over/under or side-by-side shotguns is the leg-of-mutton type. Cheap canvas or plastic offers little protection. The best cases are leather. English cases—they are rare in this type—are very costly. Ones about equally as good, but made in Spain, sell for much less. Price differential is accounted for by labor costs. The standard case has a partition to separate the stock from the barrels. Cases are also available for guns with a second set of barrels.

The major disadvantage in the past of the leather leg-of-mutton case, as compared to the traditional British trunk case, was that no snap caps, shot cartridges, or cleaning gear could be toted along with the shotgun.

Today, the major disadvantage of the leg-of-mutton case is its readily recognizable appearance. Thieves among baggage smashers easily spot the case as a gun container. Most of the author's shotguns have trunk cases.

Rectangular trunk cases don't look like a trunk. They have room for a spare box of shot cartridges, cleaning rods, snap caps, gun oil, patches, and so on.

The British trunk case, like the leg-of-mutton type, costs at least twice as much as a similar Spanish case of about equal quality.

Today, most shooters settle for the far less expensive synthetic cases, and these cases may be more practical than the beautiful leather ones.

Leather requires a certain amount of attention, particularly in climates with high humidity. Any leather, including camera cases, shoes, belts, and gun slings, should be stored in air-conditioned spots in such climates.

APPENDIX

U.S. ARMS MANUFACTURERS

A-J ORDNANCE, INC., (Alexander-James), 1066 E. Edna Pl., Covina, CA 91722

A.R. SALES CO., 9624 Alpaca St., South El Monte, CA 91733

AMERICAN HERITAGE ARMS, INC., Rte. 44 P.O. Box 95, West Willington, CT 06279

ARMALITE, 118 E. 16th St., Costa Mesa, CA 92627

APOLLO CUSTOM RIFLES, INC., 1235 Cowles St., Long Beach, CA 90813

ARTISTIC ARMS, INC., Box 23, Hoagland, IN 46745

AUTO MAG CORP. (See Lee E. Jurras & Assoc., Inc.)

AUTO-ORDNANCE CORP., Box ZG, West Hurley, NY 12491

BAUER FIREARMS, 34750 Klein Ave., Fraser, MI 48026

CHALLANGER MFG. CORP., 118 Pearl St., Mt. Vernon, NY 10550

CHAMPLIN FIREARMS, INC., Box 3191, Enid, OK 73701

CHARTER ARMS CORP., 430 Sniffens Ln., Stratford, CT 06497

CLASSIC ARMS INTL., INC., 20 Wilbraham St., Palmer, MA 01069

CLERKE PRODUCTS, 2219 Main St., Santa Monica, CA 90405

COLT, 150 Huyshope Ave., Hartford, CT 06102

COMMANDO ARMS, INC., Box 10214, Knoxville, TN 37919

CUMBERLAND ARMS, 1222 Oak Dr., Manchester, TN 37355

DAY ARMS CORP., 2412 S.W. Loop 410, San Antonio, TX 78227

DUBIEL ARMS CO., P.O. Box 856, Denison, TX 75020

EE-DA-HOW LONG RIFLES, INC., 3318 Camrose Lane, Boise, ID 83705

EMF CO. INC., Box 1248, Studio City, CA 91604

FALLING BLOCK WORKS, P.O. Box 22, Troy, MI 48084

FIREARMS DEVELOPMENT, INC. (See Hi-Shear Corp.)

FIREARMS IMP. & EXP. CO., 2470 N.W. 21st St., Miami, FL 33142

FIREARMS INTL. CORP. (See: Garcia)

4 ACE MFG. INC., P.O. Box 3820, Brownsville, TX 78520

GOLDEN AGE ARMS CO., 14 W. Winter St., Delaware, OH 43015

HARRINGTON & RICHARDSON, INDUSTRIAL ROWE, Gardner, MA 01440

A.D. HELLER, INC., Box 268, Grand Ave., Baldwin, NY 11510

HI-SHEAR CORP., AD-TECH DIV., 2830 Lomita Blvd., Torrance, CA 90505

HIGH STANDARD MFG. CO., 1817 Dixwell Ave., Hamden, CT 06514

HOPKINS & ALLEN, (See: High Standard)

HYPER-SINGLE PRECISION SS RIFLES, 520 E. Beaver, Jenks, OK 74037

ITHACA GUN CO., Terrace Hill, Ithaca, NY 14850

IVER JOHNSON ARMS & CYCLE WORKS, Fitchburg, MA 01420

J & R CARBINE (See: PJK, Inc.)

LEE E. JURRAS & ASSOC., INC., P.O. Box 846, Roswell, NM 88201

LJUTIC IND., INC., P.O. Box 2117, Yakima WA 98902

MB ASSOCIATES (See: Intercontinental Arms)

MANCHESTER ARMS, INC., 6858 Manchester Rd., Rte. 2, Clinton, OH 44216

MARLIN FIREARMS CO., 100 Kenna Dr., New Haven, CT 06473

MERRILL CO. INC., Box West High, Rockwell City, IA 50579

O.F. MOSSBERG & SONS, INC., 7 Grasso St., New Haven, CT 06473

W.L. MOWREY GUN WORKS, INC., Box 28, Iowa Park, TX 76367

NATL. ORDNANCE INC., 9643 Alpaca, S. El Monte, CA 91733

NAVY ARMS CO., 689 Bergen Blvd., Ridgefield, NJ 07657

NORARMCO, 41471 Irwin, Mt. Clemens, MI 48043

NORTH AMERICAN ARMS, P.O. Box 158, Freedom, WY 83120

NORTH STAR ARMS, R.2, Box 74A, Ortonville, MN 56278

NUMRICH ARMS CORP., W. Hurley, NY 12491

OMEGA (See: Hi-Shear Corp.)

PJK, INC., 1527 Royal Oak Dr., Bradbury, CA 91010

PLAINFIELD MACHINE CO., INC., Box 447, Dunellen, NJ 08812

PLAINFIELD ORDNANCE CO., P.O. Box 251, Middlesex, NJ 08846

POTOMAC ARMS CORP., P.O. Box 35, Alexandria, VA 22313

RG INDUSTRIES, 2485 N.W. 20th S.E., Miami, FL 33142

REMINGTON ARMS CO., Bridgeport, CT 06602

RIEDL RIFLES, 15124 West State St., Westminster, CA 92683

ROCKY MOUNTAIN ARMS CORP., Box 224, Salt Lake City, UT 84110

RUGER (See: Sturm, Ruger & Co.)

SAVAGE ARMS CORP., Westfield, MA 01085

SEARS, ROEBUCK & CO., 825 S. St. Louis, Chicago, IL 60607

SECURITY INDUSTRIES OF AMERICA, INC., 31 Bergen Turnpike, Little Ferry, NJ 07643

SEVENTREES LTD., 315 W. 39th St., New York, NY 10018

U.S. ARMS MANUFACTURERS (continued)

SHILOH PRODUCTS, 37 Potter St., Farmingdale,
NY 11735

SMITH & WESSON, INC., 2100 Roosevelt Ave.,
Springfield, MA 01101

SPORTING ARMS, INC., 9643 Alpaca St., So. El Monte,
CA 91733

SPRINGFIELD ARMORY, 111 E. Exchange St.,
Geneseo, IL 61254

STERLING ARMS CORP., 4436 Prospect St., Gasport,
NY 14067

STURM, RUGER & CO., Southport, CT 06490

TDE MARKETING CORP., 11658 McBean Dr.,
El Monte, CA 91732

THOMPSON-CENTER ARMS, Box 2405, Rochester,
NH 03867

TINGLE, 1125 Smithland Pike, Shelbyville, Ind. 46176

TRAIL GUNS ARMORY, 2115 Lexington, Houston,
TX 77006

TRIPLE-S DEVELOPMENT CO., INC.,
1450 E. 289th St., Wickliffe, OH 44092

UNITED STATES ARMS CORP.,
Doctors Path and Middle Road, Riverhead, NY 11901

UNIVERSAL SPTG. GOODS, INC., 7920 N.W. 76th,
Miami, FL 33166

UNORDCO, P.O. Box 15723, Nashville, TN 37215

WARD'S, 619 W. Chicago, Chicago, IL 60607

WEATHERBY'S 2781 E. Firestone Blvd., South Gate,
CA 90280

DAN WESSON ARMS, 293 So. Main St., Monson,
MA 01057

WILKINSON ARMS, 1841 Merced, So. El Monte,
CA 91733

WINCHESTER REPEATING ARMS CO., New Haven,
CT 06504

WINSLOW ARMS CO., P.O. Box 578, Osprey, FL 33595

FOREIGN ARMS MANUFACTURERS

ALASKAN RIFLES, Box 30, Juneau, Alaska 99801

ARMI FABBRI, Casella 206, Brescia, Italy 25100

ARMI FAMARS, Via Cinelli 33, Gardone V.T. (Brescia),
Italy 25063

ASTRA-UNCESTA Y COMPANIA S.A., Guernica, Spain

AYA (AGUIRRE Y ARANZABAL) See: Ventura Imports
(Spanish shotguns)

BLASER/VINZENZ HUBER GMBH, P.O. Box 2245,
D-7900 Ulm, W. Germany

BRETTON, 21 Rue Clement Forissier, 42-St. Etienne,
France

CARL GUSTAV FABRIKEN, Eskistuna, Sweden

CARL WALTHER WAFFENFABRIK, Ulm/Donau,
W. Germany

ERMA-WERKE, Dachau, W. Germany

EUROARMS, Via Solferino 13/A, 25100 Brescia, Italy

J. FANZOJ, P.O. Box 25, Ferlach, Austria 9170

A. FRANCOTTE & CIE., 61 rue Mont St. Clair, Liege,
Belgium

RENATO GAMBA, Fabbrica d'Armi, via Petrarca,
25060 Ponte Zanano di Sarezzo (Brescia), Italy

ARMAS GARBI, Fundidores 4, Eibar, Spain (shotguns)

HAMMERLI, Lenzburg, Switzerland

GEVELOT OF CAN. LTD., Box 1593, Saskatoon, Sask.,
Canada

GEORGES GRANGER, 66 Cours Fauriel, 42 St. Etienne,
France

HECKLER & KOCH, Oberndorf am Neckar, W. Germany

ITALGUNS, Via Leonardo da Vinci 169, 20090 Trezzano,
(Milano), Italy

LLAMA GABILILONDA Y CIA, Elgoibar, Spain

LEVER ARMS SERV. LTD., 771 Dunsmuir, Vancouver,
B.C., Canada V6C 1M9

MCQUEEN SALES CO. LTD., 1760 W. 3rd Ave.,
Vancouver, B.C., Canada V6J 1K5

MANU-ARM, St. Etienne, France

MANUFRANCE, 100 Cours Fauriel, 42 St. Etienne,
France

MERKURIA, P.O. Box 18, 17005 Prague,
Czechoslovakia (BRNO)

MAUSER-WERKE, Obendorf an Neckar, W. Germany

MUSGRAVE & SONS, Bloemfontein,
Union of South Africa

PARKER-HALE, Bisleyworks, Golden Hillock Rd.,
Sparbrook, Birmingham B11 2PZ, England

PICARD-FAYOLLE, 42-rue du Vernay,
42100 Saint Etienne, France

LEONARD PUCCINELLI CO., Casella 309,
25100 Brescia, Italy (Fabbri)

SIG (Schweizerishe Industrie Gesellschaft)
Neuhausen an Reinfalls, Schaufhausen, Switzerland

SKINNER'S GUN SHOP (see Alaskan Rifles)

STATE ARSENAL, Izhevsk, U.S.S.R.

FRANZ SODIA JAGDGEWEHRFABRIK,
Schulhausgasse 14, 9170 Ferlach, Austria

STAR-B ECHEVARRIA, Eibar, Spain

STEYR-DAIMLER-PUCH, A4400 Steyr, Austria

UBERTI, ALDO & CO., Via G. Carducci 41 or 39,
Ponte Zanano (Brescia), Italy

IGNACIO UGARTECHEA, Eibar, Spain

UNION ARMERIA, Eibar, Spain

VERNEY-CARRON, 17 Cours Fauriel,
42010 St. Etienne Cedex, France

WAFFEN-FRANKONIA, Box 380, 87 Wurzburg,
W. Germany

WEBLEY & SCOTT, Park Lane, Handsworth,
Birmingham, England

WESTLEY RICHARDS & CO., LTD., Grange Road,
Bournebrook, Birmingham, England

ZAVODI CRVENA ZASTAVA, 29 Novembra St.,
No. 12, Belgrade, Yugoslavia

ARMS IMPORTERS

ABERCROMBIE & FITCH, Madison at 45th, New York, NY 10017

AMERICAN IMPORT CO., 1167 Mission St., San Francisco, CA 94103

AMERICAN INTERNATIONAL, 103 Social Hall Ave., Salt Lake City, UT 84111

AYA (AGUIRRE Y ARANZABAL) See: Ventura Imports (Spanish shotguns)

ARMOURY INC., Rte. 25, New Preston, CT 06777

ARMSPORT, INC., 2811 N.W. 75th Ave., Miami, FL 33122

BROWNING, Rte. 4, Box 624-B, Arnold, MO 63010

CENTENNIAL ARMS CORP., 3318 W. Devon, Chicago, (Lincolnwood) IL 60645

CENTURY ARMS CO., 3-5 Federal St., St. Albans, VT 05478

CHAMPLIN FIREARMS, INC., Box 3191, Enid, OK 73701 (Gebruder Merkel)

CONNECTICUT VALLEY ARMS CO., Saybrook Rd., Haddam, CT 06438 (CVA)

CONTINENTAL ARMS CORP., 697 Fifth Ave., New York, NY 10022

W.H. CRAIG, Box 927, Selma, AL 36701

CREIGHTON & WARREN, P.O. Box 15723, Nashville, TN 37215 (Krieghoff combination guns)

MORTON CUNDY & SON, LTD., 413 6th Ave., E. Kalispell, MT 59901

DAIWA, 14011 Normandie Ave., Gardena, CA 90247

DAVIDSON FIREARMS CO., 2703 High Pt. Rd., Greensboro, NC 27403 (shotguns)

DAVIS GUN SHOP, 7213 Lee Highway, Falls Church, VA 22046 (Fanzoj, Ferlach; Spanish guns)

DIANA CO., 842 Vallejo St., San Francisco, CA 94133 (Benelli, Breda Shotguns)

DIXIE GUN WORKS, INC., Hwy 51, South Union City, TN 38261 ("Kentucky" rifles)

EASTERN SPORTS DISTRIBUTORS CO., INC., P.O. Box 28, Milford, NH 03055 (Rottweil; Geco)

EXCAM INC., 4480 E. 11th Ave., P.O. Box 3483, Hialeah, FL 33013

FERLACH (AUSTRIA) OF NORTH AMERICA, P.O. Box 430435, S. Miami, FL 33143

R.C. FESSLER & CO., 1634 Colorado Blvd., Los Angeles, CA 90041

FIREARMS CENTER INC., (FCI), 113 Spokane, Victoria, TX 77901

FIREARMS IMP. & EXP. CO., 2470 N.W. 21st St., Miami, FL 33142

FIREARMS INTERNATIONAL CORP., 17801 Indian Head Hwy., Accokeek, MD 20607

FLAIG'S LODGE, Millvale, PA 15209

FLORIDA FIREARMS CORP., 555 N.W. 36th Ave., Hialeah, FL 33142

FREELAND'S SCOPE STANDS, INC., 3737 14th Ave., Rock Island, IL 61201

J.L. GALEF & SON, INC., 85 Chambers, New York, NY 10007

GARCIA SPTG. ARMS CORP., 329 Alfred Ave., Teaneck, NJ 07666

HAWES NATIONAL CORP., 1524 Cabrito Rd., Van Nuys, CA 91406

HEALTHWAYS, Box 45055, Los Angeles, CA 90061

GIL HEBARD GUNS, Box 1, Knoxville, IL 61448 (Hammerli)

A.D. HELLER, INC., Box 268, 2322 Grand Ave., Baldwin, NY 11510

HERTER'S, Waseca, MN 56093

INTERARMCO (See: Interarms Walther)

INTERARMS LTD., 10 Prince St., Alexandria, VA 22313 (Mauser, Valmet M-62/S)

INTERNATIONAL DISTR., INC., 7290 S.W. 42nd St., Miami, FL 33155 (Taurus rev.)

ITHACA GUN CO., Terrace Hill, Ithaca, NY 14850 (Perazzi)

PAUL JAEGER INC., 211 Leedom St., Jenkintown, PA 19046

JANA INTL. CO., Box 1107, Denver, CO 80201 (Parker-Hale)

J.J. JENKINS, 375 Pine Ave., No. 25, Goleta, CA 93017

GUY T. JONES IMPORT CO., 905 Gervais St., Columbia, SC 29201

KANEMATSU-GOSHO USA INC., 543 W. Algonquin Rd., Arlington Heights, IL 60005 (Nikko)

KASSNAR IMPORTS, P.O. Box 3895, Harrisburg, PA 17105

KERR'S SPORT SHOP, INC., 9584, Wilshire Blvd., Beverly Hills, CA 90212

KIMEL INDUSTRIES, P.O. Box 335, Matthews, NC 28105

KLEINGUENTHER'S, P.O. Box 1261, Seguin, TX 78155

KNIGHT & KNIGHT, 5930 S.W. 48th St., Miami, FL 33155 (made to order only)

KRIEGHOFF GUN CO., P.O. Box 48-1367, Miami, FL 33148

L.A. DISTRIBUTORS, 4 Centre Market Pl., New York, NY 10013

L.E.S. 3640 Dempster, Skokie, IL 60076 (Steyr, Mannlicher-Schönauer)

S.E. LASZLO, 200 Tillary St., Brooklyn, NY 11201

LIBERTY ARMS ORGANIZATION, Box 306, Montrose, CA 91020

MCKEOWN'S GUNS, R.R.1, Pekin, IL 61554

MANDALL SHOOTING SUPPLIES CORP., 7150 E. 4th St., Scottsdale, AZ 85252

MARS EQUIPMENT CORP., 3318 W. Devon, Chicago, IL 60645

NAVY ARMS CO., 689 Bergen Blvd., Ridgefield, NJ 07657

NIKKO SPORTING FIREARMS, 543 W. Algonquin Rd., Arlington Heights, IL 60005

HARRY OWEN, P.O. Box 774, Sunnyvale, CA 94088

PACHMAYR GUN WORKS, 1220 S. Grand Ave., Los Angeles, CA 90015

PACIFIC INTL. MERCH. CORP., 2215 "J" St., Sacramento, CA 95816

ED PAUL SPTG. GOODS, 172 Flatbush Ave., Brooklyn, NY 11217 (Premier)

PRECISE, 3 Chestnut, Suffern, NY 10901

PREMIER SHOTGUNS, 172 Flatbush Ave., Brooklyn, NY 11217

RG INDUSTRIES, INC., 2485 N.W. 20th St., Miami, FL 33142 (Erma)

ARMS IMPORTERS (continued)

RICHLAND ARMS CO., 321 W. Adrian St., Blissfield, MI 49228

ROTTWEIL (See: Eastern)

SANDERSON'S 724 W. Edgewater, Portage, WI 53901

SAVAGE ARMS CORP., Westfield, MA 01085 (Anschutz)

SECURITY ARMS CO., 1815 No. Ft. Myer Dr., Arlington, VA 22209 (Heckler & Koch)

SERVICE ARMAMENT, 689 Bergen Blvd., Ridgefield, NJ 07657 (Greener Harpoon Gun)

SHERWOOD DIST., INC., 18714 Parthenia St., Northridge, CA 91324

SIMMONS SPEC., INC., 700 Rogers Rd., Olathe, KS 66061

SLOAN'S SPTG., GOODS, INC., 10 South St., Ridgefield, CT 06877

STOEGER ARMS CO., 55 Ruta Ct., S. Hackensack, NJ 07606

TRADEWINDS, INC., P.O. Box 1191, Tacoma, WA 98401

TWIN CITY SPTG. GDS., 217 Ehrman Ave., Cincinnäti, OH 45220

UNIVERSAL SPTG. GOODS, INC., 7920 N.W. 76th Ave., Medley, FL 33166

VALOR IMP. CORP., 5555 N.W. 36th Ave., Miami, FL 33142

VENTURA IMPORTS, P.O. Box 2782, Seal Beach, CA 90740 (European shotguns)

WEATHERBY'S 2781 Firestone Blvd., So. Gate, CA 90280 (Sauer)

DAN WESSON ARMS, 293 So. Main, Monson, MA 01057

AMMUNITION (*Commercial*)

ALCAN SHELLS (See: Smith & Wesson Ammunition Co.)

AMRON CORP., 525 Progress Ave., Waukesha, WI 53186

CASCADE CARTRIDGE INC. (See: Omark)

DWM (See RWS)

DYNAMIT NOBEL OF AMERICA, INC., 910, 17th St. NW, Suite 709, Washington, DC 20006

FEDERAL CARTRIDGE CO., 2700 Foshay Tower, Minneapolis, MN 55402

FRONTIER CARTRIDGE CO., INC., Box 1848, Grand Island, NE 68801

LEE E. JURRAS & ASSOC., INC., P.O. Box 846, Roswell, NM 88201

OMARK-CCI, INC., Box 856, Lewiston, ID 83501

OMARK-SPEER-CCI, INC., Box 896, Lewiston, ID 83501

RWS (See Dynamit Nobel)

REMINGTON ARMS CO., Bridgeport, CT 06602

SERVICE ARMAMENT, 689 Bergen Blvd., Ridgefield, NJ 07657

SMITH & WESSON AMMUNITION CO., 2399 Forman Rd., Rock Creek, OH 44084

WEATHERBY'S 2781 E. Firestone Blvd., South Gate, CA 90280

WINCHESTER-WESTERN, East Alton, IL 62024

AMMUNITION (*Custom*)

BILL BALLARD, P.O. Box 656, Billings, MT 59103

BALLISTEK, Box 459, Laconia, NH 03246

BEAL'S BULLETS, 179 W. Marshall Rd., Lansdowne, PA 19050

BELL'S GUN & SPORT SHOP, 3309-19 Mannheim Rd., Franklin Park, IL 60131

BRASS EXTRUSION LABS. LTD., 800 W. Maple Lane, Bensenville, IL 60106

RUSSELL CAMPBELL, 219 Leisure Dr., San Antonio, TX 78201

COLLECTORS SHOTSHELL ARSENAL, 16425 Old South Golden Rd., Golden, CO 80401

AMMUNITION (*Custom*)

CROWN CITY ARMS, P.O. Box 1126 Cortland, NY 13045

CUMBERLAND ARMS, 1222 Oak Dr., Manchester, TN 37355

E.W. ELLIS SPORT SHOP, RFD 1, Box 139, Corinth, NY 12822

ELLWOOD EPPS (ORILLIA) LTD., Hwy. 11 North, Orillia Ont., Canada

RAMON B. GONZALEZ, P.O. Box 370, Monticello, NY 12701

GUSSERT BULLET & CARTRIDGE CO., 1868 Lenwood Ave., Green Bay, WI 54303

HUTTON RIFLE RANCH, 619 San Lorenzo St., Santa Monica, CA 90402

J-4, INC., 1700 Via Burton, Anaheim, CA 92806

R.H. KEELER, 1304 S. Oak, Port Angeles, WA 98362

KTW INC., 710 Foster Park Rd., Lorain, OH 44053

DEAN LINCOLN, P.O. Box 1886, Farmington, NM 87401

LOMONT PRECISION BULLETS, 4421 S. Wayne Ave., Ft. Wayne, IN 46807

MANSFIELD GUNSHOP, Box 83, New Boston, NH 03070

NUMRICH ARMS CORP., 203 Broadway, W. Hurley, NY 12491

THE OUTRIDER, INC., 3288 LaVenture Dr., Chamblee, GA 30341

ROBERT POMEROY, Morison Ave., Corinth, ME 04427

PRECISION AMMUNITION & RELOADING, 122 Hildenboro Square, Agincourt, Ont. M1W 1Y3, Canada

ANTHONY F. SAILER-AMMUNITION, P.O. Box L, Owen, WI 54460

SANDERS CUST. GUN SERV., 2358 Tyler Lane, Louisville, KY 40205

SHOTSHELL COMPONENTS, 16425 Old South Golden Rd., Golden, CO 80401

GEO. SPENCE, P.O. Box 222 Steele, MO 63877

H. WINTER CAST BULLETS, 422 Circle Dr., Clarksville, TN 37040

AMMUNITION (Foreign)

ABERCROMBIE & FITCH, Madison at 45th St., New York, NY 10017

AMMODYNE, Box 1859, Los Angeles, CA 90053 (RWS)

CANADIAN IND. LTD. (C.I.L.), Ammo Div., Howard House, Brownsburg, Que., Canada JOV 1AO

CENTENNIAL ARMS CO., 3318 W. Devon Ave., Chicago, IL 60645

COLONIAL AMMUNITION CO., Box 8511, Auckland, New Zealand

DYNAMIT NOBEL OF AMERICA, INC., 910, 17th St. NW, Suite 709, Washington, DC 20006

EASTERN SPORTS DISTRIBUTORS CO., P.O. Box 28, Milford, NH 03055 (RWS; Geco)

GEVELOT OF CANADA, Box 1593, Saskatoon, Sask., Canada

HIRTENBERGER PATRONEN-, ZÜNDHÜTCHEN- & METALLWARENFABRIK, A.G. Leobersdorfer Str. 33, A2552 Hirtenburg, Austria

HY-SCORE ARMS CO., 200 Tillary, Brooklyn, NY 11201

JAMES C. TILLINGHAST, Box 568, Marlow, NH 03456

NORMA-PRECISION, South Lansing, NY 14882

OREGON AMMO SERVICE, Box 19341, Portland, OR 97219

PAUL JAEGER INC., 211 Leedom St., Jenkintown, PA 19046

S.E. LASZLO, 200 Tillary, Brooklyn, NY 11201

STOEGER ARMS CORP., 55 Ruta Ct., S. Hackensack, NJ 07606

THE OUTRIDER, INC., 3288 LaVenture Dr., Chamblee, GA 30341

RWS (RHEINISCHE-WESTFÄLISCHE SPRENGSTOFF) (See: Eastern)

OPTICAL EQUIPMENT—Scopes, Mounts, Accessories

ABERCROMBIE & FITCH, 45th & Madison Ave., New York, NY 10017

ALLEY SUPPLY CO., Carson Valley Industrial Park, Gardnerville, NV 89410

AMERICAN IMPORT CO., 1167 Mission, San Francisco, CA 94103

ANDERSON & CO., 1203 Broadway, Yakima, WA 98902

ARMSPORT, INC., 2811 N.W. 75th Ave., Miami, FL 33122

AVERY CORP., P.O. Box 99 Electra, TX 76360

B-SQUARE CO., Box 11281, Ft. Worth, TX 76109

BAUSCH & LOMB INC., 635 St. Paul St., Rochester, NY 14602

BENNETT, 561 Delaware, Delmar, NY 12054

BRIDGE MOUNT CO., Box 3344, Lubbock, TX 79410

BROWNING ARMS, Rte. 4, Box 624-B, Arnold, MO 63010

MAYNARD P. BUEHLER, INC., 17 Orinda Highway, Orinda, CA 94563

BURRIS CO., 351 E. 8th St., Greeley, CO 80631

BUSHNELL OPTICAL CO., 2828 E. Foothill Blvd., Pasadena, CA 91107

BUTLER CREEK CORP., Box GG, Jackson Hole, WY 83001

KENNETH CLARK, 18738 Highway 99, Madera, CA 93637

CLEARVIEW MFG. CO., INC., 23702 Crossley, Hazel Park, MI 48030

CLEAR VIEW SPORTS SHIELDS, P.O. BOX 255, Wethersfield, CT 06107

COLT'S, Hartford, CT 06102

COMPASS INSTR. & OPTICAL CO., INC., 104 E. 25th St., New York, NY 10010

CONETROL SCOPE MOUNTS, Hwy 123 South, Seguin, TX 78155

CONTINENTAL ARMS CORP., 697-5th Ave., New York, NY 10022

DAVIS OPTICAL CO., P.O. Box 6, Winchester, IN 47934

DEL-SPORTS INC., Main St., Margaretville, NY 12455

M.B. DINSMORE, Box 21, Wyomissing, PA 19610

EDER INSTRUMENT CO., 5115 N. Ravenswood, Chicago, IL 60640

FLAIG'S LODGE, Babcock Blvd., Millvale, PA 15209

FREELAND'S SCOPE STANDS, INC., 3734 14th, Rock Island, IL 61201

OPTICAL EQUIPMENT (continued)

GRIFFIN & HOWE, INC., 589-8th Ave., New York, NY 10017

H.J. HERMANN LEATHER CO., Rte. 1, Skiatook, OK 74070

HERTER'S INC., Waseca, MN 56093

J.B. HOLDEN CO., 295 W. Pearl, Plymouth, MI 48170

THE HUTSON CORP., P.O. 1127, Arlington, TX 76010

HY-SCORE ARMS CORP., 200 Tillary St., Brooklyn, NY 11201

INTERARMS, 10 Prince St., Alexandria, VA 22312

PAUL JAEGER, 211 Leedom St., Jenkintown, PA 19046

JANA INTL. CO., Box 1107, Denver, CO 80201

JASON EMPIRE INC., 9200 Cody, Overland Park, KS 66214

JEFFREDO GUNSIGHT CO., 1629 Via Monserate, Fallbrook, CA 92028

KESSELRING GUN SHOP, 400 Pacific Hway 99, No. Burlington, WA 98283

KRIS MOUNTS, 108 Lehigh St., Johnstown, PA 15905

KUHARSKY BROS. (See: Modern Industries)

KWIK-SITE, 27367 Michigan Ave., Inkster, MI 48141

LANDAV, 7213 Lee Highway, Falls Church, VA 22046

S.E. LASZLO HOUSE OF IMPORTS, 200 Tillary St., Brooklyn, NY 11201

L.E.S., 3640 Dempster, Skokie, IL 60076

LEATHERWOOD BROS., Rte. 1, Box 111, Stephenville, TX 76401

T.K. LEE, Box 2123, Birmingham, AL 35201

E. LEITZ, INC., Rockleigh, NJ 07647

LEUPOLD & STEVENS, INC., P.O. Box 688, Beaverton, OR 97005

JAKE LEVIN AND SON, INC., 9200 Cody, Overland Park, KS 66214

W.H. LODEWICK, 2816 N.E. Halsey, Portland, OR 97232

LYMAN GUN SIGHT PRODUCTS, Rte. 147, Middlefield, CT 06455

MANDALL SHOOTING SUPPLIES, 7150 E. 4th St., Scottsdale, AZ 85252

MARBLE ARMS CO., 420 Industrial Park, Gladstone, MI 49837

MARLIN FIREARMS CO., 100 Kenna Dr., New Haven, CT 06473

MITCHELL'S SHOOTING GLASSES, Box 539, Waynesville, MO 65583

MODERN INDUSTRIES, INC., 613 W-11, Erie, PA 16501

O.F. MOSSBERG & SONS, INC., 7 Grasso Ave., North Haven, CT 06473

NIKKO (KANEMATSU-GOSHO USA INC.), 543 W. Algonquin Rd., Arlington Heights, IL 60005

NORMARK CORP., 1710 E. 78th St., Minneapolis, MN 55423

NUMRICH ARMS, West Hurley, NY 12491

NYDAR (See: Swain Nelson Co.)

PEM'S MOUNTS, 6063 Waterloo, Atwater, PA 44201

PGS, PETERS' INC., 622 Gratiot Ave., Saginaw, MI 48602

PACHMAYR GUN WORKS, 1220 S. Grand Ave., Los Angeles, CA 90015

PACIFIC TOOL CO., P.O. Drawer 2048, Ordnance Plant Rd., Grand Island, NB 68801

ED PAUL'S SPTG. GOODS, INC., 172 Flatbush Ave., Brooklyn, NY 11217

PRECISE, 3 Chestnut, Suffern, NY 10901

RANGING INC., 90 N. Lincoln Rd., East Rochester, NY 14445

RAY-O-VAC, WILLSON PROD. DIV., P.O. Box 622, Reading, PA 19603

REALIST, INC., N. 93 W. 16288, Megal Dr., Menomonee Falls, WI 53051

REDFIELD GUN SIGHT CO., 5800 E. Jewell Ave., Denver, CO 80222

S&K MFG. CO., Box 247, Pittsfield, PA 16340

SANDERS CUST. GUN SERV., 2358 Tyler Lane, Louisville, Ky 40205

SAUNDERS GUN & MACHINE SHOP, 145 Delhi Rd., Manchester, IA 52057

SAVAGE ARMS, Westfield, MA 01085

SEARS, ROEBUCK & CO., 825 S. St. Louis, Chicago, IL 60607

SHERWOOD DIST., INC., 18714 Parthenia St., Northridge, CA 91324

W.H. SIEBERT, 22720 S.E. 56th Pl., Issaquah, WA 98027

SINGLEPOINT (See: Normark)

SOUTHERN PRECISION INST. CO., 3419 E. Commerce St., San Antonio, TX 78219

SPACETRON INC., Box 84, Broadview, IL 60155

STOEGER ARMS CO., 55 Ruta Ct., S. Hackensack, NJ 07606

SUPREME LENS COVERS, Box GG, Jackson Hole, WY 83001

SWAIN NELSON CO., Box 45, 92 Park Dr., Glenview, IL 60025

SWIFT INSTRUMENTS, INC., 952 Dorchester Ave., Boston, MA 02125

TASCO, 1075 N.W. 71st, Miami, FL 33138

THOMPSON-CENTER ARMS, P.O. Box 2405, Rochester, NH 03867

TRADEWINDS, INC., Box 1191, Tacoma, WA 98401

JOHN UNERTL OPTICAL CO., 3551-5 East St., Pittsburgh, PA 15214

UNITED BINOCULAR CO., 9043 S. Western Ave., Chicago, IL 60620

UNIVERSAL SPORTING GOODS INC., 7920 N.W. 76th Ave., Miami, FL 33166

VISSING (See: Supreme Lens Covers)

WEATHERBY'S, 2781 Firestone, South Gate, CA 90280

W.R. WEAVER CO., 7125 Industrial Ave., El Paso, TX 79915

WEIN PRODS. INC., 115 W. 25th St., Los Angeles, CA 90007

WILLIAMS GUN SIGHT CO., 7389 Lapeer Rd., Davison, MI 48423

BOYD WILLIAMS INC., 8701-14 Mile Rd. (M-57), Cedar Springs, MI 49319

WILLRICH PRECISION INSTRUMENT CO., 37-13 Broadway, Rte. 4, Fair Lawn, NJ 07410

CARL ZEISS INC., 444 Fifth Ave., New York, NY 10018

BALLISTICS CHARTS

Ballistics for Standard Centerfire Rifle Ammunition
Produced by the Major U. S. Manufacturers

Cartridge	Wt. Grs.	Bullet Type(g)	Velocity (fps) Muzzle	100 yds.	200 yds.	300 yds.	Energy (ft. lbs.) Muzzle	100 yds.	200 yds.	300 yds.	Mid-Range Trajectory 100 yds.	200 yds.	300 yds.
218 Bee	46	HP	2860	2160	1610	1200	835	475	265	145	0.7	3.8	11.6
22 Hornet	45	SP	2690	2030	1510	1150	720	410	230	130	0.8	4.3	13.0
22 Hornet (c, d)	45	HP	2690	2030	1510	1150	720	410	230	130	0.8	4.3	13.0
22 Hornet	46	HP	2690	2030	1510	1150	740	420	235	135	0.8	4.3	13.0
222 Remington (e)	50	PSP, MC, PL	3200	2660	2170	1750	1140	785	520	340	0.5	2.5	7.0
222 Remington Magnum (c, d)	55	SP, PL	3300	2800	2340	1930	1330	955	670	455	0.5	2.3	6.1
223 Remington (c, d, e)	55	SP, PL	3300	2800	2340	1930	1330	955	670	455	0.5	2.1	5.4
22-250 Remington (a, c, d)	55	PSP, PL	3760	3230	2745	2305	1730	1275	920	650	0.4	1.7	4.5
225 Winchester (a, b)	55	PSP	3650	3140	2680	2270	1630	1200	875	630	0.4	1.8	4.8
243 Winchester (e)	80	PSP, PL	3500	3080	2720	2410	2180	1690	1320	1030	0.4	1.8	4.7
243 Winchester (e)	100	PP, CL, PSP	3070	2790	2540	2320	2090	1730	1430	1190	0.5	2.2	5.5
6mm Remington (c, d)	80	PSP, HP, PL	3450	3130	2750	2400	2220	1740	1340	1018	0.4	1.8	4.7
6mm Remington (c, d)	100	PCL	3190	2920	2660	2420	2260	1890	1570	1300	0.5	2.1	5.1
244 Remington (c, d)	90	PSP	3200	2850	2530	2230	2050	1630	1280	995	0.5	2.1	5.5
25-06 Remington (c, d)	87	HP	3500	3070	2680	2310	2370	1820	1390	1030	Not Available		
25-06 Remington (c, d)	120	PSP	Not Available				Not Available				Not Available		
25-20 Winchester	86	L, Lu	1460	1180	1030	940	405	265	200	170	2.6	12.5	32.0
25-20 Winchester	86	SP	1460	1180	1030	940	405	265	200	170	2.6	12.5	32.0
25-35 Winchester	117	SP, CL	2300	1910	1600	1340	1370	945	665	465	1.0	4.6	12.5
250 Savage	87	PSP, SP	3030	2660	2330	2060	1770	1370	1050	820	0.6	2.5	6.4
250 Savage	100	ST, CL, PSP	2820	2460	2140	1870	1760	1340	1020	775	0.6	2.9	7.4
256 Winchester Magnum (b)	60	OPE	2800	2070	1570	1220	1040	570	330	200	0.8	4.0	12.0
257 Roberts (a, b)	87	PSP	3200	2840	2500	2190	1980	1560	1210	925	0.5	2.2	5.7
257 Roberts	100	ST, CL	2900	2540	2210	1920	1870	1430	1080	820	0.6	2.7	7.0
257 Roberts	117	PP, CL	2650	2280	1950	1690	1820	1350	985	740	0.7	3.4	8.8
6.5 Remington Magnum (c)	100	PSPCL	3450	3070	2690	2320	2640	2090	1610	1190	Not Available		
6.5mm Remington Magnum (c)	120	PSPCL	3030	2750	2480	2230	2450	2010	1640	1330	0.6	2.3	5.7
264 Winchester Magnum	100	PSP, CL	3700	3260	2880	2550	3040	2360	1840	1440	0.4	1.6	4.2
264 Winchester Magnum	140	PP, CL	3200	2940	2700	2480	3180	2690	2270	1910	0.5	2.0	4.9
270 Winchester	100	PSP	3480	3070	2690	2340	2690	2090	1600	1215	0.4	1.8	4.8
270 Winchester (e)	130	PP, PSP	3140	2880	2630	2400	2850	2390	2000	1660	0.5	2.1	5.3
270 Winchester	130	ST, CL, BP, PP	3140	2850	2580	2320	2840	2340	1920	1550	0.5	2.1	5.3
270 Winchester (c, d)	150	CL	2800	2440	2140	1870	2610	1980	1520	1160	0.6	2.9	7.6
270 Winchester (a, b, e)	150	PP	2900	2620	2380	2160	2800	2290	1890	1550	0.6	2.5	6.3
280 Remington (c, d)	125	PCL	3190	2880	2590	2320	2820	2300	1860	1490	0.5	2.1	5.3
280 Remington (c, d)	150	PCL	2900	2670	2450	2220	2800	2370	2000	1640	0.6	2.5	6.1
280 Remington (c, d)	165	CL	2820	2510	2220	1970	2910	2310	1810	1420	0.6	2.8	7.2
284 Winchester (a, b)	125	PP	3200	2880	2590	2310	2840	2300	1860	1480	0.5	2.1	5.3
284 Winchester (a, b)	150	PP	2900	2630	2380	2160	2800	2300	1890	1550	0.6	2.5	6.3
7mm Mauser (e)	175	SP	2490	2170	1900	1680	2410	1830	1400	1100	0.8	3.7	9.5
7mm Remington Magnum	125	CL	3430	3080	2750	2450	3260	2630	2100	1660	0.6	1.8	4.7
7mm Remington Magnum (e)	150	PP, CL	3260	2970	2700	2450	3540	2940	2430	1990	0.4	2.0	4.9
7mm Remington Magnum (e)	175	PP	3070	2720	2400	2120	3660	2870	2240	1750	0.5	2.4	6.1
7mm Remington Magnum (c, d)	175	PCL	3070	2860	2660	2460	3660	3170	2740	2350	0.5	2.1	5.2
30 Carbine (e)	110	HSP, SP	1980	1540	1230	1040	950	575	370	260	1.4	7.5	21.7
30-30 Winchester (c, d)	150	CL	2410	1960	1620	1360	1930	1280	875	616	0.9	4.5	12.5
30-30 Winchester (e)	150	HP	2410	2020	1700	1430	1930	1360	960	680	0.9	4.2	11.0
30-30 Winchester (a, b)	150	PP, ST, OPE	2410	2020	1700	1430	1930	1360	960	680	0.9	4.2	11.0
30-30 Winchester (a)	170	PP, HP, CL, ST, MC	2220	1890	1630	1410	1860	1350	1000	750	1.2	4.6	12.5
30 Remington	170	ST, CL	2120	1820	1560	1350	1700	1250	920	690	1.1	5.3	14.0
30-06 Springfield	110	PSP	3370	2830	2350	1920	2770	1960	1350	900	0.5	2.2	6.0
30-06 Springfield	125	PSP	3200	2810	2480	2200	2840	2190	1710	1340	0.5	2.2	5.6
30-06 Springfield (c, d)	150	BP	2970	2710	2470	2240	2930	2440	2030	1670	0.5	2.4	6.0
30-06 Springfield (e)	150	PP	2970	2620	2300	2010	2930	2280	1760	1340	0.6	2.5	6.5

(a) — Winchester only; (b) — Remington only; (c) — Peters only; (d) — Speer DWM; (e) — Cartridges also available from Federal; (f) — Not safe in Winchester 1873 rifle or handguns; (g) — HP-Hollow Point; SP-Soft Point; PSP-Pointed Soft Point; PP-Winchester Power Point; L-Lead; Lu-Lubaloy; ST-Silvertip; HSP-Hollow Soft Point; MC-Metal Case; BT-Boat Tail; MAT-Match; BP-Bronze Point; CL-Core Lokt; PCL-Pointed Core Lokt; OPE-Open Point Expanding; PL-Power-Lokt.

Ballistics for Standard Centerfire Rifle Ammunition
Produced by the Major U. S. Manufacturers (continued)

Cartridge	Bullet Wt. Grs.	Type (g)	Velocity (fps) Muzzle	100 yds.	200 yds.	300 yds.	Energy (ft. lbs.) Muzzle	100 yds.	200 yds.	300 yds.	Mid-Range Trajectory 100 yds.	200 yds.	300 yds.
30-06 Springfield	150	ST, PCL, PSP	2970	2670	2400	2130	2930	2370	1920	1510	0.6	2.4	6.1
30-06 Springfield	180	PP, CL, PSP	2700	2330	2010	1740	2910	2170	1610	1210	0.7	3.1	8.3
30-06 Springfield (e)	180	ST, BP, PCL	2700	2470	2250	2040	2910	2440	2020	1660	0.7	2.9	7.0
30-06 Springfield	180	MCBT, MAT	2700	2520	2350	2190	2910	2540	2200	1900	0.6	2.8	6.7
30-06 Springfield	220	PP, CL	2410	2120	1870	1670	2830	2190	1710	1360	0.8	3.9	9.8
30-06 Springfield (a, b)	220	ST	2410	2180	1980	1790	2830	2320	1910	1560	0.8	3.7	9.2
30-40 Krag	180	PP, CL	2470	2120	1830	1590	2440	1790	1340	1010	0.8	3.8	9.9
30-40 Krag	180	ST, PCL	2470	2250	2040	1850	2440	2020	1660	1370	0.8	3.5	8.5
30-40 Krag	220	ST	2200	1990	1800	1630	2360	1930	1580	1300	1.0	4.4	11.0
300 Winchester Magnum	150	PP, PCL	3400	3050	2730	2430	3850	3100	2480	1970	0.4	1.9	4.8
300 Winchester Magnum	180	PP, PCL	3070	2850	2640	2440	3770	3250	2790	2380	0.5	2.1	5.3
300 Winchester Magnum (a, b)	220	ST	2720	2490	2270	2060	3620	3030	2520	2070	0.6	2.9	6.9
300 H & H Magnum (a, b)	150	ST	3190	2870	2580	2300	3390	2740	2220	1760	0.5	2.1	5.2
300 H & H Magnum	180	ST, PCL	2920	2670	2440	2220	3400	2850	2380	1970	0.6	2.4	5.8
300 H & H Magnum	220	ST, CL	2620	2370	2150	1940	3350	2740	2260	1840	0.7	3.1	7.7
300 Savage (e)	150	PP	2670	2350	2060	1800	2370	1840	1410	1080	0.7	3.2	8.0
300 Savage	150	ST, PCL	2670	2390	2130	1890	2370	1900	1510	1190	0.7	3.0	7.6
300 Savage (c, d)	150	CL	2670	2270	1930	1660	2370	1710	1240	916	0.7	3.3	9.3
300 Savage (e)	180	PP, CL	2370	2040	1760	1520	2240	1660	1240	920	0.9	4.1	10.5
300 Savage	180	ST, PCL	2370	2160	1960	1770	2240	1860	1530	1250	0.9	3.7	9.2
303 Savage (c, d)	180	CL	2140	1810	1550	1340	1830	1310	960	715	1.1	5.4	14.0
303 Savage (a, b)	190	ST	1980	1680	1440	1250	1650	1190	875	660	1.3	6.2	15.5
303 British (e)	180	PP, CL	2540	2300	2090	1900	2580	2120	1750	1440	0.7	3.3	8.2
303 British (c, d)	215	SP	2180	1900	1660	1460	2270	1720	1310	1020	1.1	4.9	12.5
308 Winchester	110	PSP	3340	2810	2340	1920	2730	1930	1349	900	0.5	2.2	6.0
308 Winchester (a, b)	125	PSP	3100	2740	2430	2160	2670	2080	1640	1300	0.5	2.3	5.9
308 Winchester (e)	150	PP	2860	2520	2210	1930	2730	2120	1630	1240	0.6	2.7	7.0
308 Winchester	150	ST, PCL	2860	2570	2300	2050	2730	2200	1760	1400	0.6	2.6	6.5
308 Winchester (e)	180	PP, CL	2610	2250	1940	1680	2720	2020	1500	1130	0.7	3.4	8.9
308 Winchester	180	ST, PCL	2610	2390	2170	1970	2720	2280	1870	1540	0.8	3.1	7.4
308 Winchester (a, b)	200	ST	2450	2210	1980	1770	2670	2170	1750	1400	0.8	3.6	9.0
32 Winchester Special (c, d, e)	170	HP, CL	2280	1920	1630	1410	1960	1390	1000	750	1.0	4.8	12.5
32 Winchester Special (a, b)	170	PP, ST	2280	1870	1560	1330	1960	1320	920	665	1.0	4.8	13.0
32 Remington (c, d)	170	CL	2120	1800	1540	1340	1700	1220	895	680	1.0	4.9	13.0
32 Remington (a, b)	170	ST	2120	1760	1460	1220	1700	1170	805	560	1.1	5.3	14.5
32-20 Winchester HV (f)	80	OPE, HP	2100	1430	1090	950	780	365	210	160	1.5	8.5	24.5
32-20 Winchester	100	SP, L, Lu	1290	1060	940	840	370	250	195	155	3.3	15.5	38.0
8mm Mauser (e)	170	PP, CL	2570	2140	1790	1520	2490	1730	1210	870	0.8	3.9	10.5
338 Winchester Magnum (a, b)	200	PP	3000	2690	2410	2170	4000	3210	2580	2090	0.5	2.4	6.0
338 Winchester Magnum (a, b)	250	ST	2700	2430	2180	1940	4050	3280	2640	2090	0.7	3.0	7.4
338 Winchester Magnum (a, b)	300	PP	2450	2160	1910	1690	4000	3110	2430	1900	0.8	3.7	9.5
348 Winchester (a)	200	ST	2530	2220	1940	1680	2840	2190	765	509	0.4	1.7	4.7
348 Winchester (c, d)	200	CL	2530	2140	1820	1570	2840	2030	1470	1090	0.8	3.8	10.0
35 Remington (c, d)	150	CL	2400	1960	1580	1280	1920	1280	835	545	0.9	4.6	13.0
35 Remington (e)	200	PP, ST, CL	2100	1710	1390	1160	1950	1300	860	605	1.2	6.0	16.5
350 Remington Magnum (c, d)	200	PCL	2710	2410	2130	1870	3260	2570	2000	1550	Not Available		
350 Remington Magnum (c, d)	250	PCL	2410	2190	1980	1790	3220	2660	2180	1780	Not Available		
351 Winchester Self-Loading	180	SP, MC	1850	1560	1310	1140	1370	975	685	520	1.5	7.8	21.5
358 Winchester (a, b)	200	ST	2530	2210	1910	1640	2840	2160	1610	1190	0.8	3.6	9.4
358 Winchester (a, b)	250	ST	2250	2010	1780	1570	2810	2230	1760	1370	1.0	4.4	11.0
375 H&H Magnum	270	PP, SP	2740	2460	2210	1990	4500	3620	2920	2370	0.7	2.9	7.1
375 H&H Magnum	300	ST	2550	2280	2040	1830	4330	3460	2770	2230	0.7	3.3	8.3
375 H&H Magnum	300	MC	2550	2180	1860	1590	4330	3160	2300	1680	0.7	3.6	9.3
38-40 Winchester	180	SP	1330	1070	960	850	705	455	370	290	3.2	15.0	36.5
44 Magnum (c, d)	240	SP	1750	1360	1110	980	1630	985	655	210	1.6	8.4	—
44 Magnum (b)	240	HSP	1750	1350	1090	950	1630	970	635	480	1.8	9.4	26.0
444 Marlin (c)	240	SP	2400	1845	1410	1125	3070	1815	1060	675	Not Available		
44-40 Winchester	200	SP	1310	1050	940	830	760	490	390	305	3.3	15.0	36.5
45-70 Government	405	SP	1320	1160	1050	990	1570	1210	990	880	2.9	13.0	32.5
458 Winchester Magnum	500	MC	2130	1910	1700	1520	5040	4050	3210	2570	1.1	4.8	12.0
458 Winchester Magnum	510	SP	2130	1840	1600	1400	5140	3830	2900	2220	1.1	5.1	13.5

(a)—Winchester only; (b)—Remington only; (c) Peters only; (d)—Speer DWM; (e)—Cartridges also available from Federal; (f)—Not safe in Winchester 1873 rifle or handguns; (g)—HP-Hollow Point; SP-Soft Point; PSP-Pointed Soft Point; PP-Winchester Power Point; L-Lead; Lu-Lubaloy; ST-Silvertip; HSP-Hollow Soft Point; MC-Metal Case; BT-Boat Tail; MAT-Match; BP-Bronze Point; CL-Core Lokt; PCL-Pointed Core Lokt; OPE-Open Point Expanding; PL-Power-Lokt.

Speer/DWM Ballistics
Ammunition Manufactured by DWM in Germany and Distributed Through Speer Outlets in This Country

Cartridge	Wt. Grs.	Bullet Type (a)	Velocity (fps) Muzzle	100 yds.	200 yds.	300 yds.	Energy (ft. lbs.) Muzzle	100 yds.	200 yds.	300 yds.	Mid-Range Trajectory 100 yds.	200 yds.	300 yds.
5.6 × 35 R Vierling	46	SP	2030	1500	1140		418	224	130		1.2	7.5	
5.6 × 50 R (Rimmed) Mag.	50	PSP	Not Available				Not Available				Not Available		
5.6 × 52 R (Savage H.P.)	71	PSP	2850	2460	2320	2200	1280	947	846	766	.3	2.3	6.5
5.6 × 61 SE	77	PSP	3700	3360	3060	2790	2350	1920	1605	1345	.1	1.1	3.4
5.6 × 61 R	77	PSP	3480	3140	2840	2560	2070	1690	1370	1120	.1	1.3	4.0
6.5 × 54 MS	159	SP	2170	1925	1705	1485	1660	1300	1025	810	.5	4.1	11.5
6.5 × 57 Mauser	93	PSP	3350	2930	2570	2260	2300	1760	1350	1040	.1	1.7	4.8
6.5 × 57 R	93	PSP	3350	2930	2570	2260	2300	1760	1350	1040	.1	1.7	4.8
7 × 57 Mauser	103	PSP	3330	2865	2450	2060	2550	1890	1380	977	.1	1.7	5.2
	162	TIG	2785	2480	2250	2060	2780	2200	1820	1520	.3	2.4	6.7
7 × 57 R	103	PSP	3260	2810	2390	2000	2430	1820	1320	920	.1	1.8	5.3
	139	SP	2550	2240	1960	1720	2000	1540	1190	910	.3	2.9	8.6
	162	TIG	2710	2420	2210	2020	2640	2120	1750	1460	.3	2.4	6.9
7 × 64	103	PSP	3572	3110	2685	2283	2930	2230	1670	1190	.1	1.4	4.4
	139	SP	3000	2570	2260	1980	2780	2040	1570	1200	.2	2.2	6.4
	162	TIG	2960	2603	2375	2200	3150	2440	2030	1740	.2	2.0	6.0
	177	TIG	2880	2665	2490	2325	3270	2820	2440	2130	.2	2.0	5.6
7 × 65 R	103	PSP	3480	3010	2590	2200	2770	2100	1540	1120	.1	1.5	4.7
	139	SP	3000	2570	2260	1980	2780	2040	1570	1200	.2	2.2	6.4
	162	TIG	2887	2540	2320	2140	3000	2320	1930	1650	.2	2.2	6.3
	177	TIG	2820	2600	2420	2255	3120	2660	2300	2000	.2	2.1	5.9
7mm SE	169	ToSto	3300	3045	2825	2620	4090	3480	3010	2600	.1	1.4	3.9
7 × 75 R SE	169	ToSto	3070	2840	2630	2430	3550	3050	2620	2240	.1	1.6	4.5
30-06	180	TUG	2854	2562	2306	2077	3261	2632	2133	1726	.2	2.2	6.3
8 × 57 JS	123	SP	2968	2339	1805	1318	2415	1497	897	477	.2	2.7	8.8
	198	TIG	2732	2415	2181	1985	3276	2560	2083	1736	.3	2.5	7.1
8 × 57 JR	196	SP	2391	1991	1742	1565	2488	1736	1316	1056	.5	3.9	11.2
8 × 57 JRS	123	SP	2970	2340	1805	1318	2415	1497	897	477	.2	2.7	8.8
	196	SP	2480	2140	1870	1640	2680	2000	1510	1165	.4	3.3	9.4
	198	TIG	2600	2320	2105	1930	2970	2350	1950	1620	.3	2.7	7.6
8 × 60 S	196	SP	2585	2162	1890	1690	2905	2030	1560	1245	.4	3.2	9.2
	198	TIG	2780	2450	2205	2010	3390	2625	2130	1770	.3	2.4	6.9
9.3 × 62	293	TUG	2515	2310	2150	2020	4110	3480	3010	2634	.3	2.8	7.5
9.3 × 64	293	TUG	2640	2450	2290	2145	4550	3900	3410	3000	.3	2.4	6.6
9.3 × 72 R	193	FP	1925	1600	1400	1245	1590	1090	835	666	.5	5.7	16.6
9.3 × 74 R	293	TUG	2360	2160	1998	1870	3580	3000	2560	2250	.3	3.1	8.7

(a) FP-flat point; SP-soft point; PSP-pointed soft point; TIG-Brenneke Torpedo Ideal; TUG-Brenneke Torpedo Universal; ToSto-Vom Hofe Torpedo Stop Ring; SM-Stark Mantel (strong jacket).

Ballistics for Standard Rimfire Ammunition
Produced by the Major U. S. Manufacturers

Cartridge	Wt. Grs.	Bullet Type(a)	Velocity (fps) Muzzle	100 yds.	Energy (ft. lbs.) Muzzle	100 yds.	Mid-Range Trajectory 100 yds.	Handgun Barrel Length	M.V. fps	M.E. ft. lbs.	
22 Short	29	C, L*	1045	810	70	42	5.6	6″	865	48	
22 Short Hi-Vel.	29	C, L	1125	920	81	54	4.3	6″	1035	69	
22 Short HP Hi-Vel.	27	C, L	1155	920	80	51	4.2	—	—	—	
22 Short	29	D	1045	—	70	—	—	—	—	—	(per 500)
22 Short	15	D	1710	—	97	—	—	—	—	—	(per 500)
22 Long Hi-Vel.	29	C, L	1240	965	99	60	3.8	6″	1095	77	
22 Long Rifle	40	L*	1145	975	116	84	4.0	6″	950	80	
22 Long Rifle	40	L*	1120	950	111	80	4.2	—	—	—	
22 Long Rifle	40	L*	—	—	—	—	—	6¾″	1060	100	
22 Long Rifle	40	C	1165	980	121	84	4.0	—	—	—	
22 Long Rifle Hi-Vel.	40	C, L	1335	1045	158	97	3.3	6″	1125	112	
22 Long Rifle HP (Hi-Vel.)	37	C, L	1365	1040	149	86	3.4	—	—	—	
22 Long Rifle HP (Hi-Vel.)	36	C	1365	1040	149	86	3.4	—	—	—	
22 Long Rifle	No	12 Shot	—	—	—	—	—	—	—	—	
22 WRF (Rem. Spl.)	45	C, L	1450	1110	210	123	2.7	—	—	—	
22 WRF Mag.	40	JHP	2000	1390	355	170	1.6	6½″	1550	213	
22 WRF Mag.	40	MC	2000	1390	355	170	1.6	6½″	1550	213	
22 Win. Auto Inside lub.	45	C, L	1055	930	111	86	4.6	—	—	—	
5mm Rem. RFM	38	PLHP	2100	1605	372	217	Not Available				

(a) C-Copper Plated; L-Lead (wax coated); D-Disintegrating; L-Lead Lubricated; MC-Metal Case; HP-Hollow Point; JHP-Jacketed Hollow Point

Ballistics of Norma-Precision Centerfire Rifle Ammunition
Manufactured in Sweden

Cartridge	Wt. Grs.	Bullet Type (a)	Velocity (fps) Muzzle	100 yds.	200 yds.	300 yds.	Energy (ft. lbs.) Muzzle	100 yds.	200 yds.	300 yds.	Max. Height of Trajectory (in.) 100 yds.	200 yds.	300 yds.
22 Hornet	45	SPS	2690	2030	1510	1150	720	410	230	130	Not Available		
220 Swift	50	PSP	4111	3611	3133	2681	1877	1448	1090	799	.2	.9	3.0
222 Remington	50	PSP	3200	2660	2170	1750	1137	786	523	340	.0	2.0	6.2
223	50	SPP	3300	2900	2520	2160	1330	1027	776	570	.4	2.4	6.8
22-250	50	SPS	3800	3300	2810	2350	1600	1209	885	613	Not Available		
	55	SPS	3650	3200	2780	2400	1637	1251	944	704	Not Available		
243 Winchester	75	HP	3500	3070	2660	2290	2041	1570	1179	873	.0	1.4	4.1
	100	PSP	3070	2790	2540	2320	2093	1729	1433	1195	.1	1.8	5.0
6mm Remington	100	SPS	3190	2920	2660	2420	2260	1890	1570	1300	.4	2.1	5.3
250 Savage	87	PSP	3032	2685	2357	2054	1776	1393	1074	815	.0	1.9	5.8
	100	PSP	2822	2514	2223	1956	1769	1404	1098	850	.1	2.2	6.6
257 Roberts	100	PSP	2900	2588	2291	2020	1868	1488	1166	906	.1	2.1	6.2
	120	PSP	2645	2405	2177	1964	1865	1542	1263	1028	.2	2.5	7.0
6.5 Carcano	156	SPRN	2000	1810	1640	1485	1386	1135	932	764	Not Available		
6.5 Japanese	139	PSPBT	2428	2280	2130	1990	1820	1605	1401	1223	.3	2.8	7.7
	156	SPRN	2067	1871	1692	1529	1481	1213	992	810	.6	4.4	11.9
6.5 × 54 MS	139	PSPBT	2580	2420	2270	2120	2056	1808	1591	1388	.2	2.4	6.5
	156	SPRN	2461	2240	2033	1840	2098	1738	1432	1173	.3	3.0	8.2
6.5 × 55	139	PSPBT	2789	2630	2470	2320	2402	2136	1883	1662	.1	2.0	5.6
	156	SPRN	2493	2271	2062	1867	2153	1787	1473	1208	.3	2.9	7.9
270 Winchester	110	PSP	3248	2966	2694	2435	2578	2150	1773	1448	.1	1.4	4.3
	130	PSPBT	3140	2884	2639	2404	2847	2401	2011	1669	.0	1.6	4.7
	150	PSPBT	2802	2616	2436	2262	2616	2280	1977	1705	.1	2.0	5.7
7 × 57	110	PSP	3068	2792	2528	2277	2300	1904	1561	1267	.0	1.6	5.0
	150	PSPBT	2756	2539	2331	2133	2530	2148	1810	1516	.1	2.2	6.2
	175	SPRN	2490	2170	1900	1680	2410	1830	1403	1097	.4	3.3	9.0
7mm Remington Magnum	150	SPSBT	3260	2970	2700	2450	3540	2945	2435	1990	.4	2.0	4.9
	175	SPRN	3070	2720	2400	2120	3660	2870	2240	1590	.5	2.4	6.1
7 × 61 S & H (26 in.)	160	PSPBT	3100	2927	2757	2595	3416	3045	2701	2393	.0	1.5	4.3
30 U.S. Carbine	110	SPRN	1970	1595	1300	1090	948	622	413	290	.8	6.4	19.0
30-30 Winchester	150	SPFP	2410	2075	1790	1550	1934	1433	1066	799	.9	4.2	11.0
	170	SPFP	2220	1890	1630	1410	1861	1349	1003	750	.7	4.1	11.9
308 Winchester	130	PSPBT	2900	2590	2300	2030	2428	1937	1527	1190	.1	2.1	6.2
	150	PSPBT	2860	2570	2300	2050	2725	2200	1762	1400	.1	2.0	5.9
	180	PSPBT	2610	2400	2210	2020	2725	2303	1952	1631	.2	2.5	6.6
	180	SPDC	2610	2400	2210	2020	2725	2303	1952	1631	.7	3.4	8.9
7.62 Russian	180	PSPBT	2624	2415	2222	2030	2749	2326	1970	1644	.2	2.5	6.6
308 Norma Magnum	180	DC	3100	2881	2668	2464	3842	3318	2846	2427	.0	1.6	4.6
30-06	130	PSPBT	3281	2951	2636	2338	3108	2514	2006	1578	.1	1.5	4.6
	150	PS	2972	2680	2402	2141	2943	2393	1922	1527	.0	1.9	5.7
	180	PSPBT, SPDC	2700	2494	2296	2109	2914	2487	2107	1778	.1	2.3	6.4
	220	SPRN	2411	2197	1996	1809	2840	2358	1947	1599	.3	3.1	8.5
300 H & H	180	PSPBT	2920	2706	2500	2297	3409	2927	2499	2109	.0	1.9	5.3
	220	SPRN	2625	2400	2170	1986	3367	2814	2301	1927	.2	2.5	7.0
7.65 Argentine	150	PSP	2920	2630	2355	2105	2841	2304	1848	1476	.1	2.0	5.8
303 British	130	PSP	2789	2483	2195	1929	2246	1780	1391	1075	.1	2.3	6.7
	150	PSP	2720	2440	2170	1930	2465	1983	1569	1241	.1	2.2	6.5
	180	PSPBT	2540	2340	2147	1965	2579	2189	1843	1544	.2	2.7	7.3
7.7 Japanese	130	PSP	2950	2635	2340	2065	2513	2004	1581	1231	.1	2.0	5.9
	180	PSPBT	2493	2292	2101	1922	2484	2100	1765	1477	.3	2.8	7.7
8 × 57 JR	196	SPRN	2362	2045	1761	1513	2428	1820	1530	996	.4	3.7	10.6
8 × 57 JS	123	PSP	2887	2515	2170	1857	2277	1728	1286	942	.1	2.3	6.8
	159	SPRN	2723	2362	2030	1734	2618	1970	1455	1062	.2	2.6	7.9
	196	SPRN	2526	2195	1894	1627	2778	2097	1562	1152	.3	3.1	9.1
358 Winchester	200	SPS	2530	2210	1910	1640	2843	2170	1621	1195	.4	3.1	8.8
	250	SPS	2250	2010	1780	1570	2811	2243	1759	1369	.6	3.9	10.4
358 Norma Magnum	250	SPS	2790	2493	2231	2001	4322	3451	2764	2223	.2	2.4	6.6
375 H & H Magnum	300	SPS	2550	2280	2040	1830	4333	3464	2773	2231	.3	2.8	7.6
44 Magnum	240	SPFP	1750				1640				Not Available		

(a) P-Pointed; SP-Soft Point; HP-Hollow Point; FP-Flat Point; RN-Round Nose; BT-Boat Tail; MC-Metal Case; DC-Dual Core; SPS-Semi-pointed Soft Point.

Ballistics for Weatherby Magnum Ammunition Supplied by Weatherby's Inc. for use in Weatherby Rifles

			Velocity (fps)				Energy (ft. lbs.)				Mid-Range Trajectory		
Cartridge	Wt. Grs.	Bullet Type (a)	Muzzle	100 yds.	200 yds.	300 yds.	Muzzle	100 yds.	200 yds.	300 yds.	100 yds.	200 yds.	300 yds.
224 Weatherby Varmintmaster	50	PE	3750	3160	2625	2140	1562	1109	1670	1250	0.7	3.6	9.0
224 Weatherby Varmintmaster	55	PE	3650	3150	2685	2270	1627	1212	881	629	0.4	1.7	4.5
240 Weatherby	70	PE	3850	3395	2975	2585	2304	1788	1376	1038	0.3	1.5	3.9
240 Weatherby	90	PE	3500	3135	2795	2475	2444	1960	1559	1222	0.4	1.8	4.5
240 Weatherby	100	PE	3395	3115	2850	2595	2554	2150	1804	1495	0.4	1.8	4.4
257 Weatherby	87	PE	3825	3290	2835	2450	2828	2087	1553	1160	0.3	1.6	4.4
257 Weatherby	100	PE	3555	3150	2815	2500	2802	2199	1760	1338	0.4	1.7	4.4
257 Weatherby	117	SPE	3300	2900	2550	2250	2824	2184	1689	1315	0.4	2.4	6.8
270 Weatherby	100	PE	3760	3625	2825	2435	3140	2363	1773	1317	0.4	1.6	4.3
270 Weatherby	130	PE	3375	3050	2750	2480	3283	2685	2183	1776	0.4	1.8	4.5
270 Weatherby	150	PE	3245	2955	2675	2430	3501	2909	2385	1967	0.5	2.0	5.0
7mm Weatherby	139	PE	3300	2995	2715	2465	3355	2770	2275	1877	0.4	1.9	4.9
7mm Weatherby	154	PE	3160	2885	2640	2415	3406	2874	2384	1994	0.5	2.0	5.0
300 Weatherby	150	PE	3545	3195	2890	2615	4179	3393	2783	2279	0.4	1.5	3.9
300 Weatherby	180	PE	3245	2960	2705	2475	4201	3501	2925	2448	0.4	1.9	5.2
300 Weatherby	220	SPE	2905	2610	2385	2150	4123	3329	2757	2257	0.6	2.5	6.7
340 Weatherby	200	PE	3210	2905	2615	2345	4566	3748	3038	2442	0.5	2.1	5.3
340 Weatherby	210	Nosler	3165	2910	2665	2435	4660	3948	3312	2766	0.5	2.1	5.0
340 Weatherby	250	SPE	2850	2580	2325	2090	4510	3695	3000	2425	0.6	2.7	6.7
378 Weatherby	270	SPE	3180	2850	2600	2315	6051	4871	4053	3210	0.5	2.0	5.2
378 Weatherby	300	SPE	2925	2610	2380	2125	5700	4539	3774	3009	0.6	2.5	6.2
460 Weatherby	500	RN	2700	2330	2005	1730	8095	6025	4465	3320	0.7	3.3	10.0

(a) PE-Pointed Expanding; SPE-Semi-Pointed Expanding; RN-Round Nose; Nosler-Nosler Partition Controlled Expansion Bullet. All velocities taken from 26-inch barrels.

Ballistics of Standard Shotshell Ammunition Loaded by the Major U. S. Manufacturers

Gauge	Length Shell Ins.	Powder Equiv. Drams	Shot Ozs.	Shot Size
MAGNUM LOADS				
10	3 1/2	5	2	2, 4
12	3	4 1/2	1 7/8	BB, 2, 4
12	3	4 1/4	1 5/8	2, 4, 6
12	2 3/4	4	1 1/2	2, 4, 5, 6
16	2 3/4	3 1/2	1 1/4	2, 4, 6
20	3	3 1/4	1 1/4	2, 4, 6, 7 1/2
20	3	Max	1 3/16	4
20	2 3/4	3	1 1/8	2, 4, 6, 7 1/2
28	2 3/4	Max	1	6, 7 1/2, 8, 9
LONG RANGE LOADS				
10	2 7/8	4 3/4	1 5/8	4
12	2 3/4	3 3/4	1 1/4	BB, 2, 4, 5, 6, 7 1/2, 9
16	2 3/4	3 1/4	1 1/8	4, 5, 6, 7 1/2, 9
16	2 3/4	3	1 1/8	4, 5, 6, 7 1/2, 9
20	2 3/4	2 3/4	1	4, 5, 6, 7 1/2, 9
28	2 3/4	2 1/4	3/4	4, 6, 7 1/2, 9
FIELD LOADS				
12	2 3/4	3 1/4	1 1/4	7 1/2, 8, 9
12	2 3/4	3 1/4	1 1/8	4, 5, 6, 7 1/2, 8, 9
12	2 3/4	3	1 1/8	4, 5, 6, 8, 9
12	2 3/4	3	1	4, 5, 6, 8
16	2 3/4	2 3/4	1 1/8	4, 5, 6, 7 1/2, 8, 9
16	2 3/4	2 1/2	1	4, 5, 6, 8, 9
20	2 3/4	2 1/2	1	4, 5, 6, 7 1/2, 8, 9
20	2 3/4	2 1/4	7/8	4, 5, 6, 8, 9
SCATTER LOADS				
12	2 3/4	3	1 1/8	8
16	2 3/4	2 1/2	1	8
20	2 3/4	2 1/4	7/8	8

Gauge	Length Shell Ins.	Powder Equiv. Drams	Shot Ozs.	Shot Size
TARGET LOADS				
12	2 3/4	3	1 1/8	7 1/2, 8, 9
12	2 3/4	2 3/4	1 1/8	7 1/2, 8, 9
16	2 3/4	2 1/2	1	8, 9
20	2 3/4	2 1/4	7/8	8, 9
28	2 3/4	2 1/4	3/4	9
410	3	Max	3/4	4, 5, 6, 7 1/2, 9
410	2 1/2	Max	1/2	4, 5, 6, 7 1/2, 9
SKEET & TRAP				
12	2 3/4	3	1 1/8	7 1/2, 8, 9
12	2 3/4	2 3/4	1 1/8	7 1/2, 8, 9
16	2 3/4	2 1/2	1	8, 9
20	2 3/4	2 1/4	7/8	8, 9
BUCKSHOT				
12	3 Mag	4 1/2	–	00 Buck – 15 pellets
12	3 Mag	4 1/2	–	4 Buck – 41 pellets
12	2 3/4 Mag	4	–	2 Buck – 20 pellets
12	2 3/4 Mag	4	–	00 Buck – 12 pellets
12	2 3/4	3 3/4	–	00 Buck – 9 pellets
12	2 3/4	3 3/4	–	0 Buck – 12 pellets
12	2 3/4	3 3/4	–	1 Buck – 16 pellets
12	2 3/4	3 3/4	–	4 Buck – 27 pellets
16	2 3/4	3	–	1 Buck – 12 pellets
20	2 3/4	2 3/4	–	3 Buck – 20 pellets
RIFLED SLUGS				
12	2 3/4	3 3/4	1	Slug
16	2 3/4	3	1 7/8	Slug
20	2 3/4	2 3/4	5/8	Slug
410	2 1/2	Max	1/5	Slug

Ballistics for Standard Pistol and Revolver Centerfire Ammunition
Produced by the Major U. S. Manufacturers

Cartridge	Bullet Grs.	Bullet Style	Muzzle Velocity	Muzzle Energy	Barrel Inches		Cartridge	Bullet Grs.	Bullet Style	Muzzle Velocity	Muzzle Energy	Barrel Inches
22 Jet	40	SP	2100	390	8³/₈		38 Special	158	MP	855	256	6
221 Fireball	50	SP	2650	780	10¹/₂		38 Special	125	SJHP		Not available	
25 (6.35mm) Auto	50	MC	810	73	2		38 Special	158	SJHP		Not available	
256 Winchester Magnum	60	HP	2350	735	8¹/₂		38 Special WC	148	Lead	770	195	6
30 (7.65mm) Luger Auto	93	MC	1220	307	4¹/₂		38 Special Match, IL	148	Lead	770	195	6
30 (7.63mm) Mauser Auto	85	MC	1410	375	5¹/₂		38 Special Match, IL	158	Lead	855	256	6
32 S&W Blank	No bullet		—	—	—		38 Special Hi-Speed	158	Lead	1090	425	6
32 S&W Blank, BP	No bullet		—	—	—		38 Special	158	RN	900	320	6
32 Short Colt	80	Lead	745	100	4		38 Colt New Police	150	Lead	680	154	4
32 Long Colt, IL	82	Lub.	755	104	4		38 Short Colt	128	Lead	730	150	6
32 Colt New Police	100	Lead	680	100	4		38 Short Colt, Greased	130	Lub.	730	155	6
32 (7.65mm) Auto	71	MC	960	145	4		38 Long Colt	150	Lead	730	175	6
32 (7.65mm) Auto Pistol	77	MC	900	162	4		38 Super Auto	130	MC	1280	475	5
32 S&W	88	Lead	680	90	3		38 Auto, for Colt 38 Super	130	MC	1280	475	5
32 S&W Long	98	Lead	705	115	4		38 Auto	130	MC	1040	312	4¹/₂
7.5 Nagant	104	Lead	722	120	4¹/₂		380 Auto	95	MC	955	192	3³/₄
32-20 Winchester	100	Lead	1030	271	6		38-40 Winchester	180	SP	975	380	5
32-20 Winchester	100	SP	1030	271	6		41 Long Colt, IL	200	Lub.	730	230	6
357 Magnum	158	SP	1550	845	8³/₈		41 Remington Magnum	210	Lead	1050	515	8³/₄
357 Magnum	158	MP	1410	695	8³/₈		41 Remington Magnum	210	SP	1500	1050	8³/₄
357 Magnum	158	Lead	1410	696	8³/₈		44 S&W Special	246	Lead	755	311	6¹/₂
357 Magnum	158	JSP	1450	735	8³/₈		44 Remington Magnum	240	SP	1470	1150	6¹/₂
9mm Luger	116	MC	1165	349	4		44 Remington Magnum	240	Lead	1470	1150	6¹/₂
9mm Luger Auto	124	MC	1120	345	4		44-40 Winchester	200	SP	975	420	7¹/₂
38 S&W Blank	No bullet		—	—	—		45 Colt	250	Lead	860	410	5¹/₂
38 Smith & Wesson	146	Lead	685	150	4		45 Colt, IL	255	Lub., L	860	410	5¹/₂
38 S&W	146	Lead	730	172	4		45 Auto	230	MC	850	369	5
380 MK II	180	MC	620	153	5		45 ACP	230	JHP	850	370	5
38 Special Blank	No bullet		—	—	—		45 Auto WC	185	MC	775	245	5
38 Special, IL	150	Lub.	1060	375	6		45 Auto MC	230	MC	850	369	5
38 Special, IL	150	MC	1060	375	6		45 Auto Match	185	MC	775	247	5
38 Special	158	Lead	855	256	6		45 Auto Match, IL	210	Lead	710	235	5
38 Special	200	Lead	730	236	6		45 Auto Rim	230	Lead	810	335	5¹/₂

IL-Inside Lubricated; JSP-Jacketed Soft Point; WC-Wadcutter; Rh-Round Nose; Hp-Hollow Point; Lub-Lubricated; MC-Metal Case; SP-Soft Point; MP-Metal Point; LGC-Lead Gas Check; JHP-Jacketed Hollow Point

Ballistics of Super Vel Cartridge
Corporation Handgun Ammunition

Cartridge	Bullet Gr. Style	Bullet Style (a)	Muzzle Velocity	Muzzle Energy	Barrel Inches
380 ACP	80	JHP	1026	188	5
9mm Luger	90	JHP	1422	402	5
9mm Luger	110	SP	1325	428	5
38 Special	110	JHP/SP	1370	458	6
38 Special	147	HBWC	775	196	6
38 Special Int.	158	Lead	1110	439	6
357 Magnum	110	JHP/SP	1690	697	6
44 Magnum	180	JHP/SP	2005	1607	6
45 Auto	190	JHP	1060	743	5

(a) JHP-Jacketed Hollow Point; JSP-Jacketed Soft Point; HBWC-Hollow Base Wad Cutter.

INDEX

ARMS INDEX

CARTRIDGE INDEX

GENERAL INDEX